I0127042

Made of Clay and Pickles:
Yorkshire to Michigan

Curt Sanders

TABLE OF CONTENTS:

COPYRIGHT MATTER

Made of Clay and Pickles:
Yorkshire to Michigan

Every attempt was to accurately recreate events, locales, notes, and conversations from reputable, original, documented sources.

Printed by lulu.com a B-corporation.

- Font, body: Book Antiqua, 10 point. COPPERPLATE for others.
- Principle software for genealogy organization: Reunion™ for Apple Macintosh.™
- Principle software for book composition: Apple Pages.™
- Cover image licensed from Canva.

International Standard Book Number: 978-1-7324538-5-2

1. Genealogy - Yorkshire, England
2. Genealogy - United States

Library of Congress Control Number: 2023922182

CITATION: Sanders, Curt. *Made of Clay and Pickles: Yorkshire to Michigan.* Harrisburg, Pennsylvania: self-published, 2024.

You may contact the author at:

Curt Sanders
4707 Hillside Road
Harrisburg, Pennsylvania 17109-5203
U.S.A.
Email: k3urt@mac.com

ACKNOWLEDGMENTS

• **Vena Emily KILBOURNE DOYLE** is sincerely thanked posthumously for preserving the family records: photographs, Bible entries, the death record of Issac Clay, and the marriage certificate of James Pickles and Issac's daughter Sally Clay — seeds planted decades ago for this book.

• Born in the Victorian Age, posthumously a special thanks to **Amelia Hannah Elizabeth PICKLES KILBOURNE TREGENZA,** who inspired the research with her parents' tales of life in Michigan. Hannah's quiet demeanor spoke little of her family, but she left a large legacy.

• Thanks to my family's curiosity, which watered the seeds of inquiry.

• Thanks to my Beta Readers, **Janelle SIMMONS** and **Kathryn Marie "Kate"** (*nee* **SANDERS**) **GLASSFORD,** for encouraging the author to weave a complex thread of these families and for taking a first look at the scribble.

• Familysearch.org, ancestry.com, newspapers.com, findmypast.UK, British Newspaper Archive, and others like them for their digitalizing records made this work more accessible to the hundreds of newspapers that were the social media of their day.

• The Calderdale [England] Family History Society: Incorporating Halifax and District. I just wish I could live for a year in the area to possibly fill-in any missing data!

• A vital acknowledgment goes to **Kathleen Marie** (*nee* **O'DELL**) **TOWNSLEY** for her years of research and photographs. Her hard work and investigations.

• And thanks to **Barbara Lucille** (*nee* **MEDD**) **MANNE STARK** (1931-2006) and her daughter **Susan R.** (*nee* **MANNE**) **CLUFF.**

• To **Tammie NEWHOUSE.**

• Lastly, many thanks to the others I may have missed — my apologies!

PREFACE

"Made of Clay and Pickles" sounds like a strange culinary concoction. But from a genealogical perspective, it is a recipe for two families that made courageous decisions in the late nineteenth century to migrate from England, cross the Atlantic Ocean, and land in the American state of Michigan and elsewhere.

As a young lad, summer travel to Michigan to visit relatives on mother's side was with an obligatory stop-over to call upon great-grandma Amelia Hannah Elizabeth nee Pickles-Kilbourne-Tregenza – better known as "Grandma Kilbourne" to us youngsters [see #14, Part I]. She was a woman of a quiet demeanor with a cold aloofness to a child in pre-teens. In hindsight, it was an acquired self-consciousness, rising from shyness from her deafness obtained from a fever at age 12. Raised in the Victorian Age (or the American Reconstruction Age) by English parents, she added to her stereotypical English reserve! Eventually, curiosity from the author would ask about family ancestry and history: Father? Mother? "Did you always live here?" "Why did your parents come to America from England?" Her answers or non-answers were vague – understandable since she was born shortly after their arrival to America and too young to remember – or feigned deafness to questions she wanted to avoid. Her children later supplied additional information.

Amateurish research of the author's family history started in his late adolescence. More earnestly, from 1975 to 1977, as a US Air Force serviceman at the Royal Air Force base at Lakenheath in County Suffolk, he navigated the United Kingdom (UK) record system when duty did not call. It was confusing, bewildering, and different from most US records – and an era long before the birth of the Internet, the vast digitalization of records, and his inexperience with the avocation.

The principal problem encountered in family research in nineteenth-century English records is the connective family details. An example would be which "John Pickles" child belonged to in an area of many "John Pickles" – often located in the same square mile and born around the same time! The introduction of UK civil record keeping in 1837 gave some details on vital information needed for identity.

Most of the subjects in this book are within 64 square miles (166 square kilometers) of each other (see Figure 2).

The author naively thought the investigation would be pretty straightforward. "Pickles" (and its variations) is a rather unique surname, making it easy to research – so he thought! It is a common surname of the Yorkshire area! Not to mention the commonality of the surname "Clay" – the other predominant family in this book.

Moreover, many used unremarkable Christian names like John, James, Hannah, Mary, and like (see **APPENDIX: WORD CLOUD** as an example) – and were often born in the same months or years and within the same families. Add to the recipe the same occupations! Many spreadsheets and analyses were needed to compile this record entirely and accurately. Of course, new data and errors inevitably will be found – genealogy is dynamic, and changes and new discoveries are inevitable.

– Curt Sanders, July 2024

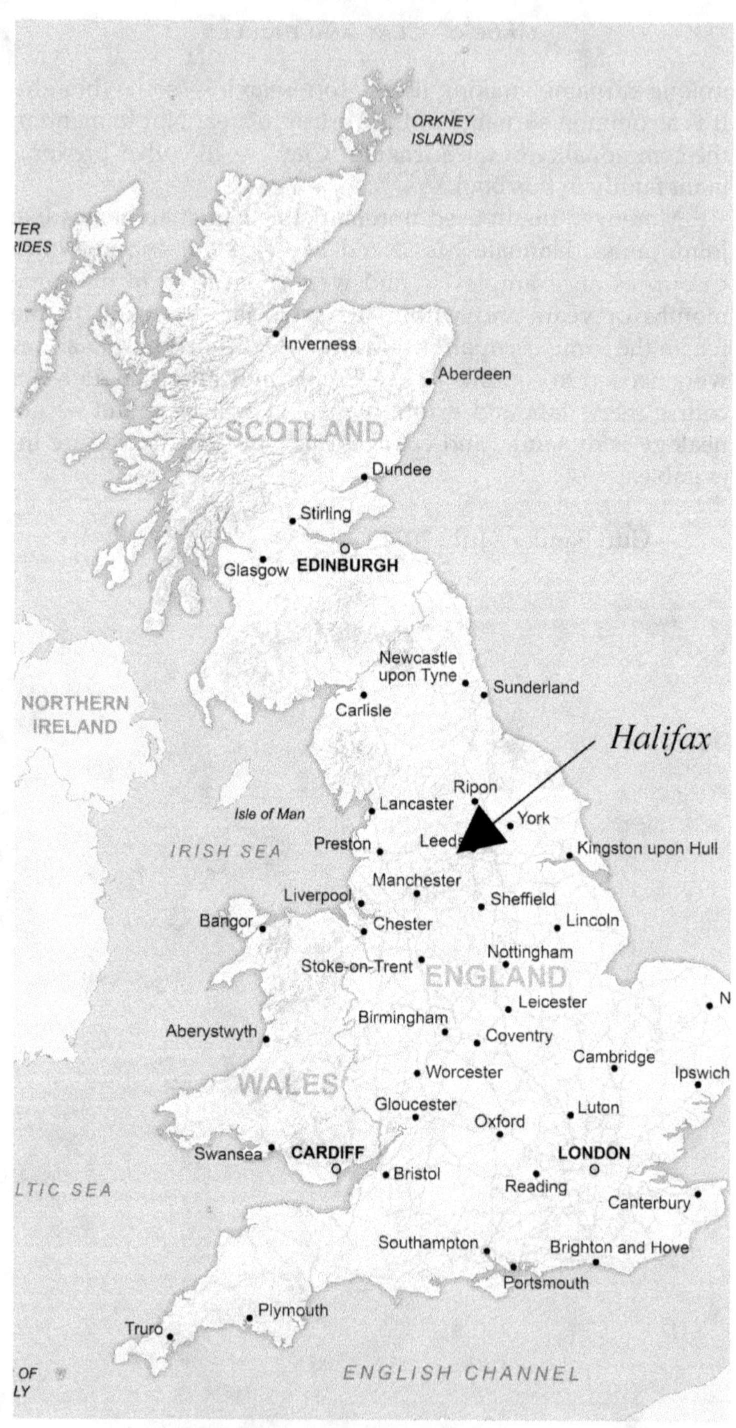

Figure 1:
UK Ordnance Survey Data Hub. 2014.
https://osdatahub.os.uk/downloads/open/GBOverviewMaps

INTRODUCTION:

THE CENTRAL RESEARCH QUESTION

Why did these connecting families of Clay and Pickles immigrate from Yorkshire, England, to Michigan in the United States of America?

THE RESEARCH CONFINES

The book attempts to cover known sources using accepted genealogical and historical practices during the approximate the late 1790s to early 1900s.

The author limited descent for the Clay and Pickles family for brevity.

- Part 1, "Abegail Clay's Children," examines the five descending generations of Abegail Clay.
- Part 2, "Made of Pickles," with three generations down from the earliest Pickles the author could reasonably undertake.

The families are connected by James Pickles (1843-1911) and his wife Hannah Clay (1838-1927).

For an understanding of the numbering system, please see **APPENDIX: NGSQ SYSTEM.**

THE STANDARDS:

o The Genealogical Proof Standard (GPS) from *Genealogy Standards*, by the Board for Certification of Genealogists.

- **Reasonably exhaustive research**

  The author utilized online resources from major databases and history (cited in the Sources).
- **Complete and accurate source citations**

  Sources are primary, original documents and cited per recognized writing style. Over 95% of the documents reviewed are digitally scanned original items. Newspaper articles, and like, are faithfully transcripted and matched to the original text by the author.
- **Analysis and correlation of the collected information**
  - Genealogy gleans its sources from documents that have no thought of recording genealogy for posterity. They record for:
    - *Religion*: consanguinity—in marriage and birth in identifying partners and their children; and in death to identify who is going to the hereafter.

  - *Civil records:* primarily to establish property rights and inheritances.
  - *Posterity*: noting one's accomplishments or passing acts that affect others.

- **Resolution of any conflicting evidence**
  - Where there is no conclusive, reasonable evidence, the author leaves the item blank and cites the omisson. For example, research by someone else giving a person's middle name without supporting documentation, the author does not use a middle name.
  - North American history is "newer," thus often having many sources to correlate conclusions.
  - The research used evidence deduction methods, spreadsheets, and other analysis techniques. The genealogist acronym FAN (Friends And Neighbors) expanded to include distant relatives in the search for verifiable information.

    English newspapers of the nineteenth century were usually business only. Birth, marriages, deaths, and obituaries were usually only associated with society's wealthy and upper classes. The families in this book are working class. (And the class bias of the newspapers did not hesitate to record the crimes of the proletariat in detail!) However, there are exceptions.
- **A soundly reasoned, coherently written conclusion**
  - Hopefully, the author has conveyed sound, evidential conclusions with a pleasant, entertaining style.
  - This narrative uses the National Genealogical Society Quarterly (NGSQ) register system. The NGSQ System assigns a number to every child, whether or not that child has progeny.

o Richard Marius and Melvin E. Page's, *A Short Guide to Writing About History*.

o All topped off with continued education and methods taught courses by Boston University, New England Historic Genealogical Society, familysearch.org, Board for Certification of Genealogists, Legacy Family Tree Webinars, and other institutions encompassing social science disciplines and more.

o Sources are all gleaned from public records.

o Living individuals will have their birthdates replaced with even when documented in a public record as "[withheld for privacy—living person]." Public records, including religious, government, and newspapers, are cited in the

SOURCES sections. Please refer to the SOURCES for additional information and documentation.

ABBREVIATIONS. The author dislikes abbreviations. Hence, unless within quoted material, abbreviations are rarely used. The exceptions are:

ED: Enumeration District

GRO: General Register Office (United Kingdom)

Rev.: Reverend

NARA: (National Archives and Records Administration, United States of America)

UK: United Kingdom

US: United States of America

For any proper recount of family history, it is necessary to background the history and sociology of the times they lived. The author includes maps and photographs as assistants. Also suggested are the GLOSSARY and the APPENDIX pages for additional understanding.

Finally, no research is ever complete. Internet-based research continues to explode with newly scanned or presented information. New discoveries in "Aunt Maude's Attic" or in local, state, and national institutions do happen.

Herein is the author's best attempt to complete evidence-based research. The author concluded research for this book for publishing preparation by July 2024 after four years work. He continues to update the files and welcomes additional information.

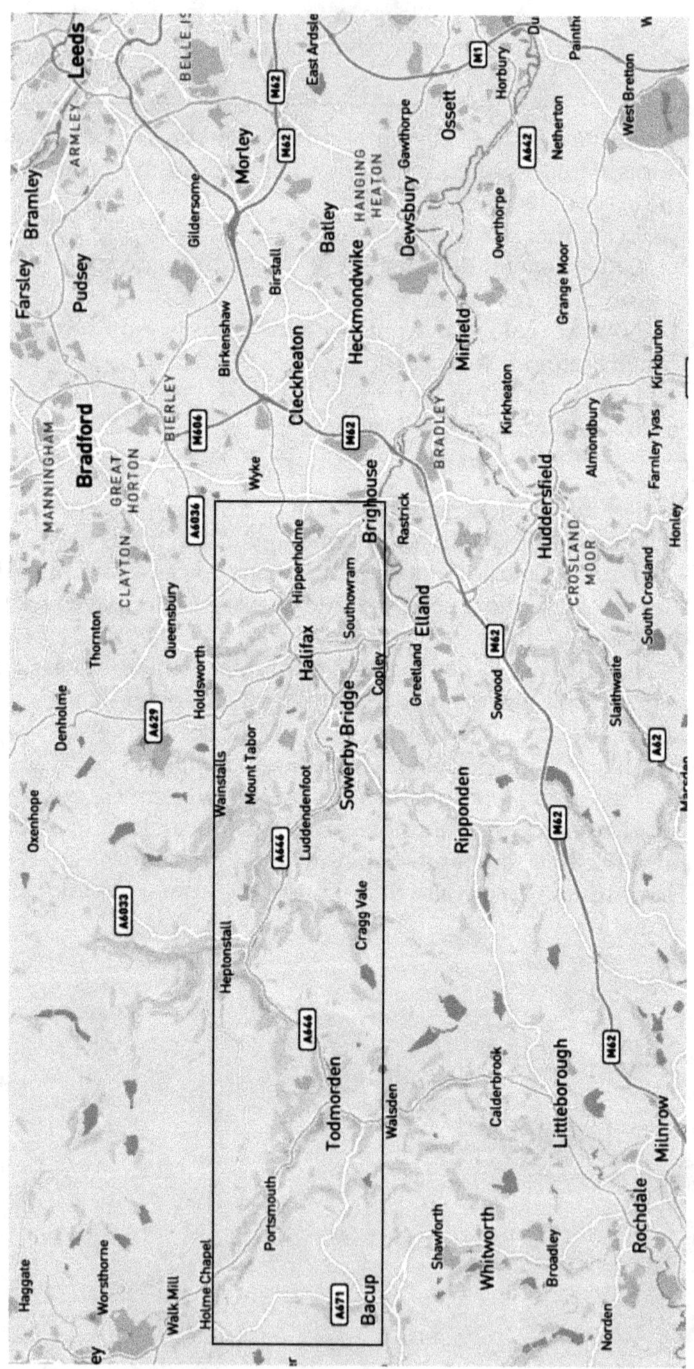

Figure 2. The area enclosed in the rectangle is the approximate area of primary interest. It generally follows the modern A646 road, then Burnley Road in the nineteenth century.

THE BIG OVERVIEW

Origins

Both families originate in the Yorkshire region of England, generally centered around Halifax and its environs. Without confusing the reader and not recanting the ever-shifting civil and ecclesiastical boundaries over the 200-plus years of this narrative, the author simplified as much as possible in descriptions.

Yorkshire is the county or "shire" of York City, divided into "ridings" – a Viking term deriving from Threthingr: a third part. The families in this book primarily originate within 64 square miles or 166 square kilometers (see *Figure* 2.)

For this narrative, both clans originate in the historic County of York, principally in the ceremonial West Yorkshire, West Riding, now Calderdale Metropolitan District. Despite the whims of time, boundaries have not radically changed overall. Because of work, religion, or seeking a mate, the families can be found also in eastern Lancashire County, particularly in Burnley, Rossendale, and Rochdale in Yorkshire, Todmorden, and Bacup areas that border West Riding and Halifax.

Surname Clay

The surname "Clay" of Yorkshire and the Midlands is probably from Old English clǣg 'clay,' applied as a name for someone who lived in an area of clay soil.[2028]

The Clay of England Society claims Yorkshire was once the Clay capital of England. They cite William de Clay (circa 1190 CE*) as an early example.[2029] Because of the commonality of "Christian" first names applied to the surname, researching early origins was difficult. However, in West Yorkshire, the surname CLAY was 798 in prevalence, with a rank of 469 in Yorkshire, making it not too uncommon but enough to cloud the genealogical research soup.[2030] According to the 1841 to 1939 UK Censuses, most Clays lived in Yorkshire, and is the 643rd most common name in the UK.[2031]

* See GLOSSARY "Common Era" for definition and use.

Surname Pickles

For this research project, the early surname was PIGHELLS – a derivative of many inventions of the name to come:

> "It is topographical for someone who lived by a small field or paddock. The name derives from the Middle English word 'pightel', meaning a small enclosure. The modern surname can be found as Pickles, Pickless, Pickle, Pickell and Pighills, and is recorded mainly in Yorkshire. The first recorded spelling of the family name is shown to be that of Richard de Righkeleys – dated 1379, in the Poll Tax Returns of Yorkshire, during the reign of King Richard, known as 'Richard of Bordeaux', 1377 - 1399."[2032,2033]

The surname is profuse in Yorkshire.

> "In 1891 there were 4,073 alive Pickles families living in Yorkshire. This was about 70% of all the recorded Pickles in United Kingdom. Yorkshire had the highest population of Pickles families in 1891."[2034]

"... and [Yorkshire] is still thought to have more residents with the name than anywhere else in the [UK]."[2035]

General Topography

Our ancestors' general residences were in the Southern Pennine chain of Hills in the west, which is of Carboniferous origin. Halifax is surrounded to the North and West by rolling hills divided by the Calder River. Yorkshire has often been described colloquially as "God's County" because of its beauty and the inhabitants' friendliness. Unfortunately, our ancestors probably did not enjoy that view. As landless folks, they generally were village or city dwellers, and the topography of industrial England was probably more barren and bleak than today.

Sheep herding denuded brush and bush for over 4,000 years, leaving rich grasslands. Sheep probably was first used as a meat source, but the value of wool quickly turned around when the Romans invaded. The Vikings followed with their breeds, and after the Norman invasion, wool-making was the backbone of the English economy. *British Sheep & Wool: A guide to British sheep breeds and their unique wool* is suggested reading.[2066]

Pre-Nineteenth History

Although out of the breath of this book, the very ancient history of our people is noteworthy. Numerous groups of denizens invaded or migrated to the region. With the retreat of the ice age around 8,000 BCE, the area became inhabited by Celtic Britons coming up from the south.

Northern England was still much the hinterland when the Romans came in 43 and left by 410 CE, leaving their legacy in the area. However, with their withdrawal, a vacuum was filled with Scheswig-Holstein Angles in the 5th and 6th centuries, introducing Christianity.

Then followed Danish Vikings, led by Ivan the Boneless, invading the Yorkshire regions by 866 CE with the sacking of Eoforwic or Jorvik, better known as "York." The Viking Danelaw dominated the region, socially and politically, in "Scandinavian York" until 1066 CE.

The invasion of Normans (also of Viking heritage) by William The Conqueror in 1066 dramatically shifted the political landscape of the British Isles. The King of Norway, Harold Hardrada, and William disputed Harold Godwinson's rule in York. The pivotal battle of Stamford Bridge ended the Viking dominance of the region with Hardrada's death in battle. Godwinson turned south to meet William's army at Hastings and was killed and defeated. The Normans rose to ascendency but contended with uprisings from the Yorkshire people until 1071.

Scots made raiding forays into the area in the 1300s, causing suffering for the region's poor peasant folks, primarily subsistence farmers with little natural resources. The common folk turned to trade crafts of which, by the nineteenth century, the West Riding communities of Yorkshire were well into the wool industries by the 1300s. Over time, the wool industry developed into a cottage industry. It evolved into small factories or guild associations by the nineteenth century.

A Guild is an association of artisans and merchants who oversee the practice of their tradecraft in a particular area. The inclusional framework of a guild differed and was comprehensive. At times, the "privilege" was that only guild members were allowed to sell their goods or practice their skills within the city. The involvement of the Clays and Pickles in the guild movement is unclear. Did they belong to local guilds? No evidence of their membership survives. Nevertheless, they were in the employ of others by the mid-nineteenth century. Moreover, as the data is glaring, they engaged in the wool industry in the region.

HALIFAX – the central conurbation for our families – was believed first recorded in 1091 as Halyfax, an Anglo-Saxon term meaning "area of coarse grass on the nook of land." [2036] Another interpretation is "holy hair." Halifax was known as a religious center by the 12th century, but its wealth was from the weaving industries, recording its first weaver in 1275. Saint John The Baptist's head is fancifully to be believed buried in the area and thus became the patron saint of weavers.

Today, Halifax, West Yorkshire is a town, a part of the modern Metropolitan Borough of Calderdale.

Up to the Industrial Revolution, the Yorkshire region had additional calamities befall it: The Black Death reached York by 1349, The War of the Roses, 1455-1487, the Yorkshire Rebellion of 1489, and like. Yorkshire was a bed of dissenters from Guy Fawkes, 1570-1606, to the Puritans who landed Plymouth Rock, Massachusetts, in 1620.

The Industrial Revolution

What was the Industrial Revolution? The textile industry in northern England was already in place and running before the academically designated era started in the 1770s. The date of the start of the epoch varies depending on the scholar. Textiles, particularly wool and cotton, were the principal industry – by far! The epoch encompassed much in a short period: a revolution in inventions, steam, mining, transportation, agriculture, technology, society, and others.

In general, our study focuses on the period from the 1770s to the decline in the 1890s – the research arc of the CLAY and PICKLES families for this narrative. Unaware at the time, these families were born into the peak and gradual decline of the IR, which eventually led to changes and immigration.

Occupationally, within the scope of this book, the CLAY family exhibited more diversity than the PICKLES family, which was deeply rooted in the woolen industries.

Wool

"Be their country hot or cold, torrid or frigid,
'tis the same thing, near the Equinox or near

the Pole, the English woollen manufacturer clothes them all..."

"By 1850, at the apogee of its power, Britain had 1.8% of world population. The area of the British Isles is only about 0.16% of the world land mass. Yet Britain then produced two-thirds of world output of coal and one half of world production of cotton textiles and iron. Output per worker was higher in Britain than in any other country."[2037]

Earlier, and already a century in the making, Edward III, in the 1337 statute, bestowed letters of entry and protection to competing foreign laborers, particularly Flemish—wool weavers, to pump up the manufacture. In 1454, Parliament declared, "...the making of cloth within all parts of the realm is the greatest occupation and living of the poor commmons of this land."

Moreover, northern England quickly became the wool industry pillar into the late nineteenth century, with the "... population, income and political power mov[ing] in favor of the north."[2038]

Wool was important for trade, and England grew a reputation of impeccable quality.

And it was largely a woolen industry until the introduction of cotton. Wool became a victim of vacillating Crown protectionist policies over the centuries, competing with a nacent cotton industry in the ninetheenth century.

Wool weaving was the principal occupation of the Pickles families — and barely any departed from the calling. We attribute this to static class mobility, limited opportunities, and family tradition. One account describes "...little employment in husbandry, except during the hay harvest, the labouring poor are very dependent on the neighbouring towns, where the cloth manufacture is carried on..."[2039]

In the mid-nineteenth century, wool became threatened with replacement by cheap cotton imported from *antebellum* America and later Egypt.

However, the wool industry continued to attract preference as the wearing apparel of choice. Statistics show the industry remained popular, adapting to a lower quality of "cheaper mixed worsteds for a much wider market," of which "France commanded the softer all-wool worsteds." These mixed worsteds were "shoddy" — now a derogatory term in modern popular context, but in the industry, it was the combination of recovered and reused wool yarn and cloth. Our Yorkshire families were skilled in the "art of combining," re-

A Wool Comber, 1804 – The Book Of Trades, part I.

taining their niche market lead.[2040]

Weaving was a laborious job, but innovations made it easier for the worker but also threatened his or her livelihood with its efficiency. Much of the spinning was done by women long before the eighteenth century and was an enterprise for the whole family. It required entire families to be devoted to the process. Many of these "spinsters" delayed seeking husbands to provide an income; hence, the term was born.[2041] But the mean age of marriage for women dropped as machines freed them, from 1610 to 1837, from 25.5 to 23.6 years of age. In 1620, 20% of women never married. By the end of the eighteenth century, about 25% of first births were "illegitimate."[2042]

Later, inventions such as coal mining, steam engines, and more water-powered efficiencies threatened the labor-intensive family profession and its social structure.

Inventions as a revolutionary force of note in the wool and cotton industry:

- Flying Shuttle by John Kay (1733)
- Spinning Engine (1738) by Lewis Paul and John Wyatt; and later refined as the "Arkwright."
- Spinning Jenny (1769) by James Hargreaves
- Power Loom (1785) by Edmund Cartwright; further refined by James Bullough and William Kenworthy by 1834
- Cotton gin by Eli Whitney (1794)
- Jacquard Loom (1803)
- Noble Machine (1854)

In 1776, Adam Smith, considered the father of capitalist economic analysis, published *The Wealth of Nations* and exclaimed that the revolution in the woolen industry was substituting the spinning wheel for the rock and spindle, fulling mills, and improvement in warp and woof. Moreover, it was the beginning of separating workers from production ownership and skill.

The mining of coal also contributed to the explosion of production for both cotton and wool in the early 1800s, along with the iron revolution going on further south. Coal demand increased dramatically from the 1840s onwards with the introduction of steam engines in the woolen textile mills. Previously, power delivery to home or factory was either by horse or mule (but too expensive due to limited land resources), by windmill (too fickle), and by water wheel (limited to a few land owners and the whims of nature). With mines nearby in this northeast England area, with technological improvements, coal was the power supply choice married to steam contraptions. The debut of the steam locomotive engine in 1804 in Wales eventually solidified the transportation revolution.

By 1787, power looms were in operation, further displacing workers of their means of production viz-a-viz automation. The resentment of displacement labor culminated in West Riding, Yorkshire with the Luddite uprising by 1812.

> "Luddites were protesting against changes they thought would make their lives much worse, changes that were part of a new market system. Before this time, craftspeople would do their work for a set price, the usual price. They did not want this new system that involved working out how much work they did, how much materials cost, and how much profit there would be for the factory owner."[2067]
>
> "By 1820 there were over 12,000 power looms in operation, and by 1833 85,000. By the 1840s they had displaced almost all the hand powered looms.
>
> This was one of the first great instances of technological unemployment. While spinning had displaced hand spinners, these had been mainly women who were not the main income source for their families. But hand weavers were mainly men (in part because hand weaving required strength)."[2043]

WORSTED WOOL - POWER LOOM

6. Drawing the worsted into slivers

Labour and the Poor in England and Wales, 1849-1851, *Letters to the Morning Chronicle, plate after,* page 42; *https://history.pictures/2020/01/22/3-4-the-worsted-industry-in-the-west-riding/*

The 1841 census of Yorkshire shows the increasing dominance of power looms: 1,398 to that of 536 hand-loom workers.[2044] New technologies in a factory meant more worker regimens but fewer workers and individual freedom in time. It appears our families retained some independence, but like the trend, they probably, by the 1840s, were employed in factories owned by others.

> "The worsted sector of the textile industry was the first to adapt the machinery developed by the Lancashire cotton industry and had become completely factory based by the 1860s including large horizontally integrated mills."[2045]

The Victorian Age (1837-1901) was not much better for the common folk than the years preceding. The epoch was dismal in working conditions, but it was an era rich in British history, advancing innovations in medicine, railroads, new ideas like evolution, in political economy, the discovery of new species, and the introduction of compulsory, non-denominational public education for children between 5-10 years of age, in 1870. Before the 1871 England and Wales census, the occupation "Scholar" was a young person generally underage, unable to work in a factory, and tutored privately. Post-1871 censuses, "Scholar" is a lad or lass in a school (private or public) between the ages of 5-10 years (in 1899, 5-13 years of age by law).

The Elementary Education Act (or Forster Act) was a blow against the abhorrent employment of young children in factories – taking many out of the labor pool. However, students *still had to pay for their schooling* unless they were too poor to pay. The census records imply that our families highly regarded education and took whatever advantage they could.

New philosophies arose concerning working people's poor living and working conditions and challenged the established order.

Robert Owen (1771-1858), a Welsh-born owner of the New Lanark cotton mill, came up from the working class, struggled to improve factory conditions, promoted utopian communities, and sought government control of education. His axiom, "the character of a man is formed for him, not by him," believed nurture formed the person contrary to the then-popular notion that one was born into one's station in life. He later emigrated to America and founded the communal colony of New Harmony. It failed, and he returned to England in 1828 and advocated for the workers until his death.

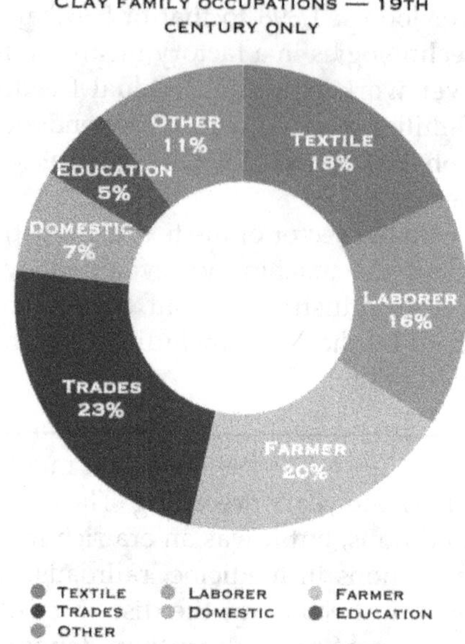

Frederich Engels was partner and operator of his father's cotton mill, Ermen & Engels, in Salford. Later, he co-authored works with philosopher Karl Marx and applied statistics and first-hand knowledge with a ready-made laboratory in his backyard from èmigrè in 1842 to his death in 1895. *The Condition of the Working Class in England,* 1845, is a detailed classic account.

Writers like Charles Dickens (1812-1870), who depicted the stark realities of England of the era, give a descriptive look at the era. (Despite Dickens' severe criticism of society, he was a self-described "Liberal" conservative. For context, a Liberal was a reformist ideologue of *laissez-faire* capitalism, but it was in opposition to staid institutional "Tory" Conservatism.)

The Chartism movement (1834-1850s), an authentic working-class protest over general conditions, and the harsh Poor Law Amendment of 1834, *et al* were immensely controversial in their time. Although mostly peaceful, Halifax was known for its more militant branch, culminating in the Plug Riots in 1842. Otherwise, meetings were picnic-like with brass bands and speakers, and included enlightened Todmorden industrialist and newspaper owner Feargus O'Connor.

There is no direct evidence that the CLAY and PICKLES families worked for others or if owning property or not. It was not until John Pickles [Part 2, #10], in the 1881 England and Wales census, that he owned "8 acres" of land—a lifelong accom-

PICKLES surname, in census years 1841, 1871 and 1891, as percent of occupation, Yorkshire:

	1841	1871*	1891
WEAVER, GENERAL	16	8	4
WEAVER, COTTON	15	24	35
WEAVER, WOOL	35	31	21
AGRICULTURAL	9	6	9
OTHER	25	31	31
TOTALS	100	100	100

**1871: less 709 "Scholars" in school as a result of the 1870 education act.*

It is easy to see that the main occupation the Pickles family seemed dedicated to, wool weaving, declined over the decades, possibly encouraging migration as the job skill became scarce. Cotton ascended over wool.

plishment from proletariat to bourgeoisie.[2027] Within 150 years, the modern textile revolution began with cottage industry artisans to alienated employees deskilled by the end of the nineteenth century. According to Iwama's description of the Halifax "middle class, distinctions between working people and owners blurred."[2046] He identifies them as "voluntary associations, domestic ideology, and entrepreneurial drive." There is little evidence that our families were a part of this yarn.[2047] It was not until our family's departure and acculturation in America that we saw changes in class arrangements.

No doubt some landowning Pickles and Clay families supplemented their income by mining coal and stone or leasing what little plots of land they had. A recount (at least to our family) of Homes and Edward Pickles in 1861 involved a convoluted public legal snafu over land rights.[2048]

For the Pickles families, weaving—and its adjunct occupations, was the leading trade. An essential fact in researching the family genealogy is that employment was a social status and often carried it for life.

> "Simplistically, there were the 'haves' and the 'have nots'. Although the distinction has since passed away, the original definition of a Gentleman or a Lady was someone not burdened with the need to work for

JOHN BULL MAKES A DISCOVERY.

John Bull Makes A Discovery.
PULL QUOTE: "Well yes! ... it is certain that Cotton is more useful to me than Wool!!" – *(Library of Congress)*

a living. In most cases, they were expected to be catered for in every way."[2049]

Our folks may have had the etiquette of a Lady or Gentleman, but not the social and political status.

The previous charts are essential to see the industry changes from 1841 to 1891 – changes that impacted the Clay and Pickles families.[2050]

Remember, our Pickles family was mainly in the woolen industry, particularly in worsted fabric, not cotton. As one can see, cotton weaving and its adjunct occupations grew from 1841 to 1891. Wool also grew but dropped post-1871. Nevertheless, today, it is still a viable, robust commodity in Yorkshire despite reaching an apex in the 1870s.

What happened to the woolen industry during the mid-nineteenth century? America. Initially imported into England in the early 1800s, cotton was an exotic textile and expensive due to transportation and labor costs. However, inventions for cotton improved its quality, the growth of cheap slave labor and a sizable sailing fleet in the US made it more feasible to import.

> "By 1820, the United States was producing about 160 million pounds of cotton a year, and cotton accounted for 32% of the nation's export revenue."[2051]

By the beginning of the American Civil War, England depended upon cotton, receiving nearly 75% of America's exports. Moreover, nearly 40% of Britain's exports were cotton textiles![2052]

> "From the 1860s, however, fashion changes perhaps partly initiated by the American Civil War, the resultant cotton famine and consequent alterations in relative raw fibre prices favoured the French, and growing German, worsted industry. Moreover tariff barriers, particularly in the United States, were most effective against lower and medium quality goods to the disadvantage of Britain. As a result the British worsted industry lost much of its home market to France and suffered a decline in trade to its major traditional markets, including the United States."[2053]

Exports of cotton from the US to English mills dropped considerably from 1861 to 1865 because of embargos from the American Civil War. England turned to Egypt and India for cotton to make up the deficit. Cotton continued its popularity and ascent in the markets worldwide.

Food: a conveyance of immigration?

Were they hungry? What did the Clays and Pickles eat? What was available to the mid-nineteenth-century working poor?

> "The working classes comprised approximately three-quarters of the Victorian population, covering a wide range of incomes and living standards though daily life was arduous and uncomfortable for most. Yet contemporary reports reveal that many women managed their families on very limited incomes without exposing them to starvation or malnutrition."[2071]

Staples were grown, determined mainly by the cool summers and mild winters of Yorkshire: onions, beets, Jerusalem artichokes, carrots, turnips, potatoes, cabbage, lettuce, and greens; some peas and beans. Fruits like apples were the most common. When they could get it, fish, particularly red herring and other species. Pork was the most common meat, free-ranged on limited land (otherwise taken up by sheep). Other meat was sometimes edible but reportedly rotten by Saturday markets when prices were cheaper. Having a few hens around came in handy. The drink was usually beer, but not like the unprocessed stuff of today, and with an alcohol content of not more than two percent, and often used in food preparations. Distilled spirits and wine were rare among the working classes.

Moreover, almost a third of the populace did not drink, reflecting religious proclivities. "Tea was the staple drink. Coffee might be consumed at breakfast even by the poorest, but in the form of chicory/coffee mixture."

However, generally for the working poor: "... a sandwich of bread and watercress was the most common. At the start of the week, porridge made with water might be possible. Lunch involved bread, combined with cheese if possible or more watercress. At the start of the week, soup could occasionally be bought as cheap street food."

Clayton/Rowbotham cheerfully conclude, "... working-class mid-Victorians ate a superior version of the Mediterranean diet, with a much higher consumption of vegetables and fruits than has hitherto been realized. ... the picture that emerges of mid-Victorian nutrition is remarkably positive, and one that matches or surpasses modern nutritional recommendations."

However, the casual perusal of local newspapers and other documents does show diets much less desirable, and people did go hungry. People experiencing poverty were under the whims of weather and wages in finding food. Indeed, the potato blight (1845-1847, *et al*) that swept Europe with massive consequences, especially for the Irish, was calamitous.

Our folks, if allowed, grew backyard gardens. However, the lands of Yorkshire were geared toward sheep grazing, leaving little room for other vegetation. Food was imported into the area, and one's ability to pay was the only barrier to obtaining it. The era's English literature by Charles Dickens, the Brontë sisters, the brother Mayhew, and others are underlying cautionary tales of pervasive hunger and the constant fear of it.

Passage across The Pond

The Clays and Pickles encountered daunting packing and selling off their possessions before moving abroad – usually a one-way ticket – and had a more significant barrier to overcome: The Pond – the Atlantic Ocean.

The cost of transportation varied over the early or late nineteenth century, whether by sail or steam. The subjects in this book went by steam. Hatton found that from 1856 to 1869, the crossing times went from 19 to 14 days for steamships from Liverpool to New York, depending upon weather. From 1890 to 1913, the passage was 5-7 days.

Fares varied: "In 1860, Cunard Line's emigrant fare, 8 pounds, 8 shillings from Liverpool, England, to New York, put you in the 'intolerably crowded, noisy, smelly and badly ventilated" steerage class...'"[2072]

Hatton's analysis suggests an "... estimate for 1863 the westward steerage fare is £3.50 for sail and £6.0 ... for steam..."[2073] Although going by sailship was cheaper, the shortened time of unpleasant steerage accommodations made the extra fee more attractive for a steamer boat. In today's US Dollar amount, that passage was around $490 to $840 or in UK Sterling £528 to £905 respectively – a large sum but not unreachable. Extrapolating from the US Bureau of Labor,[2074] juxtaposition of an English 1871 wool washer working 60 hours per week at $.73 per hour, made an annual wage of around $2,277. Saving up money plus help from friends, relatives, and church put transportation within reach.

It is worth noting that the "word-of-mouth" correspondence between the Michigan and Yorkshire families probably convinced others to come. Indeed, as late as 1892: "Fred Clay favors us with copies of a Great Britain paper, the *Halifax Courier,* containing excellent accounts of the recent English election."[2076] (see Frederic Clay, #4)

Religion as a factor of migration

Most of the Pickles and Clay families were non-conformist worshipers (those outside the established Church Of England) who embraced the fundamental doctrine of John Wesley's Methodism.

Like most theologies, over time, a dogma off-shoot developed. The Methodist New Connexion, or Kilhamite Methodism – was formed in 1797 by secession from the Wesleyan Methodists and merged in 1907 with other like-minded Methodist churches to form the United Methodist Church. The secession was led by Alexander Kilham and William Thom in 1797, resulting from a dispute regarding the position and rights of the laity, which were held high in their view. This branch of Methodism was more bent toward the working class and their needs. Otherwise, the church doctrine remained essentially unchanged. With their overwhelming participation in non-conformist denominations, the Clay and Pickles families were very much a part of this movement.

William "Prophet of the Poor" Booth (1829-1912), founder of the Salvation Army in 1865, was a celebrity of the Methodist New Connexion and an ordained minister in 1858.

Fred Clay (SEE APPENDIX: JOHN C. CLAY, EARLY TO AMERICA) would have been comfortable with the Methodists in America in the 1850s, who comprised over 34% of the adherents.

Ellen Gould (*nee* Harmon) White (1827-1915) was a devout Methodist in her youth but was forced out of the church when her family embraced William Miller's Parousia dogma of the imminent return of The Lord. Eventually, with her husband James, she moved to Battle Creek, Calhoun County, Michigan, in 1855 and founded the Seventh Day Adventist Church in 1863 with others. White was probably attracted to the area as early adherents were religious non-conformists like themselves, i.e., The Quakers. Also, it was a hotbed of abolitionism that squared with the church's teachings. Sojourner Truth was the town residence from 1856 until she died in 1883.

However, as explained by White:

> "In 1855 the brethren in Michigan opened the way for the publishing work to be removed to Battle Creek. At that time my husband was owing between two and three thousand dollars; and all he had, besides a small lot of books, was accounts for books, and some of these were doubtful. The cause had apparently come to a standstill. Orders for publications were very few and small. My husband's health was very poor. He was troubled with cough and soreness of lungs, and his nervous system was prostrated. We feared that he would die while still in debt."[2054]

Early Battle Creek was a crossroads for farmers selling and milling cereal grains. White was an avid health practitioner and vegetarian who founded the Battle Creek Sanitarium in 1866. White's dietary reforms and area staples dovetailed into her healthcare thinking.

John Harvey Kellogg and his brother Will Keith Kellogg, both from a Seventh-day Adventist family in Battle Creek, furthered White's vegetarianism and omission of alcohol, tobacco, tea, coffee, and dairy products. He later founded the Sanitas Food Company, evolving into the corporate behemoth Kellogg's of Battle Creek – a well-known cereal maker in the nineteenth to the twenty-first centuries.

Sally Tidswell Book
She was Born March 17th
1813

"Sally Tidswell Book
She was Born March 17th
1813"
– inscription in her book.

Sally TIDSWELL, the wife of **Isaac CLAY** (Part 1, #2), no doubt had some influence on the family's religious life. She treasured a book copy of *The New Methodist Magazine* of 1833, with possessive remarks in the front free endpaper.[2055]

Sally was part of the Primitive Methodist movement of the era and probably shaped her daughter Hannah's beliefs. These beliefs were bestowed to the Michigan Methodists, who further evolved into the Seventh Day Adventists, which many descendants still practice today.

The Fashions of the Day... The Year (1808) Lady's Undress of Bumbe-seen *by George Murgatroyd Woodward. Extract: Wikimedia Commons as part of a project by the New York Metropolitan Museum of Art.*

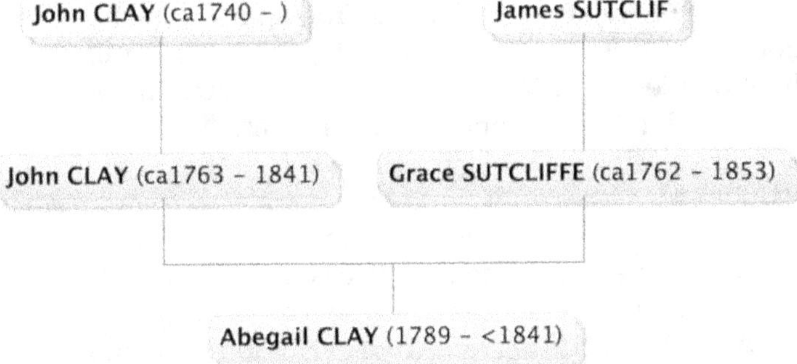
John CLAY (ca1740 -)
James SUTCLIF
John CLAY (ca1763 - 1841)
Grace SUTCLIFFE (ca1762 - 1853)
Abegail CLAY (1789 - <1841)

Part 1. Abegail Clay's Children

First Generation

Every story begins with someone. Our beginning is with an uncommon single mother of three known children:

---

1. **Abegail CLAY** is the daughter of John CLAY (ca1763-1841) and Grace SUTCLIFFE (ca1762-1853).

Abegail was born in 1789, in Yorkshire, England, and infant baptized in Ovenden, Yorkshire, on December 6, 1789, at the Zion Methodist New Connexion – a church predominately featured in the Clay and Pickles families.[1-4]

Abegail likely died in Yorkshire before 1841. The UK General Records Office (GRO) has only one death record: "Abigel Clay" in 1843.[2026] Unfortunately, the record makes her age 71, thus born circa 1772.[5] The evidence is more clear she was born in 1789, and having her first child, Isaac, at age 17.

A 1843 civil death record has a "Widow of John Clay[,] Weaver,"[6] suggesting she was married. However, a search for a marriage record under John Clay and Abegail Clay is not found. Nor was she found under her surname or with a "John Clay" in the 1841 census (or thereafter).

No church burial record is found.

We assumed she never married but used her CLAY surname in registering her children's births. Fathers were usually recorded in this patriarchial society. However, none of the records of the three known children reveal a father. Indeed, Abegail apparently refused to acknowledge who the father was. It would have made life very difficult for her.

Nevertheless, more importantly, ***none*** of Abegail's children were stigmatized as *filius nullius* in the church records.

> "If a marriage was not forthcoming (and up to 1844 a fair element of coercion could be used) the father, or his father or mother, would be forced to enter into a bond to pay for the lying-in and subsequent maintenance of the child, indemnifying the parish against any future costs."[2068]

Between 1750 and 1850 there was a rise in "out-of-wedlock births." The percentage per the population is still debated, but one source conservatively suggests (and probably underestimates):

> "Illegitimacy in England was never common, the number of such births in the past usually being under two per cent... It rose to three per cent again about 1750, slowly increased to seven per cent in the 1840s..."[2056]
>
> "Illegitimates were tolerated as long as they did not seek equality, limiting their agency and ultimately facilitating their continued legal exclusion."[2069]

Abegail's children would encounter a harsh life in this social climate.

The reasons for the rise of children born out of wedlock — possibly the pressures of rapid industrialization — are still being researched today. Women were liberated from conventional cultural restraints — learning trades, making them somewhat independent of men. On the converse side, women were open to labor abuse from male overseers.

The term "spinster" originated during the late 18th century — meaning one who spun cloth — and carried over to meaning an unmarried woman. By the 1851 census of England, women in occupations comprised 51.1% of the workforce in the textile and clothing industries — a significant rise from previous decades. Women still comprised 85.5% of "domestic services."[2057]

The ascent of Queen Victoria ushered in a perceived socially conservative "Victorian Age" (1837-1901) with a more classed-structured society of women dependent upon patriarchy, but with some responsibility by the male partners. There was some financial support from the Poor Laws (1834-1865) for women having no husband, but no record for Abegail can be found. The Bastardy Clause prohibited parishes from granting unwed mothers any relief. The law forced women and their children, without fathers, to enter workhouses that granted them a horrible reputation.[2058]

No parish record survives that we know of showing any support to Abegail, but she must have had some. She was living independently with her children from about 1805 up to 1837. In context to the era, it is doubtful that she would financially make it on her own. We do not know her occupation because she disappeared by the first UK civil census in 1841 - unless she married under another name - not to be found. Her father stated he was a weaver in his 1786 marriage record. Abegail's mother, Grace, before marriage, was convicted under the Worsted Act in 1784:

"The following Perfons have been feverally convicted under the Worfted Act: ... June ... 26th, Before Wm. Walker, Efq. Grace Sutcliffe, of Heptonstall."[2062]

The Act was "... for more effectually preventing Frauds and Abuses committed by Persons employed in the Manufacture of Combing Wool, Worsted Yarn, and Goods made from Worsted in the Counties of York, Lancaster, and Chester."[2063] A further reading of the Act suggests manufacturers, not the workers, were the instigators of the legislation, claiming workers were shorting or stealing material thus establishing penalties. Conveniently, it was the manufacturers who sat judge and jury on who was the guilty party.[2064]

Therefore, Abegail probably worked in the woolen textile industry in this context — as many did in Yorkshire then. Otherwise, we do not know what type of limited employment was open to her.

Abegail probably ended up in a workhouse with her children unless she and the children traditionally ended up in the mother's family by custom. But we do know "Abigal Clay" was admitted to the Halifax Ovenden Workhouse 25 April 1837, age 48. She was discharged for "Went out" 8 May 1837.[2160]

It is possible Abegail had more than three children. In the research of **Kathleen Marie O'DELL Townsley**, a descendent, the Halifax Antiquarian Society and staff member Sheila Bye replied to the Removal Order document, 2 August 1817:

> "... Basically, the Churchwardens and Overseers of the Poor at Ovenden had complained to the 2 local Justices of the Peace that Abigail Clay had come to live in Ovenden without having legal settlement there. People at that time had to have 'legal settlement' in the place where they lived, and if they wanted to move somewhere else they had to apply for settlement there. It was all to do with the Poor Laws, which made the settlement place responsible for providing care for the people living there, if they became ill or unable to provide for themselves, so they were very keen to stop any strays turning up and needing help from the parish purse!
>
> Abigail was 'pregnant with child', and chargeable to Ovenden if she stayed there. Her last lawful place of settlement was Warley, and the Justices were now ordering the Churchwardens and Overseers of the

Poor at Ovenden to convey Abigail to Warley and deliver her..."[2075]

So, how did Abegail buck the era's social norms without any apparent sigma of unmarried motherhood? We may never know. Abegail's reasons or circumstances surrounding her and her children may be lost to history.

Was Abegail "married" to **John FARRAR**[7], son of John FARRAR, born circa 1787 in Yorkshire? Who was baptized in Ovenden, Yorkshire, on 1 April 1787,[8,9] at the South Parade Wesleyan, Zion Chapel (New Methodist Connextion)?

Was John the father of at least two of the known CLAY children? He is listed on Isaac's marriage record as "overseer." "Overseer" in context to this era, would usually mean a person who was a financial governor of the poor and usually with no relation to them. No records can be found, but Isaac, by inference with his mother and the Overseer connotation, was probably in a workhouse at an early age. The Poor Act of 1834 would strongly suggest so.

> "...it shall be lawful for the said Commissioners, by such Rules, Orders, or Regulations as they may think fit, to declare to what Extent and for what Period the Relief to be given to able-bodied Persons or to their Families in any particular Parish or Union may be administered out of the Workhouse of such Parish or Union, by Payments in Money, or with Food or Clothing in Kind..."

The law gave enormous power to the local administrators:

> "...Overseers or Guardians of any: Parish or Union to which such Orders or Regulations shall be addressed or directed, shall, upon Consideration of the special Circumstances of such Parish or Union, or of any Person or Class of Persons therein, *be of opinion [italics, ed.]* that the Application and enforcing of such Orders or Regulations, or of any Part thereof, at the Time or in the Manner prescribed by the said Commissioners, would be inexpedient, it shall be lawful for such Overseers or Guardians to delay the Operation of such Orders or Regulations, or of any Part thereof..."[2065]

Of course, the Act limited application for relief for able-bodied individuals.

There are too many "John Farrar's" born approximately the same year and location to fully discern who is who, although the 1787 baptism (John Farrar, father) is more likely.[8] The non-conformist register has other family names: Horsfel, Clay, Robertshaw, Sutcliff, etc.

Other possible suspects:

- "July 21st [1787] John son of Joseph Farrar and Hannah his Wife of Wakefield was born June 24th and baptized this day by me Wm. Turner Protestant Difsenting Minister."[10] The baptism was performed at the West Gate Presbyterian Church in Wakefield.
- "John [son of] Joshua Farrer [baptized] Dec. 9 [1788]"[11] The baptism was performed at St. Matthew Church of England, Lightcliffe, Yorkshire.
- "John Farrar Son to James Farrar and his wife Judith of Bingley in the parish of Bingley and county of York was born Febr: 17 [1788] and baptized March 10th [1789] By me Thos. Lillie Protestant dissenting Minister] at Bingley"[12] This is at the Bingley Presbyterian or Independant Chapel.
- John Farrar son of Simeon Farrar, born 24 May 1788 at Woodhouse, baptized 22 June 1788, at St. Peter Church, Leeds.[13]

Moreover, there are at least four more similarities living in Yorkshire during this period (1786-1788) – more if you expand the period.

> SIDE NOTE: Possibly, by age and location deduction, he was the John Farrar imprisoned 2 March 1803, at age 14, with two other boys (both 12 years of age) at the West Riding House of Correction for "... felon [illegible] Stealing 1/2 [illegible] Weight of Cocao." Described as "Four feet 6 Brown Brown Eye [illegible]." Behavior in prison was noted as "less than good." They were released on 16 July 1803.[14]

There is no marriage record for John Farrar and Abigel Clay. There is no census with a Farrar surname attached to her. There is no known associations between John Farrar and Abegail Clay other than the instance mentioned of John in Isaac's marriage record. We must reasonably conclude that John Farrar is ***not*** Isaac or Edward Clay's father.

Abegail had the following known children:

2 i. **Isaac CLAY**. Born on 19 October 1806, in Ovenden, Yorkshire. Isaac died in Halifax, Yorkshire, on 13 March 1871; he was 64.

3 ii. **Edward CLAY**. Born in November 1811, in Ovenden, Yorkshire, Edward died in Ovenden, Yorkshire, on 16 January 1812. He was two months old.

4 iii. **Fredric "Fred" CLAY**. Born on 9 October 1826, in Ovenden, Yorkshire. Fredric "Fred" died in Michigan in 1898; he was 71.

Some Early Clay Immigrants to North America

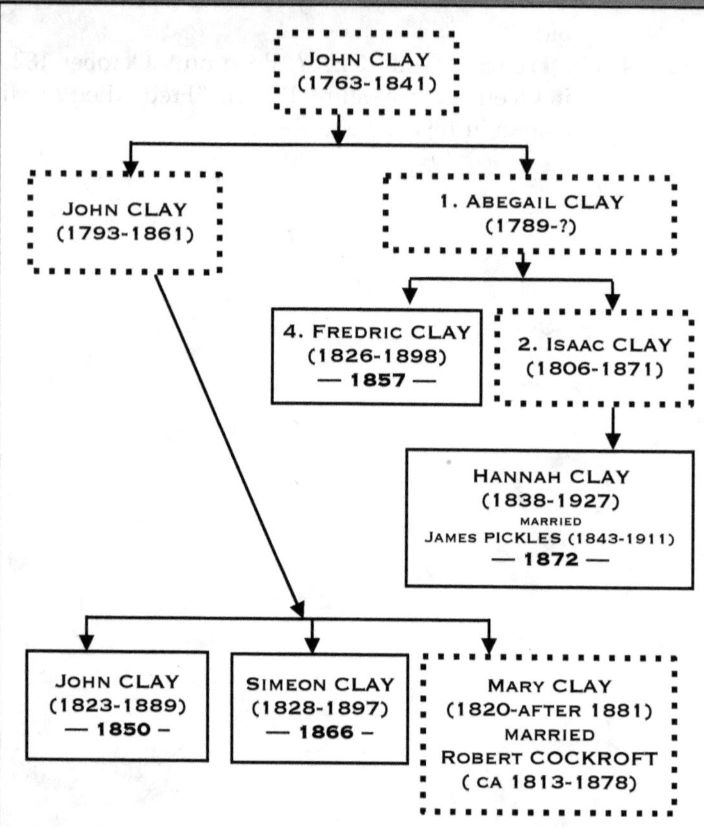

LEGEND: SOLID BOX LINES ARE THE IMMIGRANTS WITH YEAR OF IMMIGRATION; DOTTED BOX LINES ARE NON-IMMIGRANTS.

NOTES:

- **John CLAY** (1823-1889) came alone in **1850**; never married and had no progeny. He was the first of his family to immigrate. (See Appendix: John Clay)
- **Fredric CLAY** (1826-1898), came in **1857** with his wife Ann ROBERTSHAW (1828-1891) and children Sophia (1847-1904), and Simeon A. (1852-1929).
- **Simeon CLAY** (1828-1897), arrived in **1866** with his wife Mary HEAP (1831-1902) and with living children at that time, Harry (1861-1935) and Sarah Ann (1865-1889).
- Fredric's niece, **Hannah CLAY** (1838-1927), immigrated with her husband, James PICKLES, and their son Samuel James (1869-1920) in **1872.**
- Although not chronicled in this book, sons of **Mary CLAY COCKROFT** (1830-after 1881) William COCKROFT (1855-1938) and Levi COCKROFT (1859-1920) both emigrated to American in 1883.

SECOND GENERATION

The Pavior worker. The Book Of Trades or Library of the Useful Arts. *London: Part II, 4th Edition, 1811, page 75; (originally London: published byTabart & Co. August 11, 1804).*

2. Isaac CLAY[15,16] (*Abegail*[1]) was the first known child born to Abegail CLAY, on 19 October 1806, in Ovenden, Yorkshire.[17]

At the age of 11, Isaac was baptized in Ovenden, Yorkshire, on 29 October 1817,[18-20] at the Zion Methodist New Connexion church.[2156]

Isaac died in Halifax, Yorkshire, on 13 March 1871; he was 64,[21,22,2161] at the Union Workshop workhouse. He was buried on 16 March 1871, in West Yorkshire,[23] Calderdale Council, Stoney Royd Cemetery.[2157]

Occupations: Farmers House (1837); Wool Comber (1838); Worster Weaver (1841); Laborer (1851); Street Pavior/Road Setter; Joiner (1871).[24-27] Isaac's occupations varied, but principally he was Pavior — a back-breaking job of tamping down flat stone on roadways, often for 12-hours a day.

The father of Isaac, like his siblings, is unknown. John FARRAR was his "overlooker" (probably meaning "overseer" — a legal term previously discussed) recorded in Issac's marriage record. And as previously discussed paternity is doubtful.[28]

Isaac Clay and his wife, Sally, were not found between the 1851 and 1861 UK censuses. Nor were they found in prison records, in forced transported immigration to another country, workhouse records, or in local newspapers during this period. With the possibility that they may have migrated to America and later returned to England, even the 1860 US census was searched, but nothing was found.

A MAD DOG AND ONE ENGLISHMAN

> "On Friday morning last, [16 April 1869] about seven o'clock, a rabid dog was discovered to be at large at Mount Zion, in Ovenden, in the parish of Halifax. It first worried a hen, and then attacked several persons both in the road and in houses. Isaac Clay, a labourer, beat the animal off with a stone, but it bit Thomas Scott, cab driver, Illingworth, and also a little girl. A woman named Mary Ann Hoyle, who had an infant in her arms, was knocked down by the animal, and severely bit about the head, the baby also being bitten on the leg. At Illingworth Moor it entered a house and bit a cat, but on going out again it was shot by a man named Brown, who, along with others, had pursued it for a considerable distance. In its running about it had bit six other dogs, some of them very

valuable ones, but these were destroyed by their owners, as was also the cat. The persons bitten all sought medical aid at once, some of them going to Colne to a medical man who has some repute for a cure for such cases."[29,30,31]

Another newspaper implied Isaac may have been bitten:

"Mad Dog Near Halifax. - Yesterday (Friday) morning, about seven o'clock, a strange dog, in a rabid state, made its appearance at Ovenden, near Halifax. It attacked a labourer on the road, named Isaac Clay, but he beat it off."[32]

These sparse but enlightening news articles seemingly verify an old family legend.

According to his death certificate, Isaac died of "Pneumonia Mitral disease of Heart Certified." Unaware of the rabies story in the newspapers and having done no research, the rabies tale was conveyed to Vena Emily Kilbourne Doyle (great-granddaughter of Isaac), who heard it from "grandma Clay" (Isaac's daughter), who claimed her father "died of rabies." For decades, the anecdote was tucked away as a dusty curio, only to come to light. Perhaps they mixed it up, but the coincidence is too rare to dismiss.

The pathogenesis of rabies is from 10 days to about 24 months, and Isaac died 23 months after the incident. His death may have been indeed caused by a heart condition, but speculatively the secondary cause may have been rabies. Rabies was a terrifying, contagious, ultimately fatal disease, and keeping a lid on this information in a hospital ward of people was important. "A serious epidemic of Smallpox and Typhus Fever broke out in 1871-2,"[33] but authorities were knowledgeable about smallpox and typhus and would have mentioned it in his death record.

The accounts in the newspapers are probably accurate because of the known facts of the area he lived in, the same period, and the same occupation he engaged in. At his death in March 1871, Isaac was 64 years old, a pauper, unable to work and impoverished. As he sickened, he was sent to the Halifax Union workhouse and died there. Wife Sally probably went to live with their only child, Hannah (#5).

Isaac's hospitalization at the Halifax workhouse was better than most:

"In 1869-70, two large 3-Storey Infirmary Pavilions were erected at the rear of the main buildings at a

Ship Tripoli *of the Cunard Line. – Image from www.norwayheritage.com, Berge Solem, webmaster.*

cost of £30,000. These wards were at that period 'the last word' in Hospital construction. They did splendid work for the suffering poor..."[34]

Isaac's death was not in vain. It was probably one factor that spurred the immigration of daughter Hannah Clay and husband James Pickles to America, who arrived in Boston on 14 March 1872, aboard the ship *Tripoli* a year after his death. James's brother, Emmanuel "Manny" Pickles, and his wife, Sarah *nee* BAGULEY, accompanied them. Other Pickles and Clay kin followed in the decades later. Hannah's uncle Fred Clay's 1857 immigration was probably another reason and deciding factor.

THE OTHER ISAAC CLAY. There are numerous references in the West Yorkshire Electoral Registers to "Isaac Clay Sr." and "Isaac Clay Jr." in the Soothill Upper, near the Dewsbury area of Halifax. However, analysis concludes they are from a different Clay family.

On 17 December 1837, when Isaac was 31, he married **Sally "Sarah" TIDSWELL**[35-38], daughter of Jonathan TIDSWELL (1785-1848) and Hannah TETLAW (1791-?), in Halifax, Yorkshire,[39-43] at the Established Parish Church, by William Rush-

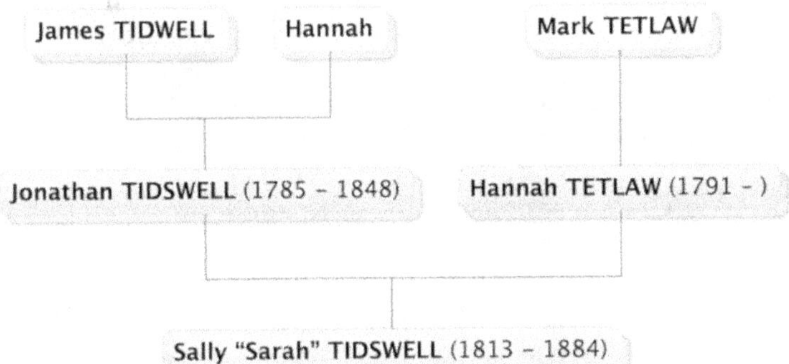

worth. At the time Isaac was residing in Sowerby.[28]

The marriage record shows her first name as "Sarah."[*,2059] She had been residing in Ovenden and was 24 years old.[28]

She was born on 17 March 1813, in Ovenden, Yorkshire,[44,45] and was baptized in Ovenden, on 4 April 1813,[46-49] at the Zion Methodist New Connexion; Zion Chapel.

---

[*] "Sally" is sobriquet for Sarah and used interchangeably.

Sally died in Ionia County, Michigan, on 13 January 1884; she was 70.[50]

Sally's Occupations: Worsted Weaver (1837, 1851); Loom Weaver (1871).[51,52]

In her youth, Sally made a tapestry typical of the young women of the era. It is currently in possession of great-great granddaughter Patricia Marie (*nee* Lang) Sanders.

Did Isaac and Sally have more than one child besides Hannah? It would seem likely over a marriage of 33 years in the era of no reputable methods of birth control. However, nothing was found in the GRO records searched from 1839 to the Census of 1851.

After her husband Isaac's death, Sally emigrated to the US between 1872 and 1880. In the 1880 US census, she lived with her daughter's family. It was always thought she came with her daughter, Hannah, and husband, James Pickles, in their migration in 1872, but there is no record.

> "Saturday, the 17th of March, [1883] being the seventieth birthday of Mrs. Sally Clay, a goodly number of friends and relatives assembled at the residence of Fred. Clay, of South Hamlin, and gave Mrs. Clay a very pleasant surprise. Twenty-eight aged people were present whose united ages were 1,553 years, making an average of nearly fifty-five years, and six months, the oldest being seventy-seven, and the youngest, thirty-five.
>
> The following presents were made:
> Easy chair - Mr. and Mrs. A. Leighton,
> Two silver dollars - Mr. John Clay,
> One silver dollar - Mrs. H. Knapp,
> Dress pattern - Mr. F. A. Clay,
> Piece Factory - Mrs. G. W. Cowan,
> Fichae - Mr. Fred. Clay,
> Necktie and apron - S. Pickles,
> Handkerchief - Mrs. H. Seeley,
> Hose and apron - Mrs. Mary Clay,
> Easy chair - Mr. and Mrs. T. H. Cowan, R. Hadley, O. Hadley, W. B. Van Allen, W. W. Reynolds, H. Seeley, H. Knapp, W. W. Wilson.
>
> After the presentations of gifts, all enjoyed a bountiful repast, at which a teacup and saucer over a hundred years old, were used by Mrs. A. Leighton.
>
> In the evening some fifteen or twenty young people had a very pleasant time singing, playing, and

listening to a very interesting declamation by Mr. W. B. Van Allen."[2155]

It is interesting to see the mixing of the two families: Clay and Pickles, in the above article. "Mr. John Clay" was Sally's first cousin (1823-1889); "Mrs. H. Knapp" was Ann Pickles (1840-1901), married to Heman Knapp, no relation other than being the brother of James who was married to Sally's daughter Hannah Clay (1838-1927); "Mr. F. A. Clay" (not identified); "Mrs. G. W. Cowen," or Sophia Robertshaw Clay was married to George W. Cowan and daughter of Ann Robertshaw previously married to a "Sim Clay," of unknown relationship; "Mr. Fred. Clay" (1825-1898) her brother; "S. Pickles" - probably Samuel Pickles (1857-1925) no relation other than being the brother of James who was married to Sally's daughter Hannah Clay; and "Mrs. Mary Clay" (unknown).

Isaac and Sally had one child:

5 i. **Hannah ("Annie") CLAY**. Born on 30 January 1838, in Brockholes, Ovenden, Halifax, Yorkshire. Hannah died in Belding, Ionia County, Michigan, on 30 May 1927; she was 89.

---

3. Edward CLAY (*Abegail*[1]) was the second child of Abegail, born in November 1811 in Ovenden, Yorkshire.[53]

Edward was baptized in Ovenden, Yorkshire, on 20 December 1811,[54,55,56] at the Zion Chapel, Methodist New Connextion. He died in Ovenden, on 16 January 1812, age two months old.[57] Buried on 19 January 1812, in Illingworth, Yorkshire,[58-61] at Saint Mary the Virgin Churchyard. His father is also unnamed in the church record.

---

4. Fredric "Fred" CLAY[62-67] (*Abegail*[1]) was born on 9 October 1826 in Ovenden, Yorkshire.[68]

Fred is the third child of Abegail and a pivotal individual in the future of the family. Fred was baptized in Ovenden, Yorkshire, on 21 February 1827,[69,70] at the Zion Chapel, Methodist New Connextion. He died in Hamilin Township, Eaton County, Michigan 16 July 1898 at age 71.[71] Buried in Springport, Jackson County, Michigan, at Griffith Cemetery.[72]

Again, like his siblings, his father is not listed in birth, baptismal or marriage records.

But the father of Fredric could well possibly be James SMITH, a weaver, named in a Filiation Order of a 9-week-old out-of-wedlock child of Abegail Clay living in Ovenden. Smith had to pay for the birth expenses, the month's lying-in, and maintenance. "Abigail herself had to pay 1/6 a week to the Church Wardens and Overseers of the Poor of Ovenden, from the child's birth for as long as it was chargeable to Ovenden. [i.e. for as long as they were providing money to keep it before it was old enough to work - maybe 4 or 5 years old at that time!]." The Filiation order of 12 December 1826 deposed James Smith to pay for the birth expenses, the month's lying in, and maintenance:

	£	s	d
p. Month	1	10	…
Expences & Orders	…	14	…
5 Weeks	…	7	6

pd p. week 1/6 [one shilling and 6 pence][2077]

Fred's occupations: Power Loom Weaver Worster (1841, 1851); Weaver (1852, 1880); Railway Porter (1854, 1857); Laborer (1857, 1860); Farmer (1870).[73-77]

Fredric is the first of this branch of the family to immigrate to America, with wife Ann, and children Sophia, age 9; and Simon, age 5; on 17 November 1857 aboard the ship *Ellen Austin* to Castle Garden, New York.[78] (Sophia was a daughter of Ann from a previous relationship to a "Sim Clay" of another Clay family not be identified.)

The *Ellen Austin* later gained notoriety when it was found in 1881 in the dreaded Bermuda Triangle, abandoned with no crew or passengers. Rather than a mythical "ghost ship," abandonment was probably "... that the officers of the *Ellen Austin* have a very unenviable notoriety for alleged cruelty to their men, and that the vessel has scarcely ever entered port without complaints being made in our Police Courts against them for cruel and inhuman treatment."[2061]

Hmm, so the crew probably mutinied and the passengers became collateral damage!

What led Fredric to immigrate? There are probably a host of reasons. Immigration in the nineteenth century was perilous. It usually was a one-way trip of no return and a decision never taken lightly. Financial reasons were paramount, but it probably was also religion for Fredric and later by his niece, Hannah Clay-Pickles.

Fredric filed an Intention to become a US citizen on 11 April 1868.[2168]

> **NOTE**: Fred's first cousin, John CLAY (1823-1889), was actually the first of this Clay clan known to have migrated in 1850 to Michigan. See **APPENDIX: JOHN C. CLAY, EARLY TO AMERICA** for his story.

Death was approaching Fred's door in June 1898: "Fred Clay is still quite low with heart trouble, his advanced aged lessons the chances for his recovery."[2107]

> *Obituary*: "Fred Clay was born in Yorkshire, England, October 15, 1826, in November 1857 he, with his wife and two children, came to America, and located in Eaton County, Mich. In 1861 he moved to the township of Springport, Jackson Co., residing there nine years, removing back into Eaton Co., in 1879, where he has since lived until his death, which occurred at his home in Hamlin, Saturday, July 16, 1898. The funeral was held at the Griffith church, Jul 17. Rev. Brown officiating and the remains laid to rest in the Griffith cemetery. Five children are left to mourn their loss. Mrs. G. W. Cowan, S. A. Clay, of Eaton Rapids; T. A. Clay, C. M. Clay, Springport and F. H. Clay of Ypsilanti."[2078]

> *Obituary*: "Fred Clay, an old resident of this vicinity, died at his home last Saturday morning of heart disease. Mr. Clay was a man of cheerful disposition and well liked by all who knew him. The funeral was held at the church Sunday afternoon."[2079]

> "Frank Clay, of Ypsilanti, was in the city over Sunday, called here by the death of his father, Frederick Clay."[2080]

On 11 July 1852, when Fred was 25, he married **Ann ROBERTSHAW**[79-83], daughter of Jonathan ROBERTSHAW (ca1806-?) and Tabitha "Dolly" WAINWRIGHT (ca1805-?), in Halifax, Yorkshire,[84,85] Parish of Halifax. She was born on 28 April 1828, in England,[86] and was baptized in Wortley, Yorkshire, on 25 May 1828,[87,88] at Saint John the Evangelist Church. She died in Hamlin Township, Eaton County, Michigan, on 27 January 1891; she was 62.[89] Buried in Springport, Jackson County, Michigan;[90] at Griffith Cemetery.
Occupation: Linen Weaver (1851).[91]

> *Obituary*: "CLAY.--At her home in Hamlin, Mrs. Ann Clay, wife of Fred Clay, on Tuesday, January 27,

1891, at the age of 62 years. Mrs. Clay was born in Yorkshire, England, on December 6, 1828 [sic] and with her husband removed to this country, locating near the place where she died, 33 years ago. She leaves a husband and five children, Mrs. Geo. W. Cowan, Simeon A., Thomas A., Cassius M., and Frank H. Clay to mourn her loss.

Mrs. Clay was in good health until last Saturday, when she was taken with pneumonia. On Saturday night she had a physician for the first time, but she failed rapidly and died within three days. The pneumonia was the result of a severe attack of the grippe. Her funeral was held yesterday from the Griffith church, the services being conducted by Rev. A. M. Griffith. Mrs. Clay was a woman beloved by all who knew her. To the sick and needy she was always a friend and a comforter. To her husband she was a helpful wife, and to her children a good adviser."[2081]

Obituary: "In the death of Ms. Fred Clay, society loses a useful member. She was a friend in need ever ready and willing to assist a neighbor in trouble. Kind and unassuming she won many warm friends. Her family mourns the loss of a beloved wife and devoted mother. As neighbors and friends, we wish to extend our kindly sympathies to those sorrow stricken hearts. It was indeed a touching scene, and one in which every tender chord vibrated in sympathy with those four heroic sons, who tenderly bore and carefully lowered to last their resting place, the earthly remains of their beloved mother."[2082]

Fredric and Ann had the following children:

6 i. **Simeon A. CLAY**. Born on 13 August 1852, in Ovenden, Halifax, Yorkshire. He died in Parma Township, Jackson County, Michigan, on 4 December 1929; he was 77.

7 ii. **John CLAY**. Born on 12 October 1854, in Bradford And North Bierley, Yorkshire.

8 iii. **Wright CLAY**. Born on 8 September 1856, in Halifax, Yorkshire, Wright died in Halifax, Yorkshire, on 1 September 1857, at Stafford House. He was just shy of a year old when he died.

9 iv. **Thomas Albert CLAY**. Born on 1 January 1859, in Barry County, Michigan. Thomas died in Friendship Township, Emmet County, Michigan, on 19 August 1921; he was 62.

10 v. **Cassius Milo CLAY**. Born on 27 March 1861, in Hamlin Township, Eaton County, Michigan. Cassius died in Lansing, Ingham County, Michigan, on 14 October 1939; he was 78.

11 vi. **Julia A. CLAY**. Born in 1862, Julia died in 1866; she was 4.

12 vii. **Frank Henry CLAY**. Born on 7 December 1864, in Eaton Rapids, Eaton County, Michigan. Frank died in Kalamazoo, Kalamazoo County, Michigan, on 4 March 1944; he was 79.

THIRD GENERATION

5. Hannah "Annie" CLAY[92-100] (*Isaac*[2], *Abegail*[1]).

Hannah* was born on 30 January 1838, in Brockholes, Ovenden, Halifax, Yorkshire.[101-103] She died in Belding, Ionia County, Michigan, on 30 May 1927; she was 89.[104,105]

She was buried on 1 June 1927, in Douglass Township, Montcalm County, Michigan,[106] at the Entrican Cemetery.

Religion: Methodist/Seventh Day Adventist.

Occupations: Nurse (1851); Farmers Wife (1871).[107,108]

She was also known as "Little Grandma" because she was under five feet tall, according to granddaughter Kathryn Angeline Kilbourne Lang who anecdotally remembers:

> "After we did our chores, Little Grandma would take us children to a nearby river during the summer months and dispense hard candy out of her huge pockets – I remember those big pockets. It was a real treat back then! I sooooo looked forward going to the river with her."

On 18 November 1866, when Hannah was 28, she married **James PICKLES**,[109-116,2158] son of John PICKLES (1816-1890) and Hannah HORSFIELD (1815-1889), in Halifax, Yorkshire,[117-119] at the South Parade Wesleyan Methodist Church.

The marriage of Hannah and James is memorialized in the local newspaper: "On Sunday, at South-parade Chapel, Halifax, by the Rev. J. A. Macdonald, Mr. James Pickles, carpet weaver, Warley, to Miss H. Clay, of Halifax."[144]

James was born on 31 May 1843 in Warley; Roils Head, Yorkshire,[120-123] and baptized in Luddenden, Yorkshire, 5 October 1843,[124-126] at the Parish of Halifax, Chapelry of Luddenden; Saint Mary's.

James died in Douglass Township, Montcalm County, Michigan, on 8 February 1911; he was 67.[127-129] He was buried on 10 February 1911 in Douglass Township, Montcalm County, Michigan,[130] at Entrican Cemetery; Lot 108, space 4.

Occupations: Wool Comber (1851); Worsted Factory Hand (1861); Carpet Weaver (1866, 1869, 1871); Laborer (1900, 1877, 1903); Farmer (1871, 1880, 1899; 1910, 1911). [131-138]

Religion: Methodist.

* "Annie" was a sobriquet she used.

James Pickles family: *(left-to-right)* **5**. *Hannah ("Annie" or "Little Grandma") CLAY; son* **13**. *Samuel James PICKLES; husband James PICKLES; sitting, front: young daughter* **14**. *Amelia Hannah Elizabeth "Minnie" PICKLES ("Grandma Kilbourne"). – photograph from the late 1880s.*

An interesting question came up decades ago about why Hannah crossed her fingers in the photograph. Was she wishing for good luck or just holding her clothing?

[See **PART 2: MADE OF PICKLES,** for his pedigree.]

This may be the "James Pickles," a bobbin-turner, who was imprisoned on 7 August 1867, at hard labor for perjury for 12 months for swearing falsely at Todmorden, 20 June 1867.[139-140]

Aside from location and approximate birth year, there is no hard evidence that this is "our" James Pickles. The newspapers and prison records give only circumstantial evidence. Sentenced to 12 months imprisonment on 20 June 1867, James's estimated release from prison was June-August 1868.

HYPOTHESIS: Right after marriage, couples of that era usually commenced having children. No children were born between late 1867 and late 1868 for James and Hannah, suggesting the couple's separation for twelve months. (The oldest known child, Samuel James, would have been conceived approximately in September 1868.) There is also in the local newspapers a "James Pickles" around the same age and time frame who was in constant trouble with the law from public drunkness and general rowdiness typical of a rudderless male of the times. Nevertheless, we cannot be positive that his identity is "our" James portrayed here. [See **APPENDIX: A ROWDY JAMES.**]

No doubt the death of Hannah's father, Isaac Clay in 1871 was one impetus for emigration out of England. James and wife Hannah, with son Samuel, and James' brother Emmanuel and wife Sarah, arrived from Liverpool, England to Boston, Massachusetts, on 14 March 1872, aboard the ship *Tripoli* of the Cunard Line.[141-143] (Later, on 17 May 1872 the ship was wrecked on Tuskar Rock, St. George's channel, Ireland, with no lives lost. It crammed-in 50 first class and 650 third class passengers into 292.5 x 38.2 feet of space.)[2060]

An anecdote about James Pickles from Vena Emily Kilbourne Doyle (granddaughter) remarked to the author in the 1970s that "Grandpa hated farming, but he couldn't find much else to do where they lived at. He did go to church, but mostly to keep grandma happy." According to census records, they were never wealthy, and, in later years, he and Hannah were boarders with his brother Samuel in the 1900 census.

James and Hannah had the following children:

13 i. **Samuel James PICKLES/PICKELL**. Born on 14 April 1869, in Halifax, Yorkshire. Samuel died in Grand Rapids, Kent County, Michigan, on 13 April 1920; he was 50.

14 ii. **Amelia Hannah Elizabeth "Minnie" PICKLES**. Born on 10 October 1877, in Hamlin Township, Eaton County, Michigan. Amelia died in Sheridan, Montcalm County, Michigan, on 13 January 1968; she was 90.

15 iii. **Fred PICKLES**. Born on 19 February 1881, in Hamlin Township, Eaton County, Michigan. Fred died in Hamlin Township, Eaton County, Michigan, on 24 February 1881, from "inflammation of Lungs" — he was five days old.

6. Simeon A. CLAY[145-154] (*Fredric*[2], *Abegail*[1]).

6. Simeon A. Clay and wife Lydia Ann Mathias.
– Photograph courtesy of Kathleen Marie O'Dell Townsley.

Born on 13 August 1852, in Ovenden, Halifax, Yorkshire,[155-157] and at the age of 4, Simeon was baptized in Illingworth, Yorkshire, on 4 January 1857,[158] at Saint Mary Church.

Simeon died in Parma Township, Jackson County, Michigan, on 4 December 1929; he was 77.[159-161] He was buried in Sandstone Township, Jackson County, Michigan,[162] at Chapel Cemetery.

Occupations: Farmer (1875-1910); Machinist (1918); Thrashing Machine (1920).[134,163-166]

He immigrated to the US, with his parents and sister Sophia, age 9: Simon, age 5; 17 November 1857 aboard the *Ellen Austin* to Castle Garden, New York.[78,167]

Circa 1875, when Simeon was 22, he first married **Lydia Ann MATHIAS,**[168-171] daughter of Lewis MATHIAS and Lydia HERB.[172] She was born on 20 June 1852, in Maryland,[173] and died at Mercy Hospital in Jackson, Jackson County, Michigan, on 21 December 1917; she was 65.[174] Buried on 23 December 1917, in Sandstone Township, Jackson County, Michigan,[175] Chapel Cemetery.

Standing in back, left to right: ***16****. Malcom and* ***17****. Fred with* ***18****. Mary Alice seated between them. Seated: Lydia Ann MATHIAS,* ***19****. "Birdie" Mabel (holding a doll),* ***6****. Simeon CLAY and* ***20****. LeRoy. – Photograph courtesy of Tammie Newhouse, ca. 1890s.*

Obituaries: "Mrs. Simeon Clay, a former well known resident of this community, died Sunday at her home in Parma, where she had resided for some time, and the funeral services were held Wednesday. William Mathias, of this city, a brother to Mrs. Clay, went to Parma to attend the funeral."[176]

"William Matthias, of this city, has been called to Parma to attend the funeral of his sister, Mrs. Simeon Clay, a former well known resident of this community."[177]

"Mrs. Lydia Ann Clay, wife of Simeon A. Clay of Parma, passed away at Mercy hospital Friday at 8 a.m., aged 65 years, 6 months. There survive her a husband, three sons, Malcolm of Onondaga, Fred of Charlotte, and Roy Clay, 326 North Gorham street; and two daughters, Mrs. Alice Krugman and Mrs. Mabel Zantop of Parma.

The funeral will be held at the home in Parma Sunday afternoon; interment at the Chapel cemetery." [178]

Simeon and Lydia had the following children:

16 i. **Malcolm J. CLAY**. Born on 29 July 1875, in Hamlin Township, Eaton County, Michigan. Malcolm died in Onondaga, Ingham County, Michigan, on 6 April 1949; he was 73.

17 ii. **Fred Henry CLAY**. Born on 5 October 1876, in Hamlin Township, Eaton County, Michigan. Fred died in Charlotte, Eaton County, on 15 April 1960; he was 83.

18 iii. **Mary Alice CLAY**. Born on 19 October 1879, in Hamlin Township, Eaton County, Michigan. Mary died in 1954; she was 74.

19 iv. **Mabel "Birdie" CLAY**. Born on 17 November 1884, in Hamlin Township, Eaton County, Michigan. Birdie died in Battle Creek, Calhoun County, Michigan, on 29 March 1978; she was 93.

20 v. **Le Roy CLAY**. Born on 17 December 1889, in Hamlin Township, Eaton County, Michigan. Le Roy died in March 1964; he was 74.

On 19 September 1918, when Simeon was 66, he second married **Emma E. SIMMONS**,[153,179,180] daughter of Tillness SIMMONS and Sarah Jane SPENCER, in Battle Creek, Calhoun County, Michigan.[181] She was born on 4 December 1865, in Fredonia, Calhoun County, Michigan. Emma died in Battle Creek, Calhoun County, Michigan, on 12 December 1944; she was 79.[182] Buried on 14 December 1944, in Battle Creek, Calhoun County, Michigan,[183] Oak Hill Cemetery.

Occupation: Domestic (1918).

They were divorced on 19 December 1921, in Battle Creek, Calhoun County, Michigan.[184] She remarried to John J. Thunder.

Obituary: "Mrs. Emma Thunder, 79, widow of John J. Thunder, died at the home of her son, Emory, of 188 North Twenty-first street, at 12:30 a. m. today.

She had been in failing health five years. She was born Dec. 4. 1865, in Fredonia township, the daughter of Mr. and Mrs. Tillness Simmons, and lived in this community all her life, residing in Battle Creek for the last 49 years. Her husband, who died in 1913, was a carpenter and contractor and was in charge of building the Grand Trunk railroad depot and the First Methodist church. Besides her son, she leaves a daughter, Mrs. Doris L. Marshall [sic] of 77 North LaVista boulevard, and a sister, Mrs Carrie Andrews of Homer."[185]

Simeon and Emma had no children.

On 28 January 1922, when Simeon was 69, he third married **Mary LEWIS** in Jackson, Jackson County, Michigan,[186] by F. S. Kenney, Methodist Episcopal Minister. She was born circa 1860 in Washington. Simeon and Mary had no children.

---

7. John CLAY[187] (*Fredric*[2], *Abegail*[1]).

Born on 12 October 1854, in Bradford And North Bierley, Yorkshire.[188,189]

So why is he not found on the immigration list like his parents and siblings? Was he too young (age 3)? He is not found in US 1860 and UK 1861 censuses, and no English death record. He's probably *not* the "John Clay" listed on the same page as the James Pickles family on the 1880 census as a 55-year-old farmer living with a servant "Lester Cole."[190] And probably *not* the "John Clay Jr." of Oneida, murder victim of 19 May 1887 near Grand Ledge, who died 19 May 1887 (shot 13 May 1887), because his tombstone is with another unrelated Clay family.

---

8. Wright CLAY (*Fredric*[2], *Abegail*[1]).

Born on 8 September 1856, in Halifax, Yorkshire.[191,192]

Wright was baptized in Illingworth, Yorkshire, on 4 January 1857,[193] at Saint Mary Church. Wright died at Stafford House, in Halifax, Yorkshire, on 1 September 1857; he was short of one year of age.[194,195]

9. Thomas Albert CLAY[196-201] (*Fredric*[2], *Abegail*[1]).

Thomas was born on 1 January 1859, in Barry County, Michigan [from death record, and implied in the 1860 census].

Thomas died in Friendship Township, Emmet County, Michigan, on 19 August 1921; he was 62.[202] Buried on 22 August 1921 in Friendship Township, Emmet County, Michigan,[203] at Friendship Cemetery.

Occupations: Servant (1880); Clerk (1885);[2083-2084] Plumber (1888); Deputy Sheriff (1896); Carpenter (1900, 1910, 1916, 1921); Farmer (1920).[204-208]

> "Albion Bartlett and Thomas A. Clay got into an altercation, Wednesday morning, and finally concluded with a knockdown argument. Bartlet had Clay arrested for assault and battery, but the matter was finally settled before Justice Hosler, both men paying an equal share of the costs."[2088]
>
> "Thomas A. Clay has again been appointed deputy sheriff for the township."[2089] There are numerous notices of arrest by Sheriff Clay in the local newspapers. At times he is referred to as the "Marshall."
>
> *Obituary*: "C. M. [Cassius M., his brother] Clay, 521 William st., was called to Harbor Springs, Saturday, by the death of his brother, Thomas Clay. The deceased was formerly a resident of Springport."[209]
>
> *Obituary*: "Whereas, It has pleased the Grand Warden of Heaven, in His infinite wisdom to call our brother, Thomas A. Clay, from his labors on earth to everlasting refreshment in the Celestial Lodge above.
>
> Resolved. That while we bow in submission to the Divine edict our hearts are heavy with sorrow and our sincere sympathy is hereby extended to his wisdom."[2090]

On 14 November 1883, when Thomas was 24, he first married **Sarah Jane "Jennie" DOAK,**[210-212] daughter of Charles R. DOAK and Mary Ann WELLINGTON, in Springport, Jackson County, Michigan,[213] by E. D. Bacon, Minister of the Gospel; witnessed by Cassius M. Clay, his brother.

Jennie was born on 14 June 1853, in Hanover Township, Jackson County, Michigan. [The tombstone says 1852; the marriage record suggests 1855; the death record is used here.]

Jennie died in Springport, Jackson County, Michigan, on 15 January 1915; she was 61.[214] Buried on 18 January 1915 in

Springport, Jackson County, Michigan,[215] at the Springport Cemetery.

Her occupation: Farmer (1894).[216]

They had no children.

Obituary: "The death of Mrs. Jennie Clay occured [sic] last Friday morning. Though she had been in very poor health for a long time, the complications following an accident of a few weeks ago, hastened her death.

The funeral was held Monday afternoon [18 January 1915] from the house. Rev. Stoffe preached the funeral sermon and the O. E. S. of which order the deceased was a charter member, conducted the burial services.

Jennie Doak was born in Hanover township, June 14, 1853. In early childhood she moved with her parents to Springport township, where most of her life was spent.

On August 15, 1871, she was united in marriage to Albion Bartlet of Eaton township. To this union was born one son, Fred I. Bartlet, whose death preceeded [sic] his mother's by but a few months.

On November 14th, 1883 she was married to Thomas A. Clay of Springport, this village being her home the greater part of her life.

For many years a sufferer, never enjoying the best of health in her later life, she yet found time to visit her relatives and friends, always enjoying their company and keenly interest in the daily life about her.

As such she will be greatly missed by those who loved her.

About the 1st of December she fell and broke her leg, the complications resulting hastening her death, which occured [sic] January 15, 1915 [illegible] age of 61 years, seven months, and 21 days.

Besides the relatives mentioned she is survived by three grand children a daughter and two sons of the late Mr. Bartlet."[2086]

Obituary: "Whereas, The Angel of Death has again entered our Chapter and taken from us our beloved sister, Jennie Clay, a charter member, who on Jan. 15, 1915, finished her journey through the labyrinth of human life, and entered the Grand Chapter on High. Again the golden chain has been broken, the golden sheaves are being garnered for the Master's use, but we humbly bow in submission to the will of our Heavenly Father, knowing that 'He doeth all things well.'"[2087]

On 30 January 1916, when Thomas was 57, he second married **Cora Elizabeth SMITH,**[217] daughter of Lorenzo N. SMITH and Bessie Stranger BROOKING, in Friendship Township, Emmet County, Michigan,[218] by the Rev. Geo. A. Weaver.

She was born on 14 January 1878, in North Adams, Hillsdale County, Michigan and died in Jefferson Township, Hillsdale County, on 5 July 1942; she was 64.[219] Buried on 9 July 1942, in Osseo, Hillsdale County,[220] East Hill Cemetery.

They also had no known children.

10. Cassius Milo CLAY[221-228,180] (*Fredric*[2], *Abegail*[1]).

Born on 27 March 1861, in Hamlin Township, Eaton County, Michigan, Cassius died at 521 William Street, Lansing, Ingham County, Michigan, on 14 October 1939; he was 78.[229] Buried on 16 October 1939 in Lansing, Ingham County, Michigan,[230] at Mount Hope Cemetery.

Occupations: Servant (1880); Farmer (1888, 1892, 1907); Day Laborer (1900); Oldsmobile Machinist (1910); Reo Motor Company (1916); Welfare Worker (1920); Automobile Factory Safety Man (1930); Reo Works (1922-1925, 1927, 1929-32); Public Works Administration (1934).[204,231-248]

Religion: Methodist.

***10**. Cassius Milo Clay*
Photograph courtesy Kathleen Marie O'Dell Townsley.

Obituary: "Cassius M. Clay, 78, of 521 William street, died at the residence Saturday morning. He was born March 27, 1861 in Hamlin township. Eaton county, and was married to Ella Schutt in Jackson county on November 14, 1888.

Besides the widow, he is survived by one son, Milo S. Clay of Dertoit, [sic] two daughters, Mrs. Mildred Fremody of Philadelphia, Pa., and Mrs. Orpha Orrison of Marshall; 10 grandchildren; five great-grandchildren, and one brother, Frank Clay of Kalamazoo. Mr. Clay was a member of the Main street Methodist church. Funeral services will be held at the Estes-Leadley funeral home Monday at 3 o'clock, the Rev. Joseph Dibley officiating. Interment will be in Mt. Hope cemetery."[249]

On 14 November 1888, when Cassius was 27, he married **Ella SCHUTT,**[250-259,180,2092] daughter of Milo SCHUTT and Dorcas L. GODFREY, in Tompkins Township, Jackson County, Michigan.[260,2091]

Ella was born in November 1865, in Michigan, and died in Birmingham, Oakland County, Michigan, on 16 May 1953; she was 87. Buried on 19 May 1953, in Lansing, Ingham County, Michigan,[261] at Mount Hope Cemetery.

Obituary: "Mrs. Ella Clay, 87, widow of Cassius M. Clay, died Saturday morning at the home of her daughter, Mrs. Howard E. Fremody at Birmingham. Other survivors are a daughter, Mrs. Jesse Orrison of Marshall and a son, Milo S. Clay of Clearwater, Fla. Funeral services will be held at Estes-Leadley Colonial chapel at 1 p. m. Tuesday.

Funeral services for Mrs. Ella Clay, former Lansing resident who died Saturday morning at Birmingham, will he held at the Estes-Leadley Colonial Chanel at 1 o'clock Tuesday. Interment will lie in Mt. Hope cemetery. Pallbearers will be Harold Schmidtman. Bruce Schmidtman, Guilford Orrison. Howard

Ella Schutt Clay
Photograph courtesy Kathleen Marie O'Dell Townsley.

Orrison, N. Keith Orrison and Jack D. Orrison."[262]

Cassius and Ella had the following children:

21 i. **Mildred L. Irene CLAY**. Born on 8 March 1890, in Parma Township, Jackson County, Michigan. Mildred died in Tarpon Springs, Pinellas County, Florida, on 31 October 1969; she was 79.

22 ii. **Orpha Zella CLAY**. Born on 10 July 1892, in Springport, Jackson County, Michigan. Orpha died in Battle Creek, Calhoun County, Michigan, on 14 May 1968; she was 75.

23 iii. **Milo Schutt CLAY**. Born on 27 November 1895, in Springport, Jackson County, Michigan. Milo died in Highlands County, Florida, on 10 March 1976; he was 80.

11. Julia A. CLAY[263] (*Fredric*[2], *Abegail*[1]).

Born in 1862, Julia died in 1866; she was four years old. Buried in Springport, Jackson County, Michigan,[264] at Griffith Cemetery.

12. Frank Henry CLAY[265-274] (*Fredric*[2], *Abegail*[1]).

Born on 7 December 1864, in Eaton Rapids, Eaton County, Michigan.[275] Frank died at the State Hospital in Kalamazoo, Kalamazoo County, Michigan, on 4 March 1944; he was 79.[276,277] Buried on 7 March 1944, in Springport, Jackson County, Michigan,[278] at Springport Cemetery.

Occupations: Salesman (1900); Commercial Travel Buggies (1910); Travel Agent (1887, 1897, 1910-11, 1913-14); Proprietor (1915-17, 1919, 1921, 1929, 1931, 1939); Auto Supply Wholesale Dealer (1920, 1924, 1926-27, 1944); Whole Merchant Radios (1930-31, 1935, 1937); General Work (1940).[279-310]

> *Obituary*: "KALAMAZOO - AP - Frank H. Clay, a past potentate of Saladin shrine and a Mason for 56 years, died at his home here after an illness of several years. He was his radio company's first distributor in the United States. He was born in Otter Creek 79 years ago."[311]

On 2 April 1890, when Frank was 25, he first married **Cora E. RODGERS**,[267,312] daughter of Thomas J. RODGERS and Elizabeth SNYDER, in Springport, Jackson County,

Michigan.[313] She was born in 1868 in Ohio, and died at 202 Parsons Street in Ypsilanti, Washtenaw County, Michigan, on 18 May 1899; she was 31.[314,315] Buried on 19 May 1899, in Springport, Jackson County, Michigan,[316] at Springport Cemetery.

Frank and Cora had the following children:

24 i. **Edith Irene CLAY**. Born on 3 October 1891, in Albion, Calhoun County, Michigan. Edith died in Kalamazoo, Kalamazoo County, Michigan, on 3 September 1986; she was 94.

25 ii. **Eldon Rodgers CLAY**. Born on 12 September 1894, in Springport, Jackson County, Michigan. Eldon died in Kandiyohi County, Minnesota, on 27 April 1975; he was 80.

On 12 June 1901, when Frank was 36, he second married **Ethel C. ROBERTS,**[317-325] daughter of Orlo N. ROBERTS and Louise ROBINSON, in Colorado Springs, El Paso County, Colorado,[326] by Benjamin Brewster, Minister.

She was born on 28 October 1873, in Otto, Cattaraugus County, New York. Ethel died at 508 Village Street, in Springport, Jackson County, Michigan, on 10 November 1959; she was 86.[327,328] Buried on 13 November 1959 in Springport, Jackson County, Michigan,[329] at Springport Cemetery.

Occupations: School Teacher (1900); Secretary/Treasurer (1929, 1931, 1934-35, 1939).[330,-336]

Frank and Ethel had no children.

FOURTH GENERATION

13. Samuel James PICKLES/PICKELL[337-342,109] (*Hannah CLAY*[3], *Isaac*[2], *Abegail*[1]).

13. *Samuel James PICKELL, and wife Julia Josephine"Josie" STEELE ca1890s.*

Samuel was born on 14 April 1869, in Halifax, Yorkshire,[343,344] and died at De Vores Hospital in Grand Rapids, Kent County, Michigan, on 13 April 1920; he was 50.[345] He was buried on 15 April 1920, in Douglass Township, Montcalm County, Michigan,[346] at the Entrican Cemetery.

Occupations: Farmer (1887); Machinist (1900, 1907, 1910); Toolmaker (1920); Mechanic (1920).[347-352]

Samuel came with his parents (he was three years old) and uncle Emmanuel and his wife Sarah, arriving from Liverpool, England to Boston, Massachusetts, 14 March 1872, aboard the ship *Tripoli* of the Cunard Line. In the 1900 US census he claims he immigrated in 1873 [sic: it actually was 1872]. Apparently he became a Naturalized US citizen by 1900, but no record is found to date.[353]

Samuel and Josephine seem to have changed their surname from PICKLES to PICKELL around the 1910-20s. There is no apparent reason other than to distinguish themselves from other families.

On 22 January 1887, when Samuel was 17, he married **Julia Josephine "Josie" STEELE,**[354-361,109] daughter of John C. STEELE and Julia A. EVERETT, in Westville, Montcalm County, Michigan.[362] She was born on 22 November 1872, in Michigan,[363] and died in Ann Arbor, Washtenaw County, Michigan, on 23 February 1938; she was 65.[364] Buried on 26 February 1938, in Douglass Township, Montcalm County, Michigan, [365] at Entrican Cemetery with her husband.

> *Obituary*: "Mrs. Josephine Pickell, 66, of Entrican, died Wednesday in Ann Arbor. She is survived by three children, Fred and James of California, and Mrs. Ruth Medd of Grand Rapids; six brothers, Dan and John Steele of Stanton, Albert, Elmer and Guy of Greenville and Sam of Grand Haven, and a sister, Mrs. Irving Beetley of Stanton. Funeral at 2 Saturday at the Entrican Methodist church. Burial in Entrican cemetery."[366]

Samuel and Josephine had the following children:

26 i. **John R. PICKLES**. Born in September 1889, in Michigan. John died in Douglass Township, Montcalm County, Michigan, on 24 November 1889; he was about three months old. He died of a burst blood vessel.

27 ii. **Ruth PICKLES**. Born on 2 September 1890, in Greenville, Montcalm County, Michigan. Ruth died in Kissimmee, Osceola County, Florida, on 28 October 1965; she was 75.

28 iii. **Frederick William "Fred" PICKLES/PICKELL.** Born on 4 December 1890, in Douglass Township, Montcalm County, Michigan. Frederick died in Orange County, California, on 29 November 1964; he was 73.

29 iv. **James Edward PICKLES/PICKELL.** Born on 27 February 1894, in Lakeview, Montcalm County, Michigan. James died at Northwest Medical Center Hospital (Houston) in Santa Rosa, Harris County, Texas, on 23 February 1974; he was 79.

---

14. Amelia Hannah Elizabeth "Minnie" PICKLES[367-376,109,180] (*Hannah CLAY*[3], *Isaac*[2], *Abegail*[1]).

Amelia was born on 10 October 1877, in Hamlin Township, Eaton County, Michigan,[377-379] and died in Sheridan, Montcalm County, Michigan, on 13 January 1968; she was 90. Buried on 16 January 1968, in Entrican, Douglass Township, Montcalm County, Michigan,[380] at the Entrican Cemetery; lot 189; space 2.

14. Amelia Hannah Elizabeth "Minnie" PICKLES ("Grandma Kilbourne" to many).

Religion: Seventh-Day Adventist.

Occupation: Boarding House (1930);[381] husband Thomas was ill by then from a stroke and work was intermittant, so she took on boarders.

After her first husband's death she lived with son Truman, at R27 Colfax NE, Grand Rapids, Kent County, Michigan in 1946.[382] [The entry incorrectly says she is the widow of "John"; probably a "typo" of the directory worker, or she didn't hear the question correctly as she was partially deaf at the time.][383]

Thomas Oscar KILBOURNE and **14**. *Amelia Hannah Elizabeth "Minnie" PICKLES with their first-born,* **30**. *Vena Emily KILBOURNE. – photograph 1899.*

Obituary: "AMELIA TREGENZA, 90 | EDMORE – Services for Mrs. Amelia Tregenza, 90, R1 Stanton, who died Saturday at Sheridan Community Hospital, will be held Tuesday at 1 p.m. at Stebbins Funeral Home, Edmore. Elder Herbert Lohr will officate [sic]. Burial will be in Entrican Cemetery.

Surviving are her husband, Charles; four daughters, Mrs. Vena Doyle and Mrs. Evelyn Knapp, Grand Rapids, Mrs. Mary Myers, Los Angeles, and Mrs. Kathryn Lang, Greenville; four sons, Raymond and

> Truman Kilbourne, Grand Rapids, Thomas, San Diego, and John, Saginaw; 28 grandchildren, 56 great grandchildren and one great great grandchild.
>
> Mrs. Tregenza was born in Eaton County Oct. 10, 1877."[384]

On 31 May 1897, when Amelia was 19, she first married a red-headed fellow named **Thomas Oscar "Tom" KILBOURNE,**[385-390,109,180] son of a Civil War veteran Churchill Vaughn KILBORN (1840-1882), and Emily Elizabeth "Libby" ALDRICH (1843-1873), in Stanton, Montcalm County, Michigan,[391,392] by Rev. W. C. Burns. The marriage was witnessed by Alice Slauker and Alice M. Bunns, but Amelia stated on record that she "didn't know her mother." (Perhaps a little tension between mother and daughter?)

Tom KILBOURNE in later years.

Born on 13 November 1868, in Montcalm County, Michigan, Tom died in Douglass Township, Montcalm County, Michigan, on 5 August 1934; he was 65.[393] Buried on 8 August 1934, in Douglass Township, Montcalm County, Michigan,[394] at the Entrican Cemetery, Lot: 189, Space: 1.

His occupations: Laborer (1897); Lumber Laborer (1900); Teamster (1900, 1902); Farmer (1910, 1920, 1930, 1934).[395-400]

Thomas was a a wrangler of horses in the nearby lumber industry. He perfected a salve for muscle strain for both horses and humans.

In 1902, he and wife were living in Jackson, Michigan with his step-grandmother, Emeline Kilbourne.

> *Obituary*: "Mrs. Clare Martin and Mrs. Milo Colburn returned Thursday from near Stanton where they attended funeral services for Mrs. Martin's brother, Thomas Kilbourne.
>
> Mr. Kilbourne, who was 65, had been ill for several years having suffered a stroke two years ago. He was able to be about the house until the last few weeks.
>
> The family home had been at Entrican for years, but about a year ago they moved to Belding. In June they went back to the old home as Mr. Kilbourne seemed so anxious to return. The death in June of a

daughter was great sorrow to the family.[*] She left six small children to mourn their mother.

Besides his widow, Mr. Kilbourne is survived by six children, three sons and a daughter at home, a daughter in Flint and one in Syracuse N. Y. Mrs. Martin is the only one left of her family, being the last of six children.

In former days three brothers and sisters frequently had gathered at the hospitable home of Dr. and Mrs. Martin and there are still a number who remember Mr. Kilbourne."[401] *[*Elizabeth Margarite Kilbourne Taylor. See number* **32** *below.]*

Amelia and Thomas had the following ten children:

30 i. **Vena Emily KILBOURNE**. Born on 12 January 1898, in Stanton, Montcalm County, Michigan. Vena died in Grand Rapids, Kent County, Michigan, on 25 September 1995; she was 97.

31 ii. **Raymond James "Ray" KILBOURNE**. Born on 11 March 1900, in Douglass Township, Montcalm County, Michigan. Raymond died in Grand Rapids, Kent County, Michigan, on 11 January 1982; he was 81.

32 iii. **Elizabeth Margarite "Bessie" KILBOURNE**. Born on 30 April 1903, in Jackson, Jackson County, Michigan. "Bessie" died in Day Township, Montcalm County, Michigan, on 23 June 1934; she was 31.

33 iv. **Harry James "Edwin" KILBOURNE**. Born on 16 February 1906, in Stanton, Montcalm County, Michigan. Harry died in Douglass Township, Montcalm County, Michigan, on 19 February 1914; he was 8.

34 v. **Kathryn Angeline "Kay" KILBOURNE**. Born on 6 June 1910, in Douglass Township, Montcalm County, Michigan. Kathryn died in Chambersburg, Franklin County, Pennsylvania, on 23 August 2000; she was 90.

35 vi. **Lillian Evelyn KILBOURNE**. Born on 1 December 1912, in Stanton, Montcalm County, Michigan. Lillian died in Winston-Salem, North Carolina, on 22 September 2005; she was 92.

36 vii. **Marie Lorraine KILBOURNE**. Born on 1 June 1915, in Douglass Township, Montcalm County, Michigan. Marie died in Los Angeles, Los Angeles County, California, on 15 September 1998; she was 83.

37 viii. **Thomas Oscar "Junior" KILBOURNE Jr.** Born on 26 September 1918, in Stanton, Montcalm County, Michigan. Junior died in Lake Vavasu City, Mohave County, Arizona, on 6 April 1993; he was 74.

38 ix. **John Churchill KILBOURNE**. Born on 29 March 1921, in Douglass Township, Montcalm County, Michigan. John died in Pontiac, Oakland County, Michigan, on 12 August 1978; he was 57.

39 x. **Truman Gordon KILBOURNE**. Born on 27 July 1923, in Stanton, Montcalm County, Michigan. Truman died in Grand Rapids, Kent County, Michigan, on 8 September 1979; he was 56.

After 1950, when Amelia was 72, she lived with another red-headed fellow **Charles Ernest "Gunzie" TREGENZA,**[402-406] son of Alfred Ernest TREGENZA (1852-?) and Elizabeth Currard REID (ca1860-?), in Michigan. He was born on 2 May 1887, in Windsor, Essex County, Ontario, Canada,[407,408] Gunzie died in Sheridan, Montcalm County, Michigan, on 18 February 1973; he was 85.[408,409] Buried on 21 February 1973, in Entrican, Douglass Township, Montcalm County, Michigan,[410] Entrican Cemetery.

Charles Ernest TREGENZA, May 1971.

Occupations: Clerk (1903); Machinist (1904, 1910); Repairman (1911, 1912, 1915, 1927); Teacher (1913); Salesman (1916, 1921); Automobile Manager (1920); Auto Service Factory/Serviceman (1930, 1932, 1939); Lathe (1945); Factory (1947); Tool Maker (1950).[411-428]

Religion: Presbyterian/Seventh Day Adventist

Gunzie had been previously married to Margaret Jane "Jennie" NICHOLS on 10 July 1909, in Windsor, Essex County, Ontario, Canada. She was born 20 February 1866, in Henrietta

The Old And The New

The Millionth Buick and one of the country's oldest valve-in-head cars in front of the General Motors building. Standing in front of the 1908, two-cylinder model, is J. A. Coy, Michigan district sales manager, while seated in the car is Charles E. Tregenza, the Detroit branch's traveling service expert. At the wheel of the millionth Buick is C. S. Mott, vice-president of the General Motors corporation in charge of production. In the rear seat is James Dickson, Jr., branch manager, and E. T. Steger, sales manager of the branch.

"Charles E. Tregenza, the Detroit branch's traveling sales manager…" 17 June 1923, Detroit Free Press, *Part 4 page 5.*

Township, Jackson County, Michigan to Emanuel Nichols, born in Pennsylvania, and Louise Hutler, born in Germany. Jennie passed away in August 1950, in Tompkins Township, Jackson County, Michigan, and is buried in Oak Grove Cemetery, Napoleon, Jackson County, Michigan. Gunzie was Jennie's third husband and she had no children by him.

Gunzie is not found in the 1900 and 1940 US censuses, or in the 1891, 1901 Canadian censuses, probably because he moved around a lot as a service repairman.

He immigrated to the US in 1898 and became a Naturalized Citizen.[429]

Border crossing from Canada to Port of Buffalo, New York, 1910:[430] "Debarred | Tregenza | Charles E. | 23 | M | 1 | Clerk | Nearest Relative: Father - Charles M. Tregenza 47 Delassare Ave., Hamilton, Ont. | Last residence: Hamilton | Final Destination: NY [State], New York"[431] There is no reason found for this "debarment" as Gunzie freely traveled across the border per other records, nor why he named his father Charles rather than Alfred.

1908, June: "Detroit [General Motors, Buick] branch's traveling service expert."[432]

Affectionally called "Gunzie" because he loved cars and liked to "gun" them hard and fast. He helped engineer automobiles in Detroit before retirement. "I remember him getting a new car every year we visited him. 'Okay laddies let's go see what she's got in her,' he would say to us impressionable little boys. Then we would go racing down the dirt roads of Michigan at top speeds, to the chagrin of our parents." Gunzie was always a gregarious, generous, and positive person and loved his baseball.

He was of a stocky, diminutive stature while Minnie stood tall and lanky 5 feet 9 inches (at least by my estimate and recollection), which made for comical comments by the grandchildren. Asked how she remained so thin all her life, her answer was to "be a farmer's wife, have ten children, and see if you have time to get fat." [author]

Military:

U.S., World War I Draft Registration Cards, 1917-1918:

Name: Charles E Tregenza |Event Type: Draft Registration; Date: 1917-1918; Place: Detroit City, Michigan | Gender: Male | Nationality: United States | Age: 30 | Race: White | Birth Date: 2d May 1887; Birthplace: Windsor, Ontario, Canada | naturalized | Occupation: Foreman of garage; Employer: Buick Motor Co., Detroit | Supporting: "mother and wife" | married | Height: 5 ft 4 in | Eyes: Brown | Hair: Red | Bald? No | Disability: "Rupture double"[433]

U.S., World War II Draft Registration Cards, 1942:

Name: Charles Earnest Tregenza | Gender: Male | Age: 56 Race: White | Height: 5' 4" | Weight: 135 | Eyes: Brown | Hair: Red Gray | Complexion: Light | Birth Date/Place: 2 May 1886 [sic], Windsor Ont. Canada | Residence Place: Tompkins, Jackson, Michigan | Military Draft Date: 1942 | Next of Kin: Charles F Clemons | Occupation: farmer[434]

Gunzie and Minnie had no children of their own. Indeed, a marriage record is not found. If married, it was after 1953, and Amelia would have been beyond the age of child bearing.

[See Amelia's diary as a 12-year old at APPENDIX: DIARY OF AMELIA PICKLES]

15. Fred PICKLES (*Hannah CLAY*[3], *Isaac*[2], *Abegail*[1]).

Born on 19 February 1881, in Hamlin Township, Eaton County, Michigan.[435-437] Fred died in Hamlin Township, Eaton County, Michigan, on 24 February 1881; he was a few days old, dying from "inflammation of Lungs."[438,439]

16. Malcolm J. CLAY[440-447] (*Simeon A.*[3], *Fredric*[2], *Abegail*[1]).

16. *Malcolm J. Clay. Photograph courtesy Kathleen Marie O'Dell Townsley.*

Born on 29 July 1875, in Hamlin Township, Eaton County, Michigan,[448] he died in Onondaga, Ingham County, Michigan, on 6 April 1949; he was 73.[449] Buried on 9 April 1949 in Onondaga, Ingham County, Michigan,[450] at the Onondaga Cemetery.

Occupations: Farm Laborer (1900); Farmer (1910, 1918, 1930); Thrasher Machine (1920).[451-454]

So where are Malcolm and Lovan's children in the 1910 census? Only he and his wife are listed, but they indicate they had three alive children in the census. Perhaps omitted by the census taker? The three children were not found elsewhere either.

> *Obituary*: "EATON RAPIDS, April 8—The body of Malcolm J. Clay, 73, of Onondaga, will be taken from the Pettit funeral home. Eaton Rapids, at 10 o'clock Saturday morning to the Onondaga church where services will be held at 2 o'clock. Rev. Dudley Mosher assisted by Rev. Mal Hoyt will officiate. Burial will be

in the Onondaga cemetery. He is survived by the widow, Lovan; two daughter, Mrs. Mina Howe of Mason and Mrs. Loretta Haaff [sic] of Detroit; two sisters, Mrs. Mable Zantop of Jackson and Mrs. Alice Krugman of Parma; two brothers, Frey [sic] Clay of Charlotte and Ray Clay of Jackson; three grandchildren, nieces and nephews."[455]

"Malcomb J. Clay, 73, of Onondaga, died very suddenly Wednesday afternoon while driving his car. Funeral services will be held Saturday afternoon at two o'clock at the Onondaga church under the direction of the Pettit Funeral home. Rev. Dudley Mosher and Rev. Mal Hoyt will officiate and interment will be in the Onondaga cemetery.

Surviving him are the widow, Lovan; two daughters, Mrs. Mina Howe of Mason and Mrs. Loretta Haass [sic] of Detroit; two sisters, Mrs. Mabel Zantop of Jackson and Mrs. Alice Krugman of Parma; two brothers, Fred Clay of Charlotte and Roy Clay of Jackson; three grandchildren and several nieces and nephews."[2093]

"Funeral services were held Saturday for Malcomb J. Clay, 73, of Onondaga who died very suddenly Wednesday afternoon while driving his car. Surviving him are the widow, Lovan; two daughters, Mrs. Mina Howe of Mason and Mrs. Loretta Haas of Detroit."[2094]

"Mr. and Mrs. Fred Clay and Mr. and Mrs. James Pasco of Fenton attended the funeral of the former's brother, Malcolm Clay of Onondaga last Saturday."[2095]

Military:

U.S., World War I Draft Registration Cards, 1917-1918:

Name: Malcolm J Clay | Age: 43 | Occupation: Farming | Race: White | Birth Date: 29 Jul 1875 | Residence Date: 1917-1918 | Street Address: Box 46 | Residence Place: Onondaga, Ingham County, Michigan | Physical Build: Medium | Height: Tall | Hair Color: Gray | Eye Color: Gray | Relative: Loran B. Clay [wife][456]

On 15 October 1902, when Malcolm was 27, he married **Lovan B. HARWOOD**[457-463], daughter of George HARWOOD and Mary E. BALDWIN, in Onondaga, Ingham County, Michigan.[464,465,2096] She was born on 21 May 1876, in Onondaga-Township, Onondaga County, Michigan. Lovan died in Mason, Ingham County, Michigan, on 18 January 1952; she was

75,[449] and was buried on 19 January 1952,[450] Onondaga Cemetery.

Obituary: "(Special to The Slate Journal)

LESLIE, Jan. 19 – Mrs. Lovan Clay, 74, widow of the late Malcomb Clay of Onondaga county, died Friday afternoon at Mason hospital after a long illness. Born on a farm, Mrs. Clay lived all her life in Onondaga township. She is by two daughters, Mrs. Herbert Howe, Mason, and Mrs. Kay Haas, Detroit. Funeral services will held it 2 P. M. at the Onondaga community church. Burial will be In Onondaga cemetery."[466]

Malcolm and Lovan had the following children:

40 i. **Laurence J. CLAY**. Born on 26 July 1903, in Michigan. Laurence died in Onondaga, Ingham County, Michigan, on 27 March 1917; he was 13.

41 ii. **Mary Loretta CLAY**. Born on 2 March 1906, in Onondaga, Ingham County, Michigan. Mary died in Polk County, Florida, on 25 November 1971; she was 65.

42 iii. **Mina Lovan CLAY**. Born on 17 November 1907, in Onondaga, Ingham County, Michigan. Mina died in Mount Pleasant, Isabella County, Michigan, on 5 February 1976; she was 68.

---

17. Fred Henry CLAY[467-475] (*Simeon A.*[3], *Fredric*[2], *Abegail*[1]).

Born on 5 October 1876, in Hamlin Township, Eaton County, Michigan,[476,477] and died in Charlotte, Eaton County, Michigan, on 15 April 1960; he was 83. Buried in Charlotte, Eaton County, Michigan,[478] at Maple Hill Cemetery.

Occupation: he was a farmer all his life.[164,479-483]

Religion: Methodist.

Obituary: "CHARLOTTE – Fred H. Clay, 83, a farmer, died of a heart ailment Friday night at his residence, 1931 S. Cochran ave., Charlotte. An Eaton Rapids native, he had been a resident here for the past 50 years. He and May Lovell were married here Dec. 22, 1901. She died June 23, 1959. He was a member of the Center Eaton Methodist Church. Surviving are a son, Morrison of Charlotte; two daughters, Mrs. Hene Lee of Jackson and Mrs. Leta Pasco of Fenton; two grandchildren; two great-grandchildren; a sister, Mrs.

Mable Zantop of East Lansing, and a brother, LeRoy of Jackson."[484,485]

Military:

U.S., World War I Draft Registration Cards, 1917-1918:

Name: Fred Henry Clay | Race: White | Age: 41 | Occupation: Farming | Birth Date: 5 Nov 1877 | Residence Date: 1917-1918 | Street Address: R. F. D. #5 | Residence Place: Charlotte, Eaton County, Michigan | Physical Build: Slender | Height: Tall | Hair Color: Black | Eye Color: Blue | Relative: N. May Clay [wife][486]

17. Fred Henry Clay. Photograph from Kathleen Marie O'Dell Townsley.

On 22 December 1901, when Fred was 25, he married **Nancy Mae LOVELL,**[487-492] daughter of Legrand De Forest "Dan" LOVELL and Sarah A. CROY, in Charlotte, Eaton County, Michigan,[493-495] at the Methodist parsonage: "It was very cold and snowy on our wedding day..."

She was born on 10 October 1877, in McComb, Hancock County, Ohio,[496] and died at the Hayes-Green-Beach Hospital, in Charlotte, Eaton County, Michigan, on 28 June 1959; she was 81. Buried on 1 July 1959 in Charlotte, Eaton County, Michigan,[497] Maple Hill Cemetery.

Occupation: Teacher (1901).

Religion: Methodist.

Obituary: "CHARLOTTE, June 29 Mrs. Mae Clay, 81, of Charlotte, died at the Hayes-Green-Beach hospital Sunday after an illness of three weeks. She is survived by her husband, Fred; a son, Morrison of Charlotte; two daughters, Mrs. Ilene Lee of Jackson and Mrs. Leta Pasco of Fenton; three sisters, two grandchildren and two great-grandchildren. Funeral services will be held Wednesday at 2 p. m. at the Burkhead-Cheney funeral home in Charlotte. Burial will be in the Maple Hill cemetery."[498]

Obituary: "CHARLOTTE Mrs. Mae Clay, 81, of 1981 S. Cochran st., Charlotte, wife of Fred H. Clay, died at Hayes-Green-Beach Hospital early Sunday where she had been a patient for three weeks. She was born in Macomb, Ohio, Oct. 10, 1877, the daughter of Daniel and Sarah (Cry) LeGrand, and came to Eaton County when a young girl. She was married to Mr. Clay, Dec. 22, 1901. Surviving are her husband: a son, Morrison, of Carmel 'Township; two daughters. Mrs. Ted (Ilene) Lee of Jackson and Mrs. James (Leta) Pasco of Fenton; two grandchildren and two great-grand-children; three sisters, Mrs. Charles Collier of Vermontville and Mrs. Myrtie Welch and Mrs. Pearl Van-Buren, both of Sunfield. Mrs. Clay was a member of the Center Eaton Methodist Church and a charter member of tire I-Go-You-Go Club." [499]

"About eighty friends and neighbors spent Friday evening at Fred Clay's playing cards and dancing."[2099]

There are numerous iotas in the newspapers of the Clay's visiting and participating in various social events.

The local papers also mention one real estate transfer: "Royal G. Cole to Fred H. Clay, about 40 acres section 26, Carmel twp., $3500."[2100]

Afflicted by a disease:

1928: "Fred Clay Given Thirty Days Term," for driving drunk; found guilty, ordered to pay a $50 fine and serve 30 days in jail, and probation for 13 months.[2101]

1935: "... Fred Clay, of Charlotte, ... arrested on drunk and disorderly charges. ...but Clay paid his fine and costs."[2102]

1936: "Fred Clay Is Found Guilty," of driving drunk.[2103]

1938 - "...Fred H. Clay of south of Charlotte, who stood mute when arraigned on a charge of drunk driving in Charlotte on March 16, last, his car crashing into a tree, this being his third offense, a pleas of not guilty being entered by direction of the court."[2104]

"Fred Clay had a serious accident Monday p. m. He got his hand in a corn husker; he lost all his fingers and thumb on his left hand. The daughters, Mrs. Ilene Lee of Jackson and Mrs. Lota [sic] Pasco of Fenton are home." He "... returned home Monday from the H.G.B. hospital after a stay of just two weeks."[2105]

Fred and Nancy had the following children:

43 i. **Morrison Legrand CLAY**. Born on 18 November 1902, in Carmel Township, Eaton County, Michigan. Morrison died in Charlotte, Eaton County, Michigan, on 14 October 1977; he was 74.

44 ii. **Ann Ilene CLAY**. Born on 20 January 1905, in Michigan. Ann died in Walled Lake, Oakland County, Michigan, in November 1993; she was 88.

45 iii. **Leta Mae CLAY**. Born on 24 April 1907, in Vermontville, Eaton County, Michigan. Leta died in Bloomfield Hills, Oakland County, Michigan, on 2 September 2003; she was 96.

46 iv. **Clifford CLAY**. Born circa 1914, in Michigan.

---

18. Mary Alice CLAY[500-506,180] (*Simeon A.*[3]*, Fredric*[2]*, Abegail*[1]).

Born on 19 October 1879, in Hamlin Township, Eaton County, Michigan,[507,508] Mary died in 1954; she was 74. Buried in Tompkins Township, Jackson County, Michigan,[509] at Fairview Cemetery.

On 24 September 1908, when Mary was 28, she married **Frederick Henry "Fred" KRUGMAN,**[510-514,180] son of Frederick KRIEGMAN and Frederica SCHULTZ, in Charlotte, Eaton County, Michigan.[515,516] He was born on 29 November 1884, in Bainbridge Township, Berrien County, Michigan,[408,2112] and died in Munith, Jackson County, Michigan, in February 1966; he was 81.[408] Buried in Tompkins Township, Jackson County, Michigan,[517] Fairview Cemetery.

Occupations: Farmer (1908); Farm Laborer (1910, 1918, 1950); Railroad Car Carpenter (1920, 1928, 1930, 1938); Auto Specialist (1938); Engineer (1942).[518-522]

> "PARMA – The father who walked out on a family of six 29 years ago and thereafter was never heard from, several days ago walked into the lives of his wife, five children and six grandchildren – and the enlarged family is happy over the unexpected reunion.
>
> It was in 1915 that Fred Krugman boarded an interurban car in Parma to go into Jackson to do some trading. All efforts to trace his movements from that day on proved futile. Suddenly last week he alighted from a bus in Parma, wearing the unifrom [sic] of an army engineer, and called at the home of his son,

Everett Krugman, production official at the Goodyear Tire and Rubber Co. of Jackson.

Giving as the reason for his sudden departure and long absence an impossible domestic discord for which he blamed neither his wife nor himself, Mr. Krugman declares that during the years which have elapsed he has worked as a construction engineer in all parts of the world, in many states of the union and in Mexico. In 1939 he enlisted in the army as a civilian engineer with 241 volunteers at San Bernardino, Calif., served 14 months on Attu and since sometime in 1940 has been located at Anchorage, Alaska, to which be he must return before the first of the year. Today he claims to be the only one of the original 241 who volunteered with him still in the service. November 29 he observed his 60th birthday, but his enlistment is for the duration of the war.

Oldest son of the Krugman family is Pfc. Laverne C, Krugman, 34, classified as 'expert infantryman and bazooka man' with General Patton's army in Germany. He was a precision instrument expert with Goodyear while that concern was manufacturing big guns for the army prior to his induction, and his wife, Margie and eight-months-old daughter, Joyce, reside in Parma[.] Everett, second son, has two sons of his own, Daryl, 3 and Ronald, 1. 'Grandfather' Krugman also returns to three daughters, two of whom have children of their own. Mrs. Annabelle Hurlburt resides In Traverse City; and Mrs. Mable Tompkins and her two children, Douglas, 7, and Constance, 3, live at Holt. Mrs. Lucille Richardson of Parma, who was born after her father left home, has a three-year-old son, Michael.

Commenting on the return of his father this morning, Everett Krugman said: 'He's a grand guy and we're all tickled to death to have him back. He says that after the war he will return to Parma and we hope that before long Vern will be back from Germany and the family circle complete again.'"[523]

Unfortunately, Fred never got to see his son Laverne, as he was killed-in-action in 17 days later.

Military:

U. S. World War I Draft Registration Cards, 1917-1918:

Name: Frederick Henry Krugman | Sex: Male | Age: 33 | Occupation: Farm laborer | Event Date: from 1917 to 1918 | Event Place (Original): United States, Michigan, Berrien County no 1 | Draft Registration | Citizenship Place: United States | Birth Date: 29 Nov 1884 | Nearest Relative: Mrs. A. G. Schwart, [sister] Watervliet, Mich | Race: White | Height: Medium | Build: Medium | Eyes: Brown | Hair: D. Gray[524]

U. S. World War II Draft Registration Cards, 1942:

Name: Fred Henry Krugman | Age: 57 | Event Date: 1942 | Event Place: Camp Anderson, Ft. Richardan, Anchorage, Alaska | Event Type: Draft Registration | Birth Date/Place: 29 Nov 1884, Bainbridge Township, Michigan | Person Who Knows You: Mrs. Chas. Molter, Benton Harbor, Michigan [sister] | Employer: U.S. Engineers, Anchorage, Alaska | Race: White | Height 5 5 | Weight: 195 | Eyes: Brown | Hair: Gray | Complexion: Light Ruddy Other: right forefinger scar[525]

Mary and Fred had the following children:

47 i. **Laverne Charles "Vern" KRUGMAN**. Born on 21 September 1909, in Parma Township, Jackson County, Michigan. Vern was killed-in-action in Germany on 21 December 1944; he was 35, at "Battle of the Bulge" and "buried in eastern France."

48 ii. **Everett Leonard KRUGMAN**. Born on 26 September 1910, in Parma Township, Jackson County, Michigan. Everett died in Albion, Calhoun County, Michigan, on 13 June 1984; he was 73.

49 iii. **Annabelle KRUGMAN**. Born on 20 March 1911, in Parma Township, Jackson County, Michigan. Annabelle died in Charlotte, Eaton County, Michigan, on 14 October 1956; she was 45.

50 iv. **Mabel Louise KRUGMAN**. Born on 20 February 1914, in Parma Township, Jackson County, Michigan. Mabel died in St. Helena, Napa County, California, on 22 April 1998; she was 84.

51 v. **Lucille Ione KRUGMAN**. Born on 30 May 1916, in Parma Township, Jackson County, Michigan. Lucille died in Ann Arbor, Washtenaw County, Michigan, on 28 November 1986; she was 70.

Apparently Fred and Mary separated after 20 February 1920. Mary referred herself as a widow in the 1930 Census, and declared deceased by Fred's daughter in 1935. However, by the 1950 Census, they apparently reunited.

19. Mabel "Birdie" CLAY[526-532,180] (*Simeon A.*[3], *Fredric*[2], *Abegail*[1]).

Born on 17 November 1884, in Hamlin Township, Eaton County, Michigan,[533,408] Birdie died at the Leila Hospital in Battle Creek, Calhoun County, Michigan, on 29 March 1978; she was 93.[408,534] Buried on 1 April 1978, in Sandstone Township, Jackson County, Michigan,[535] Chapel Cemetery.

Obituary: "ZANTOP | MABLE B., formerly of Parma, Mich., age 93, died at Battle Creek Hospital on March 29, 1978. A major part of her life was spent in Parma, Mich., where she was affiliated with the Parma United Church, was a past Noble Grand Matron of the Parma Rebekah Lodge, and a former member of the Parma Review Club. Survivors include two daughters, Mrs. Thelma Lamb (Milton) of Okemos, with whom she made her home tor over 20 years, and Mrs. Anita Kelly (Owen) of Burlington, who cared for her in her last two years of illness; three sons, Howard of Allen Park, Duane of Ypsilanti, and Lloyd of Allen Park; 17 grandchildren and 26 great grandchildren. Funeral services will be held at Spencer Funeral Home, Athens, Mich., on Saturday, April 1, at 2 p.m., with the Rev. Dr. John Cermak of the Okemos Community Church officiating. Grandsons will act as pallbearers. Interment will be at the chapel cemetery In Parma."[538,539]

Obituary: "BURLINGTON – Mrs. Mable B. (Clay) Zantop, 93, of 7900 N Drive S., died Wednesday in Leila Hospital. Battle Creek.

She was born in Eaton Rapids, [sic] and resided for many years in Parma. She was a member of the Parma United Church, a member and past noble grand of the Parma Rebekah Lodge and a former member of the Parma Review Club.

She is survived by daughters, Mrs. Milton (Thelma) Lamb of Okemos, and Mrs. Owen (Anita) Kelly of Burlington; sons, Howard Zantop of Allen Park, Duane of Ypsilanti, and Lloyd of Allen Park; 17 grandchildren, and 26 great-grandchildren.

Services will be held at 2 p.m. Saturday at Spencer Funeral Home, Athens."[540]

On 4 April 1905, when Birdie was 20, she first married **Irving William GUNNELL,**[541,180] son of William GUNNELL and Alvira MOORE, in Charlotte, Eaton County, Michigan.[542,543] He was born on 19 October 1879, in Eaton Rapids, Eaton County, Michigan. (His second marriage record says he was born in 1880.) Irving died in Michigan on 17 January 1956; he was 76. Buried in Portland, Ionia County, Michigan,[544] at the Portland Cemetery.

> *1907, January:* "Charlotte – Irving Gunnell, and Eaton Rapids man, was fined $25 for beating his wife. The wife was the only witness. Gunnell has appealed." 536
>
> *1907, April:* "CHARLOTTE – Irving Gunnell, of Eaton Rapids, found guilty of assault and battery on complaint of his wife last January, and appealed the case to the April term of circuit court, was found guilty of non-support before the same justice this afternoon. The proofs show that Gunnell had only given $2 toward the support of his wife since January."[537]

Irving's occupations: Farmer (1905, 1912); Grocery Store Clerk (1907); Plumber (1918, 1955).[545]

They were divorced on 20 March 1909 in Jackson County, Michigan.[546]

> "A warranty deed given by the late William Gunnell of Eaton Rapids township to his son, Irving Gunnell for forty acres of land, is the basis of a suit started in circuit court at Charlotte by the six brothers and sisters of Irving Gunnell, who claim that undue influence was used in securing the deed. Those who are behind the suit include Mrs. Fannie Lee of Marshall." 547

Military:

U.S., World War I Draft Registration Cards, 1917-1918:

Name: Irving William Gunnell | Age: 38 | Birth Date: 19 Oct 1879 | Residence Date: 1917-1918; Place: 342 Main, Eaton Rapids, Eaton County, Michigan | Occupation: Plumbing | Employer: Minnie V Ramsey | Build: Medium | Height: Medium | Hair Color: Brown | Eye Color: Grey | Race: White | Nearest Relative: Alice Gunnell, wife, 816 So. Main, Eaton Rapids, Eaton County, Michigan[548]

U.S., World War II Draft Registration Cards, 1942:

Name: Irving William Gunnell | Gender: Male | Age: 62 Birth Date: 19 Oct 1879 | Place of Birth: Eaton Rapids, Mich. | Residence Place: 332 West Jefferson, Grand Ledge, Eaton, Michigan | Military Draft Date: 1942 | Person Who Knows You: Mrs. Glenn Lee, Kalamazoo, Mich. Gull Road | Race: White Height: 5-8 | Eyes: Gray | Weight: 185 | Hair: Brown | Complexion: Ruddy | Scar on neck & right hand[549]

They had one child:

52 i. **Thelma Clay GUNNELL**. Born on 21 June 1907, in Parma Township, Jackson County, Michigan. Thelma died in Okemos, Ingham County, Michigan, on 21 October 1993; she was 86.

On 25 March 1911, when Birdie was 26, she second married **August William ZANTOP**,[550-553] son of August ZANTOP and Louise BRAUT, in Jackson, Jackson County, Michigan.[554,555] He was born on 12 August 1889, in Jackson, Jackson County, Michigan.[408] August died in Miami-Dade County, Florida, on 20 March 1973; he was 83.[556,408] Buried in North Miami, Miami-Dade County, Florida, Southern Memorial Park.[557]

Occupations: Farmer (1911, 1950); Tractor Engineer (1920); Thrasher (1918; 1923, 1930); General Trucking (1940, 1942); School Bus Driver (1950).[558-562]

They were divorced on 27 May 1943, in Jackson County, Michigan.[563]

Obituary: "ZANTOP, AUGUST W., 83, of 12720 NE 13 Ave., passed away March 20, 1973. He came here in 1956 from Parma, Mich., and was a member of First Church of N. Miami, Congregational. He retired in 1962 from the Engineering Dept. of the Americana Hotel. Survived by wife Grace of N. Miami, 3 sons, Howard, Duane and Lloyd of Allen Park, Mich. Daughter Mrs. Owen Kelly, Burlington, Mich. Stepson Robert Grady, Detective with the N. Miami Police Dept. 22 grandchildren, 22 great-grandchildren, 2 sisters, Mrs. Anna Haase, Jackson, Mich., Mrs. Clara Inman, Pompano Beach, Fla., and brother Leo Zantop, Paradise, Mich. Funeral services Fri. 2 P.M. at JOSEPH B. COFER & SON MIAMI SHORES FUNERAL HOME 10931 NE 6 Ave. where friends may call Thurs. 7-9 P.M. Interment Southern Memorial Park."[564,565]

Obituary: "PARMA – Services were held today for August W. Zantop, 83, a former Parma resident, who died Tuesday in North Miami. Fla.

Zantop retired in 1962 from the engineering department of the Americana Hotel in Florida. He was a member of the First Congregational Church of North Miami.

Surviving are his widow, Grace; sons. Howard, Duane and Lloyd Zantop, all of Allen Park; a daughter, Mrs. Owen Kelly of Burlington; a stepson, Robert Grady of North Miami; 22 grandchildren; 22 great-grandchildren; a brother, Leo Zantop of Paradise; and sisters, Mrs. Anna Haase of Jackson and Mrs. Clara Inman of Pompano Beach. Fla."[566]

Military:

U.S., World War I Draft Registration Cards, 1917-1918:
Name: August William Zantop | Marital Status: Married | Birth Date/Place: 12 Aug 1889, Jackson, Michigan, U.S. | Residence Date: 1917-1918 | Street Address: Parma, Michigan | Residence Place: Jackson County, Michigan | Race: German |Physical Build: Medium | Height: Tall | Hair Color: Light Brown | Eye Color: Blue | Occupation: Grain Threasher (self) | Support? Wife and 3 children | Married[456]

U.S., World War II Draft Registration Cards, 1942:
Name: August W Zantop | Gender: Male | Age: 52| Race: White | Height: 6-1.5 | Eyes: Blue | Weight: 182 | Hair: Brown | Complexion: Light | Birth Date/Place: 12 Aug 1889, Jackson Mich | Residence Place: 2701 County House Rd, Blackman, Jackson, Mich | Military Draft Date: 1942 | Person Who Knows You: Clara I. Inman, R 8 Jackson Mich [Local Board No. 1 Draft Registrar] | Occupation: Self Agricultural trucking[549]

Bertie and August had the following children:

53 i. **Howard William ZANTOP**. Born on 1 October 1911, in Jackson County, Michigan. Howard died in Detroit, Wayne County, Michigan, on 18 April 1982; he was 70.

54 ii. **Naomi Alice ZANTOP**. Born on 4 January 1913, in Michigan. Naomi died in Parma Township, Jackson County, Michigan, on 12 January 1914; she was 1.

55 iii. **Harold Lyle ZANTOP**. Born on 9 March 1916, in Parma Township, Jackson County, Michigan. Harold died in Parma Township, Jackson County,

Michigan, on 3 August 1916; he was just shy of five months old.

56 iv. **Anita Mae ZANTOP**. Born on 18 April 1917, in Parma Township, Jackson County, Michigan. Anita died in Burlington, Calhoun County, Michigan, on 23 December 1995; she was 78.

57 v. **Duane August ZANTOP**. Born on 19 November 1918, in Jackson County, Michigan. Duane died in Superior Township, Washtenaw County, Michigan, on 13 April 2006; he was 87.

58 vi. **Stanley Elroy ZANTOP**. Born on 15 March 1920, in Parma Township, Jackson County, Michigan. Stanley died in Jackson, Jackson County, on 9 March 1953; he was 32.

59 vii. **Lloyd Avery ZANTOP**. Born on 10 January 1922, in Parma Township, Jackson County, Michigan. Lloyd died in Fort Lauderdale, Broward County, Florida, on 5 December 2002; he was 80.

60 viii. **Geraldine ZANTOP**. Born on 15 June 1929, in Michigan. Geraldine died in Jackson, Jackson County, Michigan, on 2 April 1936; she was 6.

"Duane A. Zantop and his three brothers [Howard William, Stanley Elroy, Lloyd Avery] formed the Zantop Flying Service in 1946. It operated as a fixed-base and charter-service, performing a limited cargo service for General Motors Corporation. It obtained a commercial operator's certificate in 1952 allowing them to expand their services to both Ford and Chrysler, as well as acquiring large aircraft. A majority of the company's contracts came from major automotive companies, and the Department of Defense. It became a supplemental air carrier in 1962 because of the Civil Aeronautics Board's approval of the transfer to Zantop of the operating certificate of Coastal Airlines. In 1966 the brothers sold their stock in Zantop air Transport, resigned, and the airline became known as Universal Airlines Inc."[2070]

20. Le Roy CLAY[567,-572] (*Simeon A.*[3], *Fredric*[2], *Abegail*[1]).

Le Roy was born on 17 December 1889, in Hamlin Township, Eaton County, Michigan,[573,408] and died in March 1964; he was 74.[408]

Occupations: Farmer (1910); Stationary/Steam Shovel Engineer (1817, 1920, 1930); Gas Engineer (1932); Shovel Operator (1935); Crane Operator (1940, 1945); Engineer (1947); Laboratory (1949); Shovel Operator (1950).[574-583]

Military:

U.S., World War I Draft Registration Cards, 1917-1918:

Name: Roy Clay | Race: Caucasian (White) | Marital Status: Married | Birth Date/Place: 17 Dec 1889, Eaton Rapids, Michigan | Residence Date: 1917-1918 | Street Address: 326 Ho Gorham | Residence Place: Jackson, Jackson, Michigan | Physical Build: Slender | Height: Tall | Hair Color: Dark | Eye Color: Blue | Bald? no | Occupation: Engine Steam Shovel | Dependents: Wife & two children, married.[584]

On 5 February 1910, when Roy was 20, he married **Cora Irene HOWE,**[585-590,180] daughter of Dewitt C. HOWE and Clara L. BERNARD, in Sandstone Township, Jackson County, Michigan.[591,592] She was born on 29 June 1889, in Sandstone Township, Jackson County, Michigan,[408] and died on 10 February 1955; she was 65.[408] Buried in Sandstone Township, Jackson County, Michigan, Chapel Cemetery.[593]

They had the following children:

61 i. **Earl Roy CLAY**. Born on 5 January 1911, in Michigan. Earl died in Jackson, Jackson County, Michigan, on 30 January 1918; he was 7.

62 ii. **Donald LaVere CLAY**. Born on 24 February 1916, in Parma Township, Jackson County, Michigan. Donald died on 18 June 1966; he was 50.

---

21. Mildred L. Irene CLAY[594-599,180] (*Cassius M.*[3], *Fredric*[2], *Abegail*[1]).

Born on 8 March 1890, in Parma Township, Jackson County, Michigan,[600] she died in Tarpon Springs, Pinellas County, Florida, on 31 October 1969; she was 79.[601] Buried on 5 September 1969 in Lansing, Ingham County, Michigan,[602] Mount Hope Cemetery.

Religion: Baptist.

Obituary: "Mrs. Mildred L. Fremody, 79 of Tarpon Springs, Fla., died Friday in Tarpon Springs.

Mrs. Fremody was a former Lansing resident who had resided in Birmingham for 30 years before moving to Florida three years ago.

Surviving are the husband, Howard; a daughter, Mrs. Mildred Schmidtman of Lansing; a brother, Milo Clay of Holiday, Fla.; six grandchildren and 11 great-grandchildren.

Funeral services will be Wednesday at 2:30 p.m. at the Gorsline-Runciman Funeral Home with burial in Mt. Hope Cemetery."[603]

"TARPON SPRINGS - Mrs. Mildred L. Fremody, 79, of 3205 Ninth St., Crestwood Gardens, died Friday. A native of Springport, Mich., she came here three years ago from Birmingham, Mich. She was a Baptist. Survivors include her husband, Howard E. Fremody; a daughter, Mrs. Mildred Schmidtman, Lansing, Mich., and a brother, Milo Clay, Holiday."[604]

On 21 July 1906, when Mildred was 16, she first married **Dr. John Frank(lin) HALE,**[605,606] son of Wallace Adonicon HALE and Sarah Jane GIFFORD, in Lansing, Ingham County, Michigan,[607] by E. M. Lake, Minister. He was born on 3 March 1888, in Ashley, Gratiot County, Michigan.[408] John died at University Hospitals, in Iowa City, Johnson County, Iowa, on 28 June 1963; he was 75.[408,608] Buried on 2 July 1963, in Northwood, Grove Township, Worth County, Iowa, at Sunset Rest Cemetery (tombstone not found).

Occupation: Carpenter (1906).

They were divorced in July 1914, in Ingham County, Michigan.[609]

Obituary: "NORTHWOOD – Funeral services for Dr. John F. Hale, 74, a longtime chiropractor, be held at 2 p.m. Tuesday the First Lutheran Church.

He died Friday at University Hospitals, Iowa City. He had been in poor health for the year.

Dr. Hale was preceded in death by a brother and a sister. Surviving are his wife, Sigrid; two sons, John W. Hale, in Indonesia, and Robert Hale Woodward; a daughter, Mrs. Harold Schmidtman, Lansing Mich.; four stepchildren, Edgar Crapser, Northwood; Donald Crapser, Boone; Lowell Crapser, Compton, Calif., and Mrs. Max (Lois) Landouw, Burbank, Calif., 20 grandchildren and five great grandchildren.

Burial will be at Sunset [Rest] Cemetery with the Connor Funeral Home in charge."[610]

Military:

U.S., World War II Draft Registration Cards, 1942:

Name: John Frank Hale | Gender: Male | Registration | Age: 54 Birth Date/Place: 3 Mar 1888, Ashley, Gratiot Co, Mich. | Residence Place: 800 2nd Ave N., Northwood, Iowa | Registration Date: abt 1942 | Military Draft Date: 1942 | Height: 5 11 Eye Color: Brown Hair Color: Brown | Weight: 180 | Complexion: Ruddy | Next of Kin: Mrs Gurena Hale [2nd wife][611]

Mildred and John had one child:

63 i. **Mildred Veralynne HALE**. Born on 20 January 1910, in Springport, Jackson County, Michigan. Mildred died in Lansing, Ingham County, Michigan, on 25 February 2002; she was 92.

On 24 December 1915, when Mildred was 25, she second married **Howard Earl FREMODY,**[612-615,180] son of Casper FREMODY and Hattie HENDRICKSON, in Lansing, Ingham County, Michigan,[616,617] by Rev. Horace Cady Wilson at his residence, 200 South Chestnut Street. Born on 18 March 1892, in Hancock, Houghton County, Michigan,[408,508] Howard died in Holiday, Pasco County, Florida, on 25 April 1975; he was 83.[408,556] Buried on 29 April 1975, in Lansing, Ingham County, Michigan, Mount Hope Cemetery.[618]

Occupations: Clerk (1915, 1916); Purchasing Agent (1917, 1919, 1920); Department Store Buyer (1930); Sales Manager (1931); Sales Engineer, Steel Rolling Mill (1940); Civil Engineer (1950); Architectural Engineer, General Motors (Death).[619-625]

Obituary: "FREMODY, HOWARD E.
Holiday, Fla.

Age 83, died April 25, 1975 in Holiday, Fla. Born Oct. 18, 1892 in Hancock, Mich. Mr. Fremody had lived in Holiday, Fla. for the past 9 yrs, and was an architectural engineer for General Motors. He is survived by a daughter Mrs. Harold (Mildred) Schmidtman of Lansing; 6 grandchildren, 13 great-grandchildren, 1 great-great-grandchild: l sister, Mrs. Tsabelle Hansen of Idaho. Funeral services will be held Tuesday, 2:30 p.m. at the Gorsline-Runciman Lansing Chapel with Rev. Keith H. Binkley of South Baptist Church officiating. Interment Mt. Hope Cemetery. Pallbearers will be Bruce Schmidtman, Davjd Schmidtman, Walter Schmidtman, Don Lehman, Charles Lehman, Dale Edgecomb. The family will receive friends Monday from 1-4 and 7-9 and Tuesday from 10-12."[626]

Military:

U.S., World War I Draft Registration Cards, 1917-1918:
Name: Howard Earl Fremody | Age: 25 | Race: caucasian | Marital Status: Married | Birth Date/Place: 18 Mar 1892, Hancock, Mich U.S.A. | Residence Date: 1917-1918 | Street Address: 430 So. Pine | Residence Place: Lansing, Ingham, Michigan | Occupation: correspondent purchase dept, Reo Motor Car Co Lansing Mich | Support? wife and child | Physical Build: Slender | Height: Medium | Hair Color: Light | Eye Color: Light Blue | Bald? slightly[627]

U.S., World War II Draft Registration Cards, 1942:
Name: Howard Earl Fremody | Gender: Male | Age: 50 | Race: White | Height 5' 10" | Eyes: Blue | Weight: 165 | Hair: Gray | Complexion: Light | Birth Date/Place: 18 Mar 1892, Hancock Michigan | Residence Place: 2184 Edgewood, West Bloomfield, Michigan | Mailing address Route #1 Birmingham Michigan | Employer: Great Lakes Steel Cor., 607 Shelby St. Detroit Wayne Mich. | Military Draft Registration Date: 27 April 1942 | Next of Kin: C. A. Fremody [father][628]

They had no children.

---

22. Orpha Zella CLAY[629-635,180] (*Cassius M.*[3], *Fredric*[2], *Abegail*[1]).

Born on 10 July 1892, in Springport, Jackson County, Michigan.[636] Orpha was baptized 3 April 1955, in Sears, Osceola County, Michigan at the Brooks Memorial Methodist Church by Howard A. Lyman, Pastor.[2116]

Orpha died at the Walter Byron Medical Facility in Battle Creek, Calhoun County, Michigan, on 14 May 1968; she was 75. Buried in Marshall, Calhoun County, Michigan,[637] Oakridge Cemetery.

Religion: Methodist.

Obituary: "MARSHALL - Mrs. Orpha Z. Orrison, 75, of 121 W. Spruce St., widow of Jesse J. Orrison, died at 6:30 a.m. today in the Walter Byron Medical Facility in Battle Creek. She had been a patient for one and one-half years.

She was born July 10, 1892, in Springport, daughter of Cassius M. and Ella (Schutt) Clay. She was married to Mr. Orrison March 14, 1913, in Jackson. He died Nov. 30, 1957.

22. *Orpha Zella Clay. Photograph courtesy of Kathleen Marie O'Dell Townsley.*

She was a member of Brooks Memorial Methodist Church, a charter member of Navy Mothers; a charter member of Women of the Moose; and a former member of the Woman's Relief Corps.

She was a graduate of the class of 1910 of Springport High School.

She is survived by a daughter, Mrs. Lawrence (Joyce) Masters of Burlington; six sons, Jack D. and Norman K., both of Marshall, Jesse E. of Tuscon, Ariz., Howard C. of Portland, Ore., Robert E. of Lompoc, Calif., and James F. of Mount Pleasant; 18 grandchildren; nine great-grandchildren; a sister, Mrs. Howard (Mildred) Fremody of Tarpon Springs, Fla.; and a brother, Milo Clay of Florida."[638,2121]

Also, "Orpha, besides being a housewife all her adult life, taught at Carverville School in Lee Twp., Calhoun Co., MI. She was a charter member of Navy Mothers (WWII) Fountain City Chapter #375, Army Mothers (WWII), 4 Star Mother (mother of 4 sons in the service) with a flag displayed in the window during WWII and Senior Regent of Moose Lodge in 1945-46."[2115] She also taught school at the Crawford School.[2117]

On 14 March 1913, when Orpha was 20, she married **Jesse John ORRISON,**[639-644,180] son of Peter ORRISON and Louisa ALLEN DODD, in Jackson, Jackson County, Michigan.[645,2118] He was born on 18 June 1889 in Clarence Township, Calhoun County, Michigan.[646]

Jesse died in Marshall, Calhoun County, Michigan, on 30 November 1957; he was 68, at the Oaklawn Hospital. Buried in Marshall, Calhoun County, Michigan,[647] at Oakridge Cemetery.

Occupations: Baggage Man (1913-1915, 1917); Grain Elevator Laborer (1917, 1920, 1923); Laborer (1926); Railroad Car

Repairer (1929, 1930); Machine Operator, Eaton Manufacturing (1931, 1934, 1940, 1950).[648-659]

1930, October: "William Desy and Jesse J. Orrison were hunting rabbitts in Marengo township yesterday afternoon. Mr. Desy was in a clump of bushes waiting for a rabbitt to come past and as it did Mr. Orrison let go. Seven of the shot struck Desy in the legs. He was taken to Dr Church's residence where the wounds were dressed. The shot could not be found at first but later it was ascertained that they had merely penetrated the clothing but had not embedded themselves in the flesh, altho the flesh had been punctured in seven places."[2121]

Obituary: "MARSHALL - Jesse J. Orrison, 68, of 124 W. Spruce St., a retired employe of Eaton Manufacturing Co. here, died at Oaklawn Hospital at 5:55 a.m. today. He had been admitted to the hospital Friday. Mr. Orrison was born June 18, 1809, in Clarence Township, son of Peter and Louisa (Allen) Orrison. He grew up in Springport where he attended school. He was married to Orpha Clay on March 14, 1913, in Jackson. Mr. Orrison retired three years ago after 24 years at the Eaton plant here. He was a member of the Loyal Order of Moose. No. 676, of Marshall. He is survived by his wife, seven sons, N. Keith and Gilford C. of Marshall, Capt. J. Eugene of Tucson, Ariz., now stationed in Japan, Capt. Howard of Williamsburg, Va., now stationed at Ft. Eustis, Va., Robert, at sea with the Navy, Jack D. of San Diego, and Pvt. James F. of Ft. Lewis, Wash.; a daughter, Mrs. Lawrence (Joyce) Masters of Burlington; 15 grandchildren; two great-grandchildren and a nephew, William Ellis of Marshall."[660]

"Jesse attended Springport, Michigan schools. He played baseball in high school. ... Jesse and Orpha were married by Rev. H.D. Allen. Work history – set type for *Springport Signal*, was a farm hand for Will Allen in Lee Township, was baggage handler for Michigan Central R.R. in Jackson, worked in the round house in Marshall for Michigan Central Railroad and retired in 1954 after 24 years at Eaton Corp., Marshall, Michigan."[2120]

Military:

U.S., World War I Draft Registration Cards, 1917-1918:
Name: Jesse John Orrison | Age: 27 | Race: Caucasian Marital Status: Married | Natural citizen | Birth Date/ Place: 18 Jun 1889, Clarence, Mich. | Residence Date: 1917-1918 | Residence Place: Springport, Mich. | Occupation: Elevator workman Support? Wife & two children | Physical Build: Medium | Height: Short | Hair Color: Light | Eye Color: Brown[456]

U.S., World War II Draft Registration Cards, 1942:
Name: Jesse John Orrison | Age: 52 | Race: White | Height: 5′ 4″ | Eyes: Brown | Weight: 130 | Hair: Brown | Complexion: Ruddy | Gender: Male | Birth Date/Place: 18 Jun 1889, Calhoun Co. Michigan | Residence Place: 402 N. Mulberry Marshall, Calhoun Michigan | Military Draft Date: 1942 | Next of Kin: Mrs Louisa Allen [mother][628]

Orpha and Jesse had the following children:

64 i. **Guilford Charles ORRISON**. Born on 14 August 1914, in Jackson, Jackson County, Michigan. Guilford died in Marshall, Calhoun County, Michigan, on 6 January 1959; he was 44.

65 ii. **Maj. Jesse Eugene ORRISON**. Born on 3 September 1916, in Jackson County, Michigan. Jesse died in Tucson, Pima County, Arizona, on 6 September 1997; he was 81.

66 iii. **Maj. Howard Clay ORRISON**. Born on 20 August 1918, in Springport, Jackson County, Michigan. Howard died in Oregon in February 2012; he was 93. *[reported, not verified]*.

67 iv. **Robert Elton ORRISON**. Born on 22 April 1923, in Lee Township, Calhoun County, Michigan. Robert died in Lompoc, Santa Barbara County, California, on 19 November 1993; he was 70.

68 v. **Norman Keith ORRISON**. Born on 28 May 1926, in Marshall, Calhoun County, Michigan. Norman died in Battle Creek, Calhoun County, Michigan, on 22 August 1986; he was 60.

69 vi. **Jack Duane ORRISON**. Born on 17 April 1928, in Lee Township, Calhoun County, Michigan. Jack died in Concord, Jackson County, Michigan, on 20 January 2012; he was 83.

70 vii. **Joyce Marie ORRISON**. Born on 18 February 1930, in Marshall, Calhoun County, Michigan. Joyce died in Sardinia, Brown County, Ohio, on 3 February 2020; she was 89.

71 viii. **James Frederick ORRISON**. Born on 2 January 1936, in Michigan. James died in Cleveland, Bradley County, Tennessee, on 17 April 2017; he was 81.

Noted from Patchin Family Association and Kathleen Marie O'Dell Townsley:

"Children, ORRISON:

2181 Jesse John, b. June 18, 1889; m. Mar. 14, 1913, Orpha, dau. Cassius and Ella (Scott) [sic] Clay, b. July 10, 1892; chn, ORRISON:

2182 Guilford Church, [sic Guilford Charles] b. Aug. 14, 1914.

2183 Jessie Eugenia, [sic Jesse Eugene] b. Sept. 3, 1916.

2184 Howard Clay, b. Aug. 20, 1918.

2185 Robert Elton, b. Apr. 22, 1923.

2186 Norma [sic Norman] Keith, b. May 28, 1926.

2187 Jack Duane, b. Apr. 17, 1928.

2188 Joyce Marie, b. Feb. 18, 1930."[212]

---

23. Milo Schutt CLAY[661-666] (*Cassius M.*[3], *Fredric*[2], *Abegail*[1]).

Born on 27 November 1895, in Springport, Jackson County, Michigan,[667,408] Milo died in Sebring, Highlands County, Florida, on 10 March 1976; he was 80.[556,408]

Occupations: Switchman, Telephone (1916); Inspector (1917); Assistant Office Manager (1936); Electrician (1919, 1920, 1942); Salesman (1938, 1940); Supervisor (1945); Building Contractor (1950).[668-678]

Religion: United Church Of Christ.

> *Obituary*: "CLAY - Milo S, passed away March 10, 1976, in Sebring, Fla. He was a resident of Holiday for the past 13 years and a member of the Holiday United Church of Christ, Holiday. He is survived by his wife, Esselteen M. Clay, of Holiday, one daughter, Mrs. John Eckhardt Jr., and one grandson, John F. Eckhardt, III. He was a member of Masonic Lodge No 192 F&AM, Dunedin, Fla. The family requests that all memorials be in the form of contributions to Holiday United Church Building Fund in memory of Milo Clay. Memorial services will be announced from the church."[679]

Military:

U.S., World War I Draft Registration Cards, 1917-1918:

Name: Milo Schutt Clay | Age: 21 | Race: Caucasian | Marital Status: Married | Support? wife | Occupation: Inspector, Reo Motor Car Co, Lansing, Mich | Birth Date/Place: 27 Nov 1895, Springport, Michigan | Residence Date: 1917-1918 | Registration Date: 5 June 1917 | Street Address: 521 William | Residence Place: Lansing, Mich. | Physical Build: Medium |Height: Medium | Hair Color: Light | Eye Color: Blue | Bald? No[456]

U.S., World War II Draft Registration Cards, 1942:

Name: Milo Schutt Clay | Age: 46 | Gender: Male | Race: White Height 5' 9" | Eyes: Blue | Weight: 170 | Hair: Brown | Complexion: Ruddy | Birth Date/Place: 27 Nov 1895, Jackson Michigan | Residence Place: 497 E Lewiston Ave Ferndale Oakland Mich | Military Draft Date: 1942 | Registration Date: 27 April 1942 | Next of Kin: Geo. K. Moore | Employer: Square D Co, Detroit, Wayne, Michigan[680]

On 17 July 1916, when Milo was 20, he married **Esselteen Mae CHURCH,**[681-683] daughter of George H. CHURCH and Ella DERMOTT, in Bay City, Bay County, Michigan,[684-687] by Rev. William Bryant, of the Presbyterian Church South Lyon, Michigan. She was born on 7 April 1893, in Bellevue, Eaton County, Michigan.[408,688] [Death record say 6 April; born in Olivet, Michigan]. Years later it was revealed they eloped.

Esselteen died at the Hendersonville Retirement Center, in Hendersonville, Henderson County, North Carolina, on 26 August 1991; she was 98.[408,689] Buried on 1 September 1991, Shepherd Memorial Park Cemetery.

Occupation: Sales Lady (1940).[690]

Religion: Baptist / Methodist.

Obituary: "BAT CAVE - Esselteen M. Clay, 98, died Monday, Aug. 26, in a Henderson County retirement center.

A native of Olivet, Mich., and a former resident of Holliday, Fla., she had been a summer resident of Henderson County since 1986. She was the wife of Milo Schutt Clay, who died in 1976.

Surviving are a daughter, Betty J. Eckhardt of Bat Cave; grandson, and two great-grandsons.

Memorial services will be at 3 p.m. Sunday in Clear Branch Baptist Church. The Rev. Houston Rider will officiate.

Memorials may be made to Clear Branch Baptist Church Building Fund, 80 Stroud Valley Road, Black Mountain 28711.

Thos. Shepherd & Son Funeral Directors is in charge of arrangements."[691]

Milo and Esselteen had the following children:

72 i. **Charlyne Ella CLAY**. Born on 15 March 1918, in Lansing, Ingham County, Michigan. Charlyn died in Detroit, Wayne County, Michigan, on 4 September 1918; she was almost 6 months old.

73 ii. **Betty Jane CLAY**. Born on 28 February 1920, in Michigan. Betty died in Asheville, Buncombe County, North Carolina, on 26 April 1999; she was 79.

24. Edith Irene CLAY[692-702] (*Frank Henry*[3], *Fredric*[2], *Abegail*[1]).

Born on 3 October 1891, in Albion, Calhoun County, Michigan,[408,703,2141] Edith died in Kalamazoo, Kalamazoo County, Michigan, on 3 September 1986; she was 94.[704,408] Buried in Springport, Jackson County, Michigan,[705] Springport Cemetery.

Occupations: Student (1910, 1911); School Teacher (1913-1955).[706-730]

On 24 August 1917, when Edith was 25, she married **Ralph Robert WALLACE** in Evanston, Cook County, Illinois.[731] Ralph was born 25 December 1886, in Elyria Township, Lorain County, Ohio, to James William WALLACE and Lydia Mary VEITS.[2142,2143] He died 8 September 1957, in Carmel, Hamilton County, Indiana, and was buried 11 September 1957, in Carmel, Hamilton County, Indiana, at the Carmel Cemetery.[2144,2145]

They were divorced in 1927, in Cleveland, Cuyahoga County, Ohio.[732]

> *Obituary*: "Robert R. Wallace, 70, Carmel, was buried today in Carmel Cemetery after services in the Smith Funeral Home. He died Sunday in his home, 410 W. Main.
>
> Born at Elyria, O., Mr. Wallace had lived at Carmel 16 years and was a retired heating engineer, having been employed by both the Hall-Neal Furnace Co. and the Round Oak Stove Co. During World War I he served in the Army.
>
> The widow, Janet Wallace, survives."[2146]

Obituary: "Funeral services have ben [sic] arranged for Robert R. Wallace, age 70, who passed away Sunday morning at his residence In Carmel where he had lived for 16 years.

Services will be held Wednesday afterrnoon at 2 o'clock at the Smith Funeral Home, Carmel, with Rev. Robert Stewart, pastor of the Orchard Park Presbyterian Church in charge. Interment will follow in Carmel Cemetery.

The deceased was a retired heating engineer with the Hall-Neal Company. He is survived by the widow Janet Wallace.

Friends wil [sic] be received at the funeral home after the noon hour, Tuesday."[2147]

Military:

U.S., World War I Draft Registration Cards, 1917-1918:

Name: Ralph R Wallace | Race: Caucasian | Marital Status: Widower | Birth Date/Place: 25 Dec 1886; Elyria Ohio, US | Residence Date: 1917-1918 | Street Address: 1610 Elmwood Ave Wilmette, Ill. | Occupation: Mgr. & part owner of garage | Employer: Central Motor Car Co, Evanston Ill. | Supporting? Mother and 2 children | Marital status: Widower | Prior Military Service? Rank: private, State National Guard for 18 months | Exemption? Business and family dependent on me | Draft Board: 3, 31 May 1917 | Physical Build: Slender | Height: Tall | Hair Color: Light | Bald? No | Eye Color: Blue[2148]

U.S., World War II Draft Registration Cards, 1942:

Name: Robert Ralph Wallace | Gender: Male | Age: 55 | Race: White | Birth Date: 25 Dec 1886 | Birth Place: Elyria, Ohio | Residence Place: Hamilton, Indiana | Military Draft Registration Date: 27 April 1942, Noblesville, Hamilton County, Indiana | Employer: Round Oak Co Dowagiac Michigan | Height: 5' 7" | Weight: 134 | Eyes: Blue | Hair: Gray | Complexion: Light | Next of Kin: Janet Wallace Carmel Ind.[2149]

Edith and Robert had one child:

74 i. **Helen Edith WALLACE**. Born on 2 June 1918, in Kalamazoo, Kalamazoo County, Michigan. Helen died in Kalamazoo, Kalamazoo County, Michigan, on 18 November 2000; she was 82.

Ralph was first married to Gertrude SLINGERLAND (1878-1912) in 1904, divorced in 1911, and had two children: James Alfred WALLACE and Eleanor L. WALLACE ROBERTS

(1907-1991). His third marriage, after Edith, was to Charlotte S. SMITH (1884-1963) in 1927, but ended in divorce in 1931. His last marriage was to Frankie Janet GUSS (1888-?) in 1941. Frankie was appointed administratrix of Ralph's will.

25. Eldon Rodgers CLAY[733-742] (*Frank Henry*[3], *Fredric "Fred"*[2], *Abegail*[1]).

Born on 12 September 1894, in Springport, Jackson County, Michigan,[408] Eldon died in Kandiyohi County, Minnesota, on 27 April 1975; he was 80.[743,408] Buried in Montevideo, Chippewa County, Minnesota,[744] Sunset Memorial Cemetery.

Occupations: Student (1910-1913); Salesman (1914, 1921, 1927, 1929, 1930, 1932, 1950); Clerk (1926); Clay Typewriter Company (1946, 1948); Gift Shop Owner (1956).[745-760]

25. *Eldon Rodgers CLAY – Photograph from Linda Johnson Klinghagen, findagrave.com*

[Not found in 1920 and 1940 US censuses.]

Military:

U.S., World War I Draft Registration Cards, 1917-1918:

Name: Eldon R Clay | Race: White | Marital Status: Single | Birth Date/Place: 12 Sep 1894, Springport, Mich. USA | Residence Date: 1917-1918 | Street Address: 706 So Rose | Residence Place: Kalamazoo, Kalamazoo, Michigan, USA | Draft Board: 2 | Physical Build: Medium | Height: Medium | Hair Color: Blonde | Eye Color: Blue | Occupation: Salesman, Harcla Research Co. | Do you claim exemption from draft? Yes - near sight defective hearing[456]

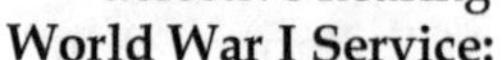

World War I Service:

Private 3rd Class; assigned 3 Company.; sent Camp McDowell, Angel Island, San Francisco.[761]

Fort McDowell, San Francisco, 3rd Recruit Company[762]

Enlistment: Army; Service: 17 October 1918 to 3 December 1918.[763]

U.S., World War II Draft Registration Cards, 1942:

Name: Eldon Rodgers Clay | Gender: Male | Registration Age: 47 | Birth Date/Place: 12 Sep 1894, Springport, Michigan, USA | Residence Place: 317 East Tenth, Winona, Winona, Minnesota | Registration Date: abt 1941 | Military Draft Date: 1942 | Height: 5 8 | Eye Color: Blue | Hair Color: Brown | Weight: 185 | Complexion: Light | Large mole on back | Spouse: Margaret J. Clay (Wife)[764]

On 25 May 1919, when Eldon Rodgers was 24, he first married **Anna Marie PETERSON**,[735,765-767] daughter of Albert John PETERSON and Christine LARSON, in Tucson, Pima County, Arizona.[768] She was born on 2 October 1897, in Somerset, Steele County, Minnesota.[769,770,408] Anna died in San Diego, San Diego County, California, on 16 March 1973; she was 75.[771,408]

Occupation: Aircraft Electronic Device Assembler (1950).[772]

They were divorced on 26 April 1922, in Kalamazoo County, Michigan.[773]

Eldon and Anna had one child:

75 i. **Kathleen Marguerite CLAY**. Born on 16 March 1920, in Owatonna, Steele County, Minnesota. Kathleen died in Oceanside, San Diego County, California, on 12 February 2000; she was 79.

On 31 December 1936, when Eldon Rodgers was 42, he second married **Margaret Estelle JOHNSON**,[774,775] daughter of John O. JOHNSON and Carrie HAGEN, in Milbank, Grant County, South Dakota,[776] by Rev. F. Wessler. She was born on 10 March 1904, in Willmar, Kandiyohi County, Minnesota.[2150,2152] Margaret died in Yellow Medicine County, Minnesota, on 30 January 1991;[2151] she was 86. Buried in Montevideo, Chippewa County, Minnesota,[777] at Sunset Memorial Cemetery.

Margaret Estelle JOHNSON. Photograph from Linda Johnson Klinghagen, findagrave.com

Religion: United Methodist Church.

Occupation: Typing, Retail Store (1950).[778]

"When she was 4, in 1908, Margaret moved with her family from the New London, MN, area to a farm homestead near Rainy Butte, ND. When she was 5, Carrie, her mother, contracted typhoid fever in 1909 and died. She was buried in North Dakota.

She moved with her family from North Dakota back to the New London area in Minnesota in 1912. Margaret would have been only 8 at the time, but there was no mention of a foster family taking care of her. Since she remained close to her cousins, Agnes and Olga, and since she was mentioned as a 'sister' in one of their obituaries, it would make sense that she probably stayed with the Elkjers, at least part of the time.

Margaret attended school in New London. In the New London History, there was a Margaret Johnson that played in the band – but I don't know if it was this Margaret or not. Her cousins, Olga and Agnes Elkjer, attended school in Willmar – so Margaret probably stayed somewhere else instead of the Elkjer's in rural Pennock, at least while she attended school.

Margaret was employed a number of years as a clerk at the Carlson Brothers Drug Store in Willmar. In a letter to her dad, John O. Johnson, written in April of 1924, with a return address for her of Willmar, MN, she said that 'I'm getting tired of just being in one place and working for years at the same thing. A change would seem so nice but one must live so I suppose it's best to stay where I am sure of a job.'

Eldon operated a typewriter shop in Winona until 1954, when they moved to Duluth, MN. From November 1955 to June 1956, they operated a gift shop in Grand Junction, CO, following which Eldon was in the real estate business for ten years in Winona, MN. In 1969, they moved to Montevideo.

Margaret and Eldon had no children – but they did have a beloved dog – a bulldog named Midge.

Following Eldon's death, Margaret lived in a retirement home with her cousins, Agnes and Olga Elkjer."[2159]

Obituary: "CLARA CITY - Margaret Clay, 86 of Montevideo died Thursday at the Clarkfield Care Center. Funeral services will be at 10 a.m. Monday at the United Methodist Church, with the Rev. Ramon Olson officiating. Interment will be in the Sunset Memorial Cemetery.

Visitation and reviewal will be one hour prior to the service on Monday at the church. Wing-Bain Funeral Home, Montevideo, is in charge of the arrangements.

Margaret Clay was born March 10, 1904 near New London to Carrie and John Johnson. On Dec. 31, 1936 she married Eldon R. Clay. They lived in Winona and moved to Montevideo in 1969. She was a member of the United Methodist Church. Surviving are one sister, Harriet Soland of New London; two sisters-in-law, Bertha Johnson of Los Angeles and Ella Johnson of Homestead, Mont.; several nieces and nephews; and a cousin, Agnes Elkjer of Montevideo. She was preceded in death by her husband, Eldon Clay, in 1975; her parents; one sister; and three brothers."[2153]

FIFTH GENERATION

26. John R. PICKLES[779] (*Samuel James PICKLES/PICKELL*[4], *Hannah CLAY*[3], *Isaac*[2], *Abegail*[1]).

Born in September 1889, in Michigan. John died in Douglass Township, Montcalm County, Michigan, on 24 November 1889; he was less than 2 months old.[780] Buried in Douglass Township, Montcalm County, Michigan,[781] Entrican Cemetery.

27. Ruth PICKLES[782-789,180] (*Samuel James PICKLES/PICKELL*[4], *Hannah CLAY*[3], *Isaac*[2], *Abegail*[1]).

Newspaper photograph:
27. *Ruth PICKLES and Ezard Percy MEDD at 50th wedding anniversary.*

Born on 2 September 1890, in Greenville, Montcalm County, Michigan, Ruth died in Kissimmee, Osceola County, Florida, on 28 October 1965; she was 75.[556] Buried in Kissimmee, Osceola County, Florida,[790] at Osceola Memory Gardens.

Religion: Methodist; Congregational.

In the 1910 census indicates she had three children of which two, Ford and Gertrude, were the only living. So, a child died between 1907-1910.

> *1913, July:* Advertisement, "Wanted—A girl or woman for general housework. Mrs. E. P. Medd, 1139 Madison Ave"[791]
>
> *1930, January:* "Mrs. E. P. Medd, Grand Rapids, Mich., will spend the season in Lake Worth, arriving here recently by motor. She lives on Pine street."[792]
>
> *Obituary*: "MRS. RUTH PICKELL MEDD, 75, 210 N. Bermuda Ave., Kissimmee, died Thursday.
>
> A native of Greenville, Mich., she moved to Kissimmee 15 years ago. She was a member of the Congregational Church.
>
> Survivors: husband, E. Percy; sons, Ford H., Kissimmee and Robert R., Grand Rapids, Mich.; daughter, Mrs. Sam Reid, Alma, Mich.; brother, James E., Paradise, Calif.; five grandchildren; 11 great-grandchildren.
>
> Riedel Funeral Home, Kissimmee, in charge."[793,794]

On 8 June 1907, when Ruth was 16, she married **Ezard Percy MEDD**,[795-801,180] son of Ezard MEDD (1849-1911) and Angeline DENNISON (1851-1907), in Grand Rapids, Kent County, Michigan.[802,803] He was born on 28 August 1883, in Howard City, Montcalm County, Michigan.[804,408] Ezard died in Orlando, Orange County, Florida, on 12 July 1967; he was 83.[408,805] Buried in Kissimmee, Osceola County, Florida,[806] at Osceola Memory Gardens.

Occupations: Machinist (1905); Electrician (1907); Restaurant (1907, 1908, 1909); Automobile Mechanic (1910-1916, 1918-1924, 1927-1930; 1933, 1936); Maintenance Man (1938, 1940).[807-835]

> *1917, February, Advertisement:* "E. P. Medd Electrician & Engineer 'The Auto Workshop' Three years trouble tester with the largest gasoline motor manufacturers in United States. 951 Madison Ave., S. E. (Rear) Citizens 32855."[836]

Percy was a collector and restorer of hundreds of clocks, dating from 1808 to 1949.[837]

Obituary: "MR. E. PERCY MEDD, 83, 201 N. Bermuda Ave., Kissimmee, died Wednesday in Orlando.

A native of Howard City, Mich., he moved to Kissimmee from Alama, Mich., upon his retirement as a maintenance engineer from the Michigan Chemical Co. His hobby was building and restoring grandfather clocks.

Survivors: sons, Ford, Kissimmee and Roberts, Grand Rapids, Mich.; sister, Mrs. Bessie Shcolosser, Grand Rapids, Mich.; five grandchildren and 11 great-grandchildren.

Conrad & Thompson Funeral Home in charge."[838]

"MEDD, MR. E. PERCY - Funeral services for Mr. E. Percy Medd, 83, Kissimmee, who died Wednesday in Orlando, will be in the chapel of Conrad & Thompson Funeral Home at 2 p.m. Sunday with the Rev. Doyle Shirley, pastor of the Woodhaven Baptist Church of Orlando, officiating. Survivors are two sons, Ford Medd of Kissimmee and Robert Medd of Grand Rapids. Mich.; one daughter, Mrs. Sam Reid of Alma, Mich.; a sister, Mrs. Bessie Scholosser, Grand Rapids; S grandchildren; 11 great-grandchildren. Interment will be at a later date. Conrad & Thompson Funeral Home, Kissimmee, in charge."[839]

Military:

U.S., World War I Draft Registration Cards, 1917-1918:

Serial Number: 3524 | Name: E Percy Medd | Race: White | Age: 35 | Birth Date: 28 Aug 1883 | Residence Date: 1917-1918 | Street Address: 951 Maclinor, Grand Rapids, Kent, Michigan | Draft Board: 3 | Occupation: Auto Repairer, Medd Garage | Physical Build: Medium | Height: Medium | Hair Color: Brown | Eye Color: Brown | "first finger crooked on right hand" | Nearest Relative: Ruth Medd, Wife[840]

U.S., World War II Draft Registration Cards, 1942:

Name: (E.) Percy Medd | 315 Orchard St, Alma, Gratiot, Mich | Age: 59 | Place of Birth: Winfield Twp. Montcalm Mich | Date of Birth: Aug 28 1883 | Person Who Knows You: Ed McCarrick - Grandville Mich | Race: White | Height: 5' 11 | Eyes: Brown Weight: - | Hair: Gray | Complexion: Ruddy | "Crippled Right Hand"[841]

Ruth and Ezard had the following children:

i. **Ford Hackley MEDD.**[842-846,180] Born on 5 June 1908, in Muskegon, Muskegon County, Michigan. Ford died in Kissimmee, Osceola County, Florida, on 24 April 1983; he was 74. He married Ruth Wilma ALLEN.

ii. [unnamed child, per 1910 census, between 1907-1910]

iii. **Gertrude Winona MEDD.**[847-854,180] Born on 28 March 1910, in Michigan. Gertrude died in Alma, Gratiot County, Michigan, on 13 December 1985; she was 75. She married Samuel Charles REID.

iv. **Robert Reginald MEDD.**[855-860] Born on 7 January 1912, in Grand Rapids, Kent County, Michigan. Robert died in Kalamazoo, Kalamazoo County, Michigan, on 9 January 1992; he was 80. He married Ethel May QUACKENBUSH.

"KISSIMMEE - Mr. and Mrs. E. P. Medd were honored on their golden wedding anniversary with an open house at the home of their son, Ford Medd, in Davis Bungalow Park.

They were married June 9, 1907 [sic] at Grand Rapids, Mich., and have three children, all of whom were here to attend the celebration. They are Ford Medd, Kissimmee; and Mrs. Sam Reed and Robert R. Medd, both of Grand Rapids.

MR. AND MRS. Medd moved to Kissimmee eight years ago to make their home at 210 Bermuda after his retirement from the Michigan Chemical Co. in St. Louis, Mich.

They have five grandchildren and five great-grandchildren.

Their son, Robert, his wife and daughters, Susan and Linda, returned to Grand Rapids this week after visiting here since May."[861]

---

28. Frederick William "Fred" PICKLES/PICKELL [862-868,180] (*Samuel James*[4]*, Hannah CLAY*[3]*, Isaac*[2]*, Abegail*[1]).

Born on 4 December 1890, in Douglass Township, Montcalm County, Michigan[353,408,869] Fred died in Orange County, California, on 29 November 1964; he was 73.[870,408] Buried in Sylmar, Los Angeles County, California,[871] at Glen Haven Memorial Park.

Occupations: Machinist (1907, 1910-1911, 1929, Airplane 1940); Repairman (1913-1915); Mechanic (1917, 1923); Electrician (1918-1920); Toolmaker (1924); Experimental Machinist (1930); Filing Station Attendant (1935); Machine Shop Proprietor (1950); Crop Duster (1955).[348,872-89]

1945, April: formed a business at "5743 Aldama Street, Los Angeles 42, California" under "Fred W. Pickles and Associates" in partnership with his spouse Lena I. Pickell.[894]

Military:

U.S., World War I Draft Registration Cards, 1917-1918:

Name: Frederic Wm Pickell | Race: Caucasian | Age: 26 | Marital Status: Married | Birth Date/Place: December 4 1890, Douglas Montcalm Co Michigan U.S.A. | Support?: wife and baby of one year | Residence Date: 1917-1918 | Street Address: 432 Graham Grand Rapids, Kent, Michigan | Occupation: gas engine mechanic | Draft Board: 3 | Physical Build: Medium | Height: Tall | Hair Color: Dark Brown | Eye Color: Grey | [previous] Military service?: Rank Private, Hospital Ward, one year, Michigan | Claim exception? Yes.[840]

U.S., World War II Draft Registration Cards, 1942:

Name: Fred William Pickell | Gender: Male | Age: 50 | Race: White | Height: 5' 10.5" | Eyes: Hazel | Weight: 168 | Hair: Brown | Complexion: Ruddy | Birth Date/Place: 4 Dec 1891, Montcalm Michigan | Residence Place: 5734 Aldama St. Los Angeles, California | Military Draft Date: 1942 | Next of Kin: Lena I. Pickell[895]

On 14 May 1913, when Fred was 22, he first married **Lena Irena RITTENHOUSE**[896-901], daughter of William Judson RITTENHOUSE and Mary Irene GARBER, in Grand Rapids, Kent County, Michigan.[902] She was born on 20 August 1891, in Big Rapids, Mecosta County, Michigan, and died in Los Angeles, Los Angeles County, California, on 27 July 1951; she was 59.[870] Buried on 31 July 1951, in Sylmar, Los Angeles County, California,[903] Glen Haven Memorial Park.

> *Obituary*: "Mrs. Lena Irena Pickell of 5074 Aldama st., died July 27 at the family residence.
>
> She was born 59 year ago in Big Rapids, Mich., and married May 14, 1913, to Fred William Pickell. She and her sister, who were married in the same double service, recently celebrated their 38th anniversary together. Memorial services were held July 31 at

In March 1907, 15-year-old [sic] **28.** *Fred wrote and article for* Popular Mechanics *magazine, "Young Mechanic Builds Successful Auto."*[2167]

Utter McKinley Highland Park chapel, with the Rev. Alden Lee Hill officiating. Interment was in Glen Haven.

She is survived by her husband, her son Philip, two daughters, Marjorie H. Fisher and Dorothy Weaver, four grandchildren, a sister, Mrs. Mae Clark and two brothers, George and Clarence Rettinhous. [sic]"[904]

Fred and Lena had the following children:

i. **Fronda Irene PICKELL.** Born on 1 June 1914, in Michigan. Fronda died in Grand Rapids, Kent County, Michigan, on 7 June 1915; she was one year old.

ii. **Marjorie Hannah PICKLES/PICKELL.**[905-909,180] Born on 10 April 1916, in Michigan. Marjorie died in Simi Valley, Ventura County, California, on 18 August 2007; she was 91. She married Capt. Stanley Frederick NAUJOKS-FISHER.

iii. **Dorothy Marie PICKLES/PICKELL.**[910-915] Born on 23 March 1918, in Howard City, Montcalm County, Michigan. Dorothy died in Bradenton Beach, Manatee County, Florida, on 22 July 2007;

she was 89. She married Forrest Lionel "Buck" WEAVER.

iv. **Milo PICKLES/PICKELL**. Born on 3 July 1923, in Michigan. Milo died a Butterworth Hospital, in Grand Rapids, Kent County, Michigan, on 19 August 1926; he was three years old.

v. **Phillip Roger PICKELL.**[916-919] Born on 12 February 1932, in Michigan. Phillip died in Las Vegas, Clark County, Nevada, on 28 June 1999; he was 67. He married Rose Marie RAWLINS.

On 29 June 1952, when Fred was 61, he second married **Mertle Marie HARDING,**[920,890,891,921,180] daughter of William Franklin HARDING and Fances G. WADE, in Los Angeles, Los Angeles County, California.[922] She was born on 24 April 1893, in Brockton, Plymouth County, Massachusetts.[923,924] Mertle died in Los Angeles, Los Angeles County, California, on 10 December 1970; she was 77.[923,925,926] Buried in Glendale, Los Angeles County, California,[927] at Forest Lawn Memorial Park.

Occupation: Typist (1953, 1958, 1959).[928-930]

Military: [Fred] Military Service Date: 30 July 1920[923]

This union had no children.

---

29. James Edward PICKLES/PICKELL[109,931-939] (*Samuel James*[4], *Hannah CLAY*[3], *Isaac*[2], *Abegail*[1]).

Born on 27 February 1894, in Lakeview, Montcalm County, Michigan,[408] James died at Northwest Medical Center Hospital, in Santa Rosa, Harris County, Texas, on 23 February 1974; he was 79.[940,408] Buried on 24 February 1974 in Paradise, Butte County, California,[941] at Paradise Cemetery.

Occupation: Draughtsman (1910); Laboratory (1910); Foundry Patternmaker (1920, 1924, 1930); Designer (1935); Pattern Inspector (1940, 1950); Wood Pattern Maker Cabinet Making (1974).[942-950]

Religion: Roman Catholic.

Obituary: "Former Paradise resident James Edward Pickell, 79, died Saturday at a hospital in Houston, Tex. He was born Feb. 27, 1894, in Entrican, Mich.

Pickell had lived in Paradise 12 years before moving to Houston. He had been a cabinet maker for 30 years and was a member of St. Thomas More Catholic Church.

Surviving are a son, James, of Houston; a daughter, Mary Cotter, of Santa Rosa; and eight grandchildren.

The Rosary was recited yesterday (Thursday) evening at 8 p.m. at Rose Chapel with Father William Storan of St. Thomas More Church officiating.

Mass will be celebrated today (Friday) at St. Thomas More Church at 10 a.m. with Msgr. Raymond Ronwald officiating. Burial will be in Paradise Cemetery."[951]

Military:

World War I Military service: 14 December 1917 to 1 August 1919.[763]

Headstone Application, 1974: Enlistment from 12 December 1917 to 22 July 1919; Private, state of South Carolina, US Army 36th Ario Squadron. Applicant: Mary Pickell Cotter [daughter][952]

U.S., World War I Draft Registration Cards, 1917-1918:

Name: James Edward Pickell | Race: Caucasian | Marital Status: Married | Birth Date/Place: 27 Feb 1894, Lake View Michigan U.S.A. | Residence Date: 1917-1918 | Street Address: 1216 Jackson Street Grand Rapids, Kent, Michigan | Occupation: garage foreman, Standard Oil Co. | Support? wife and mother | Former Military Service: first class private; field hospital, 1.5 years, M. N. G. [Michigan National Guard] Draft Board: 1 | Physical Build: Medium | Height: Tall | Hair Color: Light Brown | Eye Color: Gray[953]

"Pickell James E | 2070814 Pvt ASSC | Grace Pickell Wife 248 Marion Ave Grand Rapids Mich"[954]

Transported to Camp Hospital 85, Reserve Camp, Morton; incoming aboard *S S Mancuria* from St Azaire [France], 14 March 1919; 36th Aero Squadron, Air Service.[955]

U.S., World War II Draft Registration Cards, 1942:

Serial Number U 1259 | Name: James E. Pickell | Place of Residence: 2311 Calif. Ave. Santa Monica, L.A. Cal. | Age: 48 | Place of Birth: Montcalm, Mich. | Date of Birth: 27 February 1894 | Person Who Knows You: F. W. Pickell, Aldamen. Highland Park [brother] | Employer: Douglas Aircraft Co, 3000 Ocean Park Blvd. L.A. Cal. | Race: White | Height: 5-10 1/2 | Eyes: Hazel | Weight: 192 | Hair: Brown | Complexion: Light | "1 short finger on left hand" | Registration date: 26 April 1942.[956]

On 10 May 1915, when James was 21, he first married **Grace E. SHARP,**[957,958,180] daughter of John SHARP and Katherine MANNING, in Detroit, Wayne County, Michigan,[959] by Justice-of-the-Peace A. F. Masschiner. She was born on 6 August 1896, in Missouri. Grace died in Grand Rapids, Kent County, Michigan, on 27 February 1963; she was 66. Buried on 2 March 1963 in Six Lakes, Belvedere Township, Montcalm County, Michigan,[960] Hillcrest Cemetery.

Occupation: Saxaphone Assembler (1924).[961]

"Pickell James E, 2070814, Pvt, Grace Pickell, Wife, 248 Marion Ave, Grand Rapids Mich"[964]

They were divorced circa 1924.[962] She later remarried to Mr. FORGAR.

> *Obituary*: "FORGAR Mrs. Grace E Forgar aged 67 of 1944 Silver Ave SE passed away unexpectedly Wednesday morning at her residence. Surviving are a brother Daniel M. Sharp of Lansing. Funeral services will be held Saturday morning at 10 o'clock at the Sullivan Funeral Home where Mrs. Forgar reposes. Rev. Charles W. Scheid officiating. Interment Hillcrest Cemetery, Six Lakes, Mich."[963]

They had no children.

On 14 May 1925, when James was 31, he second married **Ann Marie WILLEMS/WILLIAMS,**[965-969] daughter of Joseph WILLEMS and Mary RADEMACHER, in Grand Rapids, Kent County, Michigan.[970] She was born on 28 February 1898, in Portland, Ionia County, Michigan. Ann Marie died in Paradise, Butte County, California, on 6 November 1967; she was 69. Buried on 8 November 1967 in Paradise, Butte County, California,[971] Paradise Cemetery.

Occupation: Nurse (1925).

Religion: Roman Catholic.

> *Obituary*: "PICKELL—in Paradise Butte County Nov. 6, 1967 Annie Marie Pickell wife of James E., mother of James J. of Midland Tex., and Mary Anne Cotter of Santa Rosa, sister of Pauline Schafer of Portland, Mich., grandmother of eight; a native of Portland, Mich., aged 69 years. The Rosary will be recited at 8 o'clock tonight in the Rose Chapel. A Requiem Mass will be offered at 9 a.m. tomorrow in the St. Thomas More Catholic Church. Burial will be in the Paradise Cemetery."[972]

They had the following children:

i. **James Joseph PICKELL Jr.**[966,973-975]. Born in November 1926, in Michigan. James died in Texas in January 2020; he was 93. He married Ellen Marie BYSHE.

ii. **Mary Anne PICKELL.**[966,976-978] Born on 20 January 1928 in Michigan. Mary died in California on 17 March 2011; she was 83. She married Daniel Sylvester COTTER.

30. Vena Emily KILBOURNE[979-985] (*Amelia Hannah Elizabeth PICKLES*[4], *Hannah CLAY*[3], *Isaac*[2], *Abegail*[1]).

Born on 12 January 1898, in Stanton, Montcalm County, Michigan,[408] Vena died in Grand Rapids, Kent County, Michigan, on 25 September 1995; she was 97.[408] Buried on 28 September 1995, in Grand Rapids, Kent County, Michigan,[986] at Woodlawn Cemetery.

30. *Vena Emily KILBOURNE*

Occupations: Nurse (1919, 1920); Businesswoman.[987]

Obituary: "Doyle – Vena E. Doyle, aged 97, of Grand Rapids, widow of Dewey I. Doyle, Sr., passed away at her home, September 25, 1995. Surviving are her son, Dewey I. 'Jack' (Georgina) Doyle, Jr. of Grand Rapids; eight grandchildren, Patricia (Christopher) Rose, Dewey I. 'Mike' (Nancee) Doyle III, Scott W. (Jill) Doyle, Joseph (Janice) Doyle, Daniel T. Doyle, and Mark (Diane) Doyle, 11 great grandchildren; and three sisters, Kathryn Lang, Evelyn L. Knapp, and Mary Myers. Funeral Services will be Thursday at 11:00 a.m. in the Metcalf & Jonkhoff Chapel. Interment Woodlawn Cemetery. Memorials to the Leukemia Foundation of Michigan are suggested. The family will receive friends Thursday 10:30 a.m. to 11 a.m. at Metcalf & Jonkhoff Funeral Service Cascade Rd. just east of I-96"[988]

Vena was a custodian of much of the genealogical information and photographs of the later Clay and Pickles families.

On 30 October 1919, when Vena Emily was 21, she married **Dewey Irwin DOYLE,**[989-995,109] son of Joseph Patrick DOYLE (1853-1922) and Rachel "Flora" SIMMONS (1858-1939), in Grand Rapids, Kent County, Michigan,[996] by J. Calvin Meese, Minister. Born on 6 February 1898, in Cedar Springs, Kent County, Michigan,[109,408] Dewey died in Grand Rapids, Kent County, Michigan, on 16 September 1978; he was 80.[408,997] He was buried in Grand Rapids, Kent County, Michigan,[998,763] Woodlawn Cemetery.

Dewey Irwin DOYLE – Photograph from school yearbook, 1917,[1031] *(member of Delta Tau Delta, Eastern Michigan University).*

Occupations: Insurance Salesman (1919); Furnace Salesman (1920); Heating Plant Salesman (1930); President, Vacuum Cleaner Company (1950); Inventor, Doyle Vacuum Cleaner Co.[999-1030]

The Doyle Vacuum Cleaner Company was founded by Dewey in 1929. The company focused on industrial and commercial applications. In 1941, it was purchased by David H. VanGorder, and the name changed in 2004 to Doyle Vacuum Systems, LLC. It continues to operate today – made in Michigan, made in the US, where it is a leading industrial manufacturer. doylevacuum.com

Education: Michigan State Normal School [Eastern Michigan University], 1917.

1922, December: Branch Manager, Homer Furnace Company, Grand Rapids, Michigan.[1032]

1923, March: Story about pet dog Wolf, a playmate of son "Little Jack Doyle."[1033]

1930, January: advertisement for Rhodes Furnace.[1034]

1959, August:

"Spending the week-end at the Dewey Doyle cottage were Mr. and Mrs. John Kilbourne of Mountainside, N. J., and the four young sons, Douglas, Jack, Ronald, and Gary.

Mr. Kilbourne is Mrs. Doyle's brother. Other guests of the Doyles recently have included their two sons and their families, Mr. and Mrs. Jack Doyle, with sons, Mike Scott and Dan, and Mr. and Mrs. Patrick Doyle and children, Patricia, Kathleen, Coleen, Joey and Mark."[1035]

1964, July: "...enjoying the company of their grandchildren, Colleen and Scott, this week. Colleen is the daughter of Mr. and Mrs. Patrick E. Doyle, Greenbrier Dr. SE. Scott's parents are Mr. and Mrs. Dewey I. Doyle Jr., Worchester Dr. NE. Sunday, Colleen's parents will come down with the rest of the family, Patricia, Kathy, Joey and Mark Kevin, to celebrate Joey's eleventh birthday."[1036]

1964, August: "... have their grandchildren, Kathleen, Joe and Mark Doyle, for several days, Mr. and Mrs. Patrick E. Doyle are parents of the children."[1037]

Military:

World War I Service: US Army:

* Squad 4; Number 25: Doyle, Dewey Irwin; Private first class; 119th Field Artillery, Battery F; Emergency Notification: Patrick J. Doyle, Father, Cedar Springs, Michigan; 26 February 1918, New York, New York.[1038]

* Embarkation *U.S.S. Frederick* to Brest, France, 22 April 1919; Number 7, Doyle, Dewey, 297740; Sergeant, Battery F, 119th Field Artillery; Emergency Notification: Patrick J. Doyle, Father, Cedar Springs, Michigan.[1039]

"Captain Writes Mrs. J. P. Doyle Son Guy Is Worthy of Decoration. Cedar Springs, Jan. 9. — Mrs. J. P. Doyle of this village has just received a letter from the captain of the company to which her son Guy belongs at Nouville, France. She and Guy's friends here are as proud of it as though he had received a medal. The letter follows:

'Now that the war has come to a successful finish there are many men in our commands who have performed deeds of valor and heroism constantly and have received little or no praise but are more deserving of mention than some of those who have been decorated.

Among these, in my estimation, is your son, Sergeant Dewey Doyle, whose unfaltering courage and devotion to duty has helped me in many a tight place and exemplified the true Americanism which has broken the Hun armies and under which pressure no armies could stand.

Had the action lasted a few weeks longer Sergeant Doyle would have been a commissioned officer as he was slated to go to school in December, and if the opportunity arises later he will be because no one that I know is more worthy of it. Harold H. Borgmah, Captain, 119th F. A.'"[1040]

"Cedar Springs, Jan. 13. Practically every resident of Cedar Springs is proud of Sergeant Dewey Doyle, almost as much so as his father and mother, Mr. and Mrs. J. P. Doyle, who last week received a letter from his captain in France informing them that he was more entitled to a decoration for bravery in action than some of those who had received them and paying high tribute to his assistance and valor. Mr. and Mrs. Doyle have two sons who have seen active service. Glen Doyle has just returned from overseas and Ferris Doyle was a dispatch rider at the front."[1041]

Concise histories of the 119th Field Artillery Regiment:

- https://en.wikipedia.org/wiki/119th_Field_Artillery_Regiment
- https://www.michigan.gov/dmva/about/history/military-events/spotlight/119th-field-artillery-in-world-war-i

Dewey told the author he was once "gassed" during a German offensive, but no medical records survive.

Served: 3 August 1917 to 15 May 1919.[763]

U.S., World War II Draft Cards Young Men, 1940-1947:
Name: Dewey Irwin Doyle | Gender: Male | Race: White | Age: 44 | Birth Date/Place: 6 Feb 1898, Cedar Springs, Kent Michigan | Residence Place: Grand Rapids, Kent, Michigan | Registration Date/Place: 15 Feb 1942, Grand Rapids, Kent, Michigan | Employer: (self) Doyle Vacuum Cleaner Co. | Height: 5 7.5 | Weight: 185 | Complexion: Ruddy | Hair Color: Brown | Eye Color: Brown | Scar Left Shin | Next of Kin: Vena E Doyle (wife)[1042]

They had the following children:

i. **Dewey Irwin "Jack" DOYLE II.**[1043-1046] Born on 12 April 1922, in Grand Rapids, Kent County, Michigan. Jack died in East Grand Rapids, Kent

County, Michigan, on 25 July 1996; he was 74. He first married Jean Mercedes PLATTS, then Georgina ROBBIE.

ii. **Patrick Edward DOYLE.**[1047-1050,180] Born on 10 October 1923, in Grand Rapids, Kent County, Michigan. Patrick died in Grand Rapids, Kent County, Michigan, on 14 August 1985; he was 61. He married Bonnie Mae MARXER.

1942, May: Vena once filed for a divorce against Dewey in court. (Apparently dropped as they were married up to his death in 1978.)[1051]

The Doyles were active in Republican politics and hosted many card games at their home. Regular guests were Gerald R. Ford and his wife Betty, before Gerald became President of the US.

"When I visited Uncle Dewey as a child, he would always give us kids a nickel and said 'you will never be poor if you have a nickel.'" [author]

---

31. Raymond "Ray" James KILBOURNE[1052-1058] (*Amelia Hannah Elizabeth PICKLES*[4], *Hannah CLAY*[3], *Isaac*[2], *Abegail*[1]).

Born on 11 March 1900, in Douglass Township, Montcalm County, Michigan,[508,408,1059,1060] Ray died in Grand Rapids, Kent County, Michigan, on 11 January 1982; he was 81.[1061,763,408] Buried on 14 January 1982, in Tallmadge Township, Ottawa County, Michigan,[763,1062] at the Rosedale Memorial Park Cemetery.

31. Raymond James KILBOURNE.

Occupation: Auto Mechanic (1921-1950); Garage Owner.[1063-1069]

Obituary: "KILBOURNE – Raymond J. Kilbourne, aged 81, of 3128 O'Brien Rd. SW., passed away Monday afternoon, Jan. 11, 1982. Surviving are his wife, Dorothy; his children, Ralph and June Sanderson, Harold and Delores Kilbourne, Robert and Leora Williams, Robert and

Rosemary Kilbourne, Richard and Louis Pattison; 23 grandchildren, and several great grandchildren, a brother, Thomas Kilbourne; his sisters, Mrs. Vena Doyle, Mrs. Evelyn Knapp, Mrs. Kathryn Lang; and several nieces and nephews. Funeral Services will be held at the funeral chapel Thursday 11 am with Rev. Rommie F. Moore officiating. Interment Rosedale Memorial Park. Those who wish, may make memorial contributions to the Michigan Heart Assoc. Friends may meet the family beginning Wednesday from 2 to 4 and 7 to 9 pm at the Shawmut Hills Funeral Home, 2120 Lake Michigan Dr. NW. A service by Posthumus-Karelse-Matthysse [Mortuaries, Inc]."[1070]

Military:

World War I Service: US Army, Private, 16th Service Comp., 221st Field Signal Battalion, Camp Vail, New Jersey from Ft. Wood, New Jersey, 11 July 1918 to 28 January 1919. Serial #3366037.[2162]

Service: 9 July 1918 to 28 January 1919.[1071]

U.S., World War II Draft Cards Young Men, 1940-1947:

Name: Ray J Kilbourne | Gender: Male | Race: White | Age: 41 | Birth Date/Place: 11 Mar 1900, Monclam, [sic] Michigan | Residence Place: Walker, Kent, Michigan | Registration Date: 16 Feb 1942 | Registration Place: Kent, Michigan, USA | Employer: Self | Height: 5 8 | Weight: 185 | Complexion: Ruddy | Hair Color: Brown | Eye Color: Blue | Next of Kin: Dorothy Kilbourne | Shot wound in Left Arm[1072]

("Shot wound in Left Arm"? No service record can be found if this was during the First World War, and no newspaper account between the wars.)

On 15 October 1921, when Raymond James was 21, he first married **Dorothy Dean HOPKINS,**[1073,1074] daughter of Squire B. HOPKINS and Sybil MORRELL, in Grand Rapids, Kent County, Michigan,[1075] by J. Calvin Meese, Minister. She was born on 26 April 1903, in Grand Rapids, Kent County, Michigan. Dorothy Dean died at Blodgett Hospital, in East Grand Rapids, Kent County, Michigan, on 6 October 1932; she was 29.[1076] Buried on 10 October 1932 in Grand Rapids, Kent County, Michigan,[1077] at the Fairplains Cemetery.

Occupation: Factory Worker (1921).

Obituary: "KILBOURNE - Dorothy Kilbourne, aged 30, of 1142 Arlington, N. E. entered into rest

Thursday morning at Blodgett hospital. She is survived by her husband, Ray Kilbourne; three sons, Harold, Stewart and Robert; three daughters, June, Leora and Lois Jane; a parent Mrs. Sybil Hopkins, all of Grand Rapids; one brother, Carl Hopkins, and one sister, Mrs John Wilcott, both of Big Rapids. The body was removed to the Clarence D. Sullivan Funeral Home. Funeral announcement later."[1078]

They had the following children (born between 1923-1932):

i. **June Mae KILBOURNE.**[1079-1083] [withheld for privacy—living person]. She married Ralph Walter SANDERSON.

ii. **Harold James KILBOURNE.**[1084-1086] Born on 17 March 1925, in Grand Rapids, Kent County, Michigan, Harold died in Grand Rapids, Kent County, Michigan, on 6 July 2011; he was 86. He married Delores June ENGEL.

iii. **Leona Dorothy KILBOURNE.**[1087-1089] [withheld for privacy—living person]. She married Dr. Robert Arthur WILLIAMS.

iv. **Stewart Carl KILBOURNE.**[1090-1094,180] Born on 27 December 1927, in Big Rapids, Mecosta County, Michigan, Stewart died in Grand Rapids, Kent County, Michigan, on 6 June 1980; he was 52. He married June Frances SHAKNIS.

v. **Robert Burns KILBOURNE.**[1095,1096,180] Born on 13 August 1930, in Grand Rapids, Kent County, Michigan, Robert died in Traverse City, Grand Traverse County, Michigan, on 13 June 2022; he was 91. He married Rosemary SNYDER.

vi. **Lois Jean KILBOURNE.**[1097,1098,180] Born on 15 July 1932, in Grand Rapids, Kent County, Michigan, Lois died in Caledonia, Kent County, Michigan, on 8 November 2001; she was 69. She married Richard Wayne PATTISON.

On 27 January 1933, when Raymond was 32, he second married **Dorothy Mildred VANDENBERG,**[1099,1100] daughter of Harry Newcomb VANDENBERGH and Minna Emilie Amanda SEHALAW, in Kent County, Michigan.[1101] She was born on 29 May 1902, in Howard City, Montcalm County, Michigan.[1102,408] Dorothy Mildred died in Grand Rapids, Kent County, Michigan, on 13 June 1999; she was 97.[408]

Obituary: "KILBOURNE - Mrs. Dorothy M. Kilbourne, aged 97, of Grand Rapids, passed away Sunday, June 13, 1999. She was precede in death by her husband, Ray and her son, Stuart Kilbourne. Surviving are her children, Harold and Dolores Kilbourne of Grand Rapids, Robert and Rosemary Kilbourne of Traverse City, June an Ralph Sanderson of Oregon, Leora and Robert Williams of Glendo, WY., and Lois and Richard Pattison of Caledonia; as well as her many grandchildren; and great grandchildren. A memorial service will be held on Saturday at 2 PM at the chapel of the Clark Retirement Community. In lieu of flowers contribution in memory of Mrs. Kilbourne may be made to the Clark Retirement Community. Expressions of sympathy may be sent to her family via Alt & Shawmut Hills Chapel 2120 Lake Michigan Dr. NW. Heritage Funeral Service www.heritagefuneralservice.com"[1103] - *undated newspaper clipping.*

They had no children from this marriage

---

32. Elizabeth Margarite "Bessie" KILBOURNE[1104-1107] (*Amelia Hannah Elizabeth PICKLES*[4], *Hannah CLAY*[3], *Isaac*[2], *Abegail*[1]).

Born on 30 April 1903, in Jackson, Jackson County, Michigan, Bessie died in Day Township, Montcalm County, Michigan, on 23 June 1934; she was 31.[1108] Buried on 26 June 1934, in McBride, Montcalm County, Michigan,[1109] at McBride's Cemetery.

Education: 10th Grade, Entrican School, Entrican, Michigan.

Occupation: Domestic (1922).

On 22 March 1922, when Bessie was 18, she married **Lloyd Everleigh TAYLOR**[1110-1114,180], son of George Franklin TAYLOR and Nellie E. SMITH, in Greenville, Montcalm County, Michigan.[1115] He was born on 17 August 1898, in Michigan.[408] Lloyd died in Loma Linda, San Bernardino County, California, on 13 January 1982; he was 83.[408,1116] Buried on 19 January 1982, in Riverside, Riverside County, California,[1117,763] at Riverside National Cemetery; Section 4 Site 1929.

Occupations: Navy Machinist (1920); Auto Mechanic (1922, 1930); Farmer (1935); Decorator (1940); US War Department Quartermaster Corps (1942); Cement Block Maker (1950); Floor Tile Manufacturer (1952).[1118-1121]

He lived with his grandparents William N. and Ida L. Smith in the 1910 and 1920 censuses.

1952, January: In partnership with Howard O. Butler, they formed a new tile company, Lanastone Products, in Ionia, Michigan.[1122]

"Kenneth Harvey Hopp | Attorney

CITATION RE WILL CONTEST AND PROOF OF SERVICE | (Probate Code, Section 370) | No. 50228

IN THE SUPERIOR COURT OF THE STATE OF CALIFORNIA IN AND FOR THE COUNTY OF SAN BERNARDINO.

In the Matter of the Estate of

LLOYD E. TAYLOR.

Deceased.

The People of the State of California to the Persons named below, Greetings:

EVA MAYE SCHNIEDER having appeared and filed written grounds for opposition to the probate of the Will or the above named decedent dated November 12, 1981; and

THOMAS TAYLOR having appeared and filed written grounds for opposition to the probate of the Will of the above named decedent dated January 6, 1981; and

The parties to said contests having entered Into a stipulation in writing for the settling of said contests;

Now, therefore, pursuant to statute, you are hereby direct to plead to said contests within 30 days after service at this citation.

WITNESS, the Honorable Rex W. Cranmer, Judge of the Superior Court or the State of California for the County of San Bernardino, with the seal of the Court affixed this tenth day of August, 1982.

Clerk

by Cynthia Cureton | Deputy Clerk | (SEAL)

KENNETH HARVEY HOPP | Attorney at Law

Post Office Box 1052 | Redlands, California 92373

714/793-2668/825-8414"[1123]

Military:

World War I Service: US Navy.

Service: 9 September 1917 to 30 September 1921.

U.S., World War II Draft Cards Young Men, 1940-1947:

Name: Lloyd E Taylor | Age: 44 | Gender: Male | Race: White Birth Date/Place: 17 Aug 1898, Clare, Clare Co. Michigan | Residence Place: Stanton, Montcalm, Michigan | Registration Date: 16 Feb 1942, Stanton, Montcalm, Michigan | Mailing Address: 4501 Monroe St. Toledo Ohio | Employer: U.S. Gov. War Dept. Q.M.C., Toledo, Ohio | Height: 5 10.5 | Weight: 158 | Complexion: Ruddy | Hair

Color: Brown | Eye Color: Blue | Next of Kin: Mrs. J. R. Kniffen, Stanton, Mich.[1124]

They had the following children:

i. **Franklin Ivan TAYLOR.**[1125,1126] Born on 9 October 1923, in Highland Park, Wayne County, Michigan, he died in New Port Richey, Pasco County, Florida, on 4 January 1999; he was 75. He first married Janice Gewell PLACE, then Sherley Evelyn MARKEL.

ii. **Leah Leona TAYLOR.**[1127-1130] Born on 6 November 1924, in Stanton, Montcalm County, Michigan, and died in Cameron County, Texas, on 26 August 1997; she was 72. She first married Frederick Charles SMITH, then William Davis GOHEEN.

iii. **Jean Elizabeth TAYLOR.**[1131-1134] Born on 23 April 1926, in Michigan, Jean died in Michigan on 14 August 2017; she was 91. She married Clayton William BUNN.

iv. **Barbara Jean TAYLOR.**[1135-1139,180] Born on 24 January 1928, in Grand Rapids, Kent County, Michigan, and died in Middleville, Barry County, Michigan, on 11 January 2022; she was 93. She married Robert Charles CLINTON.

v. **Thomas Loren TAYLOR.**[1140,1141] Born on 20 January 1929, in Michigan, and died in September 2014; he was 85. [Reported deceased by family]. He first married Avis M. WILLIAMS, then Betty Jean CROSBY.

vi. **Nonda E. TAYLOR.**[1142,1143,180] Born on 21 May 1931, in Stanton, Montcalm County, Michigan, and died at Metron, in Greenville, Montcalm County, Michigan, on 30 August 2014; she was 83. She married Delbert Lavern GARDNER, Sr.

---

33. Harry James "Edwin" KILBOURNE[1144,1145] (*Amelia Hannah Elizabeth PICKLES*[4]*, Hannah CLAY*[3]*, Isaac*[2]*, Abegail*[1]).

Born on 16 February 1906, in Stanton, Montcalm County, Michigan, Harry died in Douglass Township, Montcalm County, Michigan, on 19 February 1914; he was eight.[1146] Buried on 21 February 1914, in Douglass Township, Montcalm County, Michigan,[1147] Entrican Cemetery.

He died from a burst appendix.

34. Kathryn Angeline "Kay" KILBOURNE[1148-1154,180] (*Amelia Hannah Elizabeth PICKLES*[4], *Hannah CLAY*[3], *Isaac*[2], *Abegail*[1]).

Born on 6 June 1910, in Douglass Township, Montcalm County, Michigan,[408,1155] Kathryn was baptized in Detroit, Wayne County, Michigan, at the Holy Redeemer Roman Catholic Church. Kathryn died in Chambersburg, Franklin County, Pennsylvania, on 23 August 2000, at the Manor Care Nursing Home, she was 90.[408] Buried on 26 August 2000 in Mercersburg, Franklin County, Pennsylvania,[1156] at Fairview Cemetery.

34. *Kathryn Angeline KILBOURNE, "Grandma Lang"*

Occupations: Nurse (1928); Unemployed (1950): Telephone Operator, Cook, Manufacturing Inspector.[1157]

Education: Finished 9th Grade.

Religion: Roman Catholic.

From an interview, she recollected residing at:

- birth to about 1925 in Stanton, Montcalm County, Michigan
- 1925-28 in Grand Rapids, Kent County, Michigan
- 1928-30 Detroit, Wayne County, Michigan
- 1930-33 Rochester, Monroe County, New York
- 1934-44 Entrican, Montcalm County, Michigan
- 1944-86 Greenville, Montcalm County, Michigan
- March 1985-98, Shippensburg, Cumberland County, Pennsylvania
- 1998-2000 (death), Chambersburg, Franklin County, Pennsylvania

Work recollections:

- 1926 housework for the Van Strein family, Grand Rapids, Kent County, Michigan
- 1928-30 Michigan Bell, Detroit, Wayne County, Michigan
- 1930-32 Rochester Bell, Rochester, Monroe County, New York (transferred)
- 1932-34 housewife
- 1934-36 cook for the Donald Belknap Wurzburg family, Grand Rapids, Kent County, Michigan. Donald (1891-1959) was the son of Frederick Adolphus Wurzburg (1865-1937) a

well-know department store operator in Grand Rapids. Kathryn remembers the house being filled with music of a Wurlitzer organ (father Frederick, when not attending his business, was a music director at Power's Opera House and a composer).

• 1936-44 houseworker

• 1944-70 Federal Mogul Corporation, Greenville, Montcalm County, Michigan; inspector of ball bearings; until retirement.

From 1985 to 1998, she resided in Shippensburg, Cumberland County, Pennsylvania, at a retirement home near her daughter, Patricia. But from 1998 to 2000, she actually resided with her daughter Patricia and her husband Bill for closer care.

> *Obituary*: "Kathryn A. Lang, 90, of 2941 Adams Drive and formerly of Shippensburg, died at 8:40 p.m. Wednesday, Aug. 23, 2000, in ManorCare Health Services. She moved to Shippensburg from Greenville, Mich., in 1985.
>
> Born June 6, 1910, in Entrican, Mich., she was a daughter of the late Thomas and Amelia Pickles Kilbourne.
>
> She was a member of Our Lady of the Visitation Catholic Church, Shippensburg, and Council of Catholic Women.
>
> In 1970, she retired from Federal-Mogul Corp., Greenville.
>
> She also was a member of Fort Morris Chapter of the American Association of Retired Persons, Shippensburg. For 11 years, while living in Michigan, she was a volunteer for Michigan Association of the Blind.
>
> She is survived by one daughter, Patricia M. (Mrs. William B.) Sanders, Chambersburg; one son, Thomas W. Lang, Sylmar, Calif.; one sister, Evelyn Knapp, Lansing, N.C.; 14 grandchildren, 27 great-grandchildren, and a number of nieces and nephews. She was preceded in death by one son, James P. Lang, one grandson, five brothers, and three sisters.
>
> A Mass of Christian Burial will be at 11 a.m. Saturday in her church. The Revs. Robert Yohe and Lawrence Sherdel will officiate. Burial will be in Fairview Cemetery, Mercersburg.
>
> Visitation will be one hour before the service in the church."[1158-1160]

On 3 November 1928, when Kathryn was 18, she married **Walter George LANG,**[1161-1168,1150] son German immigrants Micheal LANG (1837-1917) and Mary Catherine YOUNG (1859-1937), in Detroit, Wayne County, Michigan,[1169] at Holy Redeemer Church, by Edward J. Dockery. He was born on 5 April 1897, in Perkinsville Village, Town Of Wayland, Steuben County, New York,[408] and was baptized in Perkinsville Village.[1170] Walter died in South Bend, Saint Joseph County, Indiana, on 4 March 1980; he was 82.[1171,408] Buried on 6 March 1980, in South Bend, Saint Joseph County, Indiana,[1172] at Riverview Cemetery.

Occupations: Railroad (1918); Truck Driver (1920); Baker (1928); Conductor); Hotel Houseman (1940); Metal Finisher (1950); Woodworker; Woodworker/Supervisor Of Studebaker Autos.[1173-1175]

Religion: Roman Catholic.

They were divorced on 31 October 1936, in Kent County, Michigan.[1176]

Walter George LANG

Obituary: "Walter G. Lang, 82, of 53950 Augustine Drive, died at 2:45 a.m. today in the Morningside Nursing Home after a lengthy illness. He was a former woodworker for the Singer Co. He was born on April 5, 1897, in Perkinsville, N.Y., and had lived in South Bend for 34 years after coming from Chicago. On Sept. 14, 1946, in Chicago, he married Helen R. Csernai, who survives. Also surviving are three sons, Walter Jr. and Robert, both of California, and Terry of South Bend, and six grandchildren.

Friends may call from 7 to 9 p.m. today and from 2 to 9 p.m. Wednesday in the Kaniewski and Sons Funeral Home, He was a member of St. John the Baptist Catholic Church and a World War I Army veteran."[1177]

Military:

U.S., World War I Draft Registration Cards, 1917-1918:

Name: Walter Lang | Event Type: Draft Registration | Event Date: 1917-1918 | Event Place: Steuben County no 2, New York, United States | Gender: Male | Nationality: United States | Birth Date/Place: 5 April 1897,

Perkinsville, New York | Father's Birthplace: Berlin, Germany | Name of Employer: P. S. & N. R. R. Co, Perkinsville, NY | Name of Nearest Relative: Mary Lang, mother | Eyes: Brown | Hair: Black | Medium height and build | Impairments: Throat trouble[1178]

New York, U.S., Abstracts of World War I Military Service, 1917-1919:

Lang Walter | 4 485 928 | White | Residence: PO Box 143 Perkinsville Steuben New York | Inducted at Hornell N Y on Sept 3 1918 | Place of birth: Perkinsville NY | Age or date of birth: Apr 5/1897 | Organizations service in with dates of assignments and transfers: Oct Aut Repl Draft Camp Jackson S Car to Dec 3/18; 156 Dep Brig to disch | Grade: Pvt | Served overseas[?]... no | Honorably discharge... Jan 2/19[1179]

1918, September: "The local exemption board has orders for the entrainment of forty-seven men ... Walter Lang, of Perkinsville. The party will go to Camp Jackson, S. C."[1180]

U.S., World War II Draft Cards Young Men, 1940-1947:

Name: Walter Lang | Race: White | Age: 44 | Birth Date/ Place: 5 Apr 1897, Perkinsville, N. Y. | Residence Place: Groveland, Livingston, N.Y. | Registration Date: 16 Feb 1942 | Registration Place: Dansville, Livingston, New York | Employer: None | Height: 5' 9" | Weight: 213 | Complexion: Dark | Hair Color: Brown | Eye Color: Brown | Person Who Knows You: Henry Swager, Groveland, N.Y.[1181]

Kathryn and Walter had the following children:

i. **Thomas Walter LANG**[1182-1184]. Born on 9 January 1931, at St. Marie Hospital, in Rochester, Monroe County, New York. Thomas died at the Veteran's Hospital in Ann Arbor, Washtenaw County, Michigan, on 1 March 2005; he was 74. He first married Juanita Mae FULLER, then common law to Jody STILL, then Shirley Marquerete SHAW.

ii. **James Patrick LANG**[1185-1187,180]. Born on 19 April 1932, in Rochester, Monroe County, New York, James died at the Veteran's Hospital in Oklahoma City, Oklahoma County, Oklahoma, on 25 December 1991; he was 59. He married Marvel Joyce DICKINSON.

iii. **Patricia Marie LANG**[1188-1200]. [withheld for privacy—living person] "Pat" married William Bertus SANDERS.

Walter George LANG had a troubled life. From the many stories, and private detective reports commissioned by his first wife, he had a mental illness. Kathryn, said he had escaped a veterans hospital after being diagnosed with what is now known as severe, sometimes violent dissociative identity disorder.

He remarried Helen Rose CSERNAI (1913-1999) in Chicago, Cook County, Illinois, in 1946, and she gave him the following children:

i. Walter G. LANG, Jr. (1947-2009)

ii. Robert M. LANG [withheld for privacy—living person]

iii. Terrance LANG [withheld for privacy—living person]

---

35. Lillian Evelyn KILBOURNE[1135,1201-1205,180] (*Amelia Hannah Elizabeth PICKLES*[4], *Hannah CLAY*[3], *Isaac*[2], *Abegail*[1]).

Born on 1 December 1912, in Stanton, Montcalm County, Michigan,[408] Evelyn, as she was preferred to be called, died at Reynolds Hospice Home, in Winston-Salem, North Carolina, on 22 September 2005; she was 92.[1206,408] Buried in Plainfield Township, Kent County, Michigan,[1206,1207] (cremated).

35. Lillian Evelyn KILBOURNE.

Occupations: Silkmill Spooler (1930); Crape Weaver (1933).[1208]

Religion: Seventh Day Adventist.

Obituary: "Evelyn Lillian Kilbourne Knapp, age 92, of Lansing, Ashe County, NC died Thursday, September 22, 2005 at the Kate B. Reynolds Hospice Home in Winston Salem, NC having been previously hospitalized at Forsyth Memorial Hospital for a stroke suffered on September 9.

She was born December 1, 1912 in Entrican, Montcalm County, Michigan of the late Thomas and

Amelia Kilbourne, early settlers to the county. Evelyn was married to Stanley C. Knapp of Belding, Michigan for 55 years until his death in 1987. Evelyn and Stanley lived in Flint, MI until 1948 when they moved to Grand Rapids, MI. Evelyn remained in Grand Rapids after her husband's death until she moved to Ashe County, NC.

In 1994, at the age of 82, she drove her motor home to Ashe County, NC and purchased a home near Lansing, to be near her son. Until recently, she spent her winters with her daughter in California. She was a member of the Warrensville, NC Seventhday Adventist Church and led an active life until her recent illness.

Survivors include son, Stanley (Charles) Knapp, Jr. and wife, Mary, of Lansing, NC; and daughter, Karen E. McFarland and husband, Jim, of Altadena, Calif. Also surviving are four grandsons, David Scott Knapp and wife, Teri, of Reston, Va.; Jay Randall Knapp and wife, Melanie, of Tampa, Fla.; Brett McFarland and wife, Heidi, of Phoenix, Ariz.; and Todd McFarland and wife, Jan, of Loma Linda, Calif. Evelyn is survived by four great grandsons, Jason, Jeremy and Joshua of Tampa, Fla. and Aden of Loma Linda, Calif.; and three great granddaughters, Samantha and Sidney of Tampa, Fla. and Emma of Phoenix, Ariz. She also has one step great granddaughter, Raven, of Charlotte, NC. Numerous nieces and nephews also survive.

Evelyn had a deeply held faith in Christ's promised second coming and a glorious resurrection of which she would be a part. A Remembrance Celebration will be held at the Knapp home, Sunday afternoon, October 23, 2005 from 2:30 – 5:30 p.m. Anyone who knew her is invited to come, meet her family and learn more of her long life.

A second Remembrance Celebration will be held in Michigan prior to internment. Place, date and time will be determined and announced.

In lieu of flowers, memorial gifts to the Adventist Development and Relief Agency International (ADRA), to benefit the Katrina hurricane relief effort will be appreciated, c/o any Seventh-day Adventist church or on line at http://www.adra.org (click on "needs") or by phone at 866-900-0123."[1209]

Stanley Charles KNAPP

On 25 November 1933, when Evelyn, as she preferred to be called, was 20, she married **Dr. Stanley Charles KNAPP**[1135,1210-1215,180], son of Charles KNAPP (1873-1952) and Ceyneth WILSON (1883-1968), in Belding, Ionia County, Michigan.[1216] Born on 27 November 1908, in Belding, Ionia County, Michigan,[408,1217] Stanley died at Bladget Hospital in Grand Rapids, Kent County, Michigan, on 26 August 1987; he was 78.[408,1218] Buried on 29 August 1987 in Plainfield Township, Kent County, Michigan,[1219] at the Plainfield Township Cemetery.

Occupations: Sheetmetal Laborer (1930); Toolmaker (1933, 1934, 1937, 1938); Auto Worker (1936); Metallurgical Engineer (1937, 1940, 1942, 1945, 1949, 1954); Research Physicist (1946); Company Chief Engineer (1948, 1950);[1220-1234] President And Director Of Industrial Testing Laboratories, Inc.

Education: University Of Michigan; University Of Chicago, Doctorate.

They were "separated" in April 1950 in Detroit, Wayne County, Michigan.[1235] "Separated" in the two census records does not mean necessarily marital separation – they were separated due to work.

> *Obituary*: "KNAPP – Mr. Stanley C. Knapp, aged 78, passed away peacefully in his sleep at Blodgett Memorial Medical Center, Wednesday, August 26, 1987. Mr. Knapp was a native of Belding and a resident of Grand Rapids for 41 years. He was an active businessman in the Northwest area of Grand Rapids for 30 years. Stan will be missed by his many friends, business acquaintances and his loving family. He is survived by his beloved wife of 54 years, Evelyn, his son Stanley C. (Mary) Knapp of Tampa, FL; his daughter, Karen (James) McFarland of Altadena, CA; his grandchildren, Scott (Teri Knapp, Jay (Traci) Knapp of Tampa, FL, Brett and Todd McFarland of Altadena, CA; and his brother, Norman L. Knapp of Belding. Funeral Services will be held Saturday at 2:30 pm at the VanStrien-Creston Chapel, 1833 Plainfield

NE. Friends may meet the family from 7 to 9 pm on Thursday and from 6 to 8 pm on Friday."[1236]

Military:

U.S., World War II Draft Cards Young Men, 1940-1947:
Name: Stanley Charles Knapp | Gender: Male | Race: White | Age: 31 | Birth Date: 27 Nov 1908, Belding, Michigan | Residence Place: 2311 Oren Avenue, Flint, Genesee, Mich. | Registration Date: 16 Oct 1940, Flint, Genesee, Michigan | Employer: Buick Motor Co. | Height: 5 11 | Weight: 170 | Complexion: Light | Hair Color: Brown | Eye Color: Hazel | Next of Kin: Mrs. Stanley C Knapp, wife[1237]

They had the following children:

i. **Col., Dr. Stanley Charles KNAPP Jr.**[1238,1239]. [withheld for privacy—living person] He is married to Mary Louise POLL.

ii. **Karen Elizabeth KNAPP.**[1135,1240] Born on 12 December 1940, in Flint, Genesee County, Michigan, Karen died in Altadena, Los Angeles County, California, on 23 June 2021; she was 80. She was married to James Robert MCFARLAND.

---

36. Marie Lorraine KILBOURNE[1135,1241-1245] (*Amelia Hannah Elizabeth PICKLES*[4], *Hannah CLAY*[3], *Isaac*[2], *Abegail*[1]).

Born on 1 June 1915, in Douglass Township, Montcalm County, Michigan.[408] Marie died in Los Angeles, Los Angeles County, California, on 15 September 1998; she was 83.[1246]

Occupation: Cook (1940).[1247]

On 23 January 1935, when Marie was 19, she first married **Lloyd Everleigh TAYLOR**[1110-1114,180], who was previously married to **#32.** Elizabeth Margarite KILBOURNE[1123,1248,1249,408,763,1116-1121], Marie's sister. He married Marie after Bessie's death in 1934, but this couple were separated in 1950.[1250]

1952, January: In partnership with Howard O. Butler, they formed a new tile company, Lanastone Products, in Ionia, Michigan.[1122,1124]

Marie and Lloyd had the following children:

i. **Therean Evereleigh TAYLOR**[1251]. [withheld for privacy—living person] He first married Helen

FAIRCHILD-KARTYCHOK, then Karen Lorraine OLSEN.

ii. **Claire Eugene TAYLOR**[1252]. Born on 5 September 1938, in Stanton, Montcalm County, Michigan. Claire died in Colorado on 21 September 2009; he was 71. He first married Jo An WIDUNAS, then Frances GORDON.

iii. **Robert Erwin TAYLOR-MYERS**[180]. Born on 17 June 1944, in Grand Rapids, Kent County, Michigan. Robert died in Canton, Cherokee County, Georgia, on 2 April 2012; he was 67. He married Therese Ann NEOLA.

Marie second married to **Joseph William MYERS** son of Charles MYERS and Mary DIOTTE. Born on 13 June 1903, in Saxon, Iron County, Wisconsin,[408] Joseph died in Phoenix, Maricopa County, Arizona, on 4 February 1960, at Good Samaritan Hospital; he was 56.[2163,408]. Buried on 9 February 1960, in Land O'Lakes, Vilas County, Wisconsin, at Oak Hill Cemetery.[2164]

Occupation: Barber (1950).[2165]

There were no children from this union.

---

37. Thomas Oscar "Junior" KILBOURNE Jr.[1253-1258,180] (*Amelia Hannah Elizabeth PICKLES*[4]*, Hannah CLAY*[3]*, Isaac*[2]*, Abegail*[1]).

Born on 26 September 1918, in Stanton, Montcalm County, Michigan,[408] Junior died in Lake Vavasu City, Mohave County, Arizona, on 6 April 1993; he was 74.[408] Buried on 10 April 1993, in Entrican, Douglass Township, Montcalm County, Michigan,[1259] Entrican Cemetery.

Occupations: Farmer (1940); Aircraft Engine Mechanic (1950); Aeronautics Industry.[1260,1261,1262,1263]

1960, January: departed on trip to Hawaii aboard *SS Matsonia* with wife Jesse.[1264]

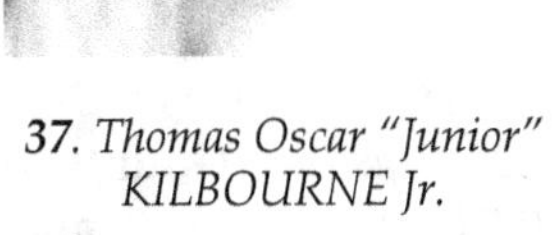

37. *Thomas Oscar "Junior" KILBOURNE Jr.*

Military:

U.S., World War II Draft Cards Young Men, 1940-1947:

Name: Thomas Junior Kilbourne | Gender: Male | Race: White | Age: 22 | Birth Date/

Place: 26 Sep 1918, Montcalm Co., Mich. | Residence Place: RR 1, Stanton, Montcalm, Mich. | Registration Date: 16 Oct 1940 | Registration Place: Stanton, Montcalm, Michigan | Employer: Self | Height: 5 11 | Weight: 150 | Complexion: Light | Hair Color: Brown | Eye Color: Blue | Next of Kin: Amelia Kilbourne Mother[1265]

World War II Army Enlistment Records, 1938-1946:

Name: Thomas J Kilbourne | Name (Original): KILBOURNE THOMAS J | Event Type: Military Service | Event Date: 12 Aug 1941 | Event Place: Detroit, Michigan, United States Race: White | Citizenship Status: citizen | Birth Year: 1918 | Birthplace: MICHIGAN | Education Level: 4 years of high school | Civilian Occupation Semiskilled painters, construction and maintenance | Marital Status: Single, without dependents | Military Rank: Private | Army Branch Air Corps, Army Component Regular Army (including Officers, Nurses, Warrant Officers, and Enlisted Men) | Source Reference: Civil Life[1266]

Service: 12 August 1941 to 5 May 1945.[763] Staff Sergeant.[901]

U.S., World War II Hospital Admission Card Files, 1942-1954:

Name: Thomas J Kilbourne | Race: White, includes Mexican (White) | Rank: Enlisted Man | Admission Age: 26 | Birth Date: abt 1918 | Admission Date: Sep 1944 | Discharge Date: May 1944 | Military Branch: Air Force, Transport/Bombardment Units | Diagnosis: Herniation, nucleus pulposus; Second Diagnosis: Dental caries | Type of Injury: Disease | Injured in Line of Duty: In line of duty | Type of Discharge: Duty Length of Service: 3 Year(s), 9, 10 OR 11 MONTHS Month(s) | Service Number: 16039018[1267]

On 7 July, Junior first married **Jessie OSBORN,**[1268,1269] daughter of Joseph OSBORN and Shirley SMAST, sometime before 1944. She was born on 27 October 1914, in Vandalia, Fayette County, Illinois.[408] Jessie died in Lake Havasu City, Mohave County, Arizona, on 28 May 1990; she was 75.[408]

Occupation: Seamstress (1950).[1270]

They had no children.

On 24 November 1990, when Junior was 72, he second married **Maxine Delores INGRAHAM**[180], daughter of William INGRAHAM and Grace KEENEY, in Lake Havasu City, Mohave County, Arizona.[1271] She was born on 3 October 1921, in Michigan, and died in Grand Rapids, Kent County, Michigan, on 31 January 2013; she was 91. Buried in Langston,

Pine Township, Montcalm County, Michigan,[1272] Riverside Cemetery.

Obituary: "Maxine Demorest age 91, formerly of the Lake Montcalm area, passed away on January 31, 2013 after a long battle with cancer, at her Grand Rapids home. She was born in Douglass Township, Michigan, on October 3, 1921, the daughter of William and Grace (Keeney) Ingraham.

Maxine is survived by her daughters, Linda Harmon and Dixie Demorest of Collinsville, Illinois; a grandson Brian (Andrea) Harmon also of Collinsville and one great-grandson, Tyler Harmon.

Maxine was preceded in death by her husbands, Nihl E. Demorest of Rockford and Thomas Kilbourne of Arizona; her parents, William and Grace Ingraham and two brothers, Lloyd Kenney of Jackson and Dennis Ingraham of Lakeview.

A graveside service will be held for Maxine in the spring at Langston Cemetery."[1273]

They had no children.

38. John Churchill KILBOURNE[1274-1277,187] (*Amelia Hannah Elizabeth PICKLES*[4]*, Hannah CLAY*[3]*, Isaac*[2]*, Abegail*[1]).

Born on 29 March 1921, in Douglass Township, Montcalm County, Michigan,[408] John died in Pontiac, Oakland County, Michigan, on 12 August 1978; he was 57.[408,1278] Buried on 15 August 1978, in Douglass Township, Montcalm County, Michigan,[1279,763] at Entrican Cemetery; Lot: 339, Space 4.

38. *John Churchill KILBOURNE*

Occupation: Bell Telephone (1941); Telephone, Office Maintenance (1950); Telephone Switchman (1953).[1280,1281]

Military:

World War II, US Navy.

U.S., World War II Draft Cards Young Men, 1940-1947:

Name: John Churchill Kilbourne | Gender: Male | Age: 20 | Race: White | Birth Date/Place: 29 Mar 1921, Stanton,

Mich. | Residence Place: 114 Green St., Flint, Genesee, Michigan | Registration Date: 16 Feb 1941 |Registration Place: Flint, Genesee, Michigan | Employer: Michigan Bell Telephone Co | Height: 5 10 | Weight: 140 | Complexion: Ruddy | Hair Color: Brown Eye Color: Gray | Next of Kin: Mrs. Stanley Knapp [sister][1282]

Aboard USS *Tautog* (SS199), 12 and 31 December 1943; 30 April 1944; 30 June 1944; 30 September 1944; 30 April 1945; 1 July 1945; 1 October 1945.[1283]

On 16 March 1946, when John Churchill was 24, he married **Ina Marie JONES,**[1284,1285,187] daughter of King JONES and Bessie ROSE, in Flushing, Genesee County, Michigan.[1286] Born on 28 September 1922, in Mount Vernon, Lawrence County, Missouri,[1287] Ina died in California on 23 December 2019; she was 97.[1288] Buried in Entrican, Douglass Township, Montcalm County, Michigan,[1289] at Entrican Cemetery.

Ina Marie JONES

Occupation: Nurse.

They had the following children:

i. **Douglas Michael KILBOURNE.**[1290] [withheld for privacy—living person]. He married Linda Kathryn MEYERS.

ii. **John Charles "Jackie" KILBOURNE**. [withheld for privacy—living person]. He first married Cynthia Ann GUDRITZ, then Beth ___.

iii. **Ronald Thomas KILBOURNE**. [withheld for privacy—living person]. He married Joyce Edna GIBSON.

iv. **Gary Alan KILBOURNE**. [withheld for privacy—living person]. He married Melody Ann Schroe HAAPALA.

---

39. Truman Gordon KILBOURNE[1291-1293] (*Amelia Hannah Elizabeth PICKLES*[4]*, Hannah CLAY*[3]*, Isaac*[2]*, Abegail*[1]).

Born on 27 July 1923, in Stanton, Montcalm County, Michigan.[408] At the age of 42, Truman was baptized in Standale, Michigan, on 10 April 1966, at Standale Reformed Church. Truman died in Grand Rapids, Kent County, Michigan, on 8

September 1979; he was 56.[408,1294] Buried on 10 September 1979 in Tallmadge Township, Ottawa County, Michigan,[763,1295] at Rosedale Memorial Park.

Occupation: Auto Mechanic (1946); Service Manager (1948); Refrigeration Mechanic (1950); Mechanic, Steam Fitter & Refrigeration And Air.[1296-1301]

Education: Davis Tech, 2 Years.

Religion: Reformed.

Obituary: "KILBOURNE – Mr. Truman G. Kilbourne, aged 56, of 3687 O'Brien Rd. SW., went to be with his Lord, Saturday, September 8, 1979. Surviving are his wife, June; his children, Diana at home, Dale and Sue of Jenison; four sisters, Mrs. Vena Doyle, Mrs. Stanley (Evelyn) Knapp both of Grand Rapids, Mrs. Kathryn Lang of Greenville, Mrs. Mary Meyers of Arizona; two brothers, Ray of Grand Rapids, and Thomas of Calif.; one sister-in-law, Mrs. Ina Kilbourne of Detroit; several nieces and nephews. Funeral services for Mr. Kilbourne will be held Monday at 1:30 PM at the Standale Reformed Church, with his pastor, The Rev. Ronald L. VerWys officiating. Interment Rosedale Memorial Park Cemetery. Friends may meet the family at the funeral chapel Sunday 2 to 4 and 7 to 9 PM. Contributions to the American Cancer Society would be appreciated. (Envelopes available at the chapel.)"[1302]

39. *Truman Gordon KILBOURNE*

Military:

U.S., World War II Draft Cards Young Men, 1940-1947:

Name: Truman Gordon Kilbourne | Gender: Male | Race: White | Age: 18 | Birth Date/Place: 25 Jul 1923, Montcalm, Michigan | Residence Place: Douglas, Montcalm, Michigan, 30 Jun 1942 | Registration Place: Douglass Township, Montcalm, Michigan | Employer: At Home | Height: 5 9 | Weight: 145 | Complexion: Light | Hair Color: Brown| Eye Color: Blue | Scar on Right Side | Next of Kin: Amelia Kilbourne [mother][1303]

World War II Army Enlistment Records, 1938-1946:

Name: Truman G Kilbourne | Name (Original): KILBOURNE TRUMAN G| Event Type: Military Service | Event Date: 01 Feb 1943 | Term of Enlistment: Enlistment for the duration of the War or other emergency, plus six months, subject to the discretion of the President or otherwise according to law | Event Place: Kalamazoo, Michigan, United States | Race: White | Height: 68 | Weight: 135 | Citizenship Status: citizen | Birth Year: 1923 | Birthplace: MICHIGAN | Education Level: 1 year of college | Civilian Occupation: Semiskilled occupations in building of aircraft, n.e.c. | Marital Status: Single, with dependents | Military Rank: Private | Army Branch: Branch Immaterial - Warrant Officers, USA | Army Component: Selectees (Enlisted Men) | Source Reference: Civil Life | Serial Number: 36424534[1304]

Service: 1 February 1943 to 12 January 1946[763]

On 7 October 1948, when Truman Gordon was 25, he married **June Louise FREVILLE,**[1305,1306] daughter of Emil Charles FREVILLE (1898-1965) and Santina B. MURRACHELLI (1901-1931), in Grand Rapids, Kent County, Michigan.[1307,1308] Born on 7 March 1926, in Grand Rapids, Kent County, Michigan; at the age of 40, June was baptized in Standale, Michigan, on 10 April 1966. June died in Clarkston, Oakland County, Michigan, at St. Joseph's Hospital, on 2 May 2015; she was 89. Buried on 6 May 2015 in Tallmadge Charter Township, Kent County, Michigan, Rosedale Memorial Park.

Occupation: Nurse; Bookkeeper (1948).[1309]

Religion: Reformed.

Obituary: "June L. Kilbourne age 89, passed away May 2, 2015. She was preceded in death by her husband Truman. June is survived by her children Dale & Sue Kilbourne, Diana & Mike Korcal; grandchildren Sarah & Josh Genereux and Kristine Kilbourne; great granddaughter Abbigal Genereux; brother Emil 'Junior' & Betty Freville; and several nieces and nephews. Her funeral service will be held on Wednesday, May 6 at 1 PM at Heritage Life Story Funeral Home - Alt & Shawmut Hills Chapel, 2120 Lake Michigan Drive NW where friends may visit with her family from 12 noon until the service. Interment in Rosedale Memorial Park. To share a memory or sign her guestbook, please visit www.lifestorynet.com."[1310]

June Louise FREVILLE

"June Kilbourne was a woman rich in the things that count in life: a strong work ethic, a devout Christian faith, and above all an unconditional love for her husband, children, grandchildren and family. She had experienced poverty and loss in her lifetime, but she never complained and appreciated all that she had. June was a loving wife, devoted mother and proud grandmother and great grandmother, who did everything she could to support and encourage her loved ones. Through her love and hard work, June provided a strong and benevolent foundation for her family.

... She was the third youngest of six children born to Emil C. and Santina (Murachelli) Freville. She had three older brothers and was later joined by another brother and sister. June's early life got off to a rough start when her mother died giving birth to her youngest sister, leaving her father with six children to raise. Circumstances would lead to the children being split up and sent to live with relatives. June and her two brothers, Emil Jr. and Howard, went to live with their grandmother, while the other three siblings went to live with an aunt. Although they were raised in different homes, she and her siblings stayed closely connected all their lives.

June grew up on the west side of Grand Rapids, where she attended the area schools and went on to graduate from Union High School in 1945. She then went to work as a bookkeeper at Kresges Five and Dime Store. It was during this time that June met the love of her life, Truman Kilbourne, while out with some of her friends. Truman was from Entrican, a small community north of Grand Rapids. He was a veteran of the U.S. Army, after serving in World War II, and was currently learning the trade of a pipefitter working for a refrigeration company. After dating for a time, the two sweethearts fell in love and were happily married on October 7, 1948, in the West Fulton Mission. After saying 'I do' the newlyweds settled into a rented home on Covey Street N.W. for a time before moving to a house on Lake Michigan Dr. N.W., near what is now known as Amen Park. ... The family later moved to a house on Maynard Street N.W. for a while, and that is when Truman decided to build their own house on O'Brian Road N.W. in Standale. The garage went up first so that the family could live in it while the rest of the house was constructed. However, June and Truman wanted to stay out of debt, so they built on only when they had the money. It was a special day when the house was completed and they could move in!

It was easy to see that June considered it pure joy to care for her husband and children. She quit working after her son Dale was born to devote herself to the role of a mother and homemaker. June was active in the lives of her children and also created a home that was a place where love was plentiful. There were so many ways that June made life around the Kilbourne home easier. She loved to cook for her family, and had a passion for collecting cookbooks and recipes, always looking for new and exciting things to make. June had a passion for gardening, where she would look forward to planting a vegetable and flower garden every summer. and canned pickles from its bounty every year. She was also an excellent seamstress, a skill she learned from her grandmother. When the children were in grade school she made most of their clothes, and her daughter Diana fondly remembers going to the local department store with her mom to pick out the fabrics she used to make new shirts and dresses. Compassionately, June touched the hearts and lives of not only the family she adored, but also their extended family. June was always willing to take in relatives, to care for them in times of sickness.

Although life was always busy, June and Truman knew the importance of being with family, and every summer they journeyed to the Upper Peninsula to go camping with Truman's family. The children have many cherished memories of time with their relatives. They also remember a 'long' trip they took out west with their pop-up camper in tow to visit some of Truman's relatives in Arizona. Sadly in the 1970s, Truman was diagnosed with cancer, and June was his loving caregiver until he passed away in 1978. After 30 years of marriage, June was alone and had to provide for herself. She decided to take the Practical Nursing Course (PCA) test and after passing, she went to work at Kent Community Hospital as a nurse. June liked being an independent woman, but she didn't drive so she relied on family and friends to get her to and from work – which they were more than happy to do! Aside from working, June kept herself busy reading devotional books, cookbooks and mystery novels. She also liked to play solitaire and doing word search games. The family always had a puzzle going, where they could just spend time together, doing the puzzle. Church was also a very important part of June's life, and she dedicated a lot of time to activities within her congregation at Standale Reformed Church, where she was a faithful member. However, nothing made June happier than spending time with her grandchildren. She always had coloring books and games for them, and gave them her undivided attention when they were there. Even after having bypass surgery, June continued to keep a busy lifestyle, babysitting her grandchildren and attending their school and sport activities. When her children took their families on vacation, they took June along too – she loved being part of the family and a help where she could. …

June was preceded in death by her husband, Truman. June is survived by her children, Dale & Sue Kilbourne, Diana & Mike Korcal; grandchildren, Sarah & Josh Genereux and Kristine Kilbourne; great granddaughter, Abbigal Genereux; brother, Emil 'Junior' & Betty Freville; and several nieces and nephews. Her funeral service will be held on Wednesday, May 6, at 1 p.m. at Heritage Life Story Funeral Home - Alt & Shawmut Hills Chapel, 2120 Lake Michigan Drive NW, where friends may visit with her family from 12 noon until the service. Interment in Rosedale Memorial Park. To share a memory or sign her guestbook, please visit www.lifestorynet.com."[1311]

They had the following children:

i. **Dale Allen KILBOURNE.**[1312] [withheld for privacy—living person]. He married Sue Ann LONGNECKER.

ii. **Diane Lynn KILBOURNE**. [withheld for privacy—living person]. She married Micheal Joseph KORCAL.

40. Laurence J. CLAY[1313] (*Malcolm J.*[4], *Simeon A.*[3], *Fredric* [2], *Abegail*[1]).

Born 26 July 1903, in Michigan,[173] Laurence died in Onondaga, Ingham County, Michigan, on 27 March 1917; he was 13 years old.[1314] Buried on 28 March 1917 in Onondaga, Ingham County, Michigan.[1315]

> "Miss Cox, a trained nurse of Lansing, is at Onondaga caring for Lawrence Clay who is suffering from an attack of diphtheria at the home of his parents, Mr. and Mrs. M. J. Clay of that village."[1316]

> "An epidemic of diphiherta [sic] has broken out in Onondaga. Lawrence Clay, age 14 [sic] years, a member of the high school, died last week Tuesday evening with the disease after a week's illness. The schools have been closed, public gatherings postponed and children ordered to stay in their own homes."[2097]

> "Lawrence Clay, son of Mr. and Mrs. M. J. Clay, of Onondaga, died Tuesday night after a week's illness with diphtheria."[2098]

41. Mary Loretta CLAY[1313,1317-1323,180] (*Malcolm J.*[4], *Simeon A.*[3], *Fredric*[2], *Abegail*[1]).

Born 2 March 1906, in Onondaga, Ingham County, Michigan,[408] Mary died in Polk County, Florida, on 25 November 1971; she was 65.[556,408] Buried in Lakeland, Polk County, Florida,[1324] at Lakeland Memorial Gardens.

Occupation: Teacher (1930, 1940).[1325,1326]

Apparently she took a cruise to Europe in 1932. She left Port of Southampton, England 31 August 1932, bound for Le Harve, France aboard the SS *Carinthia*.[1328] She arrived back from Le Harve, France, 22 August 1932, aboard the *SS Carinthia*, to the port of New York.[1329]

On 14 April 1934, when Mary was 28, she first married **Donald L. CUFF**, son of Norman CUFF and Bessie SNOW, in La Grange County, Indiana.[1330] He was born on 9 September 1905, in Jackson County, Michigan. Donald died in Pompano Beach, Broward County, Florida, on 24 March 1970; he was 64. Buried in Saginaw, Saginaw County, Michigan, Oakwood Memorial Mausoleum.

***41**. Mary Loretta CLAY. Photograph from high school yearbook, 1925.*[1327]

They were divorced on 5 December 1936, in Ingham County, Michigan.[1331]

They had no children.

On 30 December 1940, when Mary was 34, she second married **Raymond Authur HAAS,**[1323-1332,180] son of Charles HAAS and Emma BAYME, in Onondaga, Ingham County, Michigan.[1334] He was born on 29 September 1906, in Detroit, Wayne County, Michigan.[408] Raymond died at the Lucerne General Hospital in Orlando, Orange County, Florida, on 30 December 1977; he was 71.[556,408] Buried on 3 January 1978, in Lakeland, Polk County, Florida,[1335] at Lakeland Memorial Gardens Cemetery.

Occupation: Detroit Fireman (1940, 1950).[1336,1337]

Religion: Presbyterian.

> *Obituary*: "Graveside services for Raymond A. Haas, retired captain in the Detroit Fire Department, will be at 2 p.m. Tuesday in Lakeland Memorial Gardens Cemetery, Lakeland, Fla.
>
> Mr. Haas, 71, of Lakeland, died Friday in Lucerne General Hospital, Orlando. He had been with the Fire Department for 33 years.
>
> He was a member of Westminister United Presbyterian Church, Lakeland Elks Lodge, Scottish Rite, Egypt Temple and the Lakeland Shrine Club.
>
> Surviving are a son, Raymond Jr.; a daughter, Mrs. Michael Cloyd, two sisters and three grandchildren."[1338]

Obituary: "Raymond A Haas, 71, 729 Wilson Ave Lakeland died Friday in Orlando. Born in Detroit he moved to Lakeland, from Detroit in 1958. He was a retired firefighter from the Detroit Fire Department a member of Westminster United Presbyterian Church; Lakeland Elk Lodge Scottish Rite, Egypt Temple and Lakeland Shrine Club. Survivors: son, Raymond A Jr., Daytona Beach, daughter, Mrs Michael Cloyd Orlando sisters, Freida Conradsen Detroit. Mrs. Charles Jones Youngstown, Ariz.; and three grand children. Heath Funeral Chapel, Lakeland."[1339]

Military:

U.S., World War II Draft Cards Young Men, 1940-1947:
Name: Raymond Authur Haas | Gender: Male | Race: White | Age: 34 | Birth Date/Place: 29 Sep 1906, Detroit, Michigan | Residence Place: 40210 W. Lafayette, Detroit, Wayne, Michigan | Registration Date: 16 Oct 1940 | Registration Place: Detroit, Wayne, Michigan | Employer: Detroit Fire Department, Ladder 13-Lawndale | Height: 5 11 | Weight: 185 | Complexion: Light brown | Hair Color: Brown | Eye | Color: Gray | Next of Kin: Freda Coneantsen, Sister[1340]

Mary and Raymond had the following children:

i. **Judith Lovan HAAS.**[1341,1342,180] Born on 26 October 1941, in Detroit, Wayne County, Michigan. Judith Lovan died in Hiawassee, Towns County, Georgia, on 13 August 2016; she was 74. She married Michael David CLOYD.

ii. **Raymond Arthur HAAS Jr.**[1343] [withheld for privacy—living person]. He married Hilda Elizabeth BELL.

---

42. Mina Lovan CLAY[1344-1348,180] (*Malcolm J.*[4], *Simeon A.*[3], *Fredric*[2], *Abegail*[1]).

Born 17 November 1907, in Onondaga, Ingham County, Michigan,[1349] Mina died in Mount Pleasant, Isabella County, Michigan, on 5 February 1976; she was 68.[1350] Buried on 9 February 1976 in Mason, Ingham County, Michigan,[1351] at Maple Grove Cemetery.

Occupation: Teacher (1929, 1930, 1940, 1950).[1352-1354]

Education: Eastern Michigan University (Formerly Michigan Normal College).

Religion: Presbyterian.

Obituary: "MONAHAN, MINA L. (HOWE) 5439 Cranberry Lake Rd. Harrison, Mich. Formerly of Mason Age 68, died Feb. 5, 1976 in Mt. Pleasant. She was born Nov. 17, 1907 in Onondaga, Mich. She was a 1925 graduate of Lansing Central High School and graduated from Eastern Michigan University (formerly Michigan Normal College). She received her life teaching certificate in June of 1927. She retired from teaching in June of 1969 after 33 years, 26 of those years in Mason. She was a member of the Alpha Sigma Tau, member of the First Presbyterian Church of Mason. Survivors include her husband Larry Monhan [sic] of Harrison; 1 son, Laurence E. Howe of Mason; 3 grandsons, Dennis Howe of Lansing, Bruce Howe and Mark Howe, both of Mason. Funeral services will be held Monday at 1 p.m. at the Ball-Dunn Chapel Gorsline-Runciman Co., Mason, with the Rev. Keith L. Hayes, Pastor of the First United Methodist Church, officiating. Interment in Maple Grove Cemetery, Mason."[1355]

42. *Mina Lovan CLAY, wedding newspaper photograph.*[2169]

On 6 July 1929, when Mina was 21, she first married **Herbert Eddy HOWE,**[1356-1358,180] son of Eddie J. HOWE and Lina WILLIAMS, in Onondaga, Ingham County, Michigan,[1359,1360] "...at the home of her parents." Born on 29 April 1906, in Petoskey, Emmet County, Michigan,[408] Herbert died in Lansing, Ingham County, Michigan, on 13 February 1971; he was 64.[408,1361] Buried on 16 February 1971, in Mason, Ingham County, Michigan,[1362] Maple Grove Cemetery.

Occupations: Student (1923); Grocery (1929-1930); Photostat Operator (1940); Salesman (1950); Driver (1953).[1363,1352-1354,1364]

Obituary: "MASON – Services for Herbert E. Howe, 64, of 446 W. Ash, will be at 2 p.m. Tuesday at Ball-Dunn Funeral Home, with burial in Maple Grove Cemetery.

He died Saturday at a Lansing hospital, following a lingering illness.

A veteran of World War II, Mr. Howe had been active in Ingham County Republican Party projects and had served in both the county clerk and register of deeds offices.

Surviving are his wife, Mina; a son, Laurence; and three grandsons, all of Mason."[1365]

Military:

U.S., World War II Draft Cards Young Men, 1940-1947:

Name: Herbert Eddy Howe | Gender: Male | Race: White | Age: 33 | Birth Date: 29 Apr 1907 [sic] | Birth Place: Petoskey, Michigan | Residence Place: 102 Cherry, Mason, Mich | Registration Date: 16 Oct 1940 | Registration Place: Mason, Ingham, Mich. | Employer: Ingham Co. Courthouse | Height: 5 6 | Weight: 132 | Complexion: Light | Hair Color: Black | Eye Color: Brown | Next of Kin: Mina Clay Howe, Wife[1366]

Served in World War II according to obituary.

Mina and Herbert had one child:

i. **Laurence Edward HOWE.**[1367,1368] Born on 22 March 1931, in Lansing, Ingham County, Michigan. Laurence died in at Bickford of Okemos, 3830 Okemos Road, Okemos, Ingham County, Michigan, on 10 August 2023; he was 92. He married Bonnie Charme JONES.

Mina Lovan second married **Larry MONAHAN**. They had no children.

---

43. Morrison Legrand CLAY[1369-1373,180] (*Fred Henry*[4], *Simeon A.*[3], *Fredric*[2], *Abegail*[1]).

Born on 18 November 1902, in Carmel Township, Eaton County, Michigan,[408,1374] Morrison died at the Eaton County Medical Care Facility in Charlotte, Eaton County, Michigan, on 14 October 1977; he was 74.[408] Buried on 17 October 1977, in Charlotte, Eaton County, Michigan,[1375] at Maple Hill Cemetery.

Occupations: Clerk (1924, 1925); Draying (1930); Truck Driver (1940); Radio & Television Factory Supervisor Of Maintenance (1950).[1376-1378,2109]

Obituary: "CHARLOTTE - Morrison L. Clay, 74, formerly of 1981 S. Cochran St., died Saturday in the

Eaton County Medical Care Facility, where he had been a patient several months.

He was born in Eaton County and had been a Charlotte area resident all his life.

He had been a farmer and was a Charlotte School District bus driver, retiring 12 years ago.

His wife, the former Sara Ledyard, died in 1969.

Clay is survived by a daughter, Mrs. Orville (Shirley) Parton of Bloomfield Hills; two grandchildren, and sisters, Mrs. Leta Pasco of Fenton and Mrs. llene Lee of Drayton Plains.

Services will be held at 2 p.m. Monday at Pray Funeral Home."[1379,1380]

Military:

U.S., World War II Draft Cards Young Men, 1940-1947:

Name: Morrison Legrande Clay | Gender: Male | Race: White | Age: 39 | Birth Date/Place: 18 Nov 1902, Eaton Rapids, Michigan | Residence Place: 215 W. Henry Charlotte, Eaton, Michigan | Registration Date: 16 Feb 1942 | Registration Place: Charlotte, Eaton, Michigan | Employer: Wilcox Gay Corp | Height: 6 | Weight: 142 | Complexion: Light | Hair Color: Brown | Eye Color: Blue| Next of Kin: Fred Clay [father][1381]

On 9 April 1924, when Morrison was 21, he married **Sara Dale LEDYARD,**[1382-1384,2109,180] daughter of Wallace William LEDYARD and Harriet CLAFLIN, in Charlotte, Eaton County, Michigan.[1385,2109] She was born on 30 August 1902, in Benton, Eaton County, Michigan.[1386,408] Sara died in Bloomfield Township, Oakland County, Michigan, on 3 November 1969; she was 67.[408] Buried in Charlotte, Eaton County, Michigan,[1387] at Maple Hill Cemetery.

Sarah Dale Ledyard, 1921 high school photograph.[2170]

Occupation: Nurse (1924, 1940).[1388]

Obituary: "CHARLOTTE Mrs. Sarah D. (Ledyard) Clay, 67, of 19S1 S. Cochran Road, who was killed in a traffic accident Monday near Pontiac, was a retired registered nurse, formerly employed at

Hayes-Green-Beach Hospital. Born in Eaton County, she was a lifelong area resident. She was a member of the Sunshine Club. Surviving are her husband, Morrison; a daughter, Mrs. Shirley Anderson of Bloomfield Hills; a brother, Albert Ledyard of Charlotte, and a sister, Mrs. Grace Green of Jackson."[1389]

They had one child:

i. **Shirley Joan CLAY.**[1390-1392] Born on 8 January 1925, in Charlotte, Eaton County, Michigan,[2110] Shirley died in Bloomfield Hills, Oakland County, Michigan, on 9 July 2010; she was 85. She first married Lt. Karl Adolphus ANDERSON, Jr., then secondly to Orvill Sylvester PARTON.

---

44. Ann Ilene CLAY[1393-1398,180] (*Fred Henry*[4], *Simeon A.*[3], *Fredric*[2], *Abegail*[1]).

Born 20 January 1905, in Michigan,[408] Ann died in Walled Lake, Oakland County, Michigan, in November 1993; she was 88.[408] Buried in Charlotte, Eaton County, Michigan,[1399] at Maple Hill Cemetery.

Occupations: Bank Bookkeeper (1925, 1930; 1940); Collections Clerk (1950).[1400-1402]

1934: "Mrs. Fred Clay received word that her daughter, Ilene Lee of Jackson, underwent an operation for appendicitis last Thursday and is still in a Jackson hospital."[2106]

On 19 December 1925, when Ann was 20, she married **Terry Franklin LEE,**[1403-1405,180] son of Oliver LEE and Elizabeth WRENN, in Charlotte, Eaton County, Michigan,[1406,2111] at the brides' parents home, by Dr. W. W. Diehl, of the Methodist Episcopal Church. Terry was born 28 February 1901, in Delphos, Van Wert County, Ohio.[408] He died in Pontiac, Oakland County, Michigan, on 15 July 1976; he was 75.[408,1407] Buried in Charlotte, Eaton County, Michigan,[1408] at Maple Hill Cemetery.

Occupations: Automobile Inspector (1925); Clerk (1935); Shoe Store Manager/Sales (1929-1956); Restaurant Owner (1960).[1409-1432]

Military:

U.S., World War II Draft Cards Young Men, 1940-1947:

Name: Terry Franklin Lee | Gender: Male | Race: White | Age: 4| Birth Date: 28 Feb 1901, Delphos - G, Ohio | Residence Place: 264 Douglas St Jackson, Michigan | Registra-

tion Date: 16 Feb 1942 | Registration Place: Jackson, Jackson, Michigan | Employer: Glasgow's Inc, Jackson, Michigan | Height: 5 8 | Weight: 200 | Complexion: Ruddy | Hair Color: Brown | Eye Color: Brown | Next of Kin: Mrs Oliver Lee 915 Merriman Jackson Mich. [mother][1433]
They had one child:

i. **Judy K. LEE.**[1434] [withheld for privacy—living person].

---

45. Leta Mae CLAY[1435-1439,180] (*Fred Henry*[4], *Simeon A.*[3], *Fredric*[2], *Abegail*[1]).

Born on 24 April 1907, in Vermontville, Eaton County, Michigan.[408] Leta died at Deaconess Hospital, in Bloomfield Hills, Oakland County, Michigan, on 2 September 2003; she was 96.[408] Buried on 13 October 2003, in Charlotte, Eaton County, Michigan,[1440] at Maple Hill Cemetery.

45. Leta Mae CLAY. Photograph from college yearbook, 1928.[1444]

Occupation: Teacher (1930, 1940, 1950).[1441-1443]

Education: Michigan State Normal College.

Obituary: "PASCO, Leta Mae - Was born April 24, 1907 and passed away September 2, 2003 at Deaconess Hospital. She was a 5 year resident at Copper Lake Retirement Village having moved from Fenton, Michigan where she was a retired teacher having taught 42 years. She was a lifetime member of the Eastern Star and the AAUW. She was preceded in death by her husband James Pasco; brother, Morrison L. Clay; and sister, Ilene C. Lee. She is survived by 2 nieces, Shirley Parton of Bloomfield Hills, MI and Judy White of Edmond, OK; 1 great-niece and 5 great-nephews. A memorial service was held in Edmond, OK September 5, 2003. A graveside service will be at Maple Hill Cemetery in Charlotte, MI October 13, 2003 at 11 a.m. A luncheon will follow. Contributions could be made to Copper Lake Retirement Village, Edmond, OK."[1445]

"PASCO, Leta Mae, 96, died Tuesday. Services 11 a.m. Friday, St. Mary's Episcopal Church of Edmond (Cremation Society, Oklahoma City)."[1446]

On 3 August 1947, when Leta Mae was 40, she married **James Mitchel PASCO,**[1439,180] son of William H. PASCO and Mary Louella DEMOREST, at the Presbyterian Church in Fenton Township, Genesse County, Michigan, by Rev. Robert Bell, a cousin of the bride.[1447,1448,2108] He was born on 1 October 1907, in Fenton Township, Genesse County, Michigan.[1449,408] James died in Flint, Genesee County, Michigan, on 21 October 1982; he was 75.[1361,763,408] Buried in Charlotte, Eaton County, Michigan,[1450] at Maple Hill Cemetery.

Education: Michigan State College.

Military:

U.S., World War II Draft Cards Young Men, 1940-1947:

Name: James Mitchel Pasco | Address: 225 So. Adelaide St. Fenton, Genesse, Michigan | Age: 33 | Place of Birth: Fenton Michigan | Date of Birth: 1 Oct. 1907 | Next of Kin: Mrs. Mary Louella Pasco, Mother | Employer: Pasco's Shell Service Race: White | Height: 5 9 | Eyes: Gray | Weight: 158 | Hair: Brown | Complexion: Light | Remarks: wears glasses & Platea[1451]

U.S., World War II Army Enlistment Records, 1938-1946:[763]

Name: James M Pasco | Race: White | Marital Status: Single, without dependents (Single) | Rank: Private | Birth Year: 1907 | Nativity State or Country: Michigan | Citizenship: Citizen | Residence: Genesee, Michigan | Education: 4 years of high school | Civil Occupation: General industry clerks | Enlistment Date: 6 Apr 1942 | Enlistment Place: Fort Custer, Michigan | Service Number: 36178764 | Branch: Branch Immaterial - Warrant Officers, USA | Component: Selectees (Enlisted Men) | Source: Civil Life | Height: 69 | Weight: 127[1452]

World War II: Corporal, US Army.

Served: 6 April 1942 to 28 July 1944[763]

They had no children.

46. Clifford CLAY[1453] (*Fred Henry*[4], *Simeon A.*[3], *Fredric "Fred"*[2], *Abegail*[1]).

Born circa 1914 in Michigan. Not found in 1920 Census. The only mention of this person, with this family, is in the 1930 census, as a "son." No other records can be found. No mentioned in father or mother obituaries, nor anywhere else with the family.

47. Laverne Charles "Vern" KRUGMAN[1454-1457,180] (*Mary Alice CLAY*[4], *Simeon A.*[3], *Fredric*[2], *Abegail*[1]).

Born on 21 September 1909, in Parma Township, Jackson County, Michigan.[1458] Vern died in Germany on 21 December 1944; he was 35.[1459-1462] He was killed-in-action at the "Battle of the Bulge" and "buried in eastern France." Later, formerly buried in Tompkins Township, Jackson County, Michigan,[1463] at Fairview Cemetery.

47. Laverne Charles "Vern" KRUGMAN, newspaper photograph.

Occupations: Saw Mill Laborer (1930); Reporter (1936); [telephone] Line Builder (1940).[1464,1465]

Obituary: "BAINBRIDGE, Jan. 27 Sergeant Laverne C. Krugman, nephew of Mrs. Charles Molter, route 1, Coloma, died three days before Christmas, from wounds received while in action in Germany.

Krugman was connected with the *Parma News* for three years before entering the service, during which time he was the author of two humorous columns, which were widely read in eastern Calhoun and western Jackson counties.

While in service, both here and overseas he penned more than 30 compositions which he called 'Fox Hole Poems', and four days before he was wounded, answered many of the questions about which wives and friends wonder pertaining to boys over there, concerning morale, experiences and fear, in a letter to the state editor of the *Enquirer and News.*

Sergeant Krugman is survived by his wife, Mrs. Margie Krugman and nine-months old daughter, Joyce, of Parma.

Also surviving is his father, who is located at Anchorage, Alaska, as engineer in a construction crew, and many other relatives."[1466]

1945, January:

"Just four days before he was wounded in Germany on December 19, last, Sergt. Laverne C. Krugman, 35, former Parma newspaperman and village clerk, wrote a letter to Rae S. Corliss, state editor of the *Enquirer and News,* in which he answered many questions about which relatives of servicemen wonder. He died three days later and was buried in eastern France. Coming up through the ranks of the infantry in General Patton's 3rd Army, Sergeant Krugman knew the life and philosophy of the foot-soldier, and in recent letters had expressed the wish that he might 'capture the color of the mud-slogger' and put it into words.

Poem to Infantryman

In October Sergeant Krugman sent home about 30 compositions which he called 'Fox Hole Poems,' explaining he had originally written them on ration boxes. Following is one which he dedicated and entitled. 'To the Infantryman:

Here's to the infantryman, the un- glamorous buck,
He's always broke and short on luck,
He's always gripping and blowing off steam,
But they made him tough and mean and lean.
He slogs in the mud and broils in the sun,
In all kinds of weather he carries on.
And if you would see him in all of his glory
Go up to the front where the fighting is gory;
Where the blast and the blaze of bursting shell.
The churning of earth and the flash of steel,
Where the dead and the dying and stench of Hell
Dismays him not nor his courage quell.
Here's to the fighting man, giving odds,
Slugging it out with the battle gods,
Bending low in the battle gloom
He makes charge to his certain doom.
Fearlessly he makes the charge
To extend the line another yard,
A yard no larger than his grave.

'Tis the bloody way to victories paved.
Peace will come again for which he died,
Let not the reason be denied:
Let peace be equitable and just.
In monumental memory keep his trust.

The physical voice of Sergeant Krugman, now stilled for all time, may yet re-echo through his latest letter the hopes and fears of his buddies still fighting in Europe when he wrote December 15: 'Our mail arrives and comes to you out of all sequence of date. I imagine this is due to the difficulties of getting it in and out. One day on a truck up on the front line would convince anyone that miracles alone move the volume of every conceivable Item in the books to supply an army. The roads alone in the night without lights plus shelling is a veritable hell to move supplies over. Where the trucks leave off the foot and back-packing begins. Mud, rain, the obstacles of war are innumerable.'

No Athiests [sic] *in Fox Holes*

'I've met the enemy, face to face, hand to hand, walked up hill into machinegun fire, had buildings blown down from over me, weathered the hells of cross fire of artillery and mortar fire while snipers kept you so low you couldn't dig in; sat in muddy fox holes with water up to the hips hours at a time, gone hungry, wet, muddy and cold; been counter-attacked by tiger tanks and had to give; walked the streets of a newly captured town clearing out snipers. I've seen our whole squad go, one by one, replacements come and go; been blown out of fox holes by close ones, felt the sting of shrapnel that got other men mighty close. Through these times a fellow does a lot of praying — nothing in the way a preacher would call proper — but I guess God is satisfied, because he answers them. I'm a better man today for having 'walked through the valley' but I don't try to kid myself it is my prayers alone God if answering. I may be a use less cuss as men come and go, but I must mean a lot to my family If I can be the kind of fellow they think I am. I'll be a success. If God will spare me for them I'll be a credit to them.

'Others have pretty aptly summed up about all men think about in trying hours. It is hard to explain how you feel. I must be a coward because I'm too scared to just be human. Someway I've come through thus far. I've had to struggle with myself to keep going almost every attack. But I've kept going. The hardest part of all is to get started. No one who has never 'jumped off' will ever know the feeling. I doubt if it is explainable.

'As for specific stories. I can't give them without reference to censorable allusions. I've tried it, but it doesn't make much sense to the reader. As I have mentioned before, I want to tell the yarn in person. I will when I get home.'

Hits 'Policy of Hate'

'No doubt you have read Secretary of the Treasury Henry Morgenthau's 'policy of hate' in regard to his proposed program for what to do about postwar Germany. Coming from the guardian of our dollar, it implies that hatred and the desire for revenge will sneak into our peace terms. Morgenthau seems to be pretty well in on these matters as far as Roosevelt is concerned. The airing of this plot, I can't help but believe, is prolonging Germany's resistance. There is no plan to convince them we don't mean to actually annihilate the 43,000,000 people of Germany. If this plan is accepted it will be the seed of another war. Before the terms are signed the preparations will be underway. How can we successfully occupy Germany if we have to enforce such terms?

'My Interest Are Vital!'

'I believe, if you have not read the article already, the October 2 issue of *Time* magazine carries the article. It will clear up my point. My interests here are vital. If this is my world, my peace, my war, I want it to be the kind of settlement to end wars. If it isn't my world, my war, my peace what in h am I fighting for?

'Rae, I've gone off the deep end again. I should leave politics to the politicians. I've got my job over here. All I want is an alert public at home. They know what the score is and how to handle the deal. Just so someone doesn't pull a ringer and muff the second chance to settle this mess for all time — that's my little worry.'

Edited Two Columns

During the three years he was connected with the *Parma News*. Sergeant Krugman was the author of two humorous columns, 'Cracker Hill Crumbs' and 'Dear

Mayor,' which wire widely read in eastern Calhoun and western Jackson counties.

Sergeant Krugman is survived by his wife, Mrs. Margie Krugman and nine-months-old daughter, Joyce; his brother, Everett Krugman, and mother, Mrs. Mary Krugman of Parma; his father, Lieut. Fred Krugman with an army engineering corps at Anchorage, Alaska; and three sisters. Mrs. Lucille Richardson, wife of Superintendent of Schools Robert Richardson of Parma, Mrs. Annabelle Hurlburt of Traverse City, and Mrs. Mable Tompkins of Holt.

The Red Cross this week advised Mrs. Krugman that a protestant chaplain was with her husband when he died three days before Christmas. The fact that he was buried in eastern France makes more pertinent these lines taken from a poem on 'Hapless France' which he penned several months ago:

'Twas first here in this luckless land that men fought to be free

When Frenchmen of long years ago lit the torch of liberty.'"[1462]

1945, February: Senator Arthur H. Vandenberg read letter from Laverne's plea for a just and honorable peace.[1467]

Military:

U.S., World War II Draft Cards Young Men, 1940-1947:

Name: Lavern Charles Krugman | Gender: Male | Race: White | Age: 31 | Birth Date: 21 Sep 1909 | Birth Place: Sandstone Township, Michigan | Residence Place: 118 S. Church St Parma, Jackson, Michigan | Registration Date: 16 Oct 1940 | Registration Place: Parma, Jackson, Michigan | Employer: Goodyear Tire And Rubber Co | Height: 5 11 | Weight: 160 | Complexion: Dark | Hair Color: Black | Eye Color: Brown | Crippled finger left hand | Next of Kin: Margie Irene Krugman wife[1468]

World War II Service: US Army, Sergeant, Company G, 319th Infantry Regiment, 30th Infantry Division; Served from 20 December 1943 to killed-in-action 21 December 1944.[1469]

On 9 May 1936, when Vern was 26, he married **Margie Irene BOXERSOX,**[1470,180] daughter of Arthur BOXERSOX and Elsie WOODLIFF, in Parma Township, Jackson County, Michigan,[1471] by Wayne D. Fleenor, Minister. She was born on 22 January 1917, in Parma Township, Jackson County, Michigan. Margie died on 18 December 1961; she was 44. Buried in Tompkins Township, Jackson County, Michigan,[1472] at Fairview Cemetery.

1945, March: "Mrs. Margie Kdugman [sic] has received the Purple Heart medal from the war department. Her husband, Sergt. Laverne Krugman was reported to have died from wounds received in action in France December 22."[1473]

They had one child:

i. **Joyce Ann KRUGMAN**. Born on 17 March 1944, in Jackson, Jackson County, Michigan. Joyce died in Stevensville, Berrien County, Michigan, on 2 December 2016; she was 72.

---

48. Everett Leonard KRUGMAN[1474-1477,180] (*Mary Alice CLAY*[4], *Simeon A.*[3], *Fredric*[2], *Abegail*[1]).

Born 26 September 1910, in Parma Township, Jackson County, Michigan,[1478,408] Everett died in Albion, Calhoun County, Michigan, on 13 June 1984; he was 73.[1479,408] Buried in Tompkins Township, Jackson County, Michigan,[1480] at Fairview Cemetery.

Occupations: Goodyear Rubber & Tire Co. Rubber Laborer (1937, 1940); Factory Worker (1942); Tire Production Control (1950).[1481,1482,1483]

Obituary: "Krugman, Everett – Aged 73, passed away unexpectedly Wednesday morning. He resided at 320 E. Grove St., Parma. Surviving are his wife, Ellarae; two sons, Daryl C. of Tucson, Ariz. and Ronald E. of Boca Raton, Fla.; eight grandchildren; one great-grandchild; two sisters, Mrs. Lyn Mable Tompkins of Fresno, Calif., Mrs. Robert (Luceli) Richardson of Oscoda. Friends may call at the Parma Chapel of Tidd-Williams Funeral Chapels Inc., Wednesday after 7:00 p.m. Services will be held Friday, 3:30 p.m. at the Parma United Church. The Reverend Jean Crabtree officiating Chapter No. 183 F. &A. M. will conduct a Memorial Graveside Service at Fairview Cemetery, Parma. Memorial contributions may be made to the Parma United Church or the Michigan Heart Fund." [1484]

Military:

U.S., World War II Draft Cards Young Men, 1940-1947:
Name: Everett Leonard Krugman | Gender: Male | Race: White | Age: 30 | Birth Date/Place: 26 Sep 1910 Jackson County, Michigan, USA | Residence Place: 915 Backus St.

Jackson, Jackson, Michigan | Registration Date/Place: 16 Oct 1940, Jackson, Jackson, Michigan | Employer: Goodyear Tire And Rubber Co | Height: 5 8.5 | Weight: 160 | Complexion: Light | Hair Color: Brown | Eye Color: Brown | Crippled finger on left hand | Next of Kin: Ella Rayola Krugman wife[1468]

On 15 January 1938, when Everett was 27, he married **Ellarae Royola MOE,**[1485,1486,180] daughter of Raynor H. MOE and Myrla GILLETT, in Eaton Rapids, Eaton County, Michigan,[1487] by Wayne F. Fleenor, Minister. She was born on 7 May 1918, in Sandstone Township, Jackson County, Michigan.[408] Ellarae died at Allegiance Health, in Jackson, Jackson County, Michigan, on 19 August 2011; she was 93.[408] She was buried on 27 August 2011, in Tompkins Township, Jackson County, Michigan,[1488] at Fairview Cemetery (cremated).

Occupation: Saleswoman (1955).[1489]

Religion: Methodist.

Obituary: "WACKENHUT (KRUGMAN), ELLARAE - Age 93, of Parma, passed away Friday, August 19, 2011 at Allegiance Health in Jackson, Michigan. She was born in May 1918 in Sandstone Township, Michigan to Raynor and Myrla (Gillett) Moe. She was first married to Everett Krugman who preceded her in death in 1984 then she married Richard Wackenhut who preceded her in death in 1992. Ellarae was a lifelong resident of Parma. She sold Real Estate for 17 years and also had worked for I.G.A. in Parma. Ellarae was a very active member of the Parma United Methodist Church and had over the years enjoyed golf, antiques and quilting. Ellarae is survived by: sons, Ron (Nina) Krugman of Ft. Myers, FL, Daryl (Mickey) Krugman of Tucson, AZ; stepdaughter, Mary (Phil) Richardson of Brooklyn; stepson, Tom (Mary Lou) Wackenhut of Cincinnati, OH; grandchildren, Clarke, Chris, Kyle, Mark, Kim, Tammy, Karen, Jenny, Jessie, Josh and Jordan; many great-grandchildren; brothers, Duane "Bud" (Joanne) Moe of Marshall; sister-in-law, Phyllis Moe of Kalamazoo. She was preceded in death by her parents, a stepdaughter, Sandra Newcomb in 1999; brother, L.D. Moe and stepson-in-law, Al Newcomb. According to her wishes, cremation has taken place and a Memorial Service will be held Saturday, August 27, 2011 at 11:00 a.m. with a gathering of friends and family starting at 10 a.m. until time of service at the Parma United Methodist Church, 100

East Main Street, Parma, Michigan 49269. Burial of Cremains will be at the Fairview Cemetery, Sandstone Township, MI. Assistance with Memorial Contributions to: Parma United Methodist Church, Food Pantry of N. Parma Church and the Haiti Hot lunch program can be directed to the Funeral home at 811 Finley Drive, Albion, MI; envelopes will be available at church. www.kevintiddfuneralhome.com www.MLive.com/obits"[1490]

Everett and Ellarae had the following children:

i. **Daryl Clarke KRUGMAN.**[1491] Born on 5 February 1941, in Jackson, Jackson County, Michigan. Daryl died in Phoenix, Maricopa County, Arizona, on 3 July 2019; he was 78. He was married to Mary Katherine PRATT.

ii. **Ronald Everett KRUGMAN.**[1492] [withheld for privacy—living person]. He married Nina Jean BUELL.

---

49. Annabelle KRUGMAN[1493-1496] (*Mary Alice CLAY*[4]*, Simeon A.*[3]*, Fredric*[2]*, Abegail*[1]).

Born 20 March 1912, in Parma Township, Jackson County, Michigan, Annabelle died in Charlotte, Eaton County, Michigan, on 14 October 1956; she was 45. Buried in Jackson, Jackson County, Michigan,[1497] at Mount Evergreen Cemetery.

Occupations: Housework, Private (1930).[1498]

Obituary: "CHARLOTTE – Mrs. Annabelle Hurlman, [sic] 44, wife of Robert Hurlman of 511 W. Henry st., died of a heart attack Sunday at her home. Mrs. Hurlman was born March 20, 1912, in Parma, the daughter of Frederick and Mary (Clay) Krugman. She had resided in Charlotte for the past five years. She married Robert Hurlman, a local trucker, in 1936. Surviving besides her husband are her father at Parma; a brother, Everett Krugman of Parma: two sisters, Mrs. Mabel Tompkins of Fresno, Calif., and Mrs. Lucille Richardson of Oscoda."[1499]

On 18 August 1936, when Annabelle was 25, she married **Robert D. HURLBUT,**[180,1495] son of John Henry HURLBUT and Mary E. FRY, in Steuben County, Indiana.[1500] He was born on 9 November 1883, in Traverse City, Grand Traverse County, Michigan.[1469,408] [Social Security say 30 November 1883; marriage record says 9 October 1882.] Robert died in Michigan on 25 December 1966; he was 83.[408] Buried in Ypsilanti, Washtenaw County, Michigan,[1469,1501] at Udell Cemetery.

Occupations: Pensioner (1932); Trucker (1936); Retired Soldier (1936).

Military:

US Navy: Service: 12 July 1918 to 18 January 1919.[1469]

Name: Robert D Hurlbert | Residence Place: Owosso, Shiawassee | Birth Date: 9 Oct 1888 | Birthplace: Traverse City, Michigan | Military Final Rank: Fireman B | Military Unit Note: 384 | Father's Name: John Henry Hurlbert | Mother's Name: Mary Elizabeth | Spouse's Name: Eunice Smith Spouse's Birth Date: 1893 | Event Type: Military Service | Event Place: Lake, Illinois, United States | Event Place (Original): Gt Lakes Naval Station, Ill[1502]

They had no children.

---

50. Mabel Louise KRUGMAN[1503-1510] (*Mary Alice CLAY*[4], *Simeon A.*[3], *Fredric*[2], *Abegail*[1]).

Born 20 February 1914, in Parma Township, Jackson County, Michigan,[408] Mabel died in St. Helena, Napa County, California, on 22 April 1998; she was 84.[408] Buried on 27 April 1998, in Fresno, Fresno County, California, at Fresno Memorial Gardens.

Occupation: Nurse (1935).

Religion: Baptist.

Obituary: "MABLE LOUISE TOMPKINS Age 84, passed away in St. Helena, CA, on April 22, 1998. She had pursued a career in Nursing, was a member of the Order of the Eastern Star, and was a life member of the International Society of Poets. Mable was a long time member and lay worker at Harvard Terrace Baptist Church in Fresno, but more recently held membership In Calvary Christian Center, St. Helena, CA, where her son is Associate Pastor. She was predeceased by her husband of 56 years, Lynn Tompkins; her brothers LaVern and Everette; sisters, Annabel and Lucille, and her granddaughter, Constance.

She is survived by her daughter, Constance Thomas; her son, Douglas; grandsons, Timothy and Kenneth; granddaughter, Melody and four great-grandchildren.

50. *Mabel Louise KRUGMAN. Photograph from high school yearbook, 1931.*[1511]

Viewing will be held at the Lisle Funeral Home on Sunday, April 26, 1998, from 12:00 Noon until 5:00 P.M.

Funeral Services will be held at the Lisle Funeral Home on Monday, April 27, 1998, at 1 :00 P.M. Interment will follow at Fresno Memorial Gardens.

The family requests that in lieu of flowers any donations be made to the Cancer Society of the donor's choice. LISLE FUNERAL HOME

1605 'L' Street, Fresno 266-0666"[1512]

On 31 August 1935, when Mabel was 21, she married **Lynn LeRoy TOMPKINS,**[1513,-1515] son of Bryon E. TOMPKINS and Daisy E. ROBBINS, in Lansing, Ingham County, Michigan,[1516,1517] by W. S. Carpenter, Presbyterian Minister, at Mt. Hope Avenue Presbyterian Church. Lynn was born on 11 August 1909, in Jackson, Jackson County, Michigan.[1518,408] Lynn died in Fresno, Fresno County, California, on 4 January 1992; he was 82.[870,408] Buried on 7 January 1992.

Occupations: Farmer (1930); Apprentice Die Sinker (1935, 1950, 1958); Die Maker (1940).[1519,1520,1510]

> *Obituary*: "Services for Lynn L Tompkins, 82, of Fresno will be held at 1 p.m. Tuesday at Lisle Funeral Home.
>
> Mr. Tompkins died Saturday. He was a retired die sinker for Jack Cartwright & Son.
>
> Surviving are his wife, Mable; a son, Douglas of Saint Helena; a daughter Constance Thomas of Oakhurst; a brother, Leland of Fresno; a sister, Crystal Markle of Michigan; and three grandchildren.
>
> Visitation will be from 10 a.m. to 7 p.m. Monday at the funeral home."[1521]

Military:

U.S., World War II Draft Cards Young Men, 1940-1947:

Name: Lynn Leroy Tompkins | Gender: Male | Race: White | Age: 31 | Birth Date/Place: 11 Aug 1909, Jackson, Michigan | Residence Place: 2132 Dean Ave., Holt, Ingham, Michigan | Registration Date: 16 Oct 1940 | Registration Place: Holt, Ingham, Michigan | Employer: Atlas Drop Forge | Height: 5 8 | Weight: 163 | Complexion: Light | Hair Color: Brown | Eye Color: Brown | Partial Stiff right hip | Next of Kin: Mable L Tompkins. Wife[1522]

Mabel and Lynn had the following children:

i. **Rev. Douglas Leland TOMPKINS**[1523,1524]. [withheld for privacy—living person]. He married Marion BATTS.

ii. **Constance Beth TOMPKINS**[1525]. [withheld for privacy—living person]. She first married Floyd Dwight SIEMENS, then Jimmy P. THOMAS.

---

51. Lucille Ione KRUGMAN[1526-1530] (*Mary Alice CLAY[4], Simeon A.[3], Fredric[2], Abegail[1]*).

Born on 30 May 1916, in Parma Township, Jackson County, Michigan,[408] Lucille died in Ann Arbor, Washtenaw County, Michigan, on 28 November 1986; she was 70.[1531,408] Buried in Oscodo, Iosco County, Michigan,[1532] at Pinecrest Cemetery.

On 30 December 1935, when Lucille was 19, she married **Robert Dean RICHARDSON,**[1533-1535,180] son of Floyd C. RICHARDSON and Edith May KNIGHT, in LaGrange County, Indiana.[1536] He was born on 8 January 1913, in Parma Township, Jackson County, Michigan.[408] Robert died in Tawas City, Iosco County, Michigan, on 17 January 1988; he was 75.[1361,408] [Reported deceased in daughter Lucille's marriage record of 1935!] He was buried in Oscodo, Iosco County, Michigan,[1537] at Pinecrest Cemetery.

Occupation: Teacher (1935); Superintendent Of Public School (1940, 1950).[1538,1539]

Military:

U.S., World War II Draft Cards Young Men, 1940-1947:

Name: Robert Dean Richardson | Gender: Male | Race: White | Age: 27 | Birth Date/Place: 8 Jan 1913, Parmel, Michigan | Residence Place: Elk Rapids, Antrim, Michigan | Registration Date: 16 Oct 1940 | Registration Place: Elk Rapids Township, Antrim, Michigan | Employer: Board Of Education | Height: 6 | Weight: 160 | Complexion: Light | Hair Color: Brown | Eye Color: Brown | Next of Kin: Lucille Ione Richardson, wife[1540]

They had the following children:

i. **Michael S. RICHARDSON**[1541] [withheld for privacy—living person].

ii. **Anothy D. RICHARDSON**[1542] [withheld for privacy—living person].

---

52. Thelma Clay GUNNELL[1543-1548,180] (*Birdie Mabel CLAY*[4], *Simeon A.*[3], *Fredric*[2], *Abegail*[1]).

Thelma was born on 21 June 1907, in Parma Township, Jackson County, Michigan[1549,408] [marriage record says born in 1908]. Thelma died in Okemos, Ingham County, Michigan, on 21 October 1993; she was 86,[1550,408] and buried on 25 October 1993 in Vermontville, Eaton County, Michigan,[1551] at Woodlawn Cemetery.

52. *Thelma Clay GUNNELL. Photograph from College yearbook.*[1556]

Occupation: School Teacher (1930, 1933, 1940, 1950).[1552,1553,1554]

Education: Michigan State Normal College, 1928; Bachelor Of Science Degree, Eastern Michigan University; Master Of Arts Degree plus a 6th Year at Michigan State University.[1555]

Obituary: "LAMB, THELMA C. | Okemos | Mrs. Lamb died on October 21, 1993. Her early life was spent in Parma, MI. She received a Bachelor of Science Degree from Eastern Michigan University and a Master of Arts Degree plus a sixth year from Michigan State University. She spent 43 years of her life as a high school teacher, librarian, principal, guidance director and counselor, the last 23 years having been spent at Okemos High School. She was a member of the Okemos Community Church, the Mary-Martha Circle, the Friends of Historic Meridian, the Historical Society of Michigan, the Okemos Woman's

Club, the Pioneers, the Friends of the Okemos Library, the Ingham County Retired School Personnel Association (which she helped organize and served as the first treasurer), a life member of Michigan Retired School Personnel Association and life member of the Eastern Star Chapter 342 of Vermontville, MI.

She was preceded in death by her husband, Milton C. Lamb, to whom she was married 57 years; and 2 brothers. Howard and Elroy Zantop. Surviving are 1 sister, Anita (Owen) Kelly of Burlington, MI; 2 brothers, Duane (Louise) Zantop of Ypsilanti and Lloyd (Glenna) Zantop of Belleville; numerous nieces, nephews and grand nieces and nephews. The family will receive friends at Gorsline-Runciman Co. East Chapel, East Lansing on Sunday, 2-4 and 7-9 p.m.

Funeral services will be held on Monday, 10 a.m. at the Okemos Community Church, 4734 N. Okemos Road, with the Rev. Charles D. Grauer, Senior Pastor officiating. Interment will be in Woodlawn Cemetery, Vermontville, MI. Those desiring may make contributions to the Okemos Community Church. P.O. Box 680. Okemos 48805, in memory of Mrs. Lamb."[1557]

On 9 December 1933, when Thelma was 26, she married **Milton C. LAMB**[1558,1559,958,180], son of Charles H. LAMB and Lena SATTERLEE, in Auburn, DeKalb County, Indiana.[1560,1561] He was born on 21 February 1912, in Vermontville, Eaton County, Michigan,[408] and died in Okemos, Ingham County, Michigan, on 8 October 1991; he was 79.[408,1361] Buried on 11 October 1991, in Vermontville, Eaton County, Michigan,[1562] Woodlawn Cemetery.

Occupations: Storekeeper (1933); Hardware Store Manager (1940); Traffic Analyst/Technician/Engineer Aide State Highway Department (1949-1959).[1563-1571]

Education: Eastern Michigan University.

Obituary: "LAMB, MILTON C | Okemos

Age 78, died October 8, 1991. Mr. Lamb was born February 21, 1913 in Vermontville where he returned after attending Eastern Michigan University, to run a Hardware and Dry Goods Store that had been in his family for seventy years. In 1948, he sold the business and moved to Meridian Township where he worked for the Michigan State Highway Department for 30 years, retiring in 1976.

Mr. Lamb also served as a part-time Ingham County Sheriffs Deputy for 18 years and was the first police officer in Meridian Township. He was a member of the Okemos Community Church; the Friends of Historic Meridian; the Hope Borbas Library; the Central Michigan Law Enforcement Association; the Michigan Knights of the Highway; a life member of the Family Motor Coach Association; the Masonic Lodge 255 of Nashville; and the Battle Creek Elks Lodge 131.

Survivors Include his wife, Thelma C; 1 sister, Mrs. Hugh Whitmore of Eagle; and 2 nieces, Mrs. Robert Moyer of Eagle and Mrs. Vern Cole fo [sic] Albuquerque, NM.

Funeral services will be Friday, 1 p.m. at Okemos Community Church, 4734 N. Okemos Road, with the Rev. Charles D. Grauer, Senior Pastor, and the Rev. Dr. David Evans, Pastor Emeritus, officiating. Interment will be in Wood Lawn Cemetery, Vermontville. The family will receive friends at the Gorsline-Runciman East Chapel, East Lansing, Thursday, 2-4 and 7-9 p.m. Those desiring may make contributions to the Church."[1572]

They had no children.

---

53. Howard William ZANTOP[1573-1576,180] (*Birdie Mabel CLAY*[4], *Simeon A.*[3], *Fredric*[2], *Abegail*[1]).

Born 1 October 1911, in Jackson County, Michigan,[408] Howard died at Henry Ford Hospital, in Detroit, Wayne County, Michigan, on 18 April 1982; he was 70.[1361,408] Buried 21 April 1982 in Sandstone Township, Jackson County, Michigan,[1577] at Chapel Cemetery.

Occupations: Sawmill Laborer (1930); Trucking (1933); Garage Proprietor (1940); Machinist (1941); Flying Service (1947-1960).[1578-1586,2114]

Obituary: "Services for air transportation executive Howard W. Zantop, a winter resident of Fort Lauderdale, will be at noon Wednesday in Allen Park, Mich.

Zantop, of 5531 NE 31st Ave., Fort Lauderdale, died Sunday in Michigan. He was 70.

The founder of Zantop International Airlines and president of Zantop Air Transport Inc., both of Detroit, Zantop had spent winters in Fort Lauderdale since 1967. He also was a resident of Allen Park.

He was a member of the Aircraft Owners and Pilots Association, and was an avid hunter, fisherman and boater.

53. *Howard William ZANTOP, newspaper photograph.*

He is survived by his wife, Patricia J. Disque of Allen Park; a son, Harold Zantop of Allen Park; four daughters, Anne Cioffi of Norwalk, Conn., Linda Clark of Ann Arbor, Mich., Sandra Sue Battle of Woodhaven, Mich., and Sandra Jean Woods of Battle Creek, Mich.; and two brothers, two sisters, 19 grandchildren and one great-grandson."[1587]

"Howard W. Zantop, 70, of Allen Park and formerly of Parma, died Sunday in Henry Ford Hospital in Detroit. A native of Jackson County, he was founder of Zantop International Airlines Inc. at Willow Run, and Zantop Air Transport Inc. at Detroit Metropolitan Airport. His firms provided air service for Battle Creek area firms for many years. Services will be 2 p.m. Wednesday at Chapel Cemetery, Sandstone Township, Jackson County. Memorial donations may be made to the Michigan Cancer Foundation Downriver Unit in Wyandotte. Arrangements are by Martinson Funeral Home, Allen Park."[1588]

Obituary: "Howard W. Zantop, a founder of Zantop International Airlines at Willow Run Airport, was a man who loved to fix things himself.

'He had been called a mechanical genius,' said his son, Harold. 'He did the work on his own plane, but it didn't have to be airplanes. When he was in the hospital, something went wrong with one of the life support machines he was on.'

'They sent for a technician, but when the technician got back, he (Mr. Zantop) had already fixed it.'

Mr. Zantop, 70, died Sunday at Henry Ford Hospital.

He was one of four brothers who formed Zantop Flying Service in Jackson in 1946. He had been a tool and die maker who helped build planes for World War II, and his brothers had been in the Air Force.

Initially, the business was to train pilots and provide charter services, but over the years it developed into an air transport service, serving the U.S. government and the auto industry.

In 1972, Mr. Zantop and two of his brothers – one had died – formed the present company. It has about 50 airplanes and provides service to about 20 cities.

Mr. Zantop had homes in Allen Park, where he had lived for many years, and in Ft. Lauderdale, Fla. He was a member of the Aircraft Owners and Pilots Association and the Masonic Lodge in Parma and was a former member of the Lakeside Country Club in Burbank, Calif.

He was an avid deer and bird hunter.

Besides his son, he is survived by his wife, Patricia; four daughters, Anne Cioffi, Linda Clark, Sandra Sue Battle and Sandra Jean Woods; two brothers; two sisters; 19 grandchildren, and a great-grandson.

Services will be at noon Wednesday at the Martenson Funeral Home, 10915 Allen Road, Allen Park. Burial service will be at 2 p.m. Wednesday at Chapel Cemetery, Parma.

Memorial contributions may be sent to the Michigan Cancer Foundation."[1589]

Obituary: "ZANTOP – Howard W Zantop, 70, of Allen Park, MI., passed away April 18, 1982. Beloved husband of Patricia, dear father of Harold, Anne Cioffi, Linda Clark, Sandra Sue Battle, Sandra Jean Woods; also survived by two brothers, Duane A. and Lloyd A.; and two sisters. Thelma Lamb and Anita Kelly; 19 grandchildren; and one great-grandson. Funeral services from the MARTENSON FUNERAL HOME, 10915 Allen Road. Allen Park, ML. Wednesday, April 21, at 12 noon. Interment service at Chapel Cemetery in Parma. ML, Wednesday. 2 PM. Memorial contributions may be made to the Michigan Cancer Foundation."[1590]

"DETROIT (AP) – Funeral services will be held Wednesday for Howard W. Zantop, founder of Zantop International Airlines and Zantop Air Transport Inc., who died Sunday at the age of 70."[1591]

Military:

U.S., World War II Draft Cards Young Men, 1940-1947:

Name: Howard William Zantop | Gender: Male | Race: White | Age: 29 | Birth Date/Place: 1 Oct 1911, Parma, Michigan | Residence Place: 415 US 12, Parma, Jackson, Michigan | Registration Date/Place: 16 Oct 1940, Parma, Jackson, Michigan | Employer: Self; Garage | Height: 6 ft 2 | Weight: 184 | Complexion: Light | Hair Color: Brown | Eye Color: Blue | Next of Kin: Alma B Zantop, Wife[1592]

On 14 June 1933, when Howard was 21, he first married **Alma Bertelle WILKINSON**[1593,1594,180], daughter of Arthur S. WILKINSON and Florence L. RHINARD, in Parma Township, Jackson County, Michigan.[1595] She was born on 14 December 1909, in Forty Four, Luzerne County, Pennsylvania.[1596] Alma died in Parma Township, Jackson County, Michigan, on 22 September 1950; she was 40.[328,1597] Buried on 24 September 1950 in Sandstone Township, Jackson County, Michigan,[1598] at Chapel Cemetery.

Occupation: School Teacher (1933, 1940).

Education: Albion College.

Obituary: "Mrs. Alma Zantop passed away at her home in Parma, Mich., Friday, Sept. 22. She was 40 years old.

Mrs Zantop was born in Forty Fort Dec. 14, 1909, the daughter of Arthur S. and Florence Wilkinson. The family moved to Town Line when she was a child, where she resided until November, 1915, when they took up residence in Parma, Mich.

Mrs. Zantop was a graduate of the Parma High School, and also Albion College. On June 14, 1933 she became the wife of Howard Zantop, who with the following children survive, Harold, Anne, Linda and Sandra, all at home. Her parents, Mr. and Mrs. Arthur S. Wilkinson, of Jackson, Mich., also survive, and the following brothers and sisters, Mrs. Lesta Milne, of Concord; Mrs. Audrey Gillett; Mrs. Shirley Bower, and Roy C. Wilkinson, all of Jackson.

Funeral services were held at the Parma Methodist Church, Sunday, Sept. 24. Interment was in Chapel cemetery."[1599]

Howard and Alma had the following children:

i. **Harold Douglas ZANTOP Sr.**[1600,1601] Born on 14 August 1934, in Parma Township, Jackson

County, Michigan. Harold died in Indiana on 11 July 2021; he was 86. He first married Barbara Graham RAILEY, then secondly to Dian Shirley PASTOR.

ii. **Anne Jeannine ZANTOP**[1602] [withheld for privacy—living person] She married television actor Charles Michael CIOFFI (see www.imdb.-com/name/nm0162541/)

iii. **Linda Lou ZANTOP**[1603] [withheld for privacy—living person] She married Daniel Mason CLARK.

iv. **Sandra Sue ZANTOP**[1604] [withheld for privacy—living person]. She married _____BATTLE.

On 8 May 1953, when Howard was 41, he second married **Mary Rita BLEVINS** in Tarrant County, Texas.[1605,1606] They were divorced in February 1956, in Texas.[1607]

They had no children.

Howard third married **Patricia Jean DISQUE**[1585,1608], daughter of Robert C. DISQUE and Myrtle A. CASEY. She was born on 26 March 1917, in Detroit, Wayne County, Michigan.[408] Patricia died in Battle Creek, Calhoun County, Michigan, on 27 January 1995; she was 77.[408]

> *Obituary*: "Patricia D Zantop, 77, of Battle Creek, MI and formerly of Ft. Lauderdale, died, January 27, 1995 in Battle Creek. She was born, March 26, 1917 in Detroit to Robert and Myrtle (Carey) Disque. She was preceded in death by husbands, Robert H. Newton in 1952 and Howard Zantop in 1984. Surviving are a daughter, Sandra N. Woods of Battle Creek; 3 grandsons and a brother, Robert C. Disque, Jr. of Plantation, FL. Memorials to St. Thomas Episcopal Church or the Battle Creek Art Center. Arrangements by Shaw-Estes Funeral Home, 2838 Capital Ave., S.W. Battle Creek, MO 49015."[1609]

They had no children from this marriage.

---

54. Naomi Alice ZANTOP[180] (*Birdie Mabel CLAY*[4], *Simeon A.*[3], *Fredric*[2], *Abegail*[1]).

Born on 4 January 1913, in Michigan. Naomi died in Parma Township, Jackson County, Michigan, on 12 January 1914; she was one year old.[1610,1611] Buried on 14 January 1914 in

Sandstone Township, Jackson County, Michigan,[1612] at Chapel Cemetery.

55. Harold Lyle ZANTOP[180] (*Birdie Mabel CLAY*[4], *Simeon A.*[3], *Fredric*[2], *Abegail*[1]).

Born on 9 March 1916, in Parma Township, Jackson County, Michigan. Harold died in Parma Township, three months later on 3 August 1916.[1613] Buried on 5 August 1916, in Sandstone Township, Jackson County, Michigan,[1614] at Chapel Cemetery.

56. Anita Mae ZANTOP[1615-1619,180] (*Birdie Mabel CLAY*[4], *Simeon A.*[3], *Fredric*[2], *Abegail*[1]).

Born on 18 April 1917, in Parma Township, Jackson County, Michigan,[408] Anita died in Burlington, Calhoun County, Michigan, on 23 December 1995; she was 78.[408,1620] Buried in Burlington, Calhoun County, Michigan,[1621] at Abscota Cemetery.

Occupation: Beauty Operator (1938, 1940).[1622,1623]

> *Obituary*: "Burlington | Anita M. (Zantop) Kelley, 78, of Burlington died Saturday, Dec 23, 1995, at her home in Burlington Township. She had suffered a stroke in February 1993.
>
> Mrs. Kelly was born on April 18, 1917, in Parma, to August and Mable (Clay) Zantop Jr.
>
> Raised in Parma, she moved to Battle Creek in 1939 and to the Athens-Union Ciry [sic] area in 1946. She operated a beauty shop in Parma and Athens and during the Korean War she worked at the former Oliver Aircraft manufacturing plant in Battle Creek. She was one of the state's first female pilots and a charter member of the first women's flying club in the United States, which was organzied [sic] in Battle Creek. Her brothers owned and operated Zantop Airways out of Willow Run Airport in Detroit.
>
> Surviving are a daughter, Patricia Kelly of Battle Creek; sons, Robert Kelly of Burlington and Dennis Kelly of Iron; seven grandchildren; seven great-grandchildren; and brothers, Duane Zantop of Ypsilanti and Lloyd Zantop of Bellevue.
>
> Her husband, Owen Kelly, died in 1992."[1624]

On 17 October 1938, when Anita was 21, she married **Owen A. KELLY,**[1625-1628,180] son of Merwin KELLY and Lillian KITLEY, in Williams County, Ohio.[1629] He was born on 15 January 1917, in Parma Township, Jackson County, Michigan.[408] Owen died in Battle Creek, Calhoun County, Michigan, on 4 June 1992; he was 75.[1361,408] Buried on 6 June 1992, in Burlington, Calhoun County, Michigan,[1630] at Abscota Cemetery.

Occupations: Machinist (1938, 1940, 1942); Factory Worker (1939); Farmer (1950).[1631-1635]

> *Obituary*: "Burlington | Owen A. Kelly, 74, of 7900 N Drive S., died Thursday, June 4, 1992, in Battle Creek Health System/Lefla Site where he had been a patient five days.
>
> Mr. Kelly was born July 15, 1917, in Parma, to Merlin and Lillian (Kitley) Kelly.
>
> He moved to the Burlington area in 1945 and had lived at his present address since 1962.
>
> A former employee of the Clark Equipment Co., he retired from the Kellogg Co. in 1975.
>
> He was an avid horseman and a member of the U.S. Trotting Association, the Michigan Harness Horseman's Association and the Wesleyan Church in Union City.
>
> Surviving are his wife, the former Anita M. Zantop; sons, Robert Kelly of Union City and Dennis Kelly of Irons; a daughter, Patricia Kelly of Battle Creek; seven grandchildren; five great-grandchildren; a brother, Leah Kelly of Albion; and a sister, Helen Ward of Litchfield.
>
> Visitation: 2 to 4 and 6 to 8 p.m. Saturday at the Putnam Funeral Home in Union City.
>
> Services: 2 p.m. Sunday at the funeral home with the Rev. Ron. Forsythe officiating.
>
> Burial: Abscota Cemetery.
>
> Memorials: American Cancer Society."[1636]

Military:

U.S., World War II Draft Cards Young Men, 1940-1947:

Name: Owen A Kelly | Gender: Male | Race: White | Age: 23 | Birth Date/Place: 15 Jul 1917, Parma, Michigan | Residence Place: 315 E Main, Parma, Jackson, Michigan | Registration Date: 16 Oct 1940, Parma, Jackson, Michigan | Employer: Clark Equipment Co, Battle Creek, Calhoun, Mich. | Height: 5 ft 10 | Weight: 145 | Complexion: Dark | Hair Color: Brown | Eye Color: Brown | Next of Kin: Lillian A Kelly, Mother[1637]

They had the following children:

i. **Robert Leonard KELLY.**[1638,1639,180] Born on 30 March 1939, in Battle Creek, Calhoun County, Michigan. Robert died in Hillsdale County, Michigan, on 17 January 2012; he was 72. His second marriage was to Mary Lee CHMIEL.

ii. **Dennis Gale KELLY.**[1640,1641,180] Born on 24 August 1943, in Battle Creek, Calhoun County, Michigan. Dennis died in Irons, Lake County, Michigan, on 29 March 2004; he was 60. His second marriage was to Paulette Dee TODD.

iii. **Patricia N. KELLY.**[1642] [withheld for privacy—living person].

---

57. Duane August ZANTOP[1643-1647,180] (*Birdie Mabel CLAY*[4], *Simeon A.*[3], *Fredric*[2], *Abegail*[1]).

Born 19 November 1918, in Parma Township, Jackson County, Michigan,[408] Duane died at Superior Woods, in Superior Township, Washtenaw County, Michigan, on 13 April 2006; he was 87.[408] Buried on 18 April 2006, in Sandstone Township, Jackson County, Michigan,[1648] at Chapel Cemetery.

Occupations: Truck Driver (1940); Flying Service (1947-1960); Airplane Mechanic (1950).[1649-1656]

Education: Hartung School Of Aviation.

Obituary: "ZANTOP DUANE A. Of Ypsilanti, MI, Age 87, passed away Thursday, April 13, 2006 at Superior Woods.

Duane was born November 19th, 1918 in Parma, Michigan. Mr. Zantop was preceded in death by his father August and mother Mabel, four sisters and four brothers.

Mr. Zantop spent most of his life in the transportation business. He often talked about dnving trucks loaded with cement at the age of 14. During World War II he entered the Army Air Corp and spent much of his military career inspecting B24 Bombers as they came off the assembly line in Tuscon, Arizona. After returning from his military duty he attended Hartung School of Aviation. Mr. Zantop and his three brothers Howard, Floyd and Elroy began their first aviation venture in Jackson, Michigan. In 1946 the brothers started Zantop Flying Service which was a charter, aviation maintenance and flight school opera-

57. *Duane August ZANTOP, newspaper photograph.*

tion. After World War II many pilots got their start at Zantop receiving training under the GI. Bill. By 1953 the fleet of aircraft had grown and the automotive cargo business caused the company to outgrow the Jackson facility and the operation moved to Detroit Wayne Major Airport, now Detroit Metro. The company changed its name to Zantop Air Transport. Zantop flew cargo for the auto companies, military and was a contractor for the construction of the DEW, line hauling supplies for radar sites in remote areas of Canada. Zantop became a leader in the aviation Industry employing over 3000 people when it was sold in 1966. In 1972 after several years of retirement Mr. Zantop learned that his former company had closed down so he decided to again get back into the Airline business. In May of 1972. with the help of his brothers and family, he contacted many of his former employees and started Zantop International Airlines. Zantop International Airlines again became a leader in the air cargo business. By 1979, Zantop had scheduled operations with facilities in 38 cities across the United States. Mr. Zantop's operations also extended to Europe and Alaska. Zantop also had a large overhaul facility in Macon, Georgia employing over 600 people. Combined operations employed approximately 1,000 people.

Duane is survived by Louise, his wife of 57 years, one daughter Karen Freitag; three sons Jim, David, Duane (Sharon), twelve grandchildren and four great-grandchildren. The family will receive friends on Sunday April 16th from 5-9 p.m., on Monday, April 17th from 2-8 p.m. at the Nie Family Funeral Home,

2400 Carpenter Rd., Ann Arbor, MI 46108. Funeral services will be held Tuesday, April 18th, 2006 at 10:30 a.m. from the funeral home with visitation from 9:30 a.m. until time of service. Rev. Ronald Fulton will officiate. Burial will be in Chapel Cemetery, Parma, MI.

Mr. Zantop loved his work and his employee's were tike family to him. Mr. Zantop worked well past his 85th birthday. In lieu of flowers the family requests donations be sent to the American Lung Association, Ann Arbor Hospice, or a chanty of your choice."[1657]

Military:

U.S., World War II Draft Cards Young Men, 1940-1947:

Name: Duane August Zantop | Gender: Male | Race: White | Age: 21 | Birth Date/Place: 19 Nov 1918, Parma, Michigan | Residence Place: 520 E. Main St. Parma, Jackson, Michigan | Registration Date/Place: 16 Oct 1940, Parma, Jackson, Michigan | Employer: R. O. Baum | Height: 6-2 | Weight: 170 | Complexion: Freckled | Hair Color: Brown | Eye Color: Blue | Forefinger on right hand off at knuckle. | Next of Kin: Mrs. Mable Zantop, Mother[1658]

World War II: US Army Air Corps, Sergeant.
Served: 26 December 1941 to 5 November 1945[763]

U.S., World War II Army Enlistment Records, 1938-1946:

Name: Duane A Zantop | Race: White | Marital Status: Single, without dependents (Single) | Rank: Private | Birth Year: 1918 | Nativity State or Country: Michigan | Citizenship: Citizen | Residence: Jackson, Michigan | Education: 4 years of high school | Civil Occupation: Semi-skilled mechanics and repairmen, motor vehicles | Enlistment Date: 26 Dec 1941 | Enlistment Place: Detroit, Michigan | Service Number: 16043404 | Branch: Air Corps | Component: Army of the United States - includes the following: Voluntary enlistments effective December 8, 1941 and thereafter; One year enlistments of National Guardsman whose State enlistment expires while in the Federal Service; Officers appointed in the Army of | Source: Civil Life | Height: 74 | Weight: 164[1659]

On 29 November 1943, when Duane was 25, he first married **Ardith DETRICK** in Phoenix, Maricopa County, Arizona.[1660,1661] She is believed to have been born 5 March 1917, in Enon, Clark County, Ohio. They were divorced on 29 March 1946, in Jackson County, Michigan.[1662] She was previously married to Robert Perry BEAUCHAMP (1915-2004) in

1940 and divorced circa 1943. After her marriage to Duane, she remarried Frederick William ASHBROOK (1916-1969). Ardith died 26 November 1986, at Fort Walton Beath, Okaloosa County, Florida.

Duane and Ardith had one child:

i. **Duane Gerald ZANTOP**[1663] [withheld for privacy—living person]. He married Sharon HEYER.

On 10 October 1946, when Duane was 27, he second married **Maybelle Elizabeth TITUS,**[1664,1665] daughter of Raymond E. TITUS and Nora CHAMPINS, in Parma Township, Jackson County, Michigan.[1666] She was born on 5 May 1921, in Mount Clemens, Macomb County, Michigan.[408] Maybelle died in Eustis, Lake County, Florida, on 13 August 1987; she was 66.[556,1667]

Occupation: Nurse.

Religion: Roman Catholic.

They were divorced on 16 January 1946, in Macomb County, Michigan.[1668]

> *Obituary*: "MAYBELLE E. SHAENING, 66, 31 Cocos Plumosa Drive, Country Club Manor, Eustis, died Thursday. Born in Mount Clemens, Mich., she moved to Eustis from Michigan in 1976. She was a retired nurse and a member of St. Mary of the Lakes Catholic Church, Eustis. Survivors: husband, John S.; brothers, Ray Titus, Wendy Titus, both of Mount Clemens, Gary Titus, Sterling Heights, Mich.; sisters, Mrs. Audrey Stapolis, Mrs. Joyce Hill, both of Mount Clemens, Mrs. Charlotte Ehrke, Eustis, Mrs. Gail Harrington, New Baltimore, Mich., Mrs. Denny Ferdig, Gladwin, Mich. Harden-Pauli Funeral Home, Eustis."[1669]

They had no children from this marriage.

On 3 April 1949, when Duane was 30, he third married **Anna Louise CULVER,**[1670,1671,1655,180] daughter of Erwin Harrison CULVER and Winifred E. WOLCOTT, in Parma Township, Jackson County, Michigan.[1672] She was born on 18 February 1925, in Michigan. Anna died in Saline, Washtenaw County, Michigan, on 1 December 2020; she was 95. Buried on 3 December 2020, in Parma Township, Jackson County, Michigan,[1673] at Chapel Cemetery.

Occupation: Clerk (1951, 1954).[1674]

> *Obituary*: "Anna Louise (Culver) Zantop passed peacefully on Tuesday, December 1, 2020 in Saline, Michigan. Anna was born on February 18, 1925 to Erwin Harrison Culver and Winnifred E. (Wolcott) Cul-

ver. Anna had four siblings: a sister, Marie, and three brothers, Westley, Lyle, and Elmer. Anna was married to Duane A. Zantop on April 3, 1949 in Parma, Michigan at the same church as where she met him while they were both standing up in a wedding together.

Duane and Anna had four children: Duane G. (Sharon) Zantop, Jim (Elaine) Zantop , David Zantop, and Karen (the late Ed) Freitag. Proud grandparents to 12 grandchildren: Duane, Renee, Nikki, Bart, Todd, Brent, Rebecca, Michelle, Elizabeth, Kaela, Addie, and Taylor, and 17 great-grandchildren.

Anna grew up in Hanover, Michigan. In her younger days, Anna worked at Aeroquip and at Sears. After marrying Duane, she tended to her family and the home in Allen Park, Michigan where they settled while he made a living as a pioneer in the aviation industry through various endeavors. Ultimately, the family founded and ran what was at one time the largest cargo airline in the United States based out of Willow Run Airport in Ypsilanti, Michigan.

Duane and Anna moved to Ypsilanti in the 1970's and purchased a second home in Sarasota, Florida in the 1980's where they would spend the cold winter months. The family enjoyed many family vacations at the home in Sarasota, where they made happy memories together. When Duane passed away in 2006, Anna continued maintaining both of the homes and the family continued to spend happy times together with her for years to come. Anna remained in relatively good health for most of her life, and was cherished by all who knew and loved her. We love you so much and miss you dearly already. Thank you for always being there for each and every one of us. You will always live on in our hearts, and we will never forget the good times we had with you.

Laid to rest at a graveside ceremony with her family near on December 3, 2020 at Chapel Cemetery in Parma, Michigan. While we could not have a funeral service due to the COVID-19 global pandemic, you are and always will be in the thoughts and prayers of the many people who knew and loved you."[1675]

Duane and Anna had the following children:

i. **James Milton ZANTOP** [withheld for privacy—living person] He first married Deborah Ann FREITAG, then secondly Elaine _____.

ii. **Karen Jeanette ZANTOP** [withheld for privacy—living person] She married Edwin William FREITAG.

iii. **David Bruce ZANTOP** [withheld for privacy—living person].

---

58. Stanley Elroy ZANTOP[1676-1679,180] (*Birdie Mabel CLAY*[4], *Simeon A.*[3], *Fredric*[2], *Abegail*[1]).

Born 15 March 1920, in Parma Township, Jackson County, Michigan,[408] Stanley died at Foote Hospital in Jackson, Jackson County, Michigan, on 9 March 1953; he was 32.[408] Buried in Sandstone Township, Jackson County, Michigan,[1680] at Chapel Cemetery.

Occupations: Truck Driver (1940-1942); Factory Worker (1942); Flying Service (1947, 1949, [Aviation Instructor 1946], 1949, 1950, 1951).[1681-1687]

> *Obituary*: "JACKSON S. Elroy Zantop, 33, pilot of a plane which crashed eight miles southeast of here the night of March 9, died Tuesday in Foote Hospital of internal injuries."[1688]

Military:

U.S., World War II Draft Cards Young Men, 1940-1947:

Name: Stanley Elroy Zantop | Gender: Male | Race: White | Age: 21 | Birth Date/Place: 15 Mar 1920, Parma, Mich. | Residence Place: 530 E. Main, Parma, Mich. | Registration Date/Place: 1 Jul 1941, Parma, Jackson, Michigan | Employer: Self | Occupation: Truck Driver | Height: 6' 4" | Weight: 185 | Complexion: Light | Hair Color: Brown | Eye Color: Brown | Next of Kin: August Zantop [father][1689]

On 27 March 1942, when Stanley Elroy was 22, he married **Fairlene Sarah Anne Amelia "Buddy" FENWICK,**[1690-1695,180] daughter of William FENWICK and Margretta WILLIAMSON, in Parma Township, Jackson County, Michigan.[1696,1697] She was born on 17 March 1920, in Owen Sound, Grey, Ontario, Canada.[408] At the age of 34, Fairlene was baptized in Burlington, Des Moines County, Iowa, on 6 May 1954,[1698] at the Messiah Lutheran Church. Fairlene died in Fresno, Fresno County, California, on 14 May 2007; she was 87.[1699] Buried on 1 June 2007 in Sandstone Township, Jackson County, Michigan,[1700] at Chapel Cemetery.

Occupations: Beauty Operator (1942); Clerk County Sheriff (1954, 1955).[1701,1702]

Naturalization Petition Record:

District: Detroit, Michigan
Name: Fairlene Sarah Zantop, nee Fenwick
Residence: 706 Bellevue, Jackson, Michigan
Occupation: housewife | Age: 30 years
Born: 17 March 1920, Owen Sound, Canada | Sex: female
eold [sic]: white | complexion: fair | eyes: blue
hair: brown | height: 5 feet 4 1/3 inches | weight: 120
Race: white | nationality: Canada | husband: Stanley
married: 27 March 1942, Parma, Michigan
husband was born at Parma, Michigan 15 March 1920

Children/birth/place: Sharon, 16 January 1943, California; Loraine, 14 February 1948, Jackson, Michigan

Entered the U.S. at Detroit, Michigan, 29 July 1938 as Fairlene Sarah Anne Amelia Fenwick[1703]

Obituary: "Elroy Zantop, 35-year-old flying instructor in Jackson, Mich. died early Tuesday morning from injuries received when he and his family crash-landed In their plane a week ego Monday night.

Mrs. Zantop the former Fairlene Fenwick of Owen Sound, remains on the critical list. She has a broken back, internal injuries and a crushed elbow.

Their two daughters Sharon 10, and Lorraine 4, both have broken backs.

They too are said to be still in a critical condition.

Owen Sound relatives of Mrs. Zantop will return to Jackson Wednesday. They are Mrs. Zantop's father, William Fenwick, her three brothers, Gordon, Harold and Albert Fenwick, and two sisters, June, Mrs. Graham Ellis and Helen, Mrs. William Harper.

The Zantop plane crashed shortly after taking off at the airport there."[1704]

Obituary: "Memorial services for Fairlene "Buddy" A. Zantop, 87, of Clovis will be at 1 p.m. June 13 at Claremont Senior Apartments. Ms. Zantop, a homemaker, died May 14. Remembrances may be sent to Presbyterian Church Deacon's Fund, 3620 N. Millbrook Ave., Fresno, CA 93726. Arrangements are by Neptune Society of Central California in Fresno."[1705]

Stanley and Fairlene had the following children:

i. **Sharon Lee ZANTOP.**[1706] [withheld for privacy – living person]

ii. **Loraine K. ZANTOP.**[1707] [withheld for privacy – living person]

59. Lloyd Avery ZANTOP[1708-1711] (*Birdie Mabel CLAY*[4], *Simeon A.*[3], *Fredric*[2], *Abegail*[1]).

59. Lloyd Avery ZANTOP, newspaper photograph.

Born on 10 January 1922, in Parma Township, Jackson County, Michigan,[408] Lloyd died in Fort Lauderdale, Broward County, Florida, on 5 December 2002; he was 80.[408] Buried at sea on 4 January 2002.

Occupation: Flying Service/Instructor (1947-1960).[1712-1719]

Obituary: "Lloyd Zantop, cofounder of Zantop Air Transport, a Detroit-based airline company that carried parts nationwide for the automotive industry, died Dec. 5 of emphysema in Ft. Lauderdale, Fla. He was 80.

'He had a huge a smile for everybody and he had an incredible zest for adventure and for life' his daughter Diane Zantop said.

Born in Parma, Mr. Zantop showed an early interest in fast vehicles. At age 14 he built an automobile engine by combining two separate four-cylinder engines to make an eight-cylinder one, his daughter said.

'He was a mechanical wizard, he could fix anything, and he was known in Parma for creating a car, ' she said. 'It was never put to mainstream use, but he drove very fast around town.'

An airplane passing over his family's home prompted Mr. Zantop to take flying lessons. He earned his flying license while still in high school, she said.

In 1942, Mr. Zantop married his high school sweetheart, Glenna Jean Trowbridge. A year later, he was commissioned a second lieutenant in the Army Air Forces, which later became the U.S. Air Force.

He instructed cadets in advanced flying techniques. His daughter said he tested nearly every type of aircraft in the Army. His flights took him over Africa, the Middle East and Europe.

Mr. Zantop returned to Michigan in 1946. He and his wife rebuilt a small Fairchild 24 aircraft; she used her sewing machine to make fabric covers for the wings. They sold it and used the profit to buy another plane, the first in the Zantop Flying Service fleet.

The company he led with his brothers, Howard, Duane, and Elroy, moved in 1953 to Wayne Major Airport, now Detroit Metro.

The company that became Zantop Air Transport was a national leader, employing more than 2,000 people when it was sold in 1966, Diane Zantop said.

Mr. Zantop's love of boating filled much of his free time. During business trips to Miami, he often traveled by boat to the Bahamas.

After a few months of early retirement in the 1960s he and his wife founded Zantop Airways, which chartered planes to serve entertainment industry figures. It was sold in 1980.

Besides his daughter, Mr. Zantop is survived by another daughter, Kim Groseclose; son Reese (Rick) Zantop; brother Duane, and three grandchildren.

A memorial service and burial at sea for Mr. Zantop is scheduled for Jan. 4 in Ft. Lauderdale."[1720]

"As a little girl, Diane Zantop loved to go to work with her father.

On Friday nights she would bring her hula-hoop and a blanket to watch her father and his men load freight on 20 or 30 of his planes.

'They were building the business when I was born, so my childhood was spent with my mother rocking me under her desk, and when I got a little older flying with my dad,' said Diane Zantop. Her father, Lloyd Zantop, co-founded Zantop Airways with her mother in Michigan.

Mr. Zantop, 80, of Lighthouse Point, died Dec. 5 after complications from emphysema.

Mr. Zantop was born Jan. 10, 1922, in Parma, Mich.

At the age of 14, he began his love affair with speed and engineering, combining two four-cylinder engines to make an eight-cylinder hot rod. Mr. Zantop later paid for his own flying lessons, receiving his pilot's license during his senior year of high school.

In 1939, he was one of 2,500 licensed pilots in the United States. He married his childhood sweetheart, Glenna Jean Trowbridge Zantop, in 1942. But less than a year later, he received a commission as a second lieutenant in the Army Air Corps, where he instructed cadets in advanced training. For the next few years he flew for the military over Africa, the Middle East and Europe

'I read all the letters that they had written back and forth. They were apart almost three years after they were married,' said Diane Zantop of her parents' 60-year marriage. But after her father left the service, the couple wasted no time in building a life together. They rebuilt a Fairchild 24, her mother using her sewing machine for the fabric-covered wings. They later sold it, buying other planes, which led to the beginning of a fleet under the name of Zantop Air Transport. During the 1950s, Mr. Zantop and his brothers worked the small family business carrying anything they could to make money. But after a few years, Mr. Zantop took an early retirement to travel on his yacht.

Then he entered the business again, starting Zantop Airways with his wife. The company's fleet of Lear and other small jets flew freight and served as an air charter company, flying many celebrities.

Mr. Zantop eventually coached many pilots, giving them a future in aviation.

'So many people have said they wouldn't be in the field of aviation if not for my dad. When he started the airline he hired a lot of people. He helped a lot people grow in their careers,' she said.

They sold the business in 1980, and Glenna Zantop died two years ago. Diane Zantop says she'll always remember her father's zest for life. 'He taught me personally to live outside the box,' she said.

Besides his daughter Diane Zantop of Boca Raton, he is survived by his son, Reese Zantop of Bloomfield

Hills, Mich.; and daughter Kim Groseclose of Fort Wayne, Ind.

There will be a memorial service and burial at sea , at 9 a.m. Jan. 4 at the Lighthouse Point Yacht and Racquet Club. Contributions may be made in Mr. Zantop's memory to HANDY, 101 NE Third St., Fort Lauderdale, FL 33301. The charity benefits abused and neglected children."[1721]

Military:

U.S., World War II Draft Cards Young Men, 1940-1947:

Name: Lloyd Avery Zantop | Gender: Male | Race: White | Age: 20 | Birth Date/Place: 10 Jan 1922, Parma, Michigan | Residence Place: Eagle Field, Dos Palos, Merced, California | Registration Date: 30 Jun 1942 | Registration Place: Dos Palos, Merced, California, USA | Employer: Palo Alto Airport Inc | Height: 5 11 | Weight: 167 | Complexion: Freckled | Hair Color: Lt Brown | Eye Color: Hazel | Scar on chin | Next of Kin: Mrs. A W Zantop, Parma, Michigan [mother][1722]

United States World War II Army Enlistment Records, 1938-1946:

Name: Lloyd A Zantop | Marital Status: Married | Event Type: Military Service | Event Date: 18 Nov 1942 | Event Place: Merced Aaf, California, United States | Race: White | Citizenship Status: citizen | Birth Year: 1922 | Birthplace: MICHIGAN | Education Level: 4 years of high school | Civilian Occupation: Aviators | Military Rank: Private | Army Branch: Air Corps | Army Component Reserves - exclusive of Regular Army Reserve and Officers of the Officers Reserve Corps on active duty under the Thomason Act (Officers and Enlisted Men -- O.R.C. and E.R.C., and Nurses-Reserve Status) | Source Reference: Civil Life | Serial Number 19167077.[1723]

Served: US Army Air Force, 6 October 1943 to 29 July 1946

1943: Commissioned as a 2nd Lieutenant

"Lloyd Zantop, husband of Mrs. Glenna Trowbridge Zantop and son of Mrs. Mable Zantop of Charlotte and August Zantop of Parma, has been promoted to the rank of lieutenant as a service pilot in the Service Command in Egypt. He was an outstanding high school athlete prior to his graduation from Parma in 1940."[1724]

In October 1942, when Lloyd was 19, he married **Glenna Jean TROWBRIDGE,**[1713,1716,1717,1725-1727] daughter of Glenn O. TROWBRIDGE and Anna SCOBIE, in California.[1728] She was born on 7 September 1923, in Montgomery, Hillsdale County, Michigan.[408] Glenna died in Belleville, Wayne County, Michigan, on 22 June 2000; she was 76.[408] Burial at sea, 8 July 2000.

Occupations: Office Worker (1951); Teacher.[1729]

Education: School Of Theology And The Institute For Advanced Pastoral Studies, Detroit.

> *Obituary*: "ZANTOP Glenna Jean, 76, of Lighthouse Point and Belleville, MI died on June 22, 2000. She and her husband, Lloyd, co-founded Zantop Flying Service in 1946 and she continued her involvement in aviation until her retirement as Vice President and Treasurer of Zantop Airways. A teacher and eternal student, she studied at the School of Theology and the Institute for Advanced Pastoral Studies in Detroit. She served on the vestry of her parish and the Town and Country Council of the Episcopal Diocese of Michigan. She was a member of the Lighthouse Paint Yacht and Racquet Club. She was the wife of Lloyd. Mother of Diane Zantop, Rick (Chris) Zantop, and Kim (Jim) Groseclose and grandmother of Lindsay Zantop, Jim and Michael Groseclose. A Memorial and Commitment at Sea will begin at 9:45 AM Saturday, July 8, 2000 at the Lighthouse Point Yacht and Racquet Club. Another memorial will be held in Detroit, MI at the Cathedral of St. Paul in July. Memorial contributions may be made to HANDY through the Corinthians of LPYRC or Hospice By The Sea, Boca Raton."[1730]

Lloyd and Glenna had the following children:

- i. **Diane Emily ZANTOP**[1731] [withheld for privacy—living person] She married David E. RADAR.
- ii. **Reese C. "Rick" ZANTOP** [withheld for privacy—living person] He married Christine A. ROCK.
- iii. **Kim Elaine ZANTOP**. Born on 1 May 1953 in Jackson County, Michigan. Kim died in Fort Wayne, Allen County, Indiana, on 29 June 2016; she was 63. She married Jim GROSECLOSE.

60. Geraldine L. ZANTOP (*Birdie Mabel CLAY[4], Simeon A.[3], Fredric[2], Abegail[1]*).

Born on 15 June 1929, in Michigan, Geraldine died in Jackson, Jackson County, Michigan, on 2 April 1936; she was six years old.[1732]

She is not found with family in the 1930 census. However, in September 1941: "STATE of Michigan - The Probate Court for the County of Jackson. In the matter of the estates of the following name **Disappeared and Missing Persons**, No. 28842... Geraldine L. Zantop..."[2113] Apparently the state was looking to "clean-up" its probate loose-ends. She apparently died at an early age.

61. Earl Roy CLAY (*Le Roy[4], Simeon A.[3], Fredric[2], Abegail[1]*).

Born on 5 January 1911, in Michigan, Earl died in Jackson, Jackson County, Michigan, on 30 January 1918; he was seven years old.[1733] Buried on 1 February 1918, in Sandstone Township, Jackson County, Michigan,[1734] at Chapel Cemetery.

62. Donald LaVere CLAY[1735-1739,180] (*Le Roy[4], Simeon A.[3], Fredric[2], Abegail[1]*).

Born on 24 February 1916, in Parma Township, Jackson County, Michigan.[408] Donald died on 18 June 1966; he was 50.[408] Buried in Jackson, Jackson County, Michigan,[1740] at Hillcrest Memorial Park.

Occupations: Steam Shovel Operator (1938, 1947); Driver (1936, 1937, 1939-1941); Crane Operator (1949-1952, 1954-1957, 1960).[1741-1756]

Military:

U.S., World War II Draft Cards Young Men, 1940-1947:

Name: Donald Lavere Clay | Gender: Male | Race: White Age: 24 | Birth Date/Place: 24 Feb 1916, Parma, Michigan | Residence Place: 27 N. Sprague, Coldwater, Branch, Michigan | Registration Date/Place: 16 Oct 1940, Coldwater, Branch, Michigan | Employer: Baum Trucking Co | Height: 5' 9.5" | Weight: 150 | Complexion: Light | Hair Color: Blonde | Eye Color: Blue | Next of Kin: Charlotte Hannah Clay, Wife[1757]

On 21 October 1938, when Donald was 22, he married **Charlotte Hannah HANNEWALD,**[1758-1760,180] daughter of

Aaron HANNEWALD and Lillian MOECKEL, in Steuben County, Indiana.[1761,1762] She was born on 20 June 1917, in Munith, Jackson County, Michigan.[408] Charlotte died in Royal Oak, Oakland County, Michigan, on 25 May 2003; she was 85.[408] Buried on 30 May 2003 in Jackson, Jackson County, Michigan,[1763] at Hillcrest Memorial Park.

Occupation: Receptionist.

Religion: Lutheran.

Obituary: "CLAY, CHARLOTTE H. (HANNEWALD) Passed away May 25, 2003 in Royal Oak, MI. She was preceded in death by her beloved husband, Donald L. in 1966 and daughter, Carol H. in 1991. Surviving are one daughter, Donna and her husband, Richard Brewer of Ferndale; two grandsons, Charles D. (Rene) of Warren and Dennis L. (Melanie) of Brighton; one son-in- law, John 'Jack' Swartz of Weston, FL; as well as by several nieces, nephews, cousins, friends and neighbors. She was a member of Immanuel Lutheran Church and a member of AARP. She worked for many years as a receptionist at Hillcrest Memorial Park and at Patience Montgomery and Burden Funeral Homes. She was a Green-Thumb worker at Crouch Center. Family will receive friends at the funeral Home tonight from 6 to 8 p.m. and Thursday from 2 to 4 and 6 to 8 p.m. Funeral services will be from Immanuel Lutheran Church, Friday at 11:00 a.m. with Paster Erick Johnson and Vicar Timothy Steele officiating. Interment will be at Hillcrest Memorial Park. Memorials may be made to the church, the American Heart Association or Cancer Fund. www.MLive.com/obits Chas. J. Burden & Son 1806 E. Michigan Ave."[1764]

Donald and Charlotte had the following children:

i. **Donna L. CLAY.**[1765,1766,1767] [withheld for privacy—living person] She married Richard BREWER.

ii. **Carol Harriet CLAY.**[1768,1769,1770] Born circa 1941 in Michigan. Carol died in 1991; she was 50. She was married to John SWARTZ.

63. Mildred Veralynne HALE[1771,1772-1775,180] (*Mildred L. Irene CLAY*[4], *Cassius M.*[3], *Fredric*[2], *Abegail*[1]).

Born 20 January 1910, in Springport, Jackson County, Michigan,[1776,408] Mildred died in Lansing, Ingham County, Michigan, on 25 February 2002; she was 92.[408] Buried on 2 March 2002 in Lansing, Ingham County, Michigan,[1777] at Mount Hope Cemetery.

63. *Mildred Veralynne HALE, newspaper photograph.*

Obituary: "SCHMIDTMAN, MILDRED V. | Lansing | Age 92, died February 25, 2002. Born January 20, 1910 in Lansing, Mrs. Schmidtman was preceded in death by her husband, Harold of 49 years and son, David (1998). Surviving are 3 daughters, Nancy Edgecomb of Lansing, Jeanine Palacios of AZ and Joan Lehman of FL; 2 sons, Bruce of Seattle, WA, and Walter of St. Johns; 13 grandchildren; 24 great-grandchildren. Funeral Services will be held Saturday, March 2, 10 AM at the Gorsline-Runciman Co. Lansing Chapel, 900 E. Michigan Avenue, Lansing, with Chaplain David Selleck of Ingham Hospice, officiating, Interment will follow in Mt Hope Cemetery, Lansing. The family will receive friends at the Chapel Friday from 2-4 and 6-8 PM. Those desiring may make contributions to Hospice of Lansing, 6035 Executive Drive, Suite 103, Lansing, MI 48911-5338 in memory of Mrs. Schmidtman." [1778]

On 2 July 1927, when Mildred Veralynne was 17, she married **Harold August SCHMIDTMAN,**[1779-1781,180] son of August George SCHMIDTMANN and Alvina AHLSWEDE, in Buchanan, Berrien County, Michigan.[1782] He was born on 2 October 1906, in Gardner, Dorr County, Wisconsin.[1783,408] Harold died in Holiday, Pasco County, Florida, on 28 November 1976; he was 70.[408,556] Buried on 2 December 1976, in Lansing, Ingham County, Michigan,[1784] at Mount Hope Cemetery.

Occupations: Machine Operator (1927); Grinder, Old Motor Works (1930, 1940, 1945); Repairman (1948); Automobile Tool Upgrader (1950); Car Repairman (1954, 1955).[1785-1791]

Religion: Baptist.

Obituary: "SCHMIDTMAN, HAROLD A.

Holiday, Florida | (Formerly of 634 Berry Ave., Lansing)

Age 70. Died November 28, 1976 in Holiday, Fla. Born October 2, 1906 in Dorr County, Wisconsin. Mr. Schmidtman was a former resident of Lansing moving to Florida 1 year ago. He was a member of the South Baptist Church and was employed with Oldsmobile 42 years, retiring 7 years ago. He was a member of the Quarter Century Club. Surviving are: the wife, Mildred V.; 3 sons, Bruce of Southfield, David of Tofte, Minn., and Walter of Olivet; 3 daughters, Mrs. Joan Lehman of Mason, Mrs. Jeanine Hawkins of Phoenix, Arizona, and Mrs. Nancy Edgecomb of Lansing; 13 grandchildren; 1 great grandchild; 4 brothers, Edgar, Raymond, Andrew and Oscar all of Benton Harbor; 1 sister, Miss Ruth Schmidtman of Benton Harbor. Funeral services will be held Thursday 2:30 p.m. at the Gorsline-Runciman Lansing Chapel with Dr. Howard Sugden of the South Baptist Church officiating. Interment will be at Mt. Hope Cemetery."[1792]

Military:

U.S., World War II Draft Cards Young Men, 1940-1947:

Name: Harold August Schmidtman | Address: 125 Berry Ave Lansing Ingham Mich | Age: 34 | Place of Birth: Dorr Co Wisconsin U.S. | Date of Birth: 2 Oct 1906 | Person Who Knows You: Mrs. Mildred Verline Schmidtman wife | Employer: Olds Motor Works | Race: White | Height: 5' 11" | Eyes: Gray | Weight: 159 | Hair: Gray | Complexion: Dark | No index finger on right hand. | Date of Registration: 16 Oct. 1940.[1793]

Mildred and Harold had the following children:

i. **Bruce Allen SCHMIDTMAN.**[1794,1795,1796] Born 5 May 1928, in Wayne County, Michigan. Bruce died in Mountlake Terrace, Snohomish County, Washington, on 28 November 2022; he was 94. He was married to Collen Joyce EADY.

ii. **Joan Elvina SCHMIDTMAN.**[1797,1798,1799] Born 12 December 1929, in Michigan. Joan died in Florida on 9 August 2009; she was 79. She was married to Donald Clinton LEHMAN.

iii. **David Matthew SCHMIDTMAN.**[1800,1801,1802,180] Born 28 March 1937, in Lansing, Ingham County, Michigan, David died in Minneapolis, Hennepin County, Minnesota, 7 December 1998; he was 61. He was married to Karen J. OLSON.

iv. **Walter Hugh SCHMIDTMAN.**[1803,1804] [withheld for privacy—living person] He married Carole S. RIVARD.

v. **Jeanine Ella SCHMIDTMAN.**[1805] [withheld for privacy—living person] She married David Lawrence NULF.

vi. **Nancy Sue SCHMIDTMAN.**[1806,180] Born on 14 September 1944 in Lansing, Ingham County, Michigan, Nancy died in Michigan on 21 November 2013; she was 69. She wasmarried to Cleo Dale EDGECOMB.

---

64. Guilford Charles ORRISON[1807-1810,180] (*Orpha Zella CLAY*[4], *Cassius M.*[3], *Fredric*[2], *Abegail*[1]).

Born 14 August 1914, in Jackson, Jackson County, Michigan, and hedied in Marshall, Calhoun County, Michigan, on 6 January 1959; he was 44. Buried on 9 January 1959, in Marshall, Calhoun County, Michigan,[1811] at Oak Ridge Cemetery.

Occupations: Student (1929, 1931); Grocery Clerk (1935, 1940, 1959); Meat Cutter, Retail Food Shop (1950).[1812-1815]

Religion: Methodist.

> *Obituary*: "MARSHALL - Guilford Charles Orrison, 44, a butcher living at 715 W. Hanover St., Marshall, was found dead last night hanging from a steel girder under a bridge on the West Girard road two miles south of here. Coroner Van B. Rogers of Bronson declared the death a suicide.
>
> Dale Barnhart, a resident of the area near the bridge, found the body about 8 p.m. He noticed Mr. Orrison's car parked near the, bridge pointing against traffic, and after observing at intervals all day, and seeing no one around it, decided to check on it.
>
> He found tracks leading down over the bank to the creek be neath the bridge. Following them, he came upon the body.

64. Guilford Charles ORRISON. Photograph from high school yearbook.[1816]

Sheriff's deputies and Mr. Rogers believe Mr. Orrison made two attempts, the first one failing when a leather belt that he used broke. The broken belt was found on an abutment of the bridge.

Mr. Orrison and his wife, Dorothy, both went to work at Freddie's Food Market in Marshall yesterday morning, but he left work about half an hour later saying he was going home to change his clothes When he failed to return, Mrs. Orrison went home to look for him. When she found her husband and the family car gone, and that he had not changed his clothes, she notified police.

Mr. Orrison had suffered a nervous breakdown, the family said, and only recently had returned home after treatment. He had shown signs of despondency.

Mr. Rogers estimated the time of death as about 10 a.m. yesterday.

Mr. Orrison was born Aug. 14, 1914, in Jackson, son of Jesse and Orpha (Clay) Orrison. He was married to the former Dorothy Sipe on Sept 1, 1935, in Marshall. He belonged to the Brooks Memorial Methodist Church and the, Knights of Pythias.

Besides his wife, Mr. Orrison is survived by his mother, now living in Marshall; two daughters, Mrs. Nolan (Donna) Gutchess and Mrs. Kenneth (Janet Ann) Embury, both living in Battle Creek; two sons, David and Michael, both at home; six brothers, Keith and James of Marshall, Eugene of Dyess Air Force Base, Tex., Howard stationed in Korea, and Robert and Jack, both of San Diego; two grandchildren and several nieces and nephews.

Funeral services will be held Friday at 4 p.m. from the Court Funeral Home in Marshall, the Rev. Carl B. Strange, pastor of Brooks Methodist Church, officiating. Burial will be at Oak Ridge Cemetery in Marshall."[1817]

"Guil attended schools in Lee Township, Calhoun County, and Marshall High School. He loved baseball and football. Graduated 1932 from M.H.S. After graduation, he worked for Harold Crosby at his grocery store on Michigan Ave, Marshall. For a time he worked for Ralph Kline at the Marshall Creamery, then worked several years for Fred Clements as a meat cutter along with his wife Dorothy, at the old Freddies Market on south Marshall St. Guil was a Chancellor Commander of the Knights of Pythias (History of Marshall by Richard Carver). Member of Brooks Memorial Methodist Church. He was buried in Oakridge Cemetery, Marshall, Michigan."[2125]

Military:

U.S., World War II Draft Cards Young Men, 1940-1947:

Name: Guilford Charles Orrison | Gender: Male | Race: White | Age: 26 | Birth Date/Place: 14 Aug 1914, Jackson, Michigan | Residence Place: 425 Locust St. Marshall, Calhoun, Mich. | Registration Date/Place: 16 Oct 1940, Marshall, Calhoun, Michigan | Employer: Martin Reedy | Height: 5 6 | Weight: 138 | Complexion: Other Hair Color: Brown | Eye Color: Gray | scar on left thumb | Next of Kin: Dorothy Cora Orrison wife[1818]

1940, November: draft list 2412.[1819]

On 1 September 1935, when Guilford was 21, he married **Dorothy Cora SIPE,**[1820-1822,180] daughter of Lawrence I. SIPE and Martha A. DEPOTTY, in Marshall, Calhoun County, Michigan,[1823,1824] by George H. Waid, Baptist Minister. Born on 21 August 1914, in Washtenaw County, Michigan,[408] Dorothy Cora died in Hastings, Barry County, Michigan, on 8 March 2002; she was 87.[408] Buried 12 March 2002, in Marshall, Calhoun County, Michigan,[1825] at Oakridge Cemetery.

Occupations: Waitress, Tasty Food Shop (1950); Grocery Clerk (1959).[1826]

Obituary: "Marshall | Dorothy C. Orrison, 87, of Marshall went to her heavenly home with the Lord, March 8, 2002.

Mrs. Orrison was born on August 21, 1914 in Clinton, Michigan to Lawrence and Martha (DePotty) Sipe. She has been a resident of Marshall and was a graduate of Marshall High School. Mrs. Orrison worked as a sales clerk until she was 72 years old, re-

Dorothy Cora SIPE. Photograph from high school yearbook.[1827]

tiring from Bill's Bi-Rite. Other places of employment included, The Dime Store, Tasty Sandwich Shop and Freddie's Market.

On September 1, 1935, she married Guilford C. Orrison. He preceded her in death in 1959.

Mrs. Orrison was a former member of the Brooks Memorial Methodist Church in Marshall. She loved her family, customers and friends dearly. She enjoyed sewing and doing needlework.

She is survived by daughters, Donna Gutchess of Hastings, Janet (Ken) Embury of Battle Creek, sons, David (Marilyn) Orrison of Potterville, Michael (Connie) Orrison of Missouri, 14 grandchildren and 16 greatgrandchildren, a great-great-granddaughter and brother Arthur Sipe of Albion.

She was also preceded by granddaughter, Karen Orrison, sister Arlene Goodman, brother Lester Sipe, and son-in-law, Nolan Gutchess.

Friends may call from 6:00-8:00 Monday at the Craig K. Kempf Funeral Home.

A service to celebrate her life will be held 1:00 p.m. Tuesday at the funeral home.

Memorials are to Calhoun County Humane Society."[1828]

Guilford and Dorothy had the following children:

i. **Donna Mae ORRISON.**[1829,1830,180] Born 9 June 1936, in Marshall, Calhoun County, Michigan, Donna died in Hastings, Barry County, Michigan, on 6 January 2019; she was 82. She was married to Nolan Richard GUTCHESS Sr.

ii. **Janet Ann ORRISON.**[1831,1832] Born 6 December 1938, Janet died in Battle Creek, Calhoun County, Michigan, on 5 July 2022; she was 83. She was married to Kenneth Clayton EMBURY.

iii. **David Jon ORRISON Sr.**[1833] Born 15 November 1941, in Marshall, Calhoun County, Michigan and died in Potterville, Eaton County, Michigan, on 20 December 2018; he was 77. He first married Margaret Mary PIERCE, then Marilyn Anne BARTLETT.

iv. **Michael Eugene ORRISON.**[1834] [withheld for privacy—living person.] He married Consuelo M. NOEDEL.

---

65. Maj. Jesse Eugene ORRISON[1835-1839,180] (*Orpha Zella CLAY*[4], *Cassius M.*[3], *Fredric*[2], *Abegail*[1]).

Born on 3 September 1916, in Jackson County, Michigan,.[408] Jesse died in Tucson, Pima County, Arizona, on 6 September 1997; he was 81.[408] Buried on 9 September 1997, in Tucson, Pima County, Arizona,[1840] at East Lawn Palms Cemetery and Mortuary.

65. *Maj. Jesse Eugene ORRISON. Photograph from Kathleen Marie O'Dell Townsley, ancestry.com, 16 March 2017.*

Occupations: Student (1929, 1931); Laboratory (1934); Machine Operator, Eaton Manufacturing (1940); Military (1941-1963); Postal Worker.[1841-1847]

Education: Western Michigan College Of Education, Kalamazoo.

Obituary: "ORRISON, Jesse Eugene, 81, of Tucson, died September 6, 1997. Survivors include his beloved wife, Doris Darling Orrison; children, Wayne (Phyllis) Orrison, Kathryn S. Plumb; daughter-in-law, Cheryll Ball Orrison; six grandchildren; one great-grandson; six brothers; one sister; plus many loving relatives and friends. He was preceded in death by his first wife, Margaret Nell, and his son, Lt. Col. Stephen L. Orrison. After serving 22 years with the USAF, Jesse retired as a Major, with time served during WWII and Korea resulting in numerous decorations. He spent 23 months as a POW. Jesse has since retired from the Postal Service and been a member of the Shriners. Friends may call at EAST LAWN PALMS MORTUARY, 5801 E. Grant Rd., Tuesday, September 9, 1997 from 6:00 to 8:00 p.m. Funeral Service will be held at EAST LAWN PALMS CHAPEL, Wednesday, at 11:00 a.m., with Burial to follow."[1848]

Eulogy, authored and read by son Wayne:

"I guess I've had a lifetime to think about what to say about my father when this time came, but it's impossible for me to do justice and summarize his life in a few short words. You all knew my father from your own perspectives, something I can't ever fully appreciate, only value out his love as well as I can. What I can do is share my perspective and tell you about the man I knew and observed as a father, grandfather, teacher, husband and friend.

I don't want to rattle on and on here and stray in every direction, so I want to share something I read some time ago that I believe is appropriate.

> 'It's not the critic who counts; not the man who points out how the strong man stumbles, or where the doer of deeds could have done them better. The credit belongs to the man who is actually in the arena, whose face is marred by dust and sweat and blood, who strives valiantly; who errs and comes up short again and again; because there is no effort without error and shortcoming; but - (it is the man) - who does actually strive to do the deeds, who knows the great enthusiasms, the great devotions; who spends himself in a worthy cause; who at the best knows at the end - the triumph of achievement, at least - fails while daring greatly, ...so that his place will never be with those cold and timid souls who knew victory or defeat.' Theodore Roosevelt said those words a century ago.

My father was a doer - who made the effort - who accepted the sacrifices and never shunned a task, but always gave it full measure. That was true of all things he was a part of - in work or play. My dad loved his family; his beloved Doris, his grandchildren. He loved many things - puttering around the house, teaching - everything from Sunday School to tutoring and history. He loved trying new things and challenging things. I think he was far more adventuresome and game than most of us would imagine. He was certainly brave - and always someone I could count on for love, support and wisdom.

So now we are one less... but united in his memory, we are more. In Matthew, chapter 5, verse 12, Jesus says to his desciples 'rejoice and be glad; for great is your reward in heaven.' My father's recent physical suffering has now ended and he has moved on to his reward. As a family we will move on in the strength of our love and his memory.

Thank you all for coming today to help us in our memory of him.

Wayne Orrison."[2126]

Military:

U.S., World War II Draft Cards Young Men, 1940-1947:

Name: Jesse Eugene Orrison | Gender: Male | Race: White | Birth Date/Place: 3 Sep 1916, Jackson, Michigan | Residence Place: 402 N Mulberry St. Marshall, Calhoun, Mich. | Registration Date/Place: 16 Oct 1940, Marshall, Calhoun, Michigan | Employer: Eaton Mfg. Co | Height: 5 8 | Weight: 150 | Complexion: Light | Hair Color: Brown | Eye Color: Brown | Next of Kin: Orpha Clay Orrison - Mother[1818]

1940, November: draft number 2161.[1849]

U.S., World War II Army Enlistment Records, 1938-1946:

Name: Jesse E Orrison | Race: White | Marital Status: Single, without dependents (Single) | Rank: Private | Birth Year: 1916 | Nativity State or Country: Michigan | Citizenship: Citizen | Residence: Calhoun, Michigan | Education: 4 years of high school | Civil Occupation: Semiskilled machine shop and related occupations, n.e.c. | Enlistment Date: 13 Apr 1942 | Enlistment Place: Grand Rapids, Michigan | Service Number: 16033483 | Branch: Branch Immaterial - Warrant Officers, US | Component: Army of the United States - includes the following: Voluntary enlistments effective December 8, 1941 and thereafter; One year enlistments of National Guardsman whose State enlistment expires while in the Federal Service; Officers appointed in the Army of | Source: Enlisted Man, Regular Army, after 3 months of Discharge | Height: 67 | Weight: 148 | Term of Enlistment: Enlistment for the duration of the War or other emergency, plus six months, subject to the discretion of the President or otherwise according to law.[1850]

U.S., World War II Prisoners of War, 1941-1945:

Name: Jesse E Orrison | Move Place: Stalag Luft 1 Barth-Vogelsang Prussia 54-12 | Race: White | Military Rank: Second Lieutenant or Ensign | Military Service Branch: Army | Military Service Place: 1 | Event Type: Military Service | Event Date: 29 Nov 1943 | Event Place: Germany | Service Number: O&685705 [sic] | Military Status: Returned to Military Control, Liberated or Repatriated | Parent Military Unit: Harbor Defense/Group Headquarters | Subordinate Military Unit: Infantry[1851]

1944, January: "MARSHALL – Lieut. Jesse Eugene Orrison, who was reported missing in action since November 29, is a prisoner of the Germans, according to a telegram from the war department received Wednesday by his parents, Mr. and Mrs. Jesse J. Orrison. North Mulberry.

The telegram stated 'A report has just been received through the International Red Cross that Lieut Jesse Eugene Orrison is a prisoner of war of the German government. Letters of information will follow from the adjutant general. Lieut. Orrison was a navigator on a bombing plane and was known to be on a mission over Europe, flying from England, when he was reported missing. Lieutenant Orrison, who is 27, has two brothers. Robert and Howard in the service. Another brother, Keith, a senior in the Marshall high school, passed a V-5 naval aviation test in Detroit. Wednesday and was accepted as a naval enlistee. He expects to be called to service about March 1." [1852,1853,1854]

"MARSHALL Mr. and Mrs. Jesse Orrison of 317 South Mulberry were pretty happy because within the week they had heard from three of their sons, each on a different fighting front. A long, newsy letter had come from Howard in Italy and 18-year-old Keith, somewhere in the south Pacific, had sent a beautiful valentine to his mother. A card in his own hand writing was received from 'Gene', which is the most they could expect for 'Gene' is a prisoner of war in Germany. They spoke wistfully of Bob, also in the south Pacific, but thought hearing from all four in one week was too much to ask, then Bob walked in to deliver his greetings in person. … Lieut. Jesse Eugene Orrison, 28, was one of the first Marshall boys to be missing in action. A navigator of a [B-17] Flying Fortress, the plane was shot down over Bremen, Germany Nov. 29, 1943. His parents were informed he was a prisoner Jan. 29, 1944 and four months later received their first personal word from him. In the year and a half that he has been a prisoner, his parents had received just four cards from him, up until two weeks ago, then within those two weeks four more cards have come, his latest saying he had just received the package that was sent to him last June.

On his return home Lieutenant Orrison will be surprised to find that his parents have been able to piece together the story of what has happened to him. From Sergt, George C. Fisher of Roslindale, Mass. an American soldier repatriated by the exchange ship Gripsholm has come the tale of Sergt. Eugene Moran of Gays Mills, Wis., who was the tail gunner on the Fortress of which Lieutenant Orrison was the navigator. They were on their fifth bombing mission, a part of one of the first big raids over Germany, when the tail of the Flying Fortress was severed by flak and fell four miles into a tree-top with Sergeant Moran trapped inside, but he escaped with only minor injuries and is now a German prisoner of war. The front half of the plane was eventually found with the pilot Lieut. Woody Langley still strapped in his seat. Mrs. Orrison corresponds with the pilot's mother, Mrs. William Langley of Pittsfield, Mass. and Eugene's wife, Nell, of San Antonio, Texas, has made the acquaintance of Lieutenant Langley's brother who at one time was stationed in Texas.

Lieutenant Orrison first entered the service in July 1941 as an aviation cadet. He trained at Cimarron Field, Okla. and was released in October 1941 to be called back when needed. He re-entered the service August 1942 and received advanced navigation training at Hondo, Texas, where he was given his wings and commission July 16, 1943. He was sent overseas with the 8th Air Force in October of the same year.

Lieutenant Orrison has been presented with the bronze star, his wife accepting it, at a ceremony at Kelly Field, Tex. In June 1944."[1855]

"When his plane was shot down in Germany, he had to parachute out and during the landing was injured. He and the tail gunner were the only survivors. The germans operated on him and then kept him as a POW for approximately 18 months in a prison camp. After the war he returned to Marshall, where he worked for a time. After a 2 year rest (approx), he rejoined the Air force and spent the rest of his twenty years there at several air bases in the U.S. and abroad during the Korean war and Viet Nam war, in the Strategic Air Command. He acted as Commanding Officer at a base in Japan during those conflicts. He retired from the Air Force a Major in 1962 after 20 years."[2127]

Service: US Army Air Force, 18 July 1941 to 13 November 1963[763]

Medals: Air Medal for completion of five mission. Purple Heart. Korea Conflict service.

On 13 October 1942, when Jesse Eugene was 26, he first married **Margaret Nell BROWN,**[1856,1857,180] daughter of Will H. BROWN and Irene L. RANDOLPH, in Bexar County, Texas.[1858] She was born on 27 September 1920, in Louisiana.[408] Margaret died in Tucson, Pima County, Arizona, on 12 February 1977; she was 56.[408] Buried on 15 February 1977, in Tucson, Pima County, Arizona,[1859] at East Lawn Palms Cemetery and Mortuary.

Obituary: "ORRISON, Margret Nell, 56, of Tucson. Died February 12th, 1977. Survived by husband, Jesse E. Orrison; two sons, Wayne J. Orrison of San Diego, California, and Stephen L. Orrison of El Paso, Texas; daughter, Kathryn S. Orrison of San Diego, California; mother, Mrs. Irene Brown of Tucson; three grandchildren all of San Diego. Funeral services 2:30 p.m., Tuesday, from the PALM'S MORTUARY CHAPEL, with the Reverend Milton R. Emmons of Christ Presbyterian Church officiating. Friends may call at PALM'S MORTUARY, 5225 E. Speedway, from 7-9 p.m., Monday. In lieu of flowers, family suggests contributions to the American Cancer Society. Burial will be in Tucson Memorial East Lawn."[1860]

Jesse and Margaret had the following children:

i. **Wayne Jeffrey ORRISON.**[1861] [withheld for privacy—living person] He married Phyllis Karen HACKFORD.

ii. **Lt. Col. Stephen Lawrence ORRISON.**[1862-1865,180] Born on 21 September 1948 in Arizona, Stephen died in Tucson, Pima County, Arizona, on 1 March 1997; he was 48. He first married Nancy Anne KNOERLE, then Cheryll Lynn BALL.

iii. **Kathryn Susan ORRISON.**[180] Born on 6 April 1951 in Tucson, Pima County, Arizona. Kathryn died in Show Low, Navajo County, Arizona, on 11 October 2015; she was 64. She first married Rick Dean TODD, then secondly Gary E. PLUMB, and third Christopher Edward MCCORMAC.

When Jesse Eugene was 74, he second married **Doris Eleanor DARLING** on 11 December 1991, in Arizona.[1866] Doris was the daughter of Charles DARLING and Vieva FORD. (Doris was first married to Charles William ROBERTS). Doris was born 26 February 1919, in Albion, Calhoun County, Michigan, and died 21 July 2012, age 93, with cremains interred at Riverside Cemetery, Albion 4 August 2012.[180,2128]

> *Obituary*: "Doris (Darling) (Roberts) Orrison Charlotte Doris (Darling) (Roberts) Orrison, age 93 of Charlotte, MI, formerly of Albion and Olivet, MI, died Saturday, July 21, 2012 at her residence. Mrs. Orrison was born Feb. 26, 1919 in Albion, MI the daughter of Charles and Vieva (Ford) Darling and was a lifelong area resident. She worked for many years as a receptionist for Dr. Ralph Cram in Albion, had been a member of the Albion Garden Club and enjoyed bird watching. She was preceded in death by husbands, Charles W. Roberts and Jesse E. Orrison; 2 sisters, Virginia King and Patricia Railer and her brother, Wendell Darling. Surviving are: her daughter, Pamela (Richard) Babcock of Olivet; grandson, James (Candy) Obrinski of Olivet; step son, Wayne (Phyllis) Orrison of Rockton, IL; and 2 great grandchildren, Tyler and Audrey McGlaughlin. Per Mrs. Orrison's request, cremation has taken place. There will be no visitation. A graveside service will be held at 2:00 P.M. Saturday, August 4, 2012 at the Riverside Cemetery in Albion, MI. Memorial contributions may go to the Great Lakes Hospice or to the American Diabetes Association. Arrangements by Burkhead-Green Funeral Home of

Charlotte, MI. www.burkhead-greenfuneralhome.-com"[2029]

---

66. Maj. Howard Clay ORRISON[1867-1872,2131] (*Orpha Zella CLAY*[4]*, Cassius M.*[3]*, Fredric*[2]*, Abegail*[1]).

66. Maj. Howard Clay ORRISON – Photograph courtesy Kathleen Townsley.

Born on 20 August 1918, in Springport, Jackson County, Michigan, Howard died in Oregon in February 2012; he was 93 [reported, not verified].

Occupations: Student (1931, 1934); Motor Vehicle Operator (1940); Cotton Farmer (1946).[1873-1875]

1936, March: "Jesse J. Orrison, 423 Monroe, reported to the sheriff's department Friday that his son, Howard Orrison, 17, was missing. The boy has been missing for three days, it developed although it was not reported to the sheriff's department until Friday. The boy is described as having brown hair, brown eyes and wearing dark blue pants, black gymnasium shoes, a red blazer and a gray felt hat, also a white scarf."[2123]

1960, September: resided in Williamsburg, Virginia.[1876] In 2002, he resided in Sitka, Alaska.

"The outfit I joined before the war was called (CCC's) Civilian Conservation Corps. It was a program disigned to help families during those tough times when there few jobs, we were paid $30 per month, $25 of which was sent home to the family, we had $5 for our use. The work we did was not only tree planting, but what was called stream improvement. This was to clean out the edges of streams so they would flow faster. Most of the time I was stationed in the Upper Peninsula up near Munising, near Lake

66. Howard Clay ORRISON and wife Naomi Ruth BRIGHT. – Photograph courtesy Kathleen Marie O'Dell Townsley.

Superior. Spent about a year doing this, it was a decent life, learned a lot."[2130]

Military: Korea
US Army: tank corps instructor; Air Corps navigator.

U.S., World War II Draft Cards Young Men, 1940-1947:

Name: Howard Clay Orrison | Gender: Male | Race: White | Age: 22 | Birth Date/Place: 20 Aug 1918, Springport, Michigan | Residence Place: 402 N. Mulberry St., Marshall, Calhoun, Michigan | Registration Date: 16 Oct 1940 | Registration Place: Marshall, Calhoun, Michigan | Employer: Marshall Furnace Co. | Height: 5 7 | Weight: 144 | Complexion: Ruddy | Hair Color: Brown | Eye Color: Brown | Next of Kin: Orpha Zella Orrison, Mother[1818]

1940, November: Draft registration number 3023.[1877]
Service: 24 May 1941 to 1961.
1943, February: Commissioned as 2nd Lieutenant in the US Cavalry at Ft. Riley.[1878,2132]
1943, December: Stationed at Fort Clark, Texas.[1879]
1943, February: "Howard C. Orrison, son of Jesse Orrison, Marshall, has received a commission as second lieutenant in the U. S. Cavalry. He has just completed a three months course in an officers training school for the cavalry at Ft.

Riley. He [Jesse, not Howard] entered the service on March 14, 1914, and has been in the cavalry since his induction. He is the first Marshall man to become a commissioned officer in the cavalry during the present war."[2119]

1944, February: Commissioned First Lieutenant.[1880]

United States World War II Army Enlistment Records, 1938-1946:

Name: Howard C Orrison | Marital Status: Married | Event Type: Military Service | Event Date: 08 Apr 1946 | Event Place: Battle Creek, Michigan, United States | Term of Enlistment: Enlistment for Hawaiian Department | Race: White Citizenship Status: citizen | Birth Year: 1918 | Birthplace: MICHIGAN | Education Level: 3 years of high school | Civilian Occupation: Cotton farmers | Military Rank: Master Sergeant | Army Branch: No branch assignment | Army Component: Regular Army (including Officers, Nurses, Warrant Officers, and Enlisted Men) | Source Reference: National Guard[1881]

1945, February: "MARSHALL Mr. and Mrs. Jesse Orrison of 317 South Mulberry were pretty happy because within the week they had heard from three of their sons, each on a different fighting front. A long, newsy letter had come from Howard in Italy and 18-year-old Keith, somewhere in the south Pacific, had sent a beautiful valentine to his mother. A card in his own hand writing was received from 'Gene', which is the most they could expect for 'Gene' is a prisoner st war in Germany. They spoke wistfully of Bob, also in the south Pacific, but thought hearing from all four in one week was too much to ask, then Bob walked in to deliver his greetings in person. ... Lieutenant Howard Orrison, entered the army March 24, 1941 presumably for a year's training. Assigned to the Cavalry, he trained at Port Riley, Kansas and entered Officer's Training school receiving his commission as a second Lieutenant in January 1943. He then, alternated his duties as an instructor between Ft. Riley, Kan. and Ft. Clark, Texas and was promoted to a first lieutenant November 1943. He was sent overseas a year ago and spent some time in Africa, from there going to northern Italy. While overseas he has seen two Marshall boys, Henry Mumaw and Clifford Weakley. His wife. Ruth, resides in Junction City, Kan."[1855]

1949, February: stationed at Fort Storcy, Virginia.[1882]

1953, December: returned from Germany with family.[1883]

1957, May: Commanded 63rd Transportation Truck Company.[1884,1885]

1960, August: Commander, 27th Tank Battalion, Fort Eustis, Virginia.[2133]

1960, September: resided in Williamsburg, Virginia.[1876]

1961, June: 48th Transportation Group, Fort Eustis, Virginia.[1886]

1961, October: Retired to Kalispell, Montana with family.[1887]

On 28 December 1941, when Howard Clay was 23, he married **Naomi Ruth BRIGHT,**[1888-1892] daughter of Willie D. BRIGHT and Beatrice Avo JEFFERS, in Junction City, Geary County, Kansas.[1880,1893] She was born on 18 May 1920, in Iola, Allen County, Kansas.[408] Naomi died in Tucson, Pima County, Arizona, on 12 June 1992; she was 72.[1894,1895,1896]

They had one child:

i. **Deborah Beth ORRISON**[1897-1899] [withheld for privacy—living person] She married Stephen Eric BELL.

---

67. Robert Elton ORRISON[1900-1903] (*Orpha Zella CLAY*[4], *Cassius M.*[3], *Fredric*[2], *Abegail*[1]).

Born on 22 April 1923, in Lee Township, Calhoun County, Michigan,[408] and died in Lompoc, Santa Barbara County, California, on 19 November 1993; he was 70.[870,408]

Occupation: Military (1950, 1959).[1904,1905]

Military:

US Navy, World War II and Korea

USS Appalachian, 14 October 1944, 31 December 1944, 31 March 1945, 1 July 1945, 1 August 1945, 1 September 1945, 1 October 1945, 1 January 1946, 1 April 1946[1906]

USS New Mexico, 31 December 1941, 2 February 1943, 31 March 1943, 30 September 1942, 31 December 1942, 30 June 1943, 30 September 1943, 31 December 1943, 16 February 1944[1907]

Service: 7 October 1941, to 1951.

> "MARSHALL Mr. and Mrs. Jesse Orrison of 317 South Mulberry were pretty happy because within the week they had heard from three of their sons, each on a different fighting front. A long, newsy letter had come from Howard in Italy and 18-year-old Keith, somewhere in the south Pacific, had sent a beautiful

67. Robert Elton ORRISON. – Photograph courtesy Kathleen Marie O'Dell Townsley.

valentine to his mother. A card in his own hand writing was received from 'Gene', which is the most they could expect for 'Gene' is a prisoner st war in Germany. They spoke wistfully of Bob, also in the south Pacific, but thought hearing from all four in one week was too much to ask, then Bob walked in to deliver his greetings in person. ... Robert Orrison, 21, ship fitter third class is home on a 19 day leave direct from the invasions of Leyte and the Philippines. Bob entered the navy Oct. 7, 1941 and now wears six battle stars, the star denoting prewar service and ribbons showing service in the American theater campaign, the Asiatic - Pacific campaign, the Philippines, the American Defense ribbon and the navy amphibian patch.

He first trained at Newport, Rhode Island and because of war being declared was not home on boot leave but was immediately assigned to duty and sent to the Pacific theater of operations, where he has crossed the equator many times and taken part in practically ever major landing operation of the Pacific war. This surprise visit is only his third leave since entering the service. Bob has many souvenirs which include a notebook filled with Japanese writing and a card written in Japanese evidently prepared for sending, also pieces of coral. Japanese coins and even a box of Japanese tooth powder. He has just brought to his mother a lovely bracelet from New Caledonia."[1855]

1951, October: Serving aboard destroyer tender *USS Piedmont* as Second Class Metalsmith.[1908]

1958, May: Returned from Western Pacific aboard destroyer *USS Southerland.*[1909]

When Robert was 23, he first married **Bernice H. FINK,**[1910] daughter of Edward Michael FINK and Wilkelmina "Minnie" Augusta RUSH. She was born on 27 April 1919, in South Dakota.[1911,408] Bernice died on 13 December 2012; she was 93.[408]

They were divorced circa 1951 in California.[1912] She later remarried to Charlie A. CLARK.

Robert and Bernice had one child:

i. **Cintra Darnell ORRISON**[1913]. Born on 18 March 1948, in Michigan, Cintra died in El Cajon, San Diego County, California, on 1 August 2008; she was 60. She was married to Dennis Allan DEMARAIS.

On 1 November 1958, when Robert was 35, he second married **Hazel Frances GILMORE,**[180] daughter of Roy Davis GILMORE and Viola Louise NEWMAN, in Nevada.[1914] She was born on 4 November 1919, in Fayette, Howard County, Missouri.[408] Hazel died in Roseville, Placer County, California, on 18 July 2007; she was 87.[408] Buried on 26 July 2007, in Bonita, San Diego County, California,[1915] at Glen Abbey Memorial Park.

> *Obituary*: "(GILMORE) Born November 4, 1919 in Fayette, MO. Passed away peacefully July 18, 2007 of heart failure at age 87, in Roseville, CA. Hazel had a career as home-maker and mother of one son and two daughters. She also worked as an aircraft assembler during WWII, telephone operator, US Postal Service employee, and a school bus driver, which she enjoyed immensely. Hazel is preceded in death by her parents Roy and Viola Gilmore of Franklin and Boonville, MO and her brothers Paul Allen Gilmore and Roy Artell Gilmore. Hazel is survived by her children, Robert Fricke, Patty Miller, and Judy Hirigoyen, all of CA; her sister Nelson (Gilmore) Nosbish of West Branch, Iowa; and sister-in-law Christine Gilmore of Danville, VA. Hazel will be laid to rest at the Glen Abbey Memorial Park, Bonita, CA on July 26, 2007 at 2:30 p.m. Please sign the guest book at obituaries.uniontrib.com."[1916]
>
> *Obituary*: "Hazel Frances Gilmore Orrison, 87, of Roseville, Calif., passed away peacefully Wednesday, July 18, 2007, of heart failure.

Hazel will be laid to rest at the Glen Abbey Memorial Park, Bonita, Calif., Thursday, July 26, 2007, at 2:30 pm.

Hazel was born Nov. 4, 1919 in Fayette, Mo. After high school, Hazel studied at Dunkle's Business School in Boonville, in 1936-37.

Hazel had a career as homemaker and mother of one son and two daughters. She also worked as an aircraft assembler during World War II, a telephone operator, a U.S. Postal Service employee, and a school bus driver, which she enjoyed immensely.

A resident of California for the past 66 years, she lived in and near San Diego until 1996, when she moved to the Sacramento area.

She spent her retirement first in El Cajon, near San Diego, then in the Sacramento area, with her beloved pet dog and constant companion, 'Brittney.'

Hazel is preceded in death by her parents Roy and Viola Gilmore of Franklin and Boonville, Mo., and her brothers Paul Allen Gilmore and Roy Artell Gilmore.

Hazel is survived by her children: Robert Fricke of Salton Sea, Calif, Patty Miller of Loomis, Calif., and Judy Hirigoyen of Lincoln, Calif.; her sister Nelson Gilmore Nosbish of West Branch, Iowa; sister-in-law Christine Gilmore of Danville, Va.; six grandchildren; three great-grandchildren; three nieces; three nephews; many great nieces and nephews; and best friend of over 50 years, Lucille Lyle of Palm Desert, Calif.

Though she is reunited with her beloved mother, father and two brothers in heaven, she will also be with us in loving memory."[1917]

They had no children.

---

68. Norman Keith ORRISON[1918-1920] (*Orpha Zella CLAY*[4], *Cassius M.*[3], *Fredric*[2], *Abegail*[1]).

Born on 28 May 1926, in Marshall, Calhoun County, Michigan,[408] Norman died in Battle Creek, Calhoun County, Michigan, on 22 August 1986; he was 60.[408,1921] Buried on 25 August 1986 in Augusta, Kalamazoo County, Michigan,[1922,1923] at Fort Custer National Cemetery.

Occupation: Butter Maker (1950).[1924]

Education: Emery And Henry College (1944).

Obituary: "MARSHALL Norman Keith Orrison, 60, died Friday in Leila Hospital after an eight-month illness.

He was born in Marshall and had lived in the area all his life. He was employed at Aero-Quip Corp. for 33 years, retiring a month ago due to ill health. He was a World War II U.S. Navy veteran, a life member of Battle Creek VFW Post 1815 and a former member of Moose Lodge No. 676.

68. Norman Keith ORRISON. Photograph from high school yearbook.[1925]

Surviving are brothers, Jesse Eugene Orrison of Tuscon, Ariz., Howard C. Orrison of Portland, Ore., Robert E. Orrison of Lompoc, Calif., Jack D. Orrison of Marshall and James F. Orrison of Fort Pierce, Fla.; and a sister, Joyce M. Blaskie of Battle Creek.

Services will be held 2 p.m. Monday in Craig K. Kempf Funeral Home. Memorial donations may be made to the oncology unit at Leila Hospital."[1926]

Military:
World War II, US Navy, Seaman 1.
On 1944 October 10; 1944 December 31; 1945 March 31; 1945 April 30; 1945 July 1; 1945 October 1; 1945 December 1; 1946 January 1: aboard the USS *Pittsburgh*[1927]

"MARSHALL Mr. and Mrs. Jesse Orrison of 317 South Mulberry were pretty happy because within the week they had heard from three of their sons, each on a different fighting front. A long, newsy letter had come from Howard in Italy and 18-year-old Keith, somewhere in the south Pacific, had sent a beautiful valentine to his mother. A card in his own hand writing was received from 'Gene', which is the most they could expect for 'Gene' is a prisoner st war in Germany. They spoke wistfully of Bob, also in the south Pacific, but thought hearing from all four in one week was too much to ask, then Bob walked in to deliver his greetings in person. ... Norman Keith Orrison, 18, seaman second class, enlisted in the 1 January 24, 1944 while a senior in high school, he received his high school diploma in February. He trained at Emery and

Henry college, Emery, Virginia and at Barnbridge, Maryland. In October 1944 he was assigned to a newly commissioned ship and is now somewhere in the south Pacific."[1855]

1945, April: Aboard the *USS* *Pittsburgh* (CA72), 30 April 1945[1928]

Service: 25 January 1944 to 20 October 1947.[763]

"Varied wartime experiences have not discouraged three of the sons of Mr. and Mrs. Jessie Orrison of 427 Monroe from continuing their careers in the armed forces. ... Norman Keith Orrison, a fourth son, also served in the navy in the South Pacific and at present is at home."[1929]

"Keith was pulled out of high school during WWII (all the students were still awarded their High School Diploma) and entered the Navy (1944-1948). He served on the heavy cruiser *USS Pittsburg* which was caught in a typhoon and was partially blown up. They managed to make it back to port.

Keith worked for Ralph Klein at the Marshall Creamery in Marshall after he returned from the service. He worked there for a time then went to work at Kennedy Automatic. His boss was Kenneth Kennedy. Later it was called Aeroquip Corp."[2134]

---

69. Jack Duane ORRISON[1930-1932,180] (*Orpha Zella CLAY*[4], *Cassius M.*[3], *Fredric*[2], *Abegail*[1]).

Born on 17 April 1928, in Lee Township, Calhoun County, Michigan,[408] Jack died in Concord, Jackson County, Michigan, on 20 January 2012; he was 83.[408] Buried in Marshall, Calhoun County, Michigan,[1933] at Oakridge Cemetery.

Occupations: Shipping Clerk (1950); Insurance (1959).[1934,1935]

Obituary: "Concord | Jack D. Orrison, 83, died January 20, 2012.

Services at a later date. www.kempffuneralhome.-com"[1937]

Obituary: "Jack D. Orrison, 83 of Concord formerly of Marshall, died on January 20, 2012, at his home surrounded by his family. Mr. Orrison was born on April 17, 1928, in Lee Township, to Jesse J. and Orpha Z. (Clay) Orrison. He graduated from Marshall High School in 1946. On August 20, 1950, he married Peggy

J. Callahan at the Wesleyan Methodist Church in Union City. Mr. Orrison retired from the Eaton Company in Marshall after working 30 years. He was a member of the Eaton 25 year Club, and the Marshall Mates Square Dance Club. After his retirement, he enjoyed traveling with his wife Peggy, but would also be found helping in her upholstery business. Mr. Orrison was a skilled woodworker and would make wooden toys for all of his grandchildren. He was proud to say he taught himself how to use the computer and his e-mail. He is survived by his wife Peggy of Concord, three children, John (Patricia) Orrison of Pulaski, Jean (Timothy) Brunt of Battle Creek, Paul (Nancy) Orrison of Newport News, Virginia, four grandchildren Tracy Orrison, Aric Ruble, Dana Moore, and Connor Orrison. He is also survived by four great-grandchildren, sister Joyce Blaskie of Battle Creek, brothers, Clay Orrison of Oregon, and James Orrison of Tennessee. He was preceded in death by his parents, an infant son Brian, brothers Norman, Jesse, Robert, and Gilford Orrison. A graveside service will take place at Oakridge Cemetery in the spring. Family requests memorial contributions be made to the Great Lakes Hospice. Assistance with memorials is available the Craig K. Kempf Funeral Home and Cremation Services."[1938]

69. Jack Duane ORRISON. Photograph from high school yearbook.[1936]

Military:

U.S., World War II Draft Cards Young Men, 1940-1947:

Name: Jack Duane Orrison | Gender: Male | Race: White | Age: 18 | Birth Date/Place: 17 Apr 1928, Lee Township, Michigan | Residence Place: 317 S. Mulberry, Marshall, Mich. | Registration Date: 18 Apr 1946, Mulberry, Lenawee, Michigan | Employer: Murray's Shoe Repair | Height: 5 2 | Weight: 112 | Complexion: Ruddy | Hair

Peggy Jane CALLAHAN. Photograph from newspaper wedding announcement, 27 August 1950.

Color: Brown | Eye Color: Brown | 2 scars on head - scar on left arm | Next of Kin: Jesse J Orrison [father][1793]

On 20 August 1950, when Jack was 22, he married **Peggy Jane CALLAHAN,**[1939,1940] daughter of Hugh David CALLAHAN and Estella May CORNELL, in Union City, Branch County, Michigan,[1941,1942,1943] at the Wesleyan Methodist Church, by Alvin C. Barker.

She died 27 July 2016, in Jackson, Jackson County, Michigan. She was cremated and the cremains interred at Marshall, Calhoun County, Michigan,[1944] at Oakridge Cemetery.

Occupation: Peg's Upholstery Shop.

She worked in the Central Store for 25 years and the Michigan National Bank for approximately 2 years. She also operated her own upholstery business as a second job."[2135]

Jack and Peggy had the following children:

i. **John Duane ORRISON**. [withheld for privacy—living person] He first married Sara Jane LEVIN, then Patricia A. FRALEY.

ii. **Jean Ann ORRISON**. [withheld for privacy—living person] She first married Roger Mas RUBLE, then Timothy L. BRUNT.

iii. **Paul Keith ORRISON**. [withheld for privacy—living person] He married Nancy Lynn ROBERTSON.

iv. **Brian Jay ORRISON.**[180] Born in 1959. Brian Jay died in 1959.

---

70. Joyce Marie ORRISON[1945-1947,180] (*Orpha Zella CLAY*[4], *Cassius M.*[3], *Fredric*[2], *Abegail*[1]).

Born on 18 February 1930, in Marshall, Calhoun County, Michigan, Joyce died in Sardinia, Brown County, Ohio, on 3 February 2020; she was 89. Buried on 14 February 2020, in Augusta, Kalamazoo County, Michigan,[1948] Fort Custer National Cemetery.

70. Joyce Marie ORRISON, photograph from newspaper.

Occupations: "...waitress, factory worker, manager for a drive-in restraurant and retired as personnel manager from K-Mart in Battle Creek, Michigan."[2136]

Religion: Roman Catholic.

Obituary: "Joyce Marie (Orrison) Blaskie, 89, of Sardinia, Ohio and formerly of Battle Creek, Michigan died peacefully at her home on February 3, 2020.

She was born February 18, 1930 in Marshall, Michigan the daughter of Jesse and Orpha Z. (Clay) Orrison. Joyce was raised in Marshall and attended Marshall High School. She was employed in the personnel department at K-Mart for 30 years, retiring in 1994.

Joyce Marie Orrison was united in marriage to Joseph Henry Blaskie on April 15, 1972 in Battle Creek. She is survived by her daughter Kathleen and son-in-law Garry Townsley; step-sons David, Dan (Deanna), Steven and Ken; grandsons Anthony (Julie) Schuler and Jason (Susan) Schuler; granddaughter Dawn Wind; great-grandchildren Tiffany Westrich, Heather, Alyssa, Cheyenne, Andrew, Kelsi, Kaine Schuler, Joseph Ford and special friend Denise Fletcher-Buroker.

She was preceded in death by her parents, beloved husband Joseph Blaskie, brothers Guilford, Jesse, Howard, Robert, Keith, Jack, James and son Arthur Eugene Masters.

Joyce was a member of St. Philip Roman Catholic Church and the Sportsman Club of Battle Creek. She enjoyed boating and fishing on their boat in Saugatuck. Joyce also enjoyed traveling and camping in their motor home.

Friends will be received 10:30 – 11:25 a.m. Friday, February 14, 2020 at St. Philip Roman Catholic Church. A Mass of Christian Burial will be celebrated by Rev. John D. Fleckenstein at St. Philip Roman Catholic Church 11:30 a.m. Friday, February 14, 2020. A committal service will follow at Fort Custer National Cemetery.

> Memorial contributions in memory of Joyce may be made to the St. Jude Children's Research Hospital. Personal messages for the family may be placed here at www.farleyestesdowdle.com."[1949]

On 19 July 1947, when Joyce Marie was 17, she first married **Arthur Eugene O'DELL,**[1950] son of Ora Dennis O'DELL and Alice Dora FISHER, in Marshall, Calhoun County, Michigan.[1951,1952] He was born on 23 May 1930, in Michigan.[408] Arthur died in Albion, Calhoun County, Michigan, on 9 April 2008; he was 77.[408] He was cremated 15 April 2008, with cremains interred at Cook's Prairie Cemetery, Clarendon, Calhoun County Michigan.[2137]

Occupations: Factory Worker (1949); Handyman (1950).[1953,1954]

They were divorced on 17 December 1951, in Calhoun County, Michigan.[1955]

> *Obituary*: "Albion | Arthur E. O'Dell, 77, of Albion, died April 9, 2008. A graveside service will be Tuesday, April 15 at 1:00 p.m. at Cook's Prairie Cemetery. Visitation 11:00 a.m. - 12:30 p.m. at J. Kevin Tidd Funeral Home, 811 Finley Drive, Albion, www.kevintiddfuneralhome.com"[1956]

> *Obituary*: "Arthur E. O'Dell, 77, of Albion died Wednesday, April 9, at his home. He is survived by five daughters, Deborah Willingham, Patty Mathis, Jeffrey O'Dell, Rhonda Wheeler and Kathy Townsley; one son, Hiram Eugene O'Dell; two sisters, Reena Snyder and Goldie Martin; two brothers Bill and Leslie O'Dell; and several grandchildren and great-grandchildren. Arrangements are by the J. Kevin Tidd Funeral Home, 811 Finley Dr., Albion."[1957]

They had the following children:

- i. **Arthur O'DELL Jr.**[1958] [withheld for privacy—living person]
- ii. **Kathleen Marie O'DELL.**[1959] [withheld for privacy—living person] She married Garry Lee TOWNSLEY.

On 9 May 1953, when Joyce was 23, she second married **Lawrence Waynard MASTERS,**[1960] son of Earl Jack MASTERS and Rachel Jane BOWMAN, in Steuben County, Indiana.[1961] He was born on 18 April 1926, in Tekonsha Township, Calhoun County, Michigan.[408] Lawrence died in Titusville, Brevard County, Florida, on 4 January 2002; he was 75.[408] Buried in Burlington, Calhoun County, Michigan,[1962] Burlington Township Cemetery.

They were divorced.

1982, May: "Lawrence W. Masters of 10505 K Drive S., Burlington, did a variety of work, including sheetmetal and production machines. He retired after 34 years of service, and plans to travel to the World's Fair in Tennessee this summer." [1963]

Military:

U.S., World War II Draft Cards Young Men, 1940-1947:

Name: Lawrence Waynard Masters | Gender: Male | Race: White | Age: 18 | Birth Date/Place: 18 Apr 1926, Newton Twp., Michigan | Residence Place: Hanover, Jackson, Michigan | Registration Date/Place: 18 Apr 1944, Hanover, Jackson, Michigan | Employer: Walter George Height: 5 7 | Weight: 140 | Complexion: Ruddy | Hair Color: Brown | Eye Color: Hazel | Next of Kin: Rachel Masters [mother][1964]

Korea: US Army, Company C, 453rd D Engineers.

Joyce and Lawrence had one child:

i. **Arthur Eugene MASTERS.**[180,1965] Born on 15 January 1948, in Albion, Calhoun County, Michigan. Arthur died in Battle Creek, Calhoun County, Michigan, on 1 February 1996; he was 48. He was married to Barbara Jo OTT.

On 15 April 1972, when Joyce was 42, she third married **Joseph Henry BLASKIE Jr.,**[180] son of Joseph Henry BLASKIE Sr. and Mary Victoria KUBIAK, in Battle Creek, Calhoun County, Michigan. [Joe's obituary says married at Middleville, Barry County; Joyce's obituary says Battle Creek, Michigan.] He was born on 27 February 1919, in Detroit, Wayne County, Michigan. Joseph died in Battle Creek, Calhoun County, Michigan, on 20 January 2017; he was 97. Buried in Augusta, Kalamazoo County, Michigan,[1966] at Fort Custer National Cemetery.

Occupations: Auto Body Mechanic; Teacher.[1967]

Religion: Roman Catholic.

Obituary: "Joseph Henry 'Joe' Blaskie, Jr.

Battle Creek | Joseph Henry 'Joe' Blaskie, Jr., age 97, of Battle Creek, MI, died Friday morning January 20, 2017 at his residence and with his loving family at his side.

Joe, the son of Joseph H. and Mary (Kubiak) Blaskie, Sr., was born in Detroit, MI on February 27, 1919 and was a graduate of St. Charles Catholic High

School of Coldwater, MI. He served his Country honorably and nobly during World War II in the United States Army as a Sergeant with the 126th Infantry (Awarded his Combat Infantry Badge) in the South Pacific Theater. Joe was an auto body mechanic, first owning his own shop and then working for Smith's Auto Body Shop. He also worked for his brother at Burt's Glass Shop and finally retiring in 1994. Joe was a member of St. Philip Roman Catholic Church; the Knights of Columbus, Third Degree having joined in Saugatuck, MI and the National Rifle Association. He enjoyed camping with their motor home, hunting and fishing. Almost every weekend possible, he went to Saugatuck to fish off their boat on the Big Lake, Lake Michigan.

Joe was united in marriage to the former Joyce M. Orrison in Middleville, MI on April 15, 1972. Surviving is his wife of 44 years, Joyce; four sons, Steven Blaskie of Phoenix, AZ, David Blaskie of Ann Arbor, MI, Dan (Deanna) Blaskie and Ken Blaskie, both of Battle Creek ; several grandchildren; a step-daughter, Kathy (Gary) Townsley of Cincinnati, OH; his sister, Ann Cuendent of Coldwater, MI and several nieces and nephews. Joe was preceded in death by his parents; two sisters and four brothers.

Mass of Christian Burial will be celebrated on Wednesday, January 25th at 10:30 a.m. at St. Philip Roman Catholic Church, 92 Capital Avenue, NE, Battle Creek with Father Robert Johanson, Celebrant. Interment will follow at Fort Custer National Cemetery, Augusta, MI with the United States Army Honor Guard and the Fort Custer Honor Guard bestowing full military honors. Joe's family will greet friends on Wednesday from 9:30 a.m. until Mass Time in the Church Vestibule. The Farley Estes Dowdle Funeral Home & Cremation Care, Battle Creek is assisting Joe's family with his arrangements."[1968]

Military:

World War II: US Army, Sergeant; Bronze Star. 126th Infantry, 32nd Division (Awarded his Combat Infantry Badge) in the South Pacific Theater, New Guinea for two years.

They had no children.

71. James Frederick ORRISON[1969,1970,2138] (*Orpha Zella CLAY*[4], *Cassius M.*[3], *Fredric*[2], *Abegail*[1]).

Born on 2 January 1936, in Michigan, James died in Cleveland, Bradley County, Tennessee, on 17 April 2017; he was 81. Buried on 13 May 2017, in Cleveland, Bradley County, Tennessee,[1971] at Sunset Memorial Gardens.

71. James Frederick ORRISON. Photograph from high school yearbook.[1972]

Education: Bachelor Of Science Business Management, Central Michigan University.

Religion: Seventh Day Adventist.

"In the fall of 1954 he enrolled at Ferris State College, leaving winter term in 1955. He worked at *Marshall Evening Chronicle* until entering the Army Nov. 1, 1956, where he served as a supply clerk, until discharged Oct. 31, 1958.

Jim had various work opportunities in Michigan, one of which was from 1970 until 1975 at Central Michigan University. He chose to attend CMU full time, graduating in 1977 with a bachelors degree in Business Administration. In 1979 they went to Massachusetts to work for Pioneer Valley Academy, a private boarding high school near Worcester. They lived in the Ft. Pierce-Vero beach area in Florida from 1983 through 2003 and then moved to Cleveland, Tennessee." In 2007 he worked part time at Southern Adventist University, Collegedale, Tennessee.[2139]

> *Obituary*: "James Orrison, 81, of Cleveland, passed away Sunday, April 16, 2017, at his home, surrounded by family.
>
> He was a member of the Seventh-day Adventist church of Cohutta, Ga., and a master guide of Pathfinders.
>
> He graduated from Central Michigan University with a bachelor of science in business management. He enjoyed bowling, golf, computers and woodworking. He loved being outdoors.
>
> He was a veteran of the United States Army.

Mary Ann SHIELS. Photograph from high school yearbook.[1975]

He was preceded in death by his parents, Jesse and Orpha Clay Orrison; and six brothers. He is survived by his wife of 59 years, Mary Ann Shiels Orrison of Cleveland; three children: Russell Orrison (Beverly) of Apison, James Michael Orrison (Lora) of Cleveland, and Jerilyn Pewsey of Collegedale; six grandchildren: Michael Orrison, Alan Orrison, Kristopher Orrison, Kevin Orrison, Heather Harding and Matthew Pewsey; five great-grandchildren: Elliot Orrison, Wesley Orrison, Olivia Orrison and Aria and Madelyn Harding; sister Joyce Balaski; and several nieces and nephews.

A Celebration of Life will be held at 3:30 p.m. on Saturday, May 13, 2017, at Cohutta Seventh-day Adventist church. A fellowship meal will immediately follow the service.

The family wishes to extend appreciation to Jill Duggan, RN, of Hospice of Chattanooga, for her devotion and loving care during a most difficult time.

Memorial donations may be made to Hospice of Chattanooga, 4411 Oakwood Drive, Chattanooga, TN 37416 or hospiceofchattanooga.org.

Ralph Buckner Funeral Home is in charge of arrangements."[1973]

Military: US Army, Private, circa 1957.

On 12 October 1957, at Fort Lewis, Pierce County, Washington[2139] when James was 21, he married **Mary Ann SHIELS**, daughter of Walter Earl SHIELS and Beulah Mae CAREY.[1974] Mary Ann was born in Michigan [dates withheld for privacy – living person].

"She worked as a telephone operator in Charlotte until marrying Jim in 1957. From 1970 to 1979 she served as a dental assistant until they moved to Massachussetts. Mary Ann then worked for Pioneer Academy from 1971 through 1983. They moved to Florida, where she helped home school her grandchildren from 1998 to 2003. She worked as a daycare teacher for two year olds."[2139]

James and Mary had the following children:

i. **Russell L. ORRISON** [withheld for privacy—living person] Married to Beverly _____.

ii. **James Michael ORRISON** [withheld for privacy—living person]. First married to Renee Lynn BROTHER, then Lora _____.

iii. **Jerilyn Dee ORRISON** [withheld for privacy—living person] Married to Charles Grant PEWSEY.

---

72. Charlyne Ella CLAY (*Milo Schutt[4], Cassius M.[3], Fredric[2], Abegail[1]*).

Born on 15 March 1918, in Lansing, Ingham County, Michigan.[1976] Charlyn died in Detroit, Wayne County, Michigan, on 4 September 1918; she was six months old.[1977,2140] Buried on 5 September 1918 in Lansing, Ingham County, Michigan, at Mount Hope Cemetery.

---

73. Betty Jane CLAY[1978-1980] (*Milo Schutt[4], Cassius M.[3], Fredric[2], Abegail[1]*).

Born on 28 February 1920, in Detroit, Wayne County, Michigan,[408] Betty died at Memorial Mission Hospital in Asheville, Buncombe County, North Carolina, on 26 April 1999; she was 79.[408,1981]

Occupations: Clerk (1940); Cashier (1942); Inspector (1945).[1982-1984]

Betty Jane married **John Fredrick ECKHARDT Jr.**,[1985,1986,180] son of John F. ECKHARDT Sr. and Emilie M. JUNKERANN. He was born on 10 October 1920, in Williamstown, Gloucester County, New Jersey.[408] John was baptized in Philadelphia, Philadelphia County, Pennsylvania, on 28 November 1920,[1987] at the Tabor Evangelical Church as "Johann Fredrick Eckhardt." John died in Inverness, Citrus County, Florida, on 2 March 2006; he was 85.[408] Buried in Inverness, Citrus County, Florida,[1988] at Oak Ridge Cemetery.

Occupations: Can Feeder (1950); Trip Acres Poultry Farm (1949-1954); Postal Worker.[1989,1990]

John was active in the local VFW and Dunedin Masonic Lodge 192.

Obituary: "ECKHARDT, JOHN FREDRICK JR., 86, of Inverness, formerly of Dunedin, died Thursday (March 2, 2006) under the care of his wife and Hospice of Citrus County. Born in Williamstown, N.J., he came here several years ago from Dunedin where he lived for 22 years. He was an Army Air Force veteran and worked at the Dunedin Post Office with 18 years of service. He was a Third Degree Mason, a member VFW and the Inverness Church of God. He enjoyed traveling. Survivors include his wife, Abbie Arnold Eckhardt; a son, John Eckhardt Bat Cave, N.C.; several stepchildren; a sister, Emelie Wolf, New Jersey; several nieces and grandnieces; two grandsons and several stepgrandchildren. Hooper Funeral Home, Inverness."[1991]

Military:

U.S., World War II Draft Cards Young Men, 1940-1947:
Name: John Frederick Eckhardt, Jr. | Place of Residence: 21 West St. Glassboro Gloucester N.J. | Age: 21 | Place of Birth: Williamstown New Jersey | Date of Birth: 10 October 1920 | Name of Person Who Knows You: Mrs. Emilie Eckhardt [mother] | Employer: Hungerford and Terry, Clayton, New Jersey | Race: White | Height: 5′ 10.5″ | Eyes: Brown | Weight: 165 | Hair: Brown | Complexion: Dark | Scar on right elbow | Registration Date: 14 March 1942.[1992]

U.S., World War II Army Enlistment Records, 1938-1946:
Name: John F Eckhardt Jr | Race: White | Marital Status: Single, with dependents (Single) | Rank: Private | Birth Year: 1920 | Nativity State or Country: New Jersey | Citizenship: Citizen | Residence: Gloucester, New Jersey | Education: 4 years of high school | Civil Occupation: Foremen, construction | Enlistment Date: 14 Jul 1942 | Enlistment Place: Camden, New Jersey | Service Number: 32075274 | Branch: Branch Immaterial - Warrant Officers, USA | Component: Selectees (Enlisted Men) | Source: Civil Life | Height: 69 Weight: 160[1993]

Service: World War II, US Army Air Force, 28 July 1942 to 14 January 1945.[763]

Betty and John had one child:

i. **John F. "Tripper" ECKHARDT III.**[1994,1995] [withheld for privacy—living person] He married Patricia L. LENTZ.

74. Helen Edith WALLACE[1996-2001] (*Edith Irene CLAY*[4], *Frank Henry*[3], *Fredric*[2], *Abegail*[1]).

Born on 2 June 1918, in Kalamazoo, Kalamazoo County, Michigan,[408] Helen died in Kalamazoo, Kalamazoo County, Michigan, on 18 November 2000; she was 82.[408] Buried in Kalamazoo, Kalamazoo County, Michigan,[2002] at Mount Ever-Rest Memorial Park South (cremated).

Occupations: Cady Shop (1940); American Airlines Reservation Agent (1950); Sales Agent (1951); The Village Shop.[2003-2005]

Education: Western Michigan University.

> *Obituary*: "Died Saturday morning, November 18, 2000 at her residence. Mrs. Pierce was born June 2, 1918, a daughter of Ralph R. and Edith C. Wallace. She attended Kalamazoo Public Schools, graduating from Kalamazoo Central in 1936. She attended Western Michigan University and worked for American Airlines for 6 years, based in Chicago. Upon leaving American Airlines, she managed an airline desk in the Morrison Hotel and Merchandise Mart. Returning to Kalamazoo she owned and operated the Village Shop, Women's Specialty shop for finer apparel. After having the shop for 17 years, she closed it at the time of her husband's retirement. He preceded her in death. In accordance with her wishes cremation has taken place. There will be no visitation. A private inurnment of cremains will be in Mt. Ever-Rest Cemetery. Arrangements were made by the Langeland Family Funeral Homes Memorial Chapel."[2006]

Helen married **Maynard Bert PIERCE,**[2007] son of Harvey B. PIERCE and Gertrude ROBINSON. He was born on 12 October 1911, in Scotts, Kalamazoo County, Michigan,[408] and died in Kalamazoo, Kalamazoo County, Michigan, on 7 July 1982; he was 70.[408,2008] Buried in Kalamazoo, Kalamazoo County, Michigan,[2009] at Mount Ever-Rest Memorial Park South.

Occupation: Service Station Attendant (Since 1931, 1935); Standard Oil Company Assistant Division Manager, Green Bay (1956).[2010,2011]

Military:

U.S., World War II Draft Cards Young Men, 1940-1947:

Name: Maynard Bert Pierce | Gender: Male | Race: White | Age: 29 | Birth Date/Place: 12 Oct 1911, Scotts, Michigan | Residence Place: 719 Cooper St. Kalamazoo, Kalamazoo, Michigan | Registration Date: 16 Oct 1940 |

Registration Place: Kalamazoo, Kalamazoo, Michigan | Employer: Self | Height: 5ft. 11 in | Weight: 172 | Complexion: Light | Hair Color: Brown | Eye Color: Gray | Next of Kin: Wayne Williams, Friend[1793]

They had no children.

---

75. Kathleen Marguerite CLAY[2012-2015] (*Eldon Rodgers*[4], *Frank Henry*[3], *Fredric "Fred"*[2], *Abegail*[1]).

Born on 16 March 1920, in Owatonna, Steele County, Minnesota,[2016,408] Kathleen died in Oceanside, San Diego County, California, on 12 February 2000; she was 79.[408] Buried [cremated] in Oceanside, San Diego County, California, at Eternal Hills Memorial Park.

Occupations: Switchboard Operator (1940); Law Office Secretary (1950).[2017,772]

Arrived in Honolulu, Hawaii September 1950: "Clay | Kathleen | Age 30 | F | Place of Birth: Owatonna, Minn" Sailing from Los Angeles Harbor.[2154]

> *Obituary*: "OCEANSIDE - Kathleen C. Pearce, 79, died Sunday, Feb. 12. 2000, at her home.
>
> Bom March 16, 1920, in Minnesota, she lived in Oceanside for 40 years.
>
> Mrs. Pearce is survived by her son, David Pearce of Oceanside.
>
> No service will be held at the request of the deceased. A private cremation is planned with inurnment to take place at a later date at Eternal Hills Memorial Park.
>
> Eternal Hills Mortuary is handling arrangements."[2018]

On 10 March 1944, when Kathleen Marguerite was 23, she first married **George Reed BEIDLER,**[180] son of Earl John BEIDLER and Chloe REED, in New York City, New York,[2019,2020] at Saint Nicholas Church. He was born on 24 March 1913, in the village of Oakville, North Newton Township, Cumberland County, Pennsylvania.[408,2021] George was baptized in Newville Township, Cumberland County, Pennsylvania, on 7 February 1914,[2022] at the Big Spring United Presbyterian Church. [Baptismal record says 21 March]. George died in Des Plaines, Cook County, Illinois, on 25 April 1988; he was 75;[408] buried in Newville Township, Cumberland County, Pennsylvania,[2023] Newville Cemetery.

Occupations: Coast Guard (1944); Sales Engineer (1948).
Religion: Presbyterian.

They were divorced on 24 June 1946, in Los Angeles County, California. [per second marriage record].

George lived in Long Island, New York, 1946; New Jersey 1950, Baltimore, Maryland in 1988.

Military:
World War II: US Coast Guard
Service: 20 March 1942 to 14 September 1945[2024]
World War II Draft Card mentions wife "Mona Rebecca Beidler"

They had no children.

On 20 September 1952, when Kathleen was 32, she second married **Frank Hill PEARCE** at Camp Pendleton in San Diego, San Diego County, California.[2025,2166] He was born 8 February 1921, at Cayce Marsha, Marshall County, Mississippi[408] to Lee Powers PEARCE and Blanch Helen HILL. Frank died 23 November 1998, age 77.[408]

Kathleen and Frank had one child:

i. **David PEARCE**.

Sources: Abegail Clay's Children

1. England & Wales, Non-Conformist and Non-Parochial Registers, 1567-1936, Registers of Births, Marriages and Deaths Surrendered to the Non-Parochial Registers Commissions of 1837 and 1857. The National Archives of the UK; Kew, Surrey, England; GRO, database with image, Class RG4; Piece Number 3407; South Parade Chapel (Wesleyan), 1772-1817. "Abagail Daughter of John and Grace Clay of Mixenden-Ings in Ovenden."
2. England and Wales Non-Conformist Record Indexes (RG4-8), 1588-1977, database, (https://familysearch.org/ark:/61903/1:1:F449-G32 : 11 December 2014) Abegail Clay, 6 Dec 1789, Baptism; citing p. 41, Ovenden, Yorkshire, record group RG4.
3. Ibid. (https://familysearch.org/ark:/61903/1:1:VWZ4-Q45 : 11 December 2014), Abagail Clay, 6 Dec 1789, Baptism; citing p. 77, Halifax, Yorkshire, record group RG4.
4. England Births and Christenings, 1538-1975, familysearch.org, database, (https://www.familysearch.org/ark:/61903/1:1:J3DF-NFZ : 5 February 2023), Abagail Clay, 1789.
5. England & Wales Civil Registration Indexes, 1837-1915, ancestry.com, UK GRO, London, database with image, "No. 2319. | Abigail Clay | Abode. Warley | When Buried. September 14 | Age. 71 yrs" New Reference Number: WDP39/11.
6. Death Certificate/Record. GRO, number 200. Death: 10 September 1843, in Midgley. "Abigel Clay 71 years Widow of John Clay Weaver"; registered 11 September 1843.
7. 1841 England and Wales Census, Northowram Township, Halifax, Yorkshire, 6 June 1841, "Stocks Buildings" ED: 10; Folio 10; Page 13; Line 8; GSU roll 464263; "Overlooker" age 53.
8. England & Wales, Non-Conformist and Non-Parochial Registers, 1567-1936, Registers of Births, Marriages and Deaths Surrendered to the Non-Parochial Registers Commissions of 1837 and 1857. Class Number: RG 4; Class Number: Rg 4; Piece Number: 3011 (ancestry.com image 70); "John Son of John Farrar of Ovenden Baptd Apr 1, 1787."
9. England, Select Births and Christenings, 1538-1975, database with no images, Ancestry.com, FHL Film Number: 0816623 (RG4 3011).
10. England & Wales, Non-Conformist and Non-Parochial Registers, 1567-1936, Registers of Births, Marriages and Deaths Surrendered to the Non-Parochial Registers Commissions of 1837 and 1857. Class Number: RG 4; Class Number: Rg 4; Piece Number: 3704; (ancestry.com image 44).
11. West Yorkshire, England, Church of England Baptisms, Marriages and Burials, 1512-1812, database with image, West Yorkshire Archive Service, ancestry.com, New Reference Number: WDP47/1/1/2; (ancestry.com image 1).
12. England & Wales, Non-Conformist and Non-Parochial Registers, 1567-1936, Registers of Births, Marriages and Deaths Surrendered to the Non-Parochial Registers Commissions of 1837 and 1857. Page 17/33; (ancestry.com image 22).
13. West Yorkshire, England, Church of England Baptisms, Marriages and Burials, 1512-1812, database with image, West Yorkshire Archive Service, Page 39; (ancestry.com image 6).

14. West Yorkshire, England, Prison Records, 1801-1914, Register of Male and Female Prisoners, West Yorkshire Archive Service; Wakefield, West Yorkshire, England, (ancestry.com image 93); Ledger Page 91; Year Range: 1801-1808; Reference Number: C118/98; West Yorkshire Prison Records. Reference C118.

15. 1841 England and Wales Census, Brock Holes, Upper, Ovenden, Yorkshire, England, 6 June 1841, Class HO107; Piece 1302; Book 7; Civil Parish: Halifax; County: Yorkshire; ED 24; Folio 41; Page 6; Line 9; GSU roll 464262; "Isaac Clay" (ancestry.com image 4).

16. 1851 Census of England and Wales, Ovenden, Yorkshire-West Riding, 30 March 1851, "94 Rocks," Class: HO107; Piece: 2301; Folio 337; Page 25; GSU roll 87509; (ancestry.com image 26); "Isaac Clay."

17. 1841 census estimates year of birth as 1821; 1851 census estimates year as 1819. But his birthdate comes from the family Bible (observed by the author in the 1970s). The death record also suggests he was born in 1806.

18. National Archives of the UK; GRO, England and Wales Non-Conformist and Non-Parochial Registers, 1567-1970, RG4; Piece Number 3408; (ancestry.com image 92); "Isaac Son of Abagail Clay of Brockholes was Bapd. Oct. 29, 1817" - no mention of his father.

19. England Births and Christenings, 1538-1975, (https://www.familysearch.org/ark:/61903/1:1:JW64-V86 : 3 February 2023), Abagial Clay in entry for Isaac Clay, 1817; RG-4 series nos. 3407-3410.

20. England and Wales Non-Conformist Record Indexes (RG4-8), 1588-1977, (https://familysearch.org/ark:/61903/1:1:F7KD-J3J : 11 December 2014), Abagail Clay in entry for Isaac Clay, 29 Oct 1817, Baptism; citing page 92, Ovenden, Yorkshire, record group RG4.

21. Death Certificate/Record. Number 463; GRO, Age: about 65 years of age making him born about 1806.

22. England and Wales Civil Death Registration Index 1837-2007, database with scanned image, familysearch.org and ancestry.com and findmypast.com, GRO. England and Wales Civil Registration Indexes. Volume 9A, Page 349, Line 41.

23. Deceased Online Burial Indexes; UK, Burial and Cremation Index, 1576-2014, Scanned image, Gower Consultants and Manuscripti Joint Enterprise, https://www.deceasedonline.com/, C/D/324.

24. Death Certificate/Record. "Street Pavior/Road Setter".

25. 1841 England and Wales Census, Brock Holes, Upper, Ovenden, Yorkshire, England, 6 June 1841, "Worsted Weaver."

26. 1851 Census of England and Wales, Ovenden, Yorkshire-West Riding, 30 March 1851, "Laborer."

27. The Book Of Trades or Library of the Useful Arts, London: Tabart And Co., Third Edition, 1806, Part II, "Paviour" page 64.

28. Marriage Certificate/Record/Application.

29. Bradford Observer, newspaper, Bradford, England, "Several Persons Bitten By A Mad Dog." 22 April 1869, page 3; "Several Person Bitten By a Mad Dog At Ovenden." 17 April 1869, page 4.

30. Bradford Daily Telegraph, newspaper, Bradford, England, "Halifax." 17 April 1869, page 2.

31. Halifax Guardian, newspaper, Halifax, England, "Ovenden. Another Mad Dog. - Several Persons Bit.-" 17 April 1869, page 5.

32. Huddersfield Examiner, newspaper, Yorkshire, England, "Halifax." 17 April 1869, page 8.

33. Higginbotham, Peter, Halifax, "West Riding of Yorkshire" www.workhouses.org.uk/Halifax/, (viewed 14 June 2023).

34. Ibid.
35. 1841 England and Wales Census, Brock Holes, Upper, Ovenden, Yorkshire, 6 June 1841, Class: HO107; Piece: 1302; Book: 7; Civil Parish: Halifax; County: Yorkshire; ED 24; Folio 41; Page 6; Line 10; GSU roll: 464262; "Salley Clay" (ancestry.com image 4).
36. 1851 Census of England and Wales, Ovenden, Yorkshire-West Riding, 30 March 1851, "94 Rocks," Class: HO107; Piece: 2301; Folio 337; Page 25; GSU roll 87509; (ancestry.com image 26); "Sally Clay."
37. 1871 Census of England and Wales, Halifax, Yorkshire, 2 April 1871, ED 32; Class RG10; Piece 4397; Folio 12; Page 18; GSU roll 848095; Line 90; "30 Hanthrpt street"; Widow; "Sarah Clay."
38. 1880 US Census, Hamlin Township, Eaton County, Michigan, June 1880, NARA T9; Roll 578; ED 78; Page 15/324; Dwelling 157; Family 171; Line 42. Residing in James Pickles household (son-in-law). "Sally Clay" "Mother-in-Law" age 62 (born circa 1818).
39. Marriage Certificate/Record/Application. West Yorkshire Archive Service; Leeds, Yorkshire; Yorkshire Parish Records; Reference Number: WDP53/1/3/30; his "father" was John Farrar, Overseer.
40. England and Wales Marriage Registration Index, 1837-2005, database, familysearch.org, Volume 22, Page 188, Line 144.
41. West Yorkshire Archive Service, West Yorkshire, Church of England Births and Baptisms, 1813-1910, Wakefield, Yorkshire, ancestry.com, Page 122, 3 December 1837; Number 244, marriage. (Original in custody of Curt Sanders.)
42. West Yorkshire Archive Service, West Yorkshire, Church of England Marriages and Banns, 1813-1935, database with image, ancestry.com, Banns: Yorkshire Parish Records; Reference Number: WDP53/1/5/9; 1836, number 1239, page 246, St. John the Baptist.
43. England & Wales, Civil Registration Marriage Index, 1837-2005, database with scanned images, ancestry.com ; findmypast.com, (ancestry.com image 15); Volume 22, Page 188.
44. From family Bible. Later records show her birth circa 1813-1818. 1841 Census says 1816; 1851 Census says 1813.
45. unknown author, New Methodist Magazine, unknown, [U.K.] 1833, (inscription inside jacket).
46. England Births and Christenings, 1538-1975, (https://www.familysearch.org/ark:/61903/1:1:J38T-58B : 3 February 2023), Sally Tidswell, 1813; RG-4 series nos. 3407-3410.
47. England and Wales Non-Conformist Record Indexes (RG4-8), 1588-1977, database, https://familysearch.org, citing page 64, Ovenden, Yorkshire, record group RG4, Public Record Office, London.
48. National Archives of the UK; GRO, England and Wales Non-Conformist and Non-Parochial Registers, 1567-1970, RG4, www.ancestry.com, Piece Number: 3408. "Sally Tidswell."
49. England & Wales, Non-Conformist and Non-Parochial Registers, 1567-1936, Registers of Births, Marriages and Deaths Surrendered to the Non-Parochial Registers Commissions of 1837 and 1857. Class Number RG 4; Piece Number 3408; (ancestry.com image 64). "Sally Dau of Jonathan and Hannah Tidswell of Sanehead Bap April 4 1813".
50. No civil or church record found. The information came from various family records.
51. 1851 Census of England and Wales, Ovenden, Yorkshire-West Riding, 30 March 1851; "Worsted Weaver."
52. 1871 Census of England and Wales, Halifax, Yorkshire, 2 April 1871; "Loom Weaver."

53. Claimed by findagrave.com.
54. England & Wales, Non-Conformist and Non-Parochial Registers, 1567-1936, Registers of Births, Marriages and Deaths Surrendered to the Non-Parochial Registers Commissions of 1837 and 1857. Class Number RG 4; Piece Number 3408. (ancestry.com image 55). "Edward Son of Abagail Clay of Brookhouse."
55. England and Wales Non-Conformist Record Indexes (RG4-8), 1588-1977, (https://familysearch.org/ark:/61903/1:1:FQ6S-JZH : 11 December 2014), Edward Clay, 20 Dec 1811, Baptism; citing p. 55, Ovenden, Yorkshire, record group RG4, Public Record Office, London.
56. England Births and Christenings, 1538-1975, (https://www.familysearch.org/ark:/61903/1:1:J38T-TZZ : 3 February 2023), Abagail Clay in entry for Edward Clay, 1811.
57. Per burial record.
58. West Yorkshire Archive Service, Yorkshire Parish Records, Wakefield, Yorkshire, England. Burial: New Reference Number: WDP53/1/1/8. "Edward [of] Abigail Clay, Ovn."
59. West Yorkshire, England, Church of England Baptisms, Marriages and Burials, 1512-1812, database with image, West Yorkshire Archive Service, (ancestry.com image 6); "1812 Jany. 19 Edward Abigail Clay Ovn."
60. England, Yorkshire, Bishop's Transcripts, 1547-1957, Borthwick Institute for Archives, (https://www.familysearch.org/ark:/61903/1:1:68ZF-3NLG : 16 August 2021), Edward Clay, 1812.
61. Find-A-Grave, (findagrave.com/memorial/221743353/edward-clay: accessed 27 July 2022). Memorial ID 221743353, citing St. Mary the Virgin Churchyard, Halifax, Metropolitan Borough of Calderdale, West Yorkshire; maintained by Glynn Thomas Helliwell (contributor 48559631).
62. 1841 Census of England and Wales, Halifax, West Riding, Yorkshire, 6 June 1841, Brook House, Page 5; Piece/Folio: 1302/6; Registration number H0107. Living with is grandmother Grace Clay; "Fredk Clay."
63. 1851 Census of England and Wales, Ovenden, Yorkshire, England, 30 March 1851, Class: HO107; Piece 2301; Folio 332; Page 14; GSU roll 87509; ED 18; Sheet 14, page 332; "53 Brookhouse" lodging with the John Hodgson family. (ancestry.com image 15); "Frederick Clay."
64. 1860 US Census, Eaton Rapids, Eaton County, Michigan, June 1860, NARA M653; Roll 542; Page 527; Dwelling 226; Family 210; Line 25; "Fred Clay."
65. 1870 US Census, Eaton Rapids, Eaton County, Michigan, June 1870, Enumerated 1 August 1870; NARA M593; Roll 670; Page 208A; Dwelling 347; Family 347; Line 28; "Fred Clay."
66. 1880 US Census, Hamlin Township, Eaton County, Michigan, June 1880, NARA T9; Roll 578; Page 322C; ED 78; Dwelling 110; Family 117; Line 11; "Fredric Clay."
67. Tombstone. (See findagrave.com; "Fred 1827-1898").
68. From baptismal record and 1851 Census.
69. England & Wales, Non-Conformist and Non-Parochial Registers, 1567-1936, Registers of Births, Marriages and Deaths Surrendered to the Non-Parochial Registers Commissions of 1837 and 1857. Class: RG 4; Piece: 3409; (ancestry.com image 103). "Frederic Son of Abagail Clay of Brookhouse in Ovenden."
70. England Births and Christenings, 1538-1975, (https://www.familysearch.org/ark:/61903/1:1:JQ1B-XJQ : 3 February 2023), Abagail Clay in entry for Fredric Clay, 1827.
71. Death record not found. Tombstone says 1898.

72. Find-A-Grave, (www.findagrave.com/memorial/16917854/fred-clay: accessed 27 July 2022); Memorial ID 16917854, citing Griffith Cemetery, Springport, Jackson County, Michigan; maintained by Deb Hayes-Wolfe (contributor 46811474).

73. 1841 Census of England and Wales, Halifax, West Riding, Yorkshire, 6 June 1841, "Worsted Weaver."

74. 1851 Census of England and Wales, Ovenden, Yorkshire, England, 30 March 1851, "Power Loom Weaver Worsted."

75. 1860 US Census, Eaton Rapids, Eaton County, Michigan, June 1860, "Laborer."

76. 1870 US Census, Eaton Rapids, Eaton County, Michigan, June 1870, "Farmer."

77. 1880 US Census, Hamlin Township, Eaton County, Michigan, June 1880, "Weaver."

78. New York, U.S., Arriving Passenger and Crew Lists (including Castle Garden and Ellis Island), 1820-1957, NARA, Washington, District of Columbia, www.ancestry.com, Microfilm Serial M237, 1820-1897; Lines 10-13; List Number 1330.

79. 1851 Census of England and Wales, Wortley Township, Leeds, Yorkshire, 30 March 1851, Class HO107; Piece 2314; Folio 287; Page 43; GSU roll 87532-87533. "Ann Robertshaw."

80. 1860 US Census, Eaton Rapids, Eaton County, Michigan, June 1860, NARA M653; Roll 542; Page 527; Dwelling 226; Family 210; Line 26; "Ann Clay."

81. 1870 US Census, Eaton Rapids, Eaton County, Michigan, June 1870, NARA M593; Roll 670; Page 208A; Dwelling 347; Family 347; Line 29; "Ann Clay."

82. 1880 US Census, Hamlin Township, Eaton County, Michigan, June 1880, NARA T9; Roll 578; Page: 322C; ED 78; Dwelling 110; Family 117; Line 12; "Ann Clay."

83. Tombstone. (See findagrave.com; "Ann 1829-1891").

84. West Yorkshire Archive Service, West Yorkshire, England, Church of England Marriages and Banns, 1813-1935, Reference Number: WD-P53/1/3/50; Page 39, number 77. (ancestry.com image 208).
"Frederick Clay his X Mark"
"Ann Robertshaw her X Mark"

85. England & Wales, Civil Registration Marriage Index, 1837-2005, 3rd Quarter; Volume 9a; Page 407; (ancestry.com image 64).

86. Date from notation on side of baptismal record.

87. England, Select Births and Christenings, 1538-1975, https://familysearch.org/ark:/61903/1:1:J3F8-85M : 19 September 2020), John Robertshaw in entry for Anne Robertshaw, 1828.

88. West Yorkshire Archive Service, West Yorkshire, England, Church of England Births and Baptisms, 1813-1910, New Reference Number: RDP111/1/1A; Number 1225, page 154. (ancestry.com image 4).

89. Eaton County, Michigan; number 225, page 247. Died from pnemonia; "62 years, 1 month, 21 days," [6 December 1828], Parents: Jonathan Robertshaw | Dolly Robertshaw"

90. Find-A-Grave, (www.findagrave.com/memorial/16917856/ann-clay: accessed 27 July 2022); Memorial ID 16917856, citing Griffith Cemetery, Springport, Jackson County, Michigan; maintained by Deb Hayes-Wolfe (contributor 46811474).

91. 1851 Census of England and Wales, Wortley Township, Leeds, Yorkshire, 30 March 1851, "Linen Weaver."

92. Family Bible. (Observed by Curt Sanders, 1970s.).

93. 1841 England and Wales Census, Brock Holes, Upper, Ovenden, Yorkshire, England, 6 June 1841, Class: HO107; Piece: 1302; Book: 7; Civil Parish: Halifax; County: Yorkshire; ED 24; Folio 41; Page 6; Line 11; GSU roll: 464262; "Hannah Clay" (ancestry.com image 4).
94. 1851 Census of England and Wales, Ovenden, Yorkshire-West Riding, 30 March 1851, "94 Rocks," Class: HO107; Piece: 2301; Folio 337; Page 25; GSU roll 87509; (ancestry.com image 26); "Hannah Clay."
95. 1871 Census of England and Wales, Hipperholme With Brighouse, Yorkshire, 2 April 1871, Class: RG10; Piece 4384; Folio 77; Page 20; GSU roll 848091; Schedule 104; Lightcliffe street; "Hannah Pickles."
96. 1880 US Census, Hamlin Township, Eaton County, Michigan, June 1880, NARA T9; Roll 578; ED 78; Page 15/324; Dwelling 157; Family 171; Line 39; "Hanah Pickle."
97. 1900 US Census, Jackson City, Jackson County, Michigan, June 1900, NARA T623; Roll 719; ED 19; Ward 8; Sheet 1A; Page 58; W. Water Lou Street; House 634; Dwelling 4; Family 4; Line 21; "Hannah Pickles."
98. 1910 US Census, Douglass Township, Montcalm County, Michigan, April 1910, NARA T624; Roll 665; ED 149; Sheet 3A; Page 131; Dwelling 36; Family 37; Line 2; "Hannah Pickles."
99. 1920 US Census, Douglass Township, Montcalm County, Michigan, January 1920, NARA T625; Roll 787; Sheet 4A; ED 113; Line 50; Dwelling 90; Family 90; Page 102; "Hannah Pickles" (living alone).
100. Tombstone. (See findagrave.com) "Hannah Pickles | 1838-1927".
101. Birth Certificate/Record. First Quarter 1838; Page 253; Volume 22; #203. GRO, registered 11 February 1838.
102. Birth record says 30th; death records says she was born 31st January 1838.
103. England & Wales Civil Registration Indexes, 1837-1915, (ancestry.com), GRO, London, database with image, Birth: First Quarter 1838; Volume 22, Page 253.
104. Michigan Death Certificates, 1921-1952, database, Michigan Division for Vital Records and Health Statistics, Lansing, familysearch.org, Belding, Ionia, Michigan, Division for Vital Records and Health Statistics, Lansing.
105. Death Certificate/Record. State of Michigan, Michigan Department Of Health, Division of Vital Statistics, Certificate Of Death, file 134 326.
106. Find-A-Grave, (www.findagrave.com/memorial/27326986/hanna-pickles : accessed 25 May 2022). Memorial ID 27326986, citing Hillside Entrican Cemetery, Entrican, Montcalm County, Michigan; maintained by Gail (contributor 47136090). Tombstone: "Hannah Pickles | 1838-1927"; visited by the author in the 1980s and earlier.
107. 1851 Census of England and Wales, Ovenden, Yorkshire-West Riding, 30 March 1851, "Nurse."
108. 1871 Census of England and Wales, Halifax, Yorkshire, 2 April 1871, "Farmers Wife."
109. Family Bible (observed in the 1970s).
110. 1851 Census of England and Wales, Green Lane, Ovenden Township, Yorkshire, 30 March 1851, Series: HO107, Line: 16, Illingworth Moor Green Lane, Piece/Folio: 2301/347; Page: 4, Ecclesiastical district: St Johns, Family: 13. "James Pickles."
111. 1861 Census of England and Wales, Luddenden (Halifax), Warley, District 6, Yorkshire, 7 April 1861, Page 26; RG 9; Piece/Folio: 3295/80; GSU roll 543109; Schedule 108; (www.familysearch.org/ark:/61903/1:1:M7ZG-NTZ : 3 March 2021); "James Pickles."

112. 1871 Census of England and Wales, Hipperholme With Brighouse, Yorkshire, 2 April 1871, Class: RG10; Piece 4384; Folio 77; Page 20; GSU roll 848091; Schedule 104; Lightcliffe street; "James Pickles."

113. 1880 US Census, Hamlin Township, Eaton County, Michigan, June 1880, NARA T9; Roll 578; ED 78; Page 15/324; Dwelling 157; Family 171; Line 38; "James Pickle."

114. 1900 US Census, Jackson City, Jackson County, Michigan, June 1900, NARA T623; Roll 719; ED 19; Ward 8; Sheet 1A; Page 58; House 634; W. Water Loo Street; Dwelling 4; Family 4; Line 20; "James Pickles."

115. 1910 US Census, Douglass Township, Montcalm County, Michigan, April 1910, NARA T624; Roll 665; ED 149; Sheet 3A; Page 131; Dwelling 36; Family 37; Line 1; "James Pickles."

116. Tombstone. (See findagrave.com); "At Rest | James Pickles, | Born May 31, 1843, | Died Feb. 8, 1911, | Aged 67 yrs. 8 ms. 8 days."

117. Marriage Certificate/Record/Application. #62, County York, England (original in possession of Curtis Daryl Sanders - gggrandson).

118. England & Wales, Civil Registration Marriage Index, 1837-2005, 1866: Oct-Nov-Dec; (ancestry.com image 9 for James; image 10 for Hannah); Volume 9a; Page 787.

119. Leeds Times, newspaper, Leeds, England, "Miscellaneous," 24 November 1866, page 8. "On Sunday, at South-parade Chapel, Halifax, by the Rev. J. A. Macdonald, Mr. James Pickles, carpet weaver, Warley, to Miss H. Clay, of Halifax."

120. Birth Certificate/Record. Birth record, 1843, Registrar District Luddenden; UK General Registration Office, 3 April 2022. Parents: "John Pickles m | Hannah Pickles formerly Horsfield"; registered 11 July 1843.

121. Baptismal record and tombstone says 31 May 1843; 1900 US Census says May 1838; death record says 1844 and calculates 30 April 1843—inconsistent with its own calculation.

122. England Births and Christenings, 1538-1975, familysearch.org, confirms born 31 May 1843.

123. West Yorkshire Archive Service, West Yorkshire, Church of England Births and Baptisms, 1813-1910, ancestry.com, Born 31 May 1843 to John and Hannah Pickles.

124. Ibid. New Reference Number: WDP39/5; (ancestry.com image 9 and 18).

125. Baptismal Certificate. West Yorkshire Archive Service; Wakefield, Yorkshire; Yorkshire Parish Records; New Reference Number: WDP39/5; Page 211; number 1685; (ancestry.com image 9).

126. England Births and Christenings, 1538-1975, familysearch.org, database, (https://familysearch.org/ark:/61903/1:1:NF3B-DL5 : 21 March 2020), Hannah Pickles in entry for James Pickles, 1843.

127. Michigan Deaths and Burials, 1800-1995, database, familysearch.org, Michigan Deaths and Burial, 1800-1995, v 2 C p 27; (https://familysearch.org/ark:/61903/1:1:FHGZ-KYH).

128. Michigan Death Records Project, Library of Michigan, Lansing, Rolls 1-302; Archive Barcode/Item Number 30000008532784; Roll Number 159; Certificate Number 2.

129. Death Certificate/Record. State Of Michigan, Department of State-Division of Vital Statistics, Certificate Of Death, Register No. 2, 6 March 1911. Mother's name not known; Informant: Mrs. James Pickles [his wife]; number 3723; death by "Bulbar paralysis."

130. Find-A-Grave, www.findagrave.com/memorial/27327015/james-pickles : accessed 23 January 2022). Memorial ID 27327015, citing Hill-

side Entrican Cemetery, Entrican, Montcalm County, Michigan; maintained by Gail (contributor 47136090).
131. 1851 Census of England and Wales, Green Lane, Ovenden Township, Yorkshire, 30 March 1851, "Wool Comber."
132. 1861 Census of England and Wales, Luddenden (Halifax), Warley, District 6, Yorkshire, 7 April 1861, "Worsted Factory hand."
133. 1871 Census of England and Wales, Hipperholme With Brighouse, Yorkshire, 2 April 1871, "Carpet Weaver."
134. 1880 US Census, Hamlin Township, Eaton County, Michigan, June 1880, "Farmer."
135. Polk's Jackson City And County Directory, 1899-1900, Detroit, Michigan: R. L. Polk & Co., Publishers, 1900, Page 396; (ancestry.com image 216); "Pickles James, farmer, bds 916 Chicago."
136. 1900 US Census, Jackson City, Jackson County, Michigan, June 1900, "day Laborer."
137. Jackson City Directory 1903, Detroit, Michigan: R. L. Polk & Co., 1903, Page 448; (ancestry.com image 244); "Pickles James, lab, bds 634 N Waterloo av."
138. 1910 US Census, Douglass Township, Montcalm County, Michigan, April 1910, "farmer | general farm."
139. Huddersfield Chronicle, newspaper, Yorkshire, England, "Perjury At Todmorden," 17 August 1867, page 7.
140. Burnley Gazette, newspaper, Burnley, England, "District News: Burnley-Valley," 17 August 1867, page 3.
141. NARA, Passenger Lists of Vessels Arriving at Boston, Massachusetts, 1820-1891; Record Group Title: Records of the U.S. Customs Service; Record Group Number 36; Series Number M277; NARA Roll Number 082.
142. 1910 US Census, Douglass Township, Montcalm County, Michigan, April 1910; confirms English nativity.
143. Massachusetts, Index to Boston Passenger Lists, 1848-1891. (https://familysearch.org/ark:/61903/1:1:Q2HV-W99S : 16 March 2018), James Pickles, 1872; citing Immigration, ship *Tripoli*, NARA M265; roll M265; (familysearch.org image 2754). .
144. Leeds Times, "Miscellaneous," 24 November 1866, page 8.
145. New York, U.S., Arriving Passenger and Crew Lists (including Castle Garden and Ellis Island), 1820-1957, NARA, (www.ancestry.com), Microfilm Serial: M237, 1820-1897; Line 13; List Number 1330.
146. 1860 US Census, Eaton Rapids, Eaton County, Michigan, June 1860, NARA M653; Roll 542; Page 527; Dwelling 226; Family 210; Line 28; "Simeon Clay."
147. 1870 US Census, Eaton Rapids, Eaton County, Michigan, June 1870, NARA M593; Roll 670; Page 208A; Dwelling 347; Family 347; Line 30; "Simeon Clay."
148. 1880 US Census, Hamlin Township, Eaton County, Michigan, June 1880, NARA T9; Roll 578; Page 327A; ED 78; Dwelling 212; Family 226; Line 1; "Simeon Clay."
149. 1880 US Selected Agricultural Census, Hamlin Township, Eaton County, Michigan, Archive Collection Number T1164; Roll 35; Page: 7; Line 7; ED 78; Schedule Type: Agriculture.
150. 1900 US Census, Eaton Rapids, Eaton County, Michigan, June 1900, NARA T623; Roll 709; Sheet 6A; ED 70; Dwelling 121; Family 121; Line 12; "Simeon A Clay."

151. 1910 US Census, Parma Township, Jackson County, Michigan, April 1910, NARA T624; Roll 653; Sheet 7B; ED 34; Dwelling 163; Family 163; Line 60; "Simeon A Clay."

152. 1920 US Census, Battle Creek, Calhoun County, Michigan, January 1920, NARA T625; Roll 759; Sheet 2A; ED 42; Dwelling 21; Family 41; Line 45; "Simon A. Clay."

153. R. L. Polk & Co.'s Battle Creek City Directory 1921, Detroit, Michigan: R. L. Polk & Co., Publishers, 1921, Page 342; (ancestry.com image 174); "Clay Simeon (Emma), res 21 Frederick."

154. Tombstone. (See findagrave.com); "S. A. Clay."

155. England and Wales Birth Registration Index, 1837-2008, database, familysearch.org and ancestry.com, UK GRO, 3rd Quarter 1852; Page 463, Volume 9A.

156. (see baptismal, death records).

157. Birth Certificate/Record. GRO number 395; Father: Frederick Clay; Mother: Ann Clay formerly Robertshaw; registered 2 September 1852.

158. West Yorkshire Archive Service, West Yorkshire, Church of England Births and Baptisms, 1813-1910, page 210. Yorkshire Parish Records; New Reference Number: WDP73/1/2/2; page 210; number 1679; D73/5; (ancestry.com image 1) "Simeon Clay."

159. Michigan Death Certificates, 1921-1952, Michigan Division for Vital Records and Health Statistics, Lansing, familysearch.org, (https://familysearch.org/ark:/61903/1:1:KF3W-572 : 13 March 2018).

160. Death Certificate/Record. Michigan Department of Community Health, Division for Vital Records and Health Statistics; Lansing; Certificate of Death; File 38 2919, "Simeon A. Clay" (widowed at death).

161. Jackson Citizen Patriot, newspaper, Jackson, Michigan, "Legals. | State of Michigan—Probate Court for the County of Jackson, 21st Day of December, A. D. 1929, "Simeon A. Clay, deceased," Administration of estate granted to Mabel Zantop (daughter); 2 January 1930, page 15.

162. Find-A-Grave, (www.findagrave.com/memorial/19540590/simeon-a-clay: accessed 28 July 2022). Memorial ID 19540590, citing Chapel Cemetery, Sandstone, Jackson County, Michigan; maintained by Deb Hayes-Wolfe (contributor 46811474).

163. 1880 US Selected Agricultural Census, Hamlin Township, Eaton County, Michigan, "Farmer" [implied].

164. 1900 US Census, Eaton Rapids, Eaton County, Michigan, June 1900, "Farmer."

165. 1910 US Census, Parma Township, Jackson County, Michigan, April 1910, "Farmer | quit farmer."

166. 1920 US Census, Battle Creek, Calhoun County, Michigan, January 1920, "[illegible] foreman assist | Thrashing Machine Co."

167. 1900 US Census, Eaton Rapids, Eaton County, Michigan, June 1900, Naturalized citizen.

168. 1880 US Census, Hamlin Township, Eaton County, Michigan, June 1880, NARA T9; Roll 578; Page 327A; ED 78; Dwelling 212; Family 226; Line 2; "Ann L Clay."

169. 1900 US Census, Eaton Rapids, Eaton County, Michigan, June 1900, NARA T623; Roll 709; Sheet 6A; ED 70; Dwelling 121; Family 121; Line 13; "Lydia A Clay."

170. 1910 US Census, Parma Township, Jackson County, Michigan, April 1910, NARA T624; Roll 653; Sheet 7B; ED 34; Dwelling 163; Family 163; Line 61; "Lydia A Clay."

171. Tombstone. (See findagrave.com); "Lydia A. wife of S. A. Clay".

172. (estimated from 1900 census).

173. (from death record).
174. Death Certificate/Record. State Of Michigan, Department of State-Division of Vital Statistics; Certificate Of Death, File 1047.
175. Find-A-Grave, (www.findagrave.com/memorial/14321321/lydia-ann-clay: accessed 28 July 2022). Memorial ID 14321321, citing Chapel Cemetery, Sandstone, Jackson County, Michigan; maintained by Frank Passic, Albion Historian (contributor 46564182).
176. The State Journal, 3 January 1918, page 7.
177. Jackson Sunday Patriot, "Eaton Rapids." 6 January 1918, page 3.
178. The Patriot, newspaper, Jackson, Michigan, "Obituary: Mrs. S. A. Clay." 22 December 1917, page 10.
179. 1920 US Census, Battle Creek, Calhoun County, Michigan, January 1920, NARA T625; Roll 759; Sheet 2A; ED 42; Dwelling 21; Family 41; Line 46. "Emma E Clay."
180. Tombstone. (See findagrave.com).
181. Marriage record/certificate/application. Number 868; Calhoun County, Michigan.
182. Death Certificate/Record. Michigan Department Of Health, Bureau of Records and Statistics, Certificate Of Death, State 13 9226, Local 106. "Emma E. Thunder" Mrs. D. L. Parshall [daughter] was informant.
183. Find-A-Grave, (www.findagrave.com/memorial/15837631/emma-e-thunder: accessed 08 November 2022). Memorial ID 15837631, citing Oak Hill Cemetery, Battle Creek, Calhoun County, Michigan; maintained by Nina (contributor 48820459).
184. Divorce Record. Michigan Department of Community Health, Division for Vital Records and Health Statistics; Lansing. Records 17, 145; granted, absolute. (ancestry.com image 545).
185. Battle Creek Enquirer And News, newspaper, Battle Creek, Michigan, "Deaths: Mrs. John J. Thunder," 12 December 1944, page 3.
186. Marriage record/certificate/application. Jackson County, Michigan; number 44; "S. A. Clay" and "Mary Lewis" (https://familysearch.org/ark:/61903/1:1:NQ99-3QF : 18 February 2021).
187. Tombstone. (see findagrave.com).
188. Birth Certificate/Record. Number 747; registered 1 November 1854; GRO, D quarter, Volume 9B, page 20.
189. England & Wales, Civil Registration Birth Index, 1837-1915, GRO. England and Wales Civil Registration Indexes, London, database with scanned image, (ancestry.com), 1854 Bradford, page 20, volume 9B; 4th Quarter.
190. 1880 US Census, Hamlin Township, Eaton County, Michigan, June 1880, Roll: 578; Page: 324C/15; ED 78; Dwelling 159; Family 173; Line 47; "John Clay" born in England.
191. (see Baptismal record).
192. England & Wales Civil Registration Indexes, 1837-1915, ancestry.com, GRO, 4th Quarter, Volume 9a, Page 361.
193. West Yorkshire Archive Service, West Yorkshire, Church of England Births and Baptisms, 1813-1910, page 210. Yorkshire Parish Records; New Reference Number: WDP73/1/2/2; page 210; number 1680; D73/5; (ancestry.com image 1) "Wright Clay."
194. Death Certificate/Record. GRO, number 439, "Wright Clay 11 months" Father: "Frederick Clay a Laborer"; Cause: "Dropsy"; Informant: "Ann Clay present at death"; registered 3 September 1857.
195. England & Wales, Civil Registration Death Index, 1837-1915, GRO. England and Wales Civil Registration Indexes, London, database with

image, (ancestry.com), Halifax, 1857, 3rd Quarter, 1857, Volume 9a, page 244.

196. 1860 US Census, Eaton Rapids, Eaton County, Michigan, June 1860, NARA M653; Roll 542; Page 527; Dwelling 226; Family 210; Line 29; "Thomas A. Clay."

197. 1870 US Census, Eaton Rapids, Eaton County, Michigan, June 1870, NARA M593; Roll 670; Page 208A; Dwelling 347; Family 347; Line 31; "Thomas Clay."

198. 1880 US Census, Hamlin Township, Eaton County, Michigan, June 1880, NARA T9; Roll 578; Sheet 9; ED 78; Page 321A; Dwelling 92; Family 100; Line 44. In the household of David How; "Thomas A Clay."

199. 1900 US Census, Springport Township, Jackson County, Michigan, June 1900, NARA T623; Roll 719; ED 30; Sheet 3B; Dwelling 81; Family 81; Line 54; "Thomas A. Clay."

200. 1910 US Census, Springport Township, Jackson County, Michigan, April 1910, NARA T624; Roll 653; Sheet 9B; ED 39; Grand Street; Dwelling 30, Family 30; Line 94; "Thomas A. Clay."

201. 1920 US Census, Friendship Township, Emmet County, Michigan, January 1920, NARA T625; Roll 763; ED 159; Sheet 5B; Dwelling 112; Family 112; Line 86; "Thomas A Clay."

202. Death Certificate/Record. Michigan Department of Community Health, Division for Vital Records and Health Statistics; Lansing. Register 6; "Thomas A. Clay."

203. Find-A-Grave, (www.findagrave.com/memorial/8804603/thomas-a-clay: accessed 9 June 2023). Memorial ID 8804603, citing Friendship Township Cemetery, Harbor Springs, Emmet County, Michigan; maintained by Nicole La Faive (contributor 17167635).

204. 1880 US Census, Hamlin Township, Eaton County, Michigan, June 1880, "Servant."

205. Jackson City and County Directory 1888, Volume 10, Detroit, Michigan: R. L. Polk & Co., Publishers, 1888, Page 399 (ancestry.com image 196); "Clay Thomas, plumber, Springport, Springport."

206. 1900 US Census, Springport Township, Jackson County, Michigan, June 1900, "Carpenter house."

207. 1910 US Census, Springport Township, Jackson County, Michigan, April 1910, "Carpenter House."

208. 1920 US Census, Friendship Township, Emmet County, Michigan, January 1920, "Farmer | General Farm."

209. The State Journal, "City In Brief," 22 August 1921, page 2.

210. 1900 US Census, Springport Township, Jackson County, Michigan, June 1900, NARA T623; Roll 719; ED 30; Sheet 3B; Dwelling 81; Family 81; Line 55; "Jennie S. Clay."

211. 1910 US Census, Springport Township, Jackson County, Michigan, April 1910, NARA T624; Roll 653; Sheet 9B; ED 39; Grand Street; Dwelling 30, Family 30; Line 95; "Jennie S Clay."

212. Tombstone. (See findagrave.com); "Jennie Doak wife of Thomas Clay 1852-1915."

213. Marriage record/certificate/application. Jackson County, Michigan; Page 66; Number 327.

214. Death Certificate/Record. State Of Michigan, Department of State-Division of Vital Statistics, Certificate Of Death; 329; "Jennie S Clay."

215. Find-A-Grave, (www.findagrave.com/memorial/22898711/jennie-clay: accessed 26 September 2022). Memorial ID 22898711, citing Springport Cemetery, Springport, Jackson County, Michigan; maintained by Deb Hayes-Wolfe (contributor 46811474).

216. Jackson City And County Directory 1894-95, Detroit, Michigan: R. L. Polk & Co., Publishers, 1894, Volume XIV, Page 467 (ancestry.com image 231); "Clay, Jennie, f, 17, 18, $1050, Springport, Springport."

217. 1920 US Census, Friendship Township, Emmet County, Michigan, January 1920, NARA T625; Roll 763; ED 159; Sheet 5B; Dwelling 112; Family 112; Line 87; "Cora E. Clay."

218. Marriage record/certificate/application. Michigan Department of Community Health, Division of Vital Records and Health Statistics; Marriage Records, 1867-1952; Film 127; Film Description: 1915 Wayne-1916 Genesee; record 7.

219. Death Certificate/Record. Michigan Department Of Health, Bureau of Records and Statistics, Certificate of Death, Local 6; State 30 6115.

220. Find-A-Grave, (www.findagrave.com/memorial/191615538/cora-elizabeth-cousins: accessed 26 September 2022). Memorial ID 191615538, citing East Hill Cemetery, Osseo, Hillsdale County, Michigan; maintained by Lori Zeiler (contributor 48040750).

221. 1870 US Census, Eaton Rapids, Eaton County, Michigan, June 1870, NARA M593; Roll 670; Page 208A; Dwelling 347; Family 347; Line 32; "Cornelius Clay."

222. 1880 US Census, Hamlin Township, Eaton County, Michigan, June 1880, NARA T9; Roll 578; Sheet 9; ED 78; Page 321A; Dwelling 92; Family 100; Line 33. In the household of Frank Brown; "Cashius Clay."

223. 1900 US Census, Springport Township, Jackson County, Michigan, June 1900, NARA T623; Roll 719; Sheet 4B; ED 30; Dwelling 111; Family 111; Line 58; "Cassius Clay."

224. 1910 US Census, Lansing, Ingham County, Michigan, April 1910, NARA T624; Roll 651; Sheet 6A; ED 66; Ward 3; Dwelling 113; Family 115; Line 29; "Cassius M Clay."

225. 1920 US Census, Lansing, Ingham County, Michigan, January 1920, NARA T625; Roll 771; Sheet 19A; ED 95; Ward 3; House 521; Dwelling 371; Family 404; Line 36; "Cassius Clay."

226. 1930 US Census, Lansing, Ingham County, Michigan, April 1930, NARA T626; Sheet 14B; ED 33-20; 3rd Precinct; 3rd Ward; House 521; Dwelling 267; Family 366; Line 74; "Cassius M. Clay."

227. Lansing And East Lansing City Directory 1938, Volume XXXVII, Lansing, Michigan: Lansing Directory Publishers, Inc., 1938, Page 108 (ancestry.com image 58); "Clay Cassius M (Ella) h 521 William."

228. Lansing And East Lansing City [Michigan] Directory 1939, Volume XXXVIII, Lansing, Michigan: Lansing Directory Publishers, Inc., 1939, Page 107 (ancestry.com image 56); "Clay Cassius M (Ella) h521 William."

229. Death Certificate/Record. Michigan Department Of Health, Bureau of Records and Statistics, Certificate Of Death, File 13314859.

230. Find-A-Grave, (www.findagrave.com/memorial/21504198/cassius-m-clay: accessed 05 October 2022). Memorial ID 21504198, citing Mount Hope Cemetery, Lansing, Ingham County, Michigan; maintained by Ed Houghtaling (contributor 46804583). "Cassius M Clay | 1861-1939."

231. 1900 US Census, Springport Township, Jackson County, Michigan, June 1900, "Day Laborer."

232. R. L. Polk & Co.'s Benton Harbor, St. Joseph, Niles and Berrien County Directory 1907-1908, Volume III, Detroit: R. L. Polk &Co., Publishers, 1907, Page 68 (ancestry.com image 40); "Clay Cassius M, farmer, res e s Cornelia, 3 s of Main."

233. 1910 US Census, Lansing, Ingham County, Michigan, April 1910, "Machinist | Olds Automobile."

234. Lansing City [Michigan] Directory 1916, Volume XVI, Lansing, Michigan: Chilson, McKinley & Co. Publishers, 1916, Page 249 (ancestry.com image 136); "Clay Cassius M (Ella), wks Reo M C Co, res 521 William."

235. Lansing City [Michigan] Directory 1919, Lansing, Michigan: Chilson McKinley & Co. Publishers, 1919, Page 284 (ancestry.com image 151); "Clay Cassius M (Ella), wks Reo, H 521 William."

236. 1920 US Census, Lansing, Ingham County, Michigan, January 1920, "Welfare Worker"

237. Lansing City [Michigan] Directory 1921, Volume XXI, Lansing, Michigan: Chilson McKinley & Co. Publishers, 1921, Page 310 (ancestry.com image 188); "Clay Cassius M (Ella), wks Reo, h 521 William."

238. Lansing City Directory [Michigan] 1922, Volume XXII, Lansing, Michigan: Chilson-McKinley Co., Publishers, 1922, Page 628 (ancestry.com image 192); "Clay Cassius M (Ella), wks Reo, h 521 William."

239. Lansing City [Michigan] Directory 1923, Lansing, Michigan: Chilson, McKinley & Co. Publishers, 1923, Page 353 (ancestry.com image 197); "Clay Cassius M (Ella), wks Reo, h 521 William."

240. Lansing City [Michigan] Directory 1924, Volume XXIV, Lansing, Michigan: McKinley-Reynolds Co. Publishers, 1924, Page 367 (ancestry.com image 213); "Clay Cassius M (Ella), wks Reo, h 521 William."

241. Lansing City [Michigan] Directory 1925, Volume XXV, Lansing, Michigan: McKinley-Reynolds Co. Publishers, 1925, Page 261 (ancestry.com image 158); "Clay Cassius M (Ella) wks Reo h521 William."

242. Lansing and East Lansing City [Michigan] Directory 1927, Volume XXVII, Lansing, Michigan: McKinley-Reynolds Company, Inc. Publishers, 1927, Page 281 (ancestry.com image 163); "Clay Cassius M (Ella) wks Reo h521 William."

243. Classified Buyers's Guide of Lansing and East Lansing [Michigan] 1929, Lansing, Michigan: McKinley-Reynolds Company, Inc., Publishers, 1929, Page 187 (ancestry.com image 99); "Clay Cassius M (Ella) wks Reo, h521 William."

244. 1930 US Census, Lansing, Ingham County, Michigan, April 1930, "Safety man | auto factory."

245. Classified Buyers' Guide of Lansing and East Lansing [Michigan] 1930, Lansing, Michigan: McKinley-Reynolds Company, Inc., Publishers, 1930, Page 167 (ancestry.com image 93); "Clay Cassius M (Ella) wks Reo h521 William."

246. Classified Buyers' Guide of Lansing and East Lansing [Michigan] 1931, Lansing, Michigan: McKinley-Reynolds Company, Inc., Publishers, 1931, Page 137 (ancestry.com image 76); "Clay Cassius M (Ella) wks Reo h521 William."

247. Classified Buyers' Guide of Lansing and East Lansing [Michigan] 1932, Lansing, Michigan: McKinley-Reynolds Company, Inc. Publishers, 1932, Page 110 (ancestry.com image 68); "Clay Cassius M (Ella) wks Reo h521 William."

248. Classified Buyers' Guide of Lansing and East Lansing [Michigan] 1934-5, Lansing, Michigan: McKinley-Reynolds Company, Inc., 1934, Page 115 (ancestry.com image 64); "Clay Cassius M (Ella) wks PWA h521 William."

249. The State Journal, "Deaths: Cassius M. Clay," 14 October 1939, page 5.

250. 1900 US Census, Springport Township, Jackson County, Michigan, June 1900, NARA T623; Roll 719; Sheet 4B; ED 30; Dwelling 111; Family 111; Line 59; "Ella Clay."

251. 1910 US Census, Lansing, Ingham County, Michigan, April 1910, NARA T624; Roll 651; Sheet 6A; ED 66; Ward 3; Dwelling 113; Family 115; Line 30; "Ella Clay."

252. 1920 US Census, Lansing, Ingham County, Michigan, January 1920, NARA T625; Roll 771; Sheet 19A; ED 95; Ward 3; House 521; Dwelling 371; Family 404; Line 37; "Ella Clay."

253. 1930 US Census, Lansing, Ingham County, Michigan, April 1930, NARA T626; Sheet 14B; ED 33-20; 3rd Precinct; 3rd Ward; House 521; Dwelling 267; Family 366; Line 75; "Ella Clay."

254. 1940 US Census, Lansing, Ingham County, Michigan, April 1940, NARA T627; ED 33-32; Sheet 17B; Line 50; "Ella Clay."

255. Lansing And East Lansing [Michigan] City Directory 1940, Lansing, Michigan: Lansing Directory Publishers, Inc., 1940, Page 110; (ancestry.-com image 59); "Clay Ella (wid Cassius M) h521 William."

256. Lansing And East Lansing [Michigan] City Directory 1941, Lansing, Michigan: Lansing Directory Publishers, Inc., 1941, Page 113; (ancestry.-com image 59); "Clay Ella (wid Cassius M) h521 William."

257. Polk's Lansing (Ingham County, Mich.) City Directory 1945, Volume XLI, Detroit: R. L. Polk & Co., Publishers, 1945, Page 140; (ancestry.com image 74); "Clay Ella Mrs h521 William."

258. Polk's Lansing (Ingham County, Mich.) City Directory 1946 Including East Lansing, Volume XLII, Detroit: R. L. Polk & Co., Publishers, 1946, Page 144; (ancestry.com image 71); "Clay Ella (wid Cassius M) h521 William."

259. Lansing And East Lansing [Michigan] City Directory 1949, Lansing, Michigan: Lansing Directory Publishers, Inc., 1949, Page 157; (ancestry.-com image 79); "Clay Ella (wid Cassius M) h521 William."

260. Marriage record/certificate/application. Michigan Department of Community Health, Division of Vital Records and Health Statistics; Lansing; Marriage Records, 1867-1952; Film 35; Film Description: 1887 Shiawasee-1888 Genesee; number 204.

261. Find-A-Grave, (www.findagrave.com/memorial/21504225/ella-clay: accessed 5 October 2022). Memorial ID 21504225, citing Mount Hope Cemetery, Lansing, Ingham County, Michigan; maintained by Ed Houghtaling (contributor 46804583); ""Ella Shutt Clay | 1865-1953."

262. The State Journal, "Deaths: Mrs. Ella Clay," 16 May 1953, page 2; "Funerals: Clay, Mrs. Ella: Birmingham, Mich.," 18 May 1953, page 18.

263. Tombstone. (See findagrave.com; engraved on father and mother's stone, plus a separate stone); "Clay | Julia A. 1862-1866."

264. Find-A-Grave, (www.findagrave.com/memorial/16917862/julia-a-clay: accessed 27 July 2022). Memorial ID 16917862, citing Griffith Cemetery, Springport, Jackson County, Michigan; maintained by Deb Hayes-Wolfe (contributor 46811474).

265. 1870 US Census, Eaton Rapids, Eaton County, Michigan, June 1870, NARA M593; Roll 670; Page 208A; Dwelling 347; Family 347; Line 33; "Frank Clay."

266. 1880 US Census, Hamlin Township, Eaton County, Michigan, June 1880, NARA T9; Roll 578; Page: 322C; ED 78; Dwelling 110; Family 117; Line 13; "Frank H Clay" at school.

267. Glen V. Mills' Ann Arbor-Ypsilanti [Michigan] Directory 1899, Ann Arbor, Michigan: Glen V. Mills, Publisher, 1899, Page 304 (ancestry.com image 191); "Clay Frank H (Cora E), (Webster, Cobb & Co), res 202 Parsons (Mich office 39, res 27, New State 131)."

268. 1900 US Census, Springport Township, Jackson County, Michigan, June 1900, NARA T623; Roll 719; Sheet 5; ED 30; Dwelling 148; Family 148;

Line 85. "Frank H. Clay" Residing in the house of his in-laws, Thomas Rodgers.

269. 1910 US Census, Kalamazoo, Kalamazoo County, Michigan, April 1910, NARA T624; Roll 654; Sheet 16A; ED 147; Ward 4; House 706; Visited 337; Family 364; Line 17; "Frank H Clay."

270. 1920 US Census, Kalamazoo, Kalamazo County, Michigan, January 1920, NARA T625; Roll 775; Sheet 8A; ED 165; Ward 3; House 447; Dwelling 124; Visited 121; Line 40; "Frank H Clay."

271. 1930 US Census, Kalamazoo Township, Kalamazoo County, Michigan, April 1930, NARA T626; Page 159; Sheet 22A; ED 39-27; Ward 3; House 508; Dwelling 520; Family 621; Line 36; "Frank H. Clay."

272. 1940 US Census, Kalamazoo, Kalamazoo County, Michigan, April 1940, NARA T627; Roll 1771; Sheet 5B; ED 39-32; House 508; Line 64. "Frank H Clay" [the census taker assumed he was born in New York].

273. US Social Security Applications and Claims Index, 1936-2007, (Social Security Numerical Identification Files-NUMIDENT), database, www.ancestry.com or www.familysearch.org, Claim Date: 7 August 1940; Notes: 19 Aug 1977: Name listed as FRANK H CLAY.

274. Tombstone. (See findagrave.com; "Frank H. Clay 1865-1944.")

275. [per death record]

276. Michigan Deaths and Burials, 1800-1995, Michigan Deaths and Burial, 1800-1995, (https://familysearch.org/ark:/61903/1:1:FHHF-59G : 23 February 2021).

277. Death Certificate/Record. Michigan Department of Health, Bureau of Records and Statistics; Lansing; Certificate Of Death number 239 4237.

278. Find-A-Grave, (www.findagrave.com/memorial/22902573/frank-h-clay: accessed 28 September 2022). Memorial ID 22902573, citing Springport Cemetery, Springport, Jackson County, Michigan; maintained by Deb Hayes-Wolfe (contributor 46811474).

279. Jackson City And County Directory for 1887, Volume IX, Detroit, Michigan: R. L. Polk & Co., 1887, Page 97 (ancestry.com image 47); "Clay Frank H, traveler Jackson Cracker Co, bds Commercial hotel."

280. Battle Creek, Albion, Marshall, and Calhoun County [Michigan] Directory 1897-98, Detroit, Michigan: R. L. Polk & Co., Publishers, 1897, Page 358 (ancestry.com image 178); "Clay Frank H, trav agt, h 409 Clinton S."

281. 1900 US Census, Springport Township, Jackson County, Michigan, June 1900, "Salesman farm."

282. Glen V. Mills' Ypsilanti City Directory 1901, Ypsilanti, Michigan: Glen V. Mills Publisher, 1901, Page 57 (ancestry.com image 35); "Clay Frank H, removed to Albion."

283. 1910 US Census, Kalamazoo, Kalamazoo County, Michigan, April 1910, "Commercial Traveler | Buggies."

284. R. L. Polk & Co.'s 1911 Grand Rapids City Directory, Grand Rapids, Michigan: The Grand Rapids Directory Company, 1911, Page 376 (ancestry.com image 191); "Clay Frank H (Ethel R), trav agt, res 706 S Rose."

285. R. L. Polk & Co.'s 1910 Kalamazoo [Michigan] City Directory, Detroit, Michigan: R. L. Polk & Co., Compilers and Publishers, 1910, Page 365 (ancestry.com image 184); "Clay Frank H (Ethel R), trav agt, res 706 S Rose."

286. Polk's 1913 Kalamazoo [Michigan] City Directory, Detroit, Michigan: R. L. Polk & Co., 1913, Page 342 (ancestry.com image 176); "Clay Frank H (Ethel) trav agt, res 706 S Rose."

287. Polk's 1914 Kalamazoo [Michigan] City and County Directory, Detroit, Michigan: R. L. Polk & Co., 1914, Page 356 (ancestry.com image 180); "Clay Frank H (Ethel), trav, res 706 S Rose."

288. Polk's 1915 Kalamazoo [Michigan] City Directory, Detroit, Michigan: R. L. Polk & Co., 1915, Page 350 (ancestry.com image 173); "Clay Frank H (Ethel), sec and treas Harda Research Co, res 706 S Rose."

289. R. L. Polk & Co.'s Kalamazoo [Michigan] City and County Directory 1916, Kalamazoo, Michigan: R. L. Polk & Co., Publishers, 1916, Page 344 (ancestry.com image 175); "Clay Frank H (Ethel), sec and treas Harcla Research Co, see Kazoo Komfort Kushion Co, res 760 S Rose."

290. R. L. Polk & Co.'s Kalamazoo [Michigan] City Directory 1917, Detroit, Michigan: R. L. Polk & Co., Publishers, 1917, Page 372 (189); "Clay Frank H (Ethel), Mnfr and Distributor of Auto Ignition, Propr of Kalamazoo Specialty Co, Sec Harcla Research Co, See Kazoo Komfort Kushion Co, Mngr Kazoo Go-Bang Co, Propr Chemical Research Co, 215 N Rose, Tel 2180, res 706 S Rose."

291. R. L. Polk & Co.'s Kalamazoo City And County Directory 1919, Detroit, Michigan: R. L. Polk & Co., Publishers, 1919, Page 360 (ancestry.com image 175); "Clay Frank H (Ethel), prop Harcla Research Co, Kalamazoo Specialty Co, Kazoo Go-Bang Co and Chemical Research Co, res 447 W Walnut."

292. 1920 US Census, Kalamazoo, Kalamazo County, Michigan, January 1920, "Wholesale Dealer | auto supplies."

293. R. L. Polk & Co.'s Kalamazoo [Michigan] City Directory 1921, Detroit, Michigan: R. L. Polk & Co., Publishers, 1921, Page 442 (ancestry.com image 225); "Clay Frank H (Ethel), prop Harcla Research Co, Kalamazoo Specialty Co, Chemical Research Co., auto accessory mfr 215 N Rose, res 447 W Walnut."

294. Polk's Kalamazoo [Michigan] City Directory 1922, Detroit, Michigan: R. L. Polk & Co., Publishers, 1922, Page 1001 (ancestry.com image 498); "Clay Frank H (whol), 215 N Rose."

295. Polk's Kalamazoo City [Michigan] Directory 1924, Detroit, Michigan: R. L. Polk & Co., Publishers, 1924, Page 382 (ancestry.com image 193); "Clay Frank H (Ethel M) whol auto accessories 215 N Rose h 447 W Walnut."

296. Polk's Kalamazoo [Michigan] City Directory 1926, Detroit, Michigan: R. L. Polk & Co., Publishers, 1926, Page 158 (ancestry.com image 80); "Clay Frank H (Ethel) who auto supplies 233 (215 N Rose h508 Village").

297. Polk's Kalamazoo (Michigan) City Directory, 1927, Detroit, Michigan: R. L. Polk & Co., Publishers, 1927, Page 150 (ancestry.com image 77); "Clay Frank H (Ethel) who auto sup 322 N Rose h508 Village."

298. Polk's Kalamazoo [Michigan] City Directory 1929, Detroit, Michigan: R. L. Polk & Co., Publishers, 1929, Page 150 (ancestry.com image 71); "Clay Frank H Co, Frank H Clay Pres, Harvey A Gridley V-Pres, Ethel Clay Sec-Treas, Wholesale Radio and Accessories 322 N Rose, Tel 2-9335."

299. Ibid. Page 150 (ancestry.com image 71); "Clay Frank H (Ethel R) pres Frank H Clay Co h508 Village."

300. 1930 US Census, Kalamazoo Township, Kalamazoo County, Michigan, April 1930, "Whol merchant | Radios."

301. Polk's Kalamazoo (Michigan) City Directory 1931, Detroit, Michigan: R. L. Polk & Co., Publishers, 1931, Page 122 (ancestry.com image 63); "Clay Frank H (Ethel) pres Frank H Clay Co h508 Village."

302. Ibid. Page 122 (ancestry.com image 63); "Clay Frank H Co, Frank H Clay Pres. Harvey A Gridley V-Pres. Ethel Clay Sec-Treas. Wholesale Radio and Accessories 322 N Rose, Tel 29335."

303. Polk's Kalamazoo (Kalamazoo County, Mich.) City Directory 1934, Detroit, Michigan: R. L. Polk & Co., Publishers, 1934, Page 107 (ancestry.com image 54); "Clay Frank H (Ethel) pres Frank H Clay Co h508 Village."

304. Ibid. Page 107 (ancestry.com image 54); "Clay Frank H Co, Frank H Clay Pres. Harvey A Gridley V-Pres, Ethel Clay Sec-Treas, Wholesale Radio and Electrical Utilities 322 N Rose, Tel 29335."

305. Polk's Kalamazoo (Kalamzoo County, Mich.) City Directory, 1935, Detroit: R. L. Polk & Co., Publishers, 1935, Page 131 (ancestry.com image 68); "Clay Frank H Co, Frank H Clay Pres. Harvey A Gridley V-Pres, Ethel R Clay Sec-Treas, Wholesale Radio and Electrical Utilities 326 W Kalamazoo, Tel 29335."

306. Ibid. Page 131 (ancestry.com image 68); "Clay Frank H (Ethel R) pres Frank H Clay Co h508 Village."

307. Polk's Kalamazoo (Kalamazoo County, Mich.) City Directory 1937, Detroit, Michigan: R. L. Polk & Co., Publishers, 1937, Page 99 (ancestry.com image 48); "Clay Frank H Co (Frank H Clay) whol radio 326 W Kalamazoo av."

308. Polk's Kalamazoo (Kalamazoo County, Mich.) City Directory 1939, Detroit: R. L. Polk & Co., Publishers, 1939, Page 94 (ancestry.com image 45); "Clay Frank H (Ethel) v-pres Frank H Clay Co h508 Village."

309. 1940 US Census, Kalamazoo, Kalamazoo County, Michigan, April 1940, "general work."

310. Polk's Kalamazoo [Michigan] City Directory 1943, Detroit, Michigan: R. L. Polk & Co., 1943, Page 93 (ancestry.com image 234); "Clay Frank H (Ethel) h508 Village."

311. Battle Creek Enquirer And News, "Kalamazoon Mason Dies." 7 March 1944, page 8.

312. Tombstone. (See findagrave.com; "Cora Rodgers wife of Frank H. Clay 1868-1899.")

313. Marriage record/certificate/application. Eaton County, Michigan; page 375, record 63; (familysearch.org image 29).

314. Michigan Deaths and Burials, 1800-1995, (https://familysearch.org/ark:/61903/1:1:FHRD-YPX : 23 February 2021), Cora Rodgers Clay, 1899.

315. Death Certificate/Record. Michigan. Department Of State-Division Of Vital Statistics. Certificate And Record Of Death. Number 37; "Cora Rodgers Clay."

316. Find-A-Grave, (www.findagrave.com/memorial/22903698/cora-clay: accessed 28 September 2022). Memorial ID 22903698, citing Springport Cemetery, Springport, Jackson County, Michigan; maintained by Deb Hayes-Wolfe (contributor 46811474).

317. 1900 US Census, Colorado Springs, El Paso County, Colorado, June 1900, NARA T623; Roll 124; Sheet 13B; Precinct 30; ED 27; Dwelling 207; Line 100; "Ethel C Roberts."

318. 1910 US Census, Kalamazoo, Kalamazoo County, Michigan, April 1910, NARA T624; Roll 654; Sheet 16A; ED 147; Ward 4; House 706; Visited 337; Family 364; Line 18; "Ethel Clay."

319. 1920 US Census, Kalamazoo, Kalamazo County, Michigan, January 1920, NARA T625; Roll 775; Sheet 8A; ED 165; Ward 3; House 447; Dwelling 124; Visited 121; Line 41; "Ethel Clay."

320. 1930 US Census, Kalamazoo Township, Kalamazoo County, Michigan, April 1930, NARA T626; Page 159; Sheet 22A; ED 39-27; Ward 3; House 508; Dwelling 520; Family 621; Line 37; "Ethel Clay."

321. 1940 US Census, Kalamazoo, Kalamazoo County, Michigan, April 1940, NARA T627; Roll 1771; Sheet 5B; ED 39-32; House 508; Line 65; "Edith [sic] Clay."

322. 1950 US Census, Kalamazoo, Kalamazoo County, Michigan, April 1950, Record Group Number 29; Roll 411; Sheet 82; ED 89-43; 508 Village; Line 20; "Ethel Clay" widowed.

323. Polk's Kalamazoo (Kalamazoo County, Mich.) City Directory 1950, Detroit: R. L. Polk & Co., Publishers, 1950, Page 89; (ancestry.com image 61); "Clay Ethel (wid Frank H) h508 Village."

324. US Social Security Applications and Claims Index, 1936-2007, 7 Dec 1983: Name listed as ETHEL ROBERTS CLAY.

325. Tombstone. (See findagrave.com); "Ethel Roberts Wife Of Frank H. Clay 1873-1959."

326. Marriage record/certificate/application. State of Colorado, Division of Vital Statistics Marriage Record Report; El Paso County, Number 1285.

327. Michigan Deaths and Burials, 1800-1995, Michigan Deaths and Burial, 1800-1995, (https:familysearch.org/ark:/61903/1:1:FHQL-TGW : 23 February 2021), Ethel Roberts Clay, 1959.

328. Michigan, U.S., Death Records, 1867-1995, Michigan Department of Vital and Health Records., ancestry.com.

329. Find-A-Grave, (www.findagrave.com/memorial/22902535/ethel-clay: accessed 28 September 2022). Memorial ID 22902535, citing Springport Cemetery, Springport, Jackson County, Michigan; maintained by Deb Hayes-Wolfe (contributor 46811474).

330. 1900 US Census, Colorado Springs, El Paso County, Colorado, June 1900, "Public School Teacher."

331. Polk's Kalamazoo [Michigan] City Directory 1929, Detroit, Michigan: R. L. Polk & Co., Publishers, 1929, Page 150; (ancestry.com image 71); "Clay Ethel Mrs. sec-treas Frank H Clay Co r508 Village."

332. Polk's Kalamazoo (Michigan) City Directory 1931, Detroit, Michigan: R. L. Polk & Co., Publishers, 1931, Page 122; (ancestry.com image 63); "Clay Ethel Mrs sec-treas Frank H Clay Co h508 Village."

333. Polk's Kalamazoo (Kalamazoo County, Mich.) City Directory 1934, Detroit, Michigan: R. L. Polk & Co., Publishers, 1934, Page 107; (ancestry.com image 54); "Clay Ethel Mrs sec-treas Frank H Clay Co h508 Village."

334. Polk's Kalamazoo (Kalamzoo County, Mich.) City Directory, 1935, Detroit: R. L. Polk & Co., Publishers, 1935, Page 131; (ancestry.com image 68); "Clay Frank H (Ethel R) pres Frank H Clay Co h508 Village."

335. Ibid. Page 131; (ancestry.com image 68); "Clay Frank H Co, Frank H Clay Pres. Harvey A Gridley V-Pres, Ethel R Clay Sec-Treas, Wholesale Radio and Electrical Utilities 326 W Kalamazoo, Tel 29335."

336. Polk's Kalamazoo (Kalamazoo County, Mich.) City Directory 1939, Detroit: R. L. Polk & Co., Publishers, 1939, Page 94; (ancestry.com image 45); "Clay Ethel Mrs sec Frank H Clay Co h 508 Village."

337. 1871 Census of England and Wales, Hipperholme With Brighouse, Yorkshire, 2 April 1871, Class: RG10; Piece 4384; Folio 77; Page 20; GSU roll 848091; Schedule 104; Lightcliffe street; "Samuel Pickles."

338. 1880 US Census, Hamlin Township, Eaton County, Michigan, June 1880, NARA T9; Roll 578; ED 78; Page 15/324; Dwelling 157; Family 171; Line 40; "Samuel Pickle."

339. 1900 US Census, Battle Creek, Calhoun County, Michigan, June 1900, NARA T623; ED 34; 3rd Ward; Sheet 17; Page 181A; Dwelling 327; Family 402; Line 46; "Samuel Pickles."
340. 1910 US Census, Grand Rapids, Kent County, Michigan, April 1910, NARA T624; Roll 656; ED 55; Sheet 11A; House 140; Dwelling 167; Family 200; Line 30; "S. James Pickles."
341. 1920 US Census, Wyoming Township, Kent County, Michigan, January 1920, NARA T625; Roll 779; Sheet 12A; ED 118; House 607; Dwelling 242; Family 242; Line 39; "Samuel Pickell Boarder."
342. Tombstone. (see findagrave.com) "Samuel J. Pickles."
343. Birth Certificate/Record. "31 Haigh Street"; UK General Registry Office, number 150; registered 22 May 1869.
344. England and Wales Birth Registration Index, 1837-2008, database, familysearch.org and ancestry.com, GRO, 1869, 2nd Quarter, Halifax, Page 422; Volume 9a.
345. Death Certificate/Record. State Of Michigan, Department of State-Division of Vital Statistics, Transcript Of Certificate Of Death; Registered No. 699; Father: James Pickell; Mother: Anna Clay.
346. Find-A-Grave, (www.findagrave.com/memorial/27327023/samuel-j-pickles : accessed 25 January 2022). Memorial ID 27327023, citing Hillside Entrican Cemetery, Entrican, Montcalm County, Michigan; maintained by Gail (contributor 47136090).
347. 1900 US Census, Battle Creek, Calhoun County, Michigan, June 1900, "Machinist."
348. 1910 US Census, Grand Rapids, Kent County, Michigan, April 1910, "Machinist | Machine Shop."
349. 1920 US Census, Wyoming Township, Kent County, Michigan, January 1920, "Tool Maker | Tool Shop."
350. <u>R. L. Polk's & Co.'s Grand Rapids City Directory 1907</u>, Grand Rapids, Michigan : Grand Rapids Directory Company, Publishers, 1907, Thirty-Fifth Edition, Page 829; (ancestry.com image 424); "Samuel J Pickles, mach Fox Typewriter Co, h 111 Scribner."
351. <u>R. L. Polk's & Co.'s 1910 Grand Rapids City Directory For Year Commencing October</u>, Grand Rapids, Michigan : Grand Rapids Directory Company, Publishers, 1910, Thirty-Eighth Edition, Page 871; (ancestry.com image 439); "Samuel J. Pickles foreman Truman M Smith Co, h 140 Lyon."
352. <u>R. L. Polk's & Co.'s 1918 Grand Rapids City Directory</u>, Forty-Sixth Edition, Grand Rapids, Michigan : Grand Rapids Directory Company, Publishers, 1920, Page 808; (ancestry.com image 406); "Samuel J Pickell, bds 951 Madison av."
353. 1900 US Census, Battle Creek, Calhoun County, Michigan, June 1900.
354. 1880 US Census, Douglass Township, Montcalm County, Michigan, June 1880, NARA T9; Roll 596; Page 10C; ED 226; Dwelling 167; Family 167; Line 13; "Josephene Steele."
355. 1900 US Census, Battle Creek, Calhoun County, Michigan, June 1900, NARA T623; ED 34; 3rd Ward; Sheet 17; Page 181A; Dwelling 327; Family 402; Line 47; "Josie J. Pickles."
356. 1910 US Census, Grand Rapids, Kent County, Michigan, April 1910, NARA T624; Roll 656; ED 55; Sheet 11A; House 140; Dwelling 167; Family 200; Line 31; "Josephine Pickles."
357. 1920 US Census, Wyoming Township, Kent County, Michigan, January 1920, NARA T625; Roll 779; Sheet 12A; ED 118; House 607; Dwelling 242; Family 242; Line 40; "Josephine Pickell Boarder."

358. 1930 US Census, Grand Rapids, Kent County, Michigan, April 1930, (then township) NARA T626; Sheet 11A; ED 41-116; North Park; House 3130; Dwelling 32; Family 33; Line 18; "Julia J. Pickell" Mother, living with her son Fred's family.

359. Polk's Grand Rapids City Directory 1923, 51st Edition, Grand Rapids, Michigan: Grand Rapids Directory Company, Publishers, 1923, Page 686; (ancestry.com image 345); "Pickell Josephine (wid Saml) r951 Madison av SE."

360. Polk's Grand Rapids (Michigan) City Directory , Volume 1929 LVII, Grand Rapids, Michigan: Grand Rapids Directory Co., Publishers, 1929, Page 711; (ancestry.com image 364); "Pickell Julia J (wid Saml J) 43130 Coit rd NE."

361. Tombstone: "Josephine Pickles."

362. Marriage Certificate/Record/Application. Michigan Department of Community Health, Division of Vital Records and Health Statistics; Lansing, Marriage Records, 1867-1952; Film 34; Film Description: 1887 Iron-1887 Schoolcraft; page 539; number 3532. "Samuel J Pickles | Jessie J. Steele."

363. 1900 US Census, Battle Creek, Calhoun County, Michigan, June 1900, Death record estimates born in 1872; 1900 Census says 1870.

364. Death Certificate/Record. Michigan Department Of Health, Bureau of Records and Statistics, Certificate Of Death, Register no. 121, state office no 381 8709; "Josephine J Pickell."

365. Find-A-Grave, (www.findagrave.com/memorial/27326991/josephine-pickles : accessed 25 January 2022). Memorial ID 27326991, citing Hillside Entrican Cemetery, Entrican, Montcalm County, Michigan; maintained by Gail (contributor 47136090).

366. Grand Rapids Press, newspaper, Grand Rapids, Kent County, Michigan, "Michigan Deaths," 24 February 1938, page 12.

367. 1880 US Census, Hamlin Township, Eaton County, Michigan, June 1880, NARA T9; Roll 578; ED 78; Page 15/324; Dwelling 157; Family 171; Line 41; "Amelia Pickle."

368. 1900 US Census, Douglass Township, Montcalm County, Michigan, June 1900, NARA T623; Roll 733; ED 125; Line 69; Sheet 3B; Page 105; Dwelling 57; Family 58; "Amelia Kilborn."

369. 1910 US Census, Douglass Township, Montcalm County, Michigan, April 1910, NARA T624; Roll 665; ED 149; Sheet 3A; Line 4; Page 131; Dwelling 36; Family 37; "Amelia H Kilbourne" Living with her father and mother with husband.

370. Michigan, Census of World War I Veterans with Card Index, 1917-1919, familysearch.org/ark:/61903/1:1:QPLQ-77GK : 8 September 2019; citing Military Service, New York, Michigan Department of State, Lansing; FHL microfilm 008461588; Fort Wood, New York; 14 July 1918. In the household of son Raymond.

371. 1920 US Census, Douglass Township, Montcalm County, Michigan, January 1920, NARA T625; Roll 787; Sheet 4A; ED 113; Line 44; Page 102; Dwelling 89; Family 89; Line 44; "Amelia Kilbourne."

372. 1930 US Census, Belding, Ionia County, Michigan, April 1930, NARA T626; ED 2; Sheet 4A; Line 19; Dwelling 89; Family 91; "Amelia Kilbourne."

373. 1940 US Census, Douglass Township, Montcalm County, Michigan, April 1940, NARA T627; Roll 1793; ED 54-11B; Sheet 1B; Line 43; "Amelia Kilbourne."

374. 1950 US Census, Tallmadge, Ottawa County, Michigan, April 1950, Enumerated 8 June 1950; Record Group Number 29; Roll 2224; Sheet 74; ED 70-65B; Line 16; "Amelia H. Kilbourne."

375. US Social Security Applications and Claims Index, 1936-2007, Claim date 2 July 1953; name listed as AMELIA H KILBOURNE on 19 May 1953.

376. Funeral Card: in possession of Curtis Daryl Sanders (author)

377. Michigan, U.S., Births and Christening Index, 1867-1911, database with images, ancestry.com and familysearch.org, FHL Film Number 966583.

378. Michigan Births and Christenings, 1775-1995, (https://familysearch.org/ark:/61903/1:1:F414-XBL : 17 January 2020), Amelia H.E. Pickle, 1877.

379. Birth Certificate/Record. Michigan, Return of Births in the County of Eaton; Page 90; Number 201; recorded 25 May 1878; familysearch.org image 467.

380. Find-A-Grave, (www.findagrave.com/memorial/27289392/amelia-h-tregenza : accessed 20 January 2022). Memorial ID 27289392, citing Hillside Entrican Cemetery, Entrican, Montcalm County, Michigan; maintained by Sherry (contributor 47725101).

381. 1930 US Census, Belding, Ionia County, Michigan, April 1930, "Boarding house at home."

382. Polk's Grand Rapids (Kent County, Mich.) City Directory Including East Grand Rapids, Grand Rapids, Michigan: Grand Rapids Directory Company, Publishers, 1946, Vol. 1946 LXVIII, Page 472; (ancestry.com image 234).

383. Polk's Grand Rapids (Kent County, Mich.) City Directory Including East Grand Rapids, Comstock Park and North Park, Vol. 1946 LXIX, Grand Rapids, Michigan: Grand Rapids Directory Company, Publishers, 1946, Page 481; (ancestry.com image 242).

384. Daily News, newspaper, Greenville, Montcalm County, Michigan; undated newspaper clipping.

385. 1870 US Census, Douglass Township, Montcalm County, Michigan, June 1870, NARA M593; Roll 692; Page 2; Dwelling 14; Family 14; Line 11; "Thomas Kilburn."

386. 1880 US Census, Douglass Township, Montcalm County, Michigan, June 1880, NARA T9; Roll 596; ED 226; Page 10B; Dwelling 76; Family 76; Line 34; "Thomas O. Kilborn."

387. 1900 US Census, Douglass Township, Montcalm County, Michigan, June 1900, NARA T623; Roll 733; ED 125; Line 68; Sheet 3B; Page 105; Dwelling 57; Family 58; "Thomas Kilborn."

388. 1910 US Census, Douglass Township, Montcalm County, Michigan, April 1910, NARA T624; Roll 665; ED 149; Sheet 3A; Line 3; Page 131; Dwelling 36; Family 38; "Thomas O Kilbourne" living in same dwelling as father-in-law James Pickles.

389. 1920 US Census, Douglass Township, Montcalm County, Michigan, January 1920, NARA T625; Roll 787; Sheet 4A; ED 113; Line 43; Page 102; Dwelling 89; Family 89; Line 43;"Thomas Kilbourne."

390. 1930 US Census, Belding, Ionia County, Michigan, April 1930, NARA T626; ED 2; Sheet 4A; Line 18; Dwelling 89; Family 91; "Thomas Kilbourne."

391. Marriage Certificate/Record/Application. Michigan Department of Community Health, Division of Vital Records and Health Statistics; Lansing; Marriage Records, 1867-1952; Film: 60; #117 Montcalm County, Michigan; Page 375; number 117.

392. Rev. Burns was from Illinois and served on the Board of Examiners of the Chicago Theological Seminary, 1896-1897.

393. Death Certificate/Record. Michigan Department of Health, Division of Vital Statistics, Certificate of Death, File 59 4152. (https://family-search.org/ark:/61903/1:1:KFQJ-D67 : 13 March 2018).

394. Find-A-Grave, (www.findagrave.com/memorial/27318717/thomas-oscar-kilbourne : accessed 20 January 2022). Memorial ID 27318717, citing Hillside Entrican Cemetery, Entrican, Montcalm County, Michigan; maintained by Gail (contributor 47136090).

395. Marriage Certificate/Record/Application; "Laborer."

396. 1900 US Census, Douglass Township, Montcalm County, Michigan, June 1900, "Laborer. (Lumber)."

397. Polk's Jackson City And County Directory, 1902, Detroit: R. L. Polk & Co., Publishers, 1902, Page 301; (ancestry.com image 166); "Kilbourne Thomas O, tmstr, res 339 Whitney."

398. 1910 US Census, Douglass Township, Montcalm County, Michigan, April 1910, "farmers general farm."

399. 1920 US Census, Douglass Township, Montcalm County, Michigan, January 1920, "Farmer General Farming."

400. 1930 US Census, Belding, Ionia County, Michigan, April 1930, "Farmer."

401. Ludington Daily News, newspaper, Ludington, Mason County, Michigan, "Return From Attending Funeral Of Relative," 11 August 1934, page 2.

402. 1891 Census of Canada, Windsor, Essex County, Ontario, Canada, Division number 6; page 38; Line 3.

403. 1910 US Census, Detroit, Wayne County, Michigan, April 1910, NARA T624; Roll 680; Sheet 6A; ED 255; Dwelling 125; Family 132; Line 41; "Charles E Tregenza"

404. 1920 US Census, Detroit, Wayne County, Michigan, January 1920, NARA T625; Roll 805; Sheet 4A; ED 112; Dwelling 48; Family 82; Line 29. "Charles Tregenza."

405. 1930 US Census, Detroit, Wayne County, Michigan, April 1930, NARA T626; Sheet 5B; ED 82-813; Dwelling 76; Family 20; Line 89; "Charles E. Tregenza."

406. 1950 US Census, Tompkins, Jackson County, Michigan, April 1950, Record Group Number 29; Sheet number 27; ED 38-142; Dwelling 234; Line 8; "Charles E Tregenza."

407. Birth Certificate/Record. Archives of Ontario; Toronto, Ontario, Canada; Registrations of Births and Stillbirths, 1869-1913; Series: Registrations of Births and Stillbirths, 1869-1913; Reel: 81; Record Group: Rg 80-2; Number 76; 8293.

408. US Social Security Death Index.

409. Michigan Death Index, 1971-1996, Michigan Department of Vital and Health Records, Lansing, database (some with scanned images), ancestry.com or familysearch.org; certificate number 10872.

410. Find-A-Grave, (www.findagrave.com/memorial/27289390/charles-e-tregenza : accessed 20 January 2022). Memorial ID 27289390, citing Hillside Entrican Cemetery, Entrican, Montcalm County, Michigan; maintained by Gail (contributor 47136090).

411. R. L. Polk & Co., Detroit City Directory For The Year Commencing August 1st., 1903, Detroit, Michigan: R. L. Polk & Co., 1903, Page 2064; (ancestry.com image 1021); "Tregenza Charles E, clk, bds 701 Clinton av." [His mother and brother reside together with him.]

412. Detroit City Directory For The Year Commencing August 1st., 1904, Detroit, Michigan: R. L. Polk & Co., 1904, Page 2305; (ancestry.com image 1103); "Tregenza Charles E, mach, bda 701 Clinton avenue." [His mother and brother were residing together.]

413. 1910 US Census, Detroit, Wayne County, Michigan, April 1910, "machinist garage."

414. Detroit City Directory For The Year August 15th., 1911, Detroit: R. L. Polk & Co., 1911, Page 2319; (ancestry.com image 1173); "Tregenza Chas E, repr. h 918 Sheridan av."

415. R. L. Polk & Co., Detroit City Directory For The Year Commencing September 1st., 1912, Detroit, Michigan: R. L. Polk & Co., 1912, Page 2488; (ancestry.com image 1287); "Tregenza Charles E. repr Buick Motor Co, h 1113 Townsend av."

416. R. L. Polk & Co., Detroit City Directory For The Year Commencing September 1st., 1913, Detroit, Michigan: R. L. Polk & Co., 1913, Page 2114; (ancestry.com image 1084); "Tregenza Chas E, tchr, h 1047 Sheridan av."

417. Detroit City Directory For The Year Commencing September 1st., 1915, Detroit: R. L. Polk & Co., 1915, Page 2350; (ancestry.com image 1211); "Tregenza Chas E, reprman, h 1676 Concord av."

418. R. L.Polk & Co's Detroit City Directory For The Year Beginning September 1916, Detroit: R. L. Polk & Co., Publishers, 1916, Page 2566; (ancestry.com image 1116); "Tregenza Chas E, slsmn Buick Motor Co, h1676 Concord av."

419. 1920 US Census, Detroit, Wayne County, Michigan, January 1920, "Manager Automobile."

420. Polk's Detroit City Directory 1921-22, Detroit: R. L. Polk & Co., Publishers, 1921, Volume LIX, Page 1935; (ancestry.com image 995); "Tregenza Chas E trav Buick Motor Co h3510 Sheridan."

421. Polk's Detroit (Michigan) City Directory 1927-1928, Detroit: R. L. Polk & Company, Publishers, 1927, Page 2150; (ancestry.com image 1048); "Tregenza Chas E service trav Buick Motor Co r4141 Drexel av."

422. Detroit, Michigan, City Directory, 1928, Detroit: 1928, Page 2016; (ancestry.com image 251); "Tregenza Chas E (Jennie) service slsmgr h4141 Drexel av."

423. 1930 US Census, Detroit, Wayne County, Michigan, April 1930, "Service Engineer | Auto Factory."

424. Polk's Detroit (Michigan) City Directory, Detroit, Michigan: R. L. Polk & Co., Publishers, 1932, Vol. 1931-32 LXIV, Page 1482; (ancestry.com image 148); "Tregenza Chas E (Jennie) servicemn h4141 Drexel av."

425. Polk's Jackson (Jackson County, Mich.) City Directory 1939, Detroit: R. L. Polk & Co., Publishers, 1939, Page 355; (ancestry.com image 174); "Tregenza Chas E (Jennie) servmn h525 Hallett."

426. Polk's Jackson (Jackson County, Mich.) City Directory 1945, Detroit: R. L. Polk & Co., Publishers, 1945, Page 372; (ancestry.com image 186); "Tregenza Chas (Jennie) lathe hd FG&F Div r RD 1 Onondaga."

427. Polk's Jackson (Jackson County, Mich.) City Directory 1947, Detroit: R. L. Polk & Co., Publishers, 1947, Page 495; (ancestry.com image 206); "Tregenza Chas fctywkr Frost Gear r Onondaga."

428. 1950 US Census, Tompkins, Jackson County, Michigan, April 1950, "Tool Maker | Gear Factory."

429. 1920 US Census, Detroit, Wayne County, Michigan, January 1920.

430. Manifests of Passengers Arriving at St. Albans, VT, District through Canadian Pacific and Atlantic Ports, 1895-1954, Manifests of Passengers Arriving at Port of Buffalo, New York, Records of the Immigration and

Naturalization Service, 1787 - 2004, NARA, database with images, Clerk; married.

431. Ibid. NARA M1464; Roll 380, Volume 499-500, September-October 1919; (https://familysearch.org/ark:/61903/1:1:QK3R-H5Q7 : 23 February 2021).

432. Detroit Free Press, "The Old And The New," 17 June 1923, Part 4 page 3.

433. US World War I Draft Registration Cards, 1917-1918, NARA, www.-familysearch.org or www.ancestry.com, "United States World War I Draft Registration Cards, 1917-1918", database with images, (www.-familysearch.org/ark:/61903/1:1:K6X7-317 : 30 December 2021), Charles E Tregenza, 1917-1918.

434. US World War II Draft Registration Cards, 1940-1947, NARA, Saint Louis, Missouri, scanned image, Selective Service Registration Cards, World War II: Fourth Registration. Records of the Selective Service System, Record Group Number 147.

435. Michigan Births and Christenings, 1775-1995, (https://familysearch.org/ark:/61903/1:1:F4BJ-69K : 17 January 2020).

436. Michigan, U.S., Births and Christening Index, 1867-1911, database with images, ancestry.com and familysearch.org, citing item 3 p 117 rn 329.

437. Birth Certificate/Record. Page 117; Number 329; recorded 28 May 1882.

438. Michigan Deaths, 1867-1897, https://familysearch.org, (https://familysearch.org/ark:/61903/1:1:N3J3-N2K : 18 February 2021), Fred Pickle, 24 Feb 1881; citing p 210 rn 168.

439. Genealogical Death Indexing System, Michigan Department of Health & Human Services; online, www.vitalstats.michigan.gov, transcription, Ledger page 210; record number 168; recorded 2 June 1882; https://vitalstats.michigan.gov/osr/gendisx/scripts/individual.asp?UniqueID=445102 (viewed 17 March 2022).

440. 1880 US Census, Hamlin Township, Eaton County, Michigan, June 1880, NARA T9; Roll 578; Page 327A; ED 78; Dwelling 212; Family 226; Line 3; "Malcom Clay."

441. 1900 US Census, Onondaga Township, Ingham County, Michigan, June 1900, NARA T623; Roll 716; Page 133; Sheet 9A; ED 55; Dwelling 227; Family 227; Line 40; "Malcom Clay" Servant in the household of his future in-laws, George Harwood family.

442. 1910 US Census, Onondaga Township, Ingham County, Michigan, April 1910, NARA T624; Roll 651; Sheet 4B; ED 90; Dwelling 124; Family 126; Line 91; "Malcolm J Clay."

443. 1920 US Census, Onondaga Township, Ingham County, Michigan, January 1920, NARA T625; Roll 771; Sheet 3A; ED 129; Dwelling 68; Family 69; Line 49; "Malcolm J Clay."

444. Lansing City [Michigan] Directory 1924, Volume XXIV, Lansing, Michigan: McKinley-Reynolds Co. Publishers, 1924, Page 367; (ancestry.-com image 213) "Clay Malcom J (Lovan), wks Van Dervoort Hdw, h 617 N. Chestnut."

445. McKinley-Reynolds Co. Lansing City Directory 1925, [Lansing, Michigan:] McKinley-Reynolds Co., 1925, Page 261 (ancestry.com image 158); "Clay Malcolm J (Lovan B) slm Van Der Voort Hdw h418 W Lapeer."

446. 1930 US Census, Onondaga Township, Ingham County, Michigan, April 1930, NARA T626; ED 33-58; Sheet 6B; Dwelling 159; Family 159; Line 54; "Malcolm Clay."

447. 1940 US Census, Onondaga Township, Ingham County, Michigan, April 1940, NARA 627; Roll 1763; Sheet 15B; ED 33-83; Line 46; "Malcolm Clay."

448. Birth Certificate/Record. Scanned image; Number 11; citing item 2 page 109 rn 11, Hamlin, Eaton, Michigan, Department of Vital Records, Lansing.

449. Death Certificate/Record. Michigan Department of Community Health, Division for Vital Records and Health Statistics; Lansing.

450. Find-A-Grave; not found.

451. 1900 US Census, Onondaga Township, Ingham County, Michigan, June 1900, "Servant" [listing under relationship to Head of household] "farmer laborer."

452. 1910 US Census, Onondaga Township, Ingham County, Michigan, April 1910, "Farmer | General farm."

453. 1920 US Census, Onondaga Township, Ingham County, Michigan, January 1920, "Thrasher Grain | Own Machine."

454. 1930 US Census, Onondaga Township, Ingham County, Michigan, April 1930, "Quadist Farmer | Farmer."

455. The State Journal, "State Deaths: Malcolm J. Clay," 8 April 1949, page 19.

456. US World War I Draft Registration Cards, 1917-1918, database with scanned images, NARA, National Archives Building, Washington, DC., (www.familysearch.org or www.ancestry.com).

457. 1900 US Census, Onondaga Township, Ingham County, Michigan, June 1900, NARA T623; Roll 716; Page 133; Sheet 9A; ED 55; Dwelling 227; Family 227; Line 39; "Leavern Harwood."

458. 1910 US Census, Onondaga Township, Ingham County, Michigan, April 1910, NARA T624; Roll 651; Sheet 4B; ED 90; Dwelling 124; Family 126; Line 92; "Lavan B. Clay."

459. 1920 US Census, Onondaga Township, Ingham County, Michigan, January 1920, NARA T625; Roll 771; Sheet 3A; ED 129; Dwelling 68; Family 69; Line 50; "Loren B Clay."

460. McKinley-Reynolds Co. Lansing City Directory 1925, [Lansing, Michigan:] McKinley-Reynolds Co., 1925, Page 261 (ancestry.com image 158); "Clay Malcolm J (Lovan B) slm Van Der Voort Hdw h418 W Lapeer."

461. 1930 US Census, Onondaga Township, Ingham County, Michigan, April 1930, NARA T626; ED 33-58; Sheet 6B; Dwelling 159; Family 159; Line 55; "Lavan Clay."

462. 1940 US Census, Onondaga Township, Ingham County, Michigan, April 1940, NARA 627; Roll 1763; Sheet 15B; ED 33-83; Line 47; "Loran Clay."

463. Not found in 1950 census.

464. Michigan Marriages, 1822-1995. This collection consists of county marriage records from various counties in Michigan, p 38 rn 55; (https://familysearch.org/ark:/61903/1:1:FCXZ-4GC : 17 January 2020).

465. Marriage record/certificate/application. Number 557; Page 303; Ingham County, Michigan; "Loren Harwood | Malcolm Clay."

466. The State Journal, "State Deaths: Mrs. Lovan Clay," 19 January 1952, page 2.

467. 1880 US Census, Hamlin Township, Eaton County, Michigan, June 1880, NARA T9; Roll 578; Page 327A; ED 78; Dwelling 212; Family 226; Line 4; "Forest H Clay."

468. 1900 US Census, Eaton Rapids, Eaton County, Michigan, June 1900, NARA T623; Roll 709; Sheet 6A; ED 70; Dwelling 121; Family 121; Line 15; "Fred. H Clay."

469. 1910 US Census, Carmel Township, Eaton County, Michigan, May 1910, NARA T624;Roll 645; Sheet 5B; ED 79; Dwelling 136; Family 136; Line 86; "Fred H. Clay."

470. 1920 US Census, Carmel Township, Eaton County, Michigan, January 1920, NARA T625; Roll 763; Sheet 2B; ED 91; Dwelling 47; Family 47; Line 91; "Fred Clay."
471. 1930 US Census, Charlotte, Eaton County, Michigan, April 1930, NARA T626; Sheet 16B; ED 23-10; Dwelling 455; Family 474; Line 73; "Fred Clay."
472. 1940 US Census, Charlotte, Eaton County, Michigan, April 1940, NARA T627; Roll 1747; Sheet 64A; ED 23-10; Line 28; "Fred Clay."
473. 1950 US Census, Charlotte, Eaton County, Michigan, April 1950, Record Group Number 29; Roll 169; Sheet 25; ED 23-16; Home 1981; Dwelling 244; Line 3; "Fred H Clay."
474. US Social Security Applications and Claims Index, 1936-2007. Claim Date 31 January 1957; 25 Jan 1957: Name listed as FRED HENRY CLAY.
475. Tombstone. (See findagrave.com) "Fred H. Clay | 1876-1960."
476. Michigan Marriages, 1822-1995, (www.familysearch.org) Record 396; citing item 2 p 98 rn 299, Hamlin, Eaton, Michigan, Department of Vital Records, Lansing.
477. World War I Draft card says 5 November 1877.
478. Find-A-Grave, (www.findagrave.com/memorial/63096677/fred-h-clay: accessed 28 July 2022). Memorial ID 63096677, citing Maple Hill Cemetery, Charlotte, Eaton County, Michigan; maintained by Woodie (contributor 46922700).
479. 1910 US Census, Carmel Township, Eaton County, Michigan, May 1910, "Farmer | General farm."
480. 1920 US Census, Carmel Township, Eaton County, Michigan, January 1920, "farmer | own farm."
481. 1930 US Census, Charlotte, Eaton County, Michigan, April 1930, "Farmer | General farm."
482. 1940 US Census, Charlotte, Eaton County, Michigan, April 1940, "farmer | farm."
483. 1950 US Census, Charlotte, Eaton County, Michigan, April 1950, "Farming chores | Farm."
484. Battle Creek Enquirer And News, "Area Obituaries," 17 April 1960, page 2.
485. The State Journal, "Area Deaths," 18 April 1960, page 15.
486. US World War I Draft Registration Cards, 1917-1918, NARA, Draft Card C.
487. 1910 US Census, Carmel Township, Eaton County, Michigan, May 1910, NARA T624;Roll 645; Sheet 5B; ED 79; Dwelling 136; Family 136; Line 87; "May N. Clay."
488. 1920 US Census, Carmel Township, Eaton County, Michigan, January 1920, NARA T625; Roll 763; Sheet 2B; ED 91; Dwelling 47; Family 47; Line 92; "Mae Clay."
489. 1930 US Census, Charlotte, Eaton County, Michigan, April 1930, NARA T626; Sheet 16B; ED 23-10; Dwelling 455; Family 474; Line 74; "Mae Clay."
490. 1940 US Census, Charlotte, Eaton County, Michigan, April 1940, NARA T627; Roll 1747; Sheet 64A; ED 23-10; Line 29;"Mae Clay."
491. 1950 US Census, Charlotte, Eaton County, Michigan, April 1950, Record Group Number 29; Roll 169; Sheet 25; ED 23-16; Home 1981; Dwelling 244; Line 4; "Mae N Clay."
492. Tombstone. (See findagrave.com) "N. Mae Clay | 1877-1959."
493. Michigan Marriages, 1822-1995, p-306-334; (https://familysearch.org/ark:/61903/1:1:FCXC-T37 : 17 January 2020).

494. Marriage record/certificate/application. Michigan Department of Community Health, Division of Vital Records and Health Statistics; Lansing. Number 334; page 653. Marriage Records, 1867-1952; Film: 71; Film Description: 1901 Clare-1901 Lake; "Fred Clay | May Lovell."

495. Battle Creek Enquirer And News, "Eaton Township Couple to Mark 50th Anniversary," 23 December 1951, page 14.

496. 1900 Census says born in Michigan.

497. Find-A-Grave, (www.findagrave.com/memorial/63096744/nancy-mae-clay: accessed 28 July 2022). Memorial ID 63096744, citing Maple Hill Cemetery, Charlotte, Eaton County, Michigan; maintained by Woodie (contributor 46922700).

498. The State Journal, "Area Deaths," 29 June 1959, page 10.

499. Battle Creek Enquirer And News, "Area Obituaries: Mrs. Fred H. Clay," 29 June 1959, page 14.

500. 1880 US Census, Hamlin Township, Eaton County, Michigan, June 1880, NARA T9; Roll 578; Page 327A; ED 78; Dwelling 212; Family 226; Line 5; "Mary A Clay."

501. 1900 US Census, Eaton Rapids, Eaton County, Michigan, June 1900, NARA T623; Roll 709; Sheet 6A; ED 70; Dwelling 121; Family 121; Line 14; "Mary A Clay."

502. 1910 US Census, Sandstone Township, Jackson County, Michigan, April 1910, NARA T624; Roll 653; Sheet 8B; ED 37; Dwelling 179; Family 189; Line 97; "Alice M Krugman."

503. 1920 US Census, Sandstone Township, Jackson County, Michigan, January 1920, Enumerated 20 February 1920; NARA T625; ED 41; Sheet 13A; Dwelling 307; Family 321; line 40; "Alice Crugman" widow.

504. 1930 US Census, Sandstone Township, Jackson County, Michigan, April 1930, NARA T626; Roll 996; ED 38-46; Sheet 3B; Dwelling 74; Family 76; Line 63; "Mary A. Krugman | Widowed."

505. 1940 US Census, Parma Township, Jackson County, Michigan, April 1940, NARA T627; ED 38-58; Sheet 2B; House 118; Line 56. "Alice Krugman" living with son Vern as a widow.

506. 1950 US Census, Sandstone Township, Jackson County, Michigan, April 1950, Record Group Number 29; Roll 4014; Sheet 9; ED 38-129; Line 19; "Mary A Kruger."

507. Birth Certificate/Record. Number 350; citing item 1 p 123 rn 350, Hamlin, Eaton, Michigan, Department of Vital Records, Lansing.

508. Michigan, U.S., Births and Christening Index, 1867-1911, database with images, ancestry.com and familysearch.org.

509. Find-A-Grave, (www.findagrave.com/memorial/20153982/mary-alice-krugman: accessed 10 August 2022). Memorial ID 20153982, citing Fairview Cemetery, Tompkins, Jackson County, Michigan; maintained by Deb Hayes-Wolfe (contributor 46811474).

510. 1910 US Census, Sandstone Township, Jackson County, Michigan, April 1910, Enumerated 3 May 1910; NARA T624; Roll 653; Sheet 8B; ED 37; Dwelling 179; Family 189; Line 96; "Fred H Krugman."

511. Polk's Jackson City And County Directory 1913, Detroit, Michigan: R. L. Polk & Co., 1913, Page 850 (ancestry.com image 434); "Krugman Fred, personal, $300, Parma, Parma (3)."

512. 1930 US Census, San Bernardino Township, San Bernardino County, California, April 1930, NARA ED 36-76; Sheet 2A; Dwelling 23; Family 39; Line 9; "Fred H Krugman."

513. Not found in the US 1940 census; possibly in military service or in Alaska.

514. 1950 US Census, Sandstone Township, Jackson County, Michigan, April 1950, Record Group Number 29; Roll 4014; Sheet 9; ED 38-129; Line 18; "Frederick H Kruger."

515. Michigan Marriages, 1868-1925, Number 349; (https://familysearch.org/ark:/61903/1:1:N3VD-ZJ6 : 18 February 2021), entry for Frederick Kriegman and Mary A. Clay; citing Marriage, Charlotte, Jackson (of record), Michigan; Secretary of State, Department of Vital Records, Lansing.

516. Michigan, County Marriage Records, 1822-1940, ancestry.com.

517. Find-A-Grave, (www.findagrave.com/memorial/20154008/fred-h-krugman: accessed 10 August 2022). Memorial ID 20154008, citing Fairview Cemetery, Tompkins, Jackson County, Michigan; maintained by Deb Hayes-Wolfe (contributor 46811474).

518. 1910 US Census, Sandstone Township, Jackson County, Michigan, April 1910.

519. California Voter Registrations, California State Library, Sacramento, California, 1928, 1930; California State Library; Sacramento, California; Great Register of Voters, 1900-1968; "Krugman, Fred H. Car Carpenter, 659 B Rex Ave Republican"; 1938: "Krugman, F. H. Car Carpenter, 671 9th St. Republican."

520. 1930 US Census, San Bernardino Township, San Bernardino County, California, April 1930.

521. Polk's St. Joseph (Berrien County, Mich.) City Directory 1938, Detroit: R. L. Polk & Co., Publishers, 1938, Page 84 (ancestry.com image 39); "Krugman Fredk emp Auto Speciallties Mfg Co r RD 2 Watervleit."

522. 1950 US Census, Sandstone Township, Jackson County, Michigan, April 1950.

523. Battle Creek Enquirer And News, "Father Returns in Uniform to Family Twice as Large as One He Left in 1915," 4 December 1944, page 8.

524. US World War I Draft Registration Cards, 1917-1918. Affiliate Publication M1509; Affiliate Publication Title: World War I Selective Service System Draft Registration Cards.

525. US World War II Draft Registration Cards, 1940-1947, Box 5; Affiliate Repository Place: Seattle, Washington.

526. 1900 US Census, Eaton Rapids, Eaton County, Michigan, June 1900, NARA T623; Roll 709; Sheet 6A; ED 70; Dwelling 121; Family 121; Line 16; "Birdie M Clay."

527. 1910 US Census, Parma Township, Jackson County, Michigan, April 1910, NARA T624; Roll 653; Sheet 7A; ED 34; Dwelling 151; Family 151; Line 19; "Mabel Gunnell," divorceds ervant in household of Andrew Holmes.

528. 1920 US Census, Sandstone Township, Jackson County, Michigan, January 1920, NARA T625; Roll 774; Sheet 11A; ED 41; Dwelling 239; Family 250; Line 6; "Mabel B Zantop."

529. 1930 US Census, Parma Township, Jackson County, Michigan, April 1930, NARA T626; Sheet 1B; ED 46; Dwelling 22; Family 23; Line 83; "Mabel Zantop."

530. 1940 US Census, Parma Township, Jackson County, Michigan, April 1940, NARA T627; Roll 1769; Sheet 2A; ED 38-62; Line 37; "Mabel B Zantop."

531. Polk's Jackson (Jackson County, Mich.) City Directory 1947, Detroit: R. L. Polk & Co., Publishers, 1947, Page 448 (ancestry.com image 228); "Zantop Mabel (wid Aug A) r1402 E North."

532. Polk's Jackson (Jackson County, Mich.) City Directory 1949, Detroit, Michigan: R. L. Polk & Co., Publishers, 1949, Page 440 (ancestry.com image 222); "Zantop Mabel B Mrs r631 Wayne."
533. Birth Certificate/Record. Number 316; citing item 2 p 124 rn 316, Hamlin, Eaton, Michigan, Department of Vital Records, Lansing.
534. Michigan Death Index, 1971-1996, Michigan Department of Vital and Health Records, Lansing, Michigan Department of Vital and Health Records. Michigan Death Index, Lansing.
535. Find-A-Grave, (www.findagrave.com/memorial/19540721/mable-birdie-zantop: accessed 22 August 2022). Memorial ID 19540721, citing Chapel Cemetery, Sandstone, Jackson County, Michigan; maintained by Deb Hayes-Wolfe (contributor 46811474).
536. Bay City Times, newspaper, Bay City, Michigan, "News Of The State," 24 January 1907, page 3.
537. Kalamazoo Gazette, newspaper, Kalamazoo, Michigan, "Brief State News," 13 April 1907, page 2.
538. Detroit Free Press, "Death Notices," 31 March 1978, page 10C.
539. The State Journal, "Deaths and Funerals," 30 March 1978, page B-2.
540. Battle Creek Enquirer And News, "Local and Area Obituaries: Mrs. Mable B. Zantop," 30 March 1978, page A-7.
541. US Social Security Applications and Claims Index, 1936-2007, 11 Feb 1955: Name listed as IRVING W GUNNELL.
542. Michigan Marriages, 1822-1995, Page 39, number 70; Volumes 7-8; (https://familysearch.org/ark:/61903/1:1:FC6Q-PSX : 17 January 2020). "Mabel Clay."
543. Marriage record/certificate/application. Number 70; Michigan Department of Community Health, Division of Vital Records and Health Statistics; Lansing, Marriage Records, 1867-1952; Film 84; Film Description: 1905 Bay-1905 Ingham.
544. Find-A-Grave, (www.findagrave.com/memorial/103703595/irving-william-gunnell: accessed 22 August 2022). Memorial ID 103703595, citing Portland Cemetery, Portland, Ionia County, Michigan; maintained by Marilynn Johnson (contributor 46963419).
545. The State Journal, Advertisement: Irving Gunnell, 501 Lincoln, Portland, Mich. 2 October 1955, page 36.
546. Michigan, Divorce records, 1897-1952, database, Michigan Department of Community Health, Division for Vital Records and Health Statistics; Lansing, www.ancestry.com, I-490; Jackson County, Michigan.
547. Evening Chronicle, newspaper, Marshall, Michigan, "Local;" 10 July 1913, page 1.
548. US World War I Draft Registration Cards, 1917-1918, Draft Card G.
549. US World War II Draft Registration Cards, 1940-1947, Record Group Number 147.
550. 1920 US Census, Sandstone Township, Jackson County, Michigan, January 1920, NARA T625; Roll 774; Sheet 11A; ED 41; Dwelling 239; Family 250; Line 5; "August W Zantop."
551. 1930 US Census, Parma Township, Jackson County, Michigan, April 1930, NARA T626; Sheet 1B; ED 46; Dwelling 22; Family 23; Line 82; "August W. Zantop."
552. 1940 US Census, Parma Township, Jackson County, Michigan, April 1940, NARA T627; Roll 1769; Sheet 2A; ED 38-62; Line 37; "August W Zantop."
553. 1950 US Census, Parma Township, Jackson County, Michigan, April 1950, Record Group Number: 29; Roll 4014; Sheet 21; ED 38-125; Line 6; "August W Zantop."

554. Michigan Marriages, 1868-1925, Number 104; (https://familysearch.org/ark:/61903/1:1:N3KG-R9Y : 18 February 2021), entry for August W. Zantop and Mabel C. Clay Gunnell, 25 Mar 1911; Citing Secretary of State, Department of Vital Records, Lansing.

555. Marriage record/certificate/application. Number 104; Jackson County, Michigan; Michigan Department of Community Health, Division of Vital Records and Health Statistics; Lansing; Film: 106; Film Description: 1911 Gogebic-1911 Macomb.

556. Florida Death Index, 1877-1998, Florida Department of Health, Office of Vital Records, 1998, Jacksonville, Florida, (familysearch.org and ancestry.com).

557. Find-A-Grave, (www.findagrave.com/memorial/177585044/august-william-zantop: accessed 22 August 2022). Memorial ID 177585044, citing Southern Memorial Park, North Miami, Miami-Dade County, Florida; maintained by J Rowan (contributor 26611594).

558. 1920 US Census, Sandstone Township, Jackson County, Michigan, January 1920, "Engineer | Traction."

559. The Farm Journal Illustrated Rural Directory of Jackson County, MI, 1918-23, Philadelphia, Pennsylvania: Wilmer Atkinson Company, 1923, August W. Zantop, spouse Mabel, 3 children, thresher, Parma, Sand.

560. 1930 US Census, Parma Township, Jackson County, Michigan, April 1930, "Thrasher | Independent."

561. 1940 US Census, Parma Township, Jackson County, Michigan, April 1940, "Proprietor | General Trucking."

562. 1950 US Census, Parma Township, Jackson County, Michigan, April 1950, "school bus driver public school | farming farm."

563. Divorce Record. Michigan Department Of Health, Bureau of Records and Statistics; Divorce Record, state 38 4936; Docket 17-583 "B. Mabel Zantop."

564. Miami News, newspaper, Miami, Dade County, Florida, "Death Notices," 22 March 1973, page 10.

565. Miami Herald, newspaper, Miami, Florida, "Death Notices," 20 March 1973, page 17-B.

566. Battle Creek Enquirer, "Local and Area Obituaries," 23 March 1973, page 8.

567. 1900 US Census, Eaton Rapids, Eaton County, Michigan, June 1900, NARA T623; Roll 709; Sheet 6A; ED 70; Dwelling 121; Family 121; Line 17; "Roy Clay."

568. 1910 US Census, Parma Township, Jackson County, Michigan, April 1910, NARA T624; Roll 653; Sheet 7B; ED 34; Dwelling 163; Family 163; Line 63; "Le Roy Clay."

569. 1920 US Census, Jackson City, Jackson County, Michigan, January 1920, NARA T625; Roll 773; Sheet 8B; ED 9; House 212; Family 218; Line 75; "Roy Clay."

570. 1930 US Census, Blackman Township, Jackson County, Michigan, April 1930, NARA T626; Sheet 14B; ED 38-1; Dwelling 292; Family 297; Line 100; "Roy Clay."

571. 1940 US Census, Jackson City, Jackson County, Michigan, April 1940, NARA T627; Roll 1768; Sheet 1A; ED 38-43; Line 2; "Le Roy Clay."

572. 1950 US Census, Jackson, Jackson County, Michigan, April 1950, Record Group Number: 29; Roll 4014; Sheet 75; ED 38-102; Line 15; "Roy C. Clay."

573. Birth Certificate/Record. Number 275; "No name - Clay"; citing item 2 p 139 rn 275, Hamlin, Eaton, Michigan, Department of Vital Records, Lansing.

574. 1910 US Census, Parma Township, Jackson County, Michigan, April 1910, "farmer | at home."

575. 1920 US Census, Jackson City, Jackson County, Michigan, January 1920, "engineer | stationary."

576. 1930 US Census, Blackman Township, Jackson County, Michigan, April 1930, "Engineer | Steam railroad."

577. Polk's Jackson (Jackson County, Mich.) City Directory 1939, Detroit: R. L. Polk & Co., Publishers, 1939, Page 89; (ancestry.com image 41); "Clay C LeRoy (Cora I) shovel opr h531 Blackman av."

578. 1940 US Census, Jackson City, Jackson County, Michigan, April 1940, "Crane operator | Limestone Co."

579. Polk's Jackson (Jackson County, Mich.) City Directory 1945, Detroit: R. L. Polk & Co., Publishers, 1945, Page 88; (ancestry.com image 43); "Clay Leroy (Cora I) crane opr h1442 1/2 Cooper."

580. Polk's Jackson (Jackson County, Mich.) City Directory 1947, Detroit: R. L. Polk & Co., Publishers, 1947, Page 90; (ancestry.com image 47); "Clay LeRoy (Cora T) eng h1442 1/2 Cooper."

581. Polk's Jackson (Jackson County, Mich.) City Directory 1949, Detroit, Michigan: R. L. Polk & Co., Publishers, 1949, Page 94; (ancestry.com image 48); "Clay LeRoy (Cora) lab Michl E Fitzsimmons h1442 1/2 Cooper."

582. 1950 US Census, Jackson, Jackson County, Michigan, April 1950, "Shovel Operator | Lime Co."

583. Polk's Jackson (Jackson County, Mich.) City Directory 1952, Detroit: R. L. Polk & Co., Publishers, 1952, Page 88; (ancestry.com image 42); "Clay LeRoy (Cora) h1442 1/2 Cooper."

584. US World War I Draft Registration Cards, 1917-1918, database with scanned images, NARA, 5 June 1917.

585. 1910 US Census, Parma Township, Jackson County, Michigan, April 1910, NARA T624; Roll 653; Sheet 7B; ED 34; Dwelling 163; Family 163; Line 63; "Cora J Clay."

586. 1920 US Census, Jackson City, Jackson County, Michigan, January 1920, NARA T625; Roll 773; Sheet 8B; ED 9; House 212; Family 218; Line 76; "Cora Clay."

587. 1930 US Census, Blackman Township, Jackson County, Michigan, April 1930, NARA T626; Sheet 15A; ED 38-1; Dwelling 292; Family 297; Line 1; "Cora Clay."

588. 1940 US Census, Jackson City, Jackson County, Michigan, April 1940, NARA T627; Roll 1768; Sheet 1A; ED 38-43; Line 3; "Cora Clay."

589. 1950 US Census, Jackson, Jackson County, Michigan, April 1950, Record Group Number: 29; Roll 4014; Sheet 75; ED 38-102; Line 16; "Cora I Clay."

590. US Social Security Applications and Claims Index, 1936-2007, Feb 1955: Name listed as CORA CLAY.

591. Michigan Marriages, 1822-1995, "Roy Clay" (https://familysearch.org/ark:/61903/1:1:FCNG-PLV : 12 March 2020).

592. Marriage record/certificate/application. Michigan Department of Community Health, Division of Vital Records and Health Statistics; Lansing, MI, USA; Michigan, Marriage Records, 1867-1952; Film 102; Film Description: 1910 Emmet-1910 Lenawee. Record 47.

593. Find-A-Grave, (www.findagrave.com/memorial/147322306/cora-i-clay: accessed 06 September 2022). Memorial ID 147322306, citing Chapel Cemetery, Sandstone, Jackson County, Michigan; maintained by Vernon W. Goodrich (contributor 46940951).

594. 1900 US Census, Springport Township, Jackson County, Michigan, June 1900, NARA T623; Roll 719; Sheet 4B; ED 30; Dwelling 111; Family 111; Line 60; "Mildred Clay."

595. 1910 US Census, Lansing, Ingham County, Michigan, April 1910, NARA T624; Roll 651; Sheet 6A; ED 66; Ward 3; Dwelling 113; Family 115; Line 33; "Mildred Hale" (residing with her parents).

596. 1920 US Census, Detroit, Wayne County, Michigan, January 1920, NARA T625; Roll 805; Sheet 2B; ED 147; House 199; Dwelling 32; Family 38; Line 54; "Mildred L. Fremody."

597. 1930 US Census, Detroit, Wayne County, Michigan, April 1930, NARA T626; Sheet 18A; Page 84; ED 82-655; House 11710; Dwelling 350; Family 65; Line 17; "Mildred L. Fremody."

598. 1940 US Census, Haverford Township, Delaware County, Pennsylvania, April 1940, NARA T627; Roll 3492; Sheet 9A; ED 23-84; Beechwood; House 633; Line 5; "Mildred Fremody."

599. 1950 US Census, West Bloomfield Township, Oakland County, Michigan, April 1950, Record Group Number 29; Roll 3561; Sheet 4; ED 63-342; Line 22; "Mildred Fremody."

600. Birth Certificate/Record. State of Michigan, Eaton County, number 248.

601. Florida Death Index, 1877-1998, Florida Department of Health, Office of Vital Records, 1998, Jacksonville, Florida, familysearch.org and Ancestry.com, Certificate 60363; "Mildred L. Fremody."

602. Find-A-Grave, (www.findagrave.com/memorial/22385941/mildred-l-fremody: accessed 06 October 2022). Memorial ID 22385941, citing Mount Hope Cemetery, Lansing, Ingham County, Michigan; maintained by Ed Houghtaling (contributor 46804583).

603. The State Journal, "Lansing, Area Deaths and Funerals: Mildred L. Fremody," 3 November 1969, page A-2.

604. Tampa Tribune, newspaper, Tampa, Florida, "Bay Area Deaths: Mrs. MIldred Fremody," 3 November 1969, page 19-A.

605. 1910 US Census, Lansing, Ingham County, Michigan, April 1910, NARA T624; Roll 651; Sheet 6A; ED 66; Ward 3; Dwelling 113; Family 115; Line 35; "John F Hale."

606. Iowa, Old Age Tax Assistance Records, 1934-1958, database, familysearch.org, (https://www.familysearch.org/ark:/61903/1:1:C3NL-KVPZ : 8 June 2020), John Frank Hale, 1934-1946.

607. Marriage record/certificate/application. State Of Michigan, Ingham County; number 2303.

608. Iowa City Press-Citizen, newspaper, Iowa City, Iowa, "Funeral Service: Hale," 1 July 1963, page 22. "…held at Northwood, Iowa."

609. Divorce Record. Michigan Department of Community Health, Division for Vital Records and Health Statistics; Lansing; Page 120; record 6079; filed 1 July 1914.

610. Globe Gazette, newspaper, Mason City, Cerro Gordo County, Iowa, "North Iowa deaths," 1 July 1963, page 13.

611. US World War II Draft Registration Cards, 1940-1947, Record Group Number 147; Box or Roll Number 088.

612. 1920 US Census, Detroit, Wayne County, Michigan, January 1920, NARA T625; Roll 805; Sheet 2B; ED 147; House 199; Dwelling 32; Family 38; Line 53; "Howard E Fremody" (in the household of his parents).

613. 1930 US Census, Detroit, Wayne County, Michigan, April 1930, NARA T626; Sheet 18A; Page 84; ED 82-655; House 11710; Dwelling 350; Family 65; Line 16; "Howard E. Fremody."

614. 1940 US Census, Haverford Township, Delaware County, Pennsylvania, April 1940, NARA T627; Roll 3492; Sheet 9A; ED 23-84; Beechwood; House 633; Line 4; "Howard Fremody."
615. 1950 US Census, West Bloomfield Township, Oakland County, Michigan, April 1950, Record Group Number 29; Roll 3561; Sheet 4; ED 63-342; Line 21; "Howard E Fremody."
616. Marriage record/certificate/application. State Of Michigan; number 8416.
617. The State Journal, "Weddings: Fremody-Hale," 27 December 1915, page 5.
618. Find-A-Grave, (www.findagrave.com/memorial/22385917/howard-e-fremody: accessed 06 October 2022). Memorial ID 22385917, citing Mount Hope Cemetery, Lansing, Ingham County, Michigan; maintained by Ed Houghtaling (contributor 46804583).
619. Lansing City [Michigan] Directory 1916, Volume XVI, Lansing, Michigan: Chilson, McKinley & Co. Publishers, 1916, Page 321 (ancestry.com image 179); "Fremody Howard E (Mildred), clk Reo M C Co, res 430 S Pine."
620. R. L. Polk & Co.'s Detroit [Michigan] City Directory 1919, Detroit: R. L. Polk & Co. Publishers, 1919, Page 948 (ancestry.com image 1194); "Fremody Howard E asst pur agt Mich Copper & Brass h199 Lothrop av."
621. 1920 US Census, Detroit, Wayne County, Michigan, January 1920, "Purchasing Agent | Brass Factory."
622. 1930 US Census, Detroit, Wayne County, Michigan, April 1930, "buyer | department store."
623. Polks's Detroit [Michigan] City Directory 1930-1931, Detroit: R. L. Polk & Co., Publishers, 1930, Page 789 (ancestry.com image 386); "Fremody Howard E (Mildred) slsmn McConnell-Kerr Co r14277 Marlowe av."
624. 1940 US Census, Haverford Township, Delaware County, Pennsylvania, April 1940, "sales engineer | steel rolling mill."
625. 1950 US Census, West Bloomfield Township, Oakland County, Michigan, April 1950, "civil engineer | engineering."
626. The State Journal, "Deaths and Funerals," 28 April 1975, page B-2.
627. US World War I Draft Registration Cards, 1917-1918. Registration State: Michigan; Registration County: Ingham.
628. US World War II Draft Registration Cards, 1940-1947, Record Group Number 147.
629. 1900 US Census, Springport Township, Jackson County, Michigan, June 1900, NARA T623; Roll 719; Sheet 4B; ED 30; Dwelling 111; Family 111; Line 61; "Orpha Z. Clay."
630. 1910 US Census, Lansing, Ingham County, Michigan, April 1910, NARA T624; Roll 651; Sheet 6A; ED 66; Ward 3; Dwelling 113; Family 115; Line 31; "Orpha Z. Clay."
631. 1920 US Census, Springport Township, Jackson County, Michigan, January 1920, NARA T625; Roll 774; Sheet 3A; Page 199; ED 43; Dwelling 85; Family 95; Line 46; "Orpha Z Orrison."
632. Eggen, Tammy, compiler, The Farm Journal Illustrated Rural Directory of Jackson County, MI, 1918-23, Philadelphia, Pennsylvania: Wilmer Atkinson Company, 1923, Jesse J. Orrison and spouse Orpha; two children, Green St., Springport.
633. 1930 US Census, Marshall, Calhoun County, Michigan, April 1930, NARA T626; ED 13-54; Sheet 10B; House 423 Monroe St; Dwelling 285; Family 306; Line 54; "Orpha Z Orrson."

634. 1940 US Census, Marshall, Calhoun County, Michigan, April 1940, NARA T627; Roll 1737; Sheet 9A; ED 13-65; Ward 2; House 402; Line 21; "Orpha Orrison."

635. 1950 US Census, Marshall, Calhoun County, Michigan, April 1950, Record Group Number: 29; Roll 2610; Sheet 16; ED 13-128; House 427; Dwelling 202; Line 27; "Orpha Z Orrison."

636. Birth Certificate/Record. County Clerk of the County of Jackson, Michigan; Page 52.

637. Find-A-Grave, (www.findagrave.com/memorial/83700281/orpha-z-orrison: accessed 08 October 2022). Memorial ID 83700281, citing Oakridge Cemetery, Marshall, Calhoun County, Michigan; maintained by Amy (Decker) Veenendall (contributor 47104012).

638. Battle Creek Enquirer And News, "Obituaries: Mrs. Jesse J. Orrison," 14 May 1968, page 7.

639. 1920 US Census, Springport Township, Jackson County, Michigan, January 1920, NARA T625; Roll 774; Sheet 3A; Page 199; ED 43; Dwelling 85; Family 95; Line 45; "Jesse J Orrison."

640. Eggen, Tammy, compiler, The Farm Journal Illustrated Rural Directory of Jackson County, MI, 1918-23, Jesse J. Orrison, laborer, and spouse Orpha; two children, Green St., Springport.

641. 1930 US Census, Marshall, Calhoun County, Michigan, April 1930, NARA T626; ED 13-54; Sheet 10B; House 423 Monroe St; Dwelling 285; Family 306; Line 53; "Jesse J Orrson."

642. 1940 US Census, Marshall, Calhoun County, Michigan, April 1940, NARA T627; Roll 1737; Sheet 9A; ED 13-65; Ward 2; House 402; Line 20; "Jesse Orrison."

643. 1950 US Census, Marshall, Calhoun County, Michigan, April 1950, Record Group Number: 29; Roll 2610; Sheet 16; ED 13-128; House 427; Dwelling 202; Line 26;"Jesse J Orrison."

644. US Social Security Applications and Claims Index, 1936-2007, 19 Aug 1977: Name listed as JESSE JOHN ORRISON; Claim Date 24 June 1954.

645. Marriage record/certificate/application. Michigan Department of Community Health, Division of Vital Records and Health Statistics; Lansing; Number 93.

646. Marriage record says Springport.

647. Find-A-Grave, (www.findagrave.com/memorial/83695951/jesse-john-orrison: accessed 08 October 2022). Memorial ID 83695951, citing Oakridge Cemetery, Marshall, Calhoun County, Michigan; maintained by Amy (Decker) Veenendall (contributor 47104012).

648. Polk's Jackson City And County Directory, 1914, Detroit, Michigan: R. L. Polk & Co., 1914, Page 513 (ancestry.com image 265); "Orrison Jesse J (Orpha Z), baggageman, res 214 Ten Eyck."

649. R. L. Polk & Co.'s Jackson City and County Directory 1915-1916, Detroit: R. L. Polk & Co., Publishers, 1915, Page 532 (ancestry.com image 287); "Orrison Jesse J (Orpha Z), baggageman, res 327 Ten-Eyck."

650. R. L. Polk & Co.'s Jackson City Directory 1917, Detroit, Michigan: R. L. Polk & Co., Publishers, 1917, Page 735 (ancestry.com image 385); "Orrison Jesse J (Orpha), baggage agt, res 214 Ten Eyck."

651. 1920 US Census, Springport Township, Jackson County, Michigan, January 1920, "laborer | grain Elevator."

652. Polk's Marshall City [Michigan] Directory 1926, Detroit: R. L. Polk & Co., Publishers, 1926, Page 84 (ancestry.com image 44); "Orrison Jesse J (Orpha Z) lab h306 S Jefferson."

653. Polk's Jackson (Michigan) City Directory 1929, Detroit, Michigan: R. L. Polk & Co., Publishers, 1929, Page 94 (ancestry.com image 51); "Orrison Jesse J (Orpha Z) car repr h423 Monroe."

654. Polk's Marshall (Michigan) City Directory 1929, Volume II, Detroit: R. L. Polk & Co., Publishers, 1929, Page 94 (ancestry.com image 51); "Orrison Jesse J (Orpha Z) car repr h 423 Monroe."

655. 1930 US Census, Marshall, Calhoun County, Michigan, April 1930, "Car repair | Rail Road."

656. Polk's Marshall (Michigan) City Directory 1931, Volume III, Detroit: R. L. Polk & Co., Publishers, 1931, Page 95 (ancestry.com image 49); "Orrison Jesse J (Orpha Z) mach hd h423 Monroe."

657. Polk's Marshall (Cahoun County, Mich.) City Directory, 1934, Detroit: R. L. Polk & Co., Publishers, 1934, Volume IV, Page 74 (ancestry.com image 39); "Orrison Jesse J (Orpha Z) mach hd r605 Monroe."

658. 1940 US Census, Marshall, Calhoun County, Michigan, April 1940, "machine operator | Eaton mfg co."

659. 1950 US Census, Marshall, Calhoun County, Michigan, April 1950, "machine operator | mfg Fuel Rungo."

660. Battle Creek Enquirer And News, "Area Obituaries," 30 November 1957, page 11.

661. 1900 US Census, Springport Township, Jackson County, Michigan, June 1900, NARA T623; Roll 719; Sheet 4B; ED 30; Dwelling 111; Family 111; Line 62; "Milo S. Clay."

662. 1910 US Census, Lansing, Ingham County, Michigan, April 1910, NARA T624; Roll 651; Sheet 6A; ED 66; Ward 3; Dwelling 113; Family 115; Line 32; "Milo S Clay."

663. 1920 US Census, Detroit, Wayne County, Michigan, January 1920, NARA T625; Roll 809; Sheet 19B; ED 324; District 13; House 41; Dwelling 280; Family 451; Line 62; "Milo S Clay."

664. Polks's Detroit [Michigan] City Directory 1930-1931, Detroit: R. L. Polk & Co., Publishers, 1930, Page 2514; (ancestry.com image 1245): "16641 Clay Milo S" [not found in 1930 US Census].

665. 1940 US Census, Ferndale, Oakland County, Michigan, April 1940, NARA T626; Roll 1799; Sheet 3A; ED 63-36; House 497; Line 37; "Milo S Clay."

666. 1950 US Census, Pinellas County, Florida, April 1950, Record Group Number 29; Roll 5900; Sheet 31; ED 52-90; Dwelling 339; Line 6; "Milo S. Clay."

667. Birth Certificate/Record. State Of Michigan, Return of Birth in the County of Jackson, Michigan; Page 182; Number 659.

668. Lansing City [Michigan] Directory 1916, Volume XVI, Lansing, Michigan: Chilson, McKinley & Co. Publishers, 1916, Page 249 (ancestry.-com image 136); "Clay Milo S. wks Cit Tel Co. res 521 William."

669. R. L. Polk & Co.'s Detroit [Michigan] City Directory 1919, Detroit: R. L. Polk & Co. Publishers, 1919, Page 738 (ancestry.com image 1081); "Clay Milo S electn h41 Whitney av."

670. 1920 US Census, Detroit, Wayne County, Michigan, January 1920, "Electrician | Music Co."

671. R. L. Polk & Co.'s 1920-21 Detroit [Michigan] City Directory, Volume LVII, Detroit: R. L. Polk & Co., Publishers, 1920, Page 1027 (ancestry.-com image 556); "Clay Milo S electn h2683 (41) Whitney av."

672. Polk's Royal Oak and Ferndale (Oakland County, Mich.) City Directory 1936, Volume VII, Detroit: R. L. Polk & Co., Publishers, 1936, Page 537 (ancestry.com image 275); "Clay Milo S (Esselteen) asst office mgr Auburn Stove Works (Detroit) h497 E Lewiston av."

673. Polks's Royal Oak and Ferndale (Oakland County, Mich.) City Directory 1938, Volume VIII, Detroit, Michigan: R. L. Polk & Co., Publishers, 1938, Page 166 (ancestry.com image 89); "Clay Milo S (Esselteen) slsmn Auburn Stoker Sales & Serv (Detroit) h497 E Lewiston av (Fern)."
674. 1940 US Census, Ferndale, Oakland County, Michigan, April 1940, "Salesman | wholesale hating & plumbing."
675. Polk's Royal Oak and Ferndale (Oakland County, Mich.) City Directory 1940, Volume IX, Detroit: R. L. Polk & Co., Publishers, 1940, Page 209 (ancestry.com image 101); "Clay Milo S (Esselteen M) slsmn Nelson Co (Det) h497 E Lewiston av (F)."
676. Polk's Royal Oak and Ferndale (Oakland County, Mich.) City Directory 1942, Volume X, Detroit: R. L. Polk & Co., Publishers, 1942, Page 124 (ancestry.com image 57); "Clay Milo S (Esselteen M) electn h497 E Lewiston av (F)."
677. Polk's Royal Oak and Ferndale (Oakland County, Mich.) City Directory 1945, Volume XI, Detroit: R. L. Polk & Co., Publishers, 1945, Page 127 (ancestry.com image 68); "Clay Milo S (Esselteen) supvr Square D (Det) h497 E Lewiston av (F)."
678. 1950 US Census, Pinellas County, Florida, April 1950, "Building | House const."
679. Tampa Bay Times, newspaper, Saint Petersburg, Pinellas County, Florida, "Obituaries: Funeral Notice," 12 March 1976, page 8.
680. US World War II Draft Registration Cards, 1940-1947. Fourth Registration. Records of the Selective Service System, Record Group Number 147.
681. 1920 US Census, Detroit, Wayne County, Michigan, January 1920, NARA T625; Roll 809; Sheet 19B; ED 324; District 13; House 41; Dwelling 280; Family 451; Line 63; "Esselteen Clay."
682. 1940 US Census, Ferndale, Oakland County, Michigan, April 1940, NARA T626; Roll 1799; Sheet 3A; ED 63-36; House 497; Line 38; "Esselteen Clay."
683. 1950 US Census, Pinellas County, Florida, April 1950, Record Group Number 29; Roll 5900; Sheet 31; ED 52-90; Dwelling 339; Line 7; "Esselteen M Clay."
684. Michigan, U.S., County Marriage Records, 1822-1940, (https://familysearch.org/ark:/61903/1:1:FCX6-2LQ : 17 January 2020), Cassius Clay in entry for Milo S. Clay, 1916.
685. Marriage record/certificate/application. Michigan Department of Community Health, Division of Vital Records and Health Statistics; Lansing; Marriage Records, 1867-1952; Film 128; Film Description: 1916 Genesee-1916 Kalkaska; Record 8917.
686. The State Journal, "Social and Personal: Reception for Mr. and Mrs. Clay," 5 August 1916, page 5.
687. Tampa Bay Times, "They Eloped In Michigan: Clays Celebrate 50th Anniversary," 18 July 1966, page 3-D.
688. Birth Certificate/Record. Record 312, "Esseltine Church."
689. Death Certificate/Record. North Caroline Department of Environment, Health, And Natural Resources Division Of Epidemiology - Vital Records Section Certificate Of Death; 036298.
690. 1940 US Census, Ferndale, Oakland County, Michigan, April 1940.
691. Asheville Citizen-Times, newspaper, Asheville, North Carolina, "Deaths/Funerals: Esselteen M. Clay," 31 August 1991, page 4B.
692. 1900 US Census, Springport Township, Jackson County, Michigan, June 1900, NARA T623; Roll 719; Sheet 5; ED 30; Dwelling 148; Family 148; Line 86;"Erdith J Clay."

693. 1910 US Census, Kalamazoo, Kalamazoo County, Michigan, April 1910, NARA T624; Roll 654; Sheet 16A; ED 147; Ward 4; House 706; Visited 337; Family 364; Line 19; "Edith Clay."

694. R. L. Polk & Co.'s 1910 Kalamazoo [Michigan] City Directory, Detroit, Michigan: R. L. Polk & Co., Compilers and Publishers, 1910, Page 365 (ancestry.com image 184); "Clay Edith I, bds 706 S Rose."

695. 1920 US Census, Evanston City, Cook County, Illinois, NARA T625; Page 65; Sheet 17A; ED 77; 552 Elmwood; Dwelling 217; Family 419; Line 10; "Edith Wallace."

696. 1930 US Census, Kalamazoo Township, Kalamazoo County, Michigan, April 1930, NARA T626; Page 159; Sheet 22A; ED 39-27; Ward 3; House 508; Dwelling 520; Family 622; Line 38; "Edith C. Wallace."

697. 1940 US Census, Kalamazoo, Kalamazoo County, Michigan, April 1940, NARA T627; Roll 1771; Sheet 5B; ED 39-32; House 508; Line 66; "Mrs Edith Wallace."

698. 1950 US Census, Kalamazoo, Kalamazoo County, Michigan, April 1950, Record Group Number 29; Roll 411; Sheet 82; ED 89-43; 508 Village; Line 22; "Edith C. Wallace" widowed.

699. Polk's Kalamazoo [Michigan], [Detroit]: R. L. Polk & Co., 1958, Page 682 (ancestry.com image 68); "Wallace Edith C (The Village Shop) h508 Village."

700. Polk's Kalamazoo (Kalamazoo County, Mich.) City Directory 1959, Detroit: R. L. Polk & Co., Publishers, 1959, Page 638 (ancestry.com image 418); "Wallace Edith C Mrs h508 Village."

701. Polk's Kalamazoo (Kalamazoo County, Mich.) City Directory 1960, Detroit, Michigan: R. L. Polk & Co., Publishers, 1960, Page 693 (ancestry.com image 445); "Wallace, Edith C Mrs h508 Village."

702. Tombstone. (See findagrave.com); "Edith Wallace Daughter of Frank & Cora Clay 1891-1986."

703. Birth Certificate/Record. Page 172; Number 42; Record of Birth, Calhoun County, Michigan. (https://www.familysearch.org/ark:/61903/1:1:QPW8-BBX8 : 19 July 2021), Edith Irene Clay, 3 Oct 1891 | Page 369, number 42.

704. Death Certificate/Record. Michigan Department of Vital and Health Records.

705. Find-A-Grave, (www.findagrave.com/memorial/22902508/edith-irma-wallace: accessed 28 September 2022). Memorial ID 22902508, citing Springport Cemetery, Springport, Jackson County, Michigan; maintained by Deb Hayes-Wolfe (contributor 46811474).

706. R. L. Polk & Co.'s 1910 Kalamazoo [Michigan] City Directory, Detroit, Michigan: R. L. Polk & Co., Compilers and Publishers, 1910, Page 865; (ancestry.com image 184); "Clay Edith I, student, bds 706 S Rose."

707. R. L. Polk & Co.'s 1911 Kalamazoo City Directory, Detroit: R. L. Polk & Co., Compilers and Publishers, 1911, Page 376; (ancestry.com image 191); "Clay Edith I, student, bds 706 S Rose."

708. Polk's 1913 Kalamazoo [Michigan] City Directory, Detroit, Michigan: R. L. Polk & Co., 1913, Page 342; (ancestry.com image 176); "Clay Edith I, tchr, bds 706 S Rose."

709. Polk's 1914 Kalamazoo [Michigan] City and County Directory, Detroit, Michigan: R. L. Polk & Co., 1914, Page 356; (ancestry.com image 180); "Clay Edith I, tchr, bds 706 S Rose."

710. Polk's 1915 Kalamazoo [Michigan] City Directory, Detroit, Michigan: R. L. Polk & Co., 1915, Page 350; (ancestry.com image 173); "Clay Edith I, tchr Burdick St School, bds 706 S Rose."

711. R. L. Polk & Co.'s Kalamazoo [Michigan] City and County Directory 1916, Kalamazoo, Michigan: R. L. Polk & Co., Publishers, 1916, Page 344; (ancestry.com image 175); "Clay Edith I, tchr Burdick St School, bds 706 S Rose."

712. 1920 US Census, Evanston City, Cook County, Illinois, "Teacher Public school."

713. Polk's Kalamazoo City [Michigan] Directory 1924, Detroit, Michigan: R. L. Polk & Co., Publishers, 1924, Page 945; (ancestry.com image 474); "Wallace Edith C Mrs tchr Lake St Sch h1406 Portage."

714. Polk's Kalamazoo (Michigan) City Directory, 1927, Detroit, Michigan: R. L. Polk & Co., Publishers, 1927, Page 504; (ancestry.com image 255); "Wallace Edith Mrs tchr Vine Sch r508 Villag.e"

715. Polk's Kalamazoo [Michigan] City Directory 1929, Detroit, Michigan: R. L. Polk & Co., Publishers, 1929, Page 486; (ancestry.com image 239); "Wallace Edith Mrs tchr Vine St Sch r508 Village."

716. 1930 US Census, Kalamazoo Township, Kalamazoo County, Michigan, April 1930, "Teacher Pub. school."

717. Polk's Kalamazoo (Michigan) City Directory 1931, Detroit, Michigan: R. L. Polk & Co., Publishers, 1931, Page 420; (ancestry.com image 212); "Wallace Edith C Mrs tchr Vine Street Sch r508 Village."

718. Polk's Kalamazoo (Kalamazoo County, Mich.) City Directory 1934, Detroit, Michigan: R. L. Polk & Co., Publishers, 1934, Page 107; (ancestry.com image 54); "Clay Edith W tchr h508 Village."

719. Polk's Kalamazoo (Kalamzoo County, Mich.) City Directory, 1935, Detroit: R. L. Polk & Co., Publishers, 1935, Page 431; (ancestry.com image 218); "Wallace Edith C tchr PS r508 Village."

720. Polk's Kalamazoo (Kalamazoo County, Mich.) City Directory 1939, Detroit: R. L. Polk & Co., Publishers, 1939, Page 423; (ancestry.com image 209); "Wallace Edith C Mrs tchr McKinley Sch h508 Village."

721. 1940 US Census, Kalamazoo, Kalamazoo County, Michigan, April 1940, "School Teacher."

722. Polk's Kalamazoo [Michigan] City Directory 1943, Detroit, Michigan: R. L. Polk & Co., 1943, Page 444; (ancestry.com image 54); "Wallace Edith C Mrs tchr PS h508 Village."

723. Ibid. Page 425; (ancestry.com image 400); "Wallace Edith C Mrs tchr PS r508 Village."

724. Polk's Kalamazoo (Kalamazoo County, Mich.) City Directory 1945, Detroit: R. L. Polk & Co., Publishers, 1945, Page 407; (ancestry.com image 198); "Wallace Edith C Mrs tchr PS r508 Village apt 1."

725. Polk's Kalamazoo (Kalamazoo County, Mich.) City Directory 1947, Detroit, Michigan: R. L. Polk & Co., Publishers, 1947, Page 541; (ancestry.com image 258); "Wallace Edith Mrs tchr PS r508 Village."

726. Polk's Kalamazoo (Kalamazoo County, Mich.), City Directory 1948, Detroit, Michigan: R. L. Polk & Co., Publishers, 1948, Page 543; (ancestry.com image 273); "Wallace Edith (wid Robt) tchr Vine Sch r508 Village."

727. Polk's Kalamazoo (Kalamazoo County, Mich.) City Directory 1950, Detroit: R. L. Polk & Co., Publishers, 1950, Page 510; (ancestry.com image 273); "Wallace Edith C Mrs tchr Vine St Sch h508 Village."

728. Polk's Kalamazoo (Kalamazoo County, Mich.) City Directory 1952, Detroit: R. L. Polk & Co., Publishers, 1952, Page 513; (ancestry.com image 271); "Wallace Edith C Mrs tchr PS h508 Village."

729. Polk's Kalamazoo (Kalamazoo County, Mich.) City Directory 1953-1954, Detroit, Michigan: R. L. Polk & Co., Publishers, 1953, Page

574; (ancestry.com image 303); "Wallace Edith Mrs tchr Vine Sch h508 Village."

730. Polk's Kalamazoo (Kalamazoo County, Mich.) City Directory 1955, Detroit: R. L. Polk & Co., Publishers, 1955, Page 605; (ancestry.com image 319); "Wallace Edith C Mrs tchr Vine School h508 Village."

731. Cook County, Illinois Marriage Indexes, 1871-1960, database, www.ancestry.com, Page 1691; Serial number 0775618.

732. 1930 US Census, Kalamazoo Township, Kalamazoo County, Michigan, April 1930, Marital status: D [divorced]. Also, 1927 from second marriage application.

733. 1900 US Census, Springport Township, Jackson County, Michigan, June 1900, NARA T623; Roll 719; Sheet 5; ED 30; Dwelling 148; Family 148; Line 87; "Elden R. Clay."

734. 1910 US Census, Kalamazoo, Kalamazoo County, Michigan, April 1910, NARA T624; Roll 654; Sheet 16A; ED 147; Ward 4; House 706; Visited 337; Family 364; Line 20; "Aldon Clay."

735. Michigan, Census of World War I Veterans with Card Index, 1917-1919, https://familysearch.org ark:/61903/1:1:QPLR-F2QT : 8 September 2019), Fort McDowell, San Francisco, California; citing Military Service, Fort McDowell, San Francisco, California.

736. Polk's Kalamazoo [Michigan] City Directory 1922, Detroit, Michigan: R. L. Polk & Co., Publishers, 1922, Page 386; (ancestry.com image 190); "Clay Eldon R, removed to Albert Lee, Minn."

737. McCoy's Cedar Rapids [Iowa] City Directory 1929, Rockford, Illinois: The McCoy Directory Co., Publishers and Compilers, 1929, Page 160; (ancestry.com image 84); "Clay Eldon R (Anna M) r 1852 D av."

738. Not found in 1920 Census.

739. 1930 US Census, Cedar Rapids, Linn County, Iowa, NARA T626; Enumerations District 57-48; Sheet 2A; Dwelling 43; Family 43; Line 34; "Eldon R Clay."

740. Not found 1940 Census.

741. 1950 US Census, Winona, Winona County, Minnesota, Record Group Number 29; Roll 4400; Sheet: 85; ED 85-37; Line 8;"Eldon R. Clay."

742. Tombstone. (See findagrave.com; "Eldon R. Clay 1894-1975.")

743. Minnesota, U.S., Death Index, 1908-2017, Minnesota Department of Health, Minneapolis, database, ancestry.com or familysearch.corg, Certificate 011915; record 2640793.

744. Find-A-Grave, (www.findagrave.com/memorial/115721199/eldon-r-clay: accessed 29 September 2022). Memorial ID 115721199, citing Sunset Memorial Cemetery, Montevideo, Chippewa County, Minnesota; maintained by Gayle (contributor 47747536).

745. R. L. Polk & Co.'s 1910 Kalamazoo [Michigan] City Directory, Detroit, Michigan: R. L. Polk & Co., Compilers and Publishers, 1910, Page 865; (ancestry.com image 184); "Clay Eldon R, student, bds 706 S Rose."

746. R. L. Polk & Co.'s 1911 Kalamazoo City Directory, Detroit: R. L. Polk & Co., Compilers and Publishers, 1911, Page 376; (ancestry.com image 191); "Clay Eldon R, student, bds 706 S Rose."

747. Polk's 1913 Kalamazoo [Michigan] City Directory, Detroit, Michigan: R. L. Polk & Co., 1913, Page 342; (ancestry.com image 176); "Clay Eldon R, student, bds 706 S Rose."

748. Polk's 1914 Kalamazoo [Michigan] City and County Directory, Detroit, Michigan: R. L. Polk & Co., 1914, Page 356; (ancestry.com image 180); "Clay Eldon R, slsmn Remington Typewriter Co, bds 706 S Rose."

749. R. L. Polk & Co.'s Kalamazoo [Michigan] City Directory 1921, Detroit, Michigan: R. L. Polk & Co., Publishers, 1921, Page 442; (ancestry.com image 225); "Clay Eldon R (Anna), trav, res 118 Millview av."

750. Polk's Kalamazoo [Michigan] City Directory 1926, Detroit, Michigan: R. L. Polk & Co., Publishers, 1926, Page 158; (ancestry.com image 80); "Clay Eldon R clk F H Clay r508 Village."

751. Polk's Jackson City Directory 1927, Detroit, Michigan: R. L. Polk & Co., Publishers, 1927, Page 150; (ancestry.com image 77); "Clay Eldon R (Anna) slsmn Frank H Clay h522 Village."

752. Polk's Kalamazoo [Michigan] City Directory 1929, Detroit, Michigan: R. L. Polk & Co., Publishers, 1929, Page 150; (ancestry.com image 71); "Clay Eldon R (Anna) trav slsmn h522 Village."

753. 1930 US Census, Cedar Rapids, Linn County, Iowa, "Typewriter Salesman Independent."

754. Minneapolis Directory Company's Minneapolis (Minnesota) City Directory 1932, Volume LX, Minneapolis: Minneapolis Directory Company, 1932, Page 238; (ancestry.com image 121); "Clay Eldon R (Anna) slsmn h3909 Aldrich av S apt 16."

755. Polk's Duluth (St. Louis County, Minn.) City Directory 1946, Saint Paul, Minnesota: R. L. Polk & Co., Publishers, 1946, Page 124; (ancestry.com image 61); "Clay Typewriter Co, Eldon R Clay Owner, Distributors for Royal Standard and Portable Typewriters, R C Allen Adding and Business Machines, Office Furniture and Supplies, 325 W 1st, Tel Melrose 157."

756. Ibid. Page 124; (ancestry.com image 61); "Clay Eldon R (Margt J; Clay Typewriter Co) h1612 E Boulevard."

757. Polk's Duluth (St. Louis County, Minn.) City Directory 1948, Saint Paul, Minnesota: R. L. Polk & Co., Publishers, 1948, Page 126; (ancestry.com image 65): "Clay Typewriter Co, Eldon R Clay Owner, Distributors for Royal Standard and Portable Typewriters, R C Allen Adding and Business Machines, Office Furniture and Supplies, 325 W 1st, Tel Melrose 157."

758. Ibid. Page 126; (ancestry.com image 65): "Clay Eldon R (Margt J; Clay Typewriter Co) h1612 E Boulevard."

759. 1950 US Census, Winona, Winona County, Minnesota, "salesman Office Equipment."

760. Polk's Grand Junction (Mesa County, Color.) City Directory 1956, Kansas City, Missouri: R. L. Polk & Co., Publishers, 1956, Page 232; (ancestry.com image 128); "Clay Eldon R (Margt J; The Grand Gift Shop) h2235 Mesa."

761. Honor Roll of Kalamazoo County, 1917, Princeton, Illinois: 1920, "An Honor Roll Containing a Pictorial Record of he War Service of the Men and Women of Kalamazoo County [Michigan] 1871-1918-1919", Page 221 (ancestry.com image 223).

762. Michigan, Census of World War I Veterans with Card Index, 1917-1919, database, familysearch.org.

763. U.S., Department of Veterans Affairs BIRLS Death File, 1850-2010, database, www.ancestry.com. (BIRLS = Beneficiary Identification Records Locator Subsystem).

764. US World War II Draft Registration Cards, 1940-1947, Record Group Number: 147; Box or Roll Number: 495.

765. 1930 US Census, Cedar Rapids, Linn County, Iowa, NARA T626; Enumerations District 57-48; Sheet 2A; Dwelling 43; Family 43; Line 35; "Anna Clay."

766. 1940 US Census, Minnesota, Hennepin County, Minnesota, NARA T627; Roll 1985; Sheet 8B; ED 89-254; Line 50. "Anna M Clay | Divorced."

767. 1950 US Census, Los Angeles, Los Angeles County, California, April 1950, Record Group Number: 29; Roll 2061; Sheet 12; ED 66-1126; Line 13; "Anna M Clay | Divorced."

768. Marriage record/certificate/application. State Of Arizona, County of Pima, Marriage Certificate. Page 220.

769. Minnesota Births and Christenings, 1840-1980, Minnesota Department of Health, Minneapolis, database, www.familysearch.org, Minnesota Births and Christenings, 1940-1980, familysearch.org.

770. Michigan, Census of World War I Veterans with Card Index, 1917-1919, (https://www.familysearch.org ark:/61903/1:1:QPLR-F2QT : 8 September 2019), Fort McDowell, San Francisco, California; citing Eldon R Clay Military Service, Fort McDowell, San Francisco, California.

771. California Death Index, 1940-1997, State of California Department of Health Services, Center for Health Statistics, index, (https://familysearch.org/ark:/61903/1:1:VPHJ-TLC : 26 November 2014), Anna M Clay, 16 Mar 1973; Department of Public Health Services, Sacramento.

772. 1950 US Census, Los Angeles, Los Angeles County, California, April 1950.

773. Michigan, Divorce records, 1897-1952, database with (sometimes) scanned image, Michigan Department of Community Health, Division for Vital Records and Health Statistics; Lansing, www.ancestry.com, Record 18-637; file 26 May 1919, withdrawn; Record 19-85; filed 10 June 1921. Reportedly still married by 1936.

774. 1950 US Census, Winona, Winona County, Minnesota, Record Group Number 29; Roll 4400; Sheet: 85; ED 85-37; Line 9; "Margaret J. Clay."

775. Tombstone. (See findagrave.com; "Margaret J. Clay 1904-1991.")

776. Marriage record/certificate/application. South Dakota State Board Of Health, Division Of Vital Statistics, number 188798.

777. Find-A-Grave, (www.findagrave.com/memorial/115721200/margaret-estelle-clay: accessed 29 September 2022). Memorial ID 115721200, citing Sunset Memorial Cemetery, Montevideo, Chippewa County, Minnesota; maintained by Gayle (contributor 47747536).

778. 1950 US Census, Winona, Winona County, Minnesota.

779. Tombstone. (See findagrave.com): "John R. Son Of | S.&J. Pickles, | Died Nov. 27, 1890, Aged 10 Weeks."

780. Death Certificate/Record. Montcalm County, Michigan; Number 142; Page 305; recorded 21 August 1890; "John R Pickle"; died from a "Bursting Blood Vessel."

781. Find-A-Grave, (www.findagrave.com/memorial/45673919/john-r-pickles: accessed 20 November 2022). Memorial ID 45673919, citing Hillside Entrican Cemetery, Entrican, Montcalm County, Michigan; maintained by John C. Anderson (contributor 47208015).

782. 1900 US Census, Battle Creek, Calhoun County, Michigan, June 1900, NARA T623; ED 34; 3rd Ward; Sheet 17; Page 181A; Dwelling 327; Family 402; Line 48; "Ruth Pickles."

783. R. L. Polk's & Co.'s Grand Rapids City Directory 1907, Grand Rapids, Michigan : Grand Rapids Directory Company, Publishers, 1907, Thirty-Fifth Edition, Page 828; (ancestry.com image 424); "Ruth Pickles, bds 111, Scribner."

784. 1910 US Census, Grand Rapids, Kent County, Michigan, April 1910, NARA T624; Roll 658; Sheet 16B; ED 114; House 48; Dwelling 340; Family 365; Line 54; "Ruth Medd."

785. 1920 US Census, Grand Rapids, Kent County, Michigan, January 1920, NARA T625; Roll 779; Sheet 1B; ED 82; House 957; "Madison Ave" Dwelling 15; Family 18; Line 66; "Ruth Medd."
786. 1930 US Census, Grand Rapids, Kent County, Michigan, April 1930, NARA T626; Sheet 2A; Page 133; ED 41-81; "Madison Avenue S.E."; House 951; Dwelling 33; Family 35; Line 24; "Ruth Medd."
787. 1940 US Census, Alma, Gratiot County, Michigan, April 1940, NARA T627; Roll 1754; Sheet 3B; ED 29-6; House 313; Line 50; "Ruth Medd."
788. 1950 US Census, Osceola County, Florida, April 1950, Record Group Number 29; Roll 3386; Sheet 4; ED 49-9; Dwelling 32; Line 4; "Ruth Medd."
789. Funeral Card: "IN MEMORY OF | Ruth Pickell Medd | Date of Birth Sept. 2, 1890 | Date of Death Oct. 28, 1965 | Services Riedel Chapel Sunday 3:00 P.M. | Clergyman Rev. Maurice Grigsby | Interment At a Later Date | Riedel Funeral Home Kissimee, Florida"
790. Find-A-Grave, (www.findagrave.com/memorial/143622406/ruth-p-medd : accessed 25 January 2022). Memorial ID 143622406, citing Osceola Memory Gardens, Kissimmee, Osceola County, Florida; maintained by FamilySleuth (contributor 48368897).
791. Evening Press, newspaper, Grand Rapids, Michigan, 19 July 1913, page 11.
792. Palm Beach Post, newspaper, West Palm Beach, Florida, "Lake Worth Personals," 19 January 1930, page 6.
793. Orlando Sentinel, "Obituaries," 30 October 1965, page 3-C.
794. Orlando Evening Star, newspaper, Orlando, Florida, "Deaths In The News," 30 October 1965, page 6-B.
795. 1894 Michigan Census, Winfield Township, Montcalm County, Michigan, June 1894, Citing page 352; Line 3; State Archives, Lansing; (familysearch.org/ark:/61903/1:1:XHKZ-G48); FHL microfilm 915,327.
796. 1900 US Census, Winfield Township, Montcalm County, Michigan, June 1900, NARA T623; ED 143; Sheet 9A; Dwelling 171; Family 72; Line 8; "Percey Medd."
797. 1910 US Census, Grand Rapids, Kent County, Michigan, April 1910, NARA T624; Roll 658; Sheet 16B; ED 114; House 48; Dwelling 340; Family 365; Line 53; "E. Percy Medd."
798. 1920 US Census, Grand Rapids, Kent County, Michigan, January 1920, NARA T625; Roll 779; Sheet 1B; ED 82; House 957; "Madison Ave" Dwelling 15; Family 18; Line 65; "Percy Medd."
799. 1930 US Census, Grand Rapids, Kent County, Michigan, April 1930, NARA T626; Sheet 2A; Page 133; ED 41-81; House 951; "Madison Ave S. E." Dwelling 33; Family 35; Line 23; "Percy E Medd."
800. 1940 US Census, Alma, Gratiot County, Michigan, April 1940, NARA T627; Roll 1754; Sheet 3B; ED 29-6; House 313; Visitation 71; Line 49; "Percy Medd."
801. 1950 US Census, Osceola County, Florida, April 1950, Record Group Number 29; Roll 3386; Sheet 4; ED 49-9; Dwelling 32; Line 3; "E. P. Medd."
802. Marriage Certificate/Record/Application. Michigan Secretary of State, Department of Vital Records; Lansing, Marriage Records, 1867-1952; Film 92; Film Description: 1907 Ionia-1907 Montcalm; page 161; number 728; Book 14; (https://familysearch.org/ark:/61903/1:1:N3JB-TZF).
803. Orlando Sentinel,"Pair Wed 50 Years Celebrates," 19 June 1957, page 1; [newspaper has 9 June 1907].

804. Birth Certificate/Record. "—Medd" Number 157; Page 391 (familysearch.org/ark:/61903/1:1:NQH3-PP1) Howard City, Mecosta, Michigan, Department of Vital Records, Lansing; FHL microfilm 2,320,697.

805. Florida Death Index, 1877-1998, Florida Department of Health, Office of Vital Records, 1998, Jacksonville, Florida, familysearch.org and Ancestry.com, Citing volume 2978, certificate number 36702, Florida Department of Health, Office of Vital Records, Jacksonville.

806. Find-A-Grave, (www.findagrave.com/memorial/143622391/ezard-percy-medd : accessed 25 January 2022). Memorial ID 143622391, citing Osceola Memory Gardens, Kissimmee, Osceola County, Florida; maintained by FamilySleuth (contributor 48368897).

807. R. L. Polk's & Co.'s Grand Rapids City Directory 1907, Grand Rapids, Michigan : Grand Rapids Directory Company, Publishers, 1907, Thirty-Fifth Edition, Page 1290; (ancestry.com image 661); "Restaurants."

808. R. L. Polk's & Co.'s Grand Rapids City Directory 1908, Grand Rapids, Michigan : Grand Rapids Directory Company, Publishers, 1908, Thirty-Sixth Edition, Page 723; (ancestry.com image 370); apparently he was a manager for his sister Bessie I. Medd's restaurant.

809. R. L. Polk & Co., Publishers, R. L. Polk's & Co.'s 1909 Grand Rapids City Directory, Grand Rapids, Michigan : Grand Rapids Directory Company, Publishers, 1909, Thirty-Seventh Edition, Page 758; (ancestry.com image 388); apparently he was a manager for his sister Bessie I. Medd's restaurant; "450 Madison av."

810. R. L. Polk's & Co.'s 1910 Grand Rapids City Directory For Year Commencing October, Grand Rapids, Michigan : Grand Rapids Directory Company, Publishers, 1910, Thirty-Eighth Edition, Page 756; (ancestry.com image 382); "mach Riley Automobile Co, h 558 S Division."

811. 1910 US Census, Grand Rapids, Kent County, Michigan, April 1910, "Machinist | Automobile."

812. R. L. Polk & Co., Publishers, R. L. Polk & Co.'s 1912 Grand Rapids Directory, [Grand Rapids, Michigan : Grand Rapids Directory Company, Publishers, 1912], Page 710; (ancestry.com image 366); "repr, h 1139 Madison av."

813. R. L. Polk & Co.'s 1913 Grand Rapids City Directory, [Grand Rapids, Michigan : Grand Rapids Directory Company, Publishers, 1913], Page 688; (ancestry.com image 354); "foreman E M Mosher, h 1139 Madison av."

814. R. L. Polk & Co.'s 1914 Grand Rapids City Directory, [Grand Rapids, Michigan : Grand Rapids Directory Company, Publishers, 1914], Page 701; (ancestry.com image 368); "(East End Garage), h 1468 Lake dr."

815. R. L. Polk & Co.'s 1915 Grand Rapids City Directory, [Grand Rapids, Michigan : Grand Rapids Directory Company, Publishers, 1915], Page 683; (ancestry.com image 349); "auto repr, h 951 Madison av."

816. R. L. Polk & Co.'s 1916 Grand Rapids City Directory, Grand Rapids, Michigan : Grand Rapids Directory Company, Publishers, 1916, Forty-Fourth Edition, Page 1478; (ancestry.com image 1538); "Automobile Garages 951 Madison av."

817. R. L. Polk's & Co.'s 1918 Grand Rapids City Directory, Forty-Sixth Edition, Grand Rapids, Michigan : Grand Rapids Directory Company, Publishers, 1920, Page 704; (ancestry.com iamge 354); "garage 951 Madison av h same."

818. 1920 US Census, Grand Rapids, Kent County, Michigan, January 1920, "Mechanic | Motor."

819. Polk's Grand Rapids City Directory 1920, Forty-Eighth Edition, Grand Rapids, Michigan: Grand Rapids Directory Company, Publishers, 1920, Page 1431; (ancestry.com image 721); "Automobile Garages."
820. R. L. Polk & Co., Publishers, R. L. Polk & Co.'s 1921 Grand Rapids City Directory, [Grand Rapids, Michigan : Grand Rapids Directory Company, Publishers, 1921], Page 713; (ancestry.com image 354); "garage 951 Madison av h same."
821. Ibid. Page 1462; (ancestry.com image 724); "Auto Garages 951 Madison av."
822. Ibid. Page 626; (ancestry.com image 321); "garage 951 Madison av SE."
823. Polk's Grand Rapids City Directory 1922, Grand Rapids, Michigan : Grand Rapids Directory Company, Publishers, 1922, Page 1136; (ancestry.com image 581); "Automobile Garages ; 951 Madison av."
824. Polk's Grand Rapids City Directory 1923, 51st Edition, Grand Rapids, Michigan: Grand Rapids Directory Company, Publishers, 1923, Page 600; (ancestry.com image 302); "garage 951 Madison av SE h do."
825. Polk's Grand Rapids (Michigan) City Directory 1927, Fifty-Fifth Edition, Grand Rapids, Michigan: The Grand Rapids Directory Co., Publishers, 1927, Page 730; (ancestry.com image 373). "Percy E Medd (Ruth) garage 951 Madison av SE h do."
826. Ibid. Page 1436; (ancestry.com image 734); "Automobile Garages" ; '951 Madison av SE."
827. R. L. Polk's & Co.'s Grand Rapids (Michigan) City Directory 1928, Fifty-Sixth Edition, Grand Rapids, Michigan: Grand Rapids Directory Company, Publishers, 1928, Page 631; (ancestry.com image 324); "garage."
828. Polk's Grand Rapids (Michigan) City Directory , Volume 1929 LVII, Grand Rapids, Michigan: Grand Rapids Directory Co., Publishers, 1929, Page 623; (ancestry.com image 320); "Medd Perry [sic] E (Ruth) auto repr 951 madison av SE h do."
829. 1930 US Census, Grand Rapids, Kent County, Michigan, April 1930, "Auto Mechanic | At home,"
830. Polks's Detroit [Michigan] City Directory 1930-1931, Detroit: R. L. Polk & Co., Publishers, 1930, Page 1316; (ancestry.com image 650); "autowkr r 1954 Clements av."
831. Polk's Grand Rapids City Directory 1933, Grand Rapids, Michigan: Grand Rapids Directory Co., 1933, Page 463; (ancestry.com image 236); "auto repr 951 Madison av SE h do."
832. Classified Buyers' Guide Of The City Of Grand Rapids (Michigan) 1933, Grand Rapids, Michigan : Grand Rapids Directory Company, Publishers, 1933, Page 1014; (ancestry.com image 514); "Automobile Repairing" ; "951 Madison av NE."
833. Polk's Grand Rapids (Kent County, Mich.) City Directory, Volume 1936 LIX, Grand Rapids, Michigan : Grand Rapids Directory Company, Publishers, 1936, Page 581; (ancestry.com image 292); "Medd's Garage."
834. Polks's Royal Oak and Ferndale (Oakland County, Mich.) City Directory 1938, Volume VIII, Detroit, Michigan: R. L. Polk & Co., Publishers, 1938, Page 548; (ancestry.com image 282); "maintenancemn Detroit Zoological Pk r Detroit."
835. 1940 US Census, Alma, Gratiot County, Michigan, April 1940, "Maintenance" "Chemical [illegible]."
836. Grand Rapids Press, 17 February 1917, page 26.
837. Orlando Sentinel, Kate Knox, "Kissimmee Resident Builds Unusual Clocks As Hobby," 19 July 1953, page 5-B.
838. Ibid. "Obituaries," 14 July 1967, page 8-C.

839. Ibid. "Obituaries," 15 July 1967, page 4-C.
840. US World War I Draft Registration Cards, 1917-1918, NARA, Registration State: Michigan; Registration County: Kent.
841. US World War II Draft Registration Cards, 1940-1947. Record Group Number: 147.
842. 1910 US Census, Grand Rapids, Kent County, Michigan, April 1910, NARA T624; Roll 658; Sheet 16B; ED 114; House 48; Dwelling 340; Family 365; Line 55; "Ford Medd."
843. 1920 US Census, Grand Rapids, Kent County, Michigan, January 1920, NARA T625; Roll 779; Sheet 1B; ED 82; House 957; "Madison Ave," Dwelling 15; Family 18; Line 67; "Ford H Medd."
844. 1930 US Census, Kalamazoo Township, Kalamazoo County, Michigan, April 1930, NARA T626; Sheet 4A; ED 39-24; House 615; Dwelling 72; Family 104; Line 47; "Ford H. Medd."
845. 1940 US Census, Grand Rapids, Kent County, Michigan, April 1940, NARA T627; Roll 1897; Sheet 3B; ED 86-10; House 1331; Dwelling 50; Line 46; "Ford Medd."
846. 1950 US Census, Grand Rapids, Kent County, Michigan, April 1950, Record Group Number 29; Roll 1268; Sheet 73; ED 87-14; "Grand Ave" House 1311; Line 9; "Ford H. Medd."
847. 1910 US Census, Grand Rapids, Kent County, Michigan, April 1910, NARA T624; Roll 658; Sheet 16B; ED 114; House 48; Dwelling 340; Family 365; Line 56; "Gertrude W. Medd."
848. 1920 US Census, Grand Rapids, Kent County, Michigan, January 1920, NARA T625; Roll 779; Sheet 1B; ED 82; House 957; "Madison Ave," Dwelling 15; Family 18; Line 68; "Gertrude W Medd."
849. <u>Polk's Grand Rapids (Michigan) City Directory 1927</u>, Fifty-Fifth Edition, Grand Rapids, Michigan: The Grand Rapids Directory Co., Publishers, 1927, Page 730; (ancestry.com image 373); "Medd Gertrude W student r951 Madison av SE."
850. <u>R. L. Polk's & Co.'s Grand Rapids (Michigan) City Directory 1928</u>, Fifty-Sixth Edition, Grand Rapids, Michigan: Grand Rapids Directory Company, Publishers, 1928, Page 631; (ancestry.com image 324); "Medd Gertrude student r951 Madison av SE."
851. <u>Polk's Grand Rapids (Michigan) City Directory</u>, Volume 1929 LVII, Grand Rapids, Michigan: Grand Rapids Directory Co., Publishers, 1929, Page 623; (ancestry.com image 320); "Medd Gertrude W student r951 Madison av SE h do."
852. 1930 US Census, Grand Rapids, Kent County, Michigan, April 1930, NARA T626; Sheet 2A; Page 133; ED 41-81; "Madison Avenue S.E"; House 951; Dwelling 33; Family 35; Line 25; "Gertrude W. Medd."
853. 1940 US Census, Alma, Gratiot County, Michigan, April 1940, NARA T627; Roll 1754; Sheet 17A; ED 29-1; House 613; Line 3; "Gertrude W. Reid."
854. 1950 US Census, Alma, Gratiot County, Michigan, April 1950, Record Group Number 29; Roll 4769; Sheet 11; ED 29-14; House 315; "Charles St," Line 29; "Gertrude W Reid."
855. 1920 US Census, Grand Rapids, Kent County, Michigan, January 1920, NARA T625; Roll 779; Sheet 1B; ED 82; House 957; "Madison Ave," Dwelling 15; Family 18; Line 69; "Robert R. Medd."
856. <u>R. L. Polk's & Co.'s Grand Rapids (Michigan) City Directory 1928</u>, Fifty-Sixth Edition, Grand Rapids, Michigan: Grand Rapids Directory Company, Publishers, 1928, Page 631; (ancestry.com image 324); "student."

857. 1930 US Census, Grand Rapids, Kent County, Michigan, April 1930, NARA T626; Sheet 2A; Page 133; ED 41-81; "Madison Avenue S.E."; House 951; Dwelling 33; Family 35; Line 26; "Robert R. Medd."
858. 1940 US Census, Grand Rapids, Kent County, Michigan, April 1940, NARA T627; Roll 1900; Sheet 61B; ED 86-112; House 527; "Wealthy" street; Line 77; "Robert R Medd."
859. 1950 US Census, Grand Rapids, Kent County, Michigan, April 1950, Record Group Number 29; Roll 417; Sheet Number 76; ED 87-217; "Madison" street; House 218; Line 6; "Robert R Medd."
860. US Social Security Applications and Claims Index, 1936-2007, Jun 1937: Name listed as ROBERT REGINALD MEDD; 03 Jun 1993: Name listed as ROBERT R MEDD.
861. Orlando Sentinel,"Pair Wed 50 Years Celebrate," 19 June 1957, page 1.
862. 1900 US Census, Battle Creek, Calhoun County, Michigan, June 1900, NARA T623; ED 34; Sheet 17; Page 181A; Dwelling 327; House 679; Family 402; Line 49; "Frederick Pickles."
863. 1910 US Census, Grand Rapids, Kent County, Michigan, April 1910, NARA T624; Roll 656; ED 55; Sheet 11A; House 140; Dwelling 167; Family 200; Line 32; "Fred W Pickles."
864. 1920 US Census, Wyoming Township, Kent County, Michigan, January 1920, NARA T625; Roll 779; Sheet 12A; ED 118; House 607; Dwelling 242; Family 242; Line 35; "Fred W. Pickell."
865. 1930 US Census, Grand Rapids, Kent County, Michigan, April 1930, (then township) NARA T626; Sheet 11A; ED 41-116; North Park; House 3130; Dwelling 32; Family 33; Line 14; "Fred W. Pickell."
866. 1935 Florida Census, Broward County, Florida, Fort Lauderdale, Precinct 4; (https://www.familysearch.org/ark:/61903/1:1:MNJN-YMX); Tenth census, Florida, 1935; (Microfilm series S 5, 30 reels); Record Group 001021; State Library and Archives, Tallahassee (ancestry.com image 13) "Mr Fred W. Pickell."
867. 1940 US Census, Los Angeles County, California, April 1940, NARA T627; Roll 389; Sheet 6A; ED 60-1167; House 5734; Line 31; "Fred W. Pickell."
868. 1950 US Census, Los Angeles, Los Angeles County, California, April 1950, Records of the Bureau of the Census, 1790-2007; Record Group Number 29; Roll 1559; Sheet Number 4; ED 66-284; Line 25; "Fred W Pickell."
869. 1900 Census says December 1891; Death record; Social Security and WWI Draft Registration say 1890.
870. California Death Index, 1940-1997, State of California Department of Health Services, Center for Health Statistics, index, familysearch.org or ancestry.com.
871. Find-A-Grave, (www.findagrave.com/memorial/103883978/fred-william-pickell : accessed 28 January 2022). Memorial ID 103883978, citing Glen Haven Memorial Park, Sylmar, Los Angeles County, California; maintained by Kaye Vensko (contributor 47049416).
872. R. L. Polk's & Co.'s Grand Rapids City Directory 1907, Grand Rapids, Michigan : Grand Rapids Directory Company, Publishers, 1907, Thirty-Fifth Edition, Page 828; (ancestry.com image 424); "Frederick W. Pickles, mach bds 111, Scribner."
873. R. L. Polk's & Co.'s 1910 Grand Rapids City Directory For Year Commencing October, Grand Rapids, Michigan : Grand Rapids Directory Company, Publishers, 1910, Thirty-Eighth Edition, Page 871; (ancestry.com image 439); "Frederick W. Pickles mach Truman M Smith Co, bds 140 Lyon."

874. R. L. Polk & Co.'s 1911 Grand Rapids City Directory, Grand Rapids, Michigan: The Grand Rapids Directory Company, 1911, Page 714; (ancestry.com image 364); "Pickles Frederick W. mach, h 458 Wealthy av."

875. R. L. Polk & Co.'s 1913 Grand Rapids City Directory, [Grand Rapids, Michigan : Grand Rapids Directory Company, Publishers, 1913], Page 795; (ancestry.com image 408); "Pickell Frederick W. repr Miller & Brown, h 701 Oakland av."

876. R. L. Polk & Co.'s 1914 Grand Rapids City Directory, [Grand Rapids, Michigan : Grand Rapids Directory Company, Publishers, 1914], Page 811; (ancestry.com image 426); "Pickell Frederick W, repr Miller Taxi and Transfer Co, bds 904 Kensington avenue."

877. R. L. Polk & Co.'s 1915 Grand Rapids City Directory, [Grand Rapids, Michigan : Grand Rapids Directory Company, Publishers, 1915], Page 791; (ancestry.com image 404); "Pickell Frederick W, repr Miller Taxi Co, bds 904 Kensington av."

878. R. L. Polk's & Co.'s 1918 Grand Rapids City Directory, Forty-Sixth Edition, Grand Rapids, Michigan : Grand Rapids Directory Company, Publishers, 1920, Page 808; (ancestry.com image 406); "Pickell Frederick W, electn Leon S Heth Co, h 228 Ives av."

879. The Buyers' Guide R. L. Polk & Co.'s Grand Rapids [Michigan] City Directory 1919, [Grand Rapids, Michigan: R. L. Polk & Co.,] 1919, Page 816; (ancestry.com image 406); "Pickell Fred W, electn Leon S Heth Co, h 607 Northgrove av."

880. 1920 US Census, Wyoming Township, Kent County, Michigan, January 1920, "Electrician | Electric Co."

881. Glendale [California] City Directory 1923, Long Beach, California: Western Directory Co., 1923, Page 313; (ancestry.com image 162); "Pickell Fred W mechanic B J Smith r Tunjunga."

882. Polk's Grand Rapids City Directory 1924, Fifty-Second Edition, Grand Rapids, Michigan: The Grand Rapids Directory Co., 1924, Page 716; (ancestry.com image 366); "Pickell Fred W toolmkr Cheney Talking Machine Co res Ada Mich R D 3."

883. R. L. Polk's & Co.'s Grand Rapids (Michigan) City Directory 1928, Fifty-Sixth Edition, Grand Rapids, Michigan: Grand Rapids Directory Company, Publishers, 1928, Page 720; (ancestry.com image 369); "Pickell Fred W (Lena I) mach G R Textile Machy Co h3130 Colt rd NE (North Park)."

884. Polk's Grand Rapids (Michigan) City Directory , Volume 1929 LVII, Grand Rapids, Michigan: Grand Rapids Directory Co., Publishers, 1929, Page 711; (ancestry.com image 364); "Pickell Fred (Lena I) mach G R Textile Machinery Co h3130 Coit rd NE."

885. 1930 US Census, Grand Rapids, Kent County, Michigan, April 1930, "Experimental machine | Machinery Co."

886. 1935 Florida Census, Gulfport, Pinellas County, Florida, "Filling Station." Florida Department of Agriculture Bulletin [new ser.] no. 193 and Mayo.

887. 1940 US Census, Los Angeles County, California, April 1940, "Machinist | Airplane."

888. 1950 US Census, Los Angeles, Los Angeles County, California, April 1950, "Proprietor | Wholesale Machine shop."

889. Polk's Glendale (Los Angeles County, California) City Directory 1954, Los Angeles: R. L. Polk & Co. Of California Publishers, 1954, Page 382; (ancestry.com image 205): "Pickell Fred W (Mertle S; Aircraft Crop Dusting & Spraying Equip) h3762 Ramsdell av."

890. Polk's Glendale (Los Angeles County, California) City Directory 1955, Los Angeles: R. L. Polk & Co., Publishers, 1955, Page 378; (ancestry.com image 203); "Pickell Fred W (Mertle S) crop duster h3762 Ramsdell av (LaC)."
891. Polk's Glendale (Los Angeles County, California) City Directory 1957, Los Angeles: R. L. Polk & Co., Publishers, 1957, Page 419; (ancestry.com image 283); "Pickell Fred W (Mertle S; Fred W. Pickell & Associates; LA) h3762 Ramsdell av (LaC)."
892. Polk's Glendale (Los Angeles County, California) City Directory 1958, Los Angeles: R. L. Polk & Co., Publishers, 1958, Page 222; (ancestry.com image 465); "3762 [Ramsetell Avenune] Pickell Fred W CH9-2105."
893. San Fernando-Sylmar [California] Including Lakeview Terrace And Kagel Canyon City Directory, 1962-1963, San Fernando, California: B & G Publications, 1962, Page 56; (ancestry.com image 58); "Pickell Fred (Mertle) 12401 Filmore, EM 6-8285."
894. Highland Park News-Herald, newspaper, Highland Park, California, "Public Notices," 27 April 1945, page 15.
895. US World War II Draft Registration Cards, 1940-1947. Records of the Selective Service System, Record Group Number 147.
896. 1920 US Census, Wyoming Township, Kent County, Michigan, January 1920, NARA T625; Roll 779; Sheet 12A; ED 118; House 607; Dwelling 242; Family 242; Line 36; "Lena Pickell."
897. 1930 US Census, Grand Rapids, Kent County, Michigan, April 1930, (then township) NARA T626; Sheet 11A; ED 41-116; North Park; House 3130; Dwelling 32; Family 33; Line 15; "Lena Pickell."
898. 1935 Florida Census, Broward County, Florida, Fort Lauderdale, Precinct 4; (https://www.familysearch.org/ark:/61903/1:1:MNJN-YMX); Tenth census, Florida, 1935; (Microfilm series S 5, 30 reels); Record Group 001021; (ancestry.com image 13) "Mrs Lena I. Pickell."
899. 1940 US Census, Los Angeles County, California, April 1940, NARA T627; Roll 389; Sheet 6A; ED 60-1167; House 5734; Line 32; "Lena I Pickell."
900. 1950 US Census, Los Angeles, Los Angeles County, California, April 1950, Records of the Bureau of the Census, 1790-2007; Record Group Number 29; Roll 1559; Sheet Number 4; ED 66-284; Line 26; "Lena I Pickell."
901. Tombstone. (See findagrave.com); "Lena I Pickell | 1891-1951."
902. Marriage Certificate/Record/Application. Michigan Department of Community Health, Division of Vital Records and Health Statistics; Lansing, Marriage Records, 1867-1952; Film 114; Film Description: 1913 Gogebic-1913 Leelanau; Number 11457, Page 44. "Frederick W. Pickell" and "Lena I. Rittinhouse."
903. Find-A-Grave, (www.findagrave.com/memorial/103883964/lena-irena-pickell : accessed 28 January 2022). Memorial ID 103883964, citing Glen Haven Memorial Park, Sylmar, Los Angeles County, California; maintained by Kaye Vensko (contributor 47049416).
904. Highland Park News-Herald, newspaper, Highland Park, California, "Lena Irena Pickell," 3 August 1951, page 6.
905. 1920 US Census, Wyoming Township, Kent County, Michigan, January 1920, NARA T625; Roll 779; Sheet 12A; ED 118; House 607; Dwelling 242; Family 242; Line 37; "Margie Pickell."
906. 1930 US Census, Grand Rapids, Kent County, Michigan, April 1930, (then township) NARA T626; Sheet 11A; ED 41-116; North Park; House 3130; Dwelling 32; Family 33; Line 16; "Margorie Pickell."

907. 1935 Florida Census, Broward County, Florida, Fort Lauderdale, Precinct 4; (https://www.familysearch.org/ark:/61903/1:1:MNJN-YMX); Tenth census, Florida, 1935; (Microfilm series S 5, 30 reels); Record Group 001021; (ancestry.com image 13) "Marjorie Pickell."

908. 1940 US Census, Los Angeles County, California, April 1940, NARA T627; Roll 389; Sheet 6A; ED 60-1167; House 5734; Line 35; "Marjorie Fisher."

909. 1950 US Census, Los Angeles, Los Angeles County, California, April 1950, Record Group Number 29; Roll 2146; Sheet Number 4; ED 66-121B; Line 2; "Marjorie H Fisher."

910. 1920 US Census, Wyoming Township, Kent County, Michigan, January 1920, NARA T625; Roll 779; Sheet 12A; ED 118; House 607; Dwelling 242; Family 242; Line 38; "Dorothy Pickell."

911. 1930 US Census, Grand Rapids, Kent County, Michigan, April 1930, (then township) NARA T626; Sheet 11A; ED 41-116; North Park; House 3130; Dwelling 32; Family 33; Line 17; "Dorothy Pickell."

912. 1935 Florida Census, Broward County, Florida, Fort Lauderdale, Precinct 4; (https://www.familysearch.org/ark:/61903/1:1:MNJN-YMX); Tenth census, Florida, 1935; (Microfilm series S 5, 30 reels); Record Group 001021; (ancestry.com image 13) "Dorothy Pickell."

913. 1940 US Census, Grand Rapids, Kent County, Michigan, April 1940, NARA T627; Roll 1899; Sheet 6B; ED 86-60; Line 45; "Dorothy M. Weaver."

914. 1950 US Census, Grand Rapids, Kent County, Michigan, April 1950, Record Group Number 29; Roll 1269; Sheet 13; ED 87-75; 447 Darrell; Line 10; "Dorothy Weaver."

915. US Social Security Applications and Claims Index, 1936-2007, Dec 1936: Name listed as DOROTHY MARIE PICKELL; 11 Aug 2007: Name listed as DOROTHY M WEAVER. Death Certificate number 07-1929.

916. 1935 Florida Census, Broward County, Florida, Fort Lauderdale, Precinct 4; (https://www.familysearch.org/ark:/61903/1:1:MNJN-YMX); Tenth census, Florida, 1935; (Microfilm series S 5, 30 reels); Record Group 001021; (ancestry.com image 13) "Philip R. Pickell."

917. 1940 US Census, Los Angeles County, California, April 1940, NARA T627; Roll 389; Sheet 6A; ED 60-1167; House 5734; Line 33; "Philip R. Pickell."

918. 1950 US Census, Los Angeles, Los Angeles County, California, April 1950, Records of the Bureau of the Census, 1790-2007; Record Group Number 29; Residence Date: 1950; Home in 1950: Los Angeles, Los Angeles, California; Roll 1559; Sheet Number 4; ED 66-284; Line 27; "Phillip R Pickell."

919. US Social Security Applications and Claims Index, 1936-2007, Mar 1951: Name listed as PHILLIP ROGER PICKELL; 16 Jul 1999: Name listed as PHILLIP R PICKELL.

920. Polk's Glendale (Los Angeles County, California) City Directory 1954, Los Angeles: R. L. Polk & Co Of California Publishers, 1954, Page 382; (ancestry.com image 205): "Pickell Fred W (Mertle S; Aircraft Crop Dusting & Spraying Equip) h3762 Ramsdell av" and Page 382; (ancestry.com image 206); "Pickell Myrtle S Mrs h3762 Ramsdell av (PO LaC)."

921. San Fernando-Sylmar [California] Including Lakeview Terrace And Kagel Canyon City Directory, 1962-1963, San Fernando, California: B & G Publications, 1962, Page 56, (ancestry.com image 58); "Pickell Fred (Mertle) 12401 Filmore, EM 6-8285."

922. California, U.S., Marriage Index, 1949-1985, (ancestry.com image 373); County 70? State file 38387. "Fred Pickell" "Mertle Sykes" "Mertle Harding."

923. U.S., Veterans Administration Master Index, 1917-1940, database, familysearch.org or ancestry.com, NAI 76193916. Record Group 15: Records of the Department of Veterans Affairs, 1773 - 2007. NARA at St. Louis, St. Louis, Missouri.

924. Birth Certificate/Record. "Myrtle Harding" Number 193; recorded 12 February 1894. (ancestry.com image 1508).

925. California Death Index, 1940-1997, State of California Department of Health Services, Center for Health Statistics, index, familysearch.org or ancestry.com, "Mertle S Pickell".

926. Los Angeles Times, newspaper, Los Angeles, California, "Vital Records: Deaths," 12 December 1970, page Part III, page 9. "PICKELL, Mertle Sykes. Forest Lawn-Glendale."

927. Find-A-Grave, (www.findagrave.com/memorial/85488585/mertle-marie-pickell : accessed 11 May 2022). Memorial ID 85488585, citing Forest Lawn Memorial Park, Glendale, Los Angeles County, California; maintained by woowoo (contributor 49949980).

928. Polk's Pasadena (Los Angeles County, California) City Directory 1953, Los Angeles: R. L. Polk & Co. Of California, 1953, Page 555; (ancestry.com image 285); "Pickell Mertle H Mrs typ County Bur Pub Assistance r La Crescenta."

929. Polk's Pasadena (Los Angeles County, Calif.) City Directory 1958, Los Angeles: R. L. Polk & Co. Publishers, 1958, Page 526; ancestry.com image 360; "Pickell Mertle H Mrs typ County Bur of Pub Assistance r La Crescenta."

930. Polk's Pasadena (Los Angeles County, Calif.) City Directory 1959, Los Angeles: R. L. Polk & Co., Publishers, 1959, Page 520; (ancestry.com image 353); "Pickell Mertle H typ County Bur of Pub Assistance r La Crescenta."

931. 1900 US Census, Battle Creek, Calhoun County, Michigan, June 1900, NARA T623; ED 34; Sheet 17; Page 181A; Dwelling 327; Family 402; Line 50;"James Pickles."

932. 1910 US Census, Grand Rapids, Kent County, Michigan, April 1910, NARA T624; Roll 656; ED 55; Sheet 11A; House 140; Dwelling 167; Family 200; Line 33; "James E. Pickles."

933. 1919 World War I Veterans Census, Kent County, Michigan, index, Western Michigan Genealogical Society, www.wmgs.org, From Department of Military Affairs War Preparedness Board, 1917-1919; RG78-92, Lot 9; Film number 3-1307-01455-3814 "10."

934. 1920 US Census, Grand Rapids, Kent County, Michigan, January 1920, NARA T625; Roll 778; Sheet 11A; ED 70; Dwelling 229; Family 275; Line 19; "James Pickell."

935. 1930 US Census, Grand Rapids, Kent County, Michigan, April 1930, NARA T626; City Ward 3; Sheet 21B; ED 41-96; Dwelling 189; Family 190; Line 67; "James Pickell."

936. 1935 Florida Census, Gulfport, Pinellas County, Florida, Precinct 8; (Microfilm series S 5, 30 reels); Record Group 001021; State Library and Archives of Florida; "5036 28th Ave S."

937. 1940 US Census, Santa Monica, Los Angeles County, California, NARA T627; Roll 257; Sheet 62A; ED 19-771; House 2311; Line 22; "James Pickell."

938. 1950 US Census, Santa Monica, Los Angeles County, California, scanned image, Bureau of the Census; Washington, D.C., Record

Group Number 29; Roll 5861; Sheet 11; ED 74-34; House 2311; Line 15; "James E. Pickell."

939. Tombstone. (See findagrave.com); "James E Pickell | South Carolina | Pvt Air Service | World War I | Feb 27 1894 | Feb 23 1974."

940. Death Certificate/Record. State Of Texas, Certificate Of Death, File 18664; "James Edward Pickell."

941. Find-A-Grave, (www.findagrave.com/memorial/96283838/james-e-pickell : accessed 3 February 2022). Memorial ID 96283838, citing Paradise Cemetery, Paradise, Butte County, California; maintained by Adriana (contributor 47328225).

942. 1910 US Census, Grand Rapids, Kent County, Michigan, April 1910, "Draughtsman."

943. R. L. Polk's & Co.'s 1910 Grand Rapids City Directory For Year Commencing October, Grand Rapids, Michigan : Grand Rapids Directory Company, Publishers, 1910, Thirty-Eighth Edition, Page 871; (ancestry.com image 439); "James E Pickles, lab, bds 140 Lyon."

944. R. L. Polk's & Co.'s 1918 Grand Rapids City Directory, Forty-Sixth Edition, Grand Rapids, Michigan : Grand Rapids Directory Company, Publishers, 1920, Page 808; (ancestry.com image 406); "James E Pickell, h 248 Marion av NW."

945. 1920 US Census, Grand Rapids, Kent County, Michigan, January 1920, "Patternmaker Foundry."

946. Polk's Grand Rapids City Directory 1924, Fifty-Second Edition, Grand Rapids, Michigan: The Grand Rapids Directory Co., 1924, Page 716; (ancestry.com image 366); "Pickell Jas ptrnmakr r951 Madison av."

947. 1930 US Census, Grand Rapids, Kent County, Michigan, April 1930, "patternmaker Textile Machine Co."

948. 1935 Florida Census, Gulfport, Pinellas County, Florida, "Designer". Florida Department of Agriculture Bulletin [new ser.] no. 193 and Mayo.

949. 1940 US Census, Santa Monica, Los Angeles County, California, "Pattern Inspector."

950. 1950 US Census, Santa Monica, Los Angeles County, California,"wood-pattern making | lumber pattern shop."

951. California, Napa and Butte Counties, Obituaries, 1866-1992, (https://familysearch.org/ark:/61903/1:1:Q2Q1-ZPJD : accessed 13 June 2022); citing Butte, California, United States, Paradise Genealogical Society, Paradise, and Napa Valley Genealogical and Biographical Society, Napa; FHL microfilm 1.

952. "United States Headstone Applications for U.S. Military Veterans, 1861-1985," (ancestry.com image 148).

953. US World War I Draft Registration Cards, 1917-1918, database with scanned images, NARA, www.familysearch.org or www.ancestry.com, registration State: Michigan; Registration County: Kent.

954. U.S. Army Transport Service Arriving and Departing Passenger Lists, 1910-1939, NARA (ancestry.com image 292) Outgoing passenger, Kelly Field June Auto Rep 1. Draft S. C. Det. #1; H. R. Mallory; sailed 26 may 1918 from Hoboken, New Jersey.

955. Ibid. (ancestry.com image 419).

956. US World War II Draft Registration Cards, 1940-1947. Fourth Registration. Records of the Selective Service System, Record Group Number 147.

957. 1920 US Census, Grand Rapids, Kent County, Michigan, January 1920, NARA T625; Roll 778; Sheet 11A; ED 70; Dwelling 229; Family 275; Line 20; "Grace Pickell."

958. US Social Security Applications and Claims Index, 1936-2007.
959. Marriage record/certificate/application. Michigan Department of Community Health, Division of Vital Records and Health Statistics; Lansing, Michigan, Marriage Records, 1867-1952; Film: 126; Film Description: 1915 Wayne; Record 116854.
960. Find-A-Grave, (www.findagrave.com/memorial/43484332/grace_e-irene-forgar : accessed 03 February 2022). Memorial ID 43484332, citing Hillcrest Cemetery, Six Lakes, Montcalm County, Michigan; maintained by allison (contributor 47161231).
961. Polk's Grand Rapids City Directory 1924, Fifty-Second Edition, Grand Rapids, Michigan: The Grand Rapids Directory Co., 1924, Page 716; (ancestry.com image 366); "Pickell Grace saxaphone asmblr r 504 Sheldon av SE."
962. Separated/divorced by 1924 per City Directory addresses and subsequent marriage to Lyle Forgar.
963. Grand Rapids Press, "Obituary," 1 March 1963, page 36.
964. U.S. Army Transport Service Arriving and Departing Passenger Lists, 1910-1939, NARA Record Group, Records of the Office of the Quartermaster General, 1774-1985; Record Group Number 92; Roll or Box Number 488. Date Range: 26 May 1918-30 May 1918.
965. 1930 US Census, Grand Rapids, Kent County, Michigan, April 1930, NARA T626; City Ward 3; Sheet 21B; ED 41-96; Dwelling 189; Family 190; Line 68; "Anne Pickell."
966. 1935 Florida Census, Gulfport, Pinellas County, Florida, Precinct 8; (Microfilm series S 5, 30 reels); Record Group 001021.
967. 1940 US Census, Santa Monica, Los Angeles County, California, NARA T627; Roll 257; Sheet 62A; ED 19-771; House 2311; Line 23; "Anne Pickell."
968. 1950 US Census, Santa Monica, Los Angeles County, California, Record Group Number 29; Roll 5861; Sheet 11; ED 74-34; House 2311; Line 15; "Anne M. Pickell."
969. Tombstone. (See findagrave.com); "Anne M. Pickell | Feb. 28, 1898 - Nov. 6, 1967."
970. Marriage Certificate/Record/Application. Michigan Department of Community Health, Division of Vital Records and Health Statistics; Lansing, Marriage Records, 1867-1952; Film 182; Film Description: 1925 Ionia-1925 Menominee; Record 4097.
971. Find-A-Grave, (www.findagrave.com/memorial/131044935/anne-m-pickell : accessed 03 February 2022). Memorial ID 131044935, citing Paradise Cemetery, Paradise, Butte County, California; maintained by Steven Goff (contributor 47520734).
972. Sacramento Bee, newspaper, Sacramento, California, "Superior California Vital Statistics," 7 November 1967, page B3.
973. 1930 US Census, Grand Rapids, Kent County, Michigan, April 1930, NARA T626; City Ward 3; Sheet 21B; ED 41-96; Dwelling 189; Family 190; Line 69; "James J. Pickell."
974. 1940 US Census, Santa Monica, Los Angeles County, California, NARA T627; Roll 257; Sheet 62A; ED 19-771; House 2311; Line 24; "James Pickell Jr."
975. 1950 US Census, Long Beach, Los Angeles County, California, scanned image, Bureau of the Census; Washington, D.C., Records of the Bureau of the Census, 1790-2007; Record Group Number 29; Residence Date: 1950; Roll 723; Sheet Number 6; ED 65-59; Line 1; "James Pickell."

976. 1930 US Census, Grand Rapids, Kent County, Michigan, April 1930, NARA T626; City Ward 3; Sheet 21B; ED 41-96; Dwelling 189; Family 190; Line 70; "Mary A. Pickell."

977. 1940 US Census, Santa Monica, Los Angeles County, California, NARA T627; Roll 257; Sheet 62A; ED 19-771; House 2311; Line 25; "Mary A. Pickell."

978. 1950 US Census, Los Angeles, Los Angeles County, California, April 1950, Record Group Number: 29; Roll: 5055; Sheet Number: 84; ED: 66-791A; "Alma Real" street; Line 20; "Mary A Cotter."

979. 1900 US Census, Douglass Township, Montcalm County, Michigan, June 1900, NARA T623; Roll 733; ED 125; Line 70; Sheet 3B; Page 105; Dwelling 57; Family 58; "Vena Kilborn."

980. 1910 US Census, Douglass Township, Montcalm County, Michigan, April 1910, NARA T624; Roll 665; ED 149; Sheet 3A; Line 5; Page 131; Dwelling 36; Family 38; "Vena E Kilbourne."

981. 1920 US Census, Cedar Springs, Nelson Township, Kent County, Michigan, January 1920, NARA T625; Roll 779; ED 101; Page 53; Sheet 5A; Dwelling 114; Family 120; Line 13. Living with husband Dewey in sister-in-laws home, Margurite McDonald.

982. 1930 US Census, Grand Rapids, Kent County, Michigan, April 1930, NARA T626; Roll 1002; ED 66; Page 20; Sheet 20A; Dwelling 418; Family 433; Line 2; "Vena Doyle."

983. 1940 US Census, Grand Rapids, Kent County, Michigan, April 1940, NARA T627; Roll 1901; ED 86-116A; Sheet 4B; Dwelling 1417; Line 59; "Vena Doyle."

984. 1950 US Census, Grand Rapids, Kent County, Michigan, April 1950, Record Group Number 29; Roll 416; Sheet Number 15; ED 87-186; House 1417; Line 12; "Vena E Doyle."

985. The author personally knew Vena - extremely lucid in family genealogy recollections - Curtis Daryl Sanders.

986. Find-A-Grave, (https://www.findagrave.com/memorial/136793928/vena-e-doyle : accessed 15 September 2021). Memorial ID 136793928, citing Woodlawn Cemetery, Grand Rapids, Kent County, Michigan; maintained by Judith D (contributor 48139146).

987. 1920 US Census, Cedar Springs, Nelson Township, Kent County, Michigan, January 1920, "Nurse private family."

988. Michigan Obituaries, 1820-2006, (https://familysearch.org/ark:/61903/1:1:QVJ1-CTGX : 1 April 2020), Dewey I Doyle in entry for Vena E Doyle, 1995; citing, Obituary, Grand Rapids Public Library, Michigan; FHL microfilm 7,593,981.

989. 1900 US Census, Nelson Township, Kent County, Michigan, June 1900, NARA T623; Roll 723; ED 97; Sheet 1B; Dwelling 23; Family 23; Line 91; "Dewey Doyle."

990. 1910 US Census, Nelson Township, Kent County, Michigan, April 1910, NARA T624; Roll 655; ED 131; Page 152; Sheet 2A; Family 38; Line 27; "Dewey Doyle."

991. 1920 US Census, Cedar Springs, Nelson Township, Kent County, Michigan, January 1920, NARA T625; Roll 779; ED 101; Page 53; Sheet 5A; Dwelling 114; Family 120; Line 13;"Dewey Doyle" living with wife Vena in his sister's home, Margurite McDonald.

992. 1930 US Census, Grand Rapids, Kent County, Michigan, April 1930, NARA T626; Roll 1002; ED 66; Page 20; Sheet 20A; Dwelling 418; Family 433; Line 1;"Dewey I. Doyle."

993. 1940 US Census, Grand Rapids, Kent County, Michigan, April 1940, NARA T627; Roll 1901; ED 86-116A; Sheet 4B; Family 73; Line 58; "Dewey Doyle."

994. 1950 US Census, Grand Rapids, Kent County, Michigan, April 1950, Record Group Number 29; Roll 416; Sheet Number 15; ED 87-186; House 1417; Line 11; "Dewey I Doyle Sr."

995. Personally knew Dewey - Curtis Daryl Sanders.

996. Marriage record/certificate/application. Michigan Department of Community Health, Division of Vital Records and Health Statistics; Lansing, Michigan, Marriage Records, 1867-1952; Film: 144; Film Description: 1919 Gratiot-1919 Kent; 9344.

997. Michigan Death Index, 1971-1996, Michigan Department of Vital and Health Records, Lansing, Michigan Department of Vital and Health Records.

998. Find-A-Grave, (https://www.findagrave.com/memorial/136792818/dewey-irwin-doyle : accessed 15 September 2021). Memorial ID 136792818, citing Woodlawn Cemetery, Grand Rapids, Kent County, Michigan; maintained by Judith D (contributor 48139146).

999. 1920 US Census, Cedar Springs, Nelson Township, Kent County, Michigan, January 1920, "Salesman Furnance."

1000. 1930 US Census, Grand Rapids, Kent County, Michigan, April 1930, "Salesman Heating Plant."

1001. Polk's Grand Rapids City Directory 1922, Grand Rapids, Michigan : Grand Rapids Directory Company, Publishers, 1922, Page 294; (ancestry.com image 151); "Doyle Dewey J, Mgr Homer Furnace Co, h 207 Sycamore."

1002. Polk's Grand Rapids City Directory 1923, 51st Edition, Grand Rapids, Michigan: Grand Rapids Directory Company, Publishers, 1923, Page 307; (ancestry.com image 152); "Doyle Dewey J, Mgr Homer Furnace Co, h207 Sycamore SE."

1003. Polk's Grand Rapids City Directory 1924, Fifty-Second Edition, Grand Rapids, Michigan: The Grand Rapids Directory Co., 1924, Page 1209; (ancestry.com image 615); "Jefferson av 207 Doyle Dewey I Homer Furnace Co"; Page 320; (ancestry.com image 165); "Doyle Dewey I, Distributor Homer Furnace Agency, h207 Sycamore SE, Auto Phone 62266."

1004. Polk's Grand Rapids City Directories 1925, Grand Rapids, Michigan: The Grand Rapids Directory Co. Publishers, 1925, Page 300; ancestry.-com image 152; "Doyle Dewey I mgr Homer Furnace Co h1429 Logan SE."

1005. Polk's Grand Rapids (Michigan) City Directory 1927, Fifty-Fifth Edition, Grand Rapids, Michigan: The Grand Rapids Directory Co., Publishers, 1927, Page 360; (ancestry.com image 184); "Doyle, Dewey I (Vena), Heating Contractor and Agent for Homer Furnace Co 1429 Logan SE, Tel 23832 (See page 69)."

1006. Ibid. Page 1462; (ancestry.com image 747); "Doyle Dewey I, 1429 Logan SE (See page 69)."

1007. R. L. Polk's & Co.'s Grand Rapids (Michigan) City Directory 1928, Fifty-Sixth Edition, Grand Rapids, Michigan: Grand Rapids Directory Company, Publishers, 1928, Pages 6, 38; (ancestry.com images 6, 38); index listing and "Dewey I. Doyle Heating Contractor" advertisement graphic.

1008. Ibid. Page 326; (ancestry.com image 169); "Doyle, Dewey I (Vena), Heating Contractor and Agent for Homer Furnace Co 1429 Logan SE, Tel 23832 (See page 66)."

1009. Polk's Grand Rapids (Michigan) City Directory , Volume 1929 LVII, Grand Rapids, Michigan: Grand Rapids Directory Co., Publishers, 1929, Page 1316; (ancestry.com image 671); "Heating and Ventilating-Contractors Doyle Dewey I 586 Jefferson av SE and 1429 Logan SE"; Page 324; (ancestry.com image 168); "Doyle Dewey I (Vena) heating contr 586 Jefferson av SE h1429 Logan SE."

1010. Polk's Grand Rapids (Michigan) City Directory, Vol. 1932 LV, Grand Rapids, Michigan: Grand Rapids Directory Company, Publishers, 1932, Page 976; (ancestry.com image 493); "Boiler Cleaners and Repairers Doyle Dewey I 1041 Hall SE."

1011. Polk's Grand Rapids City Directory 1933, Grand Rapids, Michigan: Grand Rapids Directory Co., 1933, Page 1020; (ancestry.com image 517); "Boiler Cleaners and Repairers Doyle Dewey I 1041 Hall SE."

1012. Polk's Grand Rapids (Kent County, Mich.) City Directory, Volume 1935 LVIII, Grand Rapids, Michigan : Grand Rapids Directory Company, Publishers, 1935, Page 259; (ancestry.com image 133); "Doyle Dewey I (Vena E) heating contr 1148 Division av S h1041 Hall SE."

1013. Polk's Grand Rapids (Kent County, Mich.) City Directory, Volume 1937 LX, Grand Rapids, Michigan: Grand Rapids Directory Co., Publishers, 1937, Page 243; (ancestry.com image 119); "Doyle Dewey I (Vena E; Grand Rapids Furnace Cleaner Co) h1041 Hall SE."

1014. 1940 US Census, Grand Rapids, Kent County, Michigan, April 1940, NARA T627; Roll 1901; ED 86-1169; Sheet 4B; Dwelling 1417; Line 58; "Dewey Doyle."

1015. Polk's Grand Rapids (Kent County, Mich.) City Directory, Volume 1940 LXIII, Grand Rapids, Michigan: Grand Rapids Directory Company, Publishers, 1940, Page 220; (ancestry.com image 116); "Doyle Vacuum Cleaner Co (Dewey I Doyle) mfrs 225 Stevens SW."

1016. Polk's Grand Rapids (Kent County, Mich.) City Directory, Grand Rapids, Michigan: Grand Rapids Directory Company, Publishers, 1941, Volume 1941 LXIV, Page 235; (ancestry.com image 122); "Doyle, Dewey I (Vena; Doyle Vacuum Clnr Co) h1417 Franklin SE."

1017. Polk's Grand Rapids (Kent County, Mich.) City Directory, Volume 1942 LXV, Grand Rapids, Michigan: Grand Rapids Directory Company, Publishers, 1942, Page 213; (ancestry.com image 105); "Doyle Dewey I (Vena; Doyle Vacuum Cleaner Co) h1417 Franklin SE."

1018. Polk's Grand Rapids (Kent County, Mich.) City Directory Including East Grand Rapids, Vol. 1943-44 LXVI, Grand Rapids, Michigan: Grand Rapids Directory Company, Publishers, Page 221; (ancestry.com image 110); "Doyle Dewey I (Vena; Doyle Vacuum Cleaner Co) h1417 Franklin SE". [second entry, same page] "Doyle Vacuum Cleaner Co (Dewey I Doyle mfrs 225 Stevens SW."

1019. Polk's Grand Rapids (Kent County, Mich.) City Directory Including East Grand Rapids, Grand Rapids, Michigan: Grand Rapids Directory Company, Publishers, 1946, Vol. 1946 LXVIII, Page 235; (ancestry.com image 126); "Doyle Dewey I (Vena E) pres Doyle Vacuum Clearner Co h1417 Franklin SE."

1020. Polk's Grand Rapids (Kent County, Mich.) City Directory, Volume 1949 LXX, Grand Rapids, Michigan: Grand Rapids Directory Company, Publishers, 1949, Page 265; (ancestry.com image 135); "Doyle Dewey I (Vena E) pres Doyle Fooundry [sic] Co h1417 Franklin SE."

1021. 1950 US Census, Grand Rapids, Kent County, Michigan, April 1950, "President vacuum cleaner mfg co" "vacuum mfg. co - ret wh."

1022. Polk's Grand Rapids (Kent County, Mich.) City Directory, Volume 1951, Grand Rapids, Michigan: Grand Rapids Directory Company,

Publishers, 1951, Page 272; (ancestry.com image 125); "Doyle Dewey I (Vena E) pres-treas Doyle Fdry Co and Doyle Vacuum Cln Co h1417 Franklin SE."

1023. Polk's Grand Rapids (Kent County, Mich.) City Directory, Volume 1954 LXXIII, Detroit, Michigan: R. L. Polk & Co., Publishers, 1954, Page 313; (ancestry.com image 172); "Doyle Dewey I jr (Jean M) v-pres Doyle Vacuum Cln Co h545 Ethel ave SE."

1024. Patent Database, IFI Claims, New Haven, Connecticut, Ancestry.com. International Patents, 1890-2020 [database on-line]. Ancestry.com, Patent Country: Canada; Publication Date: 20 November 1956; Publication Number CA533422A "Dust Collector For Vacuum Cleaners Blowers And Other Dust Filters": Doyle Vacuum Cleaner Co Dewey I Doyle Sr.

1025. Ibid. Patent Country: Canada; Publication Date: 5 February 1957; Publication Number CA536822A "Vacuum Cleaner Implement and Handle Coupling" "CA548345A "Centrifugal Fan Wheel": Doyle Vacuum Cleaner Co, Dewey I Doyle.

1026. Polk's Grand Rapids (Kent County, Mich.) City Directory, Vol. 1960 LXXVIII, Detroit, Michigan: R. L. Polk & Co., Publishers, 1960, Page 249; (ancestry.com image 231); "Doyle I (Vena E) pres & treas Doyle Foundry Co h1417 Franklin SE."

1027. Patent Database, IFI Claims, Patent Country: Canada; Publication Date: 16 August 1960; "Vacuum Cleaning Tool": Doyle Vacuum Cleaner Co Dewey I Doyle.

1028. Ibid. Patent Country: Canada; Publication Date: 18 April 1961; Publication Number CA618471A; "Motor For Vacuum Producing Machines": Doyle Vacuum Cleaner Co Dewey I Doyle.

1029. Ibid. Patent Country: Canada; Publication Date: 8 April 1969; Publication Number CA809856A; "Vacuum Cleaner Unit" : Doyle Vacuum Cleaner Co Dewey I Doyle.

1030. The Patent Examination Data System, United States Patent and Trademark Office, Washington, D.C.: United States Patent and Trademark Office, 2020. Name: Dewey Doyle; Residence Place: Grand Rapids, Michigan, USA; Certificate Numbers: 12043390; 60893236.

1031. Aurora, Ypsilanti, Michigan: Michigan State Normal College [Eastern Michigan University], 1917, Vol. 24, Page 191.

1032. Grand Rapids Press, "Advertisement," 16 December 1922, page 24.

1033. Ibid. "'Strongheart' Is Uncle Of This Dog That Loves Babe," 16 March 1923, page 19.

1034. Ibid. 13 January 1930, page 13.

1035. Ibid. "Last Days of Summer Attract Many to Ridge," 15 August 1959, page 18.

1036. Ibid. "Cottagers busy at Ridge," 17 July 1964, page 27.

1037. Ibid. 9 August 1964, page 69.

1038. U.S. Army Transport Service Arriving and Departing Passenger Lists, 1910-1939, NARA; Record Group, database with image, Records of the Office of the Quartermaster General, 1774-1985; Record Group Number 92; Roll or Box Number 515.

1039. Ibid. Records of the Office of the Quartermaster General, 1774-1985; Record Group Number 92; Roll or Box Number 100.

1040. Grand Rapids Press, "Lauds Bravery Of Cedar Springs Boy," 9 January 1919, page 4.

1041. Ibid. "Whole Village Proud of Doyle," 13 January 1919, page 4.

1042. US World War II Draft Registration Cards, 1940-1947. WWII Draft Registration Cards for Michigan, 10/16/1940-03/31/1947; Record Group: Records of the Selective Service System, 147; Box 309.
1043. 1930 US Census, Grand Rapids, Kent County, Michigan, April 1930, NARA T626; Roll 1002; ED 66; Page 20; Sheet 20A; Dwelling 418; Family 433; Line 3; "Dewey Jr."
1044. 1940 US Census, Grand Rapids, Kent County, Michigan, April 1940, NARA T627; Roll 1901; ED 86-116A; Sheet 4B; Dwelling 1417; Line 60. "Dewey Doyle Jr."
1045. US Social Security Applications and Claims Index, 1936-2007, Jul 1940: Name listed as DEWEY IRWIN DOYLE JR; 02 Aug 1996: Name listed as DEWEY I DOYLE.
1046. Funeral Card.
1047. 1930 US Census, Grand Rapids, Kent County, Michigan, April 1930, NARA T626; Roll 1002; ED 66; Page 20; Sheet 20A; Dwelling 418; Family 433; Line 4; "Patrick Doyle."
1048. 1940 US Census, Grand Rapids, Kent County, Michigan, April 1940, NARA T627; Roll 1901; ED 86-116A; Sheet 4B; Dwelling 1417; Family 73; Line 61. Listed as daughter "Patricia Doyle."
1049. 1950 US Census, Grand Rapids, Kent County, Michigan, April 1950, Record Group Number 29; Roll 416; Sheet Number 20; ED 87-185; "Bemis St"; Dwelling 1324; Line 2. "Patrick E Doyle"
1050. US Social Security Applications and Claims Index, 1936-2007, Mar 1942: Name listed as PATRICK EDWARD DOYLE; 30 Dec 1987: Name listed as PATRICK DOYLE.
1051. Grand Rapids Press, 7 May 1942, page 6.
1052. 1900 US Census, Douglass Township, Montcalm County, Michigan, June 1900, NARA T623; Roll 733; ED 125; Line 71; Sheet 3B; Page 105; Dwelling 57; Family 58; "Raymond Kilborn."
1053. 1910 US Census, Douglass Township, Montcalm County, Michigan, April 1910, NARA T624; Roll 665; ED 149; Sheet 3A; Line 6; Page 131; Dwelling 36; Family 38; "Raymond J Kilbourne."
1054. Michigan, Census of World War I Veterans with Card Index, 1917-1919, familysearch.org/ark:/61903/1:1:QPLQ-77GK : 8 September 2019; citing Military Service, New York, Michigan Department of State, Lansing; FHL microfilm 008461588; Fort Wood, New York; 14 July 1918.
1055. Not found in the 1920 US Census.
1056. 1930 US Census, Grand Rapids, Kent County, Michigan, April 1930, NARA T626; ED 41-30; Sheet 15A; Page 214; Dwelling 203; Family 204; Line 35; "Ray J. Kilbourne."
1057. 1940 US Census, Walker Township, Kent County, Michigan, April 1940, NARA T627; Roll 1176; ED 41-47B; Sheet 10B; Family 210; Line 69; "Raymond J. Kilbourne."
1058. 1950 US Census, Walker, Kent County, Michigan, April 1950, Enumerated 2 May 1950; Record Group Number 29; Roll 2858; Sheet Number 13; ED 41-95B; "O Brian Rd SW" House number 3128; Dwelling 131; Line 15; "Ray Kilbourne."
1059. Birth Certificate/Record. To the County Clerk of the County of Jackson; Return of Births. (https://familysearch.org/ark:/61903/1:1:NQFZ-JVD : 20 February 2021), Raymond Kilbourne, 11 Mar 1900; citing item 2 page 164, Number 441.
1060. Stanton, Michigan by his recollection.

1061. Michigan Death Index, 1971-1996, Michigan Department of Vital and Health Records, Lansing, Michigan Department of Vital and Health Records; Certificate 2777.

1062. Find-A-Grave, (www.findagrave.com/memorial/219295482/raymond-kilbourne : accessed 07 February 2022). Memorial ID 219295482, citing Rosedale Memorial Park, Tallmadge Township, Ottawa County, Michigan; maintained by j.a.pruis-steere (contributor 47169073).

1063. Polk's Grand Rapids (Michigan) City Directory 1927, Fifty-Fifth Edition, Grand Rapids, Michigan: The Grand Rapids Directory Co., Publishers, 1927, Page 1436; (ancestry.com image 734); "Automobile Garages" | "58 Commerce av SW."

1064. 1930 US Census, Grand Rapids, Kent County, Michigan, April 1930, "Mechanic auto Garage."

1065. Grand Rapids Press, 15 November 1932, page 15: "Ray Kilbourne Garage, | 237 Ghilda Place, N. E. 9-2643."

1066. Classified Buyers' Guide Of The City Of Grand Rapids (Michigan) 1933, Grand Rapids, Michigan : Grand Rapids Directory Company, Publishers, 1933, Page 1014; (ancestry.com image 514); "Ray J Kilbourne" ; "Automobile Repairing" ; "237 Ghilda pl NE."

1067. Polk's Grand Rapids (Kent County, Mich.) City Directory, Grand Rapids, Michigan: Grand Rapids Directory Company, Publishers, 1941, Volume 1941 LXIV, Page 439; (ancestry.com image 224); "Kilbourne Harold mech Ray J Kilbourne r RD 5."

1068. 1940 US Census, Walker Township, Kent County, Michigan, April 1940, "Owner of garage" | "car & truck repair."

1069. 1950 US Census, Walker, Kent County, Michigan, April 1950, "Body Mechanic Automotive."

1070. Grand Rapids Press, 12 January 1982, page 5C.

1071. U.S., Department of Veterans Affairs BIRLS Death File, 1850-2010, www.ancestry.com, Page 1.

1072. US World War II Draft Registration Cards, 1940-1947. WWII Draft Registration Cards for Michigan, 10/16/1940-03/31/1947; Record Group: Records of the Selective Service System, 147; Box 622.

1073. 1930 US Census, Grand Rapids, Kent County, Michigan, April 1930, NARA T626; ED 41-30; Sheet 15A; Page 214; Dwelling 203; Family 204; Line 36; "Dorothy B. Kilbourne."

1074. Her middle name was verified to me in an interview with her husband; "D" in 1910 Census. —Curtis Daryl Sanders.

1075. Michigan Marriages, 1868-1925, database with images, familysearch.org, Return of Marriages, Kent County; Record 14095. "Dorothy V. Hopkins" and "Ray J. Kilbourne"; witnessed by Daisy B. Palmer and James Edward Pickell.

1076. Michigan Death Certificates, 1921-1952, database, Michigan Division for Vital Records and Health Statistics, Lansing, familysearch.org, Michigan Department of Health, Certificate of Death. State 341 277.

1077. Find-A-Grave, (www.findagrave.com/memorial/9214868/dorothy-kilbourne: accessed 21 June 2023). Memorial ID 9214868, citing Fairplains Cemetery, Grand Rapids, Kent County, Michigan; maintained by Judith D (contributor 48139146). Plot 1.117.

1078. Grand Rapids Press, "Obituary," 6 October 1932, page 21.

1079. 1930 US Census, Grand Rapids, Kent County, Michigan, April 1930, NARA T626; ED 41-30; Sheet 15A; Page 214; Dwelling 203; Family 204; Line 37; "June M. Kilbourne."

1080. 1940 US Census, Walker Township, Kent County, Michigan, April 1940, NARA T627; Roll 1176; ED 41-47B; Sheet 10B; Family 210; Line 71; "June M. Kilbourne."

1081. Polk's Saginaw (Saginaw County, Mich.) City Directory, Volume 1944 LVII, Detroit, Michigan: R. L. Polk & Co., Publishers, 1944, Page 286; (ancestry.com image 118); "Sanderson Ralph W (June; Sanderson's Service Station) r StCharles RD2."

1082. Polk's Saginaw (Saginaw County, Mich.) City Directory, Volume 1946 LVIII, Detroit, Michigan: R. L. Polk & Co., Publishers, 1946, Page 365; (ancestry.com image 184); "Sanderson Ralph W (June; Sanderson's Service Sta) 2211 Holland av."

1083. 1950 US Census, Grand Rapids, Kent County, Michigan, April 1950, Record Group Number 29; Roll 2856; Sheet 40; ED 41-37; Line 28; "June Sanderson."

1084. 1930 US Census, Grand Rapids, Kent County, Michigan, April 1930, NARA T626; ED 41-30; Sheet 15A; Page 214; Dwelling 203; Family 204; Line 38; "Harold J. Kilbourne."

1085. 1940 US Census, Walker Township, Kent County, Michigan, April 1940, NARA T627; Roll 1176; ED 41-47B; Sheet 10B; Family 210; Line 72; "Harold J. Kilbourne."

1086. 1950 US Census, Walker, Kent County, Michigan, April 1950, Record Group Number 29; Roll 2858; Sheet Number 14; ED 41-95B; House 455; Line 10; "Harold Kilbourne."

1087. 1930 US Census, Grand Rapids, Kent County, Michigan, April 1930, NARA T626; ED 41-30; Sheet 15A; Page 214; Dwelling 203; Family 204; Line 39; "Leora D. Kilbourne."

1088. 1940 US Census, Walker Township, Kent County, Michigan, April 1940, NARA T627; Roll 1176; ED 41-47B; Sheet 10B; Family 210; Line 73; "Leora D. Kilbourne."

1089. 1950 US Census, Traverse City, Grand Traverse County, Michigan, Record Group Number 29; Roll 461; Sheet 14; ED 28-30; Line 2; "Leora Williams."

1090. 1930 US Census, Grand Rapids, Kent County, Michigan, April 1930, NARA T626; ED 41-30; Sheet 15A; Page 214; Dwelling 203; Family 204; Line 40; "Stewart C. Kilbourne."

1091. 1940 US Census, Walker Township, Kent County, Michigan, April 1940, NARA T627; Roll 1176; ED 41-47B; Sheet 10B; Family 210; Line 74; "Stuart C Kilbourne."

1092. Polk's Grand Rapids (Kent County, Mich.) City Directory, Volume 1949 LXX, Grand Rapids, Michigan: Grand Rapids Directory Company, Publishers, 1949, Page 493; (ancestry.com image 249); "Kilbourne Stewart (June) h817 Hancock SE."

1093. US Social Security Applications and Claims Index, 1936-2007, Feb 1944: Name listed as STEWART CARL KILBOURNE; 30 Dec 1987: Name listed as STEWART KILBOURNE.

1094. 1950 US Census, Grand Rapids, Kent County, Michigan, April 1950, Record Group Number 29; Roll 417; Sheet 7; ED 87-225; Line 22; "Stewart Kilburn."

1095. 1940 US Census, Walker Township, Kent County, Michigan, April 1940, NARA T627; Roll 1176; ED 41-47B; Sheet 10B; Family 210; Line 75; "Robert B. Kilbourne."

1096. 1950 US Census, Traverse City, Grand Traverse County, Michigan, scanned image, Bureau of the Census; Washington, D.C., Record Group Number 29; Roll 461; Sheet 14; ED 28-30; Line 4; "Robert Kilburn" living with sister Leora Williams family.

1097. 1940 US Census, Walker Township, Kent County, Michigan, April 1940, NARA T627; Roll 1176; ED 41-47B; Sheet 10B; Family 210; Line 77; "Lois J. Kilbourne."

1098. 1950 US Census, Walker, Kent County, Michigan, April 1950, Enumerated 2 May 1950; Record Group Number 29; Roll 2858; Sheet Number 13; ED 41-95B; "O Brian Rd SW"' House number 3128; Dwelling 131; Line 17; "Lois Kilbourne."

1099. 1940 US Census, Walker Township, Kent County, Michigan, April 1940, NARA T627; Roll 1176; ED 41-47B; Sheet 10B; Family 210; Line 70; "Dorthy M. Kilbourne."

1100. 1950 US Census, Walker, Kent County, Michigan, April 1950, Enumerated 2 May 1950; Record Group Number 29; Roll 2858; Sheet Number 13; ED 41-95B; "O Brian Rd SW"' House number 3128; Dwelling 131; Line 16; "Dorothy Kilbourne."

1101. Marriage record/certificate/application. Michigan Department of Community Health, Division of Vital Records and Health Statistics; Lansing, Marriage Records, 1867-1952; Film 122; Film Title: 41 Kent 42030-45329; Kent (1947-1948); County 91-421; State 41 44474.

1102. Michigan Births, 1867-1902, (https://familysearch.org/ark:/61903/1:1:NQF6-52B : 20 February 2021), Dorethea Vandenbergh, 29 May 1902; citing item 2 p 109, number 1692, Howard City, Montcalm, Michigan.

1103. Michigan Obituaries, 1820-2006, database with images, FamilySearch.org.

1104. 1910 US Census, Douglass Township, Montcalm County, Michigan, April 1910, NARA T624; Roll 665; ED 149; Sheet 3A; Line 7; Page 131; Dwelling 36; Family 38; "Bessie M. Kilbourne."

1105. 1920 US Census, Douglass Township, Montcalm County, Michigan, January 1920, NARA T625; Roll 787; Sheet 4A; ED 113; Line 45; Page 102; Dwelling 89; Family 89; Line 45; "Bessie Kilbourne."

1106. 1930 US Census, Grand Rapids, Kent County, Michigan, April 1930, NARA T626; Roll 1004; ED 41-116; Sheet 5A; Dwelling 91; Family 91; Line 13; "Elizabeth Taylor."

1107. Tombstone. (See findagrave.com) "Bessie M. Taylor."

1108. Death Certificate/Record. Michigan Department Of Health, Division of Vital Statistics, Certificate Of Death; state 59 4096.

1109. Find-A-Grave, (www.findagrave.com/memorial/53516233/elizabeth-marguerite-taylor : accessed 14 February 2022). Memorial ID 53516233, citing McBride Cemetery, McBride, Montcalm County, Michigan; maintained by John C. Anderson (contributor 47208015).

1110. 1910 US Census, Day Township, Montcalm County, Michigan, April 1910, Enumerated 12 May 1910; NARA T624; Roll 665; ED 148; Sheet 20B; Dwelling 242; Family 243; Line 68; "Loyd Taylor" grandson living under William Smith family.

1111. 1920 US Census, Day Township, Montcalm County, Michigan, January 1920, NARA T625; Roll 787; ED 112; Sheet 3B; Dwelling 63; Family 64; Line 62; "Lloyd E Taylor" grandson living under William M Smith family.

1112. 1930 US Census, Grand Rapids, Kent County, Michigan, April 1930, NARA T626; Roll 1004; ED 41-116; Sheet 5A; Dwelling 91; Family 91; Line 12; "Loyd Taylor."

1113. 1940 US Census, Day Township, Montcalm County, Michigan, April 1940, NARA T627; Roll 1793; ED 59-10; Sheet 7B; Line 52; "Lloyd Taylor."

1114. 1950 US Census, Stanton, Montcalm County, Michigan, April 1950, Record Group Number 29; Roll 2221; Sheet: 31; ED 59-45; Line 59. Roomer and maritally separated; "Lloyd E. Taylor."

1115. Marriage record/certificate/application. Michigan Department of Community Health, Division of Vital Records and Health Statistics; Lansing; Marriage Records, 1867-1952; Film 163; Film Description: 1922 Kent-1922 Muskegon; record 5516.

1116. California Death Index, 1940-1997, State of California Department of Health Services, Center for Health Statistics, index, familysearch.org or ancestry.com, "Lloyd Everleigh Taylor."

1117. Find-A-Grave, (www.findagrave.com/memorial/3853300/lloyd-e-taylor : accessed 14 February 2022). Memorial ID 3853300, citing Riverside National Cemetery, Riverside, Riverside County, California; maintained by Doug B (contributor 102).

1118. 1920 US Census, Day Township, Montcalm County, Michigan, January 1920, "Machinist" | "Navy."

1119. 1930 US Census, Grand Rapids, Kent County, Michigan, April 1930, "Auto Mechanic" | "Garage."

1120. 1940 US Census, Day Township, Montcalm County, Michigan, April 1940, "Decorator" | "private practice."

1121. 1950 US Census, Stanton, Montcalm County, Michigan, April 1950, "Cement block maker."

1122. <u>The State Journal</u>, "Ionia Businessman Buried Saturday," 27 January 1952, page 35.

1123. <u>San Bernardino County Sun</u>, newspaper, San Bernardino, California, 1 November 1982, page D-2.

1124. US World War II Draft Registration Cards, 1940-1947. Records of the Selective Service System, 147; Box 1188.

1125. 1930 US Census, Grand Rapids, Kent County, Michigan, April 1930, NARA T626; Roll 1004; ED 41-116; Sheet 5A; Dwelling 91; Family 91; Line 14; "Ivan Taylor."

1126. US Social Security Applications and Claims Index, 1936-2007, Jan 1941: Name listed as FRANKLIN IVAN TAYLOR; 15 Jan 1999: Name listed as FRANK I TAYLOR.

1127. 1930 US Census, Grand Rapids, Kent County, Michigan, April 1930, NARA T626; Roll 1004; ED 41-116; Sheet 5A; Dwelling 91; Family 91; Line 15; "Leah Taylor."

1128. 1940 US Census, Day Township, Montcalm County, Michigan, April 1940, NARA T627; Roll 1793; ED 59-10; Sheet 7B; Line 54; "Leah Taylor."

1129. 1950 US Census, San Mateo, San Mateo County, California, April 1950, Record Group Number 29; Roll 6101; Sheet Number 75; ED 41-153; House 138; Line 10; "Leah L. Smith."

1130. US Social Security Applications and Claims Index, 1936-2007, Claim Date 23 Feb 1974.

1131. 1930 US Census, Grand Rapids, Kent County, Michigan, April 1930, NARA T626; Roll 1004; ED 41-116; Sheet 5A; Dwelling 91; Family 91; Line 16; "Jeanne Taylor."

1132. Missed in the 1940 census with the family.

1133. 1950 US Census, Scholfield Barracks Military Reservation, Honolulu County, Hawaii, April 1950, Record Group Number 29; Roll 6305; Sheet Number 3; ED 2-449; House 28; Line 15; "Jean E. Bunn."

1134. Tombstone: see findagrave.com for husband.

1135. Personal knowledge from family members, Various interviews or correspondence over years by Curtis Daryl Sanders.

1136. 1930 US Census, Grand Rapids, Kent County, Michigan, April 1930, NARA T626; Roll 1004; ED 41-116; Sheet 5A; Dwelling 91; Family 91; Line 17; "Barbara Taylor."

1137. 1940 US Census, Day Township, Montcalm County, Michigan, April 1940, NARA T627; Roll 1793; ED 59-10; Sheet 7B; Line 55; "Barbara Taylor."

1138. Polk's Grand Rapids (Kent County, Mich.) City Directory, Volume 1942 LXV, Grand Rapids, Michigan: Grand Rapids Directory Company, Publishers, 1942, Page 697; (ancestry.com image 349); "Taylor Barbara J student r641 Charles av SE."

1139. 1950 US Census, Bowne, Kent County, Michigan, April 1950, Record Group Number 29; Roll 2856; Sheet: 11; ED 41-10; Line 9; "Barbara J Clinton."

1140. 1930 US Census, Grand Rapids, Kent County, Michigan, April 1930, NARA T626; Roll 1004; ED 41-116; Sheet 5A; Dwelling 91; Family 91; Line 18; "Thomas Taylor."

1141. 1940 US Census, Day Township, Montcalm County, Michigan, April 1940, NARA T627; Roll 1793; ED 59-10; Sheet 7B; Line 56; "Thomas Taylor."

1142. Ibid. NARA T627; Roll 1793; ED 59-10; Sheet 2A; Line 7. Living with Carl E. and Ruby A. Willis as a "lodger."

1143. 1950 US Census, Greenville, Montcalm County, Michigan, April 1950, Record Group Number 29; Roll 2220; Sheet: 74; ED 59-29; Line 9; "Nonda E Gardner."

1144. 1910 US Census, Douglass Township, Montcalm County, Michigan, April 1910, NARA T624; Roll 665; ED 149; Sheet 3A; Line 8; Page 131; Dwelling 36; Family 38;"Harry E Kilbourne."

1145. Tombstone. (see findagrave.com); "Harry E. Kilbourne."

1146. Death Certificate/Record. State Of Michigan, Department of State-Division of Vital Statistics, Certificate of Death, number 3; "Harry James Kilbourne;" Died from appendicitis per family members.

1147. Find-A-Grave, (www.findagrave.com/memorial/27318690/harry-e-kilbourne : accessed 28 February 2022). Memorial ID 27318690, citing Hillside Entrican Cemetery, Entrican, Montcalm County, Michigan; maintained by Gail (contributor 47136090).

1148. Information from various interviews and correspondence to grandson Curtis Daryl Sanders since 1968-2000.

1149. 1920 US Census, Douglass Township, Montcalm County, Michigan, January 1920, NARA T625; Roll 787; Sheet 4A; ED 113; Line 46; Page 102; Dwelling 89; Family 89; Line 46; "Kathryn Kilbourne."

1150. Not found in 1930 US census.

1151. 1940 US Census, Entrican, Douglass Township, Montcalm County, Michigan, April 1940, NARA T627; Roll 1793; ED 59-11A; Sheet 1B; Line 59; "Katherine Lang."

1152. 1950 US Census, Greenville, Montcalm County, Michigan, April 1950, NARA T628; ED 59-24; Sheet 2; South Clay Street, Dwelling 16; Line 17; "Kathryn A Lang."

1153. US Social Security Applications and Claims Index, 1936-2007, Claim Date 30 April 1970.

1154. Funeral Card (in possession by grandson Curtis Daryl Sanders).

1155. Birth Certificate/Record. Montcalm County, Michigan; number 7130, F-102.

1156. Find-A-Grave, (www.findagrave.com/memorial/175920042/kathryn-angeline-lang : accessed 14 September 2021). Memorial ID

175920042, citing Fairview Cemetery, Mercersburg, Franklin County, Pennsylvania; maintained by Sherry (contributor 47725101).

1157. 1950 US Census, Greenville, Montcalm County, Michigan, April 1950, unemployed.

1158. Public Opinion, newspaper, Chambersburg, Franklin County, Pennsylvania, 26 August 2000.

1159. The Sentinel, newspaper, Carlisle, Cumberland County, Pennsylvania, "Obituaries." 25 August 2000, page B12.

1160. Michigan Obituaries, 1820-2006, database with images, FamilySearch.org, (https://familysearch.org/ark:/61903/1:1:QVPK-PB8X : 1 April 2020).

1161. Personal knowledge of Kathryn Angeline Kilbourne Lang.

1162. Wayland Register, newspaper, Wayland, Steuben County, New York, (mother's obituary notice); "George"; 6 May 1937.

1163. 1900 US Census, Wayland Township, Steuben County, New York, June 1900, NARA T623; Roll 1164; Sheet 1A; Page 187; ED 111; Dwelling 7; Family 8; Line 30; "Walter Lang."

1164. 1905 New York State, Enumeration of the Inhabitants, Wayland, Steuban County, New York, 1 June 1905, Election District A.D. 02 E.D. 02; Line 27; "George W."

1165. 1910 US Census, Wayland Town, Steuben County, New York, April 1910, NARA T624; Roll 1080; ED 163; Sheet 7B; Dwelling 156; Family 159; Line 59; "Walter Long."

1166. 1920 US Census, Detroit, Wayne County, Michigan, January 1920, NARA T625; Roll 815; ED 497; Sheet 8; Ward 16; Page 63; "Morrell Street" House 706; Dwelling 165; Line 33; "Walter Lang."

1167. 1940 US Census, Detroit, Wayne County, Michigan, April 1940, NARA T627; Roll 1845; Sheet 10B; ED 84-183; Line 44; "Lang, George" residing the house of Viola Bailey and others.

1168. 1950 US Census, Center, Marshall County, Indiana, April 1950, Record Group Number 29; ED 60-6; Sheet 7; "North Walnut" House 701; Line 23; "Walter Lang."

1169. Marriage record/certificate/application. Marriage License, Wayne County, Michigan; Number 356212; State file 82 48708.

1170. Reported by his first spouse, Kathryn Angeline Kilbourne.

1171. Death Certificate/Record. Indiana State Board Of Health, Medical Certificate of Death. Local 522; State 80-011246.

1172. Ibid.

1173. 1920 US Census, Detroit, Wayne County, Michigan, January 1920, "Truck driver" | "Cement Black Co."

1174. 1940 US Census, Detroit, Wayne County, Michigan, April 1940, "hotel houseman."

1175. 1950 US Census, Center, Marshall County, Indiana, April 1950, "metal finisher automobile factory."

1176. Divorce Record. Michigan Department of Health, Bureau of Records and Statistics, Kent County, Docket Number 39509; state number 41 7030.

1177. South Bend Tribune, newspaper, South Bend, Indiana, "Local Obituaries: Walter G. Lang," 4 March 1980, page 34.

1178. US World War I Draft Registration Cards, 1917-1918, Steuben County no 2, New York, United States, NARA M1509; Affiliate Publication Number M1509; GS Film Number 1818990; Digital Folder Number 5266143; Image Number 4770.

1179. New York, U.S., Abstracts of World War I Military Service, 1917-1919, New York State Archives, Albany, database with images, (ancestry.com image 1081); Adjutant General's Office; Series B0808.

1180. Democrat and Chronicle, newspaper, Rochester, Monroe County, New York, "Twp Quotas Leave Hornell This Week," 2 September 1918, page 7.

1181. US World War II Draft Registration Cards, 1940-1947. Order number T10751; WWII Draft Registration Cards for New York State, 10/16/1940 - 03/31/1947; Record Group: Records of the Selective Service System, 147.

1182. 1940 US Census, Entrican, Douglass Township, Montcalm County, Michigan, April 1940, NARA T627; Roll 1793; ED 59-11A; Sheet 1B; Line 60;"Thomas Lang."

1183. US Social Security Applications and Claims Index, 1936-2007, Mar 1947: Name listed as THOMAS WALTER LANG; 27 Apr 2005: Name listed as THOMAS W LANG.

1184. Information from various interviews by Curtis Daryl Sanders, 1968-2005.

1185. 1940 US Census, Entrican, Douglass Township, Montcalm County, Michigan, April 1940, NARA T627; Roll 1793; ED 59-11A; Sheet 1B; Line 61; "James Lang."

1186. US Social Security Applications and Claims Index, 1936-2007, Nov 1948: Name listed as JAMES PATRICK LANG; 22 May 1998: Name listed as J P LANG.

1187. 1950 US Census, Fort Ord, Monterey County, California, April 1950, ED 27-98; Military Installation; Sheet 27; Line 22; "James P. Lang."

1188. 1940 US Census, Entrican, Douglass Township, Montcalm County, Michigan, April 1940, NARA T627; Roll 1793; ED 59-11A; Sheet 1B; Line 62; "Patrice Lang."

1189. 1950 US Census, Greenville, Montcalm County, Michigan, April 1950, NARA T628; ED 59-24; Sheet 2; South Clay Street, Dwelling 16; Line 18; "Patricia M Lang."

1190. 1960 US Census, Saint Thomas Township, Franklin County, Pennsylvania, April 1960.

1191. 1970 US Census, Mercersburg, Franklin County, Pennsylvania.

1192. 1980 US Census, Mercersburg, Franklin County, Pennsylvania.

1193. 1990 US Census, Mercersburg, Franklin County, Pennsylvania.

1194. Mercersburg Journal, newspaper, Mercersburg, Franklin County, Pennsylvania, 19 August 1992, page A8.

1195. Public Opinion, 29 August 1992, page 6B.

1196. Ibid. 20 December 1972, "Mommy's Helper."

1197. Ibid. 21 January 1993, grandson Christopher Shane Eckstine's birth announcement.

1198. 2000 US Census, Greene Township, Franklin County, Pennsylvania, April 2000.

1199. 2010 US Census, Greene Township, Franklin County, Pennsylvania. April 2010.

1200. 2020 US Census, Chambersburg, Franklin County, Pennsylvania, April 2020.

1201. 1920 US Census, Douglass Township, Montcalm County, Michigan, January 1920, NARA T625; Roll 787; Sheet 4A; ED 113; Line 47; Page 102; Dwelling 89; Family 89; Line 47; "Evelyn Kilbourne."

1202. 1930 US Census, Belding, Ionia County, Michigan, April 1930, NARA T626; ED 2; Sheet 4A; Line 20; Dwelling 89; Family 91; "Evelyn Kilbourne."

1203. 1940 US Census, Flint, Genesse County, Michigan, NARA T627; Roll 1894; Sheet 4B; ED 85-82A; Line 74; "Evelyn Knapp."

1204. 1950 US Census, Paris, Kent County, Michigan, April 1950, Record Group Number 29; Roll 2857; Sheet Number 8; ED 41-62; House 2621 "Buxton Street"; Line 2; "Evelyn Knapp."

1205. US Social Security Applications and Claims Index, 1936-2007, Claim Date 24 Dec 1974; "Evelyn R Knapp."

1206. Knapp, Charles, Evelyn Died, 22 Sep 2005, email.

1207. Find-A-Grave, (www.findagrave.com/memorial/19148414/evelyn-l-knapp : accessed 9 March 2022). Memorial ID 19148414, citing Plainfield Cemetery, Plainfield Township, Kent County, Michigan; maintained by Carol Lee Weber (contributor 46956116).

1208. 1930 US Census, Belding, Ionia County, Michigan, April 1930, "Spooler silk mill."

1209. Jefferson Post, newspaper, Ashe County, North Carolina, 27 September 2005; page A2.

1210. 1910 US Census, Belding, Ionia County, Michigan, NARA T624; Roll 650; Sheet 2A; ED 2; Dwelling 36; Family 48; Line 33; "Stanley C. Knapp."

1211. 1920 US Census, Belding, Ionia County, Michigan, NARA T625; Roll 772; Sheet 9A; ED 62; Dwelling 169; Family 177; Line 50; "Stanley Knapp."

1212. 1930 US Census, Belding, Ionia County, Michigan, April 1930, NARA T626; Sheet 3B; ED 34-1; Dwelling 77; Family 85; Line 74; "Stanley C Knapp."

1213. 1940 US Census, Flint, Genesse County, Michigan, NARA T627; Roll 1894; Sheet 4B; ED 85-82A; Line 73; "Stanley Knapp."

1214. 1950 US Census, Detroit, Wayne County, Michigan, April 1950, Record Group Number 29; Roll 5841; Sheet 11; ED 85-310; House 5545; Line 30; living as a lodger with his brother-in-law John Churchill Kilbourne family; "Stanley C Knapp."

1215. 1950 US Census, Paris, Kent County, Michigan, April 1950, Record Group Number 29; Roll 2857; Sheet Number 8; ED 41-62; House 2621 "Buxton Street"; Line 1; "Stanley Knapp."

1216. Marriage record/certificate/application. Ionia County, number 34 1892; Michigan Department of Community Health, Division of Vital Records and Health Statistics; Lansing, Michigan.

1217. Michigan, County Births, 1867-1917, (https://www.familysearch.org/ark:/61903/1:1:QGSD-WR3Z : 19 July 2021), Stanley Charles Knapp, 27 Nov 1908; citing Birth, various county courts, Michigan.

1218. Michigan Death Index, 1971-1996, Michigan Department of Vital and Health Records, Lansing, database (https://www.familysearch.org/ark:/61903/1:1:VZ1R-LXJ : 10 August 2022), Stanley C Knapp, 1987. Certificate 48210.

1219. Find-A-Grave, (www.findagrave.com/memorial/19148418/stanley-charles-knapp : accessed 9 March 2022). Memorial ID 19148418, citing Plainfield Cemetery, Plainfield Township, Kent County, Michigan; maintained by Carol Lee Weber (contributor 46956116).

1220. 1930 US Census, Belding, Ionia County, Michigan, April 1930, "Sheet-metal worker" "Refrigerator factory"

1221. Polks's Flint (Genesse County, Mich.) City Directory 1934, Detroit: R. L. Polk & Co., Publishers, 1934, Page 401; (ancestry.com image 205); "Knapp Stanley C (Evelyn L) tool mkr r1303 Mason."

1222. Polk's Flint (Genesee County, Mich.) City Directory 1936, Detroit: R. L. Polk & Co., Publishers, 1936, Page 442; (ancestry.com image 224); "Knapp Stanley (Evelyn) autowkr h2311 Oren."

1223. Polk's Flint (Genesee County, Mich.) City Directory 1937, Detroit: R. L. Polk & Co., Publishers, 1937, Page 515; (ancestry.com image 260); "Knapp Stanley (Evelyn) toolmkr Buick h2311 Oren av."

1224. Polk's Flint (Genesse County, Mich.) City Directory 1938, Detroit: R. L. Polk & Co., Publishers, 1938, Page 507; (ancestry.com image 255; "Knapp Stanley (Evelyn) toolmkr Buick h 2311 Oren av."

1225. Polk's Flint (Genesee County, Mich.) City Directory 1939, Detroit: R. L. Polk & Co., Publishers, 1939, Page 477; (ancestry.com image 236); "Knapp Stanley C (Evelyn L) metallurgist Buick h2311 Oren av."

1226. 1940 US Census, Flint, Genesse County, Michigan, "metallurgical engineer" | "automobile".

1227. Polk's Flint (Genesee County, Mich.) City Directory 1942, Detroit: R. L. Polk & Co., Publishers, 1942, Page 448; (ancestry.com image 227); "Knapp Stanley (Evelyn) supt Buick Motor h 1119 Flushing rd."

1228. Polk's Flint (Genesse County, Mich.) City Directory 1945, Detroit: R. L. Polk & Co., Publishers, 1945, Page 313; (ancestry.com image 156); "Knapp Stanley C (Evelyn L) metallurgist Buick h1119 Flusing rd."

1229. Polk's Flint (Genesee County, Mich.) City Directory 1946, Detroit: R. L. Polk & Co., Publishers, 1946, Page 330; (ancestry.com image 174); "Knapp Stanley C (Evelyn L) research physicist Buick h1119 Flushing rd."

1230. Polk's Grand Rapids (Kent County, Mich.) City Directory 1948, Volume 1948 LXIX, Grand Rapids, Michigan: Grand Rapids Directory Company, Publishers, 1948, Page 491; (ancestry.com image 247); "Knapp Stanley C (Evelyn L) chf eng Doyle Vacuum Clnr h2621 Burton SW."

1231. Polk's Grand Rapids (Kent County, Mich.) City Directory, Volume 1949 LXX, Grand Rapids, Michigan: Grand Rapids Directory Company, Publishers, 1949, Page 503; (ancestry.com image 254); "Knapp Stanley C (Evelyn L) metallurgical eng h2621 Burton SE."

1232. 1950 US Census, Detroit, Wayne County, Michigan, April 1950, "Cheif [sic] Engineer Brass Industry."

1233. 1950 US Census, Paris, Kent County, Michigan, April 1950, "Chief Engineer Brass Mfg."

1234. Polk's Grand Rapids (Kent County, Mich.) City Directory, Volume 1954 LXXIII, Detroit, Michigan: R. L. Polk & Co., Publishers, 1954, Page 627; (ancestry.com image 330); "Knapp Stanley C (Evelyn L) consulting eng 2621 Burton SE h do."

1235. 1950 US Census, Detroit, Wayne County, Michigan, April 1950, Detroit census: "Marital Status: Sep[arated]" The Paris census reports both together and "Mar[ried]." They were united until their deaths. [Source 1233 above]

1236. Grand Rapids Press, 27 August 1987, page E11.

1237. US World War II Draft Registration Cards, 1940-1947. Serial Number 2405; Order Number 1904; Records of the Selective Service System, 147; Box 636.

1238. 1940 US Census, Flint, Genesse County, Michigan, NARA T627; Roll 1894; Sheet 4B; ED 85-82A; Line 75; "S. Charles Knapp."

1239. 1950 US Census, Paris, Kent County, Michigan, April 1950, Record Group Number 29; Roll 2857; Sheet Number 8; ED 41-62; House 2621 "Buxton Street"; Line 3; "Stanley Charles Knapp."

1240. Ibid. Record Group Number 29; Roll 2857; Sheet Number 8; ED 41-62; House 2621 "Buxton Street"; Line 5; "Karen Knapp."

1241. 1920 US Census, Douglass Township, Montcalm County, Michigan, January 1920, NARA T625; Roll 787; Sheet 4A; ED 113; Line 48; Page 102; Dwelling 89; Family 89; Line 48; "Marie Kilbourne."

1242. 1930 US Census, Belding, Ionia County, Michigan, April 1930, NARA T626; ED 2; Sheet 4A; Line 21; Dwelling 89; Family 91; Line 21; "Marie Kilbourne."

1243. 1940 US Census, Day Township, Montcalm County, Michigan, April 1940, NARA T627; Roll 1793; ED 59-10; Sheet 7B; Line 53; "Marie Taylor."

1244. US Social Security Applications and Claims Index, 1936-2007, Oct 1939: Name listed as MARIE KILBOURNE TAYLOR; Nov 1956: Name listed as MARIE L MYERS; May 1961: Name listed as MARY L MYERS.

1245. Not found in 1950 census.

1246. US Social Security Death Index; "Mary L. Myers."

1247. 1940 US Census, Day Township, Montcalm County, Michigan, April 1940, "Cook" "[illegible] school FWA."

1248. Marriage record/certificate/application. Montcalm County, Michigan; County 8187; State 59 2085.

1249. Personal knowledge from family members, Various interviews or correspondence over years by Curtis Daryl Sanders; from the diary of her mother.

1250. 1950 US Census, Stanton, Montcalm County, Michigan, April 1950, "Separated."

1251. 1940 US Census, Day Township, Montcalm County, Michigan, April 1940, NARA T627; Roll 1793; ED 59-10; Sheet 7B; Line 57;"Thereon E. Taylor."

1252. Ibid. NARA T627; Roll 1793; ED 59-10; Sheet 7B; Line 58; "Clarir Taylor."

1253. 1920 US Census, Douglass Township, Montcalm County, Michigan, January 1920, NARA T625; Roll 787; Sheet 4A; ED 113; Line 49; Page 102; Dwelling 89; Family 89; Line 49; "Thomas Kilbourne Jr."

1254. 1930 US Census, Belding, Ionia County, Michigan, April 1930, NARA T626; ED 2; Sheet 4A; Line 22; Dwelling 89; Family 91; Line 22; "Thomas Kilbourne Jr."

1255. 1940 US Census, Douglass Township, Montcalm County, Michigan, April 1940, NARA T627; Roll 1793; ED 54-11B; Sheet 1B; Line 42; "Thomas Kilbourne Jr."

1256. 1950 US Census, Maricopa County, Arizona, April 1950, Record Group Number 29; Roll 4698; Sheet 74; ED 7-163; House 2236; Line 25; "Thomas J Kilbourne."

1257. Phoenix Arizona ConSurvey City Directory 1951, Phoenix, Arizona: Baldwin ConSurvey Company, 1951, Volume 17, Page 1781; (ancestry.com image 433); "Kilbourne Thos (Jessie) H h 2236 E Monterosa."

1258. US Social Security Applications and Claims Index, 1936-2007, Jan 1939: Name listed as THOMAS JUNIOR KILBOURNE; 13 Apr 1993: Name listed as THOMAS J KILBOURNE.

1259. Find-A-Grave, (www.findagrave.com/memorial/27318711/thomas-oscar-kilbourn : accessed 9 March 2022). Memorial ID 27318711, citing Hillside Entrican Cemetery, Entrican, Montcalm County, Michigan; maintained by Gail (contributor 47136090).

1260. 1940 US Census, Douglass Township, Montcalm County, Michigan, April 1940.

1261. 1950 US Census, Maricopa County, Arizona, April 1950, "aircraft engine mechanic" | "aircraft Wholesale Industries."
1262. The Mullin-Kille and Baldwin Phoenix Arizona ConSurvey City Directory 1952, Volume 18, Phoenix: Mullin-Kille Company and Baldwin ConSurvey Company, 1952, Page 1836; (ancestry.com image 493); "Kilbourne Thos J (Jessie) H mech A & E Air Craft h 2236 E Monte Rosa [Telephone] 5-6214."
1263. The Mullin-Kille Phoenix Arizona ConSurvey City Directory 1956, Phoenix, Arizona: Mullin-Kille Company, 1956, Volume 21, Page 1326; (ancestry.com image 517); "Kilbourne Thos J (Jessie) H pres Paradise Airport Inc & treas N Phx Aircraft Sls h 7743 N 17th Ave [Telephone] WI 3-3663."
1264. Arizona Republic, newspaper, Phoenix, Arizona, "Hawaiian Trip," 11 January 1960, page 14.
1265. US World War II Draft Registration Cards, 1940-1947. Records of the Selective Service System, 147; Box 622.
1266. U.S. World War II Army Enlistment Records, 1938-1946, NARA, serial Number 16039018; Affiliate ARC Identifier 1263923; Box Film Number 02102.67; "Electronic Army Serial Number Merged File, ca. 1938-1946," database, Access to Archival Databases (AAD); NARA NAID 126323.
1267. U.S., World War II Hospital Admission Card Files, 1942-1954, NARA. Hospital Admission Card Files, ca. 1970 - ca. 1970; NAI 570973; Record Group Number: Records of the Office of the Surgeon General (Army), 1775-1994; Record Group Title 112.
1268. 1950 US Census, Maricopa County, Arizona, April 1950, Record Group Number 29; Roll 4698; Sheet 74; ED 7-163; House 2236; Line 26; "Jessie Kilbourne."
1269. US Social Security Applications and Claims Index, 1936-2007, Oct 1937: Name listed as JESSIE AUSBORN SKUSA; Oct 1949: Name listed as JESSIE KILBOURNE.
1270. 1950 US Census, Maricopa County, Arizona, April 1950, "alteration seamstress" | "Retail Department Store."
1271. As reported to family members.
1272. Find-A-Grave, (www.findagrave.com/memorial/6208660/maxine-demorest : accessed 9 March 2022). Memorial ID 6208660, citing Riverside Cemetery, Langston, Montcalm County, Michigan; maintained by Anonymous (contributor 24254493).
1273. Ibid.
1274. 1930 US Census, Belding, Ionia County, Michigan, April 1930, NARA T626; ED 2; Sheet 4A; Line 23; Dwelling 89; Family 91; Line 23; "Johnnie C. Kilbourne."
1275. 1940 US Census, Fairplain Township, Montcalm County, Michigan, April 1940, NARA T627; Roll 1793; Sheet 2B; ED 59-16; Line 54; "hired hand" living with the Eddie and Enah Phillips family; "John Kilbourne."
1276. 1950 US Census, Detroit, Wayne County, Michigan, April 1950, Record Group Number 29; Roll 5841; Sheet 11; ED 85-310; House 5545; Line 22; "John C Kilbourne."
1277. US Social Security Applications and Claims Index, 1936-2007, Nov 1940: Name listed as JOHN CHURCHILL KILBOURNE; 30 Dec 1987: Name listed as JOHN KILBOURNE.
1278. Michigan Death Index, 1971-1996, Michigan Department of Vital and Health Records, Lansing, database; Certificate Number 47295.
1279. Find-A-Grave, (www.findagrave.com/memorial/27318704/john-churchill-kilbourn : accessed 9 March 2022). Memorial ID 27318704,

citing Hillside Entrican Cemetery, Entrican, Montcalm County, Michigan; maintained by Gail (contributor 47136090).

1280. 1950 US Census, Detroit, Wayne County, Michigan, April 1950, "office maintenance" | "Telephone Co."

1281. Polk's Lincoln Park, Allen Park and Melvindale (Wayne County, Mich.) Directory 1953, Detroit, Michigan: R. L. Polk & Co., Publishers, 1953, Page 380; (ancestry.com image 192); "Kilborne, John C (Ina M) swtchman TelCo (Det) h14841 Thomas (AP)."

1282. US World War II Draft Registration Cards, 1940-1947. Records of the Selective Service System, 147; Box 622.

1283. US World War II Navy Muster Rolls, 1938-1949, NARA, Record Group: 24, Records of the Bureau of Naval Personnel, 1798 - 2007; Series ARC ID: 594996; Series MLR Number: A1 135.

1284. 1940 US Census, Flushing, Genesee County, Michigan, NARA T627; Roll 1749; Sheet 5B; ED 25-18A; Line 51; "Ina Jones."

1285. 1950 US Census, Detroit, Wayne County, Michigan, April 1950, Record Group Number 29; Roll 5841; Sheet 11; ED 85-310; House 5545; Line 23. "Ina M Kilbourne"

1286. Michigan Marriages, 1867-1952, database, ancestry.com and familysearch.org, Genesse County, Michigan; County number 47534; State 25 37248.

1287. Missouri, Birth Registers, 1847-1910, database with images, www.ancestry.com.

1288. San Diego Union-Tribune, newspaper, San Diego, California, Online, 29 December 2019; https://www.legacy.com/us/obituaries/sandiegouniontribune/name/ina-kilbourne-obituary?pid=194852804 (viewed 10 March 2022); no obituary - just a listing.

1289. Find-A-Grave, (www.findagrave.com/memorial/27318695/ina-marie-kilbourn : accessed 10 March 2022). Memorial ID 27318695, citing Hillside Entrican Cemetery, Entrican, Montcalm County, Michigan; maintained by Gail (contributor 47136090).

1290. 1950 US Census, Detroit, Wayne County, Michigan, April 1950, Record Group Number 29; Roll 5841; Sheet 11; ED 85-310; House 5545; Line 24; "Douglas M Kilbourne."

1291. 1930 US Census, Belding, Ionia County, Michigan, April 1930, NARA T626; ED 2; Sheet 4A; Line 24; Dwelling 89; Family 91; Line 24; "Truman Kilbourne."

1292. 1940 US Census, Douglass Township, Montcalm County, Michigan, April 1940, NARA T627; Roll 1793; ED 54-11B; Sheet 1B; Line 45; "Truman G. Kilbourne."

1293. 1950 US Census, Tallmadge, Ottawa County, Michigan, April 1950, Record Group Number 29; Roll 2224; Sheet 1; ED 70-65B; House 1934; Line 27; "Truman G Kilbourne."

1294. Michigan Death Index, 1971-1996, Michigan Department of Vital and Health Records, Lansing, Certificate Number 50334.

1295. Find-A-Grave, (www.findagrave.com/memorial/222477403/truman-g-kilbourne : accessed 10 March 2022). Memorial ID 222477403, citing Rosedale Memorial Park, Tallmadge Township, Ottawa County, Michigan; maintained by j.a.pruis-steere (contributor 47169073).

1296. Polk's Grand Rapids (Kent County, Mich.) City Directory Including East Grand Rapids, Grand Rapids, Michigan: Grand Rapids Directory Company, Publishers, 1946, Vol. 1946 LXVIII, Page 471; (ancestry.com image 234); "R27 Colfax NE" Grand Rapids, Michigan.

1297. Polk's Grand Rapids (Kent County, Mich.) City Directory Including East Grand Rapids, Comstock Park and North Park, Vol. 1946 LXIX,

Grand Rapids, Michigan: Grand Rapids Directory Company, Publishers, 1946, Page 481; (ancestry.com image 242); R27 Colfax NE" Grand Rapids, Michigan; "Kool-Rite Co."

1298. Polk's Grand Rapids (Kent County, Mich.) City Directory, Volume 1949 LXX, Grand Rapids, Michigan: Grand Rapids Directory Company, Publishers, 1949, Page 493; (ancestry.com image 249); "Kilbourne Truman G (June) hlpr Udell Refrig Co r1934 Lake Michigan dr NW."

1299. 1950 US Census, Tallmadge, Ottawa County, Michigan, April 1950, "Refrigeration Mechanic" | "Wholesale & Repair Refrigeration Co."

1300. Polk's Grand Rapids (Kent County, Mich.) City Directory, Volume 1951, Grand Rapids, Michigan: Grand Rapids Directory Company, Publishers, 1951, Page 507; (ancestry.com image 244); "Kilbourne Truman G (June) servmn Udell Refrigeration Co r1934 Lake Michigan dr NW."

1301. Polk's Grand Rapids (Kent County, Mich.) City Directory, Volume 1954 LXXIII, Detroit, Michigan: R. L. Polk & Co., Publishers, 1954, Page 614; (ancestry.com image 324); "Kilbourne Truman G servmn Udell Refgr Co r1934 Lake Michigan dr NW."

1302. Grand Rapids Press, 9 September 1979, page F1. Also 8 September 1979, page 8B.

1303. US World War II Draft Registration Cards, 1940-1947. Records of the Selective Service System, 147; Box 622; Serial number N326; Order Number 11840.

1304. U.S. World War II Army Enlistment Records, 1938-1946, Affiliate Publication Title: Electronic Army Serial Number Merged File, ca. 1938-1946; Affiliate ARC Identifier 1263923; Box Film Number 10805.142; NARA NAID 126323.

1305. 1930 US Census, Grand Rapids, Kent County, Michigan, April 1930, NARA T626; Enumeration district 24; Sheet 16A; Family 374; Line 27.

1306. 1950 US Census, Tallmadge, Ottawa County, Michigan, April 1950, Record Group Number 29; Roll 2224; Sheet 1; ED 70-65B; House 1934; Line 28; "June L. Kilbourne."

1307. Grand Rapids Press, "Marriage License Seekers." 20 September 1948, page 14.

1308. Michigan Marriages, 1867-1952, database, ancestry.com and familysearch.org, Michigan Department of Community Health, Division of Vital Records and Health Statistics; Lansing; Marriage Records, 1867-1952; Film: 123; Film Title: 41 Kent 45330-48599; Film Description: Kent (1948-1949); county 95-528; state 41 46829.

1309. Polk's Grand Rapids (Kent County, Mich.) City Directory 1948, Volume 1948 LXIX, Grand Rapids, Michigan: Grand Rapids Directory Company, Publishers, 1948, Page 315; (ancestry.com image 159); "Freville June L bkpr GRIndusrialElec r736 Emperor SW."

1310. Grand Rapids Press, 2 May 2015; online, (www.genealogybank.com/doc/obituaries/obit/1551A8C8D51AA620 -1551A8C8D51AA620 : accessed 9 February 2022).

1311. Heritage Life Story Funeral Home, Grand Rapids, Kent County, Michigan, https://heritagelifestory.com/obituaries/june-kilbourne.107301, (Viewed 10 July 2022).

1312. 1950 US Census, Tallmadge, Ottawa County, Michigan, April 1950, Record Group Number 29; Roll 2224; Sheet 1; ED 70-65B; House 1934; Line 29; "Dale A Kilbourne."

1313. Not found in 1910 census.

1314. Death Certificate/Record. Michigan Department of Community Health, Division for Vital Records and Health Statistics; Lansing; Certificate of Death; Number 177.
1315. Find-A-Grave, Not found in Onondaga, Michigan area cemeteries.
1316. The State Journal, "Diphtheria Hits Onondaga Village," 28 March 1917, page 7.
1317. 1920 US Census, Onondaga Township, Ingham County, Michigan, January 1920, NARA T625; Roll 771; Sheet 3B; ED 129; Dwelling 68; Family 69; Line 51; "Loretta M Clay."
1318. 1930 US Census, Jackson City, Jackson County, Michigan, April 1930, NARA T626; Sheet 37A; ED 22; House 128; Dwelling 837; Family 893; Line 21; "Mary L Clay;" residing as a boarder with Herbert Storey family.
1319. 1940 US Census, Alpena Township, Alpena County, Michigan, April 1940, NARA T627; Roll 1722; Sheet 64B; ED 4-1; Line 46; "Mary Loretta Clay."
1320. 1950 US Census, Detroit, Wayne County, Michigan, April 1950, Record Group Number: 29; Roll 4116; Sheet 5; ED 85-2579; Line 19; "Mary L Haas."
1321. Polk's Lakeland (Polk County, Florida) City Directory 1956, Richmond, Virginia: R. L. Polk & Co., Publishers, 1956, Page 158 (ancestry.-com image 204); "Haas Raymond A (Mary L) h729 Wilson."
1322. Polk's Lakeland (Polk County, Florida) City Directory 1959, Richmond, Virginia: R. L. Polk & Co., Publishers, 1959, Page 150 (ancestry.-com image 204); "Haas Raymond A (Mary L) h729 Wilson av."
1323. Polk's Lakeland (Polk County, Florida) City Directory 1960, Richmond, Virginia: R. L. Polk & Co., Publisher, 1960, Page 159 (ancestry.-com image 210); "Haas Raymond A (Mary L) h729 Wilson av."
1324. Find-A-Grave, (www.findagrave.com/memorial/114026022/mary-l-haas: accessed 30 July 2022). Memorial ID 114026022, citing Lakeland Memorial Gardens, Lakeland, Polk County, Florida; maintained by Donna McPherson (contributor 46906329).
1325. 1930 US Census, Jackson City, Jackson County, Michigan, April 1930.
1326. 1940 US Census, Alpena Township, Alpena County, Michigan, April 1940.
1327. Oracle Nineteen Twenty-Five: The Oracle of Lansing Senior High School - 1925, Lansing, Michigan: Lansing Senior High School, 1925, Volume 35, Page 27 (ancestry.com image 35).
1328. UK and Ireland, Outward Passenger Lists, 1890-1960, The National Archives; Kew, Surrey, England; BT27 Board of Trade: Commercial and Statistical Department and Successors: Outwards Passenger Lists, database, ancestry.com and familysearch.org, Contract ticket 38553; Series BT27-147318; (ancestry.com image 31).
1329. New York, U.S., Arriving Passenger and Crew Lists (including Castle Garden and Ellis Island), 1820-1957, database with images, NARA, www.ancestry.com, Microfilm Serial: T715, 1897-1957; Line 26; Page Number 47.
1330. Indiana Marriages, 1810-2019, database, familysearch.org or ancestry.-com, Page 119.
1331. Divorce Record. Michigan Department Of Health, Bureau Of Records And Statistics, Lansing. File 33 4056; Docket 18183.
1332. 1940 US Census, Detroit, Wayne County, Michigan, April 1940, NARA T627; Roll 1863; ED 84-756; Sheet 84A; Ward 14 "Hotel Yorba Lafayette Blvd." Line 38; "Raymond A Haas."

1333. 1950 US Census, Detroit, Wayne County, Michigan, April 1950, Record Group Number: 29; Roll 4116; Sheet 5; ED 85-2579; Line 18;"Raymond A Haas."

1334. Marriage record/certificate/application. Michigan Department of Community Health, Division of Vital Records and Health Statistics; Lansing; Film 304; Film Title: 82 Wayne 240060-243299; number 240172. (Licensed in Wayne County, but married in Ingham.)

1335. Find-A-Grave, (www.findagrave.com/memorial/114025997/raymond-a-haas: accessed 30 July 2022). Memorial ID 114025997, citing Lakeland Memorial Gardens, Lakeland, Polk County, Florida; maintained by Donna McPherson (contributor 46906329).

1336. 1940 US Census, Detroit, Wayne County, Michigan, April 1940, "Fireman Detroit Fire Department."

1337. 1950 US Census, Detroit, Wayne County, Michigan, April 1950, "Sgt. of Engine Co. City Line Dept."

1338. Detroit Free Press, "Raymond A. Haas, Retired Fire Captain," 1 January 1978, page 16-D.

1339. Orlando Sentinel, "Obituaries," 1 January 1978, page 11-E.

1340. US World War II Draft Registration Cards, 1940-1947. Records of the Selective Service System, 147; Box 462.

1341. 1950 US Census, Detroit, Wayne County, Michigan, April 1950, Record Group Number: 29; Roll 4116; Sheet 5; ED 85-2579; Line 20; "Judith L Haas."

1342. Polk's Lakeland (Polk County, Florida) City Directory 1960, Richmond, Virginia: R. L. Polk & Co., Publisher, 1960, Page 159 (ancestry.com image 210); "Haas Judith L studt r729 Wilson av."

1343. 1950 US Census, Detroit, Wayne County, Michigan, April 1950, Record Group Number: 29; Roll 4116; Sheet 5; ED 85-2579; Line 21; "Raymond A Haas."

1344. 1920 US Census, Onondaga Township, Ingham County, Michigan, January 1920, NARA T625; Roll 771; Sheet 3B; ED 129; Dwelling 68; Family 69; Line 52; "Mina L Clay."

1345. McKinley-Reynolds Co. Lansing City Directory 1925, [Lansing, Michigan:] McKinley-Reynolds Co., 1925, Page 261 (ancestry.com image 158); "Clay Mina L student h418 Lapeer."

1346. 1930 US Census, Delhi Township, Ingham County, Michigan, April 1930, NARA T626; ED 33-4; Sheet 13B; Dwelling 324; Family 325; Line 55; "Mina L. Howe."

1347. 1940 US Census, Mason Township, Ingham County, Michigan, April 1940, NARA T627; Roll 1763; Sheet 61B; ED 33-79; Line 52; "Mina E. Howe."

1348. 1950 US Census, Mason Township, Ingham County, Michigan, April 1950, Record Group Number 29; Roll 4780; ED 33-89; "Mina C. Howe."

1349. Michigan, County Births, 1867-1917, database with images, www.familysearch.org, Page 291; Record 5155.

1350. Michigan Death Index, 1971-1996, Michigan Department of Vital and Health Records, Lansing; Certificate 8853.

1351. Find-A-Grave, (www.findagrave.com/memorial/37565036/mina-l-howe: accessed 31 July 2022). Memorial ID 37565036, citing Maple Grove Cemetery, Mason, Ingham County, Michigan; maintained by Sandra Moore (contributor 47025864).

1352. 1930 US Census, Delhi Township, Ingham County, Michigan, April 1930. "Teacher."

1353. 1940 US Census, Mason Township, Ingham County, Michigan, April 1940. "Teacher."

1354. 1950 US Census, Mason Township, Ingham County, Michigan, April 1950. "Teacher."

1355. The State Journal, "Deaths and Funerals," 7 February 1976, page A-2.

1356. 1930 US Census, Delhi Township, Ingham County, Michigan, April 1930, NARA T626; ED 33-4; Sheet 13B; Dwelling 324; Family 325; Line 54; "Herbert E. Howe."

1357. 1940 US Census, Mason Township, Ingham County, Michigan, April 1940, NARA T627; Roll 1763; Sheet 61B; ED 33-79; Line 51; "Herbert E. Howe."

1358. 1950 US Census, Mason Township, Ingham County, Michigan, April 1950, Record Group Number 29; Roll 4780; ED 33-89; "Herbert E. Howe."

1359. The State Journal, "Onondaga Girl Is Recent Bride," 10 July 1929, page 13.

1360. Marriage record/certificate/application. Michigan Department of Community Health, Division of Vital Records and Health Statistics; Lansing. Film: 96; Film Title: 38 Jackson 01331-04599. Numer 38 2695. (License was for Jackson County, but married in Ingham.)

1361. Michigan Death Index, 1971-1996, Michigan Department of Vital and Health Records, Lansing.

1362. Find-A-Grave, (www.findagrave.com/memorial/37565019/herbert-e-howe: accessed 31 July 2022). Memorial ID 37565019, citing Maple Grove Cemetery, Mason, Ingham County, Michigan; maintained by Sandra Moore (contributor 47025864).

1363. Lansing City [Michigan] Directory 1923, Lansing, Michigan: Chilson, McKinley & Co. Publishers, 1923, Page 546; (ancestry.com image 320); "Howe Herbert E. student, h 433 N Butler blvd."

1364. Polk's Lansing (Ingham County, Mich.) City Directory, 1953, Volume XLXI, Detroit, Michigan: R. L. Polk & Co., Publishers, 1953, Page 359; (ancestry.com image 196); "Howe Herbert driver Kirksey Mtr Frt r Leslie."

1365. The State Journal, "Deaths and Funerals," 15 February 1971, page A-2.

1366. US World War II Draft Registration Cards, 1940-1947,. Registration Cards for Michigan, 10/16/1940-03/31/1947; Record Group: Records of the Selective Service System, 147; Box 543.

1367. 1940 US Census, Mason Township, Ingham County, Michigan, April 1940, NARA T627; Roll 1763; Sheet 61B; ED 33-79; Line 53; "Laurence E. Howe."

1368. Polk's Lansing (Ingham County, Mich.) City Directory 1956, Detroit, Michigan: R. L. Polk & Co., Publishers, 1956, Volume 1956 XLXIV, Page 480 (ancestry.com image 380); "Howe Laurence E (Bonnie) teller First Natl Bank of East Lansing r Mason Mich."

1369. 1910 US Census, Carmel Township, Eaton County, Michigan, May 1910, NARA T624;Roll 645; Sheet 5B; ED 79; Dwelling 136; Family 136; Line 88; "Morrison L. Clay."

1370. 1920 US Census, Carmel Township, Eaton County, Michigan, January 1920, NARA T625; Roll 763; Sheet 2B; ED 91; Dwelling 47; Family 47; Line 93; "Morrison Clay."

1371. 1930 US Census, Charlotte, Eaton County, Michigan, April 1930, NARA T626; ED 23-8; Page 133; Sheet 5A; House 225; Dwelling 123; Family 137; Line 12; "Morrison L Clay."

1372. 1940 US Census, Charlotte, Eaton County, Michigan, April 1940, NARA T627; Roll 1747; Sheet 4B; ED 23-9; House 214; Line 75; "Morrison Clay."

1373. 1950 US Census, Carmel Township, Eaton County, Michigan, April 1950, Record Group Number 29; Roll 169; Sheet 7; ED 23-8; Dwelling 45; Line 15; "Morrison L. Clay."

1374. Note. (WWII Draft registration says Eaton Rapids).

1375. Find-A-Grave, (www.findagrave.com/memorial/63096728/morrison-legrand-clay: accessed 28 July 2022). Memorial ID 63096728, citing Maple Hill Cemetery, Charlotte, Eaton County, Michigan; maintained by Woodie (contributor 46922700).

1376. 1930 US Census, Charlotte, Eaton County, Michigan, April 1930, "Draying" | "general work."

1377. 1940 US Census, Charlotte, Eaton County, Michigan, April 1940, "Truck driver" | "wholesale Cavalry Co."

1378. 1950 US Census, Carmel Township, Eaton County, Michigan, April 1950, "Supervisor Maintenance" | "Radio & Television Factory."

1379. Battle Creek Enquirer And News, "Local and Area Obituaries," 16 October 1977, page 6.

1380. The State Journal, "Death and Funerals." 16 October 1977, page B-2.

1381. US World War II Draft Registration Cards, 1940-1947. Record Group: Records of the Selective Service System, 147; Box 212.

1382. 1930 US Census, Charlotte, Eaton County, Michigan, April 1930, NARA T626; ED 23-8; Page 133; Sheet 5A; House 225; Dwelling 123; Family 137; Line 13; "Sara D Clay."

1383. 1940 US Census, Charlotte, Eaton County, Michigan, April 1940, NARA T627; Roll 1747; Sheet 4B; ED 23-9; House 214; Line 76; "Sara Clay."

1384. 1950 US Census, Carmel Township, Eaton County, Michigan, April 1950, Record Group Number 29; Roll 169; Sheet 7; ED 23-8; Dwelling 45; Line 16; "Sara D Clay."

1385. Marriage record/certificate/application. Michigan Department of Community Health, Division of Vital Records and Health Statistics; Lansing. Number 65. Film 174; Film Description: 1924 Alcona-1924 Emmet.

1386. Michigan Births, 1867-1902, familysearch.org, Record 325; (https://familysearch.org/ark:/61903/1:1:NQ6T-C7X : 20 February 2021), Sarah Dale Ledyard, 30 Aug 1902; citing item 2 p 167 rn 325, Benton, Eaton, Michigan, Department of Vital Records, Lansing; FHL microfilm 2,363,037.

1387. Find-A-Grave, (www.findagrave.com/memorial/63096750/sara-dale-clay: accessed 06 June 2023); Memorial ID 63096750, citing Maple Hill Cemetery, Charlotte, Eaton County, Michigan; maintained by Woodie (contributor 46922700).

1388. 1940 US Census, Charlotte, Eaton County, Michigan, April 1940, "nurse" | "private home."

1389. Battle Creek Enquirer And News, "Area Obituaries: Mrs. Morrison Clay," 5 November 1969, page A-8.

1390. 1930 US Census, Charlotte, Eaton County, Michigan, April 1930, NARA T626; ED 23-8; Page 133; Sheet 5A; House 225; Dwelling 123; Family 137; Line 14; "Shirley Clay."

1391. 1940 US Census, Charlotte, Eaton County, Michigan, April 1940, NARA T627; Roll 1747; Sheet 4B; ED 23-9; House 214; Line 77; "Shirley Jonane Clay."

1392. Polk's Birmingham (Oakland County, Mich.) City Directory 1960, Volume 1960 XXI, Detroit, Michigan: R. L. Polk & Co., Publishers, 1960, Page 151 (ancestry.com image 182); "Anderson Karl A (Shirley G) coml illustrator LaDriere Studio (Det) h925 Dedham ct (B'fieldTwp)."

1393. 1910 US Census, Carmel Township, Eaton County, Michigan, May 1910, NARA T624;Roll 645; Sheet 5B; ED 79; Dwelling 136; Family 136; Line 89; "Ilene A. Clay."

1394. 1920 US Census, Carmel Township, Eaton County, Michigan, January 1920, NARA T625; Roll 763; Sheet 2B; ED 91; Dwelling 47; Family 47; Line 94; "Ilene Clay."

1395. 1930 US Census, Jackson City, Jackson County, Michigan, April 1930, NARA T626; ED 38-24; Sheet 24B; House 906; Dwelling 652; Family 782; Line 88; "Ileen A. Lee."

1396. 1940 US Census, Jackson City, Jackson County, Michigan, April 1940, NARA T627; Roll 1768; Sheet 6B; ED 38-26; House 264; Line 76; "Ilene C Lee."

1397. 1950 US Census, Jackson, Jackson County, Michigan, April 1950, Record Group Number 29; Roll 4013; Sheet 5; ED 38-61; House 264; Line 18; "Ilene C. Lee."

1398. US Social Security Applications and Claims Index, 1936-2007, (Claim Date 2 May 1968.

1399. Find-A-Grave, (www.findagrave.com/memorial/64837565/ann-ilene-lee: accessed 28 July 2022). Memorial ID 64837565, citing Maple Hill Cemetery, Charlotte, Eaton County, Michigan; maintained by Woodie (contributor 46922700).

1400. 1930 US Census, Jackson City, Jackson County, Michigan, April 1930, "Bookkeeper" | "Bank."

1401. 1940 US Census, Jackson City, Jackson County, Michigan, April 1940, "Bookkeeper" | "Bank."

1402. 1950 US Census, Jackson, Jackson County, Michigan, April 1950, "Collections Clerk" | "Bank."

1403. 1930 US Census, Jackson City, Jackson County, Michigan, April 1930, NARA T626; ED 38-24; Sheet 24B; House 906; Dwelling 652; Family 782; Line 87; "Terry F. Lee."

1404. 1940 US Census, Jackson City, Jackson County, Michigan, April 1940, NARA T627; Roll 1768; Sheet 6B; ED 38-26; House 264; Line 75; "Terry F. Lee."

1405. 1950 US Census, Jackson, Jackson County, Michigan, April 1950, Record Group Number 29; Roll 4013; Sheet 5; ED 38-61; House 264; Line 17; "Terry F. Lee."

1406. Marriage record/certificate/application. Eaton County, Michigan. Number 227; (https://familysearch.org/ark:/61903/1:1:NQ7Q-YML : 18 February 2021).

1407. Michigan Death Index, 1971-1996, Michigan Department of Vital and Health Records, Lansing.

1408. Find-A-Grave, (www.findagrave.com/memorial/64863461/terry-f-lee: accessed 28 July 2022). Memorial ID 64863461, citing Maple Hill Cemetery, Charlotte, Eaton County, Michigan; maintained by Woodie (contributor 46922700).

1409. Polk's Jackson (Michigan) City Directory 1929, Detroit, Michigan: R. L. Polk & Co., Publishers, 1929, Page 320 (ancestry.com image 166); "Lee Terry F slsmn L H Field Co r906 Orchard pl."

1410. 1930 US Census, Jackson City, Jackson County, Michigan, April 1930, "Manager" | "Shoestore."

1411. Polk's Jackson Michigan City Directory 1930, Detroit, Michigan: R. L. Polk & Co., Publishers, 1930, Page 290 (ancestry.com image 147); "Lee Terry F dept mgr L H Field Co h906 Orchard pl."

1412. Polk's Jackson (Michigan) City Directory 1931, Detroit, Michigan: R. L. Polk & Co., Publishers, 1931, Page 259 (ancestry.com image 135); "Lee Terry F (Ilene) asst mgr L H Field Co h906 Orchard pl."
1413. Polk's Jackson (Michigan) City Directory 1932, Detroit, Michigan: R. L. Polk & Co., Publishers, 1932, Page 246 (ancestry.com image 125); "Lee Terry F (Ilene) dept mgr L H Field Co h906 Orchard pl."
1414. Polk's Jackson (Jackson County, Mich.) City Directory 1933, Detroit, Michigan: R. L. Polk & Co., Publishers, 1933, Page 231 (ancestry.com image 121); "Lee Terry F (Ilene A) dept mgr L H Field Co h906 Orchard pl."
1415. Polk's Jackson (Jackson County, Mich.) City Directory 1935, Detroit: R. L. Polk & Co., Publishers, 1935, Page 265 (ancestry.com image 136); "Lee Terry F (Eileen A) clk r915 Merriman."
1416. Polk's Jackson (Jackson County, Mich.) City Directory 1936, Detroit: R. L. Polk & Co., Publishers, 1936, Page 269 (ancestry.com image 138); "Lee Terry F (Ileen) mgr Jay's Shoe Shop r915 Merriman."
1417. Polk's Jackson (Jackson County, Mich.) City Directory 1937, Detroit: R. L. Polk & Co., Publishers, 1937, Page 236 (ancestry.com image 115); "Lee Terry F (Ilene A) slsmn Arch Preserver Shop h 17107 4th."
1418. Polk's Jackson (Jackson County, Mich.) City Directory 1938, Detroit, Michigan: R. L. Polk & Co., Publishers, 1938, Page 242 (ancestry.com image 123); "Lee Terry F (Ilene A) slsmn Selby Shoes h264 Douglas."
1419. 1940 US Census, Jackson City, Jackson County, Michigan, April 1940, "Salesman" | "Retail Shoe Store."
1420. Polk's Jackson (Jackson County, Michigan) City Directory 1940, Detroit, Michigan: R. L. Polk & Co., Publishers, 1940, Page 228 (ancestry.com image 112); "Lee Terry F (Ilene A) slsmn Selby Shoes h264 Douglas."
1421. Polk's Jackson (Jackson County, Mich.) City Directory 1941, Detroit, Michigan: R. L. Polk & Co., Publishers, 1941, Page 230 (ancestry.com image 114); "Lee Terry F (Ilene C) slsmn Glasgow's Inc h264 Douglas."
1422. Polk's Jackson City Directory 1942, [Detroit, Michigan:] R. L. Polk & Co. 1942, Page 215 (ancestry.com image 262); "Lee Terry F (Ilene C) slsmn Glasgow's h264 Douglas."
1423. Polk's Jackson (Jackson County, Mich.) City Directory 1943, Detroit, Michigan: R. L. Polk & Co., Publishers, 1943, Page 226 (ancestry.com image 112); "Lee Terry F (Ilene C) slsmn h264 Douglas."
1424. Polk's Jackson (Jackson County, Mich.) City Directory 1945, Detroit: R. L. Polk & Co., Publishers, 1945, Page 230 (ancestry.com image 114); "Lee Terry (Ilene A) mgr shoe dept Rackley & Strom h264 Douglas."
1425. Polk's Jackson (Jackson County, Mich.) City Directory 1946, Detroit, Michigan: R. L. Polk & Co., Publishers, 1946, Page 250 (ancestry.com image 133); "Lee Terry F (Ilene) dept mgr Glasgow's Inc h264 Douglas."
1426. Polk's Jackson (Jackson County, Mich.) City Directory 1947, Detroit: R. L. Polk & Co., Publishers, 1947, Page 246 (ancestry.com image 125); "Lee Terry F (Eileen) slsmn h264 Douglas."
1427. Polk's Jackson (Jackson County, Mich.) City Directory 1949, Detroit, Michigan: R. L. Polk & Co., Publishers, 1949, Page 247 (ancestry.com image 125); "Lee Terry F (Eileen) slsmn h264 Douglas."
1428. 1950 US Census, Jackson, Jackson County, Michigan, April 1950, "Shoe salesman" | "retail dry goods store"
1429. Polk's Jackson (Jackson County, Mich.) City Directory 1951, Detroit, Michigan: R. L. Polk & Co., Publishers, 1951, Page 239 (ancestry.com

image 118); "Lee Terry F (Ilene C) slsmn Rackley & Strom Shoe h264 Douglas."

1430. Polk's Jackson (Jackson County, Mich.) City Directory 1952, Detroit: R. L. Polk & Co., Publishers, 1952, Page 227 (ancestry.com image 111); "Lee T F (Ilene) dept mgr Glasgow's r732 Woodlawn."

1431. Polk's Jackson (Jackson County, Mich.) City Directory 1956, Detroit, Michigan: R. L. Polk & Co., Publishers, 1956, Page 357 (ancestry.com image 198); "Lee Terry F (Ilene C) dept mgr L H Field Co h732 Woodlawn."

1432. Polk's Jackson (Jackson County, Mich.) City Directory 1960, Detroit: R. L. Polk & Co., Publishers, 1960, Page 312 (ancestry.com image 248); "Lee Terry F (Ilene C; Dog & Suds Drive In Restr) h732 Woodlawn av."

1433. US World War II Draft Registration Cards, 1940-1947, NARA. Record Group: Records of the Selective Service System, 147; Box 693.

1434. 1950 US Census, Jackson, Jackson County, Michigan, April 1950, Record Group Number 29; Roll 4013; Sheet 5; ED 38-61; House 264; Line 19; "Judy K. Lee."

1435. 1910 US Census, Carmel Township, Eaton County, Michigan, May 1910, NARA T624;Roll 645; Sheet 5B; ED 79; Dwelling 136; Family 136; Line 90; "Leta M. Clay."

1436. 1920 US Census, Carmel Township, Eaton County, Michigan, January 1920, NARA T625; Roll 763; Sheet 2B; ED 91; Dwelling 47; Family 47; Line 95; "Leta Clay."

1437. 1930 US Census, Sandusky, Sanilac County, Michigan, NARA T626; ED 76-30; Sheet 8A; Page 237; Dwelling 176; Family 180; Line 20; Boarder in the house of William H. Watson; "Leaty M Clay."

1438. 1940 US Census, Fenton Township, Genesse County, Michigan, NARA T627; Roll 1749; Sheet 1B; ED 25-12; House 306; Line 77. Lodger in the house of Ray B. Smith; "Leta Mae Clay."

1439. 1950 US Census, Fenton Township, Genesse County, Michigan, Record Group Number 29; Roll 4981; ED 25-32; Dwelling 124; "Leta Pasco."

1440. Find-A-Grave, (www.findagrave.com/memorial/67510140/leta-mae-pasco: accessed 08 August 2022); memorial ID 67510140, citing Maple Hill Cemetery, Charlotte, Eaton County, Michigan; maintained by Woodie (contributor 46922700).

1441. 1930 US Census, Sandusky, Sanilac County, Michigan. "Teacher."

1442. 1940 US Census, Fenton Township, Genesse County, Michigan, "Teacher."

1443. 1950 US Census, Fenton Township, Genesse County, Michigan, "Teacher."

1444. Ostrander, Evah, editor, Michigan State Normal College, 1928, Ypsilanti, Michigan: Michigan State Normal College, 1928, Page 141.

1445. Flint Journal, newspaper, Flint, Michigan, Online 3 October 2003; https://obits.mlive.com/us/obituaries/flint/name/leta-pasco-obituary?id=14929173 (viewed 8 August 2022).

1446. Daily Oklahoman, newspaper, Oklahoma City, Oklahoma, "Deaths: Edmond," 4 September 2003, page 14.

1447. Battle Creek Enquirer And News, "Pasco-Clay Wedding Set Aug. 3 at Fenton Church," 28 July 1947, page 3.

1448. Michigan Marriages, 1867-1952, County File Number 52452; State File Number 25 42516.

1449. Michigan, County Births, 1867-1917, database with images, www.familysearch.org, Genesee County, Michigan; Record 1357.

1450. Find-A-Grave, (www.findagrave.com/memorial/67510126/james-m-pasco: accessed 08 August 2022). Memorial ID 67510126, citing Maple

Hill Cemetery, Charlotte, Eaton County, Michigan; maintained by Woodie (contributor 46922700).

1451. US World War II Draft Registration Cards, 1940-1947, NARA, Records of the Selective Service System, 147; Box 911.

1452. U.S. World War II Army Enlistment Records, 1938-1946, NARA.

1453. 1930 US Census, Charlotte, Eaton County, Michigan, April 1930, NARA T626; Sheet 16B; ED 23-10; Dwelling 455; Family 474; Line 75; Son, "Clifford Clay,"

1454. 1910 US Census, Sandstone Township, Jackson County, Michigan, April 1910, Enumerated 3 May 1910; NARA T624; Roll 653; Sheet 8B; ED 37; Dwelling 179; Family 189; Line 98; "Vern C Krugman."

1455. 1920 US Census, Sheridan Township, Calhoun County, Michigan, January 1920, NARA T625; Roll 760; ED 84; Sheet 2A; Institution: Starr Commonwealth For Boys Incorporated" Dwelling 28; Family 29; Line 26; "Vern Krugman," Inmate.

1456. 1930 US Census, Parma Township, Jackson County, Michigan, April 1930, NARA T626; Sheet 1B; ED 46; Dwelling 22; Family 23; Line 89; "Vern C Krugman" (living with his aunt Mabel Zantop and family).

1457. 1940 US Census, Parma Township, Jackson County, Michigan, April 1940, NARA T627; ED 38-58; Sheet 2B; House 118; Line 54; "Vern C Krugman."

1458. Michigan, County Births, 1867-1917, (www.familysearch.org/ark:/61903/1:1:CSH9-CQ2M : 19 July 2021); Registered number 9.

1459. U.S., Rosters of World War II Dead, 1939-1945, United States. Army. Quartermaster General's Office, Washington, D.C., database with images, (ancestry.com image 654).

1460. News-Palladium, newspaper, Benton Harbor, St. Joseph, Michigan, "307 Berrien Youths Gave Lives For Victory," 31 December 1945, page 5. ".. reported to have died Dec. 22, 1944 in Germany."

1461. Loomis, Frances, Michigan casualties, World War, (ancestry.com image 1987); listing has him killed "4-2-1945".

1462. Battle Creek Enquirer And News, "Philosophy of Infantryman Reflected In Letter from Dead Parma Sergeant," 21 January 1945, page 18.

1463. Find-A-Grave, (www.findagrave.com/memorial/20153916/laverne-c-krugman: accessed 15 August 2022). Memorial ID 20153916, citing Fairview Cemetery, Tompkins, Jackson County, Michigan; maintained by Deb Hayes-Wolfe (contributor 46811474).

1464. 1930 US Census, Parma Township, Jackson County, Michigan, April 1930, "Laborer | Saw Mill."

1465. 1940 US Census, Parma Township, Jackson County, Michigan, April 1940, "Line Builder."

1466. Herald-Palladium, "Nephew Of Bainbridge Woman Dies In France," 27 January 1945, page 10.

1467. Battle Creek Enquirer And News, "Senator Vandenberg Moved by Plea from Dead Parma Sergeant," 14 February 1945, page 10.

1468. US World War II Draft Registration Cards, 1940-1947, NARA. Records of the Selective Service System, 147; Box 659.

1469. "United States Headstone Applications for U.S. Military Veterans, 1925-1970," database with images, www.ancestry.com or familysearch.org.

1470. 1940 US Census, Parma Township, Jackson County, Michigan, April 1940, NARA T627; ED 38-58; Sheet 2B; House 118; Line 55; "Margie Krugman."

1471. Marriage record/certificate/application. Jackson County, Michigan; Certificate of Marriage, number 185; State number 38 6390 1936.

1472. Find-A-Grave, (www.findagrave.com/memorial/20154476/margie-i-krugman_weaver: accessed 15 August 2022). Memorial ID 20154476, citing Fairview Cemetery, Tompkins, Jackson County, Michigan; maintained by Deb Hayes-Wolfe (contributor 46811474).

1473. Battle Creek Enquirer And News, "Parma Boy Wins Silver Star for Gallant Action," 1 March 1945, page 16.

1474. 1920 US Census, Sheridan Township, Calhoun County, Michigan, January 1920, NARA T625; Roll 760; ED 84; Sheet 2A; Institution: Starr Commonwealth For Boys Incorporated" Dwelling 28; Family 29; Line 25; "Everett Krugman," inmate.

1475. Not found in 1930 US census.

1476. 1940 US Census, Jackson City, Jackson County, Michigan, April 1940, NARA T627; Roll 1768; ED 38-27; Sheet 3A; Dwelling 911; Family 70; Line 28; "Everett L. Krugman."

1477. 1950 US Census, Parma Township, Jackson County, Michigan, April 1950, Record Group Number: 29; Roll 4014; Sheet 5; ED 38-124; House 320; Line 2; "Everett L Krugman."

1478. Michigan, County Births, 1867-1917, (www.familysearch.org/ark:/61903/1:1:QGDP-6V5M : 19 July 2021); Registered number 15.

1479. Michigan Death Index, 1971-1996, Michigan Department of Vital and Health Records, Lansing, (https://www.familysearch.org/ark:/61903/1:1:VZBL-NV1 : 10 August 2022); "Everett Krugman."

1480. Find-A-Grave, (www.findagrave.com/memorial/132011546/everett-l-krugman: accessed 15 August 2022). Memorial ID 132011546, citing Fairview Cemetery, Tompkins, Jackson County, Michigan; maintained by April May (contributor 47106490).

1481. 1940 US Census, Jackson City, Jackson County, Michigan, April 1940, "Rubber Laborer."

1482. Polk's Jackson City Directory 1942, [Detroit, Michigan:] R. L. Polk & Co. 1942, Page 208 (ancestry.com image 259); "Krugman Everett L fctywkr Macklin Co r308 Grace."

1483. 1950 US Census, Parma Township, Jackson County, Michigan, April 1950, "Tire Production Control."

1484. Jackson Citizen Patriot, 13 June 1984; (from the McKune Memorial Library).

1485. 1940 US Census, Jackson City, Jackson County, Michigan, April 1940, NARA T627; Roll 1768; ED 38-27; Sheet 3A; Dwelling 911; Family 70; Line 29; "Ellarae Krugman."

1486. 1950 US Census, Parma Township, Jackson County, Michigan, April 1950, Record Group Number: 29; Roll 4014; Sheet 5; ED 38-124; House 320; Line 3; "Ellarae Krugman."

1487. Marriage record/certificate/application. Jackson County, Michigan; Certificate of Marriage, number 654, state number 38 7518 1937.

1488. Find-A-Grave, (www.findagrave.com/memorial/132011472/ellarae-krugman: accessed 15 August 2022). Memorial ID 132011472, citing Fairview Cemetery, Tompkins, Jackson County, Michigan; maintained by April May (contributor 47106490).

1489. Polk's Jackson (Jackson County, Mich.) City Directory 1955, Detroit: R. L. Polk & Co., Publishers, 1955, Page 231 (ancestry.com 119); "Krugman Ellarae Mrs slswn W B Dunn & Son r Parma Mich."

1490. Jackson Citizen Patriot, Online, 22 August 2011; https://obits.mlive.com/us/obituaries/jackson/name/ellarae-wackenhut-obituary?id=21811107 (viewed 15 August 2022).

1491. 1950 US Census, Parma Township, Jackson County, Michigan, April 1950, Record Group Number 29; Roll 4014; Sheet 5; ED 38-124; House 320; Line 4; "Daryl C Krugman."

1492. Ibid. Record Group Number: 29; Roll 4014; Sheet 5; ED 38-124; House 320; Line 5;"Ronald E. Krugman."

1493. 1920 US Census, Sandstone Township, Jackson County, Michigan, January 1920, NARA T625; ED 41; Sheet 13A; Dwelling 307; Family 321; line 41; "Anna B Crugman."

1494. 1930 US Census, Sandstone Township, Jackson County, Michigan, April 1930, NARA T626; Roll 996; ED 38-46; Sheet 3B; Dwelling 74; Family 76; Line 64; "Annabelle Krugman."

1495. Not found in the 1940 and 1950 US censuses.

1496. Tombstone: (See findagrave.com); "1912-1959."

1497. Find-A-Grave, (www.findagrave.com/memorial/202235945/annabella-hurlbut: accessed 16 August 2022). Memorial ID 202235945, citing Mount Evergreen Cemetery, Jackson, Jackson County, Michigan; maintained by D. Fritz (contributor 46604229).

1498. 1930 US Census, Sandstone Township, Jackson County, Michigan, April 1930.

1499. Battle Creek Enquirer And News, "Regional Deaths: Mrs. Robert Hurlman," 15 October 1956, page 7.

1500. Indiana Marriages, 1810-2019, database, familysearch.org or ancestry.-com, (https://www.familysearch.org/ark:/61903/1:1:K3L8-8K8 : 3 August 2022).

1501. Find-A-Grave, (www.findagrave.com/memorial/55752925/robert-d-hurlbut: accessed 10 August 2022). Memorial ID 55752925, citing Union-Udell Cemetery, Ypsilanti, Washtenaw County, Michigan; maintained by Old Bones (contributor 47251769).

1502. Michigan, Census of World War I Veterans with Card Index, 1917-1919, (https://familysearch.org/ark:/61903/1:1:QPTW-BS15 : 8 September 2019).

1503. 1920 US Census, Sandstone Township, Jackson County, Michigan, January 1920, NARA T625; ED 41; Sheet 13A; Dwelling 307; Family 321; line 42; "Mabel Crugman."

1504. 1930 US Census, Sandstone Township, Jackson County, Michigan, April 1930, NARA T626; Roll 996; ED 38-46; Sheet 3B; Dwelling 74; Family 76; Line 65; "Maebelle Krugman."

1505. Polk's Ann Arbor (Washtenaw County, Mich.) City Directory 1933, Detroit, Michigan: R. L. Polk & Co., Publishers, 1933, Page 312 (ancestry.com image 159); "Krugman Mabel L student r Couzens Hall."

1506. Polk's Ann Arbor (Washtenaw County, Mich.) City Directory 1934, Detroit, Michigan: R. L. Polk & Co., Publishers, 1934, Page 345 (ancestry.com image 173); "Krugman Mable L student U of M r Couzens Hall."

1507. 1940 US Census, Holt, Delhi Township, Ingham County, Michigan, April 1940, Enumerated 1 June 1940; NARA T627; Roll 1759; Sheet 24B; ED 33-4; Line 77; "Mable L Tompkins."

1508. 1950 US Census, Onondaga Township, Ingham County, Michigan, April 1950, Record Group Number 29; Roll 4784; ED 33-99; Sheet 13408; "Mable L Tompkins."

1509. US Social Security Applications and Claims Index, 1936-2007, Jul 1957: Name listed as MABLE LOUISE TOMPKINS; 07 May 1998: Name listed as MABLE L TOMPKINS.

1510. Polk's Fresno (Fresno County, Calif.) City Directory 1958, San Francisco: R. L. Polk & Co., Publishers, 1958, Page 672 (ancestry.com image

245); "Tompkins Lynn L (Mable L) die sinker Jock Cartwright h2505 Flora av."

1511. The Reflector 1931, Volume VII, Jackson, Michigan: Jackson High School, June 1931, Page 61 (ancestry.com image 65).

1512. Fresno Bee, newspaper, Fresno, California, "Obituary Tributes • Services & Announcements," 24 April 1998, page 35.

1513. 1940 US Census, Holt, Delhi Township, Ingham County, Michigan, April 1940, Enumerated 1 June 1940; NARA T627; Roll 1759; Sheet 24B; ED 33-4; Line 76; "Lynn L. Tompkins."

1514. 1950 US Census, Onondaga Township, Ingham County, Michigan, April 1950, Record Group Number 29; Roll 4784; ED 33-99; Sheet 13408; "Lynn L Tompkins."

1515. US Social Security Applications and Claims Index, 1936-2007, Claim Date: 9 Nov 1972.

1516. Marriage record/certificate/application. Ingham County, Michigan; Marriage License, number A-833; State number 33 10294 1935.

1517. The State Journal, "Announce Marriage," 3 September 1935, page 9.

1518. Birth Certificate/Record. Jackson County, Michigan; number 291.

1519. 1940 US Census, Holt, Delhi Township, Ingham County, Michigan, April 1940.

1520. 1950 US Census, Onondaga Township, Ingham County, Michigan, April 1950.

1521. Fresno Bee, "Obituaries: Lynn L. Tompkins," 5 January 1992, page B4.

1522. US World War II Draft Registration Cards, 1940-1947, NARA. Records of the Selective Service System, 147; Box 1210.

1523. 1940 US Census, Holt, Delhi Township, Ingham County, Michigan, April 1940, Enumerated 1 June 1940; NARA T627; Roll 1759; Sheet 24B; ED 33-4; Line 78; "Douglas L Tompkins."

1524. 1950 US Census, Onondaga Township, Ingham County, Michigan, April 1950, Record Group Number 29; Roll 4784; ED 33-99; Sheet 13408; "Douglas L Tompkins."

1525. Ibid. Record Group Number 29; Roll 4784; ED 33-99; Sheet 13408; "Constance B. Tompkins."

1526. 1920 US Census, Sandstone Township, Jackson County, Michigan, January 1920, NARA T625; ED 41; Sheet 13A; Dwelling 307; Family 321; line 43; "Locele Crugman."

1527. 1930 US Census, Sandstone Township, Jackson County, Michigan, April 1930, NARA T626; Roll 996; ED 38-46; Sheet 3B; Dwelling 74; Family 76; Line 66; "Lucille Krugman."

1528. 1940 US Census, Elk Rapids Township, Antrim County, Michigan, April 1940, NARA T627; Roll 1723; Sheet 5A; ED 5-7; Line 13; "Lucille Richardson."

1529. 1950 US Census, Sandstone Township, Jackson County, Michigan, April 1950, Record Group Number: 29; Roll 4014; Sheet 9; ED 38-129; Line 15; "Lucille I. Richardson."

1530. Tombstone: (See findagrave.com) "Ceil I. Richardson."

1531. Michigan Death Index, 1971-1996, Michigan Department of Vital and Health Records, Lansing, "Luceil I Richardson," Certificate 77052.

1532. Find-A-Grave, (www.findagrave.com/memorial/107390852/ceil-i-richardson: accessed 18 August 2022). Memorial ID 107390852, citing Pinecrest Cemetery, Oscoda, Iosco County, Michigan; Maintained by mulrichosc (contributor 47861915).

1533. 1940 US Census, Elk Rapids Township, Antrim County, Michigan, April 1940, NARA T627; Roll 1723; Sheet 5A; ED 5-7; Line 12;"Robert Richardson."

1534. 1950 US Census, Sandstone Township, Jackson County, Michigan, April 1950, Record Group Number: 29; Roll 4014; Sheet 9; ED 38-129; Line 14; "Robert D. Richardson."
1535. US Social Security Applications and Claims Index, 1936-2007, Claim Date 2 January 1974.
1536. Marriage record/certificate/application. State Of Indiana; LaGrange County; page 27.
1537. Find-A-Grave, (www.findagrave.com/memorial/107390835/robert-d-richardson: accessed 18 August 2022). Memorial ID 107390835, citing Pinecrest Cemetery, Oscoda, Iosco County, Michigan; maintained by mulrichosc (contributor 47861915).
1538. 1940 US Census, Elk Rapids Township, Antrim County, Michigan, April 1940, "Superintendent | Public School."
1539. 1950 US Census, Sandstone Township, Jackson County, Michigan, April 1950, " Superintendent" | "High School."
1540. US World War II Draft Registration Cards, 1940-1947, NARA. Records of the Selective Service System, 147; Box 996.
1541. 1950 US Census, Sandstone Township, Jackson County, Michigan, April 1950, Record Group Number: 29; Roll 4014; Sheet 9; ED 38-129; Line 16; "Michael S. Richardson."
1542. Ibid. Record Group Number: 29; Roll 4014; Sheet 9; ED 38-129; Line 17; " Anothy D. Richardson."
1543. 1910 US Census, Parma Township, Jackson County, Michigan, April 1910, NARA T624; Roll 653; Sheet 7A; ED 34; Dwelling 151; Family 151; Line 20; "Thelma Gunnell" boarder with mother in household of Andrew Holmes.
1544. 1920 US Census, Sandstone Township, Jackson County, Michigan, January 1920, NARA T625; Roll 774; Sheet 11A; ED 41; Dwelling 239; Family 250; Line 7; "Thelma C Zantop."
1545. 1930 US Census, River Rouge, Wayne County, Michigan, April 1930, NARA T626; Sheet 2A; Page 129; ED 82-1043; Dwelling 16; Family 34; Line 32; "Thelma Zantop," Lodger with Ruth Peabody.
1546. 1940 US Census, Vermontville, Eaton County, Michigan, April 1940, NARA T627; Roll 1747; Sheet 3A; ED 23-27; Line 30;"Thelma Lamb."
1547. 1950 US Census, Ingham County, Michigan, April 1950, Record Group Number 29; Roll 4781; ED 33-92A; Dwelling 274; "Thelma C. Lamb."
1548. US Social Security Applications and Claims Index, 1936-2007, Claim Date 6 May 1971.
1549. Birth Certificate/Record. Jackson County, Michigan; number 11; Page 56 Return of Births.
1550. Michigan Death Index, 1971-1996, Michigan Department of Vital and Health Records, Lansing, database; Certificate 061761; (https://www.-familysearch.org/ark:/61903/1:1:VZTC-7SY : 10 August 2022).
1551. Find-A-Grave, (www.findagrave.com/memorial/150295867/thelma-c-lamb: accessed 22 August 2022). Memorial ID 150295867, citing Woodlawn Cemetery, Vermontville, Eaton County, Michigan; maintained by Scout (contributor 47319613).
1552. 1930 US Census, River Rouge, Wayne County, Michigan, April 1930, "Teacher" | "Public School."
1553. 1940 US Census, Vermontville, Eaton County, Michigan, April 1940, "Teacher" | "Public School."
1554. 1950 US Census, Ingham County, Michigan, April 1950, "Teacher" | "Public School."
1555. M S N C 1928, Ypsilanti, Michigan: Michigan State Normal College, 1928, Page 123.

1556. Ibid. Page 123; "Thelma Zantop."

1557. The State Journal, "Deaths And Funerals," 24 October 1993, page 2B.

1558. 1940 US Census, Vermontville, Eaton County, Michigan, April 1940, NARA T627; Roll 1747; Sheet 3A; ED 23-27; Line 30; "Milton Lamb."

1559. 1950 US Census, Ingham County, Michigan, April 1950, Record Group Number 29; Roll 4781; ED 33-92A; Dwelling 274; "Milton C. Lamb."

1560. Marriage record/certificate/application. State of Indiana, DeKalb County. Application for Marriage License. (https://www.familysearch.org/ark:/61903/1:1:XXTB-XSY : 3 August 2022); Page 259.

1561. Indiana Marriages, 1810-2019, database, familysearch.org or ancestry.com, page 60.

1562. Find-A-Grave, (www.findagrave.com/memorial/150295880/milton-c-lamb: accessed 22 August 2022). Memorial ID 150295880, citing Woodlawn Cemetery, Vermontville, Eaton County, Michigan; maintained by Scout (contributor 47319613).

1563. 1940 US Census, Vermontville, Eaton County, Michigan, April 1940, "Manager" | "R Hardware Store."

1564. 1950 US Census, Ingham County, Michigan, April 1950, "Traffic Analyst" | "State Highway Dept."

1565. Polk's Lansing (Ingham County, Mich.) City Directory 1949-50, Volume XLIV, Detroit, Michigan: R. L. Polk & Co., Publishers, 1949, Page 427 (ancestry.com image 215); "Lamb Milton C (Thelma) traffic analyst State Hwy Dept r6415 Reynolds rd."

1566. Polk's Lansing (Ingham County, Mich.) City Directory, 1951, Volume 1951-52 XLV, Detroit, Michigan: R. L. Polk & Co., Publishers, 1951, Page 365 (ancestry.com image 196): "Lamb Milton C (Thelma) analyst State Hwy Dept r6415 Reynolds rd (EL)."

1567. Polk's Lansing (Ingham County, Mich.) City Directory, 1953, Volume XLXI, Detroit, Michigan: R. L. Polk & Co., Publishers, 1953, Page 427 (ancestry.com image 230); "Lamb Milton C (Thelma) eng aide State Hwy Dept r6415 Reynolds rd (EL)."

1568. Polk's Lansing (Ingham County, Mich.) City Directory, 1954, Volume 1954, XLXII, Detroit, Michigan: R. L. Polk & Co., Publishers, 1954, Page 488 (ancestry.com image 260); "Lamb Milton C (Thelma) traffic techn State Hwy Dept r6415 Reynold rd (EL)."

1569. Polk's Lansing (Ingham County, Mich.) City Directory 1955, Detroit: R. L. Polk & Co., Publishers, 1955, Volume XLXIII, Page 500 (ancestry.com image 268); "Lamb Milton C hwy traffic eng State Hwy Dept r Haslett Mich."

1570. Polk's Lansing (Ingham County, Mich.) City Directory 1956, Detroit, Michigan: R. L. Polk & Co., Publishers, 1956, Volume 1956 XLXIV, Page 573 (ancestry.com image 426); "Lamb Milton C (Thelma) tech State Hwy Dept r Haslett Michigan."

1571. Polk's Lansing (Ingram County, Mich.) City Directory 1959, Volume 1959 LVI, Detroit, Michigan: R. L. Polk & Co., Publishers, 1959, Page 750 (ancestry.com image 542); "Lamb Milton C (Thelma) traffic tech State Hwy Dept r Haslett Mich."

1572. The State Journal, "Deaths And Funerals," 10 October 1991, page 2B.

1573. 1920 US Census, Sandstone Township, Jackson County, Michigan, January 1920, NARA T625; Roll 774; Sheet 11A; ED 41; Dwelling 239; Family 250; Line 8. "Howard W Zantop"

1574. 1930 US Census, Parma Township, Jackson County, Michigan, April 1930, NARA T626; Sheet 1B; ED 46; Dwelling 22; Family 23; Line 84; "Howard V. Zantop."

1575. 1940 US Census, Parma Township, Jackson County, Michigan, April 1940, NARA T627; Roll 1769; Sheet 2B; ED 38-62; Dwelling 415; Line 44; "Howard W Zantop."
1576. 1950 US Census, Parma Township, Jackson County, Michigan, April 1950, Record Group Number 29; Roll 4014; Sheet 3; ED 38-124; Serial 34; Line 11; "Howard W. Zantop."
1577. Find-A-Grave, (www.findagrave.com/memorial/147450939/howard-william-zantop: accessed 23 August 2022). Memorial ID 147450939, citing Chapel Cemetery, Sandstone, Jackson County, Michigan; maintained by Vernon W. Goodrich (contributor 46940951).
1578. 1930 US Census, Parma Township, Jackson County, Michigan, April 1930, "Laborer" | "Saw Mill."
1579. 1940 US Census, Parma Township, Jackson County, Michigan, April 1940, "Proprietor" | "Garage."
1580. Polk's Jackson (Jackson County, Mich.) City Directory 1949, Detroit, Michigan: R. L. Polk & Co., Publishers, 1949, Page 440 (ancestry.com image 222); "Zantop Howard W (Alma; Zantop Flying Serv) r Parma."
1581. Polk's Jackson (Jackson County, Mich.) City Directory 1947, Detroit: R. L. Polk & Co., Publishers, 1947, Page 448 (ancestry.com image 228); "Zantop Howard W (Alma; Zantop Flying Serv) r Parma."
1582. 1950 US Census, Parma Township, Jackson County, Michigan, April 1950, "Flying service operator" | "Aviation."
1583. Polk's Jackson (Jackson County, Mich.) City Directory 1951, Detroit, Michigan: R. L. Polk & Co., Publishers, 1951, Page 427 (ancestry.com image 212); "Zantop Howard W (Zantop Flying Service) r Parma."
1584. Polk's Jackson (Jackson County, Mich.) City Directory 1954, Detroit, Michigan: R. L. Polk & Co., Publishers, 1954, Page 403 (ancestry.com image 204); "Zantop Howard (Zantop Flying Serv) r Parma Mich."
1585. Polk's Lincoln Park, Allen Park and Melvindale (Wayne County, Mich.) Directory 1960, Detroit, Michigan: R. L. Polk & Co., Publishers, 1960, Page 463 (ancestry.com image 282); "Zantop Howard W (Patricia) pres Zantop Air Transport Inc h 15281 Pleasant av (AP)."
1586. Polk's Lincoln Park, Allen Park and Melvindale (Wayne County, Mich.) Directory 1957, Detroit, Michigan: R. L. Polk & Co., Publishers, 1957, Page 459 (ancestry.com image 285; "Zantops Howard (Aeroplane Transportation; W) h15270 Philomene (AP)."
1587. Fort Lauderdale News, newspaper, Fort Lauderdale, Florida, "Deaths: Airline executive Howard W. Zantop," 20 April 1982, page 4B.
1588. Battle Creek Enquirer And News, "Local/State Report: Obituaries," 20 April 1982, page B-2.
1589. Detroit Free Press, "He was a true do-it-yourselfer," 20 April 1982, page 2C.
1590. Fort Lauderdale News, "Death Notices," 21 April 1982, page 4B.
1591. Herald-Palladium, newspaper, Benton Harbor, St. Joseph, Michigan, "Airman Dies," 20 April 1982, page 12.
1592. US World War II Draft Registration Cards, 1940-1947, NARA. Records of the Selective Service System, 147; Box 1345.
1593. 1940 US Census, Parma Township, Jackson County, Michigan, April 1940, NARA T627; Roll 1769; Sheet 2B; ED 38-62; Dwelling 415; Line 45; "Alma B Zantop."
1594. 1950 US Census, Parma Township, Jackson County, Michigan, April 1950, Record Group Number 29; Roll 4014; Sheet 3; ED 38-124; Serial 34; Line 12; "Alma B. Zantop."
1595. Marriage record/certificate/application. Certificate of Marriage, Jackson County, Michigan; number 38 4553 1933.

1596. Birth Certificate/Record. Commonwealth of Pennsylvania, Bureau of Vital Statistics, Certificate of Birth, file 196444.

1597. Michigan Death Certificates, 1921-1952, database, Michigan Division for Vital Records and Health Statistics, Lansing, (https://familysearch.org/ark:/61903/1:1:KF34-FG4 : 13 March 2018).

1598. Find-A-Grave, (www.findagrave.com/memorial/147450909/alma-bertell-zantop: accessed 23 August 2022). Memorial ID 147450909, citing Chapel Cemetery, Sandstone, Jackson County, Michigan; maintained by Vernon W. Goodrich (contributor 46940951).

1599. Mountain Echo, newspaper, Shickshinny, Luzerne County, Pennsylvania, "Mrs. Alma Zantop Died At Parma, Mich," 6 October 1950, page 1.

1600. 1940 US Census, Parma Township, Jackson County, Michigan, April 1940, NARA T627; Roll 1769; Sheet 2B; ED 38-62; Dwelling 415; Line 46; "Harold Douglas Zantop."

1601. 1950 US Census, Parma Township, Jackson County, Michigan, April 1950, Record Group Number 29; Roll 4014; Sheet 3; ED 38-124; Serial 34; Line 13; "Harold D. Zantop."

1602. Ibid. Record Group Number 29; Roll 4014; Sheet 3; ED 38-124; Serial 34; Line 14; "Anne J. Zantop."

1603. Ibid. Record Group Number 29; Roll 4014; Sheet 3; ED 38-124; Serial 34; Line 15; "Linda L. Zantop."

1604. Ibid. Record Group Number 29; Roll 4014; Sheet 3; ED 38-124; Serial 34; Line 16; "Sandra S. Zantop."

1605. Star-Telegram, newspaper, Fort Worth, Texas, "Marriage Licenses," 10 May 1953, page 3 Sec. 6. "Howard Zantop, Parma, Mich, and Mary Rita Blevins, 4032 Rufe Snow Dr."

1606. Texas, U.S., Select County Marriage Records, 1837-1965, ancestry.com, Johnson County Clerk's Office; Denton, Texas; Smith County Marriage Records.

1607. Star-Telegram, "Legal Records." 1 September 1955, page 21. "Mary R. Zantop v. Howard W. Zantop, divorce." | "Legal Records." 19 February 1956, Section 4, Page 4; "Mary R. Zantop vs. Howard W. Zantop, divorce granted."

1608. US Social Security Applications and Claims Index, 1936-2007, PATRICIA DISQUE NEWTON (Apr 1937), Application: PATRICIA DISQUE ZANTOP (Nov 1960), Death: PATRICIA J ZANTOP (Jan 1995).

1609. South Florida Sun-Sentinel, newspaper, Fort Lauderdale, Florida, 2 February 1995, obit for ZANTOP - Patricia D., GenealogyBank.com (https://www.genealogybank.com/doc/obituaries/obit/103B0013D983C719-103B0013D983C719 : accessed 8 June 2023).

1610. Michigan Deaths and Burials, 1800-1995, (https://familysearch.org/ark:/61903/1:1:FHYM-642 : 23 February 2021).

1611. Death Certificate/Record. State Of Michigan, Department of State-Division of Vital Statistics, Certificate Of Death. (ancestry.com image 685, scanned image).

1612. Find-A-Grave, (www.findagrave.com/memorial/52116928/naomi-alice-zantop: accessed 29 August 2022). Memorial ID 52116928, citing Chapel Cemetery, Sandstone, Jackson County, Michigan; maintained by Cammy (contributor 47038505).

1613. Death Certificate/Record. State Of Michigan, Department of State - Division of Vital Statistics, Certificate Of Death; file 334.

1614. Find-A-Grave, (www.findagrave.com/memorial/52116899/harold-lyle-zantop: accessed 29 August 2022). Memorial ID 52116899, citing

Chapel Cemetery, Sandstone, Jackson County, Michigan; maintained by Cammy (contributor 47038505)

1615. 1920 US Census, Sandstone Township, Jackson County, Michigan, January 1920, NARA T625; Roll 774; Sheet 11A; ED 41; Dwelling 239; Family 250; Line 9; "Anita Mae Zantop."

1616. 1930 US Census, Parma Township, Jackson County, Michigan, April 1930, NARA T626; Sheet 1B; ED 46; Dwelling 22; Family 23; Line 85; "Anita M. Zantop."

1617. 1940 US Census, Battle Creek, Calhoun County, Michigan, April 1940, NARA T627; Roll 1735; Sheet 6B; ED 13-16; Line 67; "Anita D Kelly."

1618. 1950 US Census, Athens, Calhoun County, Michigan, April 1950, Record Group Number 29; Roll 2606; Sheet 15; ED 13-16; Line 16; "Anita M Kelly."

1619. US Social Security Applications and Claims Index, 1936-2007, Jan 1953: Name listed as ANITA MAE KELLY; 13 Jan 1996: Name listed as ANITA M KELLY.

1620. Michigan Death Index, 1971-1996, Michigan Department of Vital and Health Records, Lansing; Certificate 081356.

1621. Find-A-Grave, (www.findagrave.com/memorial/12678296/anita-m-kelly: accessed 29 August 2022). Memorial ID 12678296, citing Abscota Cemetery, Burlington, Calhoun County, Michigan; maintained by KimTisha (contributor 47493469).

1622. 1940 US Census, Battle Creek, Calhoun County, Michigan, April 1940, "Operator" | "Beauty Shop."

1623. Polk's Battle Creek (Calhoun County, Mich.) City Directory 1940, Detroit, Michigan: R. L. Polk & Co., Publishers, 1940, Page 181; (ancestry.com image 90); "Kelly Owen A (Anita M) mach h57 N Wood."

1624. Battle Creek Enquirer And News, "Obituaries." 25 December 1995, page 4A.

1625. 1940 US Census, Battle Creek, Calhoun County, Michigan, April 1940, NARA T627; Roll 1735; Sheet 6B; ED 13-16; Line 66; "Owen Kelly."

1626. Polk's Battle Creek (Calhoun County, Mich.) City Directory 1945, Detroit: R. L. Polk & Co., Publishers, 1945, Page 214; (ancestry.com image 106); "Kelly Owen h57 N Wood."

1627. 1950 US Census, Athens, Calhoun County, Michigan, April 1950, Record Group Number 29; Roll 2606; Sheet 15; ED 13-16; Line 15; "Owen A Kelly."

1628. US Social Security Applications and Claims Index, 1936-2007, Claim Date 4 January 1972.

1629. Marriage record/certificate/application. Williams County, Ohio; Number 488.

1630. Find-A-Grave, (www.findagrave.com/memorial/8213324/owen-a-kelly: accessed 29 August 2022). Memorial ID 8213324, citing Abscota Cemetery, Burlington, Calhoun County, Michigan; maintained by Graveaddiction (contributor 46528400).

1631. Polk's Battle Creek (Calhoun County, Mich.) City Directory 1939, Detroit: R. L. Polk & Co., Publishers, 1939, Page 182 (ancestry.com image 90;"Kelly Owen A (Anita M) fctywkr h57 N Wood."

1632. 1940 US Census, Battle Creek, Calhoun County, Michigan, April 1940, "Machinist" | "Tractor Factory."

1633. Polk's Battle Creek (Calhoun County, Mich.) City Directory 1940, Detroit, Michigan: R. L. Polk & Co., Publishers, 1940, Page 181 (ancestry.com image 90); "Kelly Owen A (Anita M) mach h57 N Wood."

1634. Polk's Battle Creek (Calhoun County, Mich.) City Directory 1942, Detroit, Michigan: R. L. Polk & Co., Publishers, 1942, Page 184 (ancestry.com image 94); "Kelly Owen (Anita) mach h57 N Wood."
1635. 1950 US Census, Athens, Calhoun County, Michigan, April 1950, "Farming" | "Farm."
1636. Battle Creek Enquirer And News, "Obituaries," 5 June 1992, page 2A.
1637. US World War II Draft Registration Cards, 1940-1947, NARA, Serial Number 983; Records of the Selective Service System, 147; Box 613.
1638. 1940 US Census, Battle Creek, Calhoun County, Michigan, April 1940, NARA T627; Roll 1735; Sheet 6B; ED 13-16; Line 68; "Robert Kelly."
1639. 1950 US Census, Athens, Calhoun County, Michigan, April 1950, Record Group Number 29; Roll 2606; Sheet 15; ED 13-16; Line 17; "Robert L Kelly."
1640. Ibid. Record Group Number 29; Roll 2606; Sheet 15; ED 13-16; Line 18; "Dennis G Kelly."
1641. US Social Security Applications and Claims Index, 1936-2007, Jan 1962: Name listed as DENNIS GALE KELLY; 23 Apr 2004: Name listed as DENNIS G KELLY.
1642. 1950 US Census, Athens, Calhoun County, Michigan, April 1950, Record Group Number 29; Roll 2606; Sheet 15; ED 13-16; Line 19; "Patricia N Kelly."
1643. 1920 US Census, Sandstone Township, Jackson County, Michigan, January 1920, NARA T625; Roll 774; Sheet 11A; ED 41; Dwelling 239; Family 250; Line 10; "Duane A Zantop."
1644. 1930 US Census, Parma Township, Jackson County, Michigan, April 1930, NARA T626; Sheet 1B; ED 46; Dwelling 22; Family 23; Line 86; "Duane A. Zantop."
1645. 1940 US Census, Parma Township, Jackson County, Michigan, April 1940, NARA T627; Roll 1769; Sheet 2A; ED 38-62; Line 39; "Duane A Zantop."
1646. 1950 US Census, Blackman Township, Jackson County, Michigan, April 1950, Record Group Number 29; Roll 4011; Sheet 4; ED 38-5; House 631; Line 26; "Duane A Zantop."
1647. US Social Security Applications and Claims Index, 1936-2007, Jun 1937: Name listed as DUANE AUGUST ZANTOP; 02 May 2006: Name listed as DUANE A ZANTOP.
1648. Find-A-Grave, (www.findagrave.com/memorial/68625188/duane-august-zantop: accessed 31 August 2022). Memorial ID 68625188, citing Chapel Cemetery, Sandstone, Jackson County, Michigan; maintained by: Find a Grave.
1649. 1940 US Census, Parma Township, Jackson County, Michigan, April 1940, "Truck driver" | "General trucking."
1650. Polk's Jackson (Jackson County, Mich.) City Directory 1949, Detroit, Michigan: R. L. Polk & Co., Publishers, 1949, Page 440 (ancestry.com image 222); "Zantop Duane A (Zantop Flying Service) h631 Wayne."
1651. Polk's Jackson (Jackson County, Mich.) City Directory 1947, Detroit: R. L. Polk & Co., Publishers, 1947, Page 448 (ancestry.com image 228); "Zantop Duane A (Maybelle; Zantop Flying Serv) h631 Wayne."
1652. 1950 US Census, Blackman Township, Jackson County, Michigan, April 1950, "Mechanic" | "Airplane."
1653. Polk's Jackson (Jackson County, Mich.) City Directory 1951, Detroit, Michigan: R. L. Polk & Co., Publishers, 1951, Page 427 (ancestry.com image 212); "Zantop Duane A (A Louise; Zantop Flying Serv) h631 Wayne."

1654. Polk's Jackson (Jackson County, Mich.) City Directory 1954, Detroit, Michigan: R. L. Polk & Co., Publishers, 1954, Page 403 (ancestry.com image 204); "Zantop Duane A (Anna L; Zantop Flying Serv) h631 Wayne (BT)."

1655. Polk's Lincoln Park, Allen Park and Melvindale (Wayne County, Mich.) Directory 1957, Detroit, Michigan: R. L. Polk & Co., Publishers, 1957, Page 459 (ancestry.com image 285; "Zantop Duane A (Anna L) with Zantop Air Transport Corp (Inkstar) h9701 Melbourne (AP)."

1656. Polk's Lincoln Park, Allen Park and Melvindale (Wayne County, Mich.) Directory 1960, Detroit, Michigan: R. L. Polk & Co., Publishers, 1960, Page 463 (ancestry.com image 282); "Zantop Duane A (Anna L) with Zantop Air Transport Inc h9701 Melbourne (AP)."

1657. Detroit Free Press, "Death Notices," 15 April 2006, page 7A.

1658. US World War II Draft Registration Cards, 1940-1947, NARA, Serial number 1445; Records of the Selective Service System, 147; Box 1345.

1659. U.S. World War II Army Enlistment Records, 1938-1946, Record Group 64; Box Number 02112; Reel 68.

1660. Marriage record/certificate/application. Marriage License/Certificate #18. "Duane A. Zantop of Parma, Michigan and Ardith Beauchamp of Tucson, Pima County, Arizona." (familysearch.org/ark:/61903/1:1:QG16-446C : 29 November 2018). Affidavit (.../ark:/61903/1:1:QG16-8DGQ : 29 November 2018).

1661. Arizona Republic, "Marriage Licenses," 30 November 1943, page 5, Section 2.

1662. Divorce Record. Michigan Department of Community Health, Division for Vital Records and Health Statistics; Lansing. State 38 6185; Docket 22-48.

1663. 1950 US Census, Blackman Township, Jackson County, Michigan, April 1950, Record Group Number 29; Roll 4011; Sheet 4; ED 38-5; House 631; Line 28; "Duane G Zantop step-son."

1664. Polk's Jackson (Jackson County, Mich.) City Directory 1947, Detroit: R. L. Polk & Co., Publishers, 1947, Page 448 (ancestry.com image 228): "Zantop Duane A (Maybelle; Zantop Flying Serv) h631 Wayne."

1665. 1950 USCensus, Shelby, Macomb County, Michigan, Bureau of the Census; Washington, D.C., Record Group Number 29; Roll 5466; Sheet 4; ED 50-150; Line 15; "May Belle Stadler."

1666. Michigan Marriages, 1867-1952, Michigan Department of Community Health, Division of Vital Records and Health Statistics; Lansing. County 27926; State 50 15604.

1667. US Social Security Death Index; "Maybell Elliott"

1668. Divorce Record. Michigan Department of Community Health, Division for Vital Records and Health Statistics; Lansing. State 50 3538; Docket 15428. "Children: 1."

1669. Orlando Sentinel, 15 August 1987, page D-8.

1670. Polk's Jackson (Jackson County, Mich.) City Directory 1951, Detroit, Michigan: R. L. Polk & Co., Publishers, 1951, Page 427 (ancestry.com image 212); "Zantop Duane A (A Louise; Zantop Flying Serv) h631 Wayne"; "Zantop Lucile H Mrs clk Jackson City Bank h1036 Avery."

1671. 1950 US Census, Blackman Township, Jackson County, Michigan, April 1950, Record Group Number 29; Roll 4011; Sheet 4; ED 38-5; House 631; Line 27; "Anna L Zantop."

1672. Michigan Marriages, 1867-1952, Michigan Department of Community Health, Division of Vital Records and Health Statistics; Lansing. County 126; State 38 17596.

1673. Find-A-Grave, (www.findagrave.com/memorial/249800279/anna-louise-zantop: accessed 08 June 2023). Memorial ID 249800279, citing Chapel Cemetery, Sandstone, Jackson County, Michigan; maintained by Wittenized (contributor 49415824).

1674. Polk's Jackson (Jackson County, Mich.) City Directory 1954, Detroit, Michigan: R. L. Polk & Co., Publishers, 1954, Page 403 (ancestry.com image 204); "Zantop Lucile H Mrs clk Jackson City Bk & Tr h1036 Avery."

1675. Obituary, funeral home. Anna Louise (Culver) Zantop. https://www.niefuneralhomes.com/memorials/anna-zantop/4443694/ (viewed 3 September 2022).

1676. 1930 US Census, Parma Township, Jackson County, Michigan, April 1930, NARA T626; Sheet 1B; ED 46; Dwelling 22; Family 23; Line 87; "Stanley E. Zantop."

1677. 1940 US Census, Parma Township, Jackson County, Michigan, April 1940, NARA T627; Roll 1769; Sheet 2A; ED 38-62; Line 40; "Stanley LeRoy Zantop."

1678. 1950 US Census, Blackman Township, Jackson County, Michigan, April 1950, Record Group Number: 29; Roll 4011; Sheet 73; ED 38-6; Line 22; "Stanley E. Zantop."

1679. US Social Security Applications and Claims Index, 1936-2007, (NUMIDENT), Claim Date 8 May 1953.

1680. Find-A-Grave, (www.findagrave.com/memorial/68659242/s-elroy-zantop: accessed 04 September 2022). Memorial ID 68659242, citing Chapel Cemetery, Sandstone, Jackson County, Michigan; maintained by: Find a Grave.

1681. 1940 US Census, Parma Township, Jackson County, Michigan, April 1940, "Truck driver" | "General hauling."

1682. Polk's Jackson City Directory 1942, [Detroit, Michigan:] R. L. Polk & Co. 1942, Page 383 (ancestry.com image 346); "Zantop Stanley E factywrk Macklin Co r Parma Mich."

1683. Polk's Jackson (Jackson County, Mich.) City Directory 1946, Detroit, Michigan: R. L. Polk & Co., Publishers, 1946, Page 446 (ancestry.com image 231); "Zantop Stanley E (Fairlene A) instr Reynolds Field h631 Wayne."

1684. Polk's Jackson (Jackson County, Mich.) City Directory 1947, Detroit: R. L. Polk & Co., Publishers, 1947, Page 448 (ancestry.com image 228): "Zantop (Fairlene A; Zantop Flying Serv) r706 Bellevue."

1685. Polk's Jackson (Jackson County, Mich.) City Directory 1949, Detroit, Michigan: R. L. Polk & Co., Publishers, 1949, Page 440 (ancestry.com image 222); "Zantop Stanley E (Fairlane A; Zantop Flying Serv) h706 Bellevue av (BT)."

1686. 1950 US Census, Blackman Township, Jackson County, Michigan, April 1950, "Instructor | Flying Service."

1687. Polk's Jackson (Jackson County, Mich.) City Directory 1951, Detroit, Michigan: R. L. Polk & Co., Publishers, 1951, Page 427 (ancestry.com image 212); "Zantop S Elroy (Fairlene A; Zantop Flying Serv) h706 Bellevue av (BT)."

1688. Detroit Free Press, "Pilot Injured In Crash Dies," 18 March 1953, page 2.

1689. US World War II Draft Registration Cards, 1940-1947, NARA. Serial number S-35; Records of the Selective Service System, 147; Box 1345.

1690. Card Manifests (Alphabetical) of Individuals Entering through the Port of Detroit, Records of the Immigration and Naturalization Service, 1787 - 2004, NARA database with images, 29 July 1938; Race: Scotch |

Nationality: Canada | Last residence: Owen Sound-Ont. | Fa. Wiliam | Occupation: Domestic | Age: 18 yrs 4 mos | Height: 5 ft 4.25 in. | Complexion: Fair | Hair: L. Brown | Eyes: Blue | Mole center of forehead.

1691. 1940 US Census, Parma Township, Jackson County, Michigan, April 1940, NARA T627; Roll 1769; Sheet 1B; ED 38-59; Line 54; "Fairlene Fenwick," Maid, living with aunt and uncle Campbell.

1692. 1950 US Census, Blackman Township, Jackson County, Michigan, April 1950, Record Group Number: 29; Roll 4011; Sheet 73; ED 38-6; Line 23; "Fairlene A. Zantop."

1693. Michigan, Eastern and Western Districts, Naturalization Records, 1837-1993, database, familysearch.org, (https://www.familysearch.org/ark:/61903/1:1:HWFJ-K8T2 : 21 July 2020).

1694. Index Cards to Naturalization Petitions for the U.S. District Court for the Eastern District of Michigan, Southern Division, Detroit, 1907-1995, NARA, Naturalization Record: Fairlene Sarah Zantop, born 17 March 1920; 18 May 1950.

1695. Polk's Reno (Washoe County, Nevada) City Directory 1964, Los Angeles, California: R. L. Polk & Co. Publishers, 1964, Page 558 (ancestry.com image 810); "Schuchman Alvin A (Fairlene) eng tech Systems Mtce Dist Ofc FAA h1942 Richards pl apt 36 (S)."

1696. Marriage record/certificate/application. Certificate of Marriage; 38 10483 1942; number 209; Jackson County, Michigan.

1697. Sun Times, newspaper, Owen Sound, Ontario, Canada, "Zantop-Fenwick Parma Nuptials: Former Owen Sound Girl Married in United States Friday," 13 April 1942, page 5.

1698. Archives of the Evangelical Lutheran Church in America, Swedish American Baptisms, Marriages, Deaths, and Burials, Elk Grove Village, Illinois, under Alvin A. Schuchmann (spouse), "Fairlene Ann" certificate 10 March 1957.

1699. US Social Security Death Index; "Fairlene A. Zantop."

1700. Find-A-Grave, www.findagrave.com/memorial/68659201/fairlene-a-zantop: accessed 04 September 2022. Memorial ID 68659201, citing Chapel Cemetery, Sandstone, Jackson County, Michigan; maintained by: Find a Grave.

1701. Polk's Jackson (Jackson County, Mich.) City Directory 1954, Detroit, Michigan: R. L. Polk & Co., Publishers, 1954, Page 403 (ancestry.com image 204); "Zantop Fairlene A (wid Elroy) clk County Sheriff's Ofc h706 Bellevue av (BT)."

1702. Polk's Jackson (Jackson County, Mich.) City Directory 1955, Detroit: R. L. Polk & Co., Publishers, 1955, Page 435 (ancestry.com image 222); "Zantop Fairlene (wid Elroy) ofc Sec County Sheriff's Ofc h706 Bellevue av (BT)."

1703. Michigan, Eastern and Western Districts, Naturalization Records, 1837-1993, database, (https://www.familysearch.org/ark:/61903/1:1:HWFJ-K8T2 : 21 July 2020); Certificate 230275.

1704. Sun Times, "Elroy Zantop, 35, Dies Of Injuries In Plane Crash," 17 March 1953, page 10.

1705. Fresno Bee, "Obituaries: Zantop, Fairlene 'Buddy' A," 23 May 2007, page B6.

1706. 1950 US Census, Blackman Township, Jackson County, Michigan, April 1950, Record Group Number: 29; Roll 4011; Sheet 73; ED 38-6; Line 24; "Sharon L. Zantop."

1707. Ibid. Record Group Number: 29; Roll 4011; Sheet 73; ED 38-6; Line 25; "Loraine K. Zantop."

1708. 1930 US Census, Parma Township, Jackson County, Michigan, April 1930, NARA T626; Sheet 1B; ED 46; Dwelling 22; Family 23; Line 88; "Lloyd A. Zantop."

1709. 1940 US Census, Parma Township, Jackson County, Michigan, April 1940, NARA T627; Roll 1769; Sheet 2B; ED 38-62; Line 41; "Llody Avery Zantop."

1710. 1950 US Census, Summit, Jackson County, Michigan, April 1950, Record Group Number: 29; Roll 4015; Sheet 72; ED 38-135; Line 10; "Lloyd A Zantop."

1711. US Social Security Applications and Claims Index, 1936-2007, Jul 1941: Name listed as LLOYD AVERY ZANTOP; 12 Dec 2002: Name listed as LLOYD A ZANTOP.

1712. Polk's Jackson (Jackson County, Mich.) City Directory 1949, Detroit, Michigan: R. L. Polk & Co., Publishers, 1949, Page 440 (ancestry.com image 222); "Zantop Lloyd A (Glenna: Zantop Flying Serv) r Parma."

1713. Polk's Jackson (Jackson County, Mich.) City Directory 1947, Detroit: R. L. Polk & Co., Publishers, 1947, Page 448 (ancestry.com image 228): "Zantop Lloyd A (Glenna; Zantop Flying Serv) r Parma."

1714. 1950 US Census, Summit, Jackson County, Michigan, April 1950.

1715. Polk's Jackson (Jackson County, Mich.) City Directory 1951, Detroit, Michigan: R. L. Polk & Co., Publishers, 1951, Page 427 (ancestry.com image 212); "Zantop Lloyd A (Glenna J; Zantop Flying Serv) h1250 Levant (ST)."

1716. Polk's Jackson (Jackson County, Mich.) City Directory 1954, Detroit, Michigan: R. L. Polk & Co., Publishers, 1954, Page 403 (ancestry.com image 204); "Zantop Lloyd A (Glenna J; Zantop Flying Serv) h1250 Levant (ST)."

1717. Polk's Lincoln Park, Allen Park and Melvindale (Wayne County, Mich.) Directory 1957, Detroit, Michigan: R. L. Polk & Co., Publishers, 1957, Page 459 (ancestry.com image 285; "Zantop Lloyd A (Glenna J; Zantop Air Transport; W) h15981 Pleasant av (AP)."

1718. Polk's Lincoln Park, Allen Park and Melvindale (Wayne County, Mich.) Directory 1958, Detroit: R. L. Polk & Co., Publishers, 1958, Page 458 (ancestry.com image 284; "Zantop Loyde A (Glenna J; Zantop Air Transport; Det) h15981 Pleasant av (AP)."

1719. Polk's Lincoln Park, Allen Park and Melvindale (Wayne County, Mich.) Directory 1960, Detroit, Michigan: R. L. Polk & Co., Publishers, 1960, Page 463 (ancestry.com image 282); "Zantop Lloyd A (Glenna J) with Zantop Air Transport Inc (Det) h15981 Pleasant ave (AP)."

1720. Detroit Free Press, "Local Death," Erik Lords, "Lloyd Zantop: Co-founded a major air cargo service," 28 December 2002, page 7B.

1721. South Florida Sun-Sentinel, "Lloyd Zantop, 80, Early Aviator The Lighthouse Point Retiree Co-founded Zantop Airways," 25 December 2002; (https://www.genealogybank.com/doc/obituaries/obit/100EE6946A6BD0B5-100EE6946A6BD0B5 : accessed 6 September 2022).

1722. US World War II Draft Registration Cards, 1940-1947, NARA, Records of the Selective Service System, 147; Box 2006.

1723. U.S. World War II Army Enlistment Records, 1938-1946, Affiliate ARC Identifier 1263923; Box Film Number 03163.38. NARA NAID 1263923, National Archives at College Park, Maryland.

1724. Battle Creek Enquirer And News, "Toes Lost by Soldier As Results of Wounds," 8 March 1945, page 16.

1725. 1950 US Census, Summit, Jackson County, Michigan, April 1950, Record Group Number: 29; Roll 4015; Sheet 72; ED 38-135; Line 11; "Glenna J. Zantop."

1726. Polk's Lincoln Park, Allen Park and Melvindale (Wayne County, Mich.) Directory 1958, Detroit: R. L. Polk & Co., Publishers, 1958, Page 458 (ancestry.com image 284); "Zantop Lloyd A (Glenna J; Zantop Air Transport; Det) h15981 Pleasant av (AP)."

1727. US Social Security Applications and Claims Index, 1936-2007, Jun 1939: Name listed as GLENNA JEAN TROWBRIDGE; 20 Jul 2000: Name listed as GLENNA J ZANTOP.

1728. Merced Express, newspaper, Merced, California, "Applications For Licenses To Wed Filed At County Clerk's Office," 24 September 1942, page 4.

1729. Polk's Jackson (Jackson County, Mich.) City Directory 1951, Detroit, Michigan: R. L. Polk & Co., Publishers, 1951, Page 427 (ancestry.com image 212); "Zantop Glenna J Mrs ofc wkr Zantop Flying Serv h1250 Levant (ST)."

1730. South Florida Sun-Sentinel, "Obituaries," 30 June 2000, page 7B.

1731. 1950 US Census, Summit, Jackson County, Michigan, April 1950, Record Group Number: 29; Roll 4015; Sheet 72; ED 38-135; Line 12; "Diane E. Zantop."

1732. Michigan Death Certificates, 1921-1952, database, Michigan Division for Vital Records and Health Statistics, Lansing, (https://family-search.org/ark:/61903/1:1:KF3H-GRW : 13 March 2018) "Geraldine Zanlap."

1733. Death Certificate/Record. State Of Michigan, Department of State-Division of Vital Statistics, File 501.

1734. Find-A-Grave, (www.findagrave.com/memorial/205939801/earl-roy-clay: accessed 06 September 2022). Memorial ID 205939801, citing Chapel Cemetery, Sandstone, Jackson County, Michigan; maintained by Charles A.Dunlap (contributor 47164122).

1735. 1920 US Census, Jackson City, Jackson County, Michigan, January 1920, NARA T625; Roll 773; Sheet 8B; ED 9; House 212; Family 218; Line 77; "Donald Clay."

1736. 1930 US Census, Blackman Township, Jackson County, Michigan, April 1930, NARA T626; Sheet 15A; ED 38-1; Dwelling 292; Family 297; Line 2; "Donald Clay."

1737. 1940 US Census, Coldwater, Branch County, Michigan, April 1940, NARA T627; Roll 1734; Sheet 13B; ED 12-10; Line 60; "Donald Clay."

1738. 1950 US Census, Jackson, Jackson County, Michigan, April 1950, Record Group Number: 29; Roll 4014; Sheet 8; ED 38-107; Line 25; "Donald L. Clay."

1739. US Social Security Applications and Claims Index, 1936-2007, Claim Date 27 Jun 1966.

1740. Find-A-Grave, (www.findagrave.com/memorial/83423199/donald-l-clay: accessed 06 September 2022). Memorial ID 83423199, citing Hill-crest Memorial Park, Jackson, Jackson County, Michigan; maintained by April May (contributor 47106490).

1741. Polk's Jackson (Jackson County, Mich.) City Directory 1936, Detroit: R. L. Polk & Co., Publishers, 1936, Page 131 (ancestry.com image 69); "Clay Donald L driver r618 Oak Hill av."

1742. Polk's Jackson (Jackson County, Mich.) City Directory 1937, Detroit: R. L. Polk & Co., Publishers, 1937, Page 93 (ancestry.com image 43); "Clay Donald L driver r518 Oak Hill av."

1743. Polk's Jackson (Jackson County, Mich.) City Directory 1939, Detroit: R. L. Polk & Co., Publishers, 1939, Page 89 (ancestry.com image 41); "Clay Donald L. (Charlotte H) driver r531 Blackman av."

1744. 1940 US Census, Coldwater, Branch County, Michigan, April 1940, "driver" | "cement hauling."

1745. Coldwater, Michigan Pictorial City Directory And Year Book January, 1941, Coldwater, Michigan: W. C. Bailey, Publisher, 1941, Page 61 (ancestry.com image 30); "Clay Donald, 27 N Sprague, tr dr."

1746. Polk's Jackson (Jackson County, Mich.) City Directory 1945, Detroit: R. L. Polk & Co., Publishers, 1945, Page 88 (ancestry.com image 43); "Clay Donald L (Charlotte T) fertilizer mfrs 1311 E North h do."

1747. Polk's Jackson (Jackson County, Mich.) City Directory 1947, Detroit: R. L. Polk & Co., Publishers, 1947, Page 90 (ancestry.com image 47); "Clay Donald L (Charlotte H) shovel opr h1311 E North."

1748. Polk's Jackson (Jackson County, Mich.) City Directory 1949, Detroit, Michigan: R. L. Polk & Co., Publishers, 1949, Page 94 (ancestry.com image 48); "Clay Donald L (Charlotte H) crane opr Glick Iron h1311 E North."

1749. 1950 US Census, Jackson, Jackson County, Michigan, April 1950, "crane operator" | "scrap iron & metal."

1750. Polk's Jackson (Jackson County, Mich.) City Directory 1951, Detroit, Michigan: R. L. Polk & Co., Publishers, 1951, Page 91 (ancestry.com image 44); "Clay Donald L (Charlotte H) crane opr h1311 E North."

1751. Polk's Jackson (Jackson County, Mich.) City Directory 1952, Detroit: R. L. Polk & Co., Publishers, 1952, Page 88 (ancestry.com image 42); "Clay Donald L (Charotte H) crane opr Dunigan Bros h1311 E North."

1752. Polk's Jackson (Jackson County, Mich.) City Directory 1954, Detroit, Michigan: R. L. Polk & Co., Publishers, 1954, Page 85 (ancestry.com image 45); "Clay Donald L (Charlotte H) opr Dunigan ros h1311 E North."

1753. Polk's Jackson (Jackson County, Mich.) City Directory 1955, Detroit: R. L. Polk & Co., Publishers, 1955, Page 90 (ancestry.com image 49); "Clay Donald L (Charlotte H) mach opr Dunigan Bros h1311 E North."

1754. Polk's Jackson (Jackson County, Mich.) City Directory 1956, Detroit, Michigan: R. L. Polk & Co., Publishers, 1956, Page 196 (ancestry.com image 118); "Clay Donald L (Charlotte H) crane opr Dunigan Bros h1311 E North."

1755. Polk's Jackson (Jackson County, Mich.) City Directory 1957, Detroit, Michigan: R. L. Polk & Co., Publishers, 1957, Detroit: R. L. Polk & Co., Publishers, 1957, Page 80; (ancestry.com image 128); "Clay Donald L (Charlotte H) crane opr Dunigan Bros h1311 E North."

1756. Polk's Jackson (Jackson County, Mich.) City Directory 1960, Detroit: R. L. Polk & Co., Publishers, 1960, Page 94 (ancestry.com image 138); "Clay Donald L (Charlotte H) crane opr Dunigan Bros h1311 E North."

1757. US World War II Draft Registration Cards, 1940-1947, NARA. Records of the Selective Service System, 147; Box 212.

1758. 1940 US Census, Coldwater, Branch County, Michigan, April 1940, NARA T627; Roll 1734; Sheet 13B; ED 12-10; Line 61; "Charlotte Clay."

1759. 1950 US Census, Jackson, Jackson County, Michigan, April 1950, Record Group Number: 29; Roll 4014; Sheet 8; ED 38-107; Line 26; "Charlotte H. Clay."

1760. US Social Security Applications and Claims Index, 1936-2007, May 1963: Name listed as CHARLOTTE H CLAY.

1761. Indiana Marriages, 1810-2019, database, familysearch.org or ancestry.-com.

1762. Marriage record/certificate/application. Steuben County, Indiana; Page 241; 1938-1939 Volume 52.

1763. Find-A-Grave, (www.findagrave.com/memorial/83423153/charlotte-h-clay: accessed 06 September 2022). Memorial ID 83423153, citing Hillcrest Memorial Park, Jackson, Jackson County, Michigan; maintained by April May (contributor 47106490).

1764. Jackson Citizen Patriot, 28 May 2003. (https://www.genealogybank.com/doc/obituaries/obit/15149F849E20F3A0-15149F849E20F3A0 : accessed 7 September 2022).

1765. 1940 US Census, Coldwater, Branch County, Michigan, April 1940, NARA T627; Roll 1734; Sheet 13B; ED 12-10; Line 62; "Donna Clay."

1766. Coldwater, Michigan Pictorial City Directory And Year Book January, 1941, Coldwater, Michigan: W. C. Bailey, Publisher, 1941, Page 61 (ancestry.com image 30); "Clay Donna Lou, 27 N Sprague, u."

1767. 1950 US Census, Jackson, Jackson County, Michigan, April 1950, Record Group Number: 29; Roll 4014; Sheet 8; ED 38-107; Line 27; "Donna L. Clay."

1768. Coldwater, Michigan Pictorial City Directory And Year Book January, 1941, Coldwater, Michigan: W. C. Bailey, Publisher, 1941, Page 61 (ancestry.com image 30); "Clay Carol, 27 N Sprague, u."

1769. 1950 US Census, Jackson, Jackson County, Michigan, April 1950, Record Group Number: 29; Roll 4014; Sheet 8; ED 38-107; Line 28; "Carol H. Clay."

1770. Tombstone: "Carol Harriet Swartz 1940-1991."

1771. 1910 US Census, Lansing, Ingham County, Michigan, April 1910, NARA T624; Roll 651; Sheet 6A; ED 66; Ward 3; Dwelling 113; Family 115; Line 34; "Mildred V. Hale."

1772. 1920 US Census, Detroit, Wayne County, Michigan, January 1920, NARA T625; Roll 805; Sheet 2B; ED 147; House 199; Dwelling 32; Family 38; Line 57; "Mildred D. Hale."

1773. 1930 US Census, Lansing, Ingham County, Michigan, April 1930, NARA T626; Roll 991; Sheet 1B; ED 33-37; Lansing Township; 6th Ward; House 1539; Dwelling 21; Family 25; Line 97; "Mildred Schmidtmann."

1774. 1940 US Census, Lansing, Ingham County, Michigan, April 1940, NARA T627; Roll 1763; Sheet 42A; ED 33-72. Line 11; "Mildred Schmidtman."

1775. 1950 US Census, Lansing, Ingham County, Michigan, April 1950, Record Group Number: 29; Roll 1102; ED 90-140; Dwelling 87; Page 04798; Box 2; "Mildred V. Schmidtman."

1776. Birth Certificate/Record. State of Michigan, Jackson County, Page 77.

1777. Find-A-Grave, (www.findagrave.com/memorial/25080575/mildred-v-schmidtman: accessed 9 June 2023). Memorial ID 25080575, citing Mount Hope Cemetery, Lansing, Ingham County, Michigan; maintained by Ed Houghtaling (contributor 46804583).

1778. The State Journal, "Deaths & Funerals," 28 February 2002, page 5B.

1779. 1930 US Census, Lansing, Ingham County, Michigan, April 1930, NARA T626; Roll 991; Sheet 1B; ED 33-37; Lansing Township; 6th Ward; House 1539; Dwelling 21; Family 25; Line 96; "Harold Schmidtmann."

1780. 1940 US Census, Lansing, Ingham County, Michigan, April 1940, Enumerated 18-20 May 1940; NARA T627; Roll 1763; Sheet 42A; ED 33-72. Line 10; "Harold Schmidtman."

1781. 1950 US Census, Lansing, Ingham County, Michigan, April 1950, Record Group Number: 29; Roll 1102; ED 90-140; Dwelling 87; Page 04798; Box 1; "Harold A. Schmidtman."

1782. Marriage record/certificate/application. Marriage License, Ingham County, Michigan, State file 33 1975; County file 5717; Certificate of Marriage.

1783. Wisconsin, U.S., Birth and Christenings Index, 1801-1928, Wisconsin Department of Health and Family Services, Vital Records Division, Madison, database, (ancestry.com), "Harold August Schmidtmann."

1784. Find-A-Grave, (www.findagrave.com/memorial/25080559/harold-a-schmidtman: accessed 9 June 2023). Memorial ID 25080559, citing Mount Hope Cemetery, Lansing, Ingham County, Michigan; maintained by Ed Houghtaling (contributor 46804583).

1785. 1930 US Census, Lansing, Ingham County, Michigan, April 1930, "Grinder" | "Olds Motor Works."

1786. 1940 US Census, Lansing, Ingham County, Michigan, April 1940, "Grinder" | "Automotive."

1787. Polk's Lansing (Ingham County, Mich.) City Directory 1945, Volume XLI, Detroit: R. L. Polk & Co., Publishers, 1945, Page 590 (ancestry.com image 299); "Schmidtman Harold A (Mildred V) fcty wkr Olds h634 Berry av."

1788. Polk's Lansing City (Ingham County, Mich.) City Directory, 1948, Volume XLIII, Detroit: R. L. Polk & Co., Publishers, 1948, Page 621; (ancestry.com image 310); "Schmidtman Harold A (Mildred) reprmn r634 Berry."

1789. 1950 US Census, Lansing, Ingham County, Michigan, April 1950, "Tool upgrader" | "auto mfg."

1790. Polk's Lansing (Ingham County, Mich.) City Directory, 1954, Volume 1954, XLXII, Detroit, Michigan: R. L. Polk & Co., Publishers, 1954, Page 761 (ancestry.com image 396); "Schmidtman Harold A (Mildred V) repr Olds h634 Berry av."

1791. Polk's Lansing (Ingham County, Mich.) City Directory 1955, Detroit: R. L. Polk & Co., Publishers, 1955, Volume XLXIII, Page 783 (ancestry.com image 410); "Schmidtman Harold A (Mildred V) reprmn Olds h634 Berry av."

1792. The State Journal, "Deaths and Funerals." 30 November 1976, page B-2.

1793. US World War II Draft Registration Cards, 1940-1947, NARA, Saint Louis, Missouri, scanned image, ancestry.com and familysearch.org.

1794. 1930 US Census, Lansing, Ingham County, Michigan, April 1930, NARA T626; Roll 991; Sheet 1B; ED 33-37; Lansing Township; 6th Ward; House 1539; Dwelling 21; Family 25; Line 98; "Bruce Schmidtmann."

1795. 1940 US Census, Lansing, Ingham County, Michigan, April 1940, NARA T627; Roll 1763; Sheet 42A; ED 33-72. Line 12; "Bruce Schmidtman."

1796. 1950 US Census, Royal Oak, Oakland County, Michigan, April 1950, Roll 3556; "E. Windmere" ED 63-216; House 614; Sheet 86; Line 14; "Bruce A Schmidtman."

1797. 1930 US Census, Lansing, Ingham County, Michigan, April 1930, NARA T626; Roll 991; Sheet 1B; ED 33-37; Lansing Township; 6th Ward; House 1539; Dwelling 21; Family 25; Line 99; "Joan Schmidtmann."

1798. 1940 US Census, Lansing, Ingham County, Michigan, April 1940, NARA T627; Roll 1763; Sheet 42A; ED 33-72. Line 13; "Joan Schmidtman."

1799. Polk's Lansing City (Ingham County, Mich.) City Directory, 1948, Volume XLIII, Detroit: R. L. Polk & Co., Publishers, 1948, Page 621; (ancestry.com image 310); "Schmidtman Joan E r634 Berry av."

1800. 1940 US Census, Lansing, Ingham County, Michigan, April 1940, NARA T627; Roll 1763; Sheet 42A; ED 33-72. Line 14; "David Schmidtman."

1801. 1950 US Census, Lansing, Ingham County, Michigan, April 1950, Record Group Number: 29; Roll 1102; ED 90-140; Dwelling 87; Page 04798; Box 3; "David M. Schmidtman."

1802. US Social Security Applications and Claims Index, 1936-2007, Jun 1953: Name listed as DAVID MATTHEW SCHMIDTMAN; 23 Dec 1998: Name listed as DAVID M SCHMIDTMAN.

1803. 1940 US Census, Lansing, Ingham County, Michigan, April 1940, NARA T627; Roll 1763; Sheet 42A; ED 33-72. Line 15; "Walter Schmidtman."

1804. 1950 US Census, Lansing, Ingham County, Michigan, April 1950, Record Group Number: 29; Roll 1102; ED 90-140; Dwelling 87; Page 04798; Box 4; "Walter H. Schmidtman."

1805. Ibid. Record Group Number: 29; Roll 1102; ED 90-140; Dwelling 87; Page 04798; Box 5; "Jeanine E. Schmidtman."

1806. Ibid. Record Group Number: 29; Roll 1102; ED 90-140; Dwelling 87; Page 04798; Box 6; "Nancy S. Schmidtman."

1807. 1920 US Census, Springport Township, Jackson County, Michigan, January 1920, NARA T625; Roll 774; Sheet 3A; Page 199; ED 43; Dwelling 85; Family 95; Line 47; "Guilford C. Orrison."

1808. 1930 US Census, Marshall, Calhoun County, Michigan, April 1930, NARA T626; ED 13-54; Sheet 10B; House 423 Monroe St; Dwelling 285; Family 306; Line 55; "Guilford C Orrson."

1809. 1940 US Census, Marshall, Calhoun County, Michigan, April 1940, NARA T627; Roll 1737; Sheet 1B; ED 13-67; House 425; Line 50; "Guilford Orson."

1810. 1950 US Census, Marshall, Calhoun County, Michigan, April 1950, Record Group Number 29; Roll 2610; Sheet 72; ED 13-127; Dwelling 62; Line 10; "Guilford Orrison."

1811. Find-A-Grave, (www.findagrave.com/memorial/83695847/guilford-charles-orrison: accessed 11 October 2022). Memorial ID 83695847, citing Oakridge Cemetery, Marshall, Calhoun County, Michigan; maintained by Amy (Decker) Veenendall (contributor 47104012).

1812. Polk's Marshall (Michigan) City Directory 1929, Volume II, Detroit: R. L. Polk & Co., Publishers, 1929, Page 94 (ancestry.com image 51); "Orrison Guilford C student r423 Monroe."

1813. Polk's Marshall (Michigan) City Directory 1931, Volume III, Detroit: R. L. Polk & Co., Publishers, 1931, Page 95 (ancestry.com image 49); "Orrison Guilford student r 423 Monroe."

1814. 1940 US Census, Marshall, Calhoun County, Michigan, April 1940, "Clerk" | "Grocery."

1815. 1950 US Census, Marshall, Calhoun County, Michigan, April 1950, "meat cutter" | "Retail Food Shop."

1816. The Dial 1933, Marshall, Michigan: Senior Class, Marshall High School, 1933, Page 9 (ancestry.com image 12); "Guilford Orrison."

1817. Battle Creek Enquirer And News, "Man Is Found Dead Under Creek Bridge," 7 January 1959, Section 2, page 6.

1818. US World War II Draft Registration Cards, 1940-1947, NARA. Records of the Selective Service System, 147; Box 893.

1819. Battle Creek Enquirer And News, "Calhoun County Draft List For Draft Board No. 1," 1 November 1940, page 17.

1820. 1940 US Census, Marshall, Calhoun County, Michigan, April 1940, NARA T627; Roll 1737; Sheet 1B; ED 13-67; House 425; Line 51; "Dorothy Orson."

1821. 1950 US Census, Marshall, Calhoun County, Michigan, April 1950, Record Group Number 29; Roll 2610; Sheet 72; ED 13-127; Dwelling 62; Line 11; "Dorothy Orrison."

1822. US Social Security Applications and Claims Index, 1936-2007, Mar 1951: Name listed as DOROTHY CORA ORRISON; Dec: Name listed as DOROTHY SIPE ORRISON; 19 Mar 2002: Name listed as DOROTHY C ORRISON.

1823. Marriage record/certificate/application. Certificate of Marriage, Calhoun County, Michigan; Record Of Marriages; page 207, record number 354, state file 13 5364.

1824. Evening Chronicle, "Quiet Wedding," 3 September 1935, page 2.

1825. Find-A-Grave, (www.findagrave.com/memorial/90697265/dorothy-cora-orrison: accessed 11 October 2022). Memorial ID 90697265, citing Oakridge Cemetery, Marshall, Calhoun County, Michigan; maintained by William Kinney (contributor 46928118).

1826. 1950 US Census, Marshall, Calhoun County, Michigan, April 1950, "waitress" | "Tasty Food Shop."

1827. The Dial 1933, Marshall, Michigan: Senior Class, Marshall High School, 1933, Page 10; (ancestry.com image 13).

1828. Battle Creek Enquirer And News, "Obituaries: Dorothy C. Orrison," 11 March 2002, page 4A.

1829. 1940 US Census, Marshall, Calhoun County, Michigan, April 1940, NARA T627; Roll 1737; Sheet 1B; ED 13-67; House 425; Line 52; "Donna Orson."

1830. 1950 US Census, Marshall, Calhoun County, Michigan, April 1950, Record Group Number 29; Roll 2610; Sheet 72; ED 13-127; Dwelling 62; Line 12; "Donna M Orrison."

1831. 1940 US Census, Marshall, Calhoun County, Michigan, April 1940, NARA T627; Roll 1737; Sheet 1B; ED 13-67; House 425; Line 53; "Janet Orson."

1832. 1950 US Census, Marshall, Calhoun County, Michigan, April 1950, Record Group Number 29; Roll 2610; Sheet 72; ED 13-127; Dwelling 62; Line 13; "Janet A Orrison."

1833. Ibid. Record Group Number 29; Roll 2610; Sheet 72; ED 13-127; Dwelling 62; Line 14; "David J Orrison."

1834. Ibid. Record Group Number 29; Roll 2610; Sheet 72; ED 13-127; Dwelling 62; Line 15; "Michael E Orrison."

1835. 1920 US Census, Springport Township, Jackson County, Michigan, January 1920, NARA T625; Roll 774; Sheet 3A; Page 199; ED 43; Dwelling 85; Family 95; Line 48; "Jesse E Orrison."

1836. 1930 US Census, Marshall, Calhoun County, Michigan, April 1930, NARA T626; ED 13-54; Sheet 10B; House 423 Monroe St; Dwelling 285; Family 306; Line 56; "Eugene J Orrson."

1837. 1940 US Census, Marshall, Calhoun County, Michigan, April 1940, NARA T627; Roll 1737; Sheet 9A; ED 13-65; Ward 2; House 402; Line 22; "J. Eugene Orrison."

1838. 1950 US Census, Brighton, Sacramento County, California, April 1950, Record Group Number 29; Roll 2645; Sheet 20; ED 70-7; House 5705; Line 30; "Jesse Orrison."

1839. US Social Security Applications and Claims Index, 1936-2007, Nov 1936: Name listed as JESSE EUGENE ORRISON; 16 Sep 1997: Name listed as JESSE E ORRISON.

1840. Find-A-Grave, (www.findagrave.com/memorial/173556119/jesse-eugene-orrison: accessed 08 October 2022). Memorial ID 173556119, citing East Lawn Palms Cemetery and Mortuary, Tucson, Pima County, Arizona; maintained by woowoo (contributor 49949980).

1841. Polk's Marshall (Michigan) City Directory 1929, Volume II, Detroit: R. L. Polk & Co., Publishers, 1929, Page 94 (ancestry.com image 51); "Orrison J Eugene student r423 Monroe."

1842. Polk's Marshall (Michigan) City Directory 1931, Volume III, Detroit: R. L. Polk & Co., Publishers, 1931, Page 95 (ancestry.com image 49); "Orrison Eug student r 423 Monroe."

1843. Polk's Marshall (Cahoun County, Mich.) City Directory, 1934, Detroit: R. L. Polk & Co., Publishers, 1934, Volume IV, Page 74 (ancestry.com image 39); "Orrison J Eug lab r605 Monroe."

1844. 1940 US Census, Marshall, Calhoun County, Michigan, April 1940, "machine operator" | "Eaton mfg. co."

1845. Polk's Belleville (St. Clair County, Ill.) City Directory 1948, St. Louis, Missouri: R. L. Polk & Co., Publishers, 1948, Page 331 (ancestry.com image 166); "Orrison Jesse E (Margt N) USA r113 East D."

1846. 1950 US Census, Brighton, Sacramento County, California, April 1950, "Armed Forces."

1847. Mullin-Kille Tucson Arizona ConSurvey City Directory 1958-59, Volume 26 ABCD No. 784, Phoenix, Arizona: Mullin-Kille Company, 1958, Page 1286 (ancestry.com image 754); "Orrison Jesse E (Margt) 3 USAF h 4614 E 16th St [Phone] EA 6-3076."

1848. Arizona Daily Star, newspaper, Tucson, Arizona, "Funeral Notices," 8 September 1997, Page 10 - Section A.

1849. Battle Creek Enquirer And News, "Calhoun County Draft List For Draft Board No. 1," 1 November 1940, page 17.

1850. U.S. World War II Army Enlistment Records, 1938-1946, 1789-ca. 2007; Record Group 64; Box Number 02092; Reel 66; Affiliate ARC Identifier 1263923; Box Film 02092.66.

1851. United States, World War II Prisoners of War, 1941-1945, (familysearch.org/ark:/61903/1:1:Q298-WXDC : 18 February 2016), Jesse E Orrison, 29 Nov 1943; citing Military Service, Germany, NARA NAID 1263907 (Washington D.C.: NARA, n.d.).

1852. Battle Creek Enquirer And News, "Marshall Flier Reported Lost," 14 December 1943; "Marshall Boy First Reported Lost, Now Located As Prisoner," 27 January 1944, page 8; "Two Prisoners Of War Visit Marshall Homes," 4 July 1945, page 8.

1853. Star-Telegram, "Texas Officer Taken Prisoner," 6 March 1944, page 2.

1854. The State Journal, "Local Man Freed From Prison Camp," 22 May 1945, page 11.

1855. Battle Creek Enquirer And News, "Marshall Home Gets Letters from 3 Sons," 25 February 1945, page 18.

1856. 1950 US Census, Brighton, Sacramento County, California, April 1950, Record Group Number 29; Roll 2645; Sheet 21; ED 70-7; House 5705; Line 1; "Margaret Orrison."

1857. US Social Security Applications and Claims Index, 1936-2007, Claim Date 17 Feb 1977.

1858. Texas, U.S., Select County Marriage Records, 1837-1965, ancestry.com, Certificate Number 141367.

1859. Find-A-Grave, (www.findagrave.com/memorial/173556058/margret-nell-orrison: accessed 08 October 2022). Memorial ID 173556058, citing East Lawn Palms Cemetery and Mortuary, Tucson, Pima County, Arizona; maintained by woowoo (contributor 49949980).

1860. Arizona Daily Star, newspaper, Tucson, Arizona, "Funeral Notices," 14 February 1977, page 5 - Section B; 15 February 1977, page 2 - section B.

1861. 1950 US Census, Brighton, Sacramento County, California, April 1950, Record Group Number 29; Roll 2645; Sheet 21; ED 70-7; House 5705; Line 2; "Wayne Orrison."

1862. Ibid. Record Group Number 29; Roll 2645; Sheet 21; ED 70-7; House 5705; Line 3; "Stephen Orrison."

1863. 1975 Honolulu (Hawaii) City and County Directory, Honolulu: R. L. Polk & Co. Publishers, 1975, Page 1152; (ancestry.com image 1518); "Orrison Stephen L r95-182 Kipapa Dr Wah 623-4184."

1864. 1976 Honolulu (Hawaii) City and County Directory, Honolulu: R. L. Polk & Co. Publishers, 1976, Page 1143; (ancestry.com image 1509); "Orrison Stephen L r95-182 Kipapa Dr Wah 623-4184."

1865. US Social Security Applications and Claims Index, 1936-2007, Apr 1964: Name listed as STEPHEN LAWRENCE ORRISON; 19 Mar 1997: Name listed as STEPHEN ORRISON.

1866. Arizona Daily Star, "Domestic Relations: Marriage licenses," 28 February 1991, Page 2 - Section B.

1867. 1920 US Census, Springport Township, Jackson County, Michigan, January 1920, NARA T625; Roll 774; Sheet 3A; Page 199; ED 43; Dwelling 85; Family 95; Line 49; "Howard C. Orrison."

1868. 1930 US Census, Marshall, Calhoun County, Michigan, April 1930, NARA T626; ED 13-54; Sheet 10B; House 423 Monroe St; Dwelling 285; Family 306; Line 57; "Howard C Orrison."

1869. 1940 US Census, Marshall, Calhoun County, Michigan, April 1940, NARA T627; Roll 1737; Sheet 9A; ED 13-65; Ward 2; House 402; Line 23; "Howard Orrison."

1870. 1942 Kansas State Census, Junction City, Geary County, Kansas, March 1942, (ancestry.com image 62); Kansas State Historical Society; Topeka; Collection Name: Population Schedules and Statistical Rolls: Cities (1919-1961); Reel Number: 31984_245865; "Howard C Orrison," 2 persons residing.

1871. 1944 Kansas State Census, Junction City, Geary County, Kansas, March 1944, (ancestry.com image 284); Kansas State Historical Society; Topeka; Collection Name: Population Schedules and Statistical Rolls: Cities (1919-1961); Reel Number: 31984_254676; Line 7. "Howard C Orrison," 2 persons residing.

1872. 1947 Kansas State Census, Junction City, Geary County, Kansas, March 1947, (ancestry.com image 188); Kansas State Historical Society; Topeka; Collection Name: Population Schedules and Statistical Rolls: Cities (1919-1961); Reel Number: 31984_254699; Line 20. "Howard Orrison," 3 persons in residence.

1873. Polk's Marshall (Michigan) City Directory 1931, Volume III, Detroit: R. L. Polk & Co., Publishers, 1931, Page 95 (ancestry.com image 49); "Orrison Howard student r 423 Monroe."

1874. Polk's Marshall (Cahoun County, Mich.) City Directory, 1934, Detroit: R. L. Polk & Co., Publishers, 1934, Volume IV, Page 74 (ancestry.com image 39); "Orrison Howard C student r605 Monroe."

1875. 1940 US Census, Marshall, Calhoun County, Michigan, April 1940, "Motor Vehicle operator."

1876. Virginia Gazette, Williamsburg, Virginia, Christine Lombard, "Penniman Communities: Junior Golf-Prospect," 9 September 1960, page 6.

1877. Battle Creek Enquirer And News, "Calhoun County Draft List For Draft Board No. 1," 1 November 1940, page 16.

1878. Ibid. 2 February 1943, page 8.

1879. Ibid. "Marshall Flier Reported Lost," 14 December 1943, page 8.

1880. Ibid. "Marshall Boy Wins First Cavalry Rating," 20 February 1944, page 12.

1881. U.S. World War II Army Enlistment Records, 1938-1946, Serial number 36153378; Affiliate ARC Identifier 1263923; Box Film Number 10395.101.

1882. Iola Register, newspaper, Iola, Kansas, "Locals," 17 February 1949, page 3.

1883. Ibid. "Locals," 7 December 1953, page 3.

1884. Daily Press, newspaper, Newport News, Virginia, "Truck Unit Set For Point Duty," 23 May 1957, page 9.

1885. Virginia Gazette, Christine Lombard, "Penniman Communities: Left For West Point, N. Y." 24 May 1957, page 7.

1886. Daily Press, "Army Observes Birthday, Flag Day At Eustis," 15 June 1961, page 11.

1887. News, newspaper, Kalispell, Montana, "Family Locates Locally After Automobile Trouble Stop," 5 October 1961, page 1.

1888. Passenger and Crew Lists of Vessels and Airplanes Departing from New York, New York, 07/01/1948-12/31/1956, Records of the Immigration and Naturalization Service, 1787-2004, database with image, ancestry.com, NAI Number: 3335533; Record Group Number: 85; Series Number: A4169; NARA Roll Number: 58; (ancestry.com image 1526). List No. 8; 30 November 1949; From New York to Bremerhaven, Germany, USAT Gen. Alexander M. Patch; Line 20 "Orrison, Ruth R."

1889. New York, New York Passenger and Crew Lists, 1909, 1917-1967 [inclusive], database with images, (https://familysearch.org/ark:/61903/1:1:QVMF-J2GY : 2 March 2021); NARA microfilm publication T715. From Frankfurt, Germany to New York, 4 May 1953; Aircraft 1220V Seaboard & Western Airlines.

1890. Passenger and Crew Lists of Vessels and Airplanes Departing from New York, New York, 07/01/1948-12/31/1956, Records of the Immigration and Naturalization Service, 1787-2004, database with image, ancestry.com, 12 November 1954, from Idlewild Airport, New York to Casablanca; NAI Number: 3335533; Record Group Title: Records of the Immigration and Naturalization Service, 1787-2004; Record Group Number: 85; Series Number: A4169; NARA Roll Number: 288.

1891. New York, New York Passenger and Crew Lists, 1909, 1917-1967 [inclusive], database with images, 11 December 1955, from Casablanca to New York; List 16; USNS George W. Goethals; (https://familysearch.org/ark:/61903/1:1:2HZF-FNZ : 2 March 2021), Ruth B Orrison.

1892. US Social Security Applications and Claims Index, 1936-2007, May 1939: Name listed as NAOMI RUTH BRIGHT; Dec 1969: Name listed as RUTH BRIGHT ORRISON; 17 Jun 1992: Name listed as RUTH B ORRISON.

1893. Iola Register, Tom Waugh, "Our Home Town: The Critics," 20 April 1942, page 3.

1894. US Social Security Death Index: "Ruth B. Orrison."

1895. Arizona Daily Star, "Public Record: Deaths," 16 June 1992, page 2B. "Orrison, Naomi R., 72, Tucson, June 12, Bring's Broadway."

1896. Tucson Citizen, newspaper, Tucson, Arizona, "Public records: Deaths," 17 June 1992, page 10C. "Naomi R. Orrison, 72, homemaker, died June 12, Bring's Broadway."

1897. Passenger and Crew Lists of Vessels and Airplanes Departing from New York, New York, 07/01/1948-12/31/1956, Records of the Immigration and Naturalization Service, 1787-2004, 30 November 1949; NAI Number: 3335533; Record Group Number: 85; Series Number: A4169; NARA Roll Number: 58; (ancestry.com image 1526). List No. 8; From New York to Bremerhaven, Germany, USAT Gen. Alexander M. Patch; Line 21 "Orrison, Deborah b."

1898. New York, New York Passenger and Crew Lists, 1909, 1917-1967 [inclusive], database with images, 4 May 1953; (https://familysearch.org/ark:/61903/1:1:QVMF-J2GY : 2 March 2021); NARA microfilm publication T715. From Frankfurt, Germany to New York; Aircraft 1220V Seaboard & Western Airlines.

1899. Ibid. 11 December 1955, from Casablanca to New York; List 16; USNS George W. Goethals; (https://familysearch.org/ark:/61903/1:1:2HZF-FNZ : 2 March 2021), Deborah B. Orrison.

1900. 1930 US Census, Marshall, Calhoun County, Michigan, April 1930, NARA T626; ED 13-54; Sheet 10B; House 423 Monroe St; Dwelling 285; Family 306; Line 58; "Robert E Orrison."

1901. 1940 US Census, Marshall, Calhoun County, Michigan, April 1940, NARA T627; Roll 1737; Sheet 9A; ED 13-65; Ward 2; House 402; Line 24; "Robert Orrison."

1902. 1950 US Census, San Diego, San Diego County, California, April 1950, Record Group Number 29; Roll 1330; Sheet 1; ED 72-133; Line 21; "Robert E. Orrison."

1903. US Social Security Applications and Claims Index, 1936-2007, Mar 1941: Name listed as ROBERT ELTON ORRISON; 03 Dec 1993: Name listed as ROBERT E ORRISON.

1904. 1950 US Census, San Diego, San Diego County, California, April 1950, "Armed Forces."

1905. Polk's San Diego (San Diego County, Calif.) City Directory 1959, Los Angeles: R. L. Polk & Co., Publishers, 1959, Page 753; (ancestry.com 993); "Orrison Robt (Hazel F) USN h4357 Olive."

1906. US World War II Navy Muster Rolls, 1938-1949, National Archives at College Park; College Park, Maryland, (ancestry.com images 317, 380, 104, 174, 194, 208, 260, 15, 93 respectively). Record Group 24, Records of the Bureau of Naval Personnel, 1798 - 2007; Series ARC ID: 594996; Series MLR: A1 135.

1907. Ibid. (ancestry.com images 502, 68, 158, 608, 809, 280, 377, 505, 84 respectively); Record Group: 24, Records of the Bureau of Naval Personnel, 1798 - 2007; Series ARC ID: 594996; Series MLR: A1 135.

1908. Battle Creek Enquirer And News, "News of Our Men In the Services: Serving in Far East," 8 October 1951, page 4. "Metalsmith Second Class Robert E. Orrison of Marshall."

1909. Ibid. "News of our Men in the Services," 2 May 1958, page 4.

1910. 1950 US Census, San Diego, San Diego County, California, April 1950, Record Group Number 29; Roll 1330; Sheet 1; ED 72-133; Line 22.; "Bernice H. Orrison."

1911. South Dakota, School Records, 1879-1970, (school census) database with images, Lead Independent School District No. 5, Lawrence County, South Dakota; Line 24; Residence: "104 S. Stone St."

1912. San Diego Union, newspaper, San Diego, California, "Vital Statistics: Divorces: Complaints Filed," 5 December 1950, page 10.

1913. 1950 US Census, San Diego, San Diego County, California, April 1950, Record Group Number 29; Roll 1330; Sheet 1; ED 72-133; Line 23; "Cintra D Orrison."

1914. Nevada Marriage Index, 1956-2005, Nevada State Health Division, Office of Vital Records. Nevada Marriage Index, 1966-2005. Carson City, database with image, ancestry.com.

1915. Find-A-Grave, (www.findagrave.com/memorial/20609251/hazel-frances-orrison: accessed 24 October 2022). Memorial ID 20609251, citing Glen Abbey Memorial Park, Bonita, San Diego County, California; maintained by Doug Daniel (contributor 49519788).

1916. San Diego Union Tribune, 24 July 2007, obit for ORRISON, HAZEL FRANCES, GenealogyBank.com (https://www.genealogybank.com/doc/obituaries/obit/11ABD016F2231540-11ABD016F2231540 : accessed 24 October 2022).

1917. Boonville Daily News, newspaper, Boonville, Missouri, obit for Hazel Orrison, 87, GenealogyBank.com (https://www.genealogybank.com/doc/obituaries/obit/158E3A50C5FDF750-158E3A50C5FDF750 : accessed 24 October 2022).

1918. 1930 US Census, Marshall, Calhoun County, Michigan, April 1930, NARA T626; ED 13-54; Sheet 10B; House 423 Monroe St; Dwelling 285; Family 306; Line 59; "Norman K Orrison."

1919. 1940 US Census, Marshall, Calhoun County, Michigan, April 1940, NARA T627; Roll 1737; Sheet 9A; ED 13-65; Ward 2; House 402; Line 25; "Norman Keith Orrison."

1920. 1950 US Census, Marshall, Calhoun County, Michigan, April 1950, Record Group Number: 29; Roll 2610; Sheet 16; ED 13-128; House 427; Dwelling 202; Line 28; "Norman Keith Orrison."

1921. Michigan Death Index, 1971-1996, Michigan Department of Vital and Health Records, Lansing, (https://www.familysearch.org/ark:/61903/1:1:VZ1X-7J2 : 10 August 2022), Norman K Orrison, 1986.

1922. Find-A-Grave, (www.findagrave.com/memorial/1050932/norman-keith-orrison: accessed 08 October 2022). Memorial ID 1050932, citing Fort Custer National Cemetery, Augusta, Kalamazoo County, Michigan; maintained by Carol Lee Weber (contributor 46956116).

1923. U.S., Veterans' Cemeteries, ca.1775-2019, National Cemetery Administration. Nationwide Gravesite Locator.

1924. 1950 US Census, Marshall, Calhoun County, Michigan, April 1950, "Butter maker" | "Dairy."

1925. The Dial 1944, Marshall, Michigan: Journalism Class of Marshall High School, 1944, Page 20; (ancestry.com image 24).

1926. Battle Creek Enquirer And News, "Obituaries: Norman Keith Orrison," 23 August 1986, page 6A.

1927. US World War II Navy Muster Rolls, 1938-1949, NARA database with images, www.ancestry.com, Page 34, 30, 30, 12, 15, 16, 33, 7 respectively.

1928. Ibid. Line 24; Muster Rolls of U.S. Navy Ships, Stations, and Other Naval Activities, 01/01/1939 - 01/01/1949; Record Group: 24, Records of the Bureau of Naval Personnel, 1798 - 2007; Series ARC ID.

1929. Battle Creek Enquirer And News, "Community News: Three Sons in Family Continue in Service," 11 March 1950, page 5.

1930. 1930 US Census, Marshall, Calhoun County, Michigan, April 1930, NARA T626; ED 13-54; Sheet 10B; House 423 Monroe St; Dwelling 285; Family 306; Line 60; "Jack D Orrison."

1931. 1940 US Census, Marshall, Calhoun County, Michigan, April 1940, NARA T627; Roll 1737; Sheet 9A; ED 13-65; Ward 2; House 402; Line 26; "Jack Orrison."

1932. 1950 US Census, Marshall, Calhoun County, Michigan, April 1950, Record Group Number: 29; Roll 2610; Sheet 16; ED 13-128; House 427; Dwelling 202; Line 29; "Jack D Orrison."

1933. Find-A-Grave, (www.findagrave.com/memorial/83910947/jack-d-orrison: accessed 08 October 2022). Memorial ID 83910947, citing Oakridge Cemetery, Marshall, Calhoun County, Michigan; maintained by David Rhodes (contributor 48628564).

1934. 1950 US Census, Marshall, Calhoun County, Michigan, April 1950, "shipping clerk cook" | "mfg display cases Refrigeration appliances Restaurant."

1935. Polk's San Diego (San Diego County, Calif.) City Directory 1959, Los Angeles: R. L. Polk & Co., Publishers, 1959, Page 753 (ancestry.com image 993); "Orrison Jack D (Peggy J) agt Natl Life & Accdt Ins h4353 Olive."

1936. The Dial 1946, Marshall, Michigan: Marshall High School, 1946, Page 21; (ancestry.com image 25).

1937. Battle Creek Enquirer And News, "Jack D. Orrison," 22 January 2012, page B2.

1938. Obituary, funeral home. Kempf Family Funeral & Cremation Services, Marshall, Michigan; https://www.legacy.com/obituaries/name/jack-orrison-obituary?pid=178746709 (viewed 25 October 2022).

1939. 1950 US Census, Union City, Branch County, Michigan, Record Group Number 29; Roll 4521; Sheet 73; ED 12-36; Line 17; "Peggy J. Callahan," age 16, lodger in the household of Ned R. Foster family.

1940. Tombstone: (See findagrave.com; with husband).

1941. Battle Creek Enquirer And News, "To Wed: Miss Peggy Jane Callahan," 23 July 1950, page 3, "…set for August 27"; 8 August 1950, page 8, "applied for a marriage license."

1942. Michigan Marriages, 1867-1952, Michigan Department of Community Health, Division of Vital Records and Health Statistics; Lansing; Marriage Records, 1867-1952; Film: 23; Film Title: 12 Branch 1610-4834; Film Description: Branch (1935-1952); County 14783; State 12 4587.

1943. Battle Creek Enquirer And News, "The Orrisons," 13 August 2000, page 4D, 50th wedding anniversary.

1944. Not deceased as of 2020.

1945. 1930 US Census, Marshall, Calhoun County, Michigan, April 1930, NARA T626; ED 13-54; Sheet 10B; House 423 Monroe St; Dwelling 285; Family 306; Line 61; "Joyce M Orrison."

1946. 1940 US Census, Marshall, Calhoun County, Michigan, April 1940, NARA T627; Roll 1737; Sheet 9A; ED 13-65; Ward 2; House 402; Line 27; "Joyce Orrison."

1947. 1950 US Census, Sheridan Township, Calhoun County, Michigan, April 1950, Record Group Number 29; Roll 2610; Sheet 71; ED 13-138; Dwelling 29; Line 17; "Joyce M. O'Dell."

1948. Find-A-Grave, (www.findagrave.com/memorial/206840831/joyce-marie-blaskie: accessed 25 October 2022). Memorial ID 206840831, citing Fort Custer National Cemetery, Augusta, Kalamazoo County, Michigan; maintained by Woolsox (contributor 47347718).

1949. Obituary, funeral home. https://farleyestesdowdle.tributes.com/obituary/show/Joyce-Marie-Orrison-Blaskie-108120803 (viewed 25 October 2022).

1950. 1950 US Census, Sheridan Township, Calhoun County, Michigan, April 1950, Record Group Number 29; Roll 2610; Sheet 71; ED 13-138; Dwelling 29; Line 16; "Arthur E. O'Dell."

1951. Michigan Marriages, 1867-1952, Michigan Department of Community Health, Division of Vital Records and Health Statistics; Lansing; Marriage Records, 1867-1952; Film: 25; Film Title: 13 Calhoun 16020-19284; Film Description: Calhoun (1946-1949); County 906; State 13 17281.

1952. Battle Creek Enquirer And News,"Marriage Licenses," 16 July 1947, page 3.

1953. Polk's Battle Creek (Calhoun County, Mich.) City Directory 1949, Detroit: R. L. Polk & Co., Publisher, 1949, Page 259; (ancestry.com image 130); "O'Dell Arth E (Joyce M) fctywkr r42 Main."

1954. 1950 US Census, Sheridan Township, Calhoun County, Michigan, April 1950.

1955. Michigan, Divorce records, 1897-1952, database with (sometimes) scanned image, Michigan Department of Community Health, Division for Vital Records and Health Statistics; Lansing, (www.ancestry.com), State 13 10519; Docket 48-51.

1956. Battle Creek Enquirer And News, "Obituaries: Arthur E. O'Dell," 12 April 2008, page 4A.

1957. Jackson Citizen Patriot, 15 April 2008, obit for Arthur E. O'Dell, GenealogyBank.com (https://www.genealogybank.com/doc/obituaries/obit/120331F3E2CD4570-120331F3E2CD4570 : accessed 25 October 2022).

1958. 1950 US Census, Sheridan Township, Calhoun County, Michigan, April 1950, Record Group Number 29; Roll 2610; Sheet 71; ED 13-138; Dwelling 29; Line 18; "Arthur Jr. O'Dell."

1959. Ibid. Record Group Number 29; Roll 2610; Sheet 71; ED 13-138; Dwelling 29; Line 19; "Kathleen M. O'Dell."

1960. US Social Security Applications and Claims Index, 1936-2007, Feb 1943: Name listed as LAWRENCE WAYNARD MASTERS; 17 Oct 2000: Name listed as LAWRENCE W MASTERS.

1961. Indiana Marriages, 1810-2019, database, (https://www.familysearch.org/ark:/61903/1:1:8NRJ-3W2M : 3 August 2022), Lawrence W. Masters, 1953.

1962. Find-A-Grave, (www.findagrave.com/memorial/91016207/lawrence-waynard-masters: accessed 25 October 2022). Memorial ID 91016207, citing Burlington Township Cemetery, Burlington, Calhoun County, Michigan; maintained by RobMinteer57 (contributor 47389024).

1963. Battle Creek Enquirer And News, "Retirements," 8 May 1982, page B-3.

1964. US World War II Draft Registration Cards, 1940-1947, NARA. Records of the Selective Service System, 147; Box 761.

1965. US Social Security Applications and Claims Index, 1936-2007, Oct 1965: Name listed as ARTHUR EUGENE MASTERS; 08 Feb 1996: Name listed as ARTHUR E MASTERS.

1966. Find-A-Grave, (www.findagrave.com/memorial/175958516/joseph-henry-blaskie: accessed 25 October 2022). Memorial ID 175958516, citing Fort Custer National Cemetery, Augusta, Kalamazoo County, Michigan; maintained by Sons of Liberty (contributor 48368710).

1967. Battle Creek Enquirer And News, Al Holczman, "Hear the Hammering? Well, that's The Sound of Men Learning," 1 November 1964, page 8, Section 3.

1968. Legacy.com, Battle Creek Enquirer, 24 January 2017; online; https://www.legacy.com/us/obituaries/battlecreek/name/joseph-blaskie-obituary?id=15945669 (viewed 21 September 2023).

1969. 1940 US Census, Marshall, Calhoun County, Michigan, April 1940, NARA T627; Roll 1737; Sheet 9A; ED 13-65; Ward 2; House 402; Line 28; "James Orrison."

1970. 1950 US Census, Marshall, Calhoun County, Michigan, April 1950, Record Group Number: 29; Roll 2610; Sheet 16; ED 13-128; House 427; Dwelling 202; Line 30; "James F Orrison."

1971. Find-A-Grave, (www.findagrave.com/memorial/178541433/james-orrison: accessed 08 October 2022). Memorial ID 178541433, citing Sunset Memorial Gardens, Cleveland, Bradley County, Tennessee; maintained by WB33 (contributor 48517718).

1972. The Dial 1954, Marshall, Michigan: Journalism Class of Marshall High School, 1954, (ancestry.com image 101).

1973. Cleveland Daily Banner, newspaper, Cleveland, Tennessee, (https://www.genealogybank.com/doc/obituaries/obit/163D9466DABEBDA0-163D9466DABEBDA0 : accessed 25 October 2022).

1974. The State Journal, "Betrothal of Charlotte Woman Is Revealed," 25 August 1957, page 32.

1975. 1955 Charhian, Charlotte, Michigan: Charlotte High School, 1955, Page 34; (ancestry.com image 38).

1976. The State Journal, "Birth Announcements," 18 March 1918, page 13. "Girl-Mr. and Mrs. Milo S. Clay, 1726 Teel ave., March 15."

1977. Death Certificate/Record. State Of Michigan, Department of State - Division of Vital Statistics, Transcript Of Certificate Of Death; file 8336; "Charlyn Ella Clay."

1978. 1940 US Census, Ferndale, Oakland County, Michigan, April 1940, NARA T626; Roll 1799; Sheet 3A; ED 63-36; House 497; Line 39; "Betty Jane Clay."

1979. 1950 US Census, Pinellas County, Florida, April 1950, Record Group Number 29; Roll 5900; Sheet 31; ED 52-90; Dwelling 339; Line 9; "Betty J. Clay."

1980. US Social Security Applications and Claims Index, 1936-2007, Jul 1937: Name listed as BETTY JANE CLAY; Jul 1943: Name listed as BETTY JANE ECKHARDT; Jul 1943: Name listed as BETTY CLAY ECKHARDT; 12 May 1999: Name listed as BETTY J ECKHARDT. Born in Detroit, Michigan.

1981. North Carolina, U.S., Death Indexes, 1908-2004, Raleigh, North Carolina, database, ancestry.com.

1982. Polk's Royal Oak and Ferndale (Oakland County, Mich.) City Directory 1940, Volume IX, Detroit: R. L. Polk & Co., Publishers, 1940, Page 209 (ancestry.com image 101); "Clay Betty J clk Neisner's r497 E Lewiston av (F)."

1983. Polk's Royal Oak and Ferndale (Oakland County, Mich.) City Directory 1942, Volume X, Detroit: R. L. Polk & Co., Publishers, 1942, Page 124 (ancestry.com image 57); "Clay Betty J asst cash Neisner's (F) r497 E Lewiston av (F)."

1984. Polk's Royal Oak and Ferndale (Oakland County, Mich.) City Directory 1945, Volume XI, Detroit: R. L. Polk & Co., Publishers, 1945, Page 127 (ancestry.com image 68); "Clay Betty inspr Woodworth (F) r2400 Rochester rd."

1985. 1950 US Census, Pinellas County, Florida, April 1950, Record Group Number 29; Roll 5900; Sheet 31; ED 52-90; Dwelling 339; Line 8; "John E Jr Eckhardt."

1986. US Social Security Applications and Claims Index, 1936-2007, Apr 1937: Name listed as JOHN FREDRICK ECKHARDT; 30 Mar 2006: Name listed as JOHN F ECKHARDT.

1987. Historical Society of Pennsylvania, Pennsylvania, Church and Town Records, 1669-2013, Philadelphia, Pennsylvania, Ancestry.com. Pennsylvania and New Jersey, U.S., Church and Town Records, 1669-2013 [database on-line]. Lehi, UT, USA: Ancestry.com Operations, Inc., 2011., Reel 337.

1988. Find-A-Grave, (www.findagrave.com/memorial/40981246/john-f-eckhardt: accessed 26 October 2022). Memorial ID 40981246, citing Oak Ridge Cemetery, Inverness, Citrus County, Florida; maintained by Tracy Pry Price (contributor 46597670).

1989. 1950 US Census, Pinellas County, Florida, April 1950.

1990. Tampa Bay Times, Steve Douglass, "Converting Hens To Egg-Laying Machines Gains Popularity," 18 April 1954, page 9-C.

1991. Ibid. "Obituaries," 4 March 2006, page 9.

1992. US World War II Draft Registration Cards, 1940-1947, NARA, Records of the Selective Service System, 147; Box 186.

1993. U.S. World War II Army Enlistment Records, 1938-1946, Record Group 64; Box Number 04623; Reel 184.

1994. 1950 US Census, Pinellas County, Florida, April 1950, Record Group Number 29; Roll 5900; Sheet 31; ED 52-90; Dwelling 339; Line 10; "John E III Eckhardt."

1995. Tampa Bay Times, "Have Your Heard?" 2 February 1956, page 21.

1996. 1920 US Census, Evanston City, Cook County, Illinois, NARA T625; Page 65; Sheet 17A; ED 77; 552 Elmwood; Dwelling 217; Family 419; Line 11; "Helen Wallace."

1997. 1930 US Census, Kalamazoo Township, Kalamazoo County, Michigan, April 1930, NARA T626; Page 159; Sheet 22A; ED 39-27; Ward 3; House 508; Dwelling 520; Family 622; Line 39; "Helen F. Wallace."

1998. 1940 US Census, Kalamazoo, Kalamazoo County, Michigan, April 1940, NARA T627; Roll 1771; Sheet 5B; ED 39-32; House 508; Line 67; "Helen Wallace."

1999. 1950 US Census, Chicago, Cook County, Illinois, Record Group Number 29; Roll 513; Sheet 81; ED 103-602; House 5528; Dwelling 234; Line 10; "Helen E Wallace."

2000. US Social Security Applications and Claims Index, 1936-2007, Nov 1936: Name listed as HELEN EDITH WALLACE; Nov 1970: Name listed as HELEN EDITH PIERCE; 19 Apr 2001: Name listed as HELEN E PIERCE.

2001. Tombstone: (See findagrave; "Helen E. Pierce 1918-."

2002. Find-A-Grave, (www.findagrave.com/memorial/140885933/helen-e-pierce: accessed 29 September 2022). Memorial ID 140885933, citing Mount Ever-Rest Memorial Park South, Kalamazoo, Kalamazoo County, Michigan; maintained by Amy Dunn Hohler (contributor 47542889).

2003. 1940 US Census, Kalamazoo, Kalamazoo County, Michigan, April 1940, "Cady Shop."

2004. 1950 US Census, Chicago, Cook County, Illinois, "American Airlines Reservation Agent."

2005. New York, New York Passenger and Crew Lists, 1909, 1925-1957, NARA microfilm publication T715, database with images, (familysearch.org), 2 November 1951; originated at Amsterdam to New York; K.L.M. Royal Dutch Airlines; Page 2; Line 8; Single; "5528 South Kenwood Av. Chivago [sic]."

2006. Michigan Obituaries, 1820-2006, database with images,"PIERCE, Mrs. Helen E. Kalamazoo, MI." (https://familysearch.org/ark:/61903/1:1:QVPB-TL7V : 1 April 2020), Edith C Wallace in entry for Mrs Helen E Pierce, 2000; citing Kalamazoo, Obituary, Grand Rapids Public Library, Michigan; FHL microfilm 7,596,621.

2007. Tombstone: (See findagrave.com); "Maynard B Pierce 1911-1982."

2008. Michigan Death Index, 1971-1996, Michigan Department of Vital and Health Records, Lansing, (https://www.familysearch.org/ark:/61903/1:1:VZB1-5QD : 10 August 2022), Maynard B Pierce, 1982. Certificate 39295.

2009. Find-A-Grave, (www.findagrave.com/memorial/140885949/maynard-b-pierce: accessed 29 September 2022). Memorial ID 140885949, citing Mount Ever-Rest Memorial Park South, Kalamazoo, Kalamazoo County, Michigan; maintained by Amy Dunn Hohler (contributor 47542889).

2010. Ironwood Daily Globe, newspaper, Ironwood, Michigan, "Division Manager," 2 June 1956, page 3.

2011. Wakefield News, newspaper, Wakefield, Michigan, "Standard Promotes M. B. Pierce," 8 June 1956, page 2.

2012. 1930 US Census, Cedar Rapids, Linn County, Iowa, NARA T626; Enumerations District 57-48; Sheet 2A; Dwelling 43; Family 43; Line 36; "Kathleen Clay."

2013. 1940 US Census, Minnesota, Hennepin County, Minnesota, NARA T627; Roll 1985; Sheet 8B; ED 89-254; Line 51; "Kathleen Clay."

2014. 1950 US Census, Los Angeles, Los Angeles County, California, April 1950, Record Group Number: 29; Residence Date: 1950; Home in 1950: Los Angeles, Los Angeles, California; Roll: 2061; Sheet Number: 12; ED: 66-1126; Line 14; "Kathleen Clay," Divorced.

2015. US Social Security Applications and Claims Index, 1936-2007, Dec 1937: Name listed as KATHLEEN MARGUERITE CLAY; Apr 1945: Name listed as KATHLEEN C BEIDLER; Oct 1952: Name listed as KATHLEEN PEARCE; 09 Mar 2000: Name listed as KATHLEEN C PEARCE.

2016. Minnesota Births and Christenings, 1840-1980, Minnesota Department of Health, Minneapolis, database, (https://familysearch.org/ark:/61903/1:1:F811-W81 : 5 February 2020), Eldon R. Clay in entry for Kathleen Marguerite Clay, 1920.

2017. 1940 US Census, Minnesota, Hennepin County, Minnesota.

2018. North County Times, newspaper, Oceanside, San Diego County, California, "Obituaries: Kathleen Pearce, 79," 16 February 2000, page B-7.

2019. Minneapolis Star, newspaper, Minneapolis, Minnesota, "Beidler-Clay," 24 March 1944, page 25.

2020. Marriage record/certificate/application. New York City Municipal Archives; New York, New York; Borough: Manhattan; Volume 10; number 6427.

2021. Birth Certificate/Record. Commonwealth of Pennsylvania, Bureau of Vital Statistics, Certificate of Birth; File 39864.

2022. Presbyterian Historical Society, U.S., Presbyterian Church Records, 1701-1947, Philadelphia, Pennsylvania, database with scanned image, Number 362; (ancestry.com image 158).

2023. Find-A-Grave, (www.findagrave.com/memorial/87440622/george-reed-beidler: accessed 27 October 2022). Memorial ID 87440622, citing Newville Cemetery, Newville, Cumberland County, Pennsylvania; maintained by Family Tree Climber (contributor 46591637).

2024. Commonwealth of Pennsylvania, World War II Veterans' Compensation Bureau, Application For World War II Compensation—To Be Used By Honorably Discharged Veteran or Person Still in Service, Pennsylvania Historical and Museum Commission, Harrisburg Pennsylvania, scanned image, Record Group 19, Series 19.92; Box 48.

2025. California, U.S., Marriage Index, 1949-1985, database with images, ancestry.com, Page 751; (ancestry.com image 366); state file 53416.

2026. GRO, Third Quarter of 1843; Volume 22; page 126; (ancestry.com image 16); (findmypast.com image 91).

2027. For definitions here: *proletariat* = working class people, usually without land ownership and not having control of the means of production or the product of their own labor; *bourgeoisie* = the class who own most of society's wealth and means of production; usually the rising oligarchy of managers and owners often lumped in with the bestowed or hereditary aristocratics.

2028. CLAY Family History: CLAY Name Meaning. www.familysearch.org/en/surname?surname=CLAY (viewed 20 October 2023).

2029. Clay of England Society: Clay of Yorkshire. sites.google.com/site/clayofengland/clay-of-yorkshire (viewed 20 October 2023).

2030. forebears.io forebears.io/surnames/clay | Dated as of 2014 CE. (viewed 20 October 2023).

2031. Origins of the Clay surname. www.findmypast.co.uk/surname/clay (viewed 20 October 2023).

2032. Name Origin Research Limited. SurnameDB: The Internet Surname Database. www.surnamedb.com/Surname/Pickles (viewed 21 July 2022). © Name Origin Research Limited. All Rights Reserved.

2033. "Grewelthorpe a North Yorkshire Village. Pickles Family." www.grewelthorpe.org.uk/family-history/pickles-family (viewed 21 July 2022).

2034. Where is the Pickles family from?" www.ancestry.co.uk/name-origin?surname=pickles (viewed 21 July 2022). © Ancestry.

2035. Paul Jackson Ribblesdale, "Scribble by the Ribble: Photos of the Yorkshire Dales" www.jacksoneditorial.co.uk/yorkshire-surnames/ (viewed 21 July 2022).

2036. Watts, Victor, ed. "Halifax" *The Cambridge Dictionary of English Place-Names,* Cambridge University Press, 2020.

2037. Clark, Dr. Gregory (1957). 2. *The British Industrial Revolution,* 1760-1860. ECN 110B, Spring 2005, World Economic History, paper.

2038. Ibid. page 2.

2039. Eden, Sir Frederick Morton. *State of the Poor,* 1797.

2040. Jenkins, David T., University of York. *Transatlantic Trade In Wollen Cloth 1850-1914: The Role Of Shoddy.* Textile Society of America Symposium Proceedings, 607. (1990), page 24.

2041. Other phrases left by the weavers lexicon were "to spin a yarn," "life is a shuttle," "to weave a tale," "to spin a yarn." Or Shakespeare's "The web of our life is of a mingled yarn, good and ill together" or later Sir Walter Scott's "Oh, what a tangled web we weave - When first we practise to deceive!"

2042. Wrigley, E. A.; Davies, R. S.; Oeppen, J. E.; Schofield, R. S. English *Population History from Family Reconstitution: 1580–1837.* New York: Cambridge University Press, 1997, page 149.

2043. Clark, page 17.

2044. *A vision of Britain Through Time.* University of Portsmouth, *et al.* www.visionofbritain.org.uk/census/table/

GB1841OCC_M%5B1%5D?u_id=10134640&show=DB (viewed 17 September 2022).

2045. en.wikipedia.org/wiki/History_of_Yorkshire#cite_ref-Hey_26-2. Referring to: Hudson, Pat. *The Genesis of Industrial Capital: A Study of West Riding Wool Textile Industry, c. 1750-1850*. Cambridge University Press (1986); page 71.

2046. Iwama, Toshihiko. *The Middle Class in Halifax, 1780-1850*. Paper, PhD candidate, University of Leeds, School of History, June 2003.

2047. Smail, John. *The Origins of Middle Class Culture: Halifax, Yorkshire, 1660-1780*. Ithaca, New York: Cornell University Press, 1994).

2048. Taggart, Michael. *Private Property and Abuse of Rights in Victorian England. The Story of Edward Pickles and the Bradford Water Supply*. New York: Oxford University Press, 2002.

2049. FamilySearch.org, "Victorian England Occupations in City and Town" www.familysearch.org/en/wiki/Victorian_England_Occupations_in_City_and_Town (viewed 20 October 2023).

2050. Gleaned from www.your-family-history.com, utilizing UK census records from 1841 to 1911.

2051. University of Oregon: "Mapping History: The Spread of Cotton and of Slavery 1790-1860—The Spread of Cotton: 1790–1860"; mappinghistory.uoregon.edu/english/US/US18-01.html

2052. Dattell, Eugene R., October 2006. Mississippi Department of Archives & History. "Mississippi History Now: Cotton in a Global Economy: Mississippi (1800-1860)" www.mshistorynow.mdah.ms.gov/issue/cotton-in-a-global-economy-mississippi-1800-1860#:~:text=Cotton accounted for over half,manufactured goods from the East.

2053. Jenkins, David T., "Transatlantic Trade In Woollen Cloth 1850-1914: The Role Of Shoddy." *Textile Society of America Symposium Proceedings*. 607. York, England: University of York, (1990), page 24.

2054. White, Ellen G. *Christian Experience and Teachings of Ellen G. White*. Nampa, Idaho: Pacific Press Publishing Association, Volume I, pages 151-155.

2055. The book, Volume I, from January 1833, is in possession of the author, and is in fragile condition. As far as known, it is the only copy to survive time. A newspaper advertisement notes "This day is Published, in Manchester, price 6d., No. I. Vol. I, of the Third Series (Vol. XXVI, since the Commencement)." Although a monthly magazine, it was compiled into a book, "Sold by W. Harding, 3, Paternoster-row, London; and by the Preachers in the Methodist New Connection." [sic] *The Patriot*, newspaper, London, 16 January 1833, page 1, (Volume II, number 52).

2056. "Illegitimacy in England"; www.familysearch.org/en/wiki/Illegitimacy_in_England

2057. B. R. Mitchell, *Abstract of British Historical Statistics*. Cambridge: Cambridge University Press, 1962; page 60.

2058. British Literature Wiki, University of Delaware. sites.udel.edu/britlitwiki/social-life-in-victorian-england/ (viewed 23 September 2023)

2059. In the front pastedown of a book she possessed in 1833, she acknowledges "Sally Tidwell['s] Book She was Born as Sarah 1813 [age] 19." See Source **2055**.

2060. www.norwayheritage.com/p_ship.asp?sh=tripo

2061. New York Times, 24 July 1860, page 4; "Letter to the Editor" from W. J. Hopkines, Presbyterian Minister, Welsh Church, Philadelphia, Pennsylvania.

2062. Leeds Intelligencer, (Vol. XXXI. No. 1584) 5 October 1784, page 1, fourth column from left.

2063. https://en.wikipedia.org/wiki/Worsted_Act_1776#cite_note-2
2064. Worsted Act 1776. https://vlex.co.uk/vid/worsted-act-1776-808244321 (17 Geo. 3) CAP. XI.
2065. *An Act for the Amendment and better Administration of the Laws relating to the Poor in England and Wales.* [14th August 1834.] Section 52: ANNO QUARTO & QUINTO| GULIELMI IV. Regis. CAP. LXXVI. (from https://www.workhouses.org.uk/poorlaws/1834act.shtm)
2066. The British Wool Marketing Board. *British Sheep & Wool: A guide to British sheep breeds and their unique wool.* Bradford, 2010; ISBN 978-3-16-14810-0.
2067. The UK National Archives. "Why did the Luddites protest?" https://www.nationalarchives.gov.uk/education/resources/why-did-the-luddites-protest/#:~:text=The Luddites have been described,of a new market system.
2068. FamilySearch.org "Illegitimacy in England: Parish Records." https://www.familysearch.org/en/wiki/Illegitimacy_in_England
2069. Gibson, Kate Louise. *Experiences of Illegitimacy in England, 1660-1834.* Thesis: University of Sheffield, March 2018, page 10.
2070. Embry-Riddle Aeronautical University, Daytona Beach, Florida, "Aviation Pioneers Association Project," https://commons.erau.edu/aviation-pioneers-association/airline/zantop-international-airlines/ (viewed 20 November 2023).
2071. Clayton, Paul, and Judith Rowbotham. "An unsuitable and degraded diet? Part two: realities of the mid-Victorian diet." *Journal of the Royal Society of Medicine* vol. 101,7 (2008): 350-7. doi:10.1258/jrsm.2008.080113 .
2072. Jane Engle, "Modern versus Civil War travel costs," Los Angeles Times, 10 April 2011; https://www.latimes.com/travel/la-xpm-2011-apr-10-la-tr-money-20110410-story.html#:~:text=In%201860%2C %20-Cunard%20Line%27s%20emigrant,in%20an%20interview%20last%20week.
2073. Timothy Hatton, University of Essex and IZA Institute of Labor Economics, Discussion Paper Series, IZA DP No. 16274, "Time on the Crossing: Emigrant Voyages across the Atlantic, 1853-1913," June 2023. https://docs.iza.org/dp16274.pdf
2074. *Fifteenth Annual Report of the Commissioner Of Labor.* Washington: Government Printing Office, U.S. Bureau of Labor, 1900. Volume 2, page 1631.
2075. Kathleen Townsley, "Descendants of John Clay" "john clay.pdf" report, page 7, November 2023, citing Halifax Antiquarian Society, Catalogue Finding Number HAS:103 (237)/126; Calderdale GB 203. (Viewed in November 2023.)
2076. Eaton Rapids Journal, newpaper, Eaton Rapids, Eaton County, Michigan. "Locals," 21 October 1892, page 5. (Courtesy of Fultonhistory.com, Thomas M. Tryniski, 309 South 4th Street, Fulton, New York 13069; viewed in November 2023.)
2077. Kathleen Townsley, "john clay.pdf" page 7-8, citing Halifax Antiquarian Society, Catalogue Finding Number HAS:104 (242)/251; Calderdale GB 203. (Viewed in November-December 2023.)
2078. Springport Signal, newspaper, Springport, Jackson County, Michigan, "Locals," 22 July 1898, page 5. (Courtesy of Fultonhistory.com, Thomas M. Tryniski, 309 South 4th Street, Fulton, New York 13069; viewed in November 2023.)
2079. Eaton Rapids Journal, "Otter Creek," 22 July 1898, page 1.
2080. Ibid., "Personals," 22 July 1898, page 5.

2081. Ibid., "Died," 30 January 1891, page 5.
2082. Ibid., "Baseline," 6 February 1891, page 1.
2083. Ibid., "Springport," 13 November 1885, page 1; "Thomas Clay has given up his position as clerk for Welllington & Co., at Deck Lake, and James M. Crosby has taken his place."
2085. Ibid., "Springport," 31 July 1885, page 1; "Thomas Clay has moved to Duck Lake to take charge of Gillette, Wellington & Co.'s store."
2086. Springport Signal, "Mrs. Jennie Clay: Passed Away Last Friday, After a Long Illness," 21 January 1915, page 1.
2087. Ibid., "Resolutions of Respect," 21 January 1915, page 1.
2088. Eaton Rapids Journal, 25 August 1882, no pagination, second column from left.
2089. Ibid., "Springport," 18 January 1895, page 1.
2090. Springport Signal, "Resolutions Of Respect," 15 September 1921, no pagination.
2091. Eaton Rapids Journal, "Forty Years Ago," 23 November 1928, no pagination; newspaper says Springport Township in contrast to Tompkins on marriage record. "…at the home of the bride's parents in Springport township…"
2092. Not found in 1950 US census.
2093. Eaton Rapids Journal, "Malcomb J. Clay, 8 April 1949, page 1.
2094. Springport Signal, 14 April 1949, no pagination.
2095. Charlotte Republican Tribune, newspaper, Charlotte, Eaton County, Michigan, "Personals," 15 April 1949, page 5.
2096. Charlotte Republican, newspaper, Charlotte, Eaton County, Michigan, "Eaton Rapids," 16 October 1902, page 8. "Miss Lou and Ethel Smoyer were in Onondaga to attend the wedding of their friend, Miss Lovan Harwood, and Mal. Clay on Wednesday evening."
2097. Charlotte Tribune, newspaper, Charlotte, Eaton County, Michigan, "Local News," 4 April 1917, page 5.
2098. Eaton Rapids Journal, "Local News," 30 March 1917, no pagination.
2099. Charlotte Republican Tribune, "County News: Rawson's Corners."30 March 1906, page 3.
2100. Ibid., "Real Estate Transfers," 24 February 1915, page 3.
2101. Ibid. "Fred Clay Given Thirty Days Term," 10 December 1928, page 1.
2102. Eaton Rapids Journal, "Court Activities," 11 October 1935, page 1.
2103. Charlotte Republican Tribune, "Fred Clay Is Found Guilty," 24 January 1936, page 1.
2104. Eaton Rapids Journal, "Court News," 6 May 1938, page 1.
2105. Charlotte Republican Tribune, "Maurer District," 5 March 1948, page 7; 12 March 1948, page 7.
2106. Ibid.,"Maurer District,"28 October 1934, page 2.
2107. Eaton Rapids Journal, "Otter Creek," 10 June 1898, page 1.
2108. Charlotte Republican Tribune, "Clay-Pasco," 29 August 1947, page 6.
2109. Ibid., 14 August 1925, no pagination. "Morrison Clay married Sarah Ledyard and they will live in the [2 words illegible]. They have one child. Morrison has a very good position in the Fred Morey drug store."
2110. Ibid., "What You Folks Talked About: Ten Years Ago," 18 January 1935, page 2. "A daughter, Shirley Joan, was born to Mr. and Mrs. Morrison Clay, Thursday, January 8th."
2111. Bellevue Gazette, newspaper, Bellevue, Eaton County, Michigan, "Marriage License Applications...," 17 December 1925, page 19. "Terry L. Lee, 24, automobile inspector, Jackson, and Miss A. Ilene Clay, 20, bookkeeper, Charlotte." And, "Other News Of The Courts," 24 De-

cember 1925, page 1. "... married Saturday at a four o'clock wedding held at the home of the bride's parents... by Dr. W. W. Diehl..."

2112. Kansas, U.S., Atchison, Topeka and Santa Fe Railway Prior Service Records, 1859-1935. (ancestry.com image 38); "Fred Krugman | 659 Ninth St., San Bernardino, Cal. | 11-29-84."

2113. Jackson Citizen Patriot, "Legals," 2 September 1941, page 2.

2114. Springport Signal, "Local Happenings," 20 November 1941; no pagination. "Parma's new machine shop is ready for production... Howard Zantop, of Parma, has been hired as a machinest and has been working during the past ten days."

2115. Kathleen Townsley, "john clay.pdf" page 315; citing Richard Carver, A History of Marshall, Marshall, Michigan, 1993. https://www.marshallmich.com/orderbook.htm#:~:text=BOOKS OF MARSHALL-,BY RICHARD CARVER,a period of seventy years.

2116. Kathleen Townsley, "john clay.pdf" page 315.

2117. Springport Signal, "Local And Personal," January 1910; no pagination.

2118. Ibid., 20 March 1918, no pagination; "Jess Orrison of Jackson and Miss Orpha Clay of Lansing, former Springport poung [sic] people, were married last week. They will live in Jackson."

2119. Ibid., "News From Our Boys In The Army," 11 February 1943, page 1.

2120. Kathleen Townsley, "john clay.pdf" page 321.

2121. Springport Signal, "Two Former Area People Died," 23 May 1968, no pagination.

2122. Evening Chronicle, Marshall, Michigan, 20 October 1930, page 2.

2123. Battle Creek Enquirer, "Boy, 17, Missing," 14 March 1936, page 3.

2124. Leggett, Grace Patchen, Jillson, Myrtle M., compiler-editor, The history and genealogy of the Patchin-Patchen family, Connecticut, Waterbury: The Patchin-En Family Association, 1952; page 405. Also cited from Kathleen Townsley, "Descendants of John Clay" page 328.

2125. Townsley, Kathleen, "john clay.pdf" page 329.

2126. Ibid., pages 330-331.

2127. Ibid., page 330.

2128. Find-A-Grave, (www.findagrave.com/memorial/94064467/doris-eleanor-roberts: accessed 13 December 2023). Memorial ID 94064467, citing Riverside Cemetery, Albion, Calhoun County, Michigan; maintained by Frank Passic, Albion Historian (contributor 46564182).

2129. Battle Creek Enquirer And News, Online, 23 July 2012; https://www.legacy.com/us/obituaries/battlecreek/name/doris-orrison-obituary?id=20634970 (viewed 13 December 2023).

2130. Townsley, Kathleen, "john clay.pdf" page 332.

2131. Note: He and wife are not found in the 1950 census.

2132. Springport Signal, "News From Our Boys In The Army," 11 February 1943, page 1.

2133. Army Times, newspaper, Washington, DC, "Top Group Named," 13 August 1960, page 26.

2134. Townsley, Kathleen, "john clay.pdf" page 334.

2135. Ibid., page 335.

2136. Ibid., page 336.

2137. Ibid.

2138. U.S., Index to Public Records, 1994-2019; ancestry.com; Voter Registration Lists, Public Record Filings, Historical Residential Records, and Other Household Database Listings. For full name.

2139. Townsley, Kathleen, "john clay.pdf" pages 337-338.

2140. Find-A-Grave (www.findagrave.com/memorial/21504216/charlyne-ella-clay: accessed 15 December 2023). Memorial ID 21504216, citing

Mount Hope Cemetery, Lansing, Ingham County, Michigan; maintained by Ed Houghtaling (contributor 46804583). Tombstone: "Charlyne Ella | Clay | Sept. 6, 1918 | Age 6 Months."

2141. "Texas, U.S., Arriving and Departing Passenger and Crew Lists, 1893-1963" (ancestry.com image 174); Passengers Embarked At Monterrey N.L. Mexico Arriving Aircraft, 28 July 1947, from El Paso, Texas. Birthplace is "Albion Mich." For her daughter, Helen Edith Wallace, birthplace is "Chicago, Ill."

2142. Ohio, U.S., Births and Christenings Index, 1774-1973, Columbus, Ohio: Ohio Vital Records Office, Ancestry.com, FHL Film Number 1294334.

2143. Viets, Francis Hubbard, A Genealogy of the Viets Family with Biographical Sketches: Dr. John Viets of Simsbury, Connecticut and his Descendants, Hartford, Connecticut: The Case, Lockwood & Brainard Company, 1902, page 125; (ancestry.com image 134).

2144. Death Certificate/Record. Indiana State Board Of Health, Division of Vital Records, Medical Certificate Of Death; State number 57 028873; Local number 211. Confirms World War I service. Informant: Mrs. Janet Wallace, wife.

2145. Find-A-Grave, (www.findagrave.com/memorial/250539675/ralph-robert-wallace: accessed 15 December 2023). Memorial ID 250539675, citing Carmel Cemetery, Carmel, Hamilton County, Indiana; Burial Details Unknown; maintained by N. Sharlene (Rice) Kent (contributor 47597667).

2146. Indianapolis News, "Robert Wallace is Buried," 11 September 1957, page 21.

2147. Noblesville Ledger, newspaper, Noblesville, Indiana, "Robert R. Wallace Dies At Carmel," 9 September 1957, page 6.

2148. US World War I Draft Registration Cards, 1917-1918, NARA, National Archives Building, Washington, DC., www.familysearch.org or www.ancestry.com.

2149. US World War II Draft Registration Cards, 1940-1947, NARA, (ancestry.com image 3564); Serial Number U1438.

2150. Web: Minnesota, U.S., Birth Index, 1900-1934, database, (ancestry.com). Original data: *Minnesota Birth Certificates Index*. Minnesota Historical Society. http://people.mnhs.org/bci/: accessed 18 Nov 2014; Certificate number 1904-11595.

2151. Minnesota, U.S., Death Index, 1908-2017; Minnesota Department of Health, Minneapolis, database, (ancestry.com). Certificate number 005277; record 2706082.

2152. Norweigian Danish Evangelical Lutheran Church, Willmar, Kandiychi County, Minnesota; (ancestry.com number 439); line 13.

2153. Kathleen Townsley, "john clay.pdf" page 368-370; citing anecdotal story and 30 January 1991 obituary, Clarkfield, Yellow Medicine County, Minnesota.

2154. Honolulu, Hawaii, U.S., Arriving and Departing Passenger and Crew Lists, 1900-1959; database with image. List 194 (ancestry.com image 590); compiled 02/13/1900 - 12/30/1953; NAI : A4156; Record Group Title: Records of the Immigration and Naturalization Service, 1787 - 2004; Record Group: RG 85.

2155. Eaton Rapids Journal, "A Pleasant Surprise," 23 March 1883, no pagination.

2156 Calderdale Family History Society, Baptisms, database; https://www.cfhsweb.com/cfhs-database/baptisms_list.php?menuItemId=2 (viewed 9 January 2024); ID 259800; Father's Abode: Warley; Trade:

Comber; Registry 1685; birth date 31 May 1843; Page 211; Parish: Luddenden St. Mary; Mother: Hannah.

2157. Calderdale Family History Society, Municipal Cemeteries, database; https://www.cfhsweb.com/cfhs-database/municipal_cemeteries_list.php (viewed 9 January 2024); ID 2968; Entry 2963; Grave C324d; Occupation: Pauper; Abode: Workhouse; Death: Workhouse; Informant: W Jas Dutton; Denomination Vicar of Pellon.

2158. Halifax Guardian, 24 November 1866, page 8; cited from Calderdale Family History Society, Newspapers, database; ID 240444; Event 12.

2159. Citing Linda Klinghagen in john clay.pdf, "Descendants of John Clay" by Kathleen Marie O'Dell Townsley, pages 368-369.

2160. West Yorkshire Archive Service. Workhouses. Database. Halifax-HAS:217; cited from Calderdale Family History Society, https://www.cfhsweb.com/cfhs-database/workhouses_list.php?q=(Surname~equals~clay); viewed 2 July 2024.

2161. Halifax Guardian, 18 March 1871, page 8; "Clay, March 13th, aged 65 Isaac Clay, joiner, workhouse, this town"; transcription from Central Library and Archives, Halifax, England.

2162. Record of Kent County soldiers and sailors in service in the Great War. Volume Ka-Kz. Grand Rapids History Center, Grand Rapids Public Library, Grand Rapids, Michigan. Original viewed by the author in the 1980's, now cited as https://archive.grpl.org/repositories/4/archival_objects/33238.

2163. Death Certificate/Record. Arizona State Department Of Health, Bureau Of Vital Statistics, Certificate Of Death, file 1503; Informant: Wife * Mary Myers.

2164. Find-A-Grave, (www.findagrave.com/memorial/184413446/joseph_william-myers: accessed July 4, 2024). Memorial ID 184413446, citing Oak Hill Cemetery, Land O' Lakes, Vilas County, Wisconsin; maintained by GeeGee (contributor 48224284).

2165. 1950 US Census, Land O'Lakes, Vilas County, Wisconsin, April 1950, "Barber | Barber Shop."

2166. Marriage record; State Of California; Certificate Of Registry Of Marriage, Book 3611, page 374; File 21616.

2167. *Popular Mechanics*, "Mechanics for Young America: Young Mechanic Builds Successful Auto"; March 1907, pages 350-351.

2168. Copy. Declaration of Intention. State of Michigan. Courtesy of Kathleen Townsley; john clay.pdf page 29.

2169. "Onondaga Girl Is Recent Bride: Mrs. Herbert E. Howe" Lansing State Journal, 10 July 1929, page 13.

2170. Delphian of 1921. Charlotte, Eaton County, Michigan: Charlotte High School Senior Class, 1921, page 21; (ancestry.com image 23). "Sarah D. Ledyard" — she apparently dropped the "h" in Sarah at a later date.

INDEX: ABEGAIL'S CHILDREN

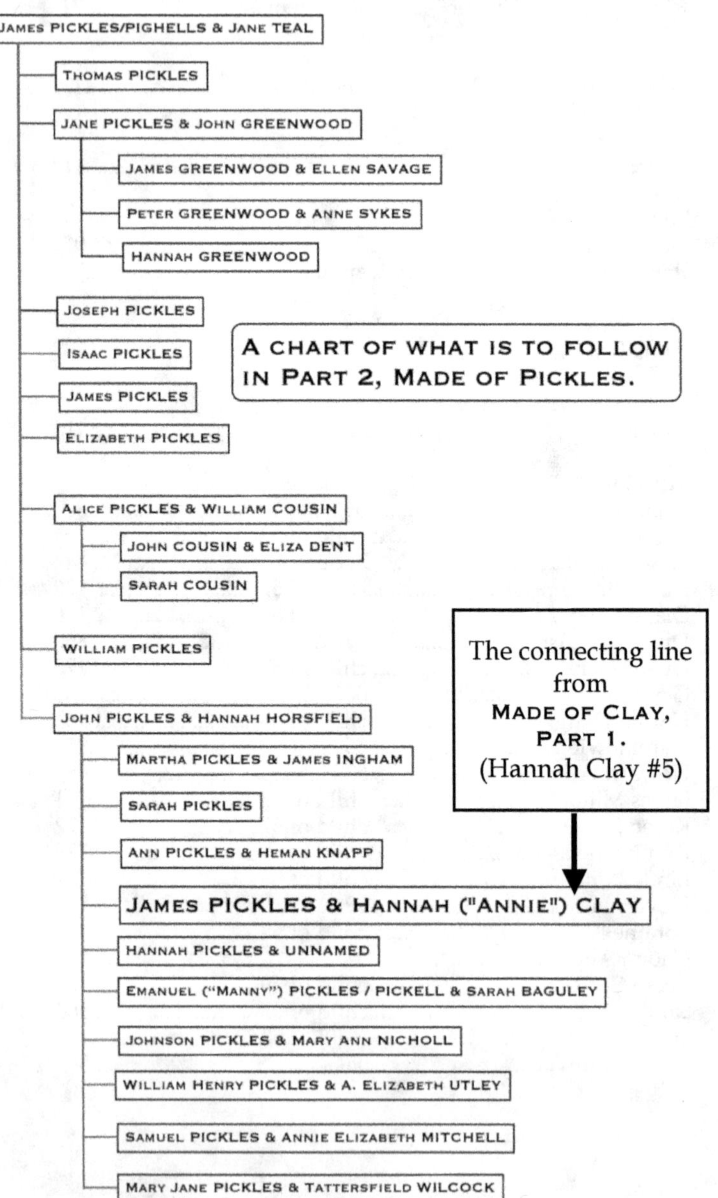

James PICKLES/PIGHELLS & Jane TEAL
Thomas PICKLES
Jane PICKLES & John GREENWOOD
James GREENWOOD & Ellen SAVAGE
Peter GREENWOOD & Anne SYKES
Hannah GREENWOOD
Joseph PICKLES
Isaac PICKLES
James PICKLES
Elizabeth PICKLES
A chart of what is to follow in Part 2, Made of Pickles.
Alice PICKLES & William COUSIN
John COUSIN & Eliza DENT
Sarah COUSIN
William PICKLES
The connecting line from Made of Clay, Part 1. (Hannah Clay #5)
John PICKLES & Hannah HORSFIELD
Martha PICKLES & James INGHAM
Sarah PICKLES
Ann PICKLES & Heman KNAPP
JAMES PICKLES & HANNAH ("ANNIE") CLAY
Hannah PICKLES & UNNAMED
Emanuel ("Manny") PICKLES / PICKELL & Sarah BAGULEY
Johnson PICKLES & Mary Ann NICHOLL
William Henry PICKLES & A. Elizabeth UTLEY
Samuel PICKLES & Annie Elizabeth MITCHELL
Mary Jane PICKLES & Tattersfield WILCOCK

PART 2: MADE OF PICKLES

FIRST GENERATION

1. James PIGHELLS.[1-5]

Born on 9 July 1778, in Whitkirk, Yorkshire.[6,7] James was baptized in Dewsbury Road, Yorkshire, on 15 July 1778,[8,9] at All Saints Church. James died in Yorkshire, in July 1820; he was 41.[10] Buried on 21 July 1820, in Whitkirk, Yorkshire,[11] at Saint Mary.

James Pickles and his wife, Jane Teal, are known from their children's church birth and marriage records. James and Jane are the earliest PICKLES family the author undertook to research. Brevity, sparse records and commonality of names and locations restricted research for earlier ancestors.

We can verify from the baptisms of the children, particularly son **10. John** (1816-1890), that the parents are James and Jane of Newsholme.* James's birth and death come nearest to other information provided, going by possible ages of having children and marriage.

SPECULATIVE: James's parents have a few suspects based upon baptismal year:

1. "1778 [July] 11 - James Son of **David Pickles** baptized." from St. Peter and St. Leonard Church, Horbury, West Yorkshire.[12] [baptized 11 July 1778]
2. First name(s): James | Last name: **Pighills** | Birth year: 1778 | Birth date: 09 Jul 1778 | Baptism date: 14 Jul 1778 | Father's first name(s): **William** | Mother's first name(s): **Hannah** | Baptism place: Whitkirk[13,14]
3. "Baptism 1778" | "July" | "James S[on] of **Mark Pickles**" | [of] "Soothill" | "Day 15"[15] [baptized 15 July 1778]
4. James Pickles, baptized 31 July 1779, Holmfirth, Yorkshire; father: **John Pickles**.[16]

*Newsholme is a hamlet in the East Riding of Yorkshire. It is approximately two miles (3.2 km) northwest of the market town of Howden. The history around 1803 is unknown. However, in 1870-72, John Marius Wilson's *The Imperial Gazetteer of England and Wales* (Volume 5, page 446) describes "NEWSHOLME, a hamlet in Keighley parish, W[est] R[iding] Yorkshire; under Blackstone Edge, near Keighley." (The most likely place of our Pickles).

5. James Pickles, baptized 25 June 1780, born 29 April 1780; [abode] = Holbeck; Leeds, St. Peter, Yorkshire; father: **Joseph Pickles**[17]

One ancestry.com researcher, Ruth Illingsworth, has convincing data that alludes James' father was **Mark Pickles**, and his mother was Elizabeth Hartley (Mark's first wife, second wife was Elizabeth Castle). Mark's alleged parents were James Pickles (1727-1800) and Martha Hargraves (1726-1760).

Available records limit the literal surname PIGHILLS to James born 1778 and married in 1800. There are no other possible suggestions when birth parameters 1770-1780 and marriage parameters 1790-1820, were performed. On findmypast.co.uk there are nine possibilities due to the known birth/baptismals of the children. Ancestry.com limits to one for a marriage record (same as findmypast), none for baptism/birth of 1778. Familysearch.org has 12 birth/baptismal possibilities with various parents; of note:

A. *[with the greatest possibility because the Pickles family frequented this church]:* "**James** Pickles, bap. 10 August 1777, Halifax, St. John the Baptist; father 'Jno' [Jonathan] Pickles"[18] *Other family names appear in the register: Clay, Ingham, Greenwood, Sutcliffe, Mitchell.* However, there is another entry (see B below) for 17 August 1783 for the same people. His possible death record: [*Most likely based upon birth and residence and burial locations]* July 1820, age 42; Abode: Leeds[22] or possibly 29 March 1856, Calderdale, Wakefield, Birchcliffe Yorkshire, number "1435 James Pickles, Foster Lane, aged 76" [born circa 1780].[23]
B. **Jonathan**, 17 August 1783 (2 records), Halifax; baptized 17 August 1783, Halifax, St. John The Baptist, "Jas. [James] Jno. [Jonathan] Pickles Sk. [believed to be of Skircoat] Weaver"[18]
C. **George**, 1 Jan 1778, Illingworth;[19]
D. **William**, 3 Feb 1779, Eastwood (2, same);[20] Another good possibility because this is from a non-conformist church.
E. **John**, 31 July 1779, Kirkburton;
F. **Joseph**, 25 June 1780, (2 records) Leeds;
G. **Eli**, 15 September 1782 (2 records), Halifax; [21]
H. **James**, 11 July 1783 (2 records), Halifax.

But we know on 5 October 1800, age 22, **James PIGHILLS** married **Jane TEAL** in Keighley, Yorkshire,[24-27] under the Church of England. *This record is verified:*

First name(s): James | Last name: Pighells
Marriage year: 1800 | Marriage date: 05 Oct 1800
Marriage place: Keighley
Spouse's first name(s): Jane | Spouse's last name: Teal
County: Yorkshire[32]

This is the only realistic marriage found since the children have the same parents.

So, who are Jane TEAL's parents?

Based upon Yorkshire listings: "Jane Daughter of Robert Teal of Sutton Woolcomber and Mary his Wife 28 Augt" [August 1782]; recorded 5 January 1783.[28,29] (However, Kildwick-in-Craven is a bit geographically north of the expected research area; but more *realistic in age* at marriage: 17, as the marriage record indicates Jane and James as minors—under 21 years of age according to the law at that time).

But also possibly: "Bapt. July 12. [1774] Jane Dau. of Joseph Teal, Weston Parish Register, Yorkshire.[30] *(more realistic based upon location)*

> DISPROVED: "Baptisms Dec 27 [1772] Jane D. of Jonathan Teal, born May 5. 1767" St. Wilfrid, Calverly, West Yorkshire[31] (making her age 33 at marriage, so we discount this because of the marriage record).

James and Jane had the following 10 children:

2 i. **Thomas PICKLES**. Born on 6 October 1801, in Keighley, Yorkshire.

3 ii. **Jane PICKLES**. Born on 24 July 1803, in Keighley. Jane died in Bradford, Yorkshire, on 1 April 1852; she was 48.

4 iii. **Joseph PICKLES**. Born on 20 December 1804, in Keighley.

5 iv. **Isaac PICKLES**. Born on 16 November 1806, in Keighley.

6 v. **James PICKLES**. Born on 28 May 1808, in Keighley.

7 vi. **Elizabeth PICKLES**. Born on 12 February 1810, in Keighley

8 vii. **Alice PICKLES**. Born on 10 February 1812, in Keighley. Alice died in Yorkshire, in July 1872; she was 60.

9 viii. **William PICKLES**. Born on 22 June 1813, in Keighley.

10 ix. **John PICKLES**. Born on 15 November 1816, in Keighley. John died in Newland Warley, Halifax, Yorkshire, on 15 June 1890; he was 73.

Pickles and Sugden. 9

1 Joseph Pickles. Son of James and Jane Pickles of Newsholm was born December the twentieth. One thousand eight hundred and four.

2 Isaac Pickles; son of James and Jane Pickles of Newsholm. Was born November the sixteenth. One thousand eight hundred and six.

3 James Pickles. son of James and Jane Pickles of Newsholm. Was born May the twenty eight, One thousand eight hundred and eight.

4 Elizabeth Pickles daughter of James and Jane Pickles of Newsholm was born February the twelfth. One thousand eight hundred and ten.

5 William Pickles Son of James and Jane Pickles of Newsholm Was born June the ~~twenty~~ One thousand eight hundred and thirteen.

6 Alice Pickles daughter of James and Jane Pickles of Newsholm was born February the tenth One thousand eight hundred and twelve.

7 John Pickles. Son of James and Jane Pickles of Newsholm. Was born November the fifteenth. One thousand eight hundred and sixteen.

1813

8 Mary Sugden. daughter of Abraham and Mary Sugden of Newsholm. Was born January the twenty second. One thousand eight hundred and nine.

9 Ann Sugden. daughter of Abraham and Mary Sugden of Newsholm. born March the twenty third. One thousand eight hundred

A page from the Keighley, Bethel Chapel (Baptist); Register of Births, Marriages and Deaths; listing the births of seven of the children of **James Pighells** and **Jane Teal**: (4) Joseph, (5) Isaac, (6) James, (7) Elizabeth, (9) William, (8) Alice and (10) John Pickles. RG4/3393; (ancestry.com image 12).

SECOND GENERATION

2. Thomas PICKLES (*James PICKLES/PIGHELLS*[1]).

Born on 6 October 1801, in Keighley, Yorkshire,[33,34] probably near Keighley, Yorkshire. Christened on 15 August 1802, in Keighley, Yorkshire;[35] Independent or Congregational Church.

Possible death: Parish of Highley; Thomas Pickles, age 31 [born 1801]; burial: 11 June 1832, Keighley; Abode: Hollings Haworth.[36]

Possible death: Parish of Dewsbury; Thomas Pickles, age 35 [born 1801]; burial: 2 June 1836; Abode: Ossett[37]

DISPROVED: 1841 Census: Thomas Pickles, 40, Worsted Weaver | Nancy Pickles [assumed wife], 35, Worsted Weaver.[38] *NOT ours!* Found a death/burial where he names his wife Nanny and mother as Betty. (There are four other records born in Yorkshire, born ca 1801.)

3. Jane PICKLES[39,40] (*James PICKLES/PIGHELLS*[1]).

Born on 24 July 1803, in Keighley, Yorkshire,[41,42] Jane was baptized in Keighley, Yorkshire, on 31 August 1803,[43-45] as a Baptist. Jane died in Bradford, Yorkshire, on 1 April 1852; she was 48.[46-48]

Occupation: Stuff Manager (1841); Stay Maker (1851).[49,50]

DOUBTFUL: married to George Lofthouse, both of the Bolton-by-Bowland parish, Lancashire, 3 January 1823. A "Thomas Pickles" (her brother?) was as witness to the marriage.[51]

She likely married **John GREENWOOD**; of Hainworth, 4 June 1827, at Bingley, All Saints Church.[52] The 1841 census has "John and Jane Greenwood" in Bingley, Yorkshire. The parents' ages were rough estimates at age "35."[39] In the 1851 census of Bingley, she clearly is born in Keighley, living on "Baptist Row" in Bingley, which is consistent with Pickles non-conformist records; but All Saints Church was Anglican.[53] (Again, the established Angelian Church required registration.) By the

1861 census, John was a widower with only Hannah, 20, living with him.

So, on 4 June 1827, when Jane was 23, she married **John GREENWOOD**[54-56] in Bingley, Yorkshire, at the All Saints Anglican Church.[52,57] He was born circa 1806 in Carlton, Yorkshire.[58] There are too many "John Greenwood" entries to ascertain who are his parents were.

Occupation: Weaver (1833); Stuff Manager (1841); Wool Handfuller (1851); Weaver (1861).[59-61]

After Jane's death he possibly married Ellen GARNET.[62]

Jane and John had the following children:

11 i. **James GREENWOOD**. Born on 20 May 1833, in Bingley, Yorkshire, James died in Keighley, Yorkshire, on 2 November 1893; he was 60.

12 ii. **Peter GREENWOOD**. Born circa 1836, in Bingley, Yorkshire.

13 iii. **Hannah GREENWOOD**. Born in November 1840, in Bingley, Yorkshire.

---

4. Joseph PICKLES (*James PICKLES/PIGHELLS*[1]).

Born on 20 December 1804, in Keighley, Yorkshire,[63-66] Joseph was baptized in Keighley, Yorkshire, at[67] Bethel Baptist.

There are too many "Joseph Pickles" in the area to ascertain his identity and life after birth and baptismal records.

---

5. Isaac PICKLES (*James PICKLES/PIGHELLS*[1]).

Born on 16 November 1806, in Keighley, Yorkshire.[63,68-71] Isaac was baptized in Keighley, Yorkshire,[67] at Bethel Baptist.

Possibly married to:

A. Rebecca Cousins, married 19 Oct. 1829, Keighley, Yorkshire.[72] "13 Rebecca d[aughter] of John & Sally Cousin born Feb. 19th [1808] Oakworth Hall The Parish"[73] Rebecca had a twin brother, Isaac, recorded on the same ledger

B. Susannah Banks, married 2 March 1828, Keighley, Yorkshire[74]

There are too many "Isaac Pickles" in the area within the same time frames to ascertain positive identity.

6. James PICKLES (*James PICKLES/PIGHELLS[1]*).

Born on 28 May 1808, in Keighley, Yorkshire.[63,75-77] James was baptized in Keighley, Yorkshire.[78]

There are too many "James Pickles" in the area to ascertain his identity and life after birth and baptismal records.

7. Elizabeth PICKLES (*James PICKLES/PIGHELLS[1]*).

Born on 12 February 1810, in Keighley, Yorkshire.[63,79,80,81] Elizabeth was baptized in Keighley, Yorkshire, at Bethel Baptist.

There are too many "Elizabeth Pickles" in the area to ascertain her identity and life after birth and baptismal records.

8. Alice PICKLES[82-85] (*James PICKLES/PIGHELLS[1]*).

Born on 10 February 1812, in Keighley, Yorkshire.[63,86-89] Alice was baptized in Keighley, Yorkshire,[67] at Bethel Baptist. Alice died in Yorkshire, in July 1872; she was 60.[90] Buried on 10 July 1872, in Ingrow And Hainworth, Yorkshire,[91] at Saint John Cemetery.

Occupations: Weaver (1841); Laborer's Wife (1861); Pauper (1871).[92-94]

On 6 September 1830, when Alice was 18, she married **William COUSIN**,[95-97] son of John COUSIN and Mary _____, in Keighley, Yorkshire.[98,99] He was born on 5 November 1811, in Keighley.[100,101] At the age of 47, William was baptized in Oakworth, West Yorkshire, on 20 June 1859,[102] at Christ Church. William died in Keighley, in January 1868; he was 56.[103] Buried on 19 January 1868 in Ingrow And Hainworth, Yorkshire,[104] at St. John Cemetery.

Occupations: Weaver (1837, 1841, 1851); Laborer (1861).[105-107]

They had the following children:

14 i. **John COUSIN**. Born on 12 August 1836, in Bingley, Yorkshire. John died in Yorkshire, in April 1875; he was 38.

15 ii. **Sarah COUSIN**. Born circa 1840, in Bingley, Yorkshire.

9. William PICKLES (*James PICKLES/PIGHELLS*[1]).

Born on 22 June 1813, in Keighley, Yorkshire.[63,108-110] William was baptized in Keighley, Yorkshire, at Bethel Baptist.

There are too many "William Pickles" in the area to further ascertain his identity and life after birth and baptismal records.

10. John PICKLES[111-118] (*James PICKLES/PIGHELLS*[1]).

Born on 15 November 1816, in the West Riding, Keighley, Yorkshire.[63,119-121] John was baptized in 1816, and died in Newland Warley, Halifax, Yorkshire, on 15 June 1890; he was 73.[122,-124]

Occupations: Wool Comber (1837-1890); Farmer (1871, 1878, 1881 "Of 8 Acres," 1888).[125-130]

Religion: Baptist.

On 21 July 1835, when John was 18, he married **Hannah HORSFIELD,**[112,132-136] daughter of Abraham HORSFIELD and Hannah BROADBENT, in Warley, Halifax, Yorkshire;[137-142] recorded in St. James Church. She was born in September 1815, in Halifax, Yorkshire.

Hannah was baptized in Sowerby, Yorkshire, on 17 September 1815,[143,144] at the Chapelry of Sowerby. She died at Standsfield, "Cross Stone-road," Yorkshire, on 3 November 1889; she was 74.[145-148]

Her *Occupation*: Wool Comber (1851); Worsted Weaver (1861).[125,149]

John and Hannah had the following 10 children:

(Four sons are uniquely recorded together for their births and baptisms: Emanuel, Johnson, William Henry, and Samuel on one page![131])

16 i. **Martha PICKLES**. Born circa 1836, in Warley; Hightown, Sub-District Of Liversedge And Heckmondwike, Yorkshire. Martha died in Halifax, Yorkshire, on 14 February 1887; she was 51.

17 ii. **Sarah PICKLES**. Born on 23 September 1837, in Ovenden, Yorkshire.

18 iii. **Ann PICKLES**. Born on 17 December 1840, in South Cloughheat, Warley, Yorkshire. Ann died in Hamlin Township, Eaton County, Michigan, on 28 January 1901; she was 60.

iv. **James PICKLES.**[150-157] Born on 31 May 1843, in Warley; Roils Head, Yorkshire.[158-161]

James was baptized in Luddenden, Yorkshire, on 5 October 1843,[162-164] Parish of Halifax, Chapelry of Luddenden; Saint Mary. James died in Douglass Township, Montcalm County, Michigan, on 8 February 1911; he was 67.[165-167] Buried on 10 February 1911 in Douglass Township, Montcalm County, Michigan,[168] at Entrican Cemetery.

This is the PICKLES record that is connected to his wife Hannah CLAY in Part 1 (see #5, Third Generation)[125,169-201]

10. *John PICKLES with daughter* **24**. *Mary Jane PICKLES.*

An interesting story involving **10**. *John Pickles and his testimony of a death of a boarder in his home.* – Bradford Observer *(Bradford, West Yorkshire), 5 April 1838, page 3.*

INQUESTS BEFORE G. DYSON, ESQ.

On Thursday last, at the house of Mr. Thomas Barraclough, the Bishop Blaize Inn, in Westgate, a highly respectable jury was summoned to inquire into the circumstances of the death of Thomas Bates, a woolcomb broachmaker, who, on the Tuesday preceding, hung himself in his lodgings in Thompson's Buildings, Silsbridge Lane. John Pickles, woolcomber, deposed: Thomas Bates came to lodge at my house on the 16th December last, and has lived with me ever since. He was a woolcomb broachmaker; he was 73 years of age; he was still able to work. He belonged to Halifax. He was poorly about six weeks, and was rather low spirited; we endeavoured to cheer him up; he got to his work again after his illness. He lost his work owing to the depression of trade. He was a good deal depressed in spirits during the last week, but he did not want for anything. I believe he received some relief from Halifax during the fortnight he was out of work. He was engaged to work with Mr. Binns in High-street, as soon as he got his shop ready. On Monday he had been with Mr. Binns's men; they had been having a footing, and he came home drunk on Monday night; he came in at about a quarter past ten, and went to bed soon after. He said Mr. Binns's men had given him drink, and they perhaps thought it would do him good, but he knew whether it would or not. At noon on Tuesday I asked him to get up and have a little broth with me, but he would not. He said he could not sup any. I left him in bed. At about half past one o'clock I went out to wash some wool, and was away about an hour and a quarter. There was no person left in the house but himself. When I came back home, I found the door shut as I left it. As soon as I got the door opened I saw his legs and feet, as I thought, on the stairs. The stairs foot door is directly opposite to the house door. I did not think he was hanging. He seemed to be resting with his arms on the chamber floor, as if he was reaching for something from the chamber. I put down my wool, and said to him, 'Thomas, do you want something; I'll come and fetch it if you do?' Receiving no answer, I went up to him, and I saw he was hanging from the stairs rail. I immediately went to the house door and gave an alarm. I did not wait of others coming in, but I cut him down directly. Sarah Warburton was the first person who came in. He was quite cold. I went for the constable. The last meal he had at my house was on Monday noon. He was a married man, but had been separated from his wife a considerable time. His wife resides in Lancashire. There was no farther evidence.—After consulting together, the jury returned a verdict—*Hanged himself whilst labouring under temporary insanity.*

19 v. **Hannah PICKLES**. Born on 31 December 1847, in Warley, Popplewells, District Of Luddenden County Of York. Superintendent Registrar District: Halifax. Hannah died at "65 Crossley Terrace" in Halifax, Yorkshire, on 13 April 1880; she was 32.

20 vi. **Emanuel "Manny" PICKLES / PICKELL**. Born on 7 January 1850, in Ovenden, Yorkshire. Emanuel died in Jackson, Jackson County, Michigan, on 6 January 1915; he was 64.

21 vii. **Johnson PICKLES**. Born on 4 February 1852, in Ovenden, Yorkshire. Johnson died in Jackson, Jackson County, Michigan, on 4 October 1917; he was 65.

22 viii. **William Henry PICKLES**. Born on 18 November 1854, in Yorkshire. William died in Jackson, Jackson County, Michigan, on 8 June 1914; he was 59.

23 ix. **Samuel PICKLES**. Born on 13 June 1857, in Ivehouse Lane, Warley, Yorkshire. Samuel died in Bowling Green, Warren County, Kentucky, on 24 May 1925; he was 67.

24 x. **Mary Jane PICKLES**. Born on 13 February 1862, in Warley, Yorkshire, at Apple House. Mary Jane died in Yorkshire, in August 1925; she was 63.

Third Generation

In Ever Loving Memory of
JAMES GREENWOOD,
of Sutton Mill,
Who Died Nov. 2nd 1893, Aged 60 Years.
Also of ELLEN, His Wife
Who Died At Steeton,
June 7th 1910, Aged 77 Years.
Also of HANNAH, Their Daughter
Who Died at Ivy Bank Terrace, Haworth,
Dec. 23rd 1877, Aged 4 Years.
And SARAH HANNAH, Their Daughter
Who Died May 8th 1883, Aged 20 Years.
Also of LILLIE, Their Daughter,
Who Died March 27th 1940, Aged 81 Years.

11. *James GREENWOOD. Photograph by Dianne Harbourne, findagrave.com*

---

11. James GREENWOOD[202-208] (*Jane PICKLES*[2], *James PICKLES/ PIGHELLS*[1]). Born on 20 May 1833, in Bingley, Yorkshire,[209]

James was baptized in Haworth, Yorkshire, on 13 October 1833,[210,211] at Saint Michael and All Angels Anglican Church. James died in Keighley, Yorkshire, on 2 November 1893; he was 60.[212] Buried in Haworth, Yorkshire,[213] at West Lane Baptist Chapel cemetery.

Occupation: Wool Sorter (1851-1891); Mill Overlooker (1893).[214-219]

On 24 March 1856, when James was 22, he married **Ellen SAVAGE,**[220-226] daughter of John SAVAGE and Ellen _____, in Bingley, Yorkshire,[227] at the Parish Church. She was born circa 1833 in Gobenorth, Lancashire,[228] and died "14 Station Road Steeton R.D." in Steeton Village, Bradford, West Yorkshire, on 7 June 1910; she was 77.[229,230] Buried in Haworth, Yorkshire, England,[231] at West Lane Baptist Chapel cemetery.

Occupation: Power Loom Weaver (1851); Spinster (1856).[232]

James and Ellen had the following nine children:

i. **Lillie GREENWOOD.**[233-239,226] Born on 9 June 1857, in Denholme, Thornton, Yorkshire. Lillie died in Bradford, Yorkshire, on 27 March 1940; she was 82. She never married.

ii. **Jane GREENWOOD.**[240-245] Born on 1 February 1859, in "Blackmires," Northowram, Halifax, Yorkshire. Jane married **George Alfred PILMOOR**. The had one known child, **Earnest Alfred PILMOOR** (1896-1984), who married **Kate WRAY**.

iii. **Lucy Ellen GREENWOOD.**[246-249] Born on 12 November 1860, in "Blackmirer," Northowram, Halifax, Yorkshire. Lucy died in Eastfield, Sutton Mill, Yorkshire, on 10 February 1893; she was 32. She married **Frederick Petty CLOUGH**, and they had three children:

- **Thomas Douglas CLOUGH** (1890-1943), Thomas married **Alice** ____, but had no known children. He was in the Merchant Navy and died in World War II, in action; buried at sea.
- **Minnie Mildred CLOUGH** (1891-1967), who apparently never married.
- **Bertram Greenwood CLOUGH** (1893-1918). Bertram died in action, at the Somme, France, during World War I; he never married. "Miss Greenwood, Station Road, Steeton, received the sad news on Wednesday morning that her nephew, Pte. Bertie

Clough, of the Tyneside Scottish, had been killed in action. An officer of the battery writes that Pte. Clough was killed instantly by an enemy shell whilst advancing. He was most willing and faithful in all he undertook, and his death is a great loss to the battery. Pte. Clough, who is the son of Mr. Frederick Clough, of Crosshills, joined the army in April, 1916. He has been wounded on three occasions, and a little over 12 months ago was seriously wounded in the leg. He only returned to France about a month ago. Previous to joining the army he was employed as a warp-dresser by Messrs. John Clough and Sons."[778]

Bertram Greenwood CLOUGH
Attributed photograph submitted by findagrave.com maintainer Coleman.

iv. **Sarah Hannah GREENWOOD.**[250,251,226] Born on 31 January 1863, in Thornton, Yorkshire, Denholme. Sarah died in Keighley, Yorkshire, on 8 May 1883; she was 20.

v. **John GREENWOOD.** [252,253] Born on 3 December 1864, in Cullingworth, Bingley, Yorkshire.

vi. **Ada GREENWOOD.**[254-256] Born on 10 April 1867, in Queensbury, Clayton, Yorkshire. Ada died in East Lee, Stansfield, Yorkshire, on 15 October 1895; she was 28.

vii. **Joseph Edward GREENWOOD.**[257-259] Born in December 1869, in Queensbury, Clayton, Yorkshire. Joseph Edward died after 1891; he was 21.

viii. **Matilda GREENWOOD.**[260-264,226] Born on 21 May 1872, in Haworth, Yorkshire, Bents. Matilda died on 19 December 1940; she was 68. She married **Frederick Charles ENTWISTLE** in 1893, they had three known children.

ix. **Hannah GREENWOOD.**[226] Born circa 1873. Hannah died in Ivy Bank Terrace, Haworth, Yorkshire, on 23 December 1877; she was four years old.

12. Peter GREENWOOD[265-272] (*Jane PICKLES*[2], *James PICKLES/PIGHELLS*[1]).

Born circa 1836, in Bingley, Yorkshire.[273]

Occupation: Worsted Spinner (1851); Overlooker (1856-1901).[274-278]

On 22 June 1856, when Peter was 20, he married **Anne SYKES,**[270,279-283] daughter of William SYKES, in Bingley, Yorkshire, England,[284,285] at All Saints Church. She was born circa 1826 in Dewsbury Road, Yorkshire. Anne died before 1911; she was 85.[286]

Occupation: Dress Maker (1861).[287]

In the 1901 census, she is living slightly different from husband Peter Greenwood. He at #68 Westminster Road, she and daughter from a previous marriage, Sarah Moulson, at #66 Westminster Road.

They had no children.

13. Hannah GREENWOOD[39,288,289] (*Jane PICKLES*[2], *James PICKLES/PIGHELLS*[1]).

Born in November 1840, in Bingley, Yorkshire. Too numerous "Hannah Greenwood" identities to confirm after her birth. The GRO does not record convincing evidence of parentage.

14. John COUSIN[290-293] (*Alice PICKLES*[2], *James PICKLES/PIGHELLS*[1]).

Born on 12 August 1836, in Bingley, Yorkshire.[294] John was baptized in Haworth, Yorkshire, on 23 February 1837,[295] at St. Michael and All Angels. John died in Yorkshire, in April 1875; he was 38.[296] Buried on 9 April 1875, in Ingrow And Hainworth, Yorkshire,[297] at St. John Cemetery.

Occupation: Tailor (1851, 1861, 1871, 1875).[298,299,300]

There is much conflicting data on his marriage and children. A closely matched marriage record says he was married to Eliza DENT, but records of the children say mothers maiden name was TAYLOR. Did John COUSIN have a previous marriage to a "Eliza Taylor"? No marriage records can confirm this. We must *tentatively identify* these children with Eliza DENT. John was unmarried as of the 1861 census.

John apparently died a month before his son Dale, in 1875. No record of his death is found in the GRO. His burial, however, was found.

In 1865, when John was 28, he married **Eliza DENT,**[301-303] daughter of George Vicars DENT and Mary _____, in Hotham, Yorkshire.[304-306] She was born circa 1845, in North Newbald, Yorkshire.[307] Eliza was baptized in North Newbald, Yorkshire, on 1 June 1845.[308]

Occupations: Servant (1861); Laundress (1881, 1891).[309-311]

The children, in their records, all say the mothers maiden name was **Taylor**. Did she marry the John Taylor, a boarder in their house in 1871? Doubtful, as this John Taylor married another person and had another life. Or did the children simply adopt TAYLOR as their surname upon John COUSIN's death?

John and Eliza had the following children:

i. **Dale COUSIN.**[312] Born circa 1864, in "Paper Mill Bridge" Bingley, Yorkshire. Dale died in Hainworth Lane Bottom, Bingley, on 23 May 1875; he was 11.

ii. **William COUSIN.**[313,314,315] Born circa 1870, in "Paper Mill Bridge" Bingley. Not much more is known of him at this time.

iii. **Stephen COUSIN.**[316] Born circa 1875, in Keighley, Yorkshire. Stephen died at Paper Mill Bridge, Bingley, on 21 April 1882; he was 7.

---

15. Sarah COUSIN[82,317-319] (*Alice PICKLES*[2], *James PICKLES/PIGHELLS*[1]).

Born circa 1840, in Bingley, Yorkshire.[320]

Occupation: Weaver (1861, 1871).[321,322]

Unmarried in 1861 an 1871 censuses.

Nothing reasonable can be found of her after 1871.

---

16. Martha PICKLES[323-326] (*John*[2], *James PICKLES/PIGHELLS*[1]).

Born circa 1836, in Warley; Hightown, Sub-District Of Liversedge And Heckmondwike, Yorkshire.[327-329] Martha was baptized in Luddenden, Yorkshire, on 15 January 1837.[330,331,779] She died in Halifax, Yorkshire, on 14 February 1887 at 51.[332,333]

Occupation: Worsted Spinner (1851, 1881).[328]

In 1857, when Martha was 21, she married **James INGHAM,**[334-340] son of William INGHAM (circa 1808->1891) and

Hannah_____ (ca1811-?), in Halifax, Yorkshire.[341,342] He was born on 24 June 1832, in Ovenden, Yorkshire.[343] James was baptized in Ovenden, Yorkshire, on 21 July 1833,[344] at the Zion Methodist New Connexion.

James "of 65 Crossley-terrace" died at Rawsons-arms Inn, Elland, in Halifax, Yorkshire, on 9 October 1901; he was 69.[345,346] Buried on 14 October 1901, in Lancashire,[347,348] at the Blackburn with Darwen Borough Council; at Blackburn Cemetery.

Occupations: Worsted Spinner (1851); Wool Warehouseman (1857); Woollen Carder (1863), Yeast Dealer Brewer/Dealer (1868-1887), General Carrier Agent (1891, 1901).[349-352]

1877, May 12:

> "The Bankruptcy Act, 1869.
>
> In the County Court of Yorkshire, holden at Halifax.
>
> In the matter of proceedings for liquidation by arrangement or composition with creditors, instituted by James Ingham, of Raglan-street and Crossley-terrace, in Halifax, in the county of York, yeast dealer and dry soap manufacturer. Notice is hereby given that a first general meeting of the creditors of the above-named person has been summoned to be held at the offices of the undersigned Joseph Walhaw, Crown-street Chambers, Halifax, aforesaid, on the 25th day of may, 1877, at eleven o'clock in the forenoon precisely. Dated this 5th day of May 1877
>
> Joseph Walshaw, solicitor for the said James Ingham.[353]

Fourteen days later, 26 May 1877, stinging from the bankruptcy:

> "James Ingham, labourer, Warley, was charged with refusing to quit the Peacock Inn, on the 15th inst. P.C. Green proved the case, and defendant had £1 2s. 6d. to pay, or ten days in prison."[354]

1887, June:

> "On Sales, by private treaty, a small Engine and Boiler nearly new, with shafting complete, suitable for either a mechanic or joiner; can be run where they now stand if required. Also, a dry soap machine, nearly new, made by James Ashbury and Sons, Bradford. – Apply James Ingham, Crossley-terrace, Halifax."[355]

1889, February: James was a member of the West Ward Halifax Liberal Association and was a signatory to:

> "That this meeting of Liberals of West Ward, condemns the brutal and vindictive treatment of the leaders of the Irish people by the Tory-Unionist Government, and expresses the hope that the Liberal Members of Parliament will do all they can to force on an appeal to the people." "...James Ingham, 65, Crossley-terrace..."[356]

1891 census: Ages, occupations and other individuals living at the same address, 65 Crossley Terrace, from other censuses highly suggest the same people. The census taker made a naming mistake, i.e. daughter Alice is now Olive? Gone from this census: Daughter Elizabeth was out of the household (married), and sons William Henry and Arthur were also probably married by 1891. Father James re-married to "Helena" after Martha's death in 1887.

1901, October obituary of James:

> "SUDDEN DEATH OF A CARRIER.—On Wednesday afternoon a carrier named James Ingham of 65, [sic 69] Crossley-terrace, Pellonlane, Halifax, was proceeding home with his waggon after carrying goods to Mirfield, and about 4-30 drew his horse and waggon under the waggon shed at the Rawson's Arms. He was seen by another carrier, who was just leaving the shed, and by him was told that some corn had been left in the stall and he could use it for his horse. This was the last time he was seen alive, for five minutes later a teamer named Wm. Burnett, of Ravenathorpe, found deceased laid face downwards in the He was dead. The body was carried into the Rawson's Arms. Ingham bad been in ill-health far some time, and had been attended by a Halifax doctor the previous week. It is supposed that he died in a fit. The circumstances have been reported to Mr. E. H. Hill, coroner, but an inquest was deemed to be unnecessary."[357]

1901, October probate: "INGHAM James of 65 Crossley-terrace Halifax carrier died 9 October 1901 at the 'Rawsons-arms' inn Elland near Halifax Probate London 20 December to Helena Ingham widow Samuel Ingham co-operative-stores-manager and George Ingham [his brother] worsted-spinner Effect £324 3s. 6d."[345]

Martha and James had the following children:

i. **William Henry INGHAM.**[358-360] Born on 18 December 1857, in Halifax, Yorkshire, at 2 Taylor Street California, Halifax. William died in Dewsbury Road, Yorkshire, in 1890; he was 32.

1884, February: "William Henry Ingham, yeast dealer..." was a witness to the murder of John Birtwhistle at the hand of John Henry Charnock at the West Ward Tavern, Crossley-terrace, Halifax" on 19 January 1884. "The murder was over a betting game of dominoes."[766]

He married **Sarah GREENWOOD** (unknown relationship to the other Greenwoods). No known children.

ii. **Elizabeth Ann INGHAM.**[361-364] Born on 5 July 1863, in Halifax, Yorkshire, on 30 Taylor Street. Elizabeth died in Halifax, in October 1903; she was 40. She married **William HIGHLEY** (1860-1924) – they had no children.

iii. **Emma Jane INGHAM.**[365-367] Born on 17 September 1868, at 38 Crossley Terrace in Halifax, Yorkshire. There are many Emma Jane Ingham's in the area. Researched was focused between 1891 (last census with her family) to 1901 when it was believed she either died or was married. Other researchers suggest her husband was William Hill. The only record linking her to her father was a West Yorkshire Banns of Marriage of Archibald Bishop, 4 June 1892, in Halifax, St. John the Baptist Church as "Mary Ann Ingham."

iv. **Arthur INGHAM.**[368] Born on 14 November 1870, in Halifax, Yorkshire, at 65 Crossley Terrace. Arthur died at 65 Crossley Terrace on 6 August 1875; he was four years old.

v. **Hannah INGHAM**. Born on 5 March 1873, at 65 Crossley Terrace in Halifax, Yorkshire. Hannah died at 65 Crossley Terrace on 9 April 1876; she was three years old.

vi. **Alice "Olive" INGHAM.**[369-372] Born on 9 July 1876, at 65 Crossley Terrace, in Halifax, Yorkshire, England. Nothing more can be definitively verified about her.

17. Sarah PICKLES[373-376] *(John[2], James PICKLES/PIGHELLS[1])*.

Born on 23 September 1837, in Ovenden, Yorkshire.[377,378,777] At the age of 11, Sarah was baptized in Luddenden, Yorkshire, on 19 November 1848,[379,380] at Saint Mary.[780]

Occupation: Wool Comber (1861); In Door Worker (1871).[127,381]

1871, April, possibly her:

> "A pauper named Sarah Pickles was reported by the Rochdale Board to be living at Blackwood, near Rochdale, and receiving relief from that Union. Mr. Bancroft said she went from this Union 2 months ago. She had been relieved by Mr. Ingham and himself in consequence of sickness, and had gone to live with a relation at Rochdale; she was not fit for any work. There was some question whether a settlement could be proved in the case in the Todmorden Union, but the Board were of the opinion that the said Sarah Pickles belonged to this Union, and made an order of 2s. a week."[382]

There are too many other "Sarah Pickles" to ascertain her positive identity.

18. Ann PICKLES[383-389] *(John[2], James PICKLES/PIGHELLS[1])*.

Born on 17 December 1840, in South Cloughheat, Warley, Yorkshire.[390] Ann died in Hamlin Township, Eaton County, Michigan, on 28 January 1901; she was 60.[391] Buried on 30 January 1901, in Springport, Jackson County, Michigan,[392] at Griffith Cemetery.

Occupation: Wool Comber (1851); Worsted Weaver (1861, 1871). [125,149,393]

She immigrated to the US in 1875,[394] arriving 16 June, in New York aboard the *SS Scythia* as "Ann Pickles age 34, spinster, born England, destination America."[395]

This was the *Scythia's* maiden voyage from Liverpool-New York, 1 May 1875. Passengers: 340 cabin and 1,100 third class. Built by James and George

18. Ann PICKLES

18. *Ann PICKLES with Husband Heman KNAPP and two of his children from previous marriage to the late Maria SMITH. (The children are believed to be Lulie (born circa 1872) and Effie (born circa 1875).*

Thomson, Clydebank, Glasgow, Scotland. Tonnage: 4,556. Dimensions: 420.8 x 42.2 feet. Single-screw, 13 1/2 knots. Compound engines. 2,780 I.H.P. Three masts and one funnel. Iron hull. Owned by the Cunard Shipping Line.[396]

On 24 June 1876, when Ann was 35, she married **Heman KNAPP,**[397-400] son of Purdy KNAPP and Rhoda HYDE, in Eaton Township, Eaton County, Michigan.[401] He was born on 22 January 1829, in Franklin County, New York.[402] Heman died in Hamlin Township, Eaton County, Michigan, on 31

March 1905; he was 76.[403,404] Buried on 2 April 1905, in Springport, Jackson County, Michigan,[405] at Griffith Cemetery.

Occupation: Farmer (1876-1901).[406,394]

Heman was previously married tro Maria SMITH, who died in child-birth.

Heman and Ann had one child:

i. **Baby KNAPP**. Born on 20 May 1877, in Hamlin Township, Eaton County, Michigan. Baby died in Hamlin Township on 22 May 1877; the male child was two days old.

---

i.v. [Birth order of the connecting child **James PICKLES** *(John[2], James PICKLES/PIGHILLS[1])* (1843-1911) previously mentioned and found in Part 1: Abegails's Children, with his wife **Hannah CLAY** (1838-1927), **#5** Third Generation), would normally be here.

---

19. Hannah PICKLES[407,134,408] (*John[2], James PICKLES/PIGHELLS[1]*).

Born on 31 December 1847, in Warley, Popplewells, District Of Luddenden, Yorkshire,[409,410] Hannah died at 65 Crossley Terrace in Halifax, Yorkshire on 13 April 1880; she was 32.[411-413] Hannah married _____ ACKROYD, son of Nathaniel ACKROYD. No further information is known about her.

Occupations: Worsted Weaver (1861, 1871); Domestic Servant (1880 -Death Record).[149,393]

> DISPROVED: John Ackroyd, age 29, Bachelor, of Skircoat, 28 April 1877 at the Parish Church, Halifax. John, son of Nathaniel Ackroyd, factory operator. Hannah, age 24, Spinster, of Halifax, daughter of John Pickles, "bloggers"[414,415] The announcement of this marriage is also found in the newspaper.[416] Also[417] Their marriage record shows her six years younger in age, making it suspect.[418] Other information disproves *19. Hannah Pickles* marriage to him.

---

20. Emanuel "Manny" PICKLES/PICKELL[419-424,226,150] (*John PICKLES[2], James PICKLES/PIGHELLS[1]*).

Born on 7 January 1850, in Ovenden, Yorkshire.[425-429] At the age of 8, Emanuel was baptized in Luddenden, Yorkshire, on 11 August 1858,[430,431] at Saint Mary.[781]

Emanuel died at the City Hospital in Jackson, Jackson County, Michigan, on 6 January 1915; he was 64.[432-434] Buried

Francis Gordon, Lillian B. and William Clarence PICKLES: children of **20.** *Emanuel PICKLES and Sarah BAGULEY, circa 1887.*

on 9 January 1915, in Jackson, Jackson County, Michigan,[435] at Woodland Cemetery.

Occupations: Worsted Factory Hand (1861) Carpenter (1871-1915); Tool Dresser (1891); Foreman (1894); Woodworker (1910); Machinist (1883-1907); Mason.[436-459]

Religion: Methodist.

Per anecdote of Vena Emily Kilbourne Doyle, he came to the US on a honeymoon, bringing his mother with them – but no immigration record of the mother is found. He also traveled with his brother James, wife Hannah, and nephew Samuel aboard the ship *Tripoli*, arriving in Boston, Massachusetts, on 14 March 1872, from Liverpool, England. Records verified immigration in 1872.[460-463]

> *Obituary*: "Emanuel Pickell, 811 North Waterloo avenue, passed away at 7:30 p. m. Wednesday, aged 65 years. There survive him a wife, two sons and a daughter, Gordon and William Pickell of Detroit, Miss Lillian Pickell of Jackson. Funeral announcement later. – Detroit paper please copy."[464]

In 1872, when Emanuel was 21, (first quarter of 1872 – January, February, or March), he married **Sarah BAGULEY,**[465-469,226] daughter of William BAGULEY and Frances BRIERLY, in Halifax, Yorkshire.[461,470] She was born on 21 November 1844, in Beeston, Nottinghamshire.[471] Sarah was baptized in Nottingham, on 25 December 1844.[472,473]

Sarah died in Jackson, Jackson County, Michigan, on 28 December 1915; she was 71.[474] Buried on 31 December 1915, in Jackson, Jackson County, Michigan,[475] at Woodland Cemetery.

She arrived in the US in 14 March 1872, with her husband Emanuel as described previously.

> *Obituary:* "Mrs. Sarah Picknell, widow of the late Emanuel Picknell, died at her home, 811 North Waterloo avenue, Tuesday, at 3 p.m., aged 71 years.
>
> The funeral will be held Friday at the North Street Methodist Episcopal church, at 10:30 a. m. Interment will be made at Woodland."[476]

For some unknown reason, this family changed their surname from PICKLES to PICKELL around the early 1880s.

They had the following children:

i. **John Henry PICKLES**. Born on 9 February 1873, in Michigan. John died in Jackson, Jackson County, Michigan, on 14 October 1878; he was five.

ii. **Charles Victor PICKLES**. Born on 19 September 1875, in Michigan.

i. John Henry PICKLES

Charles died in Jackson, Jackson County, Michigan, on 29 October 1878; he was three years old.

iii. **Francis Gordon PICKLES/PICKELL.**[477t-481] Born on 3 February 1881, in Jackson, Jackson County, Michigan. Francis Gordon died at Palm Beach Hospital, Palm Beach, Palm Beach County, Florida, on 27 March 1949; he was 68.

iii. Francis Gordon PICKLES/PICKELL

Obituary: "F. GORDON PICKELL Founder and first president of the Michigan Society of Architects, Mr. Pickell, 68, of 5545 Second, died Sunday in West Palm Beach, Fla.

Born in Jackson, Mr. Pickell studied architecture in New York, Philadelphia and London before moving to Detroit. Surviving are six cousins.

Services will be at 10 a. m. Thursday at the William R. Hamilton Co. Burial will be in Woodlawn [sic] Cemetery, Jackson."

Gordon (his preferred name) was married first to **Luzette E. OOSTDYKE** (1885-1981), then to **Mary Marusha MATIN** (1901-1994). He had no children from any of those marriages.

iv. **William Clarence "Willie" PICKLES/PICKELL.**[466,482-488,226] Born on 10 May 1882, in Jackson, Jackson County, Michigan, Willie died in Sandstone Township, Jackson County, Michigan, on 8 April 1939; he was 56.

Obituary: "Coroner John Pulling of Jackson was called to the home of William Pickell, a mile northeast of Parma Late Saturday to investigate the death of Pickell, 57. His

Third Generation Pickles Brothers:

(sons of 10. John Pickles and Hannah Horsfield): *First row seated, left-to-right:* ***20****. Emmanual and* ***iv.*** *James Pickles. Rear standing: strongly believed to be* ***21****. Johnson Pickles, and* ***23****. Samuel Pickles. Photograph circa 1890s.*

sister, Lillian, who had been caring for him for two weeks, said her brother had been ill for some time with influenza. Death was found to be due to a weakened heart condition, Pulling said.

Besides the sister, Pickell is survived by a brother in Detroit. No inquest will be held."[767]

Willie was first married to **Geneva ELIG** (1895-after 1951), then to **Madge E. LUSCOMB** (1891-1978). He had no children from those marriages.

v. **Lillian B. PICKLES/PICKELL.**[226,489-498] Born on 22 August 1883, in Jackson, Jackson County, Michigan. She died in Flint, Genesee County, Michigan, on 7 February 1941; she was 57. She never married and had no children.

v. Lillian B. PICKLES/PICKELL

21. Johnson PICKLES[499-505,226] (*John*[2], *James PICKLES/PIGHELLS*[1]).

Born on 4 February 1852, in Ovenden, Yorkshire.[506,507] At the age of 6, Johnson was baptized at St. Mary's in Luddenden, Yorkshire, on 11 August 1858.[508,509,782]

Johnson died in Jackson, Jackson County, Michigan, on 4 October 1917; he was 65.[510] Buried on 8 October 1917, in Jackson, Jackson County, Michigan,[511] at Woodlawn Cemetery.

Occupation: Worsted Factory Hand (1861); Stone Mason (1871-Death); Farmer (1910).[512-521,447,450]

According to the 1900 census, he immigrated to the US in 1887 and became a citizen, but this is incorrect.[522] He sailed on the *SS Germanic* from Liverpool, England, 23 February 1883, as verified by wife's US Passport.

1888, October: "Johnson Pickles, a subject of the queen of Great Britain, renounced his allegiance this morning to that country at the clerk's office."[523] Johnson was naturalized 12 October 1896, Jackson County, Michigan.[524]

> *Obituary*: "The funeral of Johnson Pickles will be held from 240 West Main street Monday at 10 a. m. Interment will be made at Woodland cemetery."[525]

SS Germanic *circa 1890-1900*
https://en.wikipedia.org/

On 24 October 1874, when Johnson was 22, he married **Mary Ann NICHOLL,**[526-529,226] daughter of William NICHOLL and Sarah_____, in Halifax, Yorkshire, at the[530] Parish Church of Halifax. She was born on 19 March 1852, in Sowerby, Yorkshire.[531-533] Mary Ann was baptized in Halifax, Yorkshire, on 1 May 1853.[534]

Mary Ann died after 1919; she was 66.[535] Buried in Jackson, Jackson County, Michigan,[536] at Woodlawn Cemetery.

According to the 1910 census she never had any children other than adopted female "Mabel." (Mabel was listed in the 1900 census, but gone from the household by 1910 census, and not convincingly found thereafter.)

Mary Ann became a Naturalized US Citizen with her husband, 12 October 1896, at the Circuit Court, Jackson County, Michigan.

After James's death, Mary Ann lived at 312 Pennsdale St, Roxborough, Philadelphia, Pa. as a "housekeeper." But she left from the port of Philadelphia on 7 August 1919, aboard "Haverford" with the intent of returning 16 September 1919, for "Health after bereavement" reasons.

Passport description: Age: 66 | Mouth: Medium | Stature: 5 feet, 3 inches, Eng. |Chin: Round | Forehead: Medium | Hair: Gray | Eyes: Blue | Complexion: Fair | Nose: Straight | Face: Oval | Sworn affidavit, 15 July 1919, widow, [illegible photograph][537]

1919, November: "The following cabin passengers sailed on the American Line steamer Haverford from Philadelphia for Liverpool yesterday: ... Miss Mary Pickles..."[538] Verified by incoming passenger list, 3 December 1919.[539] In this record she shows intentions of residing in England in the future.

1926, May: "Germantown Y. W. C. A. will have spring festival... Mary Pickles..."[540] Is she the same person?

Possibility: returned to England permanently as she had no children. Findagrave.com has death in 1925; with burial at Halifax, Metropolitan Borough of Calderdale, West Yorkshire, at Mount Zion Methodist Chapelyard. It is alluded she came from Calderdale.[541]

They had one child:

i. **Mabel PICKLES**[542] *(Adopted)*. Born in October 1887 in Michigan. Anecdote says she married a CANFIELD, but no further information can be found about her.

---

22. William Henry PICKLES[543-549] (*John*[2], *James PICKLES/ PIGHELLS*[1]).

Born on 18 November 1854, in Yorkshire.[550,551] At the age of 3, William was baptized in Luddenden, Yorkshire, on 11 August 1858,[552] at Saint Mary.[783]

William died at 320 West Franklin Street, in Jackson, Jackson County, Michigan, on 8 June 1914; he was 59.[553,554] Buried on 10 June 1914, in Jackson, Jackson County, Michigan,[555] at Woodland Cemetery.

Occupations: Cart Driver (1871); Cotton Spinner (1892); Labourer (1892); Weaver (1892); Mason/Stone Cutter (1878-1914); House Painter (1900).[556-563,448,447,564,450,565-571]

May 1891:

> "Yesterday morning a fire broke out in the carding room at Bottoms Mill, Salterhebble, near Halifax. The mill is owned by the Honourable Mrs. Meynell-Ingham, of Temple Newsam, and is occupied by Mr. William Henry Pickles, cotton spinner. In the middle room were four double carding machines, and in the room above this cotton spinning was carried on. It was at one of the carding engines that the fire commenced, a youth being in charge at the time. How the outbreak occurred is not known, but it is thought to have been by something hard getting into one of the

engines. The mill was practically destroyed. In the building alone there will be several hundred pounds loss. Mr. Pickles estimates his damage at £1,700, of which £1,000 is covered by insurance."[572-575]

"A fire broke out yesterday at Bottoms Mill, Siddal, near Halifax, occupied by Mr William Henry Pickles, cotton spinner, and owned by Lady Ingham. The mill was completely gutted and the damage is estimated at about £1,000, whilst the machinery and stock, valued at £1,700 were destroyed."[576]

Almost a year later after the fire, the family immigrated to US[577,578]. An outbound passenger list from Liverpool of the whole family is noted.[579] Inbound list: from Liverpool, England aboard the *Umbria*; arriving in New York in March 1892 (7 March 1892 sworn manifest).[580]

Apparently they moved to Kentucky with his brother Samuel and family to work the quarry (1910 census). By the 1920 census he was back in Michigan.

Obituaries: "William Henry Pickles, 58, died at the home of his son, Samuel Pickles, 320 West Franklin street, Monday, evening, June 8. He is survived by a wife; three sons and two daughters. Samuel and Arthur, of Jackson, and James H., Elizabeth and Emily, of Kentucky.

The funeral will be held at the home at 2 p.m., Thursday."[581]

Obituary: "Bowling Green, Ky., June 11. – (Spl.) – A telegram to J. H. Pickels [sic] announced the death of his father, W. H. Pickles, 59 years old, at Jackson, Mich. The elder Pickels was born in England, but came to the United States a number of years ago. Pickles had lived with his wife in this city for several years, and was connected with the Pickles Stone Quarries near the city. He had been in ill health for some time and left with Mrs. Pickles for Jackson for the benefit of his health. He is survived by his wife and the following children: J Harry Pickles and Miss Emily Pickles, of this city; Mrs. Harry Rigglewood, of the White Stone Quarry neighborhood, and Samuel and Arthur Pickles, of Jackson, Mich. He leaves also three brothers, Samuel Pickles, of this city; Emmanuel and Johnson Pickles, of Jackson, Mich."[582]

On 26 September 1878, when William was 23, he married **A. Elizabeth UTLEY,**[583-593,226] daughter of John UTLEY and Elizabeth KITCHEN, in Halifax, Yorkshire,[594] at the Halifax

RMS Umbria
https://en.wikipedia.org/wiki/RMS_Umbria

Parish Church. She was born on 28 March 1853, in Yorkshire.[595] At the age of 9, Elizabeth was baptized in Hebden Bridge, Yorkshire, on 2 November 1862.[596]

Elizabeth died in Bowling Green, Warren County, Kentucky, on 8 May 1931; she was 78.[597] Buried on 10 May 1931, in Bowling Green, Warren County, Kentucky,[598] at Fairview Cemetery.

Religion: Christ Scientist.

She had 6 children; one had died by 1900.[577] Confirmed again in the 1910 US census that she had 6 children, of which 5 were living.[599]

She became a US citizen: 1891[599] – 1892.[600]

Immigration: from Liverpool, England aboard the *Umbria*; arriving in New York in March 1892, with her husband [sic: March 1891][601]

1903, October: held a reception for Rev. and Mrs. Curry at their home. "…vocal solo, Elizabeth Pickles… duet, … Mrs. W. H. Pickles… vocal solo, Arthur Pickles…"[602]

Obituary:

> "Native of England Succumbs At Home of Her Daughter.
>
> *Special to The Courier-Journal.*
>
> Bowling Green, Ky., May 8. – Mrs. Elizabeth Pickles, 78 years old, died at 5:15 o'clock this morning at the I home of her daughter, Mrs. Harry A. Ricklewood, in the White Stone Quarry neighborhood, six miles west of here. Mrs. Pickles was born in Yorkshire, England. She married W. H. Pickles in Halifax, England, in 1874 [sic: 1878]. He died in Jackson, Mich., in

1913 [sic: 1914]. In addition to Mrs. Rigglewood, she is survived by another daughter, Mrs. Emily Pence of Denver, Col., and three sons, J. H. Pickles of Bowling Green, Arthur Pickles and Samuel of Jackson, Mich. Mrs. Pickles was a member of the First Church of Christ Scientist."[603]

Obituary: "Aged Women Expires Early This Morning In Quarry Section

Mrs. Elizabeth Pickles, 78 years of age, died this morning at 5:15 o'clock at the home of her daughter, Mrs. Harry A. Rigelwood, in the White Stone Quarry neighborhood. Funeral arrangements have not been completed. Mrs. Pickles called to members of the family this morning at 4 o'clock saying she was ill. A physician was called but she lived only an hour and fifteen minutes.

Mrs Pickles was born in Yorkshire, England, March 28, 1853 and was the daughter of the late John and Elizabeth Kitchen Uttley, also of English birth. She married W. H. Pickles in Halifax, England in 1874. [sic] Mr. Pickles died in Jackson Mich., in 1913. [sic] Before going to Jackson he resided in Bowling Green.

Mrs. Pickles spent about 25 years of her life here.

In addition to Mrs. Rigelwood, she is survived by another daughter Mrs. Emily Pence, of Denver Colo., and three sons J. H. Pickles, secretary and treasurer of the Southern Cut Stone Company, of this city and Arthur Pickles and Samuel Pickles, both of Jackson Mich. She is also survived by twelve grandchildren and three great grandchildren.

Mrs Pickles was a member of the First Church of Christ Scientist."[604]

William and Elizabeth had the following children:

i. **James Harry "Henry" PICKLES.**[579,587,605-613,226] Born on 25 December 1876, in Halifax, Yorkshire. James died in Bowling Green, Warren County, Kentucky, on 2 April 1960; he was 83. James was married to Helen Esther WHEDON and they had six children who had children and 13 grandchildren.

ii. **Arthur PICKLES.**[579,614-623,226] Born on 6 June 1879, in Edge and Warley, Yorkshire. Arthur died in Jackson, Jackson County, Michigan, on 17 October 1950; he was 71. He was married to **Edith L. SCHEURER**, and they had no children.

iii. **Samuel PICKLES.**[579,624-631,226] Born on 27 June 1881, in Edge End and Warley, Halifax, Yorkshire. Samuel died in Jackson, Jackson County, Michigan, on 22 February 1951; he was 69. He was married to **Erma G. WOODS** and they had three children and five grandchildren.

iv. **Bertha PICKLES.**[632,579,226] Born on 13 April 1884, in Edge and Worley, Halifax, Yorkshire. Bertha died in Jackson, Jackson County, Michigan, on 18 March 1897; she was 12 years of age.

v. **Hannah Elizabeth PICKLES.**[579,633-641,226] Born on 23 June 1887, at "7 Halifax Lane, Ludenden Warley U.S.H." Hannah died in Bowling Green, Warren County, Kentucky, on 14 March 1952; she was 64. She was married to **Harry Albert RIGELWOOD**. They had three children and three known grandchildren.

vi. **Emily PICKLES**[642-647,226]. Born on 23 May 1894, in Jackson, Jackson County, Michigan. Emily died in Fulshear, Fort Bend County, Texas, on 8 April 1983; she was 88. She was married to **John W. PENCE**, and they had one known child, and three grandchildren.

---

23. Samuel PICKLES[648-654,226] (*John*[2], *James PICKLES/PIGHELLS*[1]).

Born on 13 June 1857, at Ivehouse Lane, Warley, Yorkshire,[655-658] Samuel was baptized in Luddenden, Yorkshire, on 11 August 1858,[657,659] at Saint Mary Church.[784]

Samuel died in Bowling Green, Warren County, Kentucky, on 24 May 1925; he was 67.[660] Buried on 26 May 1925 in Bowling Green, Warren County, Kentucky,[658,661] at Fairview Cemetery.

Occupations: Woolen Miller (1871); Mason (1857, 1878); Slaterer & Plasterer (1881); Stone Cutter/Contractor (1887-1920); Travel Agent (1907); Mason & Owner Of Limestone Quarries, Bowling Green, Kentucky.[447,450,662-680]

Samuel immigrated to the US in 1880,[599] arriving at Castle Garden, New York, 12 April 1880, aboard the *SS City of Richmond*, Age 26, as a Laborer.[681]

City of Richmond, of the Inman Line, was a relatively new ship; launched from Glasgow, Scotland in 1873. It was 440.8 x

SS City of Richmond – Library of Congress

43.5 feet in dimension.[768] Four years later, the ship would bring the famous inventor Nikola Tesla to America.[769]

In October 1888: "Samuel Pickles, late of England, declared his intention to-day of becoming an American citizen, before the county clerk."[523]

Samuel quickly became an industrious individual. In 1898, as a construction as contractor, finished the Christ Episcopal Church in Adrian.[682,683]

1900, August: "The contract for building a fourth fire engine house was awarded to Samuel Pickles at $5,700." [For Jackson City, Michigan][684]

1901, July: all bidders (5) for the Ionia Asylum were rejected: "Samuel Pickles ... of Jackson" – the bids were too high.[685]

1902, April: Elected Mayor of Jackson, Michigan on the Republican ticket.[686,687]

1903, March: "Jackson, Mich., March 26. - (Special.) - The Republican city convention tonight nominated Samuel Pickles, the present incumbent, for mayor..."[688]

1903: Mayor of Jackson, Michigan:

> "'Success treads on the heels of every right effort' said Samuel Smiles, and amid all the theorizing as to the cause of success, there can be no doubt that this aphorism has its origin in the fact, that character is the real basis of success in any field of thought or action. He of whom we now write is the present mayor of Jackson and his administration has shown fideli-

CONTRACTOR COMPLIMENTED.

Samuel Pickles, Who Built a Church for the Baptist Denomination at Adrian, Praised Highly for the Excellence of the Work Performed.

Monday evening, at Adrian, was dedicated by the Baptists the new church which was erected for them by Samuel Pickles, of this city. At the dedicatory services Mr. Pickles received many compliments and a large measure of praise for the high quality of the work preformed, and for the rapidity with which the edifice was erected.

The report of the building committee, read at the services, has this to say of Mr. Pickles: * *

"The revised bids were received Wednesday, Aug. 2, and that evening, three days only after the committee was appointed, the contract was let to Mr. Samuel Pickles, of Jackson, and the committee is glad for this occasion of paying him a compliment (we have paid him about everything else) for his fairness and for giving us a chapel which we believe is first class in every particular, and which could not be duplicated for much more money than it has cost us. We found him a gentleman at all times, and commend him to any others who may be contemplating improvements either here or elsewhere. * * The first shovel of dirt was thrown out Aug. 10, the painters finished their work and turned the improvement over to us completed Dec. 11. Time, four months and one day."

The edifice, which will be known as the Dorcas Memorial chapel, cost to complete, about $7,000.

The above is taken from an extended write-up of the new church and dedication services, which appeared in the Adrian Tri-Weekly Telegram.

Jackson Citizen Patriot. *11 January 1900, page 6.*

Proclamation by the Mayor.

Whereas, It has been made to appear to me that hydrophobia exists in the city of Jackson and township of Blackman, and that dogs in the city of Jackson have such disease and are liable to be attacked by the same; now, therefore,

I, Samuel Pickles, mayor of the city of Jackson, do hereby require that all dogs running at large in the city of Jackson, for the period of forty days from and after the first day of August, A. D. 1902, shall be provided with and wear constantly while at large a good and substantial wire gauze or leather muzzle, securely put on and fastened so as to prevent every such dog going at large from biting any person or animal during such period; and all owners of dogs are hereby warned that in default of providing said muzzle or tying up or confining all dogs, that the same will be killed and buried, if found running at large within the limits of the city of Jackson, at the expiration of forty-eight hours from the 1st day of August, at 12 o'clock p. m. of said day.

Dated Jackson, Aug. 1, 1902.

SAMUEL L. PICKLES, Mayor.

Jackson Citizen Patriot, 1 August 1902, page 7.

ty, business acumen and progressive policy. His is a well rounded character and fully justifies the reputation of inflexible integrity, keen business ability, broad and liberal views and distinct individuality.

In regard to Mr. Pickles' career in Jackson a somewhat facetious, though signally appreciative, article was published in the *Jackson Morning Patriot* of comparatively recent date, and is well worthy of reproduction in full in this connection: 'In 1882 Samuel Pickles came to Jackson from England. Last April he may have disappointed some folk by being elected mayor of this city. If this was rather more rapid action than was to be expected of a former British subject, there was no one to blame but Samuel Pickles. He is not a man given to talking very much of himself. For three days last week a *Patriot* interviewer was on the lookout for FHs Honor, with the intention of asking him some questions of a personal nature. It was finally ascertained that he had taken to the tall timber, and this compelled the substitution in the matter of interviewing, of a man who has known him for many years.'

Sam Pickles is as square a man as ever stood in shoe-leather was the response to the first interrogation. There isn't a particle of meanness in his composition. He is the style of man who gets the good will of people because he deserves it. Ever since he came to Jackson he has had a hand in about all of the first-class buildings which have been erected not only in this city but also in the tributary territory. When he came to Jackson he at first followed his trade of stone-cutter. He is a native of the old Yorkshire town of Halifax, where he was born on the 13th of June, 1858. His first work in Jackson was as foreman for a Fort Wayne firm, Geek & Company. This is the firm which built the Bloomfield House, and Mr. Pickles had charge of the work. When this job was finished he formed a partnership with Andrew Butler and purchased the interests of Geek & Company in this city. A few years later he bought out Mr. Butler and since that time he has been about the only stone contractor of the first class between Chicago and Detroit. Some of the buildings he has put up? As I said, he has had something to do with the building of pretty much every first-class structure in this territory. The Carter Building, the postoffice, the Atheneum building, the Brooks-Eslow block and the parish house of St. Paul's church are some of them in this city. He has had the contracts for stone work on many of the new buildings of the University of Michigan, at Ann Arbor; and the State School for Feeble Minded, at Lapeer, the new jail and court house at Paw Paw, St. Joseph's academy at Adrian, and the court house at Mason, are some of the important contracts which he has had, either for the stone work or for the entire structure.

'I can't imagine how Sam ever got into politics. Possibly it was an accident, but he gradually became entangled. First he was chosen supervisor of the eighth ward, then he was elected alderman, then school trustee in old district No. 17, and then he was elected mayor. Mr. Pickles may have been a Republican nominee, but he has not been a mayor for the people of that party any more than for the people who didn't vote for him. He has been the mayor of the whole city of Jackson, and he will be so as long as he holds down the job.'

The foregoing colloquial account indicates in a quite effective way the standing of the mayor in the city of his home, and yet it is incumbent that the same be supplemented with other data. Mr. Pickles was reared in his native city, where he received his educational discipline and where also he learned the trade of stone-cutting, becoming an expert artisan and developing his executive and business talents, which have brought him to the forefront in connection with this same line of industrial enterprise.

He continued to be employed as a journeyman at his trade in his native land until 1882, when he came to the United States and first located in Jackson, as has been previously noted. He is a Republican in his political proclivities and takes a deep interest in the questions and issues of the hour, while it needs scarcely to be said that he has his views and convictions at all times amply fortified."[689]

"Mason, Mich., July 22[, 1903]. - The stonecutters at worked on the new county building in this city went on a strike today. They were receiving 42 1/2 cents an hour and asked for 45 cents. The men were working for Samuel Pickles, of Jackson, who has the contract for the stone work. There were twenty-five of the men at work here, most of whom have left the city."[690]

1904, November:

"Ex-Mayor Samuel Pickles, who disappeared from Jackson some six weeks ago, is still missing. He was last heard of in Chicago and Kansas City. He was sub-contractor for the stone work of the new Shiawassee county court house at Corunna, where he is aid to have left his work without a word of explanation. Rickman Bros., the contractors, have taken the work in hand and will complete the contract. His friends say there is nothing in the affairs of the company to cause him to want to disappear, but it is thought he was in financial straits from having trusted his friends too fully."[691]

In March 1911, his wife Annie died.

Last Will:

"I, Samuel Pickles, of Bowling Green, Warren County, Kentucky, being of sound mind and disposing memory, do make, publish and declare this to be my last will and testament.

First. I desire all my just debts and funeral expenses to be paid.

Second. I will, bequeath and devise unto my nephew J. H. Pickles, all my stock of the par value of $5,000.00 in the Tanksley-Trumright Cut Stone Co., Incorporated, of Nashville, Tenn.

Third. I will, bequeath and devise all the residue of my estate, both real and personal, of every kind and description, to my wife, Louise Pickles, and to my adopted daughter, Violet Pickles Newton, in equal shares, share and share alike.

Fourth: I hereby name, nominate and appoint my nephew J. H. Pickles, [John Henry PICKLES, son of **#22. William Henry PICKLES]** the executor of this my last will and testament and hereby clothe him with full power to wind up and settle my estate, to sell any real estate owned by me at the time of my death, to make conveyance of same by deed and to do any other act necessary to settle my said estate. In Witness Whereof, I have hereunto set my hand and name on this October 23rd. 1918.

Sam'l. Pickles.

Witnesses: R. C. P. Thomas

Nannie Stout.

State of Kentucky, County of Warren. SS. May term, 1925.

The foregoing will was on this day produced in open Court and proven by the oaths of the two subscribing witnesses thereto and the same is ordered probated and record, and is, with this certificate duly recorded in my office.

Given under my hand, this 27th day of May, 1925.

H. Lee Kelley, Clerk."[692]

Obituary: "Samuel Pickles died at: 5:30 o'clock Sunday morning at his residence, 1148 Laurel avenue.

The funeral services will be conducted from the residence at 10 o'clock Tuesday morning by Dr. J. E. Hampton and the burial will be in Fairview Cemetery.

Mr. Pickles was born in Yorkshire, England, on June 13, 1857. He was first married to Miss Annie Mitchell in England. She died fifteen years ago. He was married the second time to Miss Louise Sweet in August, 1913 at Chattanooga, Tenn. His last wife survives him, with one daughter Mrs. G. A. Smith of Gallatin, Tenn. He also leaves one sister Mrs. T. Wilcox, [sic Wilcock] who lives in England. He was a member of Bowling Green Lodge, No. 220, B. P. O. E.

Mr. Pickles was engaged In the stone business for a great many years and had been very active in developing the stone interests of Warren County. He was for a long time superintendent of the White Stone Quarry and later organized the Bowling Green Quarries Company, which is still one of the county's most important stone plants. He sold out his holdings in the company twelve mouths ago, his health becoming poor, and had since lived the life of a retired business man. He was prominent In Bowling Green's industrial life and will be sadly missed."[693]

On 18 March 1878, when Samuel was 20, he first married **Annie Elizabeth MITCHELL**[694-696,226], daughter of William Cockroft MITCHELL, in Halifax, Yorkshire,[697] at the Parish Chapel, Saint John the Baptist. She was born on 9 October 1855 in Thornhill, Yorkshire.[698,699]

Annie died in Douglass Township, Montcalm County, Michigan, on 9 March 1911; she was 55.[700,701] Buried on 12 March 1911 in Douglass Township, Montcalm County, Michigan,[702] at Entrican Cemetery; Lot 108, Space 1.

She also immigrated in 1880, with her husband.[599]

She died in Michigan after attending the funeral of her brother-in-law **James PICKLES.** She caught pnemonia, according to family anecdote, but the death record says she died of "Acute Nephritis."[703]

They had no children.

In August 1913, when Samuel was 56, he second married **Louise WARREN**[658,704-721,226], daughter of George WARREN and Louisa YOUNGMAN, in Chattanooga, Hamilton County, Tennessee. She was born on 2 January 1866, in Adelaide, South Australia, Australia.[722] Louise died at Mercy Hospital in Jackson, Jackson County, Michigan, on 5 October 1953; she was 87.

Buried in Bowling Green, Warren County, Kentucky,[658,723] at the Fairview Cemetery.

Her Will:

Louise WARREN.
(unknown source of photograph)

"Know all men by these presents: That I, Louise Pickles, widow of Samuel Pickles, deceased, do hereby renounce the provisions of the will of my said husband, Samuel Pickles, who died a resident of and domiciled in Warren County, Kentucky, on the 24th day of May, 1925, and which will was on the 27th day of May, 1925, admitted to probate by the Warren County Court, and established as the last Will and testament of said Samuel Pickles; and I hereby relinquish the provisions of said will for my benefit, and elect to take my dower and distribute share of my said husband's estate as if no will had been made by him.

Witness my hand this 18th day of July, 1925.

Mrs. Louise Pickles.

State of Kentucky, County of Warren. Sct.

I. Marian Fortune, a Notary Public in and for Warren County, Kentucky, do hereby certify that the foregoing instrument of writing as this day produced before me inmy [sic] said County by Louise Pickles, and acknowledged by her to be her act and deed.

Given under my hand, this July 18, 1925.

My commission expires August 25, 1926.

Marian Fortune, Notary Public, Warren County, Kentucky."[724]

Obituary: "MRS LOUISE PICKLES, 86, widow of the late Samuel Pickles, City, died at 5:15 a. m. today at Mercy Hospital, Jackson, Mich., She had been ill for several weeks. Funeral services will be held at Jackson and the body will arrive here on the Pan American at 1:35 p.m. Thursday for burial in Fairview Cemetery, beside her husband, who died May 24, 1925. A short graveside service is planned here. She Is survived by three daughters Mrs. Blanch Walker, Jackson, Mich., Mrs. Mabel Canberg, Lansing, Mich., and Mrs. George A. Smith, Buechel, Ky.; two sons Claude L. Sweet, Seabrook, Texas, and Carroll W. Sweet, Ojai, Calif., and 12 grandchildren and seven great grandchildren She had made her home with Mrs. Walker since leaving Bowling Green."[725]

Samuel and Louise had no children together.

At first glance of the 1900 US census, Samuel and Annie had a daughter named Violet. After investigation, this daughter is actually Violet M. SWEET (1894-1990) daughter of Charles L. SWEET and **Louise WARREN.** Violet later married Olon NEWTON, and then George A. SMITH. Later, Samuel names Violet as an "adopted daughter" in his Will of 1925.

24. Mary Jane PICKLES[726-730] (*John*[2], *James PICKLES/ PIGHELLS*[1]).

Born on 13 February 1862, in Apple House, Warley, Yorkshire.[731-734] At the age of three, Mary Jane was baptized in Luddenden, Yorkshire, on 21 June 1865.[735,734,785]

Mary Jane died in Yorkshire, in August 1925; she was 63.[736] Buried on 18 August 1925, in Dewsbury Road, Yorkshire,[737] at Alverthorpe, Saint Paul.

Occupation: Woolen Weaver (1881).[738]

In the 1871 census she was listed as "Grand Dau" age 10, Spinner in a Worsted Mill, born Yorkshire, Warley, but she was actually their daughter, in the household of John Pickles.[739]

According to brother Samuel's obituary (May 1925) she is the "Wilcox" [sic] sister still living in England.

On 3 November 1888, when Mary Jane was 26, she married **Tattersfield WILCOCK**[740-744], son of Carter WILCOCK and Mary EXLEY, in Halifax, Yorkshire,[745] at the Parish Church of Halifax, Saint John The Baptist. He was born on 23 April 1863, in Mirfield, Yorkshire.[746,747] Tattersfield was baptized in Dewsbury Road, Yorkshire, on 11 January 1864,[748] at the Dewsbury Parish.

Tattersfield died in Haslingden, Lancashire, on 9 August 1932; he was 69,[749,750] and was buried in Bacup, Haslingden, Rossendale Borough, Lancashire,[751] at Bacup Cemetery.

Occupations: Scholar (1871); Woolen Silver Tenter (1881); Woolen Carder (1888-1911).[752-756]

Probate: England & Wales, National Probate Calendar (Index of Wills and Administrations), 1858-1995:

> "Wilcock Tatterfield of 13 Unsworth-street Stacksteads Lancashire died 9 August 1932 at 38 Cutler-lane Stacksteads Probate London 5 September to Emily Pilling [his daughter] (wife of Ingham Read Pilling). Effects £815 13s. 4d."[757]

Mary Jane and Tattersfield had the following children:

i. **Rev. Etson WILCOCK.**[758-761] Born in 1889 in Stacksteads, County Lancaster, Etson died in Accrington, Lancashire, on 21 June 1925; he was 36.

Etson studied for the ministry from Brighton Grove College, but first preached at the age of 14.[770] In January 1912, at the Acre Mill Baptist Chapel, Bacup, Lancashire.[771] In August of that year, still a student, he preached at Waterbarn Baptist Church, Stacksteads, Lancashire.[772] He was later appointed to his first church in January 1924, at the Bethel Baptist Barnes Street Chapel.[773,774]

Etson was a veteran of World War I. His obituary tells his story and his narrow escape from certain death:

> "We regret to say that after being pastor of Barnes-street Baptist Chapel for short of a year and a half, the Rev. Etson Wilcock passed away on Sunday afternoon, at the early age of 36.
>
> The rev. gentleman had been ill since Easter, and it was realised for some time that his condition was serious. He resided in Windsor Place, Burnley-road, and left a widow and one young son, to whom deep sympathy is extended.
>
> Mr. Wilcock entered upon his ministry at Barnes-street in February, last year, [1924] filling a pulpit that had been vacant since 1914. He was born in Stacksteads, and both he and his wife come from Baptist families. His father, Mr. Tattersall [sic] Wilcock, was deacon of the Stacksteads Baptist Church for 27 years, and Sunday school superintendent for 35 years, while Mrs. Wilcock's father, Mr. R. H. [sic] Ashworth, held the position of organist at the church for 41 years. her mother was also one of the most respected church workers in the district, and for nearly twenty years was teacher of a class of young ladies numbering about 70.
>
> In early life Mr. Wilcock decided upon a ministerial career, and when only fourteen years of age occu-

pied the pulpit at Stacksteads Baptist Church. On that occasion the appointed preacher failed to arrive in time for the service, and in the anticipation that he would turn up later, young Wilcock was asked to deputise until his arrival. It so happened, however, that the minister missed not only his first train, but also the second, and Mr. Wilcock had to conduct the entire service, and preach the sermon.

i. Rev. Etson WILCOCK – newspaper photograph

For nearly five years before the war Mr Wilcock studied at Owens' College, and the Manchester Baptist College, but then the great world upheaval interfered, and he responded to his country's call by joining the Royal Garrison Artillery as a private. Opportunities were open to him to join higher branches of the service or the Y.M.C.A., but to quote his own words, he wished 'to get close to the men, ' and he felt he could understand them better by sharing their hardships and difficulties in the ranks. He served as a gunner all through the war in Belgium and Germany. When the Armistice was signed he was with the advanced columns, and the last eighteen months of his army career was spent in Germany. He was twice wounded, and had to undergo an operation after returning home, which was followed by an attack of pneumonia.

Mr. Wilcock had a miraculous escape from death during the retreat from Cambriai, due to the fact that he carried in the left pocket of his tunic a Bible. Describing the incident at the time he accepted the call to Harnes street, he said: 'We were pretty well on the run when I was knocked down by something and stunned. I did not know where I was, and it was a long time before anyone found what had caught me. What had happened was that I had been struck by a piece of German shell, but the Bible I carried in my pocket had received the force of the impact and, as I believe, saved my life.' The Bible, with its pages all torn, was one of Mr. Wilcok's [sic] treasured possessions.

After returning to civil life, Mr. Wilcock resumed his college career, and three years ago took charge of the Baptist Church at Sale. At that time the Sale Baptist Church was derelict. The cause had to dwindled that only about a dozen members of the congregation remained, and arrangements had actually been made for holding the last Communion service when Mr. Wilcock set himself to the task of rebuilding the church's life. It was an enterprise which demanded both courage and ability, but Mr. Wilcock succeeded admirably, and the church is now a very active organisation. His personality impressed itself on the whole district, and Nonconformity generally in that part of Manchester owes much to his energy.

Mr. Wilcock first preached at Barnes-street as pastor on the third Sunday in February, 1924, and his recognition service was held on March 15th.[775] A splendid tribute was paid to his worth on the occasion by Dr. H. Townsend, of the Baptist College, Manchester, and other ministers.

The interment took place at the Bacup Cemetery on Thursday, and was preceded by service at the Barnes-street Baptist Chapel."[776]

Etson married the worsted and cotton spinner and weaver, **Elizabeth Ellen ASHWORTH**, in June 1915, in Halifax, Yorkshire. She was the daughter of James Lawrence ASHWORTH and Sara Jane _____.

Etson and Sarah had one known child, **Fred WILCOCK**, born 21 July 1915. Unfortunately not much more is known of him.

ii. **Emily WILCOCK.**[762-765] Born on 13 May 1891, at "52 Acre Mill Bacup," in Bacup, Haslingden, Rossendale Borough, Lancashire. Emily died at the Rawtenstall Hospital in Lancashire, on 25 September 1957; she was 66. Emily married **Ingham Read PILLING** (1890-1971) in 1920. No known children from this union.

SOURCES: MADE OF PICKLES

1. England, Select Births and Christenings, 1538-1975, database with no images, Ancestry.com, (From the marriage of his son John.).
2. UK National Archives; GRO, England and Wales Non-Conformist and Non-Parochial Registers, 1567-1970, RG4, database with images, www.ancestry.com, From the Non-Conformist birth registry of the children: Joseph, Isaac, James, Elizabeth, William, John – all on one page. Piece 3393, Keighley, Bethel Chapel (Baptist), Yorkshire, 1791-1837' "Pickles and Lugden." Page 9.
3. England and Wales Non-Conformist Record Indexes (RG4-8), 1588-1977, database, https://familysearch.org, From daughter Jane's baptism record: (familysearch.org/ark:/61903/1:1:FWG7-54N : 11 December 2014), James Pickles in entry for Jane Pickles, 31 Aug 1803, Baptism; citing p. 54, Keighley, Yorkshire, record group RG4, Public Record Office, London.
4. England Births and Christenings, 1538-1975, familysearch.org, database, From son James's baptismal record: (familysearch.org/ark:/61903/1:1:NYBT-74F : 21 September 2020), James Pickles in entry for Thomas Pickles, 1802.
5. Ibid. From daughter Alice's birth record: (familysearch.org/ark:/61903/1:1:NPK6-BL2 : 18 September 2020), James Pickles in entry for Alice Pickles, 1812.
6. Findmypast.co.uk.
7. "James of Wm Pighills of Crofsgates Husbandman by Hannah his wife was born the 9th & baptized the 14th of July" (closest to surname) (over 4,000 with variations from Lancashire and Yorkshire).
8. England, Select Births and Christenings, 1538-1975, Father: Mark Pickles; FHL Film Number 307747; Reference ID 2:1Z9MFXL.
9. West Yorkshire, England, Church of England Baptisms, Marriages and Burials, 1512-1812, database with image, West Yorkshire Archive Service, "James S[on] of Mark Pickles Soothill 15"; (ancestry.com image 4).
10. (See burial reference).
11. West Yorkshire, England, Church of England Deaths and Burials, 1813-1985, West Yorkshire Archive Service; Wakefield, Yorkshire, Ancestry.com, database with images, Number 329; Abode: Leeds; buried 21 July 1820; age 42 [born 1778]; Saint Mary, Whitkirk, West Yorkshire. (ancestry.com image 3).
12. West Yorkshire, England, Church of England Baptisms, Marriages and Burials, 1512-1812, (ancestry.com image 1).
13. Findmypast.co.uk. Transcript. Image 400. Archive: Borthwick Institute for Archives | Record type: Bishop's transcripts | Register type: Baptisms, marriages & burials | Register year range: 1600-1812 | Record set: Yorkshire Baptisms | Collections from: England, Great Britain
14. West Yorkshire, England, Church of England Baptisms, Marriages and Burials, 1512-1812,
    "Baptisms at Whitkirk Anno 1778"
    "James of William Pighills of Crofsgates Husbandman by Hannah his wife was born the 9th & baptized the 14 of July 1778." (ancestry.com image 3).
15. Ibid. (ancestry.com image 4).
16. England & Wales, Christening Index, 1530-1980, database with no images, ancestry.com, Original: Genealogical Society of Utah. British

Isles Vital Records Index, 2nd Edition. Salt Lake City, Utah: Intellectual Reserve, © 2002.

17. West Yorkshire, England, Church of England Baptisms, Marriages and Burials, 1512-1812, "Baptisms June 1780" (ancestry.com image 7).

18. Ibid. "10 Jas [James] of Jno [Jonathan] Pickles H__comber" (ancestry.-com image 9).

19. England, Select Births and Christenings, 1538-1975, database with no images, Ancestry.com, FHL Film Number 990597. Original data: England, Births and Christenings, 1538-1975. Salt Lake City, Utah: FamilySearch, 2013.

20. Ibid. "James Pickles" Baptized 3 Feb. 1779, Myrtle Grove Independent, Eastwood, Todmorden, York. Father: Wm. Pickles; FHL Film Number 0816619 (RG4 3156).

21. West Yorkshire, England, Church of England Baptisms, Marriages and Burials, 1512-1812,
"Baptized" | "Jas. [James] Eli. Pickles [illegible] Mason"
Page 190; (ancestry.com image 1).

22. West Yorkshire, England, Church of England Deaths and Burials, 1813-1985, Number 329; Whitkirk, St. Mary, Yorkshire.

23. West Yorkshire, Non-Conformist Records, 1646-1985, West Yorkshire Archive Service, database with image, (ancestry.com images 79) Birchcliffe, Bridge, Heptonstall Slack, Lindwell Elland, Luddenden, Rishworth; CR29; (ancestry.com image 497) Birchcliffe, Wakefield; WC44.

24. West Yorkshire Archive Service, West Yorkshire, England, Church of England Marriages and Banns, 1813-1935, Number 7; Banns of Marriage; 9 January; 10 January; 17 January; Yorkshire Parish Records; Reference Number: WDP83/5/1.

25. West Yorkshire, England, Church of England Baptisms, Marriages and Burials, 1512-1812, database with image, West Yorkshire Archive Service, Banns of Marriage; number 544; (ancestry.com image 25); Keighley, "James Pighells Bachelor and Minor and Jane Teal Spinster both of this Parish" Sundays: 7, 14, 21 September 1800.

26. Marriage record/certificate/application. Page 192, number 557; (ancestry.com image 20). West Yorkshire Archive Service; Wakefield, Yorkshire; Yorkshire Parish Records.

27. England, Select Marriages, 1538–1973, database, https://www.familysearch.org/ark:/61903/1:1:N22M-KQM ; James Pighells, 1800.

28. Yorkshire, England, Church of England Parish Records, 1538-1873, database with image, ancestry.com, Birth; (ancestry.com image 122); transcript page 234; Kildwick-in-Craven 1744-1789.

29. England, Select Births and Christenings, 1538-1975, database with no images, Ancestry.com, Birth: 28 August 1782; Baptism: 5 January 1783 at Kildwick, York; Father: Robert Teal; Mother: Mary; FHL Film Number: 0496813, 0496814, 0599995, 0599997.

30. Yorkshire, England, Church of England Parish Records, 1538-1873, (ancestry.com image 33); page 59 [transcript of the original] Yorkshire Parish Register Section; Leeds, England, United Kingdom; Yorkshire: Weston Parish Register, 1639-1812.

31. West Yorkshire, England, Church of England Baptisms, Marriages and Burials, 1512-1812, (ancestry.com image 1); P17/1/3.

32. Findmypast.co.uk. Transcript of record, 25 November 2022. Country: England; Record set: England Marriages 1538-1973; Category: Birth,

Marriage, Death & Parish Records; Subcategory: Parish Marriages; Collections from: England, Great Britain

33. England Births and Christenings, 1538-1975, database, (https://familysearch.org/ark:/61903/1:1:NYBT-74F : 21 September 2020), James Pickles in entry for Thomas Pickles, 1802.

34. England & Wales, Non-Conformist and Non-Parochial Registers, 1567-1936, Registers of Births, Marriages and Deaths Surrendered to the Non-Parochial Registers Commissions of 1837 and 1857, GRO, database with image, (ancestry.com image 51); Class RG4; Piece 3394. (Birth and Baptism given); "Thomas son of James & Jane Pickles, Newsholm."

35. England and Wales Non-Conformist Record Indexes (RG4-8), 1588-1977, database, (https://familysearch.org/ark:/61903/1:1:FWX3-WYL : 11 December 2014), James Pickles in entry for Thomas Pickles, 15 Aug 1802, Baptism; citing p. 51, Keighley, Yorkshire, record group RG4, Public Record Office, London.

36. West Yorkshire, England, Church of England Deaths and Burials, 1813-1985, West Yorkshire Archive Service; Wakefield, Yorkshire, Ancestry.com, database with images, Number 1073; (ancestry.com image 15).

37. Ibid. Number 706 (ancestry.com image 12); New Reference Number: WDP9/50.

38. 1841 England and Wales Census, Bradford, Haworth, Yorkshire, District 3; (ancestry.com image 5); Class: HO107; Piece: 1295; Book: 6; Civil Parish: Bradford; County: Yorkshire; ED 3; Folio: 43; Page: 7; Line: 13; GSU roll: 464255.

39. 1841 Census of England & Wales, Bingley, Yorkshire, 6 June 1841, Page 16; "Mills St"; (ancestry.com image 13); HO 107 / 1312/8.

40. 1851 Census of England and Wales, Bingley, Yorkshire, 30 March 1851, Page 49; Schedule 179, "Baptist Row"; H.O. 107 2286; "Jane Greenwood."

41. England & Wales, Non-Conformist and Non-Parochial Registers, 1567-1936, Registers of Births, Marriages and Deaths Surrendered to the Non-Parochial Registers Commissions of 1837 and 1857, UK National Archives; GRO, database with image, (ancestry.com image 54); Class Number: RG 4; Piece Number: 3394.

42. Circa 1806 per 1841 census; 1804 in 1851 census.

43. England Births and Christenings, 1538-1975, familysearch.org, database, (https://familysearch.org/ark:/61903/1:1:JM2X-8F4 : 21 September 2020), James Pickles in entry for Jane Pickles, 1803.

44. England and Wales Non-Conformist Record Indexes (RG4-8), 1588-1977, database, (https://familysearch.org/ark:/61903/1:1:FWG7-54N : 11 December 2014), James Pickles in entry for Jane Pickles, 31 Aug 1803, Baptism; citing page 54, Keighley, Yorkshire, record group RG4, Public Record Office, London.

45. England & Wales, Non-Conformist and Non-Parochial Registers, 1567-1936, Registers of Births, Marriages and Deaths Surrendered to the Non-Parochial Registers Commissions of 1837 and 1857, Class Number: RG 4; Piece Number: 3394; (ancestry.com image 54); "Jane daughter of James & Jane Pickles. Newsholme…"

46. England & Wales, Civil Registration Death Index, 1837-1915, GRO. England and Wales Civil Registration Indexes, London, database with image, (ancestry.com), 1861, M Quarter in CHIPPING SODBURY, Volume 6A, Page 121.

47. Preston Chronicle and Lancashire Advertiser, newspaper, Yorkshire, England: "Deaths," 19 January 1861, page 5, "…Jane Greenwood, Canal-street, 58…"; GRO number 317, wife of George Greenwood, Farmer.

48. West Yorkshire, Non-Conformist Records, 1646-1985. Most probable: (ancestry.com image 321); "Jane Greenwood Wife of Jno. G. Sun St Cullinworth 49yr Brain Fever April 1st 1852 April 4th [no. of grave] 81 5/57 [Connection to the Chapel] Member."

49. 1841 Census of England & Wales, Bingley, Yorkshire, 6 June 1841, "Stuff Maney."

50. 1851 Census of England and Wales, Bingley, Yorkshire, 30 March 1851, "Stay Maker."

51. Lancashire Anglican Parish Registers, Lancashire Archives, Preston, Lancashire, England, Church of England Marriages and Banns, 1754-1936, Number 86; (ancestry.com image 86).

52. West Yorkshire, England, Church of England Deaths and Burials, 1813-1985, Number 807; (ancestry.com image 3).

53. Church of All Saints, Bingley, https://en.wikipedia.org/wiki/Church_of_All_Saints,_Bingley, (viewed 4 August 2023).

54. 1841 Census of England & Wales, Bingley, Yorkshire, 6 June 1841, Page 16; "Mills St"; (ancestry.com image 13); HO 107 / 1312/8; "John Greenwood."

55. 1851 Census of England and Wales, Bingley, Yorkshire, 30 March 1851, Page 49; Schedule 179, "Baptist Row"; H.O. 107 2286; "John Greenwood."

56. 1861 Census of England and Wales, Bingley, Yorkshire, 7 April 1861, Page 44; Schedule 245; R.G. 9 3220; Hamlet of Harden; "John Greenwood Widdower."

57. England, Select Marriages, 1538–1973, database, FHL Film Number 919129.

58. Note. Circa 1806 in 1841 census; 1804 in 1851 census; 1803 in 1861 census.

59. 1841 Census of England & Wales, Bingley, Yorkshire, 6 June 1841, "Stuff Maneg."

60. 1851 Census of England and Wales, Bingley, Yorkshire, 30 March 1851. Not clearly legible or found in trade books. See Fuller.

61. 1861 Census of England and Wales, Bingley, Yorkshire, 7 April 1861, "Weaver."

62. 1871 Census of England and Wales, Halifax, Yorkshire, 2 April 1871, Southowram district; Page 15/90; Schedule 66, in the household of his brother-in-law William Garnet; "John Greenwood" age 52; with "Ellen Greenwood" age 65. His occupation is "waste dealer" but scratched over.

63. UK National Archives; GRO, England and Wales Non-Conformist and Non-Parochial Registers, 1567-1970, RG4, database with images, www.ancestry.com, Piece 3393, Keighley, Bethel Chapel (Baptist), Yorkshire, 1791-1837; "Pickles and Lugden," page 9.

64. West Yorkshire, Non-Conformist Records, 1646-1985, BK16/1/1/1; Reel: Keighley, Oakworth, Sutton; BNC19; Line 8; recorded 1807; (ancestry.com image 34); "8 Joseph Pickles Son of James and Jane Pickles Newsholme was born December the twentieth One thousand eight hundred and four."

65. England & Wales, Non-Conformist and Non-Parochial Registers, 1567-1936, Registers of Births, Marriages and Deaths Surrendered to the Non-Parochial Registers Commissions of 1837 and 1857, UK National Archives; GRO, database with image, "Pickles and Lugden." Page 9 (ancestry.com image 12); "1 Joseph Pickles, Son of James and Jane Pickles of Newsholm was born…"
66. England Births and Christenings, 1538-1975, database, (https://familysearch.org/ark:/61903/1:1:JM2X-ZX5 : 18 September 2020), James Pickles in entry for Joseph Pickles, 1804.
67. England, Select Births and Christenings, 1538-1975, database with no images, Ancestry.com, FHL Film Number 0828136 (RG4 3393).
68. West Yorkshire, Non-Conformist Records, 1646-1985, BK16/1/1/1; Reel: Keighley, Oakworth, Sutton; BNC19; recorded 1807; Line 9; (ancestry.com image 34).
69. England Births and Christenings, 1538-1975, (https://familysearch.org/ark:/61903/1:1:JM2X-8Q8 : 18 September 2020), James Pickles in entry for Isaac Pickles, 1806.
70. England & Wales, Non-Conformist and Non-Parochial Registers, 1567-1936, Registers of Births, Marriages and Deaths Surrendered to the Non-Parochial Registers Commissions of 1837 and 1857, GRO, "Pickles and Lugden." Page 9 (ancestry.com image 12); "2 Isaac Pickles, son of James and Jane Pickles of Newsholm. Was born…"
71. West Yorkshire, Non-Conformist Records, 1646-1985, West Yorkshire Archive Service, database with image, ancestry.com, BK16/1/1/1; Reel: Keighley, Oakworth, Sutton; BNC19; Line 8; recorded 1807; "9 Isaac Pickles, Son of James and Jane Pickles of Newsholme was born November the thirteenth, one thousand eight hundred and six." (ancestry.com image 34).
72. West Yorkshire Archive Service, West Yorkshire, England, Church of England Marriages and Banns, 1813-1935; Page 55; (ancestry.com image 15).
73. West Yorkshire, England, Church of England Baptisms, Marriages and Burials, 1512-1812. Recorded in May 1808 (ancestry.com image 10). Haworth, St. Michael and All Angels.
74. West Yorkshire Archive Service, West Yorkshire, England, Church of England Marriages and Banns, 1813-1935, Page 102; (ancestry.com image 27).
75. England & Wales, Non-Conformist and Non-Parochial Registers, 1567-1936, Registers of Births, Marriages and Deaths Surrendered to the Non-Parochial Registers Commissions of 1837 and 1857, "Pickles and Lugden." Page 9 (ancestry.com image 12); "3 James Pickles, son of James and Jane Pickles of Newsholm. Was born…"
76. West Yorkshire, Non-Conformist Records, 1646-1985, BK16/1/1/1; Reel: Keighley, Oakworth, Sutton; BNC19; recorded 1808; (ancestry.com image 34); "10 James Pickles Son of James and Jane Pickles of Newsholme was born May the twenty eight One thousand eight hundred and eight."
77. England Births and Christenings, 1538-1975, familysearch.org, database, (https://familysearch.org/ark:/61903/1:1:JWD2-YZ2 : 18 September 2020), James Pickles in entry for James Pickles, 1808.
78. England, Select Births and Christenings, 1538-1975, database with no images, Ancestry.com, FHL Film Number 0828136 (RG4 3393).
79. West Yorkshire, Non-Conformist Records, 1646-1985, BK16/1/1/1; Reel: Keighley, Oakworth, Sutton; BNC19; recorded 1810; (ancestry.com image 34); "12 Elizabeth Pickles Daughter of James and Jane

Pickles of Newsholme Wasborn February the twelweth one thousand eight hundred and ten."

80. England & Wales, Non-Conformist and Non-Parochial Registers, 1567-1936, Registers of Births, Marriages and Deaths Surrendered to the Non-Parochial Registers Commissions of 1837 and 1857, "Pickles and Lugden." Page 9 (ancestry.com image 12); "4 Elizabeth Pickles, daughter of James and Jane Pickles of Newsholm was born..."

81. England Births and Christenings, 1538-1975, (https://familysearch.org/ark:/61903/1:1:JM2X-8QT : 18 September 2020), James Pickles in entry for Elizabeth Pickles, 1810.

82. 1841 Census of England & Wales, Bingley, Yorkshire, 6 June 1841, Enumeration Schedule 51; Page 13; Bocking; "Sarah Cousen."

83. 1851 Census of England and Wales, Bingley, Yorkshire, 30 March 1851, Page 41; (ancestry.com image 42); Schedule 142 "Brocking"; "Alice Cousin."

84. 1861 Census of England and Wales, Bingley, Yorkshire, 7 April 1861, Page 44; Schedule 116 "Meadowfield House"; "Alice Cousin."

85. 1871 Census of England and Wales, Bingley, Yorkshire, 2 April 1871, Page 14; Schedule 68; Cockshells House; "Alice Cousin" (widow).

86. West Yorkshire, Non-Conformist Records, 1646-1985, Baptist: BK16/1/1/1; Reel: Keighley, Oakworth, Sutton; BNC19; recorded 1818; (ancestry.com image 34); "24 Alice Pickles Daughter of James and Jane Pickles of Newsholm was born February the tenth, one thousand eight hundred and twelve."

87. England & Wales, Non-Conformist and Non-Parochial Registers, 1567-1936, Registers of Births, Marriages and Deaths Surrendered to the Non-Parochial Registers Commissions of 1837 and 1857. Baptist: "Pickles and Lugden." Page 9 (ancestry.com image 12); "6 Alice Pickles, daughter of James and Jane Pickles of Newsholm was born..."

88. England Births and Christenings, 1538-1975, (https://familysearch.org/ark:/61903/1:1:NPK6-BL2 : 18 September 2020), James Pickles in entry for Alice Pickles, 1812.

89. Born circa 1816 per 1841 census; born in Bingley, Yorkshire per 1861 census.

90. England & Wales, Civil Registration Death Index, 1837-1915, GRO. England and Wales Civil Registration Indexes, London, database with image, (ancestry.com), volume 9a, page 118; 3rd quarter.

91. West Yorkshire, England, Church of England Deaths and Burials, 1813-1985, Number 1868; (ancestry.com image 4); Abode: Paper Mill Bridge.

92. 1841 Census of England & Wales, Bingley, Yorkshire, 6 June 1841, "Worsted Weaver" [ditto from husband's trade].

93. 1861 Census of England and Wales, Bingley, Yorkshire, 7 April 1861, "Laborers Wife."

94. 1871 Census of England and Wales, Bingley, Yorkshire, 2 April 1871, "Pauper."

95. 1841 Census of England & Wales, Bingley, Yorkshire, 6 June 1841, Enumeration Schedule 51; Page 13; Bocking; "William Cousen."

96. 1851 Census of England and Wales, Bingley, Yorkshire, 30 March 1851, Page 41; (ancestry.com image 42); Schedule 142 "Brocking"; "William Cousin."

97. 1861 Census of England and Wales, Bingley, Yorkshire, 7 April 1861, Page 44; Schedule 116 "Meadowfield House"; "William Cousin."

98. England, Select Marriages, 1538–1973, database, FHL Film Number 0919144-146.

99. West Yorkshire Archive Service, West Yorkshire, England, Church of England Marriages and Banns, 1813-1935, Page 71; number 212; "William Cousin, Bachelor, Alice Pickles, Spinster".

100. West Yorkshire Archive Service, West Yorkshire, England, Church of England Births and Baptisms, 1813-1910, (birth date is recorded at the side of the ledger – apparently baptized several years later).

101. Circa 1816 in 1841 and 1851 censuses; ca 1813 in 1861 census.

102. West Yorkshire Archive Service, West Yorkshire, England, Church of England Births and Baptisms, 1813-1910, "Abode: Bockin Hall; Profession: weaver; Parents: John and Mary Cousin"; Number 282; (ancestry.com image 1).

103. England and Wales Civil Death Registration Index 1837-2007, database with scanned image, familysearch.org and ancestry.com and findmypast.com, GRO. England and Wales Civil Registration Indexes. London, Volume 9a; Page 119; 1st quarter, 1868.

104. West Yorkshire, England, Church of England Deaths and Burials, 1813-1985, Number 1504; Page 188; Reference 52D84/1/2; (ancestry.-com image 1); Abode: Paper Mill Bridgeslaw; Age 56 yrs.

105. 1841 Census of England & Wales, Bingley, Yorkshire, 6 June 1841, "Worsted Weaver."

106. 1851 Census of England and Wales, Bingley, Yorkshire, 30 March 1851, "Hand Loom Worsted Weaver."

107. 1861 Census of England and Wales, Bingley, Yorkshire, 7 April 1861, "Labourer in Iron Foundry."

108. West Yorkshire, Non-Conformist Records, 1646-1985, BK16/1/1/1; Reel: Keighley, Oakworth, Sutton; BNC19; recorded 1818; (ancestry.-com image 34); "23 William Pickles Son of James and Jane Pickles of Newsholme was born June the twenty second One thousand eight hundred and thirteen."

109. England & Wales, Non-Conformist and Non-Parochial Registers, 1567-1936, Registers of Births, Marriages and Deaths Surrendered to the Non-Parochial Registers Commissions of 1837 and 1857, "Pickles and Lugden." Page 9 (ancestry.com image 12); "6 William Pickles, Son of James and Jane Pickles of Newsholm was born…"

110. England Births and Christenings, 1538-1975, familysearch.org, database, (https://familysearch.org/ark:/61903/1:1:JM2X-83T : 18 September 2020), James Pickles in entry for William Pickles, 1813.

111. Family Bible. (Observed by Curt Sanders in 1970s.)

112. Birth Record, 30 Jun 1843, Dewsbury, County of York, England, From son James.

113. 1841 Census of England and Wales, Halifax, West Riding, Yorkshire, 6 June 1841, "Halifax St James" HO107; Piece/Folio: 1306/26; Book 5; line 5; Page 4; citing PRO HO 107; (familysearch.org/ark:/61903/1:1:MQ5X-KVV); residence: Clough Head, South. "John Pickles."

114. 1851 Census of England and Wales, Green Lane, Ovenden Township, Yorkshire, 30 March 1851, Series: HO107, Line: 16, Illingworth Moor Green Lane, Piece/Folio: 2301/347; Page: 4, Ecclesiastical district: St Johns, Family: 13. "John Pickles."

115. 1861 Census of England and Wales, Luddenden (Halifax), Warley, District 6, Yorkshire, 7 April 1861, UK National Archives; Page 26; RG 9; Piece/Folio: 3295/80; GSU roll: 543109; Schedule 108; (www.familysearch.org/ark:/61903/1:1:M7ZG-NTZ : 3 March 2021); "John Pickles."

116. The 1861 Census has his grandson William H. Ingham, age 3, living with him.

117. 1871 Census of England and Wales, Warley Township, Luddenden, Yorkshire, 2 April 1871, Class RG10; Piece 4416; Folio 29; Page 2; GSU roll 847116; ED 3; Schedule 6, Upper Edge end; "John Pickles."

118. 1881 Census of England and Wales, Warley Township, Luddenden, Yorkshire, 3 April 1881, ED 3; Schedule 5; "Lower Edge End" street; Class: RG11; Piece: 4417; Folio: 29; Page: 1; GSU roll: 1342056; "John Pickles."

119. England Births and Christenings, 1538-1975, (www.familysearch.org/ark:/61903/1:1:NPK6-YP2), John Pickles, 1816.

120. West Yorkshire, Non-Conformist Records, 1646-1985, BK16/1/1/1; Reel: Keighley, Oakworth, Sutton; BNC19; recorded 1818; (ancestry.com image 34); "25 John Pickles, Son of James and Jane Pickles of Newsholm was born November the fifteenth, one thousand eight hundred and sixteen."

121. England & Wales, Non-Conformist and Non-Parochial Registers, 1567-1936, <u>Registers of Births, Marriages and Deaths Surrendered to the Non-Parochial Registers Commissions of 1837 and 1857</u>, "Pickles and Lugden." Page 9 (ancestry.com image 12); "7 John Pickles, Son of James and Jane Pickles of Newsholm was born…" Bethel Chapel Baptist church register.

122. England & Wales Civil Registration Indexes, 1837-1915, (ancestry.com image 10); Volume 9A; Page 349.

123. Death Certificate/Record. GRO; Halifax District; sub-district Luddenden, County of York; registered 16 June 1890, John Wormald, Registrar, number 372. Signed by son Wm. H. Pickles.

124. Note: "Old Age Cardiac Failure Certified by Astley B. Crorother L.S.A." | "W. H. Pickles Son Present at the death Newlands Warley."

125. 1851 Census of England and Wales, Green Lane, Ovenden Township, Yorkshire, 30 March 1851, "Wool Comber."

126. 1854: "Comber" from son William Henry Pickles' birth record.

127. 1861 Census of England and Wales, Luddenden (Halifax), Warley, District 6, Yorkshire, 7 April 1861, The National Archives; Kew, London, "Wool Comber."

128. 1871 Census of England and Wales, Warley Township, Luddenden, Yorkshire, 2 April 1871, "Farmer."

129. 1878: "Farmer" from son William Henry Pickle's marriage record.

130. 1881 Census of England and Wales, Warley Township, Luddenden, Yorkshire, 3 April 1881, "Farmer of 8 Acres."

131. West Yorkshire Archive Service, West Yorkshire, England, Church of England Births and Baptisms, 1813-1910, Yorkshire Parish Records; New Reference Number: WDP39/6; (ancestry.com image 22).

132. 1841 Census of England and Wales, Halifax, West Riding, Yorkshire, 6 June 1841, "Halifax St James" HO107; Piece/Folio: 1306/26; Book 5; line 5; Page 4; citing PRO HO 107; (familysearch.org/ark:/61903/1:1:MQ5X-KVV); residence: Clough Head, South; "Hannah Pickles."

133. 1851 Census of England and Wales, Green Lane, Ovenden Township, Yorkshire, 30 March 1851, Series: HO107, Line: 16, Illingworth Moor

Green Lane, Piece/Folio: 2301/347; Page: 4, Ecclesiastical district: St Johns, Family: 13 Green Lane; "Hannah Pickles."

134. 1861 Census of England and Wales, Luddenden (Halifax), Warley, District 6, Yorkshire, 7 April 1861, UK National Archives, Page 26; RG 9; Piece/Folio: 3295/80; GSU roll: 543109; Schedule 108; (ancestry.com image 25); (https://www.familysearch.org/ark:/61903/1:1:M7ZG-NTZ : 3 March 2021); "Hannah Pickles."

135. 1871 Census of England and Wales, Warley Township, Luddenden, Yorkshire, 2 April 1871, Class RG10; Piece 4416; Folio 29; Page 2; GSU roll 847116; ED 3; Schedule 6, Upper Edge end; "Hannah Pickles."

136. 1881 Census of England and Wales, Warley Township, Luddenden, Yorkshire, 3 April 1881, ED 3; Schedule 5; "Lower Edge End" street; Class RG11; Piece 4417; Folio 29; Page 1; GSU roll 1342056; "Hannah Pickles."

137. England, Select Marriages, 1538–1973, database, (https://family-search.org/ark:/61903/1:1:NJ2Z-W9C : 13 March 2020), Hannah Horsfield in entry for John Pickles, 1835. Page 109, 327.

138. England, Yorkshire, Bishop's Transcripts, 1547-1957, Borthwick Institute for Archives, (https://www.familysearch.org/ark:/61903/1:1:68ZH-S6QK : 16 August 2021), Hannah Horsfield, 1835; Page 109.

139. West Yorkshire Archive Service, West Yorkshire, England, Church of England Marriages and Banns, 1813-1935, (ancestry.com image 126); Page 109; number 327; Yorkshire Parish Records; Reference Number: WDP53/1/3/28. "John Pickles of Warley... comber, bachelor and Hannah Horsfield of Warley... Spinster..."

140. Ibid. (ancestry.com image 297); Page 47; number 231; "John Pickles comber & Hannah Horsfield Spinster both of Warley in this Parish" St John the Baptist; Banns 26 June, 5 and 12 July 1835.

141. England, Yorkshire, Bishop's Transcripts, 1547-1957, Borthwick Institute for Archives, (https://www.familysearch.org/ark:/61903/1:1:68ZH-S6QK : 4 August 2022).

142. Horsfield residence, Warley; recorded as Halifax.

143. West Yorkshire Archive Service, West Yorkshire, England, Church of England Births and Baptisms, 1813-1910, Yorkshire Parish Records; New Reference Number: WDP138/1/2/1; number 518; (ancestry.com image 20).

144. England Births and Christenings, 1538-1975, (https://www.family-search.org/ark:/61903/1:1:J7W1-V5Z : 5 February 2023).

145. Death Certificate/Record. GRO, number 303, "Wife of John Pickles formerly a Wool Comber" | "William Henry Pickles Son In attendance"

146. England and Wales Civil Death Registration Index 1837-2007, GRO. England and Wales Civil Registration Indexes. (www.family-search.org/ark:/61903/1:1:2JB8-VSW), findmypast (www.findmy-past.com : 2012); citing Death, Halifax, Yorkshire, England, GRO.

147. England & Wales Civil Registration Indexes, 1837-1915, GRO, (ancestry.com image 11); DEATHS registered in October, November, and December 1889; Page 388; Volume 9A.

148. Halifax Courier, newspaper, Halifax, West Yorkshire, "Deaths," 9 November 1889, page 8; "Cross Stone-road, Standsfield."

149. 1861 Census of England and Wales, Luddenden (Halifax), Warley, District 6, Yorkshire, 7 April 1861, UK National Archives.

150. Family Bible.

151. 1851 Census of England and Wales, Green Lane, Ovenden Township, Yorkshire, 30 March 1851, Series HO107, Line 16, Illingworth Moor Green Lane, Piece/Folio 2301/347; Page 4, Ecclesiastical district: St Johns, Family: 13; "James Pickles."

152. 1861 Census of England and Wales, Luddenden (Halifax), Warley, District 6, Yorkshire, 7 April 1861, Page 26; RG 9; Piece/Folio 3295/80; GSU roll 543109; Schedule 108; (www.familysearch.org/ark:/61903/1:1:M7ZG-NTZ : 3 March 2021); "James Pickles."

153. 1871 Census of England and Wales, Hipperholme With Brighouse, Yorkshire, 2 April 1871, Class RG10; Piece 4384; Folio 77; Page 20; GSU roll 848091; Schedule 104; Lightcliffe street; "James Pickles."

154. 1880 US Census, Hamlin Township, Eaton County, Michigan, June 1880, NARA T9; Roll 578; ED 78; Page 15/324; Dwelling 157; Family 171; Line 38; "James Pickle."

155. 1900 US Census, Jackson City, Jackson County, Michigan, June 1900, NARA T623; Roll 719; ED 19; Ward 8; Sheet 1A; Page 58; House 634; W. Water Loo Street; Dwelling 4; Family 4; Line 20; "James Pickles."

156. 1910 US Census, Douglass Township, Montcalm County, Michigan, April 1910, NARA T624; Roll 665; ED 149; Sheet 3A; Page 131; Dwelling 36; Family 37; Line 1; "James Pickles."

157. Tombstone (See findagrave.com): "At Rest | James Pickles, | Born May 31, 1843, | Died Feb. 8, 1911, | Aged 67 yrs. 8 ms. 8 days."

158. Birth Certificate/Record. Birth record, 1843, Registrar District Luddenden; GRO, 3 April 2022. Parents: "John Pickles… Hannah Pickles formerly Horsfield"; registered 11 July 1843.

159. Baptismal record and tombstone says 31 May 1843; 1900 US census says May 1838; death record says 1844 and calculates 30 April 1843—which is inconsistent with its own calculation!

160. England Births and Christenings, 1538-1975, familysearch.org, database, confirms born 31 May 1843.

161. West Yorkshire Archive Service, West Yorkshire, England, Church of England Births and Baptisms, 1813-1910, Born 31 May 1843 to John and Hannah Pickles.

162. Ibid. New Reference Number: WDP39/5; (ancestry.com images 9, 18).

163. Baptismal Certificate. West Yorkshire Archive Service; Wakefield, Yorkshire, England; Yorkshire Parish Records; New Reference Number: WDP39/5; Page 211; number 1685; (ancestry.com image 9).

164. England Births and Christenings, 1538-1975, (https://familysearch.org/ark:/61903/1:1:NF3B-DL5 : 21 March 2020), Hannah Pickles in entry for James Pickles, 1843.

165. Michigan Deaths and Burials, 1800-1995, Michigan Deaths and Burial, 1800-1995, v 2 C p 27; (https://familysearch.org/ark:/61903/1:1:FHGZ-KYH).

166. Michigan Death Records Project, Library of Michigan, Lansing, Rolls 1-302; Archive Barcode/Item Number 30000008532784; Roll Number 159; Certificate Number 2.

167. Death Certificate/Record. State Of Michigan, Department of State-Division of Vital Statistics, Certificate Of Death, Register No. 2, 6 March 1911. Mother's name not known; Informant: Mrs. James Pickles [his wife]; number 3723; "Bulbar paralysis."

168. Find-A-Grave, (www.findagrave.com/memorial/27327015/james-pickles : accessed 23 January 2022). Memorial ID 27327015, citing

Hillside Entrican Cemetery, Entrican, Montcalm County, Michigan; maintained by Gail (contributor 47136090).

169. 1861 Census of England and Wales, Luddenden (Halifax), Warley, District 6, Yorkshire, 7 April 1861, "Worsted Factory hand."

170. 1871 Census of England and Wales, Hipperholme With Brighouse, Yorkshire, 2 April 1871, "Carpet Weaver."

171. 1880 US Census, Hamlin Township, Eaton County, Michigan, June 1880, "Farmer."

172. Polk's Jackson City And County Directory, 1899-1900, Detroit, Michigan: R. L. Polk & Co., Publishers, 1900, Page 396; (ancestry.com image 216); "Pickles James, farmer, bds 916 Chicago."

173. 1900 US Census, Jackson City, Jackson County, Michigan, June 1900, "day Laborer."

174. Jackson City Directory 1903, Detroit, Michigan: R. L. Polk & Co., 1903, Page 448; (ancestry.com image 244); "Pickles James, lab, bds 634 N Waterloo av."

175. 1910 US Census, Douglass Township, Montcalm County, Michigan, April 1910, "farmer" | "general farm."

176. Huddersfield Chronicle,"Perjury At Todmorden," 17 August 1867, page 7.

177. Burnley Gazette, "District News: Burnley-Valley," 17 August 1867, page 3.

178. NARA, Passenger Lists of Vessels Arriving at Boston, Massachusetts, 1820-1891; Record Group Title: Records of the U.S. Customs Service; Record Group Number 36; Series Number M277; Roll Number 082.

179. 1910 US Census, Douglass Township, Montcalm County, Michigan, April 1910.

180. Massachusetts, Index to Boston Passenger Lists, 1848-1891. (https://familysearch.org/ark:/61903/1:1:Q2HV-W99S : 16 March 2018), James Pickles, 1872; citing Immigration, ship *Tripoli*, NARA M265; roll M265; (familysearch.org image 2754).

181. Family Bible. (Observed by Curt Sanders, 1970s.)

182. 1841 Census of England and Wales, Brock Holes, Upper, Ovenden, Yorkshire, England, 6 June 1841, Class HO107; Piece 1302; Book 7; Civil Parish: Halifax; ED 24; Folio 41; Page 6; Line 11; GSU roll: 464262; "Hannah Clay" (ancestry.com image 4).

183. 1851 Census of England and Wales, Ovenden, Yorkshire-West Riding, 30 March 1851, "94 Rocks," Class HO107; Piece 2301; Folio 337; Page 25; GSU roll 87509; (ancestry.com image 26); "Hannah Clay."

184. 1871 Census of England and Wales, Hipperholme With Brighouse, Yorkshire, 2 April 1871, Class RG10; Piece 4384; Folio 77; Page 20; GSU roll 848091; Schedule 104; Lightcliffe street; "Hannah Pickles."

185. 1880 US Census, Hamlin Township, Eaton County, Michigan, June 1880, NARA T9; Roll 578; ED 78; Page 15/324; Dwelling 157; Family 171; Line 39; "Hanah Pickle."

186. 1900 US Census, Jackson City, Jackson County, Michigan, June 1900, NARA T623; Roll 719; ED 19; Ward 8; Sheet 1A; Page 58; W. Water Lou Street; House 634; Dwelling 4; Family 4; Line 21; "Hannah Pickles."

187. 1910 US Census, Douglass Township, Montcalm County, Michigan, April 1910, NARA T624; Roll 665; ED 149; Sheet 3A; Page 131; Dwelling 36; Family 37; Line 2; "Hannah Pickles."

188. 1920 US Census, Douglass Township, Montcalm County, Michigan, January 1920, NARA T625; Roll 787; Sheet 4A; ED 113; Line 50; Dwelling 90; Family 90; Page 102; "Hannah Pickles" [living alone].

189. Tombstone (See findagrave.com): "Hannah Pickles | 1838-1927."

190. Marriage Certificate/Record/Application. #62, County York, England (original in possession of Curtis Daryl Sanders, great-great-grandson).

191. England & Wales, Civil Registration Marriage Index, 1837-2005, findmypast.com, 1866: Oct-Nov-Dec; (ancestry.com image 9 for James; image 10 for Hannah); Volume 9a; Page 787.

192. Leeds Times, "Miscellaneous,"24 November 1866, page 8. "On Sunday, at South-parade Chapel, Halifax, by the Rev. J. A. Macdonald, Mr. James Pickles, carpet weaver, Warley, to Miss H. Clay, of Halifax."

193. Birth Certificate/Record. First Quarter 1838; Page 253; Volume 22; #203. GRO, registered 11 February 1838.

194. Birth record says 30th; death records says she was born 31st January 1838.

195. England & Wales Civil Registration Indexes, 1837-1915, Birth: First Quarter 1838; Volume 22, Page 253.

196. Michigan Death Certificates, 1921-1952, database, Michigan Division for Vital Records and Health Statistics, Lansing, familysearch.org, Belding, Ionia, Michigan, United States.

197. Death Certificate/Record. State of Michigan, Michigan Department Of Health, Division of Vital Statistics, Certificate Of Death, file 134 326.

198. Find-A-Grave, (www.findagrave.com/memorial/27326986/hanna-pickles : accessed 25 May 2022). Memorial ID 27326986, citing Hillside Entrican Cemetery, Entrican, Montcalm County, Michigan; maintained by Gail (contributor 47136090).

199. 1851 Census of England and Wales, Ovenden, Yorkshire-West Riding, 30 March 1851, "Nurse."

200. 1871 Census of England and Wales, Halifax, Yorkshire, 2 April 1871, National Archives, Richmond, Surrey, "Farmers Wife."

201. Leeds Times, "Miscellaneous," 24 November 1866, page 8.

202. 1841 Census of England and Wales, Bingley, Yorkshire, 6 June 1841, Page 16; "Mills St"; (ancestry.com image 13); HO 107 / 1312/8; "James Greenwood."

203. 1851 Census of England and Wales, Bingley, Yorkshire, 30 March 1851, Page 50; Schedule 179, "Village of Cullingworth"; H.O. 107 2286; "James Greenwood."

204. 1861 Census of England and Wales, Northowram, Yorkshire, 7 April 1861, Page 14; Schedule 85; "Black Mires"; R.G. 9/3302; "James Greenwood."

205. 1871 Census of England and Wales, Clayton, Yorkshire, 2 April 1871, Class Rg 10; Piece 4493; Folio 14; Page 21; GSU roll 847126; Schedule 127 "Victoria Street"; "James Greenwood."

206. 1881 Census of England and Wales, Howarth, Yorkshire, 3 April 1881, Class RG11; Piece 4352; Folio 34; Page 14; GSU roll 1342039; Schedule 80 "Ivy Bank Lane"; "James Greenwood."

207. 1891 Census of England and Wales, Sutton, Yorkshire, 5 April 1891, Class: RG12; Piece 3536; Folio 50; Page 24; GSU roll 6098646; Schedule 182 "East Field Pl" Sutton Hill, Keighley; "James Greenwood."

208. Tombstone. (See findagrave.com.)

209. (See baptismal data.)

210. West Yorkshire Archive Service, West Yorkshire, England, Church of England Births and Baptisms, 1813-1910, Number 1241; "James Son of John & Jane Greenwood [Abode] Bingley"; Birthdate is noted under baptismal date.

211. England, Select Births and Christenings, 1538-1975, database with no images, Ancestry.com, FHL Film Number 6358439; Reference ID yr 1829-1837 p 156.

212. England & Wales, Civil Registration Death Index, 1837-1915, 1893; Keighley, Volume 9a; Page 152; 3rd Quarter.

213. Find-A-Grave, (www.findagrave.com/memorial/241924449/james-greenwood: accessed 05 August 2023). Memorial ID 241924449, citing West Lane Baptist Chapel, Haworth, Borough of Bradford, West Yorkshire, England; maintained by Dianne Harbourne (contributor 50043574).

214. 1851 Census of England and Wales, Bingley, Yorkshire, 30 March 1851, "woolsorter."

215. 1861 Census of England and Wales, Northowram, Yorkshire, 7 April 1861, "Wool Sorter."

216. 1871 Census of England and Wales, Clayton, Yorkshire, 2 April 1871, "Woolsorter."

217. 1881 Census of England and Wales, Howarth, Yorkshire, 3 April 1881, "Woolsorter."

218. 1891 Census of England and Wales, Sutton, Yorkshire, 5 April 1891, "Woolsorter."

219. Other years are from children's birth records.

220. 1851 Census of England and Wales, Bingley, Yorkshire, 30 March 1851, Class HO107; Piece 2286; Folio 273; Page 25; GSU roll 87474-87475; Schedule 91; "Spring House" village of Harden. "Ellen Savage" living with her brother Richard Savage.

221. 1861 Census of England and Wales, Northowram, Yorkshire, 7 April 1861, Page 14; Schedule 85; "Black Mires"; R.G. 9/3302; "Ellen Greenwood."

222. 1871 Census of England and Wales, Clayton, Yorkshire, 2 April 1871, Class Rg 10; Piece 4493; Folio 14; Page 21; GSU roll 847126; Schedule 127 "Victoria Street"; "Ellen Greenwood."

223. 1881 Census of England and Wales, Howarth, Yorkshire, 3 April 1881, Class RG11; Piece 4352; Folio 34; Page 14; GSU roll 1342039; Schedule 80 "Ivy Bank Lane"; "Elen Greenwood."

224. 1891 Census of England and Wales, Sutton, Yorkshire, 5 April 1891, Class RG12; Piece 3536; Folio 50; Page 24; GSU roll 6098646; Schedule 182 "East Field Pl" Sutton Hill, Keighley; "Ellen Greenwood."

225. 1901 Census of England and Wales, Steeton, Yorkshire, 31 March 1901, Class RG13; Piece 4073; Folio 18; Page 28; Schedule 190, "14, Station Rd."; Keighley; "Ellen Greenwood" widow.

226. Tombstone. (See findagrave.com).

227. West Yorkshire Archive Service, West Yorkshire, England, Church of England Marriages and Banns, 1813-1935, Number 190; "James… [of] Cullingworth.." "Ellen… [of] Harden"; both "official age"; brother Peter Greenwood was a witness.

228. Marriage circa 1835; 1861 and 1871 censuses circa 1833.

229. Death Certificate/Record. GRO number 167; "widow of James Greenwood a Wool Sorter"; Informant: Lillie Greenwood [daughter] In attendance 14 Station Road Steeton"; Registered: 8 June 1910.

230. England & Wales, Civil Registration Death Index, 1837-1915, GRO Reference: 1910 J Quarter in KEIGHLEY Volume 9A Page 131.

231. Find-A-Grave, (www.findagrave.com/memorial/241924460/ellen-greenwood: accessed 05 August 2023). Memorial ID 241924460, citing

West Lane Baptist Chapel, Haworth, Borough of Bradford, West Yorkshire; maintained by Dianne Harbourne (contributor 50043574).

232. 1851 Census of England and Wales, Bingley, Yorkshire, 30 March 1851, "Power Loom Weaver."

233. 1861 Census of England and Wales, Northowram, Yorkshire, 7 April 1861, Page 14; Schedule 85; "Black Mires"; R.G. 9/3302; "Lillie Greenwood."

234. 1871 Census of England and Wales, Clayton, Yorkshire, 2 April 1871, Class Rg 10; Piece 4493; Folio 14; Page 21; GSU roll 847126; Schedule 127 "Victoria Street"; "Liley Greenwood."

235. 1881 Census of England and Wales, Howarth, Yorkshire, 3 April 1881, Class RG11; Piece 4352; Folio 34; Page 14; GSU roll 1342039; Schedule 80 "Ivy Bank Lane"; "Lillie Greenwood."

236. 1891 Census of England and Wales, Sutton, Yorkshire, 5 April 1891, Class: RG12; Piece 3536; Folio 50; Page 24; GSU roll 6098646; Schedule 182 "East Field Pl" Sutton Hill, Keighley; "Lillie Greenwood."

237. 1901 Census of England and Wales, Steeton, Yorkshire, 31 March 1901, Class RG13; Piece 4073; Folio 18; Page 28; Schedule 190, "14, Station Rd."; Keighley; "Lillie Greenwood."

238. 1911 Census of England and Wales, Steeton, Yorkshire, 2 April 1911, Schedule 67; Line 1; "Lillie Greenwood"; her nephew Bertram, residing with her.

239. 1939 England and Wales Register [Census], 29 September 1939, Bradford, Yorkshire; House 11; "Lily Greenwood."

240. 1861 Census of England and Wales, Northowram, Yorkshire, 7 April 1861, Page 14; Schedule 85; "Black Mires"; R.G. 9/3302. "Jane Greenwood."

241. 1871 Census of England and Wales, Clayton, Yorkshire, 2 April 1871, Class Rg 10; Piece 4493; Folio 14; Page 21; GSU roll 847126; Schedule 127 "Victoria Street"; "Jane Greenwood."

242. 1881 Census of England and Wales, Howarth, Yorkshire, 3 April 1881, Class RG11; Piece 4352; Folio 34; Page 14; GSU roll 1342039; Schedule 80 "Ivy Bank Lane"; "Jane Greenwood."

243. 1901 Census of England and Wales, York, Yorkshire, 31 March 1901, Class RG13; Piece 4448; Folio 72; Page 25; Page 18/96; Schedule 97; "8 Lockwood Street"; "Jane Pilmoor."

244. 1911 Census of England and Wales, York, Yorkshire, 2 April 1911, PRO RG14; Page 1; York East; Folio 691; Schedule 345; District 517; "Jenny Pilmoor."

245. 1939 England and Wales Register [Census], 29 September 1939, York County Borough; West Riding; Rg 101/3894h; "4 Belle Vue St. Heslington Rd"; Schedule 178; "Jane Pilmoor."

246. 1861 Census of England and Wales, Northowram, Yorkshire, 7 April 1861, Page 14; Schedule 85; "Black Mires"; R.G. 9/3302; "Lucy Ellen Greenwood."

247. 1871 Census of England and Wales, Clayton, Yorkshire, 2 April 1871, Class Rg 10; Piece 4493; Folio 14; Page 21; GSU roll 847126; Schedule 127 "Victoria Street"; "Lucy Ellen Greenwood."

248. 1881 Census of England and Wales, Howarth, Yorkshire, 3 April 1881, Class RG11; Piece 4352; Folio 34; Page 14; GSU roll 1342039; Schedule 80 "Ivy Bank Lane"; "Lucy Ellen Greenwood."

249. 1891 Census of England and Wales, Sutton, Yorkshire, 5 April 1891, Class RG12; Piece 3536; Folio 41; Page 5; GSU roll 6098646; Schedule 40 "Main St."; "Lucy E. Clough."

250. 1871 Census of England and Wales, Clayton, Yorkshire, 2 April 1871, Class Rg 10; Piece 4493; Folio 14; Page 21; GSU roll 847126; Schedule 127 "Victoria Street"; "Sarah Hannah Greenwood."

251. 1881 Census of England and Wales, Howarth, Yorkshire, 3 April 1881, Class RG11; Piece 4352; Folio 34; Page 14; GSU roll 1342039; Schedule 80 "Ivy Bank Lane"; "Sarah H. Greenwood."

252. 1871 Census of England and Wales, Clayton, Yorkshire, 2 April 1871, Class Rg 10; Piece 4493; Folio 14; Page 21; GSU roll 847126; Schedule 127 "Victoria Street"; "John Greenwood."

253. 1881 Census of England and Wales, Howarth, Yorkshire, 3 April 1881, Class RG11; Piece 4352; Folio 34; Page 14; GSU roll 1342039; Schedule 80 "Ivy Bank Lane"; "John Greenwood."

254. 1871 Census of England and Wales, Clayton, Yorkshire, 2 April 1871, Class Rg 10; Piece 4493; Folio 14; Page 21; GSU roll 847126; Schedule 127 "Victoria Street"; "Ada Greenwood."

255. 1881 Census of England and Wales, Howarth, Yorkshire, 3 April 1881, Class RG11; Piece 4352; Folio 34; Page 14; GSU roll 1342039; Schedule 80 "Ivy Bank Lane"; "Ada Greenwood."

256. 1891 Census of England and Wales, Sutton, Yorkshire, 5 April 1891, Class: RG12; Piece 3536; Folio 50; Page 24; GSU roll 6098646; Schedule 182 "East Field Pl" Sutton Hill, Keighley; "Ada Greenwood."

257. 1871 Census of England and Wales, Clayton, Yorkshire, 2 April 1871, Class Rg 10; Piece 4493; Folio 14; Page 21; GSU roll 847126; Schedule 127 "Victoria Street"; "Joseph Edward Greenwood."

258. 1881 Census of England and Wales, Howarth, Yorkshire, 3 April 1881, Class RG11; Piece 4352; Folio 34; Page 14; GSU roll 1342039; Schedule 80 "Ivy Bank Lane"; "Joseph Ed. Greenwood."

259. 1891 Census of England and Wales, Sutton, Yorkshire, 5 April 1891, Class: RG12; Piece 3536; Folio 50; Page 24; GSU roll 6098646; Schedule 182 "East Field Pl" Sutton Hill, Keighley; "Joseph E. Greenwood."

260. 1881 Census of England and Wales, Howarth, Yorkshire, 3 April 1881, Class RG11; Piece 4352; Folio 34; Page 14; GSU roll 1342039; Schedule 80 "Ivy Bank Lane"; "Matilda Greenwood."

261. 1891 Census of England and Wales, Sutton, Yorkshire, 5 April 1891, Class RG12; Piece 3536; Folio 50; Page 24; GSU roll 6098646; Schedule 182 "East Field Pl" Sutton Hill, Keighley; "Matilda Greenwood."

262. 1901 Census of England and Wales, Sale, Cheshire, 31 March 1901, Class RG13; Piece 3325; Folio 156; Page 27; Schedule 197, "16 Abington Road"; "Matilda Entwistle."

263. 1911 Census of England and Wales, Marple, Cheshire, 2 April 1911, Schedule 63; Line 2; "Matilda Entwistle."

264. 1939 England and Wales Register [Census], 29 September 1939, Caernarvonshire, Penmaenmawr Ud, Wales; ED ZDIA 632-4; Schedule 305; Line 1; "Matilda Entwistle."

265. 1841 Census of England & Wales, Bingley, Yorkshire, 6 June 1841, Page 16; "Mills St"; (ancestry.com image 13); HO 107 / 1312/8; "Peter Greenwood."

266. 1851 Census of England and Wales, Bingley, Yorkshire, 30 March 1851, Page 50; Schedule 179, "Village of Cullingworth"; H.O. 107 2286; "Peter Greenwood."

267. 1861 Census of England and Wales, Horton, Bradford, Yorkshire, Class RG 9; Piece 3331; Folio 62; Page 28; GSU roll 543115; Schedule 168; "526 Little Horton Lane"; "Peter Greenwood."
268. 1871 Census of England and Wales, Horton, Bradford, Yorkshire, 2 April 1871, Class RG10; Piece 4474; Folio 21; Page 36; GSU roll 847122; Schedule 177; "528 Little Horton Lane"; "Peter Greenwood."
269. 1881 Census of England and Wales, Gomersal, Yorkshire, 3 April 1881, Class RG11; Piece 4552; Folio 59; Page 20; GSU roll 1342096; Schedule 97; "Bottoms West View Terrace."
270. Missing from the 1891 England and Wales census.
271. 1901 Census of England and Wales, Poulton, bare and Torrishome, lancashire, 5 April 1901, Class RG13; Piece 3985; Folio 67; Page 38; Schedule 247; "68 Westminster Road"; "Peter Greenwood."
272. 1911 Census of England and Wales, Poulton, bare and Torrishome, Lancashire, 2 April 1911, Schedule 49; Line 2 (residing with step-daughter Sarah Moulson); "Peter Greenwood widower; old age pensioner, formerly overlooker in Worsted Mill."
273. Claims born in Cullingworth, Yorkshire in 1881 census.
274. 1851 Census of England and Wales, Bingley, Yorkshire, 30 March 1851, "Worsted Spinner."
275. 1861 Census of England and Wales, Horton, Bradford, Yorkshire, "Spinning Overlooker Master Yarn."
276. 1871 Census of England and Wales, Horton, Bradford, Yorkshire, 2 April 1871, "Worsted Spinning Overlooker."
277. 1881 Census of England and Wales, Gomersal, Yorkshire, 3 April 1881, "Manager Worsted Spinning."
278. 1901 Census of England and Wales, Poulton, Bare and Torrishome, Lancashire, 5 April 1901, "Waste & Spinning Overlooker."
279. 1851 Census of England and Wales, Rawdon, Yorkshire, 30 March 1851, Class HO107; Piece 2285; Folio 271; Page 67; GSU roll 87473; Schedule 251; "Apperly lane Acacia Lodge"; "Ann Clegg."
280. 1861 Census of England and Wales, Horton, Bradford, Yorkshire, Class RG 9; Piece 3331; Folio 62; Page 28; GSU roll 543115; Schedule 168; "526 Little Horton Lane"; "Anne Greenwood."
281. 1871 Census of England and Wales, Horton, Bradford, Yorkshire, 2 April 1871, Class RG10; Piece 4474; Folio 21; Page 36; GSU roll 847122; Schedule 177; "528 Little Horton Lane"; "Annie Greenwood."
282. 1881 Census of England and Wales, Gomersal, Yorkshire, 3 April 1881, (http://www.findmypast.com : n.d.); citing p. 20, Piece/Folio 4552/59; RG11; FHL microfilm 101,775,277;"Anne Greenwood."
283. 1901 Census of England and Wales, Poulton, bare and Torrishome, lancashire, 5 April 1901, Class RG13; Piece 3985; Folio 67; Page 38; Schedule 247; "66 Westminster Road"; "Annie Greenwood."
284. West Yorkshire Archive Service, West Yorkshire, Church of England Marriages and Banns, 1813-1935, Number 208; "Ann Clegg widow" (ancestry.com image 15).
285. England & Wales Civil Registration Marriage Indexes, 1837-1915, 1856: 2nd Quarter, Volume 9a, Page 193.
286. Too many "Anne Greenwood" and similar variations to verify identity.
287. 1861 Census of England and Wales, Horton, Bradford, Yorkshire, "Dress Maker."

288. 1851 Census of England and Wales, Bingley, Yorkshire, 30 March 1851, Page 50; Schedule 179, "Village of Cullingworth"; H.O. 107 2286; "Hannah Greenwood."

289. 1861 Census of England and Wales, Bingley, Yorkshire, 7 April 1861, Page 44; Schedule 245; R.G. 9 3220; Hamlet of Harden; "Hannah Greenwood."

290. 1841 Census of England & Wales, Bingley, Yorkshire, 6 June 1841, Enumeration Schedule 51; Page 13; Bocking; "John Cousen."

291. 1851 Census of England and Wales, Bingley, Yorkshire, 30 March 1851, Page 42; (ancestry.com image 43); Schedule 142 "Brocking"; "John Cousin."

292. 1861 Census of England and Wales, Bingley, Yorkshire, 7 April 1861, Page 44; Schedule 116 "Meadowfield House"; "John Cousin."

293. 1871 Census of England and Wales, Bingley, Yorkshire, 2 April 1871, Page 13; Schedule 52; "Cockshells House"; "John Cousin."

294. West Yorkshire Archive Service, Church of England Births and Baptisms, 1813-1910, Page 272; (ancestry.com image 7); number 2175; "John son of William & Alice Cousin, Abode: Bingley; Trade: Weaver."

295. See birth note.

296. Not found in the GRO records.

297. West Yorkshire, England, Church of England Deaths and Burials, 1813-1985, Page 256; number 2041; (ancestry.com image 3); "Abode: Paper Mill Bridge | Age: 39 years"

298. 1851 Census of England and Wales, Bingley, Yorkshire, 30 March 1851, "Tailor (ap.) [apprentice]."

299. 1861 Census of England and Wales, Bingley, Yorkshire, 7 April 1861, "Tailor."

300. 1871 Census of England and Wales, Bingley, Yorkshire, 2 April 1871, "Tailor."

301. Ibid. Page 13; Schedule 52; "Cockshells House"; "Eliza Cousin."

302. 1881 Census of England and Wales, Bingley Towship, Yorkshire, 3 April 1881, Class RG11; Piece 4345; Folio 26; Page 25; GSU roll 1342038; Schedule 125; "Cockshell House" "Eiza Cousins," widow.

303. 1891 Census of England and Wales, Bingley, Yorkshire, 5 April 1891, Class RG12; Piece 3535; Folio 39; Page 17; GSU roll 6098645; "9 Wood View Ter"; Schedule 110; "Eliza Cousins" widow.

304. England and Wales Marriage Registration Index, 1837-2005, database, familysearch.org, Page 207; volume 9d, 4th quarter "John Cousens" and "Eliza Dent."

305. England, Yorkshire, Parish Registers, 1538-2016, database, familysearch.org, Marriage Banns; page 22; reference E-PE20-12; East Riding Archives & Local Studies Service. 12 November 1865 at Hotham, Yorkshire (East Riding).

306. Her father was "Vickers Dent" ?

307. England & Wales, Civil Registration Birth Index, 1837-1915: 1845, 2Q, V23, P12, Beverley.

308. England, Select Births and Christenings, 1538-1975, database with no images, Ancestry.com, FHL Film Number 991078.

309. 1861 Census of England and Wales, Leven, Yorkshire, 7 April 1861, R.G. 9/3573; Schedule 8, Low Boswick, "Servant" in the household of John Elridge.

310. 1881 Census of England and Wales, Bingley Towship, Yorkshire, 3 April 1881, "Laundrefs."

311. 1891 Census of England and Wales, Bingley, Yorkshire, 5 April 1891, "Laundress."

312. 1871 Census of England and Wales, Bingley, Yorkshire, 2 April 1871, Page 13; Schedule 52; "Cockshells House"; "Dale Cousin."

313. Ibid. Page 13; Schedule 52; "Cockshells House"; "Wm. Cousin."

314. 1881 Census of England and Wales, Bingley Towship, Yorkshire, 3 April 1881, Class RG11; Piece 4345; Folio 26; Page 25; GSU roll 1342038; Schedule 125; "Cockshell House"; "William Cousins."

315. 1891 Census of England and Wales, Bingley, Yorkshire, 5 April 1891, Class RG12; Piece 3535; Folio 39; Page 17; GSU roll 6098645; "9 Wood View Ter"; Schedule 110; "William Cousins."

316. 1881 Census of England and Wales, Bingley Towship, Yorkshire, 3 April 1881, Class RG11; Piece 4345; Folio 26; Page 25; GSU roll 1342038; Schedule 125; "Cockshell House"; "Stephen Cousins."

317. 1851 Census of England and Wales, Bingley, Yorkshire, 30 March 1851, Page 42; (ancestry.com image 43); Schedule 142 "Brocking"; "Sarah Cousin."

318. 1861 Census of England and Wales, Bingley, Yorkshire, 7 April 1861, Page 44; Schedule 116 "Meadowfield House"; "Sarah Cousin."

319. 1871 Census of England and Wales, Bingley, Yorkshire, 2 April 1871, Page 14; Schedule 68; Cockshells House; "Sarah Cousin."

320. 1st Quarter Volume 23 Page 245 ? Searched GRO using COUSEN.

321. 1861 Census of England and Wales, Bingley, Yorkshire, 7 April 1861, "Power loom Worsted Weaver."

322. 1871 Census of England and Wales, Bingley, Yorkshire, 2 April 1871, "Worsted Weaver."

323. 1841 Census of England and Wales, Halifax, West Riding, Yorkshire, 6 June 1841, "Halifax St James" HO107; Piece/Folio: 1306/26; Book 5; line 5; Page 4; citing PRO HO 107; (familysearch.org/ark:/61903/1:1:MQ5X-KVV); residence: Clough Head, South. "Martha Pickles."

324. 1851 Census of England and Wales, Green Lane, Ovenden Township, Yorkshire, 30 March 1851, Series: HO107, Line: 16, Illingworth Moor Green Lane, Piece/Folio: 2301/347; Page: 4, Ecclesiastical district: St Johns, Family: 13;"Martha Pickles."

325. 1871 Census of England and Wales, Halifax, Yorkshire, 2 April 1871, Schedule 36; 65 Crossley Terrace; Class RG10; Piece 4395; Folio 78; Page 8; GSU roll 848095; (ancestry.com image 9); "James Ingham."

326. 1881 Census of England and Wales, Halifax, Yorkshire, Yorkshire West Riding, 3 April 1881, Schedule 81; 65 Crossley Ter; Class RG11; Piece: 403; Folio 60; Page 13; GSU roll 1342052; (ancestry.com image 14). "Marth Ingham."

327. Note: born before national registration was implemented; no church record found other than her baptism.

328. 1851 Census of England and Wales, Green Lane, Ovenden Township, Yorkshire, 30 March 1851.

329. 1881 Census of England and Wales, Halifax, Yorkshire, Yorkshire West Riding, 3 April 1881, UK National Archives.

330. West Yorkshire Archive Service, West Yorkshire, Church of England Births and Baptisms, 1813-1910, Number 1097; Yorkshire Parish Records; New Reference Number: WDP39/5. Saint Mary; chapelry of Luddenden.

331. Findmypast.co.uk. Transcript from Calderdale Family History Society. Father: John, Comber, residing in Warley; Mother: Hannah.

332. England & Wales Civil Registration Indexes, 1837-1915, Page 178; referencing District: Halifax; Volume 9a.; Page 351, "Martha Ingham [age] 50."

333. Death Certificate/Record. GRO, 3 April 2022; number 374; 65 Crossley Terrace, Halifax; sub-district Halifax.

334. Dyson, Gordon, Pickles/Ingram, 9 August 2006, email. There is a marriage at Halifax, 3rd quarter, 1857 ref 9a/522 – James INGHAM to Martha PICKLES. Tried to find them in 1861 census, but not found.

335. 1841 Census of England and Wales, Halifax, West Riding, Yorkshire, 6 June 1841, Class HO107; Piece 1302; Book 1; Civil Parish: Halifax; ED: 1; Folio 6; Page 5; Line 19; GSU roll 464262. "James Ingham."

336. 1851 Census of England and Wales, Halifax, Yorkshire, England, 30 March 1851, Page 29, Registration HO107; (familysearch.org/ark:/61903/1:1:SPMC-8Z4); Page 29; Piece/Folio 2301/339; (ancestry.com image 30); "James Ingham."

337. Not found in 1861 census after extensive search.

338. 1881 Census of England and Wales, Halifax, Yorkshire, Yorkshire West Riding, 3 April 1881, Schedule 81; 65 Crossley Ter; Class RG11; Piece 4403; Folio 60; Page 13; GSU roll 1342052; (ancestry.com image 14). "James Ingham."

339. 1891 Census of England and Wales, Halifax, Yorkshire, 5 April 1891, Class RG12; Piece 3591; Folio 78; Page 17; GSU roll 6098701. ED 33; Schedule 132, 65 Crossley Ter; "James Ingham."

340. 1901 Census of England and Wales, Halifax, Yorkshire, 31 March 1901, UK National Archives, Class RG13; Piece 4123; Folio 143; Page 9; ED 40; 65 Crossley Ter.; "James Ingham."

341. England and Wales Marriage Registration Index, 1837-2005, Volume 9A, Page 552, Line 12; 3rd Quarter (July-August-September); (familysearch.org/ark:/61903/1:1:26HS-3FK : 13 December 2014).

342. Findmypast.co.uk. (Image 1389).

343. England & Wales, Non-Conformist and Non-Parochial Registers, 1567-1936, <u>Registers of Births, Marriages and Deaths Surrendered to the Non-Parochial Registers Commissions of 1837 and 1857</u>, Class Number RG 4; Piece Number 3410; "James Son of William and Hannah Ingham of Lane Bottom in Ovenden was born June 24th 1832, and was Bap. July 21, 1833."

344. England Births and Christenings, 1538-1975, (familysearch.org/ark:/61903/1:1:JQ1B-XQ5), James Ingham, 1833.

345. England & Wales, National Probate Calendar (Index of Wills and Administrations), 1858-1995, Principal Probate Registry. Calendar of the Grants of Probate and Letters of Administration made in the Probate Registries of the High Court of Justice in England, ancestry.com, Page 270; (ancestry.com image 136).

346. England and Wales Civil Death Registration Index 1837-2007, Volume 9a; page 296; index page 172; October, November, and December 1901 register; "Ingham, James, 69 Halifax" (ancestry.com image 1).

347. Find-A-Grave, (findagrave.com/memorial/222188418/james-ingham : accessed 05 May 2022). Memorial ID 222188418, Mount Zion Methodist Chapelyard, Halifax, Metropolitan Borough of Calderdale, West Yorkshire; maintained by Baby Stegosaurus (contributor 49885654).

348. Deceased Online Burial Indexes; UK, Burial and Cremation Index, 1576-2014, https://www.deceasedonline.com/.

349. 1851 Census of England and Wales, Halifax, Yorkshire, England, 30 March 1851, "Worsted Spinner."

350. 1871 Census of England and Wales, Halifax, Yorkshire, 2 April 1871, National Archives, Kew, Richmond, Surrey, "Yeast Dealer."

351. 1881 Census of England and Wales, Halifax, Yorkshire, Yorkshire West Riding, 3 April 1881, UK National Archives, "Yeast Dealer."

352. 1891 Census of England and Wales, Halifax, Yorkshire, 5 April 1891.

353. Halifax Courier, "Public Notices," 12 May 1877, column 1, page 4.

354. Ibid. "Halifax West Riding Court," 26 May 1877, column 1, page 6.

355. Ibid. "Sales by Private Contract," 9 June 1977, column 3, page 8.

356. Ibid. "Halifax Liberal Association: Ward Meetings," 16 February 1889, column 3, page 3.

357. Brighouse and District News, Brighouse, England, "Southowram," 25 October 1901, page 5.

358. 1861 Census of England and Wales, Luddenden (Halifax), Warley, District 6, Yorkshire, 7 April 1861, Page 26; RG 9; Piece/Folio: 3295/80; GSU roll 543109; Schedule 108; (ancestry.com image 25); (www.familysearch.org/ark:/61903/1:1:M7ZG-NTZ : 3 March 2021). "William H Ingham" living with his Pickles grandparents.

359. 1871 Census of England and Wales, Halifax, Yorkshire, 2 April 1871, Schedule 36; 65 Crossley Terrace; Class RG10; Piece 4395; Folio 78; Page 8; GSU roll 848095; (ancestry.com image 9). "William Henry Ingham" living with his parents.

360. 1881 Census of England and Wales, Halifax, Yorkshire, Yorkshire West Riding, 3 April 1881, Schedule 81; 65 Crossley Ter; Class RG11; Piece 4403; Folio 60; Page 13; GSU roll 1342052; (ancestry.com image 14). "William Henry Ingham" living with his parents; marital status is blank.

361. 1871 Census of England and Wales, Halifax, Yorkshire, 2 April 1871, Schedule 36; 65 Crossley Terrace; Class RG10; Piece 4395; Folio 78; Page 8; GSU roll 848095; (ancestry.com image 9); "Elizabeth Ann Ingham."

362. 1881 Census of England and Wales, Halifax, Yorkshire, Yorkshire West Riding, 3 April 1881, Schedule 81; 65 Crossley Ter; Class RG11; Piece 4403; Folio 60; Page 13; GSU roll 1342052; (ancestry.com image 14); "Elizabeth Ann Ingham."

363. 1891 Census of England and Wales, Halifax, Yorkshire, 5 April 1891, Ovenden Parish. Class RG12; Piece 3603; Folio 66; Page 15; GSU roll 6098713; ED 4; Schedule 110; "302 Ovenden Rd," (ancestry.com image 16); living in her mother-in-law's household.

364. 1901 Census of England and Wales, Halifax, Yorkshire, 31 March 1901, Ovenden Parish. Class RG13; Piece 4136; Folio 66; Page 15. Schedule 117; "302 Ovenden Rd."; "E. Ann Highley" (ancestry.com image 16).

365. 1871 Census of England and Wales, Halifax, Yorkshire, 2 April 1871, Schedule 36; 65 Crossley Terrace; Class RG10; Piece 4395; Folio 78; Page 8; GSU roll 848095; (ancestry.com image 9); "Emma Jane Ingham."

366. 1881 Census of England and Wales, Halifax, Yorkshire, Yorkshire West Riding, 3 April 1881, Schedule 81; 65 Crossley Ter; Class RG11; Piece 4403; Folio 60; Page 13; GSU roll 1342052; (ancestry.com image 14); "Emma Jane Ingham."

367. 1891 Census of England and Wales, Halifax, Yorkshire, 5 April 1891, Class: RG12; Piece: 3591; Folio 78; Page 17; GSU roll 6098701; (ancestry.com image 18); ED 33; Schedule 132, 65 Crossley Ter, "Emma Jane Ingham."

368. 1871 Census of England and Wales, Halifax, Yorkshire, 2 April 1871, Schedule 36; 65 Crossley Terrace; Class RG10; Piece 4395; Folio 78; Page 8; GSU roll 848095; (ancestry.com image 9); "Arthur Ingham."

369. 1881 Census of England and Wales, Halifax, Yorkshire, Yorkshire West Riding, 3 April 1881, Schedule 81; 65 Crossley Ter; Class RG11; Piece 4403; Folio 60; Page 13; GSU roll 1342052; (ancestry.com image 14); "Olive Ingham."

370. 1891 Census of England and Wales, Halifax, Yorkshire, 5 April 1891, Class RG12; Piece 3591; Folio 78; Page 17; GSU roll 6098701. ED 33; Schedule 132, 65 Crossley Ter.; "Alice Ingham."

371. 1901 Census of England and Wales, Halifax, Yorkshire, 31 March 1901, Class RG13; Piece 4124; Folio 147; Page 27; Schedule 157 "West Mount"; living in employer household of James M. Bowman as "Alice Ingham" (ancestry.com image 28).

372. 1911 Census of England and Wales, Leeds, West Riding, Yorkshire, England, 2 April 1911, ED 20; Schedule 49; Series RG14, 1911; Line 2; (ancestry.com image 2626); "Alice Ingham."

373. 1841 Census of England and Wales, Halifax, West Riding, Yorkshire, 6 June 1841, "Halifax St James" HO107; Piece/Folio 1306/26; Book 5; line 5; Page 4; citing PRO HO 107; (familysearch.org/ark:/61903/1:1:MQ5X-KVV); residence: Clough Head, South; "Sarah Pickles."

374. 1851 Census of England and Wales, Green Lane, Ovenden Township, Yorkshire, 30 March 1851, Series: HO107, Line 16, Illingworth Moor Green Lane; Piece/Folio 2301/347; Page 4, Ecclesiastical district: St Johns; Family 13; "Sarah Pickles."

375. 1861 Census of England and Wales, Luddenden (Halifax), Warley, District 6, Yorkshire, 7 April 1861, Class: RG10; Piece: 4416; Folio 29; Page 2; GSU roll 847116; ED 3; Schedule 6, Upper Edge end; "Sarah Pickles."

376. 1871 Census of England and Wales, Warley Township, Luddenden, Yorkshire, 2 April 1871; Parish: Warley; Series RG10; Piece 4416; ED 3; Page 29; Page 2; Line 1.

377. West Yorkshire Archive Service, West Yorkshire, England, Church of England Births and Baptisms, 1813-1910, Number 2055; Yorkshire Parish Records; New Reference Number: WDP39/5.

378. England and Wales Birth Registration Index, 1837-2008, GRO Quarter: October-November-December 1837; Volume 22; Page 204; Halifax, Yorkshire West Riding registration. Index page 420; (ancestry.com image 21).

379. England Births and Christenings, 1538-1975, (https://familysearch.org/ark:/61903/1:1:J7JP-PS4 : 19 September 2020), Hannah Pickles in entry for Sarah Pickles, 1848.

380. West Yorkshire Archive Service, West Yorkshire, England, Church of England Births and Baptisms, 1813-1910, (ancestry.com image 6); "No. 2055. | Sarah | John and Hannah | Pickles | Warley."

381. 1871 Census of England and Wales, Warley Township, Luddenden, Yorkshire, 2 April 1871, "In Door Worker."

382. Todmorden and Hebden-Bridge Weekly Advertiser, newspaper, Todmorden, 22 April 1871, page 3.

383. 1841 Census of England and Wales, Halifax, West Riding, Yorkshire, 6 June 1841, "Halifax St James" HO107; Piece/Folio: 1306/26; Book 5; line 5; Page 4; citing PRO HO 107; (familysearch.org/ark:/

61903/1:1:MQ5X-KVV); residence: Clough Head, South. "Ann Pickles."

384. 1851 Census of England and Wales, Green Lane, Ovenden Township, Yorkshire, 30 March 1851, Series: HO107, Line: 16, Illingworth Moor Green Lane, Piece/Folio 2301/347; Page 4, Ecclesiastical district: St Johns, Family 13. "Ann Pickles."

385. 1861 Census of England and Wales, Luddenden (Halifax), Warley, District 6, Yorkshire, 7 April 1861, Page 26; RG 9; Piece/Folio 3295/80; GSU roll 543109; Schedule 108; (ancestry.com image 25); and (https://www.familysearch.org/ark:/61903/1:1:M7ZG-NTZ : 3 March 2021); "Ann Pickles."

386. 1871 Census of England and Wales, Halifax, Yorkshire, 2 April 1871, RG10; Piece: 4395; Folio: 77; Page: 6; GSU roll: 848095; Schedule 26 "Crossley Terrace Court" (Head); "Ann Pickles."

387. 1880 US Census, Hamlin Township, Eaton County, Michigan, June 1880, NARA T9; Roll 578; Page 322C; ED 78; Dwelling 112; Family 119; Line 17; "Ann Knapp."

388. 1900 US Census, Hamlin Township, Eaton County, Michigan, June 1900, NARA T623; Roll 709; Sheet 1A; Page 202A; ED 74; Dwelling 8; Family 8; Line 32; "Ann Knapp."

389. Funeral Card

390. Birth record, 1841, Registrar District Luddenden; digital image GRO, 3 April 2022. Parents: "John Pickles… Hannah Pickles formerly Horsfield"; registered 22 January 1841.

391. Death Certificate/Record. Michigan Department Of State, Lansing, Vital Statistics Division, Certificate And Record Of Death, Register number 2. Father: John Pickles, Mother: Hannah Horsfield, both born in England.

392. Find-A-Grave, (www.findagrave.com/memorial/126603235/ann-knapp : accessed 29 March 2022). Memorial ID 126603235, citing Griffith Cemetery, Springport, Jackson County, Michigan; maintained by Dorothy (contributor 47601262).

393. 1871 Census of England and Wales, Halifax, Yorkshire, 2 April 1871, UK National Archives.

394. 1900 US Census, Hamlin Township, Eaton County, Michigan, June 1900.

395. New York, U.S., Arriving Passenger and Crew Lists (including Castle Garden and Ellis Island), 1820-1957, database with images, NARA, Year: 1875; Arrival: Castle Garden, New York, New York; Microfilm Serial: M237, 1820-1897; Line: 1; List Number 510; Ship *Scythia*, "Ann Pickles 34 F Spinster England."

396. Caledonia Maritime Research Trust, Scottish Built Ships, https://www.clydeships.co.uk/view.php?ref=22318, (viewed 29 November 2022).

397. Walworth, Reuben H., LL.D., Hyde Genealogy; or The Descendants, In The Female As Well As In The Male Lines, From William Hyde, Of Norwich, Albany, New York: J. Munsell, 1864, Volume I, (ancestry.com image 258); page 242; under entry 2772 Rhoda.

398. 1880 US Census, Hamlin Township, Eaton County, Michigan, June 1880, NARA T9; Roll 578; Page 322C; ED 78; Dwelling 112; Family 119; Line 16; "Herman Knapp."

399. 1880 US Census, (Non-Population, Agricultural), Hamlin Township, Eaton County, Michigan, Archive Collection Number: T1164; Roll 35; Page 10; Line 7; Schedule Type: Agriculture; "Herman Knapp."

400. 1900 US Census, Hamlin Township, Eaton County, Michigan, June 1900, NARA T623; Roll 709; Sheet 1A; Page 202A; ED 74; Dwelling 8; Family 8; Line 31; "Heman Knapp."

401. Marriage record/certificate/application. Michigan Department of Community Health, Division of Vital Records and Health Statistics; Lansing, Marriage Records, 1867-1952; Film: 12; Film Description: 1875 Mackinac-1876 Genesee; Number 127, Page 225, Eaton County, Michigan.

402. Per marriage record.

403. Michigan Deaths and Burials, 1800-1995, database, familysearch.org.

404. Death Certificate/Record. State Of Michigan, Department Of State, Division of Vital Statistics, Certificate Of Death, File 408.

405. Find-A-Grave, (www.findagrave.com/memorial/126602096/heman-knapp : accessed 29 March 2022). Memorial ID 126602096, citing Griffith Cemetery, Springport, Jackson County, Michigan; maintained by Dorothy (contributor 47601262).

406. 1880 US Census, Hamlin Township, Eaton County, Michigan, June 1880.

407. 1851 Census of England and Wales, Green Lane, Ovenden Township, Yorkshire, 30 March 1851, Series HO107, Line 16, Illingworth Moor Green Lane, Piece/Folio 2301/347; Page 4, Ecclesiastical district: St Johns; Family 13; "Hannah Pickles."

408. 1871 Census of England and Wales, Halifax, Yorkshire, 2 April 1871, Class RG10; Piece 4395; Folio 77; Page 6; GSU roll 848095; Schedule 26 "Crossley Terrace Court" (sister Ann is Head); "Hannah Pickles."

409. England & Wales Civil Registration Indexes, 1837-1915, (ancestry.com image 117); Volume XXII; Page 203 or 218. Registered in the first quarter of 1848, January-February-March.

410. Birth Certificate/Record. GRO: Number 170; under 1848 Births. Father: "John Pickles"; Mother: "Hannah Pickles formerly Horsfield"; registered 3 February 1848.

411. Dewsbury Chronicle and West Riding Advertiser, Dewsbury, Yorkshire. Refuted relationship: "Deaths: On the 22nd inst., age 29 years, Sarah Hannah Ackroyd, George-street, Heckmondwike." 28 September 1878, page 8.

412. Death Certificate/Record. GRO, number 162; "Domestic Servant"; death reported by "James Ingham Brother-in-law In attendance" recorded 15 April 1880.

413. England & Wales, Civil Registration Death Index, 1837-1915, GRO. England and Wales Civil Registration Indexes, London, database with image, (ancestry.com), 2nd Quarter 1880; Volume 9a; page 312.

414. Marriage record/certificate/application. Number 184 (ancestry.com image 127).

415. England and Wales Marriage Registration Index, 1837-2005, database, familysearch.org, (https://familysearch.org/ark:/61903/1:1:2DP1-QRV : 13 December 2014); citing 1877, quarter 2, volume 9A, page 626, Halifax, Yorkshire.

416. Halifax Courier, newspaper, "Marriages And Deaths: Marriages," 5 May 1877, page 8. "Ackroyd-Pickles-April 28, at our Parish Church, Mr. John Ackroyd, plumber, of Skircoat, to Miss Hannah Pickles, of Halifax."

417. England and Wales Marriage Registration Index, 1837-2005, 2nd Quarter, Volume 9A, Page 626; https://familysearch.org/ark:/61903/1:1:2DP1-QRV.

418. West Yorkshire Archive Service, West Yorkshire, England, Church of England Marriages and Banns, 1813-1935, married 28 April 1877, Halifax; John is 29 years old, father Nathaniel Ackroyd; Hannah is 24, father John Pickles, Blogger.

419. 1851 Census of England and Wales, Green Lane, Ovenden Township, Yorkshire, 30 March 1851, Series: HO107, Line 16, Illingworth Moor Green Lane, Piece/Folio 2301/347; Page 4, Ecclesiastical district: St Johns, Family 13; "Emanuel Pickles."

420. 1861 Census of England and Wales, Luddenden (Halifax), Warley, District 6, Yorkshire, 7 April 1861, Page 26; RG 9; Piece/Folio 3295/80; GSU roll 543109; Schedule 108; (ancestry.com image 25); and (www.-familysearch.org/ark:/61903/1:1:M7ZG-NTZ : 3 March 2021); "Emanuel Pickles."

421. 1871 Census of England and Wales, Halifax, Yorkshire, 2 April 1871, RG10; Piece 4395; Folio 77; Page 6; GSU roll 848095; Schedule 26 "Crossley Terrace Court" (sister Ann is Head); "Emanuel Pickles."

422. 1880 US Census, Jackson County, Michigan, June 1880, NARA T9; ED 124; 8th Ward; Page 18; Sheet 434B; Dwelling 165; Family 172; Line 5; "Emanuel Pickles."

423. 1900 US Census, Jackson City, Jackson County, Michigan, June 1900, NARA T623; 2nd precinct; ED 20; Sheet 5B; Dwelling 104; Family 109; Line 63; "Emanuel Pickles."

424. 1910 US Census, Jackson, Jackson County, Michigan, April 1910, NARA T624; Roll 653; ED 27; Ward 8; Sheet 7B; Dwelling 161; Family 161; Line 58; "Emanuel Pickles."

425. Birth Certificate/Record. "Immanuel Pickles"; 1850, Registrar District Ovenden; GRO, 7 April 2022. Parents: "John Pickles… Hannah Pickles formerly Horsfield"; registered 16 February 1850. (Also see baptism record.)

426. England & Wales, Civil Registration Birth Index, 1837-1915, GRO. England and Wales Civil Registration Indexes, (ancestry.com), Volume 22, page 251 (ancestry.com image 117). "Immanuel Pickles"; District: Halifax; 1st Quarter.

427. England, Select Births and Christenings, 1538-1975, database with no images, Ancestry.com, FHL Film Number: 1542111-Reference ID: Ln #11.

428. West Yorkshire Archive Service, West Yorkshire, England, Church of England Births and Baptisms, 1813-1910, Number 428; New Reference Number: WDP39/6. (ancestry.com image 41).

429. Liverpool, England, Church of England Births and Baptisms, 1813-1919, 1850: First Quarter, "Halifax," Volume XXII 251; "Immanuel."

430. England Births and Christenings, 1538-1975, St. Mary, Luddenden; (https://familysearch.org/ark:/61903/1:1:NF3Y-H2Q : 21 March 2020), Emanuel Pickles, 1858.

431. West Yorkshire Archive Service, Church of England Births and Baptisms, 1813-1910, Number 428, Page 54, Yorkshire Parish Records; New Reference Number: WDP39/6. (ancestry.com images 22 and 41) "Manuel Pickles Abode: Warley."

432. Michigan Deaths and Burials, 1800-1995, Michigan Deaths and Burial, 1800-1995, "Michigan Deaths and Burials, 1800-1995", (https://familysearch.org/ark:/61903/1:1:FHV3-Z2Q : 23 February 2021), "Emanual Pickell, 1915."

433. R. L. Polk & Co.'s Jackson City and County Directory 1915-1916, Detroit: R. L. Polk & Co., Publishers, 1915, Page 553; (ancestry.com image 297); "Pickell Emanuel (aged 65), died Jan 6, 1915."

434. Death Certificate/Record. State of Michigan, Department of State—Division of Vital Statistics, Certificate of Death, Registered 7/841 "Emanuel Piskell" parents "unknown."

435. Find-A-Grave, (www.findagrave.com/memorial/19958450/emanuel-pickell : accessed 17 March 2022). Memorial ID 19958450, citing Woodland Cemetery, Jackson, Jackson County, Michigan; maintained by Deb Hayes-Wolfe (contributor 46811474).

436. 1861 Census of England and Wales, Luddenden (Halifax), Warley, District 6, Yorkshire, 7 April 1861, UK National Archives, "Worsted factory hand."

437. 1871 Census of England and Wales, Halifax, Yorkshire, 2 April 1871, "joiner and Builder" [carpenter].

438. Brown, C. Exera, Jackson City Directory For 1872-3., Jackson, Michigan: Van Dyne's Printing House, 1872, Volume: August And September, 1872, Page 133; (ancestry.com image 143); "Pickles Emanuel, carpenter, J F C Co."

439. 1880 US Census, Jackson County, Michigan, June 1880, "Carp[enter] for Buck & Tail Co."

440. Jackson City Directory for 1883, Detroit, Michigan: R. L. Polk & Co., 1883, Volume VI, Page 212; (ancestry.com image 119); "Pickles Emmanuel, machinist Bennett Sewer Pipe Co, res 835 Waterloo ave."

441. Jackson City And County Directory for 1885-6, Detroit, Michigan: R. L. Pok & Co., 1885, Volume VIII, Page 226; (ancestry.com image 112); "Pickles Emanuel, carpenter, res 835 Waterloo ave n."

442. Jackson City And County Directory for 1887, Volume IX, Detroit, Michigan: R. L. Polk & Co., 1887, Page 231; (ancestry.com image 115); "Pickles Emanuel, laborer Bennett Sewe Pipe Co, res 835 Waterloo ave."

443. Jackson City Directory 1890, Detroit, Michigan: R. L. Polk & Co., Publishers, 1890, Volume XI, Page 275; (ancestry.com image 143); "Pickles Emanuel, carp, res 835 N Waterloo av."

444. Jackson City And County Directory 1891, Detroit, Michigan: R. L. Polk & Co., Publishers, 1891, Volume: XII, Page 277; (ancestry.com image 153); "Pickles Emanuel, tool dresser, 305 S Water, res 835 N Waterloo ave."

445. Jackson City Directory 1893, Detroit, Michigan: R. L. Polk & Co., Publishers, 1893, Volume XIII, Page 292; (ancestry.com image 144); "Pickles Emanuel, carpenter, res 807 N Waterloo av."

446. Jackson City And County Directory 1894-95, Detroit, Michigan: R. L. Polk & Co., Publishers, 1894, Volume XIV, Page 285; (ancestry.com image 139); "Pickles Emanuel, foreman S Pickles, res 807 N Waterloo av."

447. Jackson City And County Directory 1897, Volume XVI, Detroit, Michigan: R. L. Polk & Co., Publishers, 1897, Page 339; (ancestry.com image 169); "Pickles Bros (Samuel, Emanuel, Johnson and Wm H), stone contractors, 303 S Water."

448. Ibid. Page 339; (ancestry.com image 169); "Pickles Wm H (Pickles Bros), res 311 Whitney."

449. Jackson City And County Directory, 1898-99, Detroit, Michigan: R. L. Polk & Co., Publishers, 1898, Volume XVII, Page 371; (ancestry.com image 184); "Pickles Emanuel, (Pickles Bros), res 807 N Waterloo av."
450. Ibid. Page 371; (ancestry.com image 184); "Pickles Bros (Samuel, Emanuel, Johnson and Wm H) stone contractors, 303 S Water. Tel 346."
451. Polk's Jackson City And County Directory, 1899-1900, Detroit, Michigan: R. L. Polk & Co., Publishers, 1900, Page 396; (ancestry.com image 216); "Pickles Emanuel, carp Bennett Sewer Pipe Co, res 809 N Waterloo av."
452. 1900 US Census, Jackson City, Jackson County, Michigan, June 1900, "carpenter."
453. Jackson City Directory 1903, Detroit, Michigan: R. L. Polk & Co., 1903, Page 448; (ancestry.com image 244); "Pickles Emanuel, mach, res 809 N Waterloo av."
454. Adrian City Directory 1903, Detroit, Michigan: R. L. Polk & Co., Publishers, 1903, Volume I, Page 164, (ancestry.com image 84); "Pickles Emanuel, carp, bds 82 233 W Maumee."
455. Polk's Jackson City And County Directory, 1904, Detroit, Michigan: R. L. Polk & Co., Publishers, 1904, Page 452; (ancestry.com image 233); "Pickles Emanuel, mach. res 809 N Waterloo av."
456. Polk's Jackson City And County Directory 1905, Detroit, Michigan: R. L. Polk & Co, Publishers, 1905, Page 465; (ancestry.com image 242); "Pickles Emanuel, mach, res 809 N Waterloo ave."
457. R. L. Polk & Co's. Jackson City And County Directory 1907, Detroit, Michigan: R. L. Polk & Co., Publishers, 1907, Page 453; (ancestry.com image 231); "Pickles Emanuel, mach, res 809 N Waterloo av."
458. 1910 US Census, Jackson, Jackson County, Michigan, April 1910, "Carpenter" | "house."
459. R. L. Polk's & Co.'s 1910 Jackson City And County Directory, Detroit, Michigan: R. L. Polk & Co., 1910, Page 505; (ancestry.com image 266); "Pickles Emanuel, woodwkr, res 811 N Waterloo av."
460. 1900 US Census, Jackson City, Jackson County, Michigan, June 1900.
461. 1910 US Census, Jackson, Jackson County, Michigan, April 1910.
462. NARA, Passenger Lists of Vessels Arriving at Boston, Massachusetts, 1820-1891; Record Group Title: Records of the U.S. Customs Service; Record Group Number: 36; Series Number: M277; NARA Roll Number: 082.
463. Massachusetts, Index to Boston Passenger Lists, 1848-1891. (https://familysearch.org/ark:/61903/1:1:Q2HV-WMZ6 : 16 March 2018), Emanuel Pickles, 1872; citing Immigration, ship *Tripoli*, NARA M265; roll M265; (familysearch.org image 2732).
464. Jackson Citizen Patriot, "Obituary," 7 January 1915, page 3.
465. 1880 US Census, Jackson County, Michigan, June 1880, NARA T9; ED 124; 8th Ward; Page 18; Sheet 434B; Dwelling 165; Family 172; Line 6; "Sarah Pickles."
466. 1884 Michigan State Census, Jackson, Jackson County, Michigan, June 1884, Archive Roll 4790.
467. 1900 US Census, Jackson City, Jackson County, Michigan, June 1900, NARA T623; 2nd precinct; ED 20; Sheet 5B; Dwelling 104; Family 109; Line 64; "Sarah Pickles."

468. 1910 US Census, Jackson, Jackson County, Michigan, April 1910, NARA T624; Roll 653; ED 27; Ward 8; Sheet 7B; Dwelling 161; Family 161; Line 59; "Sarah Pickles."

469. R. L. Polk & Co.'s Jackson City and County Directory 1915-1916, Detroit: R. L. Polk & Co., Publishers, 1915, Page 553; (ancestry.com image 297); "Pickell Sarah (wid Emanuel), res 811 N Waterloo av."

470. England & Wales, Civil Registration Marriage Index, 1837-2005, (ancestry.com image 7); District: Halifax; Volume 9a; Page 700. AUS-BAI index page 7 and PIC-PIT index page 153.

471. England and Wales Birth Registration Index, 1837-2008, database, familysearch.org and ancestry.com, GRO. (https://familysearch.org/ark:/61903/1:1:26BW-ZQ6 : 1 October 2014), Sarah Baguley, 1844; from "England & Wales Births, 1837-2006," database, findmypast; Page 413; Volume 15; affiliate line 7; 4th Quarter.

472. England Births and Christenings, 1538-1975, familysearch.org, database.

473. England, Select Births and Christenings, 1538-1975, database with no images, Ancestry.com, FHL Film Number: 1470917.

474. Death Certificate/Record. State of Michigan, Department of State — Division of Vital Statistics, Certificate of Death; registered 528/864 "Sarah Pickell"; informant F Gordon Pickell.

475. Find-A-Grave, (www.findagrave.com/memorial/19958455/sarah-pickell: accessed 14 November 2022). Memorial ID 19958455, citing Woodland Cemetery, Jackson, Jackson County, Michigan; maintained by Deb Hayes-Wolfe (contributor 46811474).

476. Jackson Citizen Patriot, 29 December 1915, page 8.

477. Polk's Jackson City And County Directory, 1904, Detroit, Michigan: R. L. Polk & Co., Publishers, 1904, Page 452; (ancestry.com image 233); "Pickles Gordon, removed to Philadelphia, Pa."

478. 1910 US Census, Detroit, Wayne County, Michigan, April 1910, NARA T624; Roll 680; Ward 17; ED 252; Sheet 2B; Dwelling 40; Family 41; Line 90; "F. Gordon Pickell" living with wife and in-laws.

479. 1920 US Census, Detroit, Wayne County, Michigan, January 1920, NARA T625; Roll 805; Ward 4; ED 155; Sheet 6A; Dwelling 129; Family 133; Line 8; "F. Gordon Pickell."

480. 1930 US Census, Detroit, Wayne County, Michigan, April 1930, NARA T626; Ward 15, Block 314; ED 82-460; Page 240; Sheet 9A; Line 10; "F. Gordon Pickell," Divorced Lodger.

481. 1940 US Census, Detroit, Wayne County, Michigan, April 1940, NARA T627; Roll 1865; Ward 15; ED 84-859; Sheet 6B; Line 41; "Gordon Pickell."

482. Michigan Births and Christenings, 1775-1995, database, familysearch.org, Wm. C. Pickles, 10 May 1882; citing item 3 p 156 rn 290, Jackson City, Jackson, Michigan, Department of Vital Records, Lansing; FHL microfilm 2,320,692.

483. 1900 US Census, Jackson City, Jackson County, Michigan, June 1900, NARA T623; 2nd precinct; ED 20; Sheet 5B; Dwelling 104; Family 109; Line 65; "Willie Pickles."

484. 1919 World War I Veterans Census, Wayne County, Michigan, index, Michigan Department of State, Lansing, "William Clarence Pickell."

485. 1920 US Census, Highland Park, Wayne County, Michigan, January 1920, NARA T625; Roll 801; ED 707; Sheet 5B; Dwelling 104; Family 114; Line 62; "William Pickrel."

486. 1930 US Census, Highland Park, Wayne County, Michigan, April 1930, NARA T626; Roll 1074; ED 82-942; Sheet 16A; Page 34; Dwelling 217; Family 12; Line 45; "William C. Pickell."

487. Polks's Detroit [Michigan] City Directory 1930-1931, Detroit: R. L. Polk & Co., Publishers, 1930, Page 1501; (ancestry.com image 744); "Pickell Wm C (Geneva) tehr h 60 Geneva av (HP)."

488. US Social Security Applications and Claims Index, 1936-2007, (NUMIDENT), Mar 1937: Name listed as WILLIAM CLARENCE PICKELL.

489. 1884 Michigan State Census, Jackson, Jackson County, Michigan, June 1884, Archive Roll 4790.

490. 1900 US Census, Jackson City, Jackson County, Michigan, June 1900, NARA T623; 2nd precinct; ED 20; Sheet 5B; Dwelling 104; Family 109; Line 66; "Lillie B Pickles."

491. Polk's Jackson City And County Directory, 1904, Detroit, Michigan: R. L. Polk & Co., Publishers, 1904, Page 452; (ancestry.com image 233); "Pickles Lillian B, student, bds 809 N Waterloo av."

492. 1910 US Census, Jackson, Jackson County, Michigan, April 1910, NARA T624; Roll 653; ED 27; Ward 8; Sheet 7B; Dwelling 161; Family 161; Line 60; "Lilian Pickles."

493. Polk's Jackson City And County Directory, 1904, Detroit, Michigan: R. L. Polk & Co., Publishers, 1904, Page 452; (ancestry.com image 233); "Pickles Lillian B, student bds 809 N Waterloo av."

494. Polk's Jackson City And County Directory 1905, Detroit, Michigan: R. L. Polk & Co, Publishers, 1905, Page 465; (ancestry.com image 242); "Pickles Lillian B, bds 809 N Waterloo ave."

495. Polk's Jackson City And County Directory 1918, Detroit, Michigan: R. L. Polk & Co., Publishers, 1918, Page 737; (ancestry.com image 391); "Pickell Lillian B, res 811 N Waterloo av."

496. 1920 US Census, Jackson City, Jackson County, Michigan, January 1920, NARA T625; Roll 774; Precinct 2; ED 30; Sheet 6A; Dwelling 113; Family 116; Line 75; "Lillian Pickell."

497. 1930 US Census, Detroit, Wayne County, Michigan, April 1930, NARA T626; Roll 1033; ED 49; Sheet 11B; Line 100; Family 16; "Lillian Pickell."

498. Not found in 1940 census.

499. 1851 Census of England and Wales, Liversedge, Yorkshire, England, 30 March 1851, Page 31, H.O. 107 2323, as "John Pickles."

500. 1861 Census of England and Wales, Luddenden (Halifax), Warley, District 6, Yorkshire, 7 April 1861, UK National Archives, Page 26; RG 9; Piece/Folio 3295/80; GSU roll 543109; Schedule 108; "Proper House cottages"; (www.familysearch.org/ark:/61903/1:1:M7ZG-NTZ : 3 March 2021); "Johnson Pickles."

501. 1871 Census of England and Wales, Warley Township, Luddenden, Yorkshire, 2 April 1871, Class RG10; Piece 4416; Folio 29; Page 2; GSU roll 847116; ED 3; Schedule 6, Upper Edge end;"Jonson Pickles."

502. 1881 Census of England and Wales, Halifax, Yorkshire, Yorkshire West Riding, 3 April 1881, UK National Archives, Class RG11; Piece 4417; Folio 81; Page 37; GSU roll 1342056; "Johnson Pickles."

503. 1900 US Census, Jackson Township, Jackson County, Michigan, June 1900, NARA T623; Roll 719; Sheet 6B; ED 20; Dwelling 135; Family 141; Line 95; "Johnson Pickles."

504. 1910 US Census, Blackman Township, Jackson County, Michigan, April 1910, Enumerated 9-10 May 1910; NARA T624; Roll 653; ED 1; Sheet 13A; Dwelling 280; Family 281; Line 8;"Jonathan Pickles."

505. Family Bible. (Observed in the early 1970s by Curtis Daryl Sanders.)

506. West Yorkshire Archive Service, Church of England Births and Baptisms, 1813-1910, Number 429. Volume 9A; Yorkshire Parish Records; New Reference Number: WDP39/6.

507. Birth record, 1852, Registrar District Ovenden; GRO, 7 April 2022. Parents: "John Pickles… [and] Hannah Pickles formerly Horsfield"; registered 10 March 1852.

508. West Yorkshire Archive Service, Church of England Births and Baptisms, 1813-1910, Number 429; Yorkshire Parish Records; New Reference Number: WDP39/6. (St. Mary's).

509. England Births and Christenings, 1538-1975, (https://familysearch.org/ark:/61903/1:1:JQ9Q-WYG : 21 March 2020), Hannah Pickles in entry for Johnson Pickles, 1858.

510. Death Certificate/Record. State of Michigan, Department of State—Division of Vital Statistics, Certificate of Death; Number 522. Father: John Pickles; Mother: Hannah Horsfield; informant Samuel Pickles (brother).

511. Find-A-Grave, (www.findagrave.com/memorial/19958484/johnson-pickles : accessed 17 March 2022). Memorial ID 19958484, citing Woodland Cemetery, Jackson, Jackson County, Michigan; maintained by Deb Hayes-Wolfe (contributor 46811474).

512. 1861 Census of England and Wales, Luddenden (Halifax), Warley, District 6, Yorkshire, 7 April 1861, UK National Archives, "worsted factory hand."

513. 1871 Census of England and Wales, Warley Township, Luddenden, Yorkshire, 2 April 1871, "Stone Mason."

514. 1881 Census of England and Wales, Halifax, Yorkshire, Yorkshire West Riding, 3 April 1881, UK National Archives, "Mason."

515. Jackson City Directory 1890, Detroit, Michigan: R. L. Polk & Co., Publishers, 1890, Volume XI, Page 275; (ancestry.com image 143); "Pickles Johnson, stone cutter Pickles & Butler, bds 317 Whitney."

516. Jackson City Directory 1893, Detroit, Michigan: R. L. Polk & Co., Publishers, 1893, Volume XIII, Page 292; (ancestry.com image 144); "Pickles Johnson, stone cutter, res 142 Burnett."

517. Jackson City And County Directory 1894-95, Detroit, Michigan: R. L. Polk & Co., Publishers, 1894, Volume XIV, Page 285; (ancestry.com image 139); "Pickles Johnson, stonecutter, res 142 Burnett."

518. Jackson City And County Directory, 1898-99, Detroit, Michigan: R. L. Polk & Co., Publishers, 1898, Volume XVII, Page 371; (ancestry.com image 184); "Pickles Johnson (Pickles Bros), res 919 E North."

519. Polk's Jackson City And County Directory, 1899-1900, Detroit, Michigan: R. L. Polk & Co., Publishers, 1900, Page 396; (ancestry.com image 216); "Pickles Johnson, stonecutter Samuel Pickles, res 919 E North."

520. 1900 US Census, Jackson City, Jackson County, Michigan, June 1900, "stone cutter."

521. 1910 US Census, Blackman Township, Jackson County, Michigan, April 1910, "Farmer | General farm."

522. 1900 US Census, Jackson Township, Jackson County, Michigan, June 1900.

523. Jackson Citizen Patriot, 27 October 1888, page 7.

524. United States Passport Applications, 1795-1925, from his wife Mary's passport. (https://familysearch.org/ark:/61903/1:1:QKDN-GPQR : 16 March 2018), Johnson Pickles in entry for Mary Pickles, 1919; source certificate #120507, January 2, 1906 - March 31, 1925, 927, NARA M1490 and M137.

525. Jackson Citizen Patriot, "Funeral Announcement," 6 October 1917, page 3; "Funeral Announcement," 7 October 1917, page 19.

526. 1881 Census of England and Wales, Warley Township, Luddenden, Yorkshire, 3 April 1881, Class RG11; Piece:4417; Folio 81; Page 37; GSU roll 1342056; "Mary Pickles."

527. 1900 US Census, Jackson Township, Jackson County, Michigan, June 1900, NARA T623; Roll 719; Sheet 6B; ED 20; Dwelling 135; Family 141; Line 96; "Mary Pickles."

528. 1910 US Census, Blackman Township, Jackson County, Michigan, April 1910, NARA T624; Roll 653; ED 1; Sheet 13A; Dwelling 280; Family 281; Line 9; "Mary Pickles."

529. Polk's Jackson City And County Directory 1918, Detroit, Michigan: R. L. Polk & Co., Publishers, 1918, Page 738; (ancestry.com image 392); "Pickles Mary (wid Johnson), res 810 N East av."

530. West Yorkshire, England, Church of England Baptisms, Marriages and Burials, 1512-1812, database with image, West Yorkshire Archive Service, Number 386. Reference Number: WDP53/1/3/87; (ancestry.com image 388).

531. 1900 US Census, Jackson Township, Jackson County, Michigan, June 1900, Nativity.

532. 1910 US Census, Blackman Township, Jackson County, Michigan, April 1910, Nativity.

533. United States Passport Applications, 1795-1925, NARA Roll 927; Certificates: 120500-120749, 23 Sep 1919-24 Sep 1919; "Mary Pickles (Ms.)" (ancestry.com image 26).

534. England Births and Christenings, 1538-1975, "England Births and Christenings, 1538-1975," database, (https://familysearch.org/ark:/61903/1:1:JSTB-FXZ : 21 March 2020), Ann Nicholl, 1853. Father: William Nicholl; Mother: Ellen.

535. Note: after 1919 (tombstone is unclear).

536. Find-A-Grave, (www.findagrave.com/memorial/111607106/mary-pickles : accessed 17 March 2022). Memorial ID 111607106, citing Woodland Cemetery, Jackson, Jackson County, Michigan; maintained by Vernon W. Goodrich (contributor 46940951).

537. United States Passport Applications, 1795-1925, NARA, Roll 927; Certificates: 120500-120749, 23 Sep 1919-24 Sep 1919; (ancestry.com images 26-27).

538. Philadelphia Inquirer, newspaper, Philadelphia, Pennsylvania, "Haverford Sails," 21 November 1919, page 10.

539. UK and Ireland, Incoming Passenger Lists, 1878-1960, UK National Archives; Board of Trade: Commercial and Statistical Department and Successors: Inwards Passenger Lists, database with images, ancestry.com, Class: BT26; Piece: 659; Item: 47; Ship *Haverford*; Line 44; Arrival: 3 December 1919 at Liverpool from Philadelphia (ancestry.com image 257).

540. Philadelphia Inquirer, "Events Of Week In Women's Clubs: Friday," 2 May 1926, page 2.

541. Find a Grave, (https://www.findagrave.com/memorial/222184306/mary-ann-pickles: accessed 16 November 2023). Memorial ID 222184306, citing Mount Zion Methodist Chapelyard, Halifax, Metropolitan Borough of Calderdale, West Yorkshire; maintained by Baby Stegosaurus (contributor 49885654).

542. 1900 US Census, Jackson Township, Jackson County, Michigan, June 1900, NARA T623; Roll 719; Sheet 6B; ED 20; Dwelling 135; Family 141; Line 97; "Mabel Pickles"; "adopt daughter."

543. 1861 Census of England and Wales, Luddenden (Halifax), Warley, District 6, Yorkshire, 7 April 1861, UK National Archives, Page 26; RG 9; Piece/Folio 3295/80; GSU roll 543109; Schedule 108; (ancestry.com image 25); (www.familysearch.org/ark:/61903/1:1:M7ZG-NTZ : 3 March 2021); "William H Pickles."

544. 1871 Census of England and Wales, Warley Township, Luddenden, Yorkshire, 2 April 1871, Class RG10; Piece 4416; Folio 29; Page 2; GSU roll 847116; ED 3; Schedule 6, Upper Edge end;"Wm H Pickles."

545. 1881 Census of England and Wales, Warley Township, Luddenden, Yorkshire, 3 April 1881, ED 3; Schedule 6; "Lower Edge End" street; Class RG11; Piece 4417; Folio 29; Page 1; GSU roll 1342056. "William H Pickles" Lived next door to his father's family.

546. 1891 Census of England and Wales, Halifax, Yorkshire, 5 April 1891, Class RG12; Piece 3592; Folio 24; Page 12; GSU roll 6098702; Schedule 81; "10 Thackrey St"; "William H Pickles."

547. 1894 Michigan Census, Jackson, Jackson County, Michigan, June 1894, Archive Roll 4792.

548. 1900 US Census, Jackson County, Michigan, June 1900, NARA T623; 8th Ward, 2nd Precinct; ED 20; Sheet 5; Page 82A; "Waterloo Ave"; Dwelling 101; Family 106; Line 42; "Wm Pickles."

549. 1910 US Census, Bowling Green, Warren County, Kentucky, April 1910, NARA T624; Roll 505; Sheet 4B; ED 120; "Adam Street"; Dwelling 55; Family 67; Line 51; "William H. Pickles."

550. West Yorkshire Archive Service, Church of England Births and Baptisms, 1813-1910, Number 430; Yorkshire Parish Records; New Reference Number: WDP39/6; "William Henry Pickles"; Abode: Warley.

551. Note: 1861 Census estimates b. 1855; 1900 Census says November 1853; church birth record says 18 November 1854; death record says 1855; not found in civil records.

552. West Yorkshire Archive Service, Church of England Births and Baptisms, 1813-1910, Number 430; Yorkshire Parish Records; New Reference Number: WDP39/6.

553. Michigan Deaths and Burials, 1800-1995, (https://familysearch.org/ark:/61903/1:1:FHV3-MSZ : 23 February 2021), Wm. H. Pickles, 1914.

554. Death Certificate/Record. State Of Michigan, Department of State—Division of Vital Statistics, Certificate of Death, Number 153.

555. Find-A-Grave, (www.findagrave.com/memorial/125935788/william-h-pickles : accessed 17 March 2022). Memorial ID 125935788, citing Woodland Cemetery, Jackson, Jackson County, Michigan; maintained by Deb Hayes-Wolfe (contributor 46811474).

556. 1871 Census of England and Wales, Warley Township, Luddenden, Yorkshire, 2 April 1871, Cart Driver.

557. Note: 1878: "Mason" from marriage record.

558. 1881 Census of England and Wales, Warley Township, Luddenden, Yorkshire, 3 April 1881, "Mason".

559. 1891 Census of England and Wales, Halifax, Yorkshire, 5 April 1891, "Mason."

560. Note: 1892: "cotton spinner" from newspaper article; "weaver" from arriving passenger at New York.
561. Ibid. 1892: "Labourer" Outbound passenger list.
562. Jackson City Directory 1893, Detroit, Michigan: R. L. Polk & Co., Publishers, 1893, Volume XIII, Page 292; (ancestry.com image 144); "Pickles Wm H, stone cutter, res e s Whitney 2 n of North."
563. Jackson City And County Directory 1894-95, Detroit, Michigan: R. L. Polk & Co., Publishers, 1894, Volume XIV, Page 285; (ancestry.com image 139); "Pickles Wm H, stonecutter, res 311 Whitney."
564. Jackson City And County Directory, 1898-99, Detroit, Michigan: R. L. Polk & Co., Publishers, 1898, Volume XVII, Page 371; (ancestry.com image 184); "Pickles Wm H (Pickles Bros), res 311 Whitney." Also: "Pickles Wm H, student, bds 809 N Waterloo av."
565. Polk's Jackson City And County Directory, 1899-1900, Detroit, Michigan: R. L. Polk & Co., Publishers, 1900, Page 396; (ancestry.com image 216); "Pickles Wm H, stonecutter, res 835 N Waterloo av." Second entry below: "Pickles Wm H, bds 809 N Waterloo av."
566. 1900 US Census, Jackson County, Michigan, June 1900, "house painter."
567. Jackson City Directory 1903, Detroit, Michigan: R. L. Polk & Co., 1903, Page 448; (ancestry.com image 244); "Pickles Wm H, stone cutter, res 835 N Waterloo av."
568. Polk's Jackson City And County Directory, 1904, Detroit, Michigan: R. L. Polk & Co., Publishers, 1904, Page 452; (ancestry.com image 233); "Pickles Wm H, stonecutter, res 835 N Waterloo av."
569. Polk's Jackson City And County Directory 1905, Detroit, Michigan: R. L. Polk & Co, Publishers, 1905, Page 465; (ancestry.com image 242); "Pickles Wm H, stone cutter Thomas M Robinson, res 835 N Waterloo av."
570. R. L. Polk & Co's. Jackson City And County Directory 1907, Detroit, Michigan: R. L. Polk & Co., Publishers, 1907, Page 453; (ancestry.com image 231); "Pickles Wm H, stone cutter, res 107 Lansing av."
571. 1910 US Census, Bowling Green, Warren County, Kentucky, April 1910, "Stone Cutter."
572. Yorkshire Herald, newspaper, Yorkshire, "Cotton Mill Burnt Down," 23 May 1891, pages 4, 5.
573. Huddersfield Chronicle, "A Cotton Mill Burned Down," 23 May 1891, page 8.
574. Leeds Times, "General And District: Serious Fire In A Cotton Mill," 23 May 1891, page 8.
575. Yorkshire Evening Post, newspaper, Yorkshire, "Cotton Mill Burned Down At Halifax," 22 May 1891, page 4.
576. Shields Daily Gazette And Shipping Telegraph, newspaper, South Shields, Durham, "News In A Nutshell," 23 May 1891, page 3.
577. 1900 US Census, Jackson County, Michigan, June 1900.
578. Note: 1910 US Census, Bowling Green, Warren County, Kentucky, April 1910: Incorrect because Passenger List shows March 1892.
579. UK and Ireland, Outward Passenger Lists, 1890-1960, UK National Archives; BT27 Board of Trade: Commercial and Statistical Department and Successors: Outwards Passenger Lists, database, ancestry.com and familysearch.org, Ticket 23682:
"W M Pickles, laborer, age 34 | Eliz Pickles, Mat, age 34
Harry Pickles, laborer, age 15 | Arthur, child, age 11

Sam, child, age 10 | Bertha, child, age 7 | Hanna [Ann Elizabeth], child, age 4."

580. New York, U.S., Arriving Passenger and Crew Lists (including Castle Garden and Ellis Island), 1820-1957, database with images, NARA, www.ancestry.com, Page 8; Year: 1892; Arrival: New York, New York; Microfilm Serial: M237, 1820-1897; Line 3:
"W H Pickles weaver" | "Elizabeth | wife" "Henry | weaver" "Arthur | Lad" "Sam | child" "Bertha | child" "Hannah | child."

581. Jackson Citizen Patriot, 10 June 1914, page 3.

582. Kentucky Post, newspaper, Covington, Kentucky, "Deaths In Ky. W. H. Pickels," 11 June 1914, page 4.

583. 1861 Census of England and Wales, Sowerby, Warley, District 1, Yorkshire, England, Class RG 9; Piece 3291; Folio 12; Page 17; GSU roll 543109; Schedule 99; "Elizabeth Utley."

584. 1871 Census of England and Wales, Warley Township, Luddenden, Yorkshire, 2 April 1871, Year: 1871; Parish: Warley; Series RG10; Piece 4416; ED 3; Page 11; Schedule 68; "Elizabeth Utley."

585. 1881 Census of England and Wales, Warley Township, Luddenden, Yorkshire, 3 April 1881, ED 3; Schedule 6; "Lower Edge End" street; Class RG11; Piece 4417; Folio 29; Page 1; GSU roll 1342056; "Elizabeth Pickles."

586. 1891 Census of England and Wales, Halifax, Yorkshire, 5 April 1891, Class RG12; Piece 3592; Folio 24; Page 12; GSU roll 6098702; Schedule 81; "10 Thackrey St"; "Elizabeth Pickles."

587. 1894 Michigan Census, Jackson, Jackson County, Michigan, June 1894, Archive Roll 4792.

588. 1900 US Census, Jackson County, Michigan, June 1900, NARA T623; 8th Ward, 2nd Precinct; ED 20; Sheet 5; Page 82A; "Waterloo Ave"; Dwelling 101; Family 106; Line 43; "Elizabeth Pickles."

589. Polk's Jackson City And County Directory 1905, Detroit, Michigan: R. L. Polk & Co, Publishers, 1905, Page 465; (ancestry.com image 242); "Pickles A Elizabeth, bds 835 N Waterloo av."

590. 1910 US Census, Bowling Green, Warren County, Kentucky, April 1910, NARA T624; Roll 505; Sheet 4B; ED 120; "Adam Street"; Dwelling 55; Family 67; Line 52; "Elizabeth Pickles."

591. 1920 US Census, Bowling Green, Warren County, Kentucky, January 1920, NARA T625; Roll 600; Sheet 9A; ED 134; "Adams St."; House 1244; Dwelling 119; Line 10. "Elizabeth Pickles | Mother | widowed."

592. Polk's Jackson, Mich. City And County Directory, 1920, Detroit, Michigan: R. L. Polk & Co., Publishers, 1920, Page 616; (ancestry.com image 320); "Pickles Elizabeth (wid Wm), dom, bds 344 2d."

593. Not found in 1930 census.

594. West Yorkshire Archive Service, Church of England Marriages and Banns, 1813-1935, Page 132; number 263. Yorkshire Parish Records; Reference Number: WDP53/1/3/94. (ancestry.com image 254).

595. Note: Birth date from death record and obituary; 1900 census says March 1852; not found in the GRO records.

596. England Births and Christenings, 1538-1975, (https://www.familysearch.org/ark:/61903/1:1:JQ97-MRH : 5 February 2023), Elizabeth Ann Uttley, 1862.

597. Death Certificate/Record. Commonwealth of Kentucky, State Board of Health, Bureau Of Vital Statistics, Certificate Of Death, File 13570. Informant: Mrs. Harry A. Rigelwood.

598. Find-A-Grave, (www.findagrave.com/memorial/121894210/elizabeth-pickles : accessed 17 March 2022). Memorial ID 121894210, citing Fairview Cemetery, Bowling Green, Warren County, Kentucky; maintained by Sam Hampton, Jr (contributor 46779675).

599. 1910 US Census, Bowling Green, Warren County, Kentucky, April 1910.

600. 1920 US Census, Bowling Green, Warren County, Kentucky, January 1920, Series T625 Roll 600 Page 174.

601. New York, U.S., Arriving Passenger and Crew Lists; Page 8; Year: 1892; Arrival: New York, New York; Microfilm Serial: M237, 1820-1897; Line 1; Page Number 1.

602. Jackson Citizen Patriot, "Society News," 24 October 1903, page 3.

603. Courier-Journal, newspaper, Louisville, Kentucky, "Mrs. E. Pickles, 78, Warren County, Dies," 9 May 1931, page 20.

604. Park City Daily News, "Mrs. Pickles, 78, Dies At Home of Daughter Today." 8 May 1931, page 8; "Pickles Rites Are To Be Held Sunday At Her Daughter's," 9 May 1931, page 8.

605. 1881 Census of England and Wales, Warley Township, Luddenden, Yorkshire, 3 April 1881, ED 3; Schedule 6; "Lower Edge End" street; Class RG11; Piece 4417; Folio 29; Page 1; GSU roll 1342056; "James H. Pickles."

606. 1891 Census of England and Wales, Halifax, Yorkshire, 5 April 1891, Class RG12; Piece 3592; Folio 24; Page 12; GSU roll 6098702; Schedule 81; "10 Thackrey St"; "James H Pickles."

607. Not found in 1900 US census.

608. 1910 US Census, Bean Blossom Township, Monroe County, Indiana, April 1910, NARA T624; Roll 371; Sheet 1A; ED 123; Dwelling 8; Family 8; Line 31; "James H Pickles."

609. 1920 US Census, Bowling Green, Warren County, Kentucky, January 1920, NARA T625; Roll 600; Sheet 7A; ED 134; "Thirteenth St."; Dwelling 119; Family 134; Line 21; "James H Pickles."

610. 1930 US Census, Bowling Green, Warren County, Kentucky, April 1930, NARA T626; Sheet 21A; Page 161; ED 114-10; Dwelling 464; Family 474; Line 15; "James H. Pickles."

611. 1940 US Census, Bowling Green, Warren County, Kentucky, April 1940, NARA T627; Roll 1360; Sheet 15A; ED 114-13; Visitation 280; Line 3; "James H Pickles."

612. 1950 US Census, Bowling Green, Warren County, Kentucky, April 1950, Record Group Number 29; Roll 6118; Sheet Number 24; ED 114-33; "Lansdale Street"; House 269; Line 26;"James H. Pickles."

613. US Social Security Applications and Claims Index, 1936-2007, 30 Sep 1977: James Henry Pickles, Birth: 25 December 1876, Halifax, United Kingdom; Name listed as JAMES HENRY PICKLES; claim date: 19 August 1944.

614. 1871 Census of England and Wales, Warley Township, Luddenden, Yorkshire, 2 April 1871, Year: 1871; Parish: Warley; Series RG10; Piece 4416; ED 3; Page 29; Page 2; Line 1.

615. 1881 Census of England and Wales, Warley Township, Luddenden, Yorkshire, 3 April 1881, ED 3; Schedule 6; "Lower Edge End" street; Class RG11; Piece 4417; Folio 29; Page 1; GSU roll 1342056; "Arthur Pickles."

616. 1891 Census of England and Wales, Halifax, Yorkshire, 5 April 1891, Class RG12; Piece 3592; Folio 24; Page 12; GSU roll 6098702; Schedule 81; "10 Thackrey St"; "Arthur Pickles."

617. 1900 US Census, Jackson County, Michigan, June 1900, NARA T623; 8th Ward, 2nd Precinct; ED 20; Sheet 5; Page 82A; "Waterloo Ave"; Dwelling 101; Family 106; Line 44; "Arthur Pickles."

618. Not found in 1910 US census.

619. 1920 US Census, Jackson City, Jackson County, Michigan, January 1920, NARA T625; Roll 774; Sheet 2B; ED 21; 5th Ward, 2nd Precinct; House 1130; Dwelling 40; Line 90; "Arthur Pickles."

620. 1930 US Census, Jackson City, Jackson County, Michigan, April 1930, NARA T626; Page 6A/106; ED 38-24; Dwelling 221; Family 289; Line 10; "Arthur Pickles."

621. 1940 US Census, Jackson City, Jackson County, Michigan, April 1940, NARA T627; Roll 1768; Sheet 4B; ED 38-21; Visitation 108; Line 76; "Arthur Pickles."

622. 1950 US Census, Jackson, Jackson County, Michigan, April 1950, Record Group Number 29; Roll 4012; Sheet 27; ED 38-40; Dwelling 313; Line 16; "Arthur Pickles."

623. US Social Security Applications and Claims Index, 1936-2007, 19 Aug 1977: Name listed as ARTHUR PICKLES; claim date: 15 July 1946.

624. 1891 Census of England and Wales, Halifax, Yorkshire, 5 April 1891, Class RG12; Piece 3592; Folio 24; Page 12; GSU roll 6098702; Schedule 81; "10 Thackrey St"; "Sam Pickles."

625. 1900 US Census, Jackson City, Jackson County, Michigan, June 1900, NARA T623; 8th Ward, 2nd Precinct; ED 20; Sheet 5; Page 82A; Dwelling 101; Family 106; Line 45; "Samuel Pickles."

626. 1910 US Census, Ypsilanti, Washtenaw County, Michigan, April 1910, NARA T624; Roll 678; Ward 2; Sheet 7B; ED 148; House 18, "Manual Street"; Dwelling 189; Family 208; Line 98; "Samuel Pickles."

627. 1920 US Census, Niles, Berrien County, Michigan, January 1920, NARA T625; Roll 757; Sheet 15A; ED 97; Dwelling 372; Family 390; Line 25; "Samuel Pickles."

628. 1930 US Census, Jackson City, Jackson County, Michigan, April 1930, NARA T626; ED 38-21; Sheet 6A; Page 28; Dwelling 90; Family 117, line 1; "Samuel Pickles."

629. 1940 US Census, Jackson City, Jackson County, Michigan, April 1940, NARA T627; Roll 1768; Ward 4; Sheet 9B; ED 38-28; Line 63; "Samuel Pickles."

630. US Social Security Applications and Claims Index, 1936-2007, Claim Date 30 January 1947; Birth Date 27 June 1881; 19 Aug 1977: Name listed as SAMUEL PICKLES.

631. 1950 US Census, Jackson, Jackson County, Michigan, April 1950, Record Group Number 29; Roll 4013; Sheet 7; ED 38-55; Dwelling 96; Line 3; "Samuel Pickles."

632. 1891 Census of England and Wales, Halifax, Yorkshire, 5 April 1891, Class: RG12; Piece: 3592; Folio: 24; Page: 12; GSU roll: 6098702; Schedule 81; "10 Thackrey St"; "Bertha Pickles."

633. Ibid. Class RG12; Piece 3592; Folio 25; Page 13; GSU roll 6098702; "Hannah E Pickles."

634. New York, U.S., Arriving Passenger and Crew Lists, NARA, Immigration: from Liverpool, England aboard the *Umbria*; arriving in New York in March 1892 (7 March 1892 sworn manifest). Listed as Hannah, age 7.

635. 1900 US Census, Jackson County, Michigan, June 1900, NARA T623; 8th Ward, 2nd Precinct; ED 20; Sheet 5; Page 82A; Dwelling 101; Family 106; Line 46; "Ann Elizabeth Pickles."
636. 1910 US Census, Bowling Green, Warren County, Kentucky, April 1910, NARA T624; Roll 505; Sheet 20A; Page 197; ED 123; "White Stone Quarry" Dwelling 338; Family 339; Line 27;"Elizabeth."
637. 1920 US Census, Bowling Green, Warren County, Kentucky, January 1920, NARA T625; Roll 600; Sheet 3B; ED 137; "White Stone Quarry" Dwelling 67; Family 72; Line 94; "Elizabeth Rigelwood."
638. 1930 US Census, Bowling Green, Warren County, Kentucky, April 1930, NARA T626; Sheet 21A; Page 184; ED 114-11; Dwelling 471; Family 471; Line 9; "Elizabeth Rigelwoo.d"
639. 1940 US Census, Bowling Green, Warren County, Kentucky, April 1940, NARA T627; Roll 1360; Sheet 4B; ED 114-15; House 94; Line 73; "Elizabeth Rigelwood."
640. 1950 US Census, Bowling Green, Warren County, Kentucky, April 1950, Record Group Number 29; Roll 6118; Sheet 9; ED 114-27; House 112; Line 22; "Elizabeth Riggelwood" living with son Earl.
641. Caron's Bowling Green (Warren County, KY.) City Directory 1952, Saint Louis, Missouri: Caron Directory Co., Publishers, 1952, Page 209; (ancestry.com image 106); "Rigelwood Eliz (wid Harry) r112 W 15th."
642. 1900 US Census, Jackson County, Michigan, June 1900, NARA T623; 8th Ward, 2nd Precinct; ED 20; Sheet 5; Page 82A; Dwelling 101; Family 106; Line 47; "Emily Pickles."
643. 1910 US Census, Bowling Green, Warren County, Kentucky, April 1910, NARA T624; Roll 505; Sheet 4B; ED 120; "Adam Street"; Dwelling 55; Family 67; Line 53; "Emily Pickles."
644. 1920 US Census, Belmont Heights, Davidson County, Tennessee, NARA T625; Roll 1736; 7th Civil District (part 7); Sheet 12A; ED 116; Dwelling 203; Family 297; Line 1; "Emily P. Pence."
645. 1930 US Census, Austin, Travis County, Texas, Although found in a 1930 city directory, John and Emily are not found in the 1930 census.
646. 1940 US Census, Austin, Travis County, Texas, NARA T627; Roll 4148; Sheet 25A; ED 227-20; Line 28; "Emily Pence."
647. 1950 US Census, University Park City, Dallas County, Texas, Record Group Number 29; Roll 2095; Sheet 83; ED 57-23A; Apartment 3016; Dwelling 407; Line 6; "Emily P. Pence."
648. Family Bible. Observed by Curtis Daryl Sanders in the 1970s.
649. 1861 Census of England and Wales, Luddenden (Halifax), Warley, District 6, Yorkshire, 7 April 1861, UK National Archives, Page 26; RG 9; Piece/Folio 3295/80; GSU roll 543109; Schedule 108; (ancestry.com image 25); and (www.familysearch.org/ark:/61903/1:1:M7ZG-NTZ : 3 March 2021); "Samuel Pickles."
650. 1871 Census of England and Wales, Warley Township, Luddenden, Yorkshire, 2 April 1871, Class RG10; Piece 4416; Folio 29; Page 2; GSU roll 847116; ED 3; Schedule 6, Upper Edge end;"Samuel Pickles."
651. 1881 Census of England and Wales, Northowram, Yorkshire, (21 Range Lane), 3 April 1881, Schedule 43. Class RG11; Piece 4421; Folio 32; Page 7; GSU roll 1342057; "Samuel Pickles."
652. 1900 US Census, Jackson City, Jackson County, Michigan, June 1900, NARA T623; Roll 719; ED 19; Ward 8; Sheet 1A; Page 58; W Water

Loo Street; House 634; Dwelling 4; Family 4; Line 17; "Samuel Pickles."

653. 1910 US Census, Bowling Green, Warren County, Kentucky, April 1910, NARA T624; Roll 505; Sheet 4B; ED 120; Dwelling 55; Family 67; Line 54; "Samuel Pickles."

654. 1920 US Census, Bowling Green, Warren County, Kentucky, January 1920, NARA T625; Roll 600; ED 132; Sheet 6B; Dwelling 150; Family 134; Laurel Avenue; Line 80; "Samuel Pickles."

655. Birth record, 1841, Registrar District Luddenden; GRO, 3 April 2022. "Samuel Pickles" Parents: "John Pickles… Hannah Pickles formerly Horsfield"; registered 27 July 1857.

656. Note: Tombstone says death in 1856. Death and birth records confirm birth as 13 June 1857.

657. West Yorkshire Archive Service, Church of England Births and Baptisms, 1813-1910, Number 431; Yorkshire Parish Records; New Reference Number: WDP39/6.

658. Sweet, C. Leonard, Latest info on Samuel Pickles, 20 April 2000, email.

659. England Births and Christenings, 1538-1975, (https://familysearch.org/ark:/61903/1:1:J9R5-8YJ : 21 March 2020), Hannah Pickles in entry for Samuel Pickles, 1858.

660. Death Certificate/Record. Commonwealth of Kentucky, State Board of Health, Bureau of Vital Statistics, Certificate of Death, File 13137. Record confirms birth at 13 June 1857. Informant: Mrs. Samuel Pickles.

661. Find-A-Grave, (www.findagrave.com/memorial/129402508/samuel-pickles : accessed 6 June 2022). Memorial ID 129402508, citing Fairview Cemetery, Bowling Green, Warren County, Kentucky; maintained by TColley (contributor 47285774).

662. 1871 Census of England and Wales, Warley Township, Luddenden, Yorkshire, 2 April 1871, "Wollen Miller."

663. 1881 Census of England and Wales, Northowram, Yorkshire, (21 Range Lane), 3 April 1881, "Slaterer & Plasterer."

664. Jackson City And County Directory for 1887, Volume IX, Detroit, Michigan: R. L. Polk & Co., 1887, Page 231; (ancestry.com image 115); "Pickles Samuel, stone cutter, res 835 Waterloo ave."

665. Jackson City Directory 1890, Detroit, Michigan: R. L. Polk & Co., Publishers, 1890, Volume XI, Page 275; (ancestry.com image 143); "Pickles Samuel (Pickles & Butler), res 317 Whitney."

666. Ibid. Page 275; (ancestry.com image 143); "Pickles & Butler (Samuel Pickles, Andrew Butler), stone yard, 220 E Wesley."

667. Jackson City Directory 1893, Detroit, Michigan: R. L. Polk & Co., Publishers, 1893, Volume XIII, Page 292; (ancestry.com image 144); "Pickles Samuel, stone yard, 303 S Water, res 835 N Waterloo av."

668. Jackson City And County Directory 1894-95, Detroit, Michigan: R. L. Polk & Co., Publishers, 1894, Volume XIV, Page 285; (ancestry.com image 139); "Pickles Samuel, stone yard, 303 S Water, res 835 N Waterloo."

669. Jackson City And County Directory 1897, Volume XVI, Detroit, Michigan: R. L. Polk & Co., Publishers, 1897, Page 339; (ancestry.com image 169); "Pickles Samuel, (Pickles & Platts and Pickles Bros), res 835 N Waterloo."

670. Jackson City And County Directory, 1898-99, Detroit, Michigan: R. L. Polk & Co., Publishers, 1898, Volume XVII, Page 371; (ancestry.com image 184); "Pickles Samuel, lab Bennett Sewer Pipe Co, bds 311 Whitney."

671. Ibid. page 371; (ancestry.com image 184); "Pickles & Platts (Samuel Pickles, Charles Platts), Fish, Oysters, Game and Poultry, 117 S Mechanic. Tel 334 (See left side lines.)."
672. Polk's Jackson City And County Directory, 1899-1900, Detroit, Michigan: R. L. Polk & Co., Publishers, 1900, Page 396; (ancestry.com image 216); "Pickles Samuel, General Contractor and Cut Stone Dealer, 303-305 S Water. Both Tels 346. Res 916 Chicago. Mich Tel 1005."
673. 1900 US Census, Jackson City, Jackson County, Michigan, June 1900, "Stone contractor."
674. DeLand, Col. Charles Victor, DeLand's History of Jackson County, Michigan, Indianapolis, Indiana: B. F. Bowen, 1903, Page 153; "1902 Mayor Samuel Pickles, R."
675. Jackson City Directory 1903, Detroit, Michigan: R. L. Polk & Co., 1903, Page 448; (ancestry.com image 244); "Pickles Hon Samuel, Mayor; General Contractor and Cut Stone Dealer, 6 Webb Blk. Both Tels 346; res 634 N Waterloo av., Both T5els 693."
676. Polk's Jackson City And County Directory, 1904, Detroit, Michigan: R. L. Polk & Co., Publishers, 1904, Page 452; (ancestry.com image 233); "Pickles Hon Samuel, Mayor; Cut Stone Contractor, 46 Sun Bldg. Both Tels 346, res 634 N Waterloo ave. Both Tels 694."
677. Polk's Jackson City And County Directory 1905, Detroit, Michigan: R. L. Polk & Co, Publishers, 1905, Page 465; (ancestry.com image 242); "Pickles Samuel, contr 634 N Waterloo av, res same."
678. R. L. Polk & Co's. Jackson City And County Directory 1907, Detroit, Michigan: R. L. Polk & Co., Publishers, 1907, Page 453; (ancestry.com image 231); "Pickles Samuel, trav agt. res 634 N Waterloo av."
679. 1920 US Census, Bowling Green, Warren County, Kentucky, January 1920, "Quarryman."
680. Bowling Green, Kentucky City Directory 1922, Bowling Green, Kentucky: 1922, Volume V, Page 247; (ancestry.com image 84); "Pickles Saml (Louise), pres Bowling Green Quarries Co, h 1148 Laurel av—Cumb phone 244."
681. New York Passenger Lists, 1820-1957; The Generations Network, Inc.; Provo, Utah, Year: 1880; Arrival: New York, New York; Microfilm Serial: M237, 1820-1897; Line: 1; List Number: 376; (ancestry.com image 11).
682. Bonner, Richard Illenden, Ed., Memoirs Of Lenawee County Michigan, Madison, Wisconsin: Western Historical Society, 1909, Page 496.
683. Knapp, John I. and R. I. Bonner, Illustrated History and Biographical Record Of Lenawee County, Mich., Adrian, Michigan: The Times Printing Company, 1903, Page 40.
684. Detroit Free Press, "Closed Competition Among The Numerous Bidders," 21 August 1900, page 7.
685. Ibid. "Were All Too High: Bids For Erecting New Buildings At The Ionia Asylum," 26 July 1901, page 7.
686. Ibid. "Perry Now A Back Number," 8 April 1902, page 1.
687. DeLand, Col. Charles Victor, DeLand's History of Jackson County, Michigan, Indianapolis, Indiana: B. F. Bowen, 1903, page 153.
688. Detroit Free Press, "G. O. P. Slate Went Through at Jackson," 27 March 1903, page 2.
689. DeLand, Col. Charles Victor, DeLand's History of Jackson County, Michigan, Indianapolis, Indiana: B. F. Bowen, 1903, Pages 1098-1099.

690. Detroit Free Press, "Stonecutters on Strike," 23 July 1903, page 2.
691. Belding Banner, newspaper, Belding, Montcalm County, Michigan, "From All Over Michigan: Mr. Pickles Still Missing," 3 November 1904, page 2.
692. Will/Probate/Letters of Administration. Probate Records; Author: Warren County (Kentucky). Clerk of the County Court; Probate Place: Warren, Kentucky; Vol D, 4-6, 1827-1927; (ancestry.com image 1174).
693. Park City Daily News, "Samuel Pickles Dead Following Extended Illness: End Comes Sunday Morning at Residence; Funeral On Tuesday Morning," 25 May 1925, page 1.
694. 1881 Census of England and Wales, Northowram, Yorkshire, (21 Range Lane), 3 April 1881, Schedule 43. Class RG11; Piece 4421; Folio 32; Page 7; GSU roll 1342057.
695. 1900 US Census, Jackson City, Jackson County, Michigan, June 1900, NARA T623; Roll 719; ED 19; Ward 8; Sheet 1A; Page 58; W Water Loo Street; House 634; Dwelling 4; Family 4; Line 18; "Annie Pickles."
696. 1910 US Census, Bowling Green, Warren County, Kentucky, April 1910, NARA T624; Roll 505; Sheet 4B; ED 120; Dwelling 55; Family 67; Line 55; "Annie E. Pickles."
697. West Yorkshire Archive Service, Church of England Marriages and Banns, 1813-1935, Number 398; Page 199; Yorkshire Parish Records; Reference Number: WDP53/1/3/93.
698. 1881 Census of England and Wales, Northowram, Yorkshire, (21 Range Lane), 3 April 1881.
699. Note: 1900 Census says 1865, age 35! Death record say 9 October 1855.
700. Death Certificate/Record. Montcalm County, Michigan; number 3755; acute nephenitis; age 55 years, 5 months. Recorded 25 April 1911. (ancestry.com image 201).
701. Tombstone.
702. Find-A-Grave, (www.findagrave.com/memorial/27326981/annie-elizabeth-pickles : accessed 06 June 2022). Memorial ID 27326981, citing Hillside Entrican Cemetery, Entrican, Montcalm County, Michigan; maintained by Gail (contributor 47136090).
703. Doyle, Vena Emily *nee* Kilbourne, Letter, 22 April 1981.
704. 1881 Census of England and Wales, Saxlingham Thorpe, Henstead, County Norfolk, 3 April 1881, Schedule 29; Class RG11; Piece 1958; Folio 17; Page 28; GSU roll 1341471. Living with her grandparent Jesse Youngman, widower.
705. Jackson City And County Directory, 1898-99, Detroit, Michigan: R. L. Polk & Co., Publishers, 1898, Volume XVII, Page 440; (ancestry.com image 219); "Sweet Louise (wid Charles), res 711 S Jackson."
706. Polk's Jackson City And County Directory, 1899-1900, Detroit, Michigan: R. L. Polk & Co., Publishers, 1900, Page 476; (ancestry.com image 234); "Sweet Louisa (wid Charles) res 711 S Jackson."
707. 1920 US Census, Bowling Green, Warren County, Kentucky, January 1920, NARA T625; Roll 600; ED 132; Sheet 6B; Dwelling 150; Family 134; Laurel Avenue; Line 81.
708. Polk's Jackson (Michigan) City Directory 1929, Detroit, Michigan: R. L. Polk & Co., Publishers, 1929, Page 407; (ancestry.com image 209); "Pickles Louise (wid Saml) r1301 Wildwood av."
709. Polk's Jackson Michigan City Directory 1930, Detroit, Michigan: R. L. Polk & Co., Publishers, 1930, Page 366; (ancestry.com image 186); "Pickles Louise (wid Saml) r1301 Wildwood av."
710. 1930 US Census, Jackson City, Jackson County, Michigan, April 1930, NARA T626; ED 38-13; Sheet 5B; Dwelling 101; Family 208; Line 70.

"Louisa Pickells" mother-in-law living with daughter Blanche Walker family.

711. Polk's Jackson (Michigan) City Directory 1931, Detroit, Michigan: R. L. Polk & Co., Publishers, 1931, Page 325; (ancestry.com image 168); "Pickles Louise (wid Saml) r429 Adams."

712. Polk's Jackson (Michigan) City Directory 1932, Detroit, Michigan: R. L. Polk & Co., Publishers, 1932, Page 310; (ancestry.com image 157); "Pickles Louise (wid Saml) r429 Adams."

713. Polk's Jackson (Jackson County, Mich.) City Directory 1935, Detroit: R. L. Polk & Co., Publishers, 1935, Page 329; (ancestry.com image 168); "Pickles Louise (wid Saml) r429 Adams."

714. 1940 US Census, Jackson City, Jackson County, Michigan, April 1940, NARA T627; Roll 1767; ED 38-13; Sheet 7A; Line 23. Living with daughter Blanch M Walker family.

715. Polk's Jackson (Jackson County, Michigan) City Directory 1940, Detroit, Michigan: R. L. Polk & Co., Publishers, 1940, Page 294; (ancestry.com image 145); "Pickles Louise (wid Saml) r429 Adams."

716. Polk's Jackson City Directory 1942, [Detroit, Michigan:] R. L. Polk & Co. 1942, Page 277; (ancestry.com image 293); "Pickles Louise (wid Saml) r429 Adams."

717. Polk's Jackson (Jackson County, Mich.) City Directory 1945, Detroit: R. L. Polk & Co., Publishers, 1945, Page 297; (ancestry.com image 148); "Pickles Loise (wid Saml) r429 Adams."

718. Polk's Jackson (Jackson County, Mich.) City Directory 1946, Detroit, Michigan: R. L. Polk & Co., Publishers, 1946, Page 322; (ancestry.com image 169); "Pickles Louise (wid Sam) r429 Adams."

719. Polk's Jackson (Jackson County, Mich.) City Directory 1949, Detroit, Michigan: R. L. Polk & Co., Publishers, 1949, Page 319; (ancestry.com image 161); "Pickles Louise (wid Saml) r585 Andrew av."

720. Polk's Jackson (Jackson County, Mich.) City Directory 1951, Detroit, Michigan: R. L. Polk & Co., Publishers, 1951, Page 309; (ancestry.com image 153); "Pickles Louise (wid Saml) r585 Andrew av."

721. Polk's Jackson (Jackson County, Mich.) City Directory 1952, Detroit: R. L. Polk & Co., Publishers, 1952, Page 292; (ancestry.com image 144); "Pickles Louise (wid Saml) r585 Andrew av."

722. South Australian Births, Index of Registrations 1842 to 1906, Compiled from publicly available sources, ancestry.com.

723. Find-A-Grave, (www.findagrave.com/memorial/129402468/louise-pickles : accessed 24 March 2022). Memorial ID 129402468, citing Fairview Cemetery, Bowling Green, Warren County, Kentucky; maintained by Anita R. Austill (contributor 47729061).

724. Will/Probate/Letters of Administration. (ancestry.com image 1176); Probate Records; Author: Warren County (Kentucky). Clerk of the County Court; Probate Place: Warren, Kentucky.

725. Park City Daily News, "Deaths-Funerals," 6 October 1953, page 5.

726. 1871 Census of England and Wales, Warley Township, Luddenden, Yorkshire, 2 April 1871, Parish: Warley; Series RG10; Piece 4416; ED 3; Page 29; Page 2; Line 1; "Mary Jane Pickles."

727. 1881 Census of England and Wales, Warley Township, Luddenden, Yorkshire, 3 April 1881, ED 3; Schedule 5; "Lower Edge End" street; Class RG11; Piece 4417; Folio 29; Page 1; GSU roll 1342056; "Mary J Pickles."

728. 1891 Census of England and Wales, Bacup Borough, Spotland Civil Parish, Municipal Ward of Brandwood, County Lancaster, 5 April 1891, Page 13; Schedule 66; "52 Greens Lane," Class RG12; Piece 3343; Folio 10; Page 13; GSU roll 6098453; "Mary J Wilcock."

729. 1901 Census of England and Wales, Backup, County Lancashire, 31 March 1901, Class RG13; Piece 3851; Folio 147; Page 28; Schedule 197; 52 Green Lane; "Mary Jane Wilcock."

730. 1911 Census of England and Wales, Backup, County Lancashire, 2 April 1911, Class: RG14; Piece: 24729; Schedule 165; Line 2; "Mary Jane Wilcock."

731. Birth Certificate/Record. Birth record, 1862, Superintendent District: Halifax; Registrar District Luddenden; digital image from GRO, 3 April 2022 (COL963805/2022); Parents: "John Pickles... Hannah Pickles formerly Horsfield"; registered 15 March 1862.

732. England & Wales Civil Registration Indexes, 1837-1915, ancestry.com, GRO, London, England; first quarter Jan-Feb-Mar 1862; Volume 9a; Page 452.

733. Note: Luddenden Foot; Stacks Lane, Yorkshire in 1911 Census.

734. West Yorkshire Archive Service, Church of England Births and Baptisms, 1813-1910, Number 970; Yorkshire Parish Records; New Reference Number: WDP39/6.

735. England Births and Christenings, 1538-1975, (https://familysearch.org/ark:/61903/1:1:N21L-QBB : 21 March 2020), Hannah Pickles in entry for Mary Jane Pickles, 1865.

736. England and Wales Civil Death Registration Index 1837-2007, GRO. England and Wales Civil Registration Indexes. London, Page 39; Volume 9C; affiliate line number 43.

737. West Yorkshire, England, Church of England Deaths and Burials, 1813-1985, West Yorkshire Archive Service; Number 2583. Abode: Dewsbury Road.

738. 1881 Census of England and Wales, Warley Township, Luddenden, Yorkshire, 3 April 1881, "Woolen weaver."

739. 1871 Census of England and Wales, Warley Township, Luddenden, Yorkshire, 2 April 1871, Class RG10; Piece 4416; Folio 29; Page 2; GSU roll 847116; ED 3; Schedule 6.

740. 1871 Census of England and Wales, Heckmondwike, Yorkshire, 2 April 1871, UK National Archives; Class RG10; Piece 4590; Folio 58; Page 12; GSU roll 847147; "Tattersfield Wilcock."

741. 1881 Census of England and Wales, Warley Township, Luddenden, Yorkshire, 3 April 1881, Class RG11; Piece 4417; Folio 63; Page 2; GSU roll 1342056. Street: Luddenden Foot; "Tattersfield Wilcock."

742. 1891 Census of England and Wales , Bacup Borough, Spotland Civil Parish, Municipal Ward of Brandwood, County Lancaster, 5 April 1891, Page 13; Schedule 66; "52 Greens Lane," Class RG12; Piece 3343; Folio 10; Page 13; GSU roll 6098453.; "Tattersfield Wilcock."

743. 1901 Census of England and Wales, Backup, County Lancashire, England, 31 March 1901, Class RG13; Piece 3851; Folio 147; Page 28; Schedule 197; 52 Green Lane; "Tattersfield Wilcock."

744. 1911 Census of England and Wales, Backup, County Lancashire, England, 2 April 1911, Class RG14; Piece 24729; Schedule 165; Line 1; "Tattersfield Wilcock."

745. West Yorkshire Archive Service, Church of England Marriages and Banns, 1813-1935, Marriage: Parish Church of Halifax, Saint John the Baptist, Yorkshire, Page 217; number 434; (ancestry.com image 272).

746. England & Wales, Non-Conformist and Non-Parochial Registers, 1567-1936, Registers of Births, Marriages and Deaths Surrendered to the Non-Parochial Registers Commissions of 1837 and 1857, GRO, database with image, (birth date written below baptismal date); Abode of parents: "Kilprin Hill In the parish of Batley".

747. Not found in civil registry; born in Staincliffe, Yorkshire per 1911 Census.

748. England & Wales, Non-Conformist and Non-Parochial Registers, 1567-1936, Registers of Births, Marriages and Deaths Surrendered to the Non-Parochial Registers Commissions of 1837 and 1857; GRO, database with image, Reel: Batley Carr, Dewsbury, Earlsheaton, Gawthorpe, Hanging Heaton, Mirfield Knowle; WC21. Page 54; number 429.

749. England and Wales Civil Death Registration Index 1837-2007, GRO. England and Wales Civil Registration Indexes; Volume 8e; page 109 (299). (ancestry.com image 32).

750. England and Wales, National Index of Wills and Administrations, 1858-1957, (https://familysearch.org/ark:/61903/1:1:7XD7-CH3Z : 27 August 2019), Tattersfield Wilcock, 5 Sep 1932; citing Probate, London, England, UK, Her Majesty's Stationery Office. Emily Pilling and Ingham Read Pilling, beneficiaries.

751. Find-A-Grave, (www.findagrave.com/memorial/229610806/tattersfield-wilcock : accessed 27 April 2022). Memorial ID 229610806, citing Bacup Cemetery, Bacup, Rossendale Borough, Lancashire, England; maintained by Baby Stegosaurus (contributor 49885654).

752. 1871 Census of England and Wales, Heckmondwike, Yorkshire, 2 April 1871, "Scholar."

753. 1881 Census of England and Wales, Warley Township, Luddenden, Yorkshire, 3 April 1881, "Wollen Silver Tenter."

754. 1891 Census of England and Wales, Lancashire, England, 5 April 1891, "Woolen Carder."

755. 1901 Census of England and Wales, Backup, County Lancashire, England, 31 March 1901, "Woolen Carder."

756. 1911 Census of England and Wales, Backup, County Lancashire, England, 2 April 1911, "Woolen Carder."

757. Will/Probate/Letters of Administration; page 408.

758. 1891 Census of England and Wales , Bacup Borough, Spotland Civil Parish, Municipal Ward of Brandwood, County Lancaster, 5 April 1891, Page 13; Schedule 66; "52 Greens Lane," Class RG12; Piece 3343; Folio 10; Page 13; GSU roll 6098453; Schedule 66; 52 Green Lane; "Etson Wilcock."

759. 1901 Census of England and Wales, Backup, County Lancashire, England, 31 March 1901, Class RG13; Piece 3851; Folio 147; Page 28; Schedule 197; 52 Green Lane; "Etson Wilcock."

760. 1911 Census of England and Wales, Backup, County Lancashire, England, 2 April 1911, Class RG14; Piece 24729; Schedule 165; Line 3; "Etson Wilcock."

761. 1921 England and Wales Census, Holley Villas Ashton Grove, Ashon upon Mersey, Cheshire, England, UK National Archives RG 15; Piece 16841; Schedule 41; type E; District reference RD 445 RS 3 ED 8; Registration District: Bucklow, number 445; sub-district 3; enumeration district 8; "Etson Wilcock."

762. 1901 Census of England and Wales, Backup, County Lancashire, England, 31 March 1901, Class RG13; Piece 3851; Folio 147; Page 28; Schedule 197; 52 Green Lane; "Emily Wilcock."

763. 1911 Census of England and Wales, Backup, County Lancashire, England, 2 April 1911, Class RG14; Piece 24729; Schedule 165; Line 4; "Emily Wilcock."

764. West Yorkshire, England, Electoral Registers, 1840-1962, ancestry.com; West Yorkshire Archive Service, Leeds, Sowerby, 1923; 417 R O Pilling, Emily, Holden Gate, Todmorden Ward 2; Polling District AI.

765. 1939 England and Wales Register [Census], 29 September 1939, Bacup Mb, Registration District Ntmc; Lancashire, England; Reference: Rg 101/4704b. Schedule 315, Sub 2; "Emily Pilling."

766. Halifax Guardian, "Alleged Manslaughter At Halifax." 16 February 1884, page 8.

767. Jackson Citizen Patriot, "Farmer Stricken By Heart Attack," 9 April 1939, page 4.

768. Reported arrived at 11 April 1880. Borge Solem, Norway-Heritage.-com http://www.norwayheritage.com/p_ship.asp?sh=ciric (viewed 14 October 2023).

769. Cameron Prince, www.teslauniverse.com "Nikola Tesla Timeline," https://teslauniverse.com/nikola-tesla/timeline/1884-tesla-arrives-new-york (viewed 14 October 2023).

770. Illustrated Leicester Chronicle, newspaper, Leicester, "From All Quarters: Bible Saves Life," 27 June 1925, page 9.

771. Rossendale Free Press, newspaper, Rawtenstall, Lancashire, "Stacksteads," 6 January 1912, page 3.

772. Ibid. "Stacksteads," 31 August 1912, page 5.

773. Lancashire Evening Post, newspaper, Lancashire, 4 June 1921, page 3.

774. Haslingden Gazette, newspaper, Lancashire, "Rev. Etson Wilcock for Accrington," 5 January 1924, page 2; 15 March 1924, page 1.

775. Ibid. "Public Notices." 15 March 1924, page 1.

776. Ibid. "Late Rev. Etson Wilcock. Brief Stay At Barnes Street. Saved By Bible In The War," 27 June 1925, page 3.

777. Birth Certificate/Record. GRO; number 51. Father: John Pickles; Mother: Hannah Pickles formerly Horsfield; Wool Comber; registered September 1837.

778. West Yorkshire Pioneer, newspaper, Lancashire, "Steeton Soldier Killed," 27 September 1918. From: https://www.suttonincraven.org.uk/pdf/thefallen/additions/BertramGreenwoodClough.pdf

779. Calderdale Family History Society, Baptisms, database; https://www.cfhsweb.com/cfhs-database/baptisms_list.php?menuItemId=2 (viewed 9 January 2024); ID 259210; Father: John; Trade: Comber; Mother: Hannah; Parish: Luddenden St Mary; Registry 1097; Page 138.

780. Ibid. https://www.cfhsweb.com/cfhs-database/baptisms_list.php?menuItemId=2 (viewed 9 January 2024); ID 260168; Parish: Luddenden St Mary; Father: John of Warley, Comber; Mother: Hannah; Registry 2055; birth date 23 September 1837; Page 257.

781. Ibid. https://www.cfhsweb.com/cfhs-database/baptisms_list.php?menuItemId=2 (viewed 9 January 2024); ID 260943; Father: John of Warley, Comber; Mother: Hannah; Parish: Luddenden St Mary; Registry 428; birth date: 7 January 1850; Page 54.

782. Ibid. https://www.cfhsweb.com/cfhs-database/baptisms_list.php?menuItemId=2 (viewed 9 January 2024); ID 260944; Father: John of

Warley, Comber; Mother: Hannah; Parish: Luddenden St Mary; Registry 429; birth date: 4 February 1852; Page 54.

783. Ibid. https://www.cfhsweb.com/cfhs-database/baptisms_list.php?menuItemId=2 (viewed 9 January 2024); ID 260945; Father: John of Warley, Comber; Mother: Hannah; Parish: Luddenden St Mary; Registry 430; birth date 18 November 1854; Page 54.

784. Ibid. https://www.cfhsweb.com/cfhs-database/baptisms_list.php?menuItemId=2 (viewed 9 January 2024); ID 260946; Father: John of Warley, Comber; Mother: Hannah; Registry 431; birth date: 13 June 1857; Page 54.

785. Ibid. https://www.cfhsweb.com/cfhs-database/baptisms_list.php?menuItemId=2 (viewed 9 January 2024); ID 261486; Father: John of Warley, Comber; Mother: Hannah; Registry 970; birth date: 12 February 1862; Page 122.

INDEX: MADE OF PICKLES

Epilogue

Alas, have we come to the end? Never the end in genealogy. People die, are born, and continue the story today.

We learned that our Clay and Pickles families lived in England for centuries before the radical move to migrate to America.

Why?

Our immigrant ancestors moved to another land out of economic necessity. The Industrial Revolution in England created a stark delineation of two classes of people: the haves and have-nots. Our folks were the have-nots. Unlike their ancestors, they were caught in an epoch of rapid change—work and labor were estranged by a mere 50 years before the decision to leave. Driven by word of mouth, the move to Michigan was about other opportunities and open land for farming.

Changes to work in the Industrial Revolution, such as the exploitation of gender, fragmentation of the division of labor, and the fracture of the family unit, despite the assault on prior traditional customs.

To a lesser extent, the political restlessness of the era also shaped family decisions despite enjoying a parliamentarian democracy with representation but befouled by upheaval from horrid working and living conditions. Maybe there was a democracy in politics, but there was no democracy in the workplace – a place occupying the center of home life.

A huge factor for our families was religion. Despite freedom of religion in England, the Clays and Pickles were nonconformists in theology. The Methodist and Baptist churches of their era were healthy and vibrant. Nevertheless, stories of America carried by letters from John Clay and Frederick Clay, early adventurers, back to relatives in England, enticed the faithful of like Christian eschatology to join like kindred souls in central Michigan, particularly in the Jackson County area.

Human movements of economic and religious flight is well known in history. Indeed, the very history of European migration to America!

APPENDIX: NGSQ SYSTEM

The numbering system used exclusively in this book is the National Genealogical Society Quarterly (NGSQ) system for descending genealogy. It is originally based on "Numbering Your Genealogy Sound and Simple Systems" by Joan Ferris Curran, Special Publication No. 59, *National Genealogical Society,* 1992. The NGSQ system is based upon the **Register Method** used by the New England Historical and Genealogical Register since 1847 (now known as AmericanAncestors.org as an Internet entity).

This system assigns a number to each person, whether or not that person is known to have left any descendants. The first person in each lineage is, by definition, "1." Each descendant child is assigned a number, in chronological order of birth, beginning with "1." "2." etc.

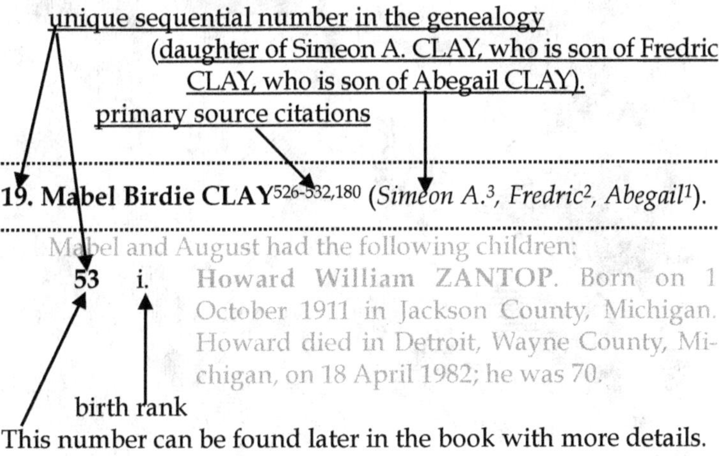

The Wool Comber.

"The attitude of the wool comber, in the plate, exhibits him in only one part of his business, the drawing out of the slivers. The wool upon which he works, is the hair or covering of the sheep, which when washed, and combed, and spun, and woven, makes worsted, many kinds of stuff and other articles of great use in the concerns of life." — *The Book of Trades or, Library of the Useful Arts,* London: 1815, 6th edition, Volume I, opposite page 1.

GLOSSARY

carpet maker/weaver

"The carpet-loom is .... placed perpendicularly, and consists principally of four pieces, two long planks or cheeks of wood, and two thick rollers or beams. The planks are set upright, and the rollers across, the one at top and the other at bottom, about a foot or more distant from the ground. They are suspended on the planks, and may be turned with bars. In each roller is a groove from one end to the other, in which the ends of the warp are so fastened that all the threads of it are kept perpendicular.

The warp is divided both before and behind into parcels of ten threads through the whole width of the piece., The weaver works on the foreside. The design or pattern is traced in its proper colours on cartons, tid about the workman, who looks at it every moment, because every stitch is marked upon it, which it is his business to imitate. By this means he always knows what colours and shades he is to use, and how many stiches of the same colour. To accomplish this, he is assisted by squares, into which the whole design is divided; each square is sub-divided into ten verticlal lines, corresponding with the parcels of ten threads of the warp; and besides, each square is ruled with ten horizontal lines, crossing the verticle lines at right angles. The workman, having placed his spindles of thread near him, begins to work on the first horizontal line of one of the squares.

The lines marked on the carton are not traced on the warp, because an iron wire, which is longer than the width of a parcel of ten threads, supplies the place of a cross line. This wire is manged by a crook at one end, at the workman's right hand; towards the other end it is flatted into a sort of knife, with a back and edge, and grows wider to the point. The weaver fixes his iron wire horizontally on the warp by twisting some turns of a suitable thread of the woof round it, which he passes forward and backward, behind a fore thread of the warp, and then behind the opposite thread, drawing them in their turn by their leishes. Afterwards, he bring the woof-thread round the wire, in order to begin again to thrust it into the warp. He continues in this manner to cover the iron rod or wire, and to fill up a line to the tenth thread of the warp. He is at liberty either to stop here, or to go on with the same cross line in the next division, according as he passes the thread of the woof round the threads of which he causes to cross one another at every instant: when he comes to the endo of the line, he takes care to strike in, or close again all the stitches with an iron reed, the teeth of which freely enter between the empty threads of the warp, and which is heavy enough to strike in the woof he has used. This row of stiches is again closed and levelled, and in the same manner the weaver proceeds; then with his left hand he lays a strong pair of sheers along the finished line, cuts off the loose hairs, and thus forms a row of tufts perfectly even, which, together with those fefore and after it, form the shag. Thus the workman follows stitch for stitch, and colour for colour, the plan of his pattern, which he is attempting to imitate; he paints magnificently, without having the least notion of painting or drawing." *The Book Of Trades, or Library of the Useful Arts. London: Tabart and Co., 1806, Part 1, pp. 30-34.*

Cart driver
A strong open vehicle with two or four wheels, typically used for carrying loads and pulled by a horse.

Clogger
Wooden shoe maker; shoes worn by the lower classes. https://www.familyresearcher.co.uk/glossary/Dictionary-of-Old-Occupations-jobs-beginning-C5.html#Clogger

Common Era Dating:
There is no biblical foundation for the Before Christ/Anno Domini, BC/AD designations. The BC/AD system was created more than 500 years after the events described in the Christian New Testament. The history recording monks Dionysius and Bede had no understanding of the concept of year zero. Nor did they know the exact year of birth of Christ. The calendar they dated events, therefore, is inaccurate. The year 1 AD would follow 1 BC without a starting point for the new chronology of events. The academic use of Common Era (CE) or Before Common Era (BCE) are considered more accurate. The author flipped the coin and uses the academic version.

Cottage industry
A business or manufacturing activity carried on in a family home.

Delver
A quarryman. *Yorkshire Historical Dictionary.* https://yorkshiredictionary.york.ac.uk/words

Doffer
Someone who removes ("doffs") bobbins, pirns or spindles holding spun fiber such as cotton or wool from a spinning frame and replaces them with empty ones.

Fruiterer A fruit seller.

Fuller
"Cleaned and thickened woven clothing to eliminate dirt, oils and impurties." – *Yorkshire Historical Dictionary.* https://www.familyresearcher.co.uk/glossary/Dictionary-of-Old-Occupations-jobs-beginning-F6.html

Fulling mill
A step in woollen clothmaking which involves the cleansing of cloth (particularly wool) to eliminate oils, dirt, and other impurities, and to make it thicker. Originally done by hand pounding the cloth requiring many workers. It was replaced by using water power.

Grippe Influenza.

Joiner Cabinet maker.

Knobstick An individual hired to be a strike-breaker; a "scab."

Loom weaver Much the same as above carpet weaver.

Methodist New Connexion
Formed from secession from the Wesleyan Methodists in 1797 at Ebenezer Chapel, Leeds, it later evolved into the present-day United Methodist Church. In England, it was a nonconformist church primarily located in the northern counties. The principal point of contention was having lay rather than ordained ministers and having a self-governing lay body. By 1848, it had over 15,000 members and 273 chapels.

Milliner A hat maker.

Non-comformist (religion)
A member of a Protestant Church which dissents from the established Church of England.

Pave setter/pavior
"The nature of the paviour's business is known to every one who has resided but a short time in any city or large town. The tools required in the work ar few, viz. a pick-axe to loosen the earth sufficiently deep to admit the stones; a large wooden hammer, such as the man in the plate is represented as holding in his hand; and a birchen broom, with which he brushes the small gravel into the joints between the stones." *The Book of Trades, Part II, p. 64.*

Publican One who owns or manages an English pub (19th century).

Reacher
"Specific occupation in the cotton/silk weaving mills. Each thread has to be Drawn through the Eye on a Heald, ready for the loom and then separately picked out from the Beam of warp threads by the Reacher." — *Hall Genealogy Website: Old Occupation Names. http://rmh-h.co.uk/occup/q-r.html#R*

Rock and spindle
(Also called a Distaff) it was designed to hold the unspun fibers, keeping them untangled and thus easing the spinning process. Fiber is wrapped around the distaff, and tied in place with a piece of ribbon or string.

Scribbler
A machine, or person, combing or preparing wool in thin, downy, translucent layers.

Shoddy
The term has acquired a derogatory meaning, but it is the use of recovered wool in yarn and cloth.

Shuttle
A tool designed to neatly and compactly store a holder that carries the thread of the warp and woof yarn while weaving with a loom.

Stay Maker
A corset maker. Later 19th century "stays" were called corsets.

Twister A machine operator for winding and twisting threads.

Victualler
One who provides food or provisions; a licensed victualler is one who possesses a license to provide alcoholic beverages. —*www.familysearch.org/en/wiki/England_Food_and_Drink_Occupations_(National_Institute)*

Warp and woof (also welf)
The warp: threads that run lengthwise; the woof: threads that run across the fabric.

Whitesmith
A whitesmith is a metalworker who does finishing work on iron and steel such as filing, lathing, burnishing or polishing.

Wool carder
Carding makes sure all the wool fibers are untangled and aligned in one direction, making it easier to spin smoothly.

Woolcomber

"The wool upon which he works is the bair or covering of the sheep, which when washed, and combed, and spun, and woven, makes worsted, many kinds of stuff, and other articles of great use in the concerns of life.

While the wool remains in the state in which it is shorn from the sheep's back, it is called a fleece. Each fleece consists of wool of different qualities and degrees of fineness, which the wool-stapler sorts, and sells at different rates. … for the making of worsted by the woolcomber. He first washes the wool in a trough, and, when very clean, puts one end on a fixed hook, and the other on moveable hook, which he turns round with a handle, till all the moisture be drained completely out. It is then thrown lightly out into the basket… The wool-comber next throws it out inot thin layers, on each of which he scatters a few drops of oil; it is then put together closely into a bin, which is placed under the bench on which he sits: at the back of woolbin is another and larger on for the noyles, that is, the part of the wool that is left on the comb after the sliver is drawn out.

….there are in each comb three rows of teeth parallel to one another. The best combs are manufactured in Halifax in Yorkshire: the teeth are made of highly tempered steel, and fixed into a very smooth stock, in which is inserted a handle nearly in a perpendiucular position. Each workman has two of these combs: theese he makes pretty hot, by putting them into a sort of jar made of clay, … called a comb-pot, in which there is a fire made of the best burnt charcoal.

When the combs are hot, he puts on each a certain quantity of wool; having first disentagnled it from all knotsm, and other obstacles that ight impede the operation. He then combs the wool from off one comb on to the other aternately, till it is exceedingly smooth; when having again heated the combs, he fixes each on an iron spike placed in the wall for the purpose, as it is represented in the plate, and draws out the wool into a fine sliver, oftentimes five or six feet in length: what is left on the comb is called anoyle, and is fit only for the manufacture of blankets and coarse cloth.

In general, four wool-combers work at the same pot, which is made large enough to admit of eight combs. There are, of course, four distinct benches and bins of both kinds in each shop. In almost every workshop is an hour-glass, by wich they measure the time: the care of this falls to the lot of a particular person. The small bottle underneath the comb is filled with oil, which is occasionally used. On the side of the wall are place two ballads, of which, in general, ther are several in every wool-comber's shop.

The journeymen work by the piece, and will earn from sixteen shillings to twenty per week. Like people in may other trades, they ofen make holidays in he early part of the week. They come on a Monday morning, and, having lighted the fire in the comb-pot, will frequently go away, and perhaps return no more till Wednesday or even Thursday. The men in this trade have curious custom: when out of work, they set out in search of a mster, with a sor of certificate from their last place; this they call going on the *tramp*; and at every shope where they call, and can get no employment, they receive one penny, which is given from a common stock raised by the men of that shop. A spare bench is always provided in the shop, upon which people on the *tramp* may rest themselves.

Wool-combing is preparatory to the manufacture of worsted yarn, and is the first process towards the making of flannels, serges, stuffs, baize, kerseys, & c. …

A pack of wool weighs 240lbs., and, it is said, will employ more thant sixty persons a week to manufacture it into cloths, viz. three men to sort, dry, mix and make it ready for the carder; five to scribble it; thirty-five women and girls to card and spin it; eitht men to weave it; four to spole it; and eight to scour, mill, pack, and press it.

When the wool is made into stuffs, serges, &c., it will employ 200 persons. And when made into stocking it will afford work for a week to 184 persons, viz. 10 combers, 102 spinners, winders &c., and 60 stocking-weavers, besides doublers, throwers, and a dryer." *The Book of Trades, Part I, pp. 1-7.*

Wollen

A fabric made of wool and especially of woolen yarns having a fuzzy or napped face (as for use in clothing or blankets)

Workhouse

A workhouse sometimes called a"union workhouse" or "spike" (a large metal nail used in crushing stones or bones) was an institution where those unable to support themselves financially were accommodated and employed—generally codified by the Act of 1834. The laws and administration of these usually miserable places were dreadful. Inmates gave up all their clothing and personal possessions, were given a uniform, and, if disciplined, often withheld food for 48 hours. They were akin to prison for the poor. Children under the age of two were allowed to remain with their mothers. Nevertheless, by entering a workhouse, inmates were considered to have forfeited responsibility to their families and were segregated by age and gender. As the 19th century wore on, workhouses increasingly became refuges for the elderly, infirm, and sick rather than the able-bodied poor.

worsted wool

Worsted wool fabric is a high-quality type of wool yarn and a yarn weight category. It is typically used in tailored garments such as suits, as opposed to woolen wool, like knitted items such as sweaters. Tropical-weighted worsteds are tightly spun, straightened wool combined with a looser weave that permits air to flow through the fabric. It has a smooth, slick, hard surface. Worsted is also used for carpets, clothing, hosiery, gloves, and baize.

Appendix: John Clay, early to America

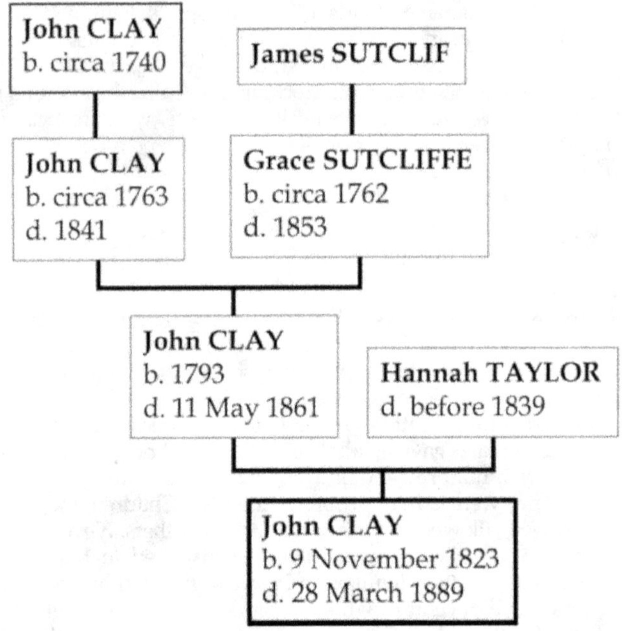

John CLAY[1-7], son of **John CLAY** and **Hannah TAYLOR**, was born on 9 November 1823, in England, and[8] baptized in Illingworth, Yorkshire, on 6 December 1823.[9,10] [No church record found of baptism with mothers name Hannah.] He died in Springport, Jackson County, Michigan, on 28 March 1889; he was 65.[11,12] Buried in Griffith Cemetery, Springport, Jackson County, Michigan.[13]

Occupations: Farmer (1841-1888);[14-17] Fancy Weaver (1850).

John is believed to be the number 104, age 25, English, from Manchester, claiming allegiance to US, aboard the merchant ship the *SS Clara Wheeler*,[27] sailing from Liverpool to Philadelphia, 15 July 1850, working as a Fancy Weaver. No other Clay members on the list.[18] For John, the *Clara Wheeler* was a new ship: built at Medford, Massachusetts in 1849. It was 995 tons and sold to British in November, 1863.[28]

In the 1860 census, his cousin **4. Fredric "Fred" Clay** (1826-1898) is a next door neighbor, and in the 1880 census cousin **5. Hannah "Annie" Clay** (1838-1927) and her husband James Pickles (1843-1911) are nearby.

SS Clara Wheeler
Naval History and Heritage Command

John served during the Civil War.

Military:

Company E, 20th Regiment Michigan Infantry

Home: Tompkins, age 37 | Wounded at Cold Harbor Clay, John, age 37.[19] Story of the 20th:[20,21] "Company E—Parma, Jackson county."[22]

United States Civil War Soldiers Index, 1861-1865:

Name: John Clay | Alias: John C. Clay

Military Beginning Rank: Private | Final Rank: Private

Side: Union | Unit: 20th Regiment, Michigan Infantry, Company E | Event Type: Military Service | Date: from 1861 to 1865 | Place: Michigan, United States[23]

U.S., Civil War Soldier Records and Profiles, 1861-1865:

Name: John Clay |Enlistment Age: 37 | Birth Date: abt 1825

Enlistment: Date: 1 Aug 1862 |Place: Tompkins, Michigan | Rank: Private | *Muster:* Date: 16 Aug 1862 | Place: Michigan Company: E | Regiment: 20th Infantry | Regiment Type: Infantry |Enlisted | *Casualty:* Date: 2 Jun 1864|Place: Cold Harbor, Virginia | Type of Casualty: Wounded |*Muster Out:* Date: 3 May 1865 |Place: Washington, District of Columbia Information: disch

Side of War: Union| Survived War? Yes

Injured in Line of Duty? Yes | *Residence Place:* Tompkins, Michigan

Death Date: 24 March 1889 | *Burial Place:* Springport, Michigan. Title: Record of Service of Michigan Volunteers 1861-65[24]

"Michigan, Grand Army of the Republic Membership Records, 1876-1945,"[25]

Name: John Clay |Age: 59 | Birth Year (Estimated): 1824 Birthplace: Yorkshire England | Residence Place: Springport

Event Type: Military ServiceEvent Date 30 Jun 1883

Event Place: Eaton Rapids, Eaton, Michigan, United States

Note: 20 Mich Infty | GAR Post 111[26]

John apparently never married and quietly farmed his land. Newspapers reveal nothing about him.

PENSION RECORD:

Dr. Amos Crosby's affidavit treated John for "Malarious or billious fever, lasting a few days," prior to military service in August 1861. When John was on leave, September 1864, John was treated by him for "chronic diarrhea or dysentery."

John's military service in the Civil War was limited by the illnesses he contracted, first in August 1862 when left for sick at Alexandria Hospital, Washington, District of Columbia. Admitted to the Mt. Pleasant General Hospital, Washington, 9 October 1862: sickness not stated. Later admitted 20 November, to the Continental Hotel General Hospital, Baltimore, Maryland, for fever.

John was taken ill on or about 30 July 1864 at Petersburg, Virginia with chronic diarrhea. It dogged him for the rest of his life and had little relief. While in the regiment he was treated at Mt. Pleasant Hospital, Washington; Halliday Hospital, Baltimore; Harwood Hospital, Washington; and lastly Finlay Hospital, Washington from which he was discharged.

In the 1880s, James McAllister, Charles Pickett, privates, and Garner A. Rose, a corporal, all who served with John, swore-out affidavits confirming his illness.

John Returns to England, 1865-1867.

In October 1865, John left for England; returning in April 1866. While in England he employed several physicians concerning his illness, but apparently they were unsuccessful. A physician wrote, "As a farmer and when he takes cold, or overdoes, or eats food that does no[t] agree with him, he is attacked by a reappearance of the said disease of chronic Diarrhoea..." John stated about one-third of his time was spent disabled.

In Dr. Josiah William's affidavit of 2 August 1883, he was acquainted with John since October 1867, then residing with the George Griffith family. "The claimant is an excentric bachelor... And for the past two years claimant has not been able to perform more than two thirds per day manual labor and much of the time not able to work at all."

It was by 1886 that John's health turned for the worse. "Tongue normal except tremulous. Bowels not bloated but tender. He has Piles - five or six large tumors down at this examination. Apex of heart is directly under nipple & valve sounds confused & undistinct. He has diarrhoea complicated with Piles. Also has organic disease of heart. ... with considerable pain in small of back extending to left side, and considerably affecting the heart causing a sense of fullness in his chest causing a shortness of breath and a sense of dizziness. Any excitement working [makes] claiment worse." It further appears from the graphic discriptions, John was probably suffering from a progressive cancer spreading throughout his body.

The last official correspondence was 16 March 1889's Declaration For The Increase Of An Invalid Pension. John was enrolled at the Detroit pension office for $10 per month for ..." chronic diarrhea disability and resulting in Piles. disease of Stomach and Heart..." On 28 March John passed away.

Sources for John Clay:

1. 1841 Census of England and Wales, Halifax, West Riding, Yorkshire, 6 June 1841, Class HO107; Piece 1304; Book 9; Civil Parish: Halifax; County: Yorkshire; ED 17; Folio 24; Page 16; Line 11; GSU roll 464264 "John Clay."

2. 1860 US Census, Eaton Rapids, Eaton County, Michigan, June 1860, NARA M653; Roll 542; Page 527; Dwelling 225; Family 209; Line 24; "John Clay" living with the Hiram Howard family.

3. 1860 US Agricultural Census (U.S. Selected Federal Census Non-Population Schedule), Eaton Rapids, Eaton County, Michigan, NARA T1164; Roll 8; Page 3; Line 29; Schedule Type: Agriculture.

4. Not found in the 1870 US census.

5. 1880 US Census, Hamlin Township, Eaton County, Michigan, June 1880, NARA T9; Roll 578; ED 78; Page 15/324; Dwelling 159; Family 173; Line 47; "John Clay."

6. Jackson City and County Directory 1888, Volume 10, Detroit, Michigan: R. L. Polk &Co., Publishers, 1888, Page 399 (ancestry.com image 196); "Clay John, f. 4. 90, $800, Springport, Springport."

7. Tombstone. (See findagrave.com) "GAR Post 111."

8. Ibid.

9. West Yorkshire Archive Service, West Yorkshire, England, Church of England Births and Baptisms, 1813-1910, Wakefield, Yorkshire, England, ancestry.com, Number 720; New Reference Number: WDP73/1/2/1.

10. England, Yorkshire, Bishop's Transcripts, 1547-1957, Borthwick Institute for Archives, database, familysearch.org, Page 90.

11. Death Certificate/Record. Michigan Department of Community Health, Division for Vital Records and Health Statistics; Lansing; Death Records; Record 447. "John Clay... Single... Age 67... [Cause of death:] Heart Disease... Birthplace: England. Farmer..." father "John Clay" mother unknown.

12. "Single 67 [born circa 1822; died from] heart disease" father John Clay others unknown; recorded 13 August 1890.
13. Find-A-Grave, (www.findagrave.com/memorial/16917853/john-clay: accessed 02 August 2022). Memorial ID 16917853, citing Griffith Cemetery, Springport, Jackson County, Michigan; maintained by Deb Hayes-Wolfe (contributor 46811474).
14. 1841 Census of England and Wales, Halifax, West Riding, Yorkshire, 6 June 1841, "farmer."
15. 1860 US Census, Eaton Rapids, Eaton County, Michigan, June 1860, "farmer."
16. 1880 US Census, Hamlin Township, Eaton County, Michigan, June 1880, "Farmer."
17. Jackson City and County Directory 1888, Volume 10, Detroit, Michigan: R. L. Polk & Co., Publishers, 1888, Page 399 (ancestry.com image 196); "Clay, John, f, 4, 90, $800, Springport, Springport."
18. Pennsylvania, U.S., Arriving Passenger and Crew Lists, 1798-1962, database with scanned image, NARA, Record Group Title: Records of the United States Customs Service, 1745-1997; Record Group Number: 36; Series: M425; Roll: 70; (ancestry.com image 413).
19. Harvey, Don, MIGenWeb: Michigan Civil War Web Site, http://www.migenweb.org/michiganinthewar/infantry/20compe.htm. Listing of men in Company E.
20. Harvey, Don, MIGenWeb: Michigan Civil War Web Site, http://www.migenweb.org/michiganinthewar/infantry/20thinf.htm. History of the regiment.
21. National Parks Service, USA, Civil War Solders and Sailors System, https://www.nps.gov/civilwar/search-soldiers-detail.htm?soldierId=57B0C88D-DC7A-DF11-BF36-B8AC6F5D926A (Private); Film Number M545 Roll 8.
22. Cutcheon, Col. Byron M., Compiler, The Story of the Twentieth Michigan Infantry, July 15th, 1862 to May 30th, 1865, Lansing, Michigan: Robert Smith Printing Co., Printers And Binders, 1904, Company E, pages 11, 16; https://babel.hathitrust.org/cgi/pt?id=wu.89062269717&view=1up&seq=40 (viewed 1 November 2022).
23. "United States Civil War Soldiers Index, 1861-1865," FamilySearch.org, database, Affiliate Film Number: 8; Affiliate Publication Number: M545; Affiliate Publication Title: Index to Compiled Service Records of Volunteer Union Soldiers Who Served in Organizations From the State of Michigan.
24. Historical Data Systems, Inc., "American Civil War Research Database," Duxbury, Massachusetts.
25. Michigan, Grand Army of the Republic Membership Records, 1876-1945, Michigan State Archives, Lansing, https://www.familysearch.org/ark:/61903/1:1:Q24T-HR1W John Clay, 30 Jun 1883; citing Eaton Rapids, Eaton; FHL microfilm 905,748.
26. Ibid. https://familysearch.org/ark:/61903/1:1:Q24T-HR1W : 7 January 2020), John Clay, 30 Jun 1883; citing Eaton Rapids, Eaton, Michigan.
27. https://www.history.navy.mil/our-collections/photography/numerical-list-of-images/nhhc-series/nh-series/NH-55000/NH-55244.html
28. Gleason, Hall. Old Ships And Ship-Building Days Of Medford 1630-1873. Massachusetts: West Medford, 1936; page 71.

APPENDIX: A ROWDY JAMES PICKLES

We can only conjecture that the following is James PICKLES (1843-1911), but there is strong circumstantial evidence suggesting it is one in the same person. See PART 1, ABEGAIL'S CHILDREN: MADE OF CLAY, spouse to **5. Hannah "Annie" CLAY** – the connecting couple of the Clay and Pickles families.

1859: "A Disorderlay Railway Passenger." At the West Riding Court, on Thursday, a person named James Pickles, residing at Sowerby Bridge, was charged with being drunk and annoying the passengers in a train on the Lancashire and Yorkshire Railway, and was fined 5s. and cost 15s." – The Bradford Observer, *22 September 1859, page 5.*

ASSAULTS ON FEMALES.—Indecent attacks on women have become very common in the villages around Halifax of late, and a case of the kind was brought before the West Riding Bench on Saturday. Three young men were concerned, namely, George Lumb, Luke Wilkinson, and James Pickles, all of Midgley, and they were charged with an assault on a young woman named Mary Ann Taylor, on the 5th inst., about eight o'clock. The defendants were fined £2 each and costs, and if not paid at once, a month's imprisonment each. In future, the Magistrates said they would impose the full penalty of £5 in all cases brought before them.

The Leeds Mercury, *(West Yorkshire), 18 December 1860, page 3.*

1863: "West Riding Spring Intermediate Sessions, Bradford. Nine months imprisonment…

James Pickles (20), fraudulently converting to his use as a bailee a coat and handkerchief, the p[roperty] of Thomas Jackson, at Wakefield." – The Bradford Observer, *28 May 1863, page 6.* Also, *"West Riding Spring Intermediate Sessions, Bradford," "Nine months imprisonment…" 22 May 1863, page 3,* The Leeds Mercury.

1863: "Drunk And Abusive In a Railway Train. – James Pickles, Sowerby Bride, was summoned before the Halifax Justices on Saturday, charge by the Lancashire and Yorkshire Railway Company with being drunk and abusive in a passenger train on the company's line. He was fined £2, including costs." – *The Leeds Mercury, 27 October 1863, page 3.*

FIGHT HE WOULD.—James Pickles and Andrew Jackson, both of Lockwood, were charged with a breach of the peace. Police-constable Redman found the defendants fighting together at the back of the Swan Inn, Lockwood, at nine o'clock on Saturday night, the 1st inst. Pickles did not appear. In defence, it was shown that on the above afternoon there had been a cricket match between two firms, and at night they had repaired to the Swan Inn, to enjoy a social glass and chat. While there Pickles quarrelled with a man named Geo. Hardy, whom he would fight. They therefore went into the back yard to have it out. Jackson went out and separated them, on which Pickles turned his attention to Jackson and struck him. In self-defence, Jackson threw his assailant, and at this moment Redman came on the scene. The case against Jackson was dismissed, and Pickles was fined 5s. and expenses, or ten days to prison.

Huddersfield Chronicle and West Yorkshire Advertiser, *15 August 1863, page 6. It is not sure if there was a relationship between Andrew Jackson and the Thomas Jackson, cited earlier.*

Below. Thereafter, he was involved in union activities when he and others mixed it up with anti-union workers and was charged and sentenced to twelve months in prison for perjury in defending another man.

PERJURY ARISING OUT OF A TRADES' UNION CASE.—*James Pickles*, 25, bobbin-turner, on bail, was charged with false swearing at Todmorden, on the 20th June. The facts were, that in consequence of some Staffordshire men having replaced some union colliers who had turned out, they were exposed to ill-treatment from other trades who sympathised with the unionists. At twelve o'clock at night, the "knobsticks" on going to work were pelted with stones, and the police saw a man named Bate pick up and throw stones. When he was before the magistrates the prisoner swore that he (Bate) did not throw stones, but the Staffordshire men were the first aggressors. Guilty.—Sentenced to twelve months' hard labour.

"District News: Burnley-Valley," Burnley Gazette, *17 August 1867, page 3.*

APPENDIX: DIARY OF AMELIA HANNAH ELIZABETH PICKLES

Young girl's diaries are often sparse and plain. **14. Amelia Hannah Elizabeth "Minnie" PICKLES** *(PART 1, MADE OF CLAY) was born five years after her parents arrival to America. She lived in the then thinly populated central Michigan flatlands with her Victorian Era farm family.*

Journals and diaries are a record of one's personal daily recollections of life, emotions, and history. In 1890, a 12-year-old girl began writing her diary. It's not an exciting diary by anyone's standards, but it gives a little insight into nineteenth-century farm life in central Michigan.

Author's note: *this is my great-grandmother's diary. I kept all the misspellings, etc., as she wrote them. I only altered where she used ditto marks – I wrote the words out – and used minor punctuation to make it understandable without compromising the content.*

In later years, her children would write their occasional entries in the diary. I have not included them here.

March through June 1890 | Excelsior Diary 1890

Amelia H Pickles | Entrican, Mich. | Age 12. 1890
"A present from my father."

MAR. 1, Sat. I went to Sabbath School;* Minnie Lewis came home from meeting with me, at night I went down to Weeks a little while. Amelia Pickles, Entrican Mich.

MAR. 2, Sun. I went to meeting at night; Mr Hipkins was here. Albert Steele and Ida Hammond was here, Henry Hammond worked here. Amelia H. Pickles, Entrican Mich. Age 12 1890

MAR. 3, Mon. I went to school.† Johnnie Steele‡ was here. Amelia H. E. Pickles. Entrican Mont - Calm Co Mich.

---

* Also known as "S.S." herein. It is unclear what church or school Amelia attended. The Seventh Day Adventist Church was organized in July 1879, but her diary does not reveal any familiar names associated with the church. Going by Amelia's family relationships, particularly with the Steele family, they probably attended the Baptist Church of Entrican. In those days the Methodist and Baptist churches worshipped in "union" until the congregations became bigger and established their own sectarianising. —John W. Dasef. *History of Montacalm County Michigan.* Indianapolis, Indiana: B.F. Bowen & Company, Inc. Volume I, pages 334, 348.

† The Entrican School, lead by Mrs. Ida M. Sadler, taught the Fall, 1889, Winter, 1890, and Spring 1890 terms. Douglass, A Michigan Township, A. M. Gustafson, 1982; page 124, quoting the *Stanton Weekly Clipper* newspaper.

‡ John C. "Johnnie" Steele (1869-1959) figures predominately in the diary, and is Minnie's contemporary. He is the son of John C. Steele, Sr. (1845-1917) and Julia A. Everett (1845-1898). Johnnie is a brother to **Julia Josephine Steele** who married Amelia's uncle **Samuel James Pickles/Pickell**. Albert Steele, in the March 2 entry, is Johnnie's brother.

MAR. 4, Tues. B. F. Lewis[§] was here to dinner. Ma and I went to meeting. "Weather." Very cold. Snow part of the time. Amelia H. E. Pickles Entrican Mich Age 12. 1890

MAR. 5, Wed. B. F. Lewis, W. Hipkins and Mr Lee all of Mc Brides was here to dinner; I went down to Mr Weeks[**] in the After Noon. Cold and Fair

MAR. 6, Thur. B. F. Lewis was here to dinner. Pa went to McBrides[††] For B. F. Lewis With a load of Vegetables.

MAR. 7, Fri. Pa went to Stanton and took a load of Wood to Mr Hill.

MAR. 8, Sat. I and Ma went to meeting. "S.S." In the After Noon Pa and I went down to Entrican. "Fine."

MAR. 9, Sun. Mr Lewis and Mrs Lewis was here to dinner. Pa drawed wood. Clear and Warm.

MAR. 10, Mon. Pa fixed the Book Cupboad. Snow and rain. Amelia H. E. Pickles, Entrican Mich.

MAR. 11, Tues. Pa was Tinkering. Cleaned out the Shop. Rain and Mild. Mr Rimes was here.

MAR. 12, Wed. Pa went to Edmore and I went down to Mr Lewis. I visited Minnie school part the day stayed all night with Minnie. Showers. Henry worked here

MAR. 13, Thur. I came back from Lewis'es. Mrs Vaughn was here to dinner. Cold and Fine. Henry worked here.

MAR. 14, FRIDAY Pa and Henry Hammond was sawing. Cold and Blustering

MAR. 15, Sat. I went to S.S. in the after-noon Pa and I went down to Entrican; At night Ma and I went down to Bro. Weeks. Cold and Fine

MAR. 16, Sun. I went up to Cora Goodno's in the after-noon. Cora came home with me. Mr Goodno[‡‡] was here at m. Pa was Drawing and Spliting wood. Fair and Warm.

MAR. 17, Mon. I went to school; Pa went to Edmore; B. F. Lewis was here; Edgar Weeks was here. "Warm."

---

§ The Lewis's are found 38 times in the diary. Believed to be Benjamin Franklin Lewis (1843-1918), a stone mason, and his wife Clara "Carrie" Smith (1836-1922). Both originally hailed from New York State. Minnie Lewis is their daughter and a favorite playmate for Amelia.

** "Mr. Weeks" Another prominent name found in her diary. Probably Albert Weeks, father of Ruby and Edgar Weeks, other playmates of Amelia.

†† Village of McBride, Day Township, Montcalm County, Michigan.

‡‡ Believed to be William Goodnoe (1853-1919) and second wife Christina Kebler (1854-1932). Olive and Fredy, young toddlers at the time for Amelia, were their children.

MAR. 18, Tues. I went to school; Pa went to Six Lakes. Mr Weeks was here. Pa sawed wood in the door-yard half day. Fair and Warm. Amelia Pickles, Entrican, Mich.

MAR. 19, Wed. I went to school; Ma went down to Mr Steeles; Mrs Weeks and Ruby Weeks[§§] was here at night, Fair and Mudy Warm.

MAR. 20, Thur. I went to school and stayed all night with Josie Swarthost. Pa went down to Mc Brides with a load of wood. "Warm"

MAR. 21, Fri. I went to school. Pa was bucking up wood. Warm. Fine.

MAR. 22, Sat. Mr and Mrs Lewis came home with us from meeting. In the after-noon, Pa went down to Entrican; In the evening Pa and I went down to Weeks. Fair & Warm. Amelia Pickles.

MAR. 23, Sun. In the forenoon Pa worked down to Weeks; In the after-noon Edgar Weeks worked here. fair and Warm. Amelia Pickles.

MAR. 24, Mon. I went to school. Mr Cook stayed all night here. Some Stormy. Amelia H. E. Pickles, Entrican, Mich.

MAR. 25, Tues. I went to school; Pa went to Stanton with C. Cook. Windy and Stormy.

MAR. 26, Wed. I went to school, Pa drawed wood; Johnnie Steele was here. Mr. C. Cook was here. Blustering. Amelia Pickles, Entrican, Mich. Age 12.

MAR. 27, Thur. It was the last day of Miss Sadler's school. Pa and Ma went to visit the school; Mr C. Cook returned to his home at Lansing. "Fine."

MAR. 28, Fri. First day of Vacation, Pa went down to Mr Weeks, North-East Blisered.

MAR. 29, Sat. I went to Sabbath School. I was nearly sick with the earache. Pa went down to Entrican in the P. M. Squally

MAR. 30, Sun. I was nearly sick with the ear ache all day. Pa was drawing manure. Fine.

MAR. 31, Mon. Pa drawing wood. Ma and I went to meeting tonight.

APR. 1, Tues. Pa drawed wood At night we went down to meeting.

APR. 2, Wed. Minnie Lewis came here. B. F. Lewis and Minnie was here to dinner. Pa & Minnie & I went down to spring at night. Fair and Warm.

---

§§ Ruby Weeks (1873-1907) was the daughter of Albert Weeks and Lydia "Adie" Valleau Weeks. Edgar Weeks is Ruby's brother.

APR. 3, Thur. I went home with Minnie Lewis. Minnie and B. F. Lewis was here to dinner. Misty & Rainy.

APR. 4, Fri. I went up to Mrs Sadlers and had a pleasant time. Mr. Weeks was here. John Steele was here. John Rummel was here. Warm.

APR. 5, Sat. I came home from Mr Lewis went to meeting. Mrs Lewis was here dinner. Mrs Pitton stayed all night here. Fine & Warm. Amelia H. E. Pickles, Entrican, Mich. Age 12, 1890.

APR. 6, Sun. Pa was tinkering. Mrs Pitton was here. Rainy at night. Amelia H. E. Pickles, Entrican, Mich., Mont Calm Co.

APR. 7, Mon. Pa was picking up stone on Mr Cook's place. I went down to Mr Weeks. Warm and Pleasant Amelia Pickles, Age 12. Entrican, Mont Calm Co., Mich.

APR. 8, Tues. Ma and I started to McBrides. Bo Dervis was here at night. Warm & Pleasant. Amelia Pickles. Entrican, Montcalm Co., Mich.

APR. 9, Wed. Pa went down to Entrican in the Afternoon. B. F. Lewis worked here. Stormy and snow some.

APR. 10, Thur. Pa & I went to Six Lakes. Fair and [illegible]

APR. 11, Fri. [illegible] to McBrides & to Mr Lewis. Minnie came along with us. Mrs Weeks and Ruby was here and Grandma Vaughn. Fine & Warm.

APR. 12, Sat. Minnie [illegible] I went to meeting at night. Ma & I went to Bro Weeks. Warm.

APR. 13, Sun. Mr & Mrs Goodno was here to supper. Mr Rime Rory was here. Olive Goodno stayed all night here. Pa commenced to dray for oats. Warm. Rain at night.

APR. 14, Mon. It was the first day of Ida. Mr. Sadlering [sp? illegible] school for third term here. Cora Goodno & Fredy & Olive Goodno was here to dinner. B. F. Lewis here to supper. Pa started to make garden. Fine & Windy.

APR. 15, Tues. Pa put his oats in. I went to school. Warm and Fair. Amelia

APR. 16, Wed. Pa put in his onions. I went to school. Warm & Fair.

APR. 17, Thur. Pa went to Edmore. I went to school. Warm.

APR. 18, Fri. Ma went to Stanton. I went to school. Quite Warm.

APR. 19, Sat. I and Ma went to Sabbath School. In the afternoon I and Pa went down to Entrican. Cool wind. Amelia Pickles, Entrican Mich. Age 12

APR. 20, Sun. I & Ma worked nearly all day in the flower garden. Pa plowed for corn. Warm & Fair.

APR. 21, Mon. I and Ma went to Bro. Forgo's place. Mr Tomkins was here. Warm and Fair.

APR. 22, Tues. I and Ma came back from Sam's. "Warm."

APR. 23, Wed. Pa draged for John Steele. I went down to Mr Weeks in the after-noon. At night Mrs & Ruby Weeks was here. Windy. Amelia H. Pickles. Age 12.

APR. 24, Thur. Ruby Weeks went to Battle Creek. I went to school. Pa went to Stanton. "Chilly"

APR. 25, Fri. I went to school. Pa plowed on the Cook place. Some Warmer.

APR. 26, Sat. I & Ma went to meeting. Ben & Minnie Lewis came home with us from meeting. "Plesent."

APR. 27, Sun. At night Pa & I went up to Mr Goodno's. Fair & Plesent

APR. 28, Mon. I went to school. Will Goodno worked here. Olive Goodno was here. "Warm."

APR. 29, Tues. I went to school. Pa was plowing on Cooks place. Warm. Amelia H. E. Pickles. Entrican, Mich.

APR. 30, Wed. I went to school & at night went after flowers was to Mr Johnson's to supper. Cool twards night.

MAY 1, Thur. It was the first day of May, we had a May party at the school house. I was made queen. I stayed all night with Paarlee Casper. Fair and Warm. Amelia H. E. Pickles, Entrican, Mich.

MAY 2, Fri. I went to school. Fair and Warm. Amelia Pickles.

MAY 3, Sat. Ma and I went to meeting. Gusta Goodno came home with me at night. Mr Charles Cook came. rain in the after-noon

MAY 4, Sun. Mr Keebler was here. Minnie Lewis was here & Pearlie Cosper. Cool.

MAY 5, Mon. I went to school. Mr and Mrs Lewis here. Ma went down to Mrs Rimes a little while. Cool towards night.

MAY 6, Tues. I went to school Papa went to Stanton. Cool. Amelia E. Pickles, Entrican, Mich. Age 12, Year 1890.

MAY 7, Wed. I went to school. Fair. Amelia Pickles.

MAY 8, Thur. I went to school. Rain.

MAY 9, Fri. I started to go to school and the rain caught me so I stayed to Josie Swarthout's. Rain.

MAY 10, Sat. It rained so hard we could not go to Sabbath School. Henry Drier [sp, illegible] stopped here as he was going back from [illegible]. Rain.

MAY 11, Sun. Pa was plowing on the Cook place. Fine. Amelia Pickles.

MAY 12, Mon. I went to school. Pa draged on the Cooks place.

MAY 13, Tues. I went to school. Pa draged on the Cooks place. Fine.

MAY 14, Wed. Iwent to school and stayed all night with Gusta Goodno. Fine and Warm.

MAY 15, Thur. I went to school. PA draged. Fine.

MAY 16, Fri. I went to school. Ma went to Edmore. Fine.

MAY 17, Sat. Ma and I went to Sabbath School. In the afternoon Pa and I went down to Entrican P. O. At night we went over to John Kublere. Fine and Warm. Amelia Pickles, Entrican, Mich.

MAY 18, Sun. Pa white-washed up stares. Ida and Addie Hammond was here. Rained part of the day.

MAY 19, Mon. I was sick with a cold. John Rummes worked here. Fair.

MAY 20, Tues. Pa finished planting his corn. Fine.

MAY 21, Wed. Pa white-washed the little room of staires. Rain.

MAY 22, Thur. Pa planted potatoes. Henry Weeks was here. Rain at night very hard. Warm in the day time.

MAY 23, Fri. Johnny Steele was to our home. Henry Weeks was here. Fine and Warm. Amelia Pickles.

MAY 24, Sat. Ma went to Greenville. I went down to Mrs Weeks. Rain first of the day.

MAY 25, Sun. Pa tinkered around we planted our peanut and muskmellons, and watermellons. Fine.

MAY 26, Mon. Ma came back from Greenville. Fine.

MAY 27, Tues. I went to school.

MAY 28, Wed. I went to school.

MAY 29, Thur. I went to school. Fine & Warm.

MAY 30, Fri. I went down to Decoration*** to Entrican and had a good time. Fine & Warm.

MAY 31, Sat. I and Ma went to meeting. Mr. and Mrs. Lewis came home with us. Fine.

JUN. 1, Sun. I was to home all day. Pa was plowing on the Cooks place. Fine and warm.

JUN. 2, Mon. Ma and I went to McBrides. I visited Minnie Lewis school. Gusta Goodnow stayed all night with me.

JUN. 3, Tues. I went to school.

JUN. 4, Wed. I went to school.

JUN. 5, Thur. I went to school and stayed all night with Imogine Covert.

JUN. 6, Fri. I went to school.

JUN. 7, Sat. I went to meeting.

*** Original name of what is now Memorial Day.

JUN. 8, Sun. I went to sunday school and stayed to Effie Bradys on the afternoon. Fine and warm.
JUN. 9, Mon. [Illegible]
[This was the last entry.]

Minnie became sick shortly after her last entry. She is believed to have caught meningitis and lost some hearing in both ears, wearing hearing aids for the rest of her life. Her whistling hearing aids (any breeze and we children would hear a whistle) and reduced ability to understand people left her self-conscious. As a child, she seemed remote and aloof to the author, but probably because of her hearing issue and upbringing by traditional and conservative English parents! But in the end, she was a sweet great-grandma.

APPENDIX: WORD-CLOUD

Common "Christian" names found in the index of this book.

CLAY WORD-CLOUD

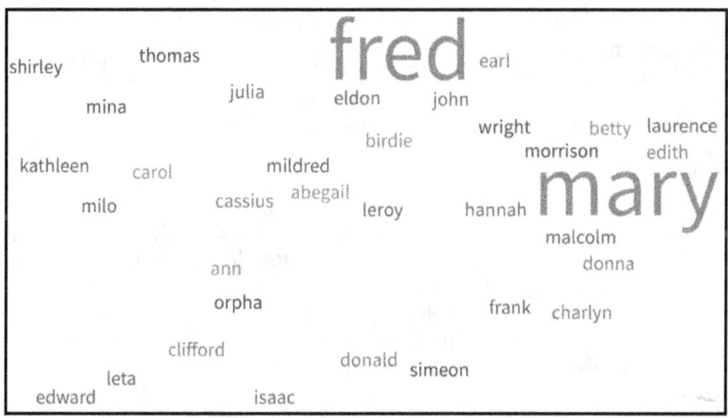

PICKLES WORD-CLOUD

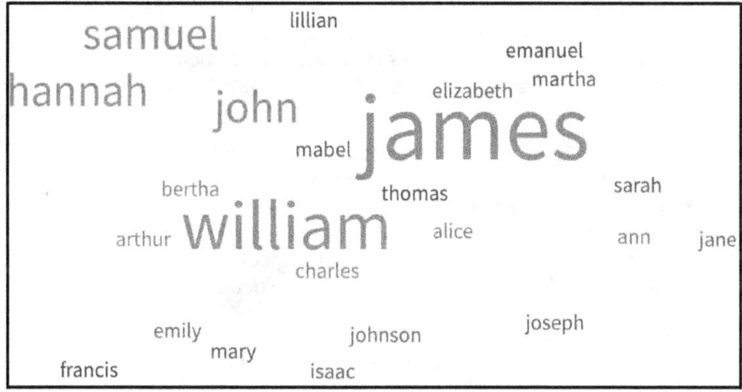

About the Author:

Curtis Daryl "Curt" Sanders – April 2023

The trek into family genealogy and history grabbed Curt early in life but solidified around age 16. After drinking-in anecdotal stories of his great-grandmother's kin pioneering in Michigan and other places, the thirst was insatiable. He wanted to know more. The beginnings were amateurish, *ad hoc,* and with the usual interfering stop-n-start ebbs of life situations and duties. While never forgetting his origins, it was not until his posting as a member of the U.S. Air Force to the United Kingdom in 1975-1977 (RAF Lakenheath) that interest was re-kindled. It was also 1976: Alex Haley published *Roots: The Saga of an American Family* and it was the bi-centennial of the United States. Curt was living in the Fenlands of the mother country, poking around the churches and cemeteries. The "locals" would often ask: "do you have roots here?" He could give some answers, but not much.

Upon military discharge in 1980, he attended college. The curriculums gave him the skills to research and write.

Curt worked in the publishing and photographic industry but also spent twenty years with the Commonwealth of Pennsylvania, retiring in 2015 as a data management analyst. The career further honed his data sifting, collection, fact-finding, and data analysis by monitoring and maintaining databases.

Today, Curt balances his busy retired life with writing and researching at his pleasure, and is a FCC licensed, amateur radio operator (K3URT).

Academia:

- Great Falls College, Montana State University, 1978.
- Harrisburg Area Community College, Associate of Liberal Arts, 1982.
- Pennsylvania State University, Bachelor of Social Science, 1984.
- Boston University, *Principles of Genealogy*, 2020.

Member of:

- Adams County [Pennsylvania] Historical Society.
- New England Historic Genealogical Society.
- Genealogy Society of Pennsylvania.
- Franklin County [Pennsylvania] Historical Society.
- South Central Pennsylvania Genealogical Society.
- Calderdale [England] Family History Society.

Other Books by the Author:

- ***Shahbaz 77.*** A personal recount of a military deployment to now de-classified exercise of the US Air Force in Shiraz, Iran, April 1977. ISBN 9781732453807; June 2018.
- ***Then Slowly Came The Aged Soldiers.*** Six essays on the authors six Civil War soldier ancestral soldiers. *(ISBN 9781732453821, June 2020, is withdrawn from publication)*; second edition published September 2023, ISBN 9781732453845.
- ***A Perfect Fit: John H. Mohn and descendants.*** A genealogy work for the Mohn family. ISBN 9781105527630; July 2021.

PEDIGREE OF THE AUTHOR.

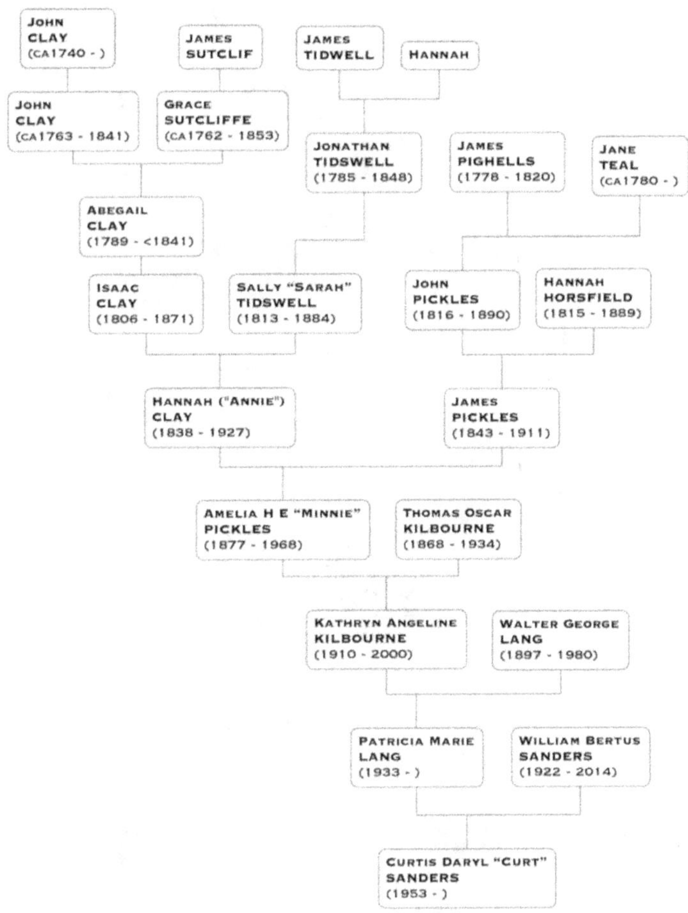

www.ingramcontent.com/pod-product-compliance
Lightning Source LLC
Chambersburg PA
CBHW071949270326
41928CB00009B/1391

* 9 7 8 1 7 3 2 4 5 3 8 5 2 *